AMERICAN FOREIGN RELATIONS SINCE INDEPENDENCE

AMERICAN FOREIGN RELATIONS SINCE INDEPENDENCE

RICHARD DEAN BURNS,
JOSEPH M. SIRACUSA,
AND
JASON C. FLANAGAN

AN IMPRINT OF ABC-CLIO, LLC
Santa Barbara, California • Denver, Colorado • Oxford, England

Copyright 2013 by Richard Dean Burns, Joseph M. Siracusa, and Jason C. Flanagan

All rights reserved. No part of this publication may be reproduced, stored in a retrieval system, or transmitted, in any form or by any means, electronic, mechanical, photocopying, recording, or otherwise, except for the inclusion of brief quotations in a review, without prior permission in writing from the publisher.

Library of Congress Cataloging-in-Publication Data

Burns, Richard Dean.
 American foreign relations since independence / Richard Dean Burns, Joseph M. Siracusa, and Jason C. Flanagan.
   pages cm
 Includes bibliographical references and index.
   ISBN 978-1-4408-0051-1 (cloth : alk. paper) — ISBN 978-1-4408-0052-8 (ebook) 1. United States—Foreign relations—History. 2. Political culture—United States—History. I. Title.
 E183.7.B88 2013
 327.73—dc23   2012036310

ISBN: 978-1-4408-0051-1
EISBN: 978-1-4408-0052-8

17 16 15 14 13   1 2 3 4 5

This book is also available on the World Wide Web as an eBook.
Visit www.abc-clio.com for details.

Praeger
An Imprint of ABC-CLIO, LLC

ABC-CLIO, LLC
130 Cremona Drive, P.O. Box 1911
Santa Barbara, California 93116-1911

This book is printed on acid-free paper ∞

Manufactured in the United States of America

To the memory of Norman A. Graebner

Contents

Preface	ix
1 The Diplomacy of the Revolution	1
2 The New Republic in a World at War	15
3 The War of 1812: Reestablishing American Independence	29
4 The Monroe Doctrine and Latin American Independence	45
5 Manifest Destiny Triumphant: Oregon, Texas, and California	57
6 A House Divided: Diplomacy during the Civil War	75
7 Territorial and Commercial Expansionism: Alaska, the Caribbean, and the Far East	87
8 War with Spain and the New Manifest Destiny	107
9 The United States Adjusts to Its New Status	125
10 Woodrow Wilson and a World at War	145
11 The Slow Death of Versailles	165
12 World War II: The Grand Alliance	185
13 A New Global Struggle: Founding of the UN to the Cold War	211
14 Crises, Conflicts, and Coexistence	237
15 The United States and Southeast Asia: Laos, Cambodia, and Vietnam	271

16 Reagan, Bush, Gorbachev, and the End of the Cold War	295
17 The United States and the Middle East: Israel, Lebanon, Iran, and Iraq	321
18 Twenty-First-Century Challenges	343
Notes	365
Selected Bibliography	407
Index	419

Preface

We have sought in the following pages to write an account at once succinct and accessible of the major events and salient ideas that have shaped the American diplomatic experience since the Revolution—historical factors that very much affect our current debates and commitments in the Middle East, as well as Europe and Asia. Contemporary public debate about the nature of U.S. foreign policy often reveals an inability—or, we believe, even an unwillingness—to remember what has happened in the past. The issues currently faced by the United States, in its attempts to further American national interests and guarantee U.S. security in the twenty-first century, can best be understood, we also believe, as simply the latest manifestation of perennial foreign policy challenges, rather than being unique to the present age. It is this sense, then, that *American Foreign Relations since Independence* explores and examines the complex relationship of American policies to national interests and the limits of the nation's power.

This relatively small one-volume history brings together the collective knowledge of three generations of diplomatic historians to create a readily accessible introduction to the subject. The authors explicitly challenge and reject the perennial debates about isolationism versus internationalism, instead asserting that American foreign relations have been characterized by the permanent tension inherent in America's desire to engage with the world, on the one hand, and the equally powerful determination to avoid undue "entanglement" in the world's troubles, on the other hand, a thread that runs like a straight line through the history of U. S. foreign relations from the Founding Fathers to the present. This work is ideally suited as a resource both for students of politics, international affairs, and history, as well as for practitioners, policymakers, and informed general interest readers.

Richard Dean Burns
Claremont

Joseph M. Siracusa
Melbourne

Jason C. Flanagan
Canberra

CHAPTER 1

The Diplomacy of the Revolution

> We ought to lay it down as a first principle and a Maxim never to be forgotten, to maintain an entire Neutrality in all future European Wars.
> —John Adams in the Continental Congress, September 1775

> As Europe is our market for trade, we ought to form no partial connection with any part of it. It is the true interest of America to steer clear of European contentions must all hang together, or assuredly we shall all hang separately.
> —Thomas Paine, *Common Sense*, January 1776

The origins of American independence can best be understood in the context of the long struggle between England and France for both domination of North America and supremacy in Europe. The conclusion in 1763 of the Seven Years' War—or the French and Indian War as it is also known—left Great Britain victorious and at the pinnacle of its power. At the same time, however, the roots of the American Revolution may be traced to this victory and the 1763 Treaty of Paris.[1] The treaty marked the beginning of increasingly divergent attitudes and confrontational policies in London and the colonies. For Britain, victory required reorganizing the vast North American territories acquired from France and Spain. Aimed at preventing frontier Indian warfare, the Proclamation of 1763 closed the trans-Appalachian area to colonial settlement. To defend and police the new territories, the British maintained an unprecedented standing army in mainland America. To meet the costs of this commitment and relieve the massive financial burden left by the war, London sought to impose new taxes and enforce imperial trade laws that had long been ignored by the colonists, ending the period of so-called salutary neglect.

These measures sought not only to bring peace and stability to North America, but also to require the colonies to share the cost of imperial defense and administration. The colonists, however, had played a vital role in the victory over the French and their Indian allies, a victory that encouraged the colonies to think of themselves as self-governing entities.[2] The removal of the French and Spanish threat to North America reinforced the notion that the colonists no longer required British protection; thus, the colonists refused to have their duties prescribed for them by Parliament and king, while Parliament and king rejected colonial self-government. Britain, consequently, found itself involved in a war not only with its colonies, but eventually most of Europe. The war, though not wholly disastrous to British arms, deprived Great Britain of the most valuable of it colonial possessions.

The initial aim of armed revolt in 1775 was not independence, but rather a recognition of what the colonials held to be their rights as British subjects that they had enjoyed prior to 1763. The colonies turned to independence when the British government adopted severe repressive measures. No one set forth the arguments for independence so persuasively as Thomas Paine, a recent immigrant from England. Paine had arrived in America in late 1774, and less than two years later, in January 1776, he published *Common Sense*. This widely read pamphlet was the single most effective articulation of the case for independence.

An Entangling Alliance with France

In asserting the benefits of independence, Paine argued that it was America's connection to Great Britain that drew it into "European wars and quarrels" and set it "at variance with nations, whom would otherwise seek our friendship, and against whom, we have neither anger nor complaint." He continued, "As Europe is our market for trade, we ought to form no partial connection with any part of it. It is the true interest of America to steer clear of European contentions." Such commerce, according to Paine, would also bring security, so far as it would "secure us the peace and friendship of all Europe; because it is in the interest of all Europe to have America a free port."[3] While such ideas would form the foundation of a basic American foreign policy principle, they were neither original nor unique to the American setting. These ideas can be traced back to earlier political debates between the English Whigs and Tories, who divided over whether England should actively participate in maintaining a continental balance of power or take advantage of its insular position and avoid European conflicts in the pursuit of trade.[4] In 1744, one pamphleteer posited a general rule that anticipated the founding fathers' views of foreign policy: "A Prince or State ought to avoid all Treaties, except such as tend towards promoting Commerce or Manufactures.... All other Alliances may be look'd upon as so many Incumbrances."[5] Such views were tempered by realistic concerns, as an "entangling alliance" with France proved essential to securing independence.

Greatly inferior to Great Britain in numbers, wealth, industry, and military and naval power, the colonies' only hope for military success depended on aid by a major European power. Months before deciding on independence, Congress had set up a secret committee to make contact with friends in Paris. The committee's agent in Paris, Silas Deane, having come to Paris in July 1776 seeking supplies and credit, discovered secret arrangements for aid had been instituted before his arrival. He found the French government's motivation in assisting the rebelling colonies was to weaken England. The celebrated French playwright and amateur diplomat Caron de Beaumarchais and French foreign minister Comte de Vergennes had persuaded King Louis XVI that aid to the colonies was in France's interest.[6] France's material aid to the colonies, managed by Beaumarchais, consisted of gunpowder and other essential supplies from French arsenals. Spain, persuaded by France, also provided aid. All in all, measured in the dollars of that day, France contributed to the American cause nearly $2 million in subsidies and over $6,350,000 in loans; Spain, approximately $400,000 and $250,000 in subsidies and loans respectively.[7]

With the Declaration of Independence, Congress sent to France the most widely admired and persuasive American of his day, Benjamin Franklin. Franklin, a celebrity in France, was regarded as the embodiment of the Enlightenment. Franklin's mission was to secure French recognition of the colonies' independence that could be accomplished by a treaty between France and the new United States. In Paris he joined Deane and Arthur Lee, who had come from London, to form an American commission. Enemy agents, however, severely compromised the commission's work, the most important of them being Deane's secretary, Dr. Edward Bancroft, secretly in the pay of the British.[8] In addition to the presence of enemy agents, Franklin frequently leaked information for political reasons, while Deane used inside information in pursuit of speculative schemes. Franklin brought with him a draft of a proposed treaty of amity and commerce, which embodied the liberal commercial principles that Congress hoped to see adopted not only by France but by the entire trading world. The Plan of Treaties of 1776, primarily authored by John Adams, was the first major state paper dealing with American foreign policy and would have influence beyond the exigencies of the Revolution.[9] Writing in June 1776, Adams made his feelings regarding the French treaty clear: "I am not for soliciting any political connection, or military assistance, or indeed naval, from France. I wish for nothing but commerce, a mere marine treaty with them."[10]

While supportive of the United States, Vergennes was initially unwilling to risk war with England by granting formal recognition to the Americans. The surrender of General Burgoyne's British army at Saratoga in October 1777 proved the colonists' determination to field a viable military force that, combined with the readiness of the French navy, encouraged a French commitment.[11] At Paris on February 6, 1778, two agreements—a Treaty of Amity and Commerce and a Treaty of Alliance—were signed, the latter to take effect if Great Britain went to war with France. Vergennes's major concern was that Britain might seek reconciliation with its former colonies. Burgoyne's surrender led Parliament in March to pass legislation repealing all bills enacted since 1763, which led to colonial resentment. In April, London dispatched a commission to America, empowered to offer to Congress virtually everything it had desired, independence alone excepted, if Americans would lay down their arms and resume their allegiance to the British Crown. The right to control their own taxation, to elect their governors and other officials formerly appointed, to be represented in Parliament if they so desired, to continue Congress as an American legislature, release from quitrents, assurance that their colonial characters would not be altered without their consent, full pardon for all who had engaged in rebellion—indicate how far Britain was willing to go to save its empire. In effect, London was offering "dominion status" to America.[12] The offer came too late. With France's recognition, the prospect of an alliance, and the promise of substantial aid, independence seemed assured. Congress ratified the treaties with France without even hesitating to parley with London's commission.

The Treaty of Amity and Commerce placed each nation on a most-favored-nation basis with reference to the liberal principles of the "Plan of 1776"—principles that would protect the interest of either signatory should it be neutral when the other was at war. The Treaty of Alliance—to go into effect should France become embroiled in the war against Great Britain—had as its object "to maintain effectually the liberty, Sovereignty, and independence absolute and unlimited" of the United States. Neither party was to make a separate peace with Great Britain nor lay down its arms until American independence was won. Both parties mutually guaranteed "from the present time and forever against all other powers" the American possessions that they then held and with which they might emerge from the war. France, in addition, undertook to guarantee the liberty, sovereignty, and independence of the United States.[13] (The Franco-American pact constituted the only "entangling alliance" in which the United States participated until the North Atlantic Treaty in 1949.[14]) The treaty proved indispensable to the winning of independence. After the British declared war on France for recognizing U.S. independence, a French army was sent to America, and French fleets operated off the American coast. The importance of French aid was illustrated in the final scene of the Revolution when, at Yorktown, a British army was trapped between a French fleet and an allied army, of which two-thirds were French.

Spain and the Revolution

Spain, though bound to France by a dynastic alliance, the "Family Compact," and though giving secret aid to the United States, refused to enter the war for over a year after France became a belligerent. The Spanish court hoped to recover Gibraltar (lost in 1713) and Florida (lost in 1763) as a reward for mediating between Great Britain and France. When London declined mediation, Spain signed a pact with France—the Convention of Aranjuez in April 1779—and declared war against Great Britain on June 21, 1779.[15] John Jay spent many bitter months in Madrid asking for recognition. Spain declined, however, to join the Franco-American alliance or, as a colonial power, to formally endorse rebellion by any colonies. Even an offer to waive the American claim of right to navigate the Mississippi River could not persuade the Spanish government to recognize the young republic. The Convention of Aranjuez pledged that France and Spain would not make peace until Spain had recovered Gibraltar. Since the United States had promised not to make peace without France, it could not, if all treaty engagements were observed, make peace until Gibraltar was restored to Spain. As Samuel Flagg Bemis put it, America found itself "chained by European diplomacy to the Rock of Gibraltar."[16]

Spanish and American interests clashed over the United States' desire for the Mississippi River as its western boundary and the right of navigation on it to the Gulf of Mexico. Spain, anxious to monopolize the navigation and commerce of both river and Gulf, was unwilling to concede either American use of the river or a foothold on its eastern bank. If the Spanish had their way, the United States' western boundary would be fixed at the summit of the Appalachians. Spain's bargaining position was strengthened by the daring of Bernardo de Galvez, the young governor of Louisiana and one of the war's most successful generals, who routed the British from West Florida.[17] He established Spain's claim to a cession of Florida at the end of the war and to full control of the lower Mississippi.

A Pawn in the European Chess Game

The young United States necessarily involved itself in the international rivalries of Europe as their politics threatened to terminate hostilities with American independence not yet achieved. Spain, reluctantly entering the war, soon grew tired of it; thus, Madrid received a British mission in 1780 anxious to discuss peace terms. For America, the Spanish ministers proposed a long truce between Great Britain and its "colonies" without specific recognition of independence and with a division of territory on the basis of the areas each party then occupied.[18] This would have left the British in control of Maine, the northern frontier, New York City, Long Island, and the principal seaports south of Virginia. While Vergennes disapproved of the Anglo-Spanish conversations, which violated the Convention of Aranjuez, he listened to a proposal for mediation from Catherine II of Russia and Austrian Emperor Joseph II, which would have had much the same effect in America. John Adams, an American peace commissioner and minister at The Hague, rejected the proposal out of hand when Vergennes laid it before him. No truce, he said, until all British troops were withdrawn from the United States; no negotiation with England without guarantees that American sovereignty and independence would be respected. But back home, Congress was more easily persuaded than was Adams. Under pressure (and in some instances monetary persuasion) from the French minister to the United States, Congress on June 15, 1781, directed its commissioners in Europe to accept the mediation of Russia and Austria and to place themselves in the hands of the French ministers, "to undertake nothing in the negotiations for peace or truce without their knowledge and concurrence," and to be governed "by their advice and opinion." Fortunately, the British government rejected the proposal for mediation.

Britain, meanwhile, was at war or on the verge of war with most of the Western world. In 1780, the Baltic countries, Russia, Denmark, and Sweden had organized a League of Armed Neutrality to protect their commerce from British naval practices. Prussia, the emperor (of the Holy Roman Empire), the Kingdom of the Two Sicilies, and even Portugal, Britain's traditional ally, had joined the league. In February 1782, following receipt of the news of the disaster at Yorktown, the British House of Commons resolved that the war ought to be terminated. In March, a new ministry headed by the Marquis of Rockingham took office and initiated peace talks by sending Richard Oswald to confer with the American representatives in Paris. After Rockingham's death in July 1782, Lord Shelburne became prime minister. He was an advocate of a generous peace, which might result in recapturing for Great Britain the bulk of American trade and at some future date, perhaps, tempt the United States back into some sort of imperial federation.[19]

The Stakes of Diplomacy

The American Congress named five peace commissioners, three of whom actually handled the negotiations. Franklin was in Paris when the talks began. John Jay, who had been in Madrid, arrived in June 1782. John Adams, who had secured recognition and a loan from the Netherlands, reached Paris in October. Franklin and Jay handled most of the discussions, with Adams providing valuable aid toward the close of the negotiations.

The American commissioners had three principal objectives: (1) recognition of independence, now assured; (2) the widest boundaries obtainable; and (3) retention of the inshore fishing privileges on the coasts of British North America the colonials had previously enjoyed. London was prepared to recognize American independence and respond generously to the other American demands. In return, it hoped to secure from the United States: (1) payment of the pre-Revolutionary debts of American planters and others to British creditors, and (2) compensation for the Loyalists (Americans who had sided with Great Britain) for the lands and other property that had been seized by the states. The most controversial American demands concerned boundaries, for their claims involved adjustments with Great Britain and Spain. Congress claimed the entire area between the Appalachian Mountains and the Mississippi River based chiefly on the sea-to-sea clauses in certain colonial charters. The British government in the years since 1763 acted as though the western lands belonged to the Crown. South of the Ohio River, American settlements in central Kentucky and eastern and central Tennessee gave the United States a solid basis for claiming those areas, but farther south the Spanish held the east bank of the Mississippi as far north as Natchez. They still hoped to deny the Americans access to the Mississippi and to draw the boundary near to the Appalachian watershed. In this endeavor they had French support.

In the summer of 1779, Congress's first step toward peace negotiations was naming John Adams a commissioner and on August 14 setting proposed boundaries that included the area claimed by the states from the mountains to the Mississippi. It added that although it was "of the utmost importance to the peace and Commerce of the United States that Canada and Nova Scotia should be ceded" and that equal rights in the fisheries should be guaranteed, a desire to terminate the war led Congress to refrain from making these objects an ultimatum. Military necessity and pressure from the French minister prompted Congress to issue new instructions on June 15, 1781, that insisted only on independence and the preservation of the treaties with France as indispensable conditions. With regard to boundaries, the commissioners were to regard the earlier instructions as indicating "the desires and expectations of Congress," but were not to adhere to them if they presented an obstacle to peace.

The Peace Negotiations

The Spanish and French erected the first obstacles encountered by the Americans. John Jay arrived in Paris suspicious of both countries after his futile mission in Madrid. The Spanish ambassador in Paris and a spokesman for Vergennes indicated to him that the Spanish, with French support, were bent on excluding the United States from the Mississippi Valley. Vergennes agreed that the American and French negotiations with the British should proceed separately, but with the understanding that neither settlement should become effective without the other. Franklin and Jay proceeded to negotiate their own preliminary terms with the British, neglecting, with considerable justification, to make those "most candid and confidential communications" to the French ministers. In their negotiations with Great Britain, they simply disregarded Spanish claims in the western country north of the 31st parallel, assuming (as did London) that that country still belonged to Great Britain.

Franklin had already informally sketched out to Oswald what, as an American, he considered the "necessary" and the "advisable" terms of a lasting settlement. Among "necessary" terms he included, after independence and withdrawal of troops, "a confinement of the boundaries of Canada" to what they had been before the Quebec Act (that is, the St. Lawrence-Nipissing line), "if not to a still more contracted state," and the retention of fishing privileges. Among "advisable" terms that might be expected to contribute to a permanent reconciliation, he mentioned indemnification by Great Britain of those persons who had been ruined through the devastations of war, admission of American ships and trade to British and Irish ports on the same terms as those of Britain, and "giving up every part of Canada." A delay now ensued, because when Oswald received his formal commission as an agent of the British government on August 8, it failed to authorize him to recognize the independence of the United States as preliminary to negotiation. It did, however, authorize him to make recognition of independence the first article of the proposed treaty. Franklin and Jay were at first inclined to insist on formal recognition of independence as a condition precedent to negotiation; but, becoming alarmed lest France use any further delay to their disadvantage, they agreed to accept recognition as stipulated in Oswald's commission.[20]

On September 1, Oswald received instructions to accept terms based on Franklin's proposed "necessary" terms, ceding to the United States the western country as far north as Canada, but rejecting payment of prewar debts or the restitution of property confiscated from the Loyalists. A draft treaty on these terms was initialed by the commissioners on October 5 and referred to London at the time news arrived that a major assault on Gibraltar had failed. With this victory, Shelburne took a firmer tone, not only insisting that something be done for British creditors and Loyalists, but attempting to hold on to the "old" Northwest territory. The Americans, reinforced by Adams, insisted on retention of the Northwest, but they agreed to inclusion in the treaty of articles in the interest of the Loyalists and the British creditors. They accepted the St. Croix River instead of the St. John, as originally proposed, as the northeastern boundary. In the West, they accepted a line through the middle of the St. Lawrence and the Great Lakes and thence via the Lake of the Woods to the Mississippi. The preliminary treaty was signed at Paris on November 30, 1782, not to become effective until France also made peace with England. The treaty was less favorable to the United States than the draft initialed on October 5. It contained troublesome provisions for Loyalists and for British creditors, and the northern boundary followed the river and lake line instead of Lake Nipissing, costing the United States the most valuable part of the modern province of Ontario.

What was remarkable about the treaty was that the United States got as much as it did, especially title to all territory east of the Mississippi between the Great Lakes and the 31st parallel. For the explanation of this one must look to the enlightened policy of the Earl of Shelburne. Desirous of a peace of reconciliation, he saw a means of achieving it at small cost to the empire. The regulation of the fur trade in that area was proving ruinously expensive to the royal treasury, and experience had seemed to show that the region was of little value without control of the mouth of the Mississippi, now firmly in the hands of Spain.

The Treaty

The principal provisions of the preliminary treaty signed on November 30, 1782, established the boundaries of the United States, several of which would be disputed for several years, but included the western territory west to the Mississippi River. Great Britain acknowledged the independence and sovereignty of the 13 states individually; promised to withdraw all its armies, garrisons, and fleets from their soil and waters "with all convenient speed"; and conceded to American fishermen the "liberty" to ply their trade much as before in the territorial waters of British North America. The United States, on its part, made certain promises in the interest of Loyalists and British creditors. The parties agreed that creditors on either side should "meet with no lawful impediment" in the recovery of the full value of bona fide debts previously contracted. The United States agreed that there should be no further prosecutions or confiscations of property against any persons for the part they had taken in the war and promised that it would "earnestly recommend" to the legislatures of the states that, with certain exceptions, rights and properties of Loyalists be restored.

The definitive treaty was signed September 3, 1783, at the same time that Great Britain made peace with its other enemies. Great Britain ceded the Floridas, with limits undefined, to Spain, which did not endorse U.S. navigation of the Mississippi or the United States' southern boundary. With both Spain and Great Britain, the United States still faced many difficulties before the stipulations of the treaty could be converted into reality.

Problems of Independence

When hostilities officially ended in 1783, France, Great Britain, the Netherlands, and Sweden had recognized the United States. Inexperienced American diplomats had previously wandered over Europe in vain to secure recognition from Russia, Prussia, Austria, Spain, and the Grand Duke of Tuscany. In these courts they had been coldly received, for few monarchs cared to countenance rebellion and the institution of republican government. A few other recognitions followed independence: in 1784, Spain sent Don Diego de Gardoqui as its first minister to the United States; Prussia signed a treaty in 1785 and Morocco in 1786. By 1787, the United States had commercial treaties with France (1778), the Netherlands (1782), and Sweden (1783), but none with Great Britain until 1794 and Spain until 1795. The British government thought so little of the importance of the United States that, though it received John Adams as minister in 1785, it did not send a full-fledged minister to Philadelphia until 1791.

The United States' temporary "underprivileged" status stemmed from it being a product of revolution, an experiment in democracy, small in population, and poor in fluid resources. But also the Articles of Confederation—a government without dependable revenue, without an army or navy, and without power to coerce the governments of the 13 individual states—lacked the respect of foreign powers. Such a government was unable to fulfill its treaty obligations, was not able to make commitments with assurance that they would be observed or threats with expectation that they would be carried out, and was incapable of securing equality of commercial treatment abroad. Additionally, it was incapable of enforcing its sovereignty over areas assigned to it or of putting an end, by either diplomacy or force, to foreign occupation of its soil. Not until after it was replaced by the more effective government provided for by the Constitution of 1787 were these pressing national problems resolved.

Independence Disrupts Trade

The lack of a commercial treaty with Britain was particularly damaging to the nation's economy. The original 13 states had, as colonies flying the British flag protected by the Royal Navy, developed a flourishing merchant marine and an extensive and profitable commerce. Colonial shipyards turned out ships more cheaply than the British. Ships built and owned in the colonies enjoyed the privileges of empire trade with American tobacco, rice, indigo, wheat, flour, meat, fish, rum, furs, and lumber finding markets in England, on the continent of Europe, in Africa, and in the West Indies. There they were exchanged for manufactured goods, sugar and molasses, coffee, rum, slaves, and specie. During the Revolution, American ships and their cargoes were excluded from British Empire ports and were at the risk of capture by British cruisers or privateers. Many American ship owners took to privateering and harried British commerce, but peace in 1783 put an end to such employment. It compelled the United States, in the exercise of its newly, won independence, to seek markets for its produce, cargoes and foreign ports for its merchantmen, and protection for ships and cargoes against the piracies of North African freebooters.

Trade with the various portions of the British Empire might have continued as before the war had the British been willing. The American peace commissioners of 1782 were instructed to secure, if possible, for citizens of the United States, "a direct commerce to all parts of the British dominions and possessions" in return for the admission of British subjects to trade with all parts of the United States. The British government at that time declined. The British Parliament was in no mood to be generous to its former colonies—least of all to encourage a rival in the American merchant marine. American ships carrying American products were admitted to ports in the British Isles on fairly liberal terms, but American ships, like other foreign ships, were excluded from trading with the British colonies. New England merchants particularly missed what had once been a profitable trade with the British West Indies; only gradually, and at considerable risk, did they succeed in reopening this trade through clandestine and illegal channels. To varying degrees, and with some exceptions, other colonial powers adhered to the same mercantilist policy of reserving trade with their colonies to their own ships.

Problems of the West

The peace treaty had assigned spacious boundaries to the United States, but American sovereignty within the boundaries was largely a legal fiction. American settlement beyond the mountains took the form of a narrow wedge, with its base stretching from Pittsburgh to the Watauga settlements in eastern Tennessee and its apex at Nashville on the Cumberland River. Within it lay the villages in the Kentucky bluegrass region and at the Falls of the Ohio (Louisville). To these should be added the old French villages on the Wabash and in the Illinois country. All told, there were perhaps 25,000 settlers between the crest of the mountains and the Mississippi. Beyond these limits, to the north, west, and south, was the country of unfriendly Indians, and the explorer or trader who penetrated the Indian barrier was likely to find garrisons of British or Spanish troops on land within the United States' treaty boundaries. The British army still occupied every strategic point on the Great Lakes, and Spanish soldiers held the Mississippi at Natchez and (a little later) at the sites of the future Vicksburg and Memphis. Moreover, both the British and Spanish had an alliance or understanding with the Indians for the purpose of preventing the United States from taking possession of its legal territory.

There was, furthermore, no assurance that the frontier settlers would be firm in their allegiance to the state governments in the East or to the weak Congress that symbolized their Union. The frontier found its natural outlets through the Ohio, Mississippi, and the St. Lawrence Rivers, and the nations that controlled those watercourses exerted a powerful influence on the settlements on their waters. Frontier leaders were not above bartering their allegiance in return for special favors from the local British and Spanish agents. Before the United States could enforce its sovereign rights, it had to accomplish three difficult, interrelated tasks: it must gain the allegiance of the frontiersmen, bring the Indian tribes under its authority, and secure from England and Spain, respectively, the execution of the terms of the Treaty of Paris. Only through ousting the British and Spanish from their footholds on its soil could the United States hope to control the Indians, and only by dealing effectively with Indians and Europeans could it win the "men of the western waters." None of these problems proved capable of solution during the period of the Articles of Confederation. The British held seven fortified posts on U.S. soil, strung out from the foot of Lake Champlain to the junction of Lakes Huron and Michigan. The British excused this violation of the peace treaty by asserting that the United States had not fulfilled its obligations. In reality, the decision to hold the posts had been taken before the treaty was formally proclaimed, for retention of the posts would maintain a valuable trade in furs and enabled the British government to meet its obligations to allied Indian tribes. British authorities encouraged these tribes, living south of the Canadian border, to resist American attempts to settle their lands. The British also hoped the dissatisfied American frontier communities in Vermont and Kentucky might detach themselves from the Confederation.

The treaty of 1783 had fixed the United States' southern boundary from the Chattahoochee to the Mississippi, at the 31st parallel, had made the middle of the Mississippi the western boundary, and had declared: "The navigation of the river Mississippi, from its source to the ocean, shall forever remain free and open to the subjects of Great Britain, and the citizens of the United States." In the contemporaneous settlement with Spain, Great Britain had ceded to that nation East and West Florida without defining their boundaries. Louisiana, embracing the region west of the Mississippi and New Orleans east of that river, had been ceded by France to Spain in 1762. After 1783, therefore, a weak and nervous Spain hemmed in the United States on both the west and the south.

Spain refused to consider itself bound by terms of the Anglo-American treaty, either as to the southern boundary of the United States or as to the free navigation of the Mississippi. As a result of the successful campaign in 1779–1781, Spain claimed a large area in the Southwest by right of conquest and denied the right of Great Britain to cede it to the United States. Holding both banks of the Mississippi from its mouth to far above New Orleans, Spain likewise denied the right of Great Britain to guarantee to citizens of the United States its free navigation. Spanish policy after 1783 included the assertion of title to a region as far north as the Tennessee and Ohio Rivers, the denial to the Americans of the use of the lower Mississippi except as a privilege granted by Spain, and the cultivation of the powerful Indian nations of the Southwest for a barrier against the Americans. From time to time, also, Spain schemed with those leaders in the American frontier communities who appeared ready to barter their allegiance for privileges or bounties conferred by the Spanish crown.

The extreme boundary claims of Spain were apparently established chiefly for bargaining purposes. Diego de Gardoqui, the first Spanish minister to the United States, was empowered to make liberal boundary concessions and to offer substantial trading privileges in return for the consent of the United States to waive its claim to the navigation of the Mississippi. John Jay, serving as secretary for foreign affairs under the direction of Congress, thought the trade offer advantageous and the navigation of the Mississippi of little immediate importance. He asked Congress for authority to consent to closure of the river for a period of 25 or 30 years. The vote on his proposal revealed sectional cleavage as Virginia, the Carolinas, and Georgia, all with land claims extending to the Mississippi, voted against his proposal. Maryland voted with its southern sisters. The seven states to the north (Delaware having no delegate in Congress) supported Jay. The majority of seven to five was sufficient to alter Jay's instructions, but any treaty that he might make would require the vote of nine states for ratification. Jay and Gardoqui continued their futile conversations. The following year (1787), however, Spanish authorities opened the river for Americans from the Kentucky settlements. One of these, Revolutionary War veteran James Wilkinson, paid for the privilege by taking a secret oath of allegiance to the Spanish Crown and advising the Spanish on the best means of winning over other Kentuckians. The establishment of satisfactory relations with Spain, as well as with Britain, awaited the formation of a more efficient American government.

A New Government for the United States

While the British and Spaniards flirted with American frontiersmen and dabbled in alliances with the Indians, the United States was establishing a new government that soon gave the country a respectable standing among the nations of the world. The Constitution written at Philadelphia, in 1787, went into effect two years later. Under it, the new government could control commerce, raise revenue, create and maintain armies and navies. Treaties, both those already made and those to be made in the future, were declared to be "the supreme law of the land," overriding state enactments and even state constitutions. Separate executive and judicial departments provided the machinery necessary for enforcement. No longer could foreign governments scorn the promises or scoff at the threats of the United States. The adoption of the Constitution inaugurated a new era in American diplomacy.

CHAPTER 2

The New Republic in a World at War

It is our true policy to steer clear of permanent alliances with any portion of the foreign world... Taking care always to keep ourselves ... on a respectable defensive posture, we may safely trust to temporary alliances for extraordinary emergencies.
—George Washington's Farewell Address, September 19, 1796

Peace, commerce, and honest friendship with all nations, entangling alliances with none.
—Thomas Jefferson, First Inaugural Address, March 4, 1801

The Constitution written at Philadelphia in 1787 offered only a vague outline of the machinery for devising American foreign policy. It was up to the first president—George Washington—to establish the basic precedents that would guide the nation's foreign affairs. Washington's administration contained, to borrow Doris Kearns Goodwin's phrase, the first and perhaps most bitter "team of rivals" in American history.[1] The appointment of Thomas Jefferson as secretary of state and Alexander Hamilton as secretary of the treasury led to a rivalry that not only divided the administration, but contributed to the formation of the nation's first political parties. The Hamilton-Jefferson divide was apparent from the first foreign policy challenge faced by the administration. In 1789, an Anglo-Spanish dispute erupted over possession of Nootka Sound in the remote Pacific Northwest. The territory was claimed by Spain, and when the British attempted to establish a post there, the Spanish drove them out and captured their ships. With both countries preparing for war, Washington was concerned the British might desire to move troops through American territory to strike at Spanish possessions in Louisiana and Florida. Since denying permission raised the specter of conflict with England, while granting such permission raised the possibility of war with Spain, he asked his advisers how the United States should respond. Jefferson essentially recommended giving no answer at all to such a request, believing that evading the question would not only guarantee American neutrality but allow time for the United States to extract some advantage from Anglo-Spanish tensions. Hamilton, on the other hand, recommended that permission be granted. Fortunately for Washington, he never had to make a decision on this matter. Spain, having lost its French ally to revolution, quickly capitulated. The unfolding French Revolution, and the war it triggered in 1792, contributed to Hamilton and Jefferson's increasingly divergent views, which would shape the American response to the unfolding international conflict.[2]

The Struggle for Neutrality

The French Revolution soon provoked a widespread conflict. The War of the First Coalition began in April 1792 when France declared war on Austria, in January the following year the French executed Louis XVI, and in February they declared war on Great Britain. The English phase of the war in 1793 launched a naval conflict that reached the shores of the United States. American popular sympathy initially favored France—a recent ally and now the exemplar of republicanism and democracy. In 1793, however, conservative Federalists recoiled at the terror in France, denying any resemblance between America's cause and that of France.[3] Jeffersonian Republicans, in contrast, formed "Jacobin Clubs," patterned after those in France, addressing one another as "citizen" and "citizeness" after the current French fashion. Popular sentiment apart, the United States had treaty obligations—obligation under certain circumstances to protect French possessions in America and to allow French naval vessels and privateers privileges denied to Great Britain. Support for France was also heightened by British interference with American trade at sea and consistent opposition to American interests on the frontier.

American officials were aware of the perils of the situation and were determined to remain neutral—on this point Jefferson and Hamilton agreed. Anticipating the arrival of the French Republic's first minister, the dashing young Edmond Genet, Washington submitted a list of 13 questions to his cabinet, consisting of Jefferson, Hamilton, Secretary of War Henry Knox and Attorney General Edmund Randolph. This list boiled down to three fundamental considerations: first, should the president issue a proclamation of neutrality; second, were the treaties made with

Louis XVI still binding on the United States, now that the monarchy had been overthrown; and finally, should Genet be received as the minister of the French Republic? The answers to these questions returned by Hamilton and Jefferson—Knox siding with Hamilton and Randolph with Jefferson—shaped the American concept of neutral rights and duties, and the rules of recognition. To the first question—issuing a proclamation of neutrality—Jefferson answered no, Hamilton yes. Jefferson argued that the question of neutrality (like that of war) was one for Congress to determine, and that the question of American neutrality should be used as a bargaining chip, not freely given. Hamilton argued that America's neutrality was not a negotiable commodity and that delaying its announcement risked America being dragged into the war.[4]

To the second question—were the treaties binding—Hamilton answered no, since the government with which they were made had been overthrown. Even if the treaties were still in force, Hamilton added, the alliance was expressly a "defensive" one, and France, having declared war against England, was the aggressor. Jefferson dissented, arguing that treaties were made by Louis XVI's government, acting as the agent of the French people, and that a change of agents did not invalidate the agreements. (Jefferson's position since has been universally accepted.) If Jefferson would not repudiate the French treaties, neither did he believe they committed the United States to join France in the war. France, he said, had not yet asked the United States to fulfill its guarantee under the alliance. Should it do so, the United States could excuse itself on the grounds that France had failed to aid in ending British occupation of the northwest posts. If Jefferson headed the pro-French faction, he was as anxious as pro-British Hamilton to preserve American neutrality. To the third question—should Genet be received—both Hamilton and Jefferson answered yes; but where Jefferson would receive him unconditionally, Hamilton would give him notice that the United States did not consider itself bound by the treaties of 1778. On April 22, 1793, Washington issued a proclamation of neutrality, avoiding the word "neutrality," declared the United States would "pursue a conduct friendly and impartial toward the belligerent Powers." He called on American citizens to avoid contrary acts and warned of the consequences of committing hostile acts against any belligerent. Offenders must expect prosecution for any violation of "the law of nations" committed "within the cognizance of the courts of the United States."

Citizen Genet arrived in the United States expecting, if not outright military alliance, at least America's active assistance in his nation's war with Britain and Spain. If he did not demand activation of the alliance, he did engage in unwarranted activities that would have compromised U.S. neutrality. Genet had landed in Charleston and only after a slow four-week journey arrived in Philadelphia. En route he used public meetings and banquets to mobilize support for the French cause, attempted to organize illegal military expeditions to seize the Spanish possessions of Florida and Louisiana, commissioned privateers to cruise under the French flag and to prey on British commerce. When Washington sought to curtail Genet's efforts, the Frenchman appealed to the American people over the president's head.[5] Genet's actions, which even Jefferson could not condone, led to a request for his recall, and the French readily agreed. France's ready acceptance was due to a desire to maintain good terms with the United States and to the new Jacobin authorities' suspicions of Genet.[6] Fearing the guillotine at home, Genet remained in the United States as a private citizen. His actions, however, were largely responsible for Congress's enactment of a landmark neutrality law on June 5, 1794.

A Crisis with England

Tensions generated by maritime grievances soon put the country at odds with Great Britain. Rejecting the Plan of 1776, the British, following the accepted law of nations, ignored the dictum "free ships make free goods"; thus, their prize courts condemned French property found on American ships. The British also seized cargoes of American wheat, corn, and flour en route to France—not for confiscation but for preemptive purchase, presumably to the injury of the shipper. Voiding the stipulation of 1776 that neutral ships were free to trade between enemy ports, the British insisted that trade illegal in peace was illegal in war. Thus France, which in peacetime limited trade between itself and its colonies to French ships, could not in wartime open that trade to neutral shipping. Neutral ships admitted to such trade, the British declared, would be subject to confiscation. But the British went further, seizing not only American ships trading between France and its colonies, but also those trading between the colonies and the United States—a trade that France permitted in peacetime—seizing some 250 ships in the West Indies.[7] British also stopped American merchant vessels on the high seas and "impressed" members of their crews, presumed to be British subjects, for service in the Royal Navy.

The tensions were further exacerbated by events on the frontier. British troops still garrisoned the Northwest posts despite the treaty of 1783, and British agents continued to encourage the Indians to resist American land claims. Viewing the Indian treaties of 1784 and later years as valid, Congress had provided for the government of the Northwest Territory in the Ordinance of 1787 and had sold large tracts of land north of the Ohio River to prospective settlers and speculators. By the spring of 1789, the settlement of the Northwest had begun, but it had become apparent that the Indians would not honor the land treaties. Two expeditions against the recalcitrant Indians in 1789 and 1791 resulted, respectively, in an inconclusive campaign and a disastrous defeat. Washington appointed "Mad" Anthony Wayne to command a third expedition. When Wayne moved into the Indian country in the fall of 1793, the United States and Great Britain were already engaged in a heated dispute over the rights of neutrals. Congress had enacted a temporary embargo on American shipping, and other measures of retaliation were introduced. Consequently, Lord Dorchester, Canadian governor general, assumed that war was inevitable and feared that Wayne, if successful against the Indians, would attack Detroit. Hence, he ordered the fortification of a strategic point at the Maumee River many miles within U.S. territory. In February 1794, Dorchester told a delegation of western Indians that the United States did not desire peace, that it had violated the 1783 treaty, and that he expected war within a year. At that time, he said, the Indians could draw a new treaty line.[8] Such was the ominous atmosphere when Wayne, by August 18, 1794, had advanced just short of the British fort on the Maumee. In a mass of fallen timber, he scattered assembled Indians, reinforced by Canadian volunteers, with a disciplined charge. The Indians fell back under the guns of the British fort, but fortunately Wayne and the British commander avoided a dangerous clash that could have started a war. Having soundly defeated the Indians, Wayne set about laying waste their villages and fields as a way of bringing them to terms.

Jay's Treaty

In April 1794, Washington had resolved to send Chief Justice John Jay to London in a final attempt to reach an agreement with England over the several matters in dispute. A staunch Federalist and experienced diplomat, Jay shared a desire for continued peace with Great Britain but understood the necessity to secure fulfillment of the treaty of 1783, including the surrender of the northwest posts. He was instructed to urge the British to accept the principles of 1776 and to seek compensation for seizures of American ships and cargoes in violation of those principles. Hamilton, in shaping Jay's instructions, had given preserving peace with Great Britain the highest priority, to continue the flow of revenue from commerce that maintained the nation's credit.[9] Negotiating in this spirit, there was little that Jay could hope to achieve. In the treaty signed on November 19, 1794, the United States agreed that enemy goods might be taken from neutral ships, that naval stores could be considered contraband, and that provisions bound for an enemy might be taken from neutral ships if paid for. The rule of 1756 remained intact; moreover, the United States was left without clarification of the definition of a legal blockade. Under the initial 1778 treaty, French ships-of-war or privateers with enemy prizes were admitted freely to American ports, but British ships with enemy prizes were excluded. The Jay treaty extended the same privilege to British ships-of-war and privateers and excluded its (French) enemies. This contradiction of the Franco-American treaty was partly nullified by a clause declaring that nothing in the treaty should "operate contrary to former and existing public treaties with other sovereigns or States."

The West fared rather better, for the treaty contained a British promise that the posts would be evacuated no later than June 1, 1796. The subjects or citizens of either country should be privileged "freely to pass and repass by land or inland navigation, into the respective territories and countries of the two parties." For the liberation of U.S. soil from British troops, Jay deserves no great credit since London had earlier decided to give up the posts. Jay attempted unsuccessfully to secure demilitarization of the lakes and an agreement that neither party would employ Indian allies in war against the other or supply the Indians with arms against the whites. Then too, Jay resisted London's attempt to secure a slice of territory reaching down the Mississippi River to navigable water near modern Minneapolis. Jay's treaty did settle, after a fashion, other controversial matters, such as the adjudication and payment, on the one side, of pre-Revolutionary debts owed by Americans to British subjects and of British claims for damages resulting from Genet's irregular activities and, on the other, of claims of illegal seizures by British cruisers of American ships and cargoes. The commercial clauses of the treaty placed the United States on a most-favored-nation basis with reference to trade with the British Isles, opened the East Indian trade to Americans on fairly liberal terms, and also opened the important West Indian trade but on so unsatisfactory terms that it was later struck from the treaty.

Jay's treaty provoked bitter controversy in Congress and a widespread and passionate public debate that heightened the emergence of a full-fledged party system.[10] In the House of Representatives, the Republican Frederick Muhlenberg cast a key vote to approve funding for the treaty. Feelings were so tense that Muhlenberg's vote destroyed his political career and led his own brother-in-law, a fellow Republican, to stab him in the streets of Philadelphia. Washington, however, skillfully managed the ratification process, giving the Federalists time to mobilize public sentiment behind the treaty.[11] Unsatisfactory in some respects, the Jay treaty not only kept the peace at a critical time, but brought about the fulfillment of the 1783 peace treaty and London's acceptance of the United States as an equal and sovereign state. Freeing the northern frontier from British garrisons led to a settlement with the Indians. Defeated by General Wayne at Fallen Timbers and deprived of British support, the tribes came to terms. At Fort Greenville on August 3, 1795, they ceded to the United States all of the future state of Ohio, except the northwest corner and a strip running along the shore of Lake Erie to the Cuyahoga River. With these two treaties, the control of the Northwest for the first time passed to the United States. Great Britain's involvement in the European war and its reluctance to take on additional enemies contributed greatly to these results.

Pinckney's Treaty with Spain

Less than a year later, Thomas Pinckney signed a treaty with Spain at Madrid that accomplished for the Southwest even greater things than Jay's treaty had achieved for the Northwest. Pinckney's treaty—the Treaty of San Lorenzo—was in many regards a by-product of the Jay Treaty. If Spain made peace with France and found itself at war with Britain, the Spanish feared an Anglo-American alliance would render Spanish colonies vulnerable, a fear heightened when Madrid learned of Jay's mission to England. Friendly relations with the United States, even at the cost of concessions, seemed the only safe policy for Spain. A hint that the Spanish might accept American claims as to the boundary line and the navigation of the Mississippi, prompted President Washington, in November 1794, to appoint Thomas Pinckney minister to Spain. As Pinckney reached Madrid in late June 1795, circumstances were ripe for a successful negotiation. When a peace treaty between Spain and France was signed in July, the news of Jay's treaty with Britain also reached Madrid. Spanish authorities decided to accept the United States' principal demands without insisting on a treaty of alliance, yet negotiations proceeded until October 27, 1795.[12]

Spain conceded America's long-standing claims to the 31st parallel of latitude from the Mississippi to the Chattahoochee as the southern boundary of the United States and to the free navigation of the Mississippi. American citizens also could enjoy for three years the privilege of landing and storing their goods at New Orleans. This "right of deposit" was important for the westerners, who brought their cargoes down the river in flatboats and needed to store them while awaiting suitable oceangoing vessels. The Spanish, however, displayed characteristic procrastination in carrying out the terms of the treaty. They did not evacuate frontier posts north of 31° until 1798, but by the end of that year all Spanish garrisons had been withdrawn and westerns were freely navigating the great river and utilizing the storage facilities of New Orleans. In the Southwest as in the Northwest, the United States had at length achieved the treaty boundaries of 1783.

A "Quasi-War" with France

While failing to promote neutral rights, Jay's treaty ushered in a decade of generally cordial relations with Great Britain.[13] But the French were upset. When Washington ratified Jay's treaty, it was seen in Paris as contrary to the spirit and the letter of the engagements with France. A South Carolina Federalist, Charles C. Pinckney (Thomas's older brother), was appointed minister to France in 1796. France, ruled now by the Directory, was elated as military successes reduced its smaller neighbors to the status of satellites and tributaries. Angered by Jay's treaty and in a heavy-handed and, at times, utterly senseless way, they sought to deal harshly with the United States. They refused to receive Pinckney; interfered in the election of 1796, hoping to put Jefferson and the Republicans in office; and by June 1797 seized over 300 American ships. French actions were aimed at damaging American commerce without provoking formal hostilities—as the French diplomat Louis-Andre Pichon said: "An open war would reunite the parties [in America]. A little clandestine war, like England made on America for three years, would produce a constructive effect."[14]

French interference in American politics actually inspired much of Washington's Farewell Address, published in September 1796.[15] In his address, Washington cautioned his fellow countrymen against "inveterate antipathies against particular nations and passionate attachments for others," and encouraged them to be "constantly awake" against the "insidious wiles of foreign influence." The address's authors, Washington and Hamilton, obviously had the initially vital but later problematic French alliance in mind when Washington declared: "it is our true policy to steer clear of permanent alliances with any portion of the foreign world" and to rely only on "temporary alliances for extraordinary emergencies." While the new republic would vigorously pursue commercial engagement with the world, it was determined to avoid permanent political and military entanglements.[16]

John Adams, elected despite French machinations, named a commission consisting of Federalist John Marshall of Virginia, Republican Elbridge Gerry of Massachusetts, and the rejected Charles Pinckney to negotiate outstanding differences with France and seek compensation for the seized ships and cargoes. Upon arrival in Paris, the commissioners were approached by three French agents—designated X, Y, and Z in the printed dispatches—as spokesmen for the French foreign minister, Charles Maurice de Talleyrand-Périgord. Talleyrand may have been "an unscrupulous, pleasure-loving aristocrat of elegant taste and loose morals,"[17] but he was also an extremely talented diplomat. The three French agents demanded a loan to France, a substantial bribe for the Directors, and an apology for some unfriendly remarks by President Adams.[18] The commissioners' rejection of the proposal was less due to moral indignation than to the fact that agreement was beyond their instructions. Publication of their correspondence set off an almost hysterical reaction in the United States. Talleyrand was burned in effigy, and the phrase "Millions for defense, but not one cent for tribute" became a popular slogan.[19] Congress authorized the president to raise a "provisional army" of 10,000 men in addition to the Regular Army and called George Washington back from retirement to command it. More significantly, they created a Navy Department, construction of warships, and authorized U.S. naval vessels and armed merchantmen to challenge armed French vessels in the western Atlantic and Caribbean. This small navy—some 15 vessels in 1798—focused on the Caribbean and cooperated closely with the British navy.[20] Although the army was not used, Congress declared the treaties of 1778 with France abrogated. This was the "quasi-war" with France of 1798 to 1800.

Neither President Adams, nor Talleyrand, nor General Napoleon Bonaparte, who, in November 1799, became the head of the French government, desired a full-scale war. Bonaparte and Talleyrand, now intent on securing Louisiana, clearly desired peace with both the United States and Great Britain. Adams declared that he would never send another minister to France without assurance that he would be "received, respected, and honored as the representative of a great, free, powerful, and independent nation."[21] Talleyrand agreed and Adams named a new commission of three men, William Vans Murray, Oliver Ellsworth, and William R. Davie, to undertake negotiations with France. The American negotiators, received in Paris with proper respect, found that Talleyrand had ordered an end to the seizure of American ships and was arranging for the release of captured American sailors. Murray and his colleagues asked indemnity for French depredations on American commerce and bilateral abrogation of the treaties of 1778—already unilaterally abrogated by an act of Congress. No agreement proving possible on the claims for indemnity, the negotiators signed on September 30, 1800, a treaty that terminated the treaties of 1778 and left the question of indemnities undetermined, both to be the subject of further negotiation "at a convenient time." As amended by the Senate and further qualified by Bonaparte before ratification, the treaty nullified the earlier treaties and cancelled the claims for indemnity.[22]

The chief importance of the treaty of 1800 with France lay in release of the United States was from all obligations that compromised its neutral position in relation to the European belligerents. The restatement of the principles of 1776 was little more than a gesture, for Napoleon Bonaparte's promises were kept only as long as they suited his convenience and, in any event, a statement of neutral rights had little importance without the concurrence of Great Britain. The treaty of 1800, followed by the election of Thomas Jefferson to the presidency later that year, marked the end of the Federalist era in American diplomacy.

The Louisiana Purchase

The Jay and Pinckney treaties of 1794 and 1795 validated the boundary provisions of the peace treaty of 1783, but these boundaries would not long hold the young republic. It was "impossible not to look forward to distant times," Jefferson wrote in 1801 "when our rapid multiplication will...cover the whole Northern, if not Southern continent with people speaking the same language, governed in similar forms, and by similar laws."[23] Spanish territories to the west and south were soon victims of such expansionist dreams. American settlers threatened to dominate Upper Louisiana and the eastern bank of the Mississippi in West Florida. At New Orleans, where the right of deposit proved a boon to the growing settlements upriver, American sailing ships far outnumbered all others. Eastward from New Orleans along the Gulf coast lay West and East Florida, sparsely inhabited but commanding the mouths of rivers that would become important as Georgia and Mississippi filled with people.

Thomas Jefferson, who became president, in March 1801, was content to let New Orleans and the Floridas remain in the hands of Spain as its rule there ceased to menace the United States. "With respect to Spain our dispositions are sincerely amicable and even affectionate," he wrote in July 1801. "We consider her possession of the adjacent country as most favorable to our interests and should see, with extreme pain any other nation substituted for them."[24] Five months later, Jefferson received evidence that by a secret treaty of October 1, 1800, Spain had retroceded Louisiana to the French Republic, headed by Napoleon Bonaparte. Originally a French colony, Louisiana had been ceded by France to Spain in 1762, but Madrid found Louisiana unprofitable and impossible to defend against intrusions from the United States and Canada. Spain returned Louisiana and provided six ships-of-war for the French navy, and, in return, Napoleon promised the nephew of the King of Spain an Italian kingdom. He also promised never to transfer Louisiana to a third party.[25]

Napoleon valued Louisiana as part of a balanced colonial empire, the heart of which would be the sugar island of Santo Domingo. But at the time of acquiring Louisiana, French authority in Santo Domingo had been substantially reduced by a violent slave revolt, and control of the island had fallen to a charismatic ex-slave Toussaint L'Ouverture. Nominally acknowledging allegiance to France, Toussaint was making himself an independent sovereign. The overthrow of Toussaint, the reestablishment of French authority in Santo Domingo, and the restoration of slavery were necessary steps in the building of the colonial empire of which Louisiana was to be a part. First, ending hostilities with England was essential; this was accomplished by the Peace of Amiens on March 27, 1802. In November 1801, Napoleon sent an army of 20,000 men to restore French rule in Santo Domingo. This expedition, which witnessed the virtual annihilation of the army, was to be followed by another to take possession of Louisiana. Due to foul weather and the collapse of the Peace of Amiens, the Louisiana expedition never sailed. The rebels' victory in Santo Domingo, encouraged by Jefferson, ended Napoleon's grand plans for France's empire in the Western Hemisphere.[26] In response to news of the defeat, Napoleon exploded: "Damn sugar, damn coffee, damn colonies!"[27]

Jefferson had been alarmed by the prospect of a vigorous and powerful France replacing Spain in New Orleans. Writing to the U.S. minister in Paris, Robert R. Livingston, Jefferson noted that New Orleans, "through which the produce of three eighths of our territory must pass to market," was the one single spot on the globe "the possessor of which is our natural and habitual enemy." He argued that French possession of New Orleans would seal "the union of two countries who in conjunction can maintain exclusive possession of the ocean. From that moment we must marry ourselves to the British fleet and nation."[28] Friends in Paris advised the president that Napoleon might be more easily swayed by money than by the threat of an Anglo-American alliance. Accordingly on May 1, 1802, Livingston was instructed to ascertain if France would sell New

Orleans. In November, Jefferson learned that Spain had transferred Louisiana to France. At almost the same time came information that the Spanish intendant at New Orleans had on October 16 withdrawn the right of deposit. The change of policy resulted from the smuggling activities of certain Americans who had abused their privileges at New Orleans. Nonetheless, the Spanish action was an undeniable violation of American treaty rights and, most alarming, seemed a foretaste of possible French policies.

Westerners were willing to leave the solution of the Mississippi question to Jefferson's diplomacy, but eastern Federalists were bellicose. Their political strategy was to force Jefferson to choose between war with France or surrender of Western interests; however, their strategy failed. Pierre Samuel DuPont de Nemours advised Jefferson that New Orleans and the Floridas might be purchased for $6 million. Jefferson resolved to follow up on DuPont's suggestion. In January 1803, he nominated James Monroe as minister extraordinary to France and Spain to assist in securing American interests. Monroe was popular in the West, and his appointment was promptly confirmed. Should the French be willing to sell New Orleans and the Floridas, the American diplomats were authorized to offer as much as $10 million to obtain them. Should France refuse to cede any territory, they were to secure and improve the right of deposit guaranteed by the Spanish treaty of 1795. If France refused even the right of deposit, they were to refer the matter to Washington, for, in addition to the $10 million carrot, there was also the familiar stick—the prospect of America's "marriage" to the British fleet. Louis Andre Pichon, the French *chargé d'affaires* in Washington, informed Talleyrand that Monroe had "carte blanche and he is to go immediately to London if he is badly received at Paris."[29]

The Purchase

Before Monroe arrived in Paris, Napoleon had decided to offer the United States not only New Orleans but all of Louisiana. On April 11, 1803, he instructed his finance minister to open negotiations with Livingston. The new proposal, however, came through Talleyrand, who that same day inquired whether the United States would care to buy all of Louisiana. Napoleon had the price at 50 million livres; the thrifty minister asked 100 million. The commissioners' instructions authorized them to purchase only New Orleans and the Floridas, but there never was any serious doubt of accepting the offer. Since the price considerably exceeded instructions, the Americans haggled to lower it, finally agreeing on

80 million livres ($15 million). Three-fourths was to be paid to France, the remainder to Americans holding damage claims against the French government. Virtual agreement was reached April 29, the treaty signed May 2, and it and the accompanying documents antedated as of April 30, 1803.

France ceded to the United States "the colony or province of Louisiana, with the same extent that it now has in the hands of Spain, and that it had when France possessed it; and such as it should be after the treaties subsequently entered into between Spain and other states." Other articles of the treaty promised the incorporation of the inhabitants of Louisiana in the Union of the United States, with all the rights of citizens, while permitting French and Spanish ships to use the ports of Louisiana for 12 years on the same terms as American ships.[30] Jefferson and his ministers had achieved an impressive diplomatic success, though the decision to sell the territory was Napoleon's alone.

But of what did Louisiana consist? To requests from the American commissioners for a more specific definition of limits, Talleyrand replied: "I can give you no direction. You have made a noble bargain for yourselves, and I suppose you will make the most of it."[31] Jefferson and James Madison, his secretary of state, claimed that all of West Florida, west of the Perdido, was part of Louisiana; henceforth, that became the official American position. Spain insisted that Louisiana was bounded on the east by the Mississippi and the Iberville; this was also the French interpretation. Weak though the U.S. claim was, the disputed strip of Gulf coast was of such potential value that Jefferson made repeated efforts to secure it—by devious methods that make up one of the least creditable chapters in American diplomacy. Jefferson tried first to bluff Spain into yielding possession of the territory; when Spain refused, he tried diplomatic persuasion. Finally, he offered Napoleon a large cash consideration if he would coerce Spain into humoring the United States. Napoleon was not above such a deal, but with his brother Joseph on the throne of Spain in 1808, he became a defender of Spanish interests.[32]

It remained for Jefferson's successor, James Madison (1809–1817), to make good the American claim to the disputed portion of West Florida. In the autumn of 1810, when revolts had begun in other Spanish colonies, the settlers along the Mississippi at the western extremity of West Florida seized the Spanish fort at Baton Rouge, proclaimed their independence, and invited the United States to annex them. President Madison acted promptly. In a proclamation of October 27, he stated anew the American claim to Florida, west of the Perdido, as a part of Louisiana and directed Governor W. C. C. Claiborne of Louisiana Territory to take possession of it without employing force against Spanish troops. The United States took formal possession of Baton Rouge on December 10, 1810, and American authority was extended eastward to the Perdido with the exception of the bay and town of Mobile. A Spanish garrison at Mobile was the sole obstacle to the acquisition by the United States of Louisiana. The removal of that garrison, in 1813, was to be an incident of a conflict with England over frontier rivalries and neutral rights.

CHAPTER 3

The War of 1812: Reestablishing American Independence

> Not content with seizing upon all our property, which falls within her rapacious grasp, the personal rights of our countrymen—rights which forever ought to be sacred, are trampled upon and violated.
> —Henry Clay on grievances against Britain, December 1811

> Whether the United States shall continue passive under these progressive usurpations and these accumulating wrongs, or, opposing force to force in defense of their national rights, shall commit a just cause into the hands of the Almighty Disposer of Events, avoiding all connections which might entangle it in the contest or views of other powers, and preserving a constant readiness to concur in an honorable re-establishment of peace and friendship, is a solemn question which the Constitution wisely confides to the legislative department of the Government.
> —James Madison calls for deliberations on the question of war, June 1812

Great Britain and France had signed a formal treaty at Amiens on March 27, 1802; however, it was broken a year later as hostilities were resumed. The United States once again looked to profit from the ongoing struggle between the major powers, while those powers gave little heed to the rights of small neutral nations. While both France and Britain were ruthless in their disregard of neutral interests, it was the offenses of Great Britain that proved in the end more offensive to the United States. Defense of neutral rights, coupled with a combination of grievances and ambitions on the American frontier, eventually led the

United States to abandon neutrality and declare war on Great Britain in 1812.

The Impressment Issue

British naval officers had long exercised the right to seize British subjects, preferably experienced seamen, afloat or ashore, and pressing them into service. The practice of impressment, however, was not limited to British vessels and subjects. Thousands of deserters left the British navy each year to join the American merchant marine, where conditions were better and wages considerably higher. In 1812, officials in London claimed that some 20,000 British sailors were serving on American vessels.[1] While this figure may have been an exaggeration, given the fact that Britain needed some 10,000 new men a year to maintain its fleet, the pressure to impress sailors from American ships was immense. To forgo the right of recovering deserters from American ships would, the British Admiralty held, imperil the efficiency of the navy in its struggle against Napoleonic France. This practice, however, predictably roused American outrage and resentment since the two nations held diametrically opposed views on the issue. These differing views revolved around differing concepts of citizenship and sovereignty. Great Britain adhered to the principle of indelible allegiance—"Once an Englishman always an Englishman." Americans believed, in the word of Thomas Jefferson, that the right of expatriation was "inherent in every man by the laws of nature."[2] Under America's liberal naturalization laws the same individual might be recognized as an American citizen and a British subject; thus, even genuine evidence of American citizenship was not adequate protection against forced service in the British fleet. Moreover, British deserters could easily obtain false certificates of U.S. citizenship.

Impressing sailors aboard American ships at sea, as the Americans saw it, was a direct violation of U.S. sovereignty, for they believed that American crews were under the protection of the American flag. The British held sovereignty rested only with naval vessels, and did not claim the right to impress British sailors aboard American warships. The notion that the flag likewise protected individuals aboard merchant vessels was labeled "too extravagant to require any serious refutation."[3] Had the British impressed only deserters, or even only British subjects, from American decks, perhaps Americans would have tolerated the practice. However, as historian Paul Varg described it, the British "resorted to the scoop rather than the tweezers."[4] Impressment carried out by naval officers who needed seamen usually arbitrarily resolved any doubt of a sailor's nationality in their favor. The only appeal was through time-consuming diplomatic channels, and if the British Foreign Office was convinced that American citizens had indeed been impressed, they were released—if still living—with regrets but no indemnification for the injury.

Attempts to settle the controversy failed. The United States offered, in 1807, to exclude British deserters from American ships in wartime if the British terminated impressment. The British Admiralty, however, refused. This issue brought the nations to the brink of war in June 1807, when the British frigate *Leopard* boarded the American frigate *Chesapeake* and removed four members of the crew, alleged to be British deserters. The unprepared American vessel put up token resistance and suffered over 20 casualties in the melee. The attack on the *Chesapeake* provoked outrage, and residents of Norfolk and Portsmouth declared their readiness to defend those "sacred rights which our forefathers purchased with their blood."[5] London, recognizing its naval agents had gone too far, disavowed the *Leopard* captain's action and made tardy amends for the injuries inflicted. Still unsettled, the impressment question temporarily dropped into the background as new controversies held the stage.

A Blow at American Commerce

In spite of the restrictions placed on neutral trade by both belligerents, American commerce flourished until 1807. The tonnage of American shipping employed in foreign trade had grown from 363,100, in 1791, to 848,300, while exports increased nearly fourfold in the same years and imports grew by 75 percent.[6] Particularly profitable was the carrying of goods between France and Spain and between the French and Spanish Caribbean colonies where they were normally excluded, since the British navy kept French and Spanish ships in port. American ship owners had circumvented the British rule of 1756 by the device of the "broken voyage," where, for example, an American ship would take on a cargo of sugar at the French island of Martinique and proceed to an American port. The ship, with sugar listed as an import but not unloaded, would receive new papers claiming the sugar as a U.S. export, and the vessel would proceed to a French port. Although neither segment of the voyage alone was forbidden by the rule of 1756, British Admiralty courts in 1805 began to challenge the reexport trade. The American merchantman *Essex* had been captured en route from Barcelona to Havana, having "broken" the voyage in Salem, Massachusetts. The British Admiralty asserted, quite rightly, that the *Essex* had not paid bona fide duties on its cargo in Salem and labeled the voyage "continuous" and prohibited by the rule of 1756. The *Essex* decision shifted the burden of proof to American shippers, now required to prove importation of enemy goods. British ships patrolling outside American ports ready to seize suspicious vessels were essentially blockading the coast.

Congress retaliated with an April 18, 1806, act prohibiting the importation of certain English manufactures, but temporarily suspended its enforcement. Jefferson sent William Pinkney to assist James Monroe, the U.S. minister in London, to settle the complex of issues involving neutral rights—blockade, contraband, the rule of 1756, the continuous voyage interpretation, and impressment. Monroe and Pinkney gained a relaxation of the rule of 1756 and the doctrine of continuous voyage, but little else. Regarding impressment, the British yielded only a promise to remedy its abuses.[7] Jefferson refused to forward the treaty Monroe and Pinkney signed on December 31 to the Senate. He instructed the envoys to add a provision limiting impressment, but Monroe and Pinkney were unsuccessful. In the meantime, the British followed the *Essex* decision with the Order-in-Council of May 16, 1806, which declared a complete blockade of Napoleonic Europe from Brest to the Elbe. As historian Marshall Smelser has observed, "paper blockades is a game that any number can play," and Napoleon, "fleetless but well-supplied with parchment and sealing wax," responded with his "Continental System."[8] Napoleon's Berlin and Milan decrees of November 21 and December 17, respectively, sought to bar British trade with continental Europe. Neutral ships that had called at British ports or submitted to search by British naval vessels were declared liable to confiscation. The British retaliated with two more Orders-in-Council, on January 7 and November 11, 1807, which forbade trade with France, its Europe allies, and colonies, and threatened confiscation of neutral vessels; but these ships might visit enemy ports if they first put in at British ports and paid duties on their merchandise. Britain's blockade was essentially designed to compel neutral vessels to pay tribute to Great Britain.

The combination of decrees and Orders-in-Council, in American eyes, constituted illegal "paper blockades," placing neutral shipping in a precarious situation. The measures, at least in theory, combined to outlaw American trade with the two empires. If an American sea captain obeyed the British orders, visiting an English port on the way to the continent, he exposed his vessel and cargo to French confiscation. If he conformed to the French decrees by avoiding contact with British ships or ports, he risked British confiscation.

Jefferson's "Peaceable Coercion"

In the wake of the 1807 *Chesapeake* affair, Jefferson wrote, "Never since the battle of Lexington, have I seen this country in such a state of exasperation as at present."[9] Unwilling to submit to the "paper blockades" and other—in American eyes—illegal infringements on American maritime rights, Jefferson was equally unwilling to go to war to defend those rights. Persuaded that American trade was vital to both France and Britain, he believed that excluding them from it could coerce them into respecting American rights. Jefferson had no real alternative to economic measures, for he recognized that the country lacked the naval and military muscle, due in part to his economic policies, to wage war.

On December 22, 1807, Congress passed the Embargo Act prohibiting the export of American goods, allowing American ships to engage only in coastal trade. When the embargo, which affected the American economy harshly, produced no change in French or British policy, it was replaced by milder measures.[10] Macon's Bill No. 2 of May 1, 1810, suggested by President James Madison, opened American ports to the commercial vessels of all nations, but provided should either England or France revoke its decrees that infringed American neutral rights, and the other belligerent failed to do likewise within three months, ships and trade of the latter would be barred from American ports. Napoleon promptly announced that the Berlin and Milan decrees, insofar as they affected American ships, would be terminated on November 1, 1810.[11] In reality, Napoleon continued to enforce the decrees against American ships; but on February 2, 1811, Madison accepted French promises as genuine and reimposed nonimportation restrictions on Great Britain.[12] London refused to revoke or modify the Orders-in-Council. The new secretary of state, James Monroe insisted that the repeal of the French decrees was genuine and demanded that England revoke its Orders-in-Council. London denied that the French decrees were really repealed and demanded that the United States give up its nonimportation policy against Great Britain.

Madison called Congress to meet in November. He complained of the unfriendly conduct of both belligerents, but reserved his ire for the British, whose practices "have the character as well as the effect of war on our lawful commerce." To resist their "hostile inflexibility in trampling on rights which no independent nation can relinquish," he asked Congress to put the United States "into an armor and an attitude demanded by the crisis."[13]

Drifting into War

This Congress failed to do, even under the whiplash of the "war hawks," a group of newly elected young representatives, most of them from western and southern states. Outstanding among them were Henry Clay of Kentucky—elected Speaker in his first session in the House—John C. Calhoun of South Carolina, John A. Harper of New Hampshire, and Peter B. Porter of western New York. They were infuriated at seeing their country mistreated year after year; such insults and injuries, they argued, must be avenged by force of arms.[14] To most war hawks, the British interference with American seaborne trade touched the pocketbook, since they were blamed for a serious decline in the prices of western products, as well as national honor. The war hawks also blamed British agents in Canada for an epidemic of Indian hostilities in the Northwest. Under the able Shawnee chieftain, Tecumseh, Indians from the Ohio River to the Mississippi had united to resist the surrender of further Indian lands. Sporadic attacks on frontier settlers were followed by a dramatic clash between Indians and General William Henry Harrison's forces near Tippecanoe Creek in Indiana, on November 7, 1811.[15] The British were known to be friendly to Tecumseh and his plans, and when British arms were found among weapons left by the Indians at Tippecanoe, many westerners were convinced that expulsion of the British from Canada was essential to peace with the Indians in the Northwest.

While for expansionists the conquest of Canada became a secondary motive for war with England, the overwhelming motive for striking Canada was the simple fact that this was the only way the United States could mount an offensive against the British enemy. As Secretary of State James Monroe observed in June 1812, "it might be necessary to invade Canada, not as an object of the war but as a means to bring it to a satisfactory conclusion."[16] As Bradford Perkins has described the causes of the War of 1812, the British Orders-in-Council were "the central structure"; others—impressments, Indian troubles, expansionist ambitions—were mere "flying buttresses."[17] It was ironic, therefore, that the central structure was being dismantled at the very time Congress declared war.

Urged on by the war hawks and by Madison, who sent in a final war message on June 1, 1812, Congress finally declared war on June 18 with large opposing minorities in both houses (79 to 49 in the House, and 19 to 13 in the Senate). Two days earlier the British government had announced its intention to repeal the Orders-in-Council, taking effect on June 23.[18] British merchants and manufacturers had been hard hit by the loss of the American market; consequently, the British expected this concession to prevent war, but the news of repeal reached America weeks after war had begun.

An Indecisive War

The War of 1812 began on June 18 and ended with the Treaty of Ghent, signed on Christmas Eve, 1814. Inadequate preparation, incompetent administrative and military leadership, and internal dissensions resulted in the United States' failure to achieve any maritime concessions or territorial gains. Though Congress had authorized a Regular Army of 35,000 men, fewer than 10,000 had been raised, mostly raw recruits, when the war began. The state militias were little better, poorly trained with incompetent officers. Senior officers, commanding the Regular Army at the beginning of the war, were, without exception, unfit. Not surprisingly, early attempts to invade and conquer Canada resulted in dismal failures. By the summer of 1814, when able officers—notably Generals Jacob Brown and Winfield Scott—had trained their little army, the opportunity for conquering Canada had vanished. With Napoleon at Elba and Wellington's veterans arriving in Canada, the problem became how to defend the United States. Meanwhile, two attempts to empower the president to take possession of East Florida were defeated in the Senate by Federalists, who opposed the war in toto, and northern Republicans, who disliked the administration's Florida policy. Mobile was occupied, but the United States had long claimed it as part of Louisiana.

On the high seas, the United States had some 17 warships in 1812, none first-class, to oppose the British navy's thousand ships. Despite a few brilliant victories in single-ship actions, before the fighting ended, virtually the entire American navy had been either captured or bottled up in port. American commerce was excluded from the seas by a tight blockade. The American naval victories that counted most took place on Lake Erie and Lake Champlain. The former, on September 10, 1813, enabled the United States to recover Detroit, lost in the first weeks of the war, but did not prevent British occupation of most of Michigan and the Wisconsin-Minnesota area. The latter, on September 11, 1814, turned back a British army intent on invading New York.[19]

The United States was fortunate in being able—except around Lake Michigan and the upper Mississippi—to defend its own territory. British forces—having burned the public buildings in Washington—were repulsed before Baltimore. It was at New Orleans, two weeks after the signing of the peace treaty, that Andrew Jackson inflicted on a British force the most crushing defeat of the war. While having no impact on the peace, that victory helped Americans believe they had won the war.[20]

The Treaty of Ghent

The defensive character that the war had assumed was evident in the final instructions to the American peace commissioners, who opened negotiations with the British at Ghent in August 1814. Earlier drafts had proposed elimination of impressment as an indispensable condition of peace and expressed a hope for a definition of legal blockade and abandonment of the rule of 1756. Indeed, Monroe's instructions of April 15, 1813, said of impressment: "If this encroachment of Great Britain is not provided against, the United States will have appealed to arms in vain. If your efforts to accomplish it should fail, all further negotiations will cease, and you will return home without delay."[21] By the summer of 1814, military failures and Napoleon's defeat had so weakened the American bargaining position that all previous conditions were dropped, and the commissioners were told to ask only a return to the status quo ante bellum. The British commissioners had come to Ghent with ambitious demands—cessions of territory in Maine, New York, and between Lake Superior and the Mississippi, and the creation of a permanent Indian buffer state embracing all or part of the present-day states of Indiana, Illinois, Ohio, Michigan, and Wisconsin.[22] The Americans immediately rejected these demands, and, with news of the American victories at Lake Champlain and Baltimore, British commissioners hesitated. The Duke of Wellington, Napoleon's conqueror, advised the British government to accept the American terms, unless it was prepared for an expensive prolongation of the war in America. The British accepted the American terms. The treaty, signed December 24, 1814, provided for restoration of all territory that had been occupied by the forces of either party. Britain's Indian allies that were still at war were to recover their land holdings of 1811. Finally, joint commissions were to settle certain boundary disputes between the United States and Canada. The United States had won not a single concession in the matter of maritime rights, not a foot of Canadian soil. Yet the treaty was greeted joyously by the American public and on February 16, 1815, was unanimously approved by the U.S. Senate.

The Treaty of Ghent did not register all the results of the war, and an awareness of some of the unregistered results may partly explain its satisfactory reception. In the Northwest, the Indian menace that had contributed to the war fever was removed or greatly reduced.[23] British support of the Indians ceased, and there was no further serious trouble in acquiring or settling Indian lands. In the South, the powerful Creek confederacy, perhaps under British influence, had gone on the warpath in 1813. Its power was broken by Andrew Jackson's Tennessee troops at Horseshoe Bend, March 27, 1814, and the Creek chieftains ceded some 23 million acres in southern Georgia and the future state of Alabama.[24] Indirectly, Indian troubles growing out of Jackson's treaty with the Creeks were to lead to the acquisition of the remainder of Florida in 1819. But the war did nothing to establish the American position on neutral maritime rights. An attempt by Secretary of State John Quincy Adams, in 1823, to secure international acceptance of a comprehensive code for the regulation of maritime war was abandoned when the British government refused to discuss the impressment issue. The Declaration of Paris of 1856, however, embodied most of the principles for which the United States had long contended.[25]

In a larger sense, however, the War of 1812 represented a kind of second war for American independence. Bradford Perkins summarized contemporary American interpretations of the nature and circumstances of the Treaty of Ghent: "Seldom has a nation so successfully practiced self-induced amnesia!"[26] While doubtless biased, Henry Clay argued that the war had delivered "respectability and character abroad [and] security and confidence at home," and had served to place the American character and constitution on "a solid basis, never to be shaken." Just as the British bombing of Fort McHenry, in 1814, would give the United States its national anthem, so too did the war reinforce national unity, identity, and confidence. Henry Adams later wrote: "In 1815, for the first time the Americans ceased to doubt the path they were to follow. Not only was the unity of the nation established, but its probable divergence from older societies was also well defined."[27] The overwhelming failures during the war and the limits of American power were quickly forgotten.

Demilitarization and Arbitration

One of the earliest American diplomatic achievements was an agreement with Great Britain, in 1817, to dismantle much of the existing naval forces on the Great Lakes and Lake Champlain. When hostilities ended, the two governments were engaged in a costly competition for naval supremacy on Lake Ontario. Negotiations in London and Washington terminated in an exchange of notes on April 28 and 29, 1817, between Richard Rush, acting secretary of state, and Charles Bagot, British minister in Washington. This agreement limited each nation on the lakes to naval vessels not exceeding 100 tons in burden nor carrying more than one 18-pound gun each.[28] Of these, each party should maintain not more than one on Lake Champlain, one on Lake Ontario, and two on the upper lakes. Either government might terminate the agreement by giving six months' notice.

The Rush-Bagot agreement, subject to some technical violations and occasional modifications or interpretations, has continued in effect to the present day. The common belief that the agreement created an "unguarded frontier" is, however, without justification. Not for over half a century did Anglo-American peace seem sufficiently secure to warrant either party's disarming the frontier. The existing naval forces on the lakes were dismantled but not destroyed, and navy yards were maintained for several years. Land fortifications were maintained and were strengthened at times of Anglo-American crises. Not until 1871 did the two governments by tacit consent gradually permit their land fortifications to decay. The "unguarded frontier" dates from 1871, not 1817.[29]

No feature of Anglo-American relations in the nineteenth century was more striking than that there were better methods than war for settling disputes between the two countries. The Jay Treaty of 1794 had provided for arbitration of four controversies: (1) the identity of the St. Croix River, designated as the boundary between Maine and Nova Scotia; (2) the amount of debts to be paid by the United States to British creditors that they had been unable to collect by reason of "lawful impediments" imposed by the states; (3) the compensation to be paid by Great Britain to American claimants for illegal seizures of vessels and other property in the Anglo-French war; and (4) the compensation to be paid by the United States to British claimants for losses resulting from violations of American neutrality by French armed vessels. Arbitration by mixed commissions adjudicated all of these controversies except the second, which in the end was settled by negotiation.

The Treaty of Ghent provided for arbitration of four boundary controversies between the United States and British Canada, embracing certain islands off the coast of Maine and the overland boundary from the head of the St. Croix (Schoodiac) River to the Lake of the Woods. Possession of the islands and the fixing of the boundary line through the St. Lawrence River and other waters to the head of Lake Huron presented no great difficulty. On the segments of the boundary from the St. Croix to the St. Lawrence and from Lake Huron to the Lake of the Woods, agreement at this time proved impossible. The line from Lake Huron to the Lake of the Woods and the line from the St. Croix to the St. Lawrence were finally settled in the Webster-Ashburton Treaty of 1842.[30]

The Northern Boundary and Oregon

The Treaty of Ghent made no provision for determining the boundary between the Lake of the Woods and the Rocky Mountains or for adjusting conflicting British and American claims to the Pacific coast region coming to be known as Oregon. The 1783 treaty had described the boundary line as running from the northwesternmost point of the Lake of the Woods due west to the Mississippi (impossible since the Mississippi rose far to the south of the Lake of the Woods), and no northern boundary had been agreed on when the United States acquired Louisiana. The American commissioners at Ghent proposed a northern boundary at the 49th parallel but dropped it when the British insisted on access to the upper Mississippi and free navigation of that river.

Also still unsettled were conflicting American and British, not to mention Spanish and Russian, claims to the Oregon country. To American claims founded on the discovery and naming of the Columbia River, in 1792, by Captain Robert Gray of Boston and the explorations of Lewis and Clark (1804–1806), there was another one based on actual settlement. In May 1811, agents of the fur merchant John Jacob Astor established a short-lived fort and trading post, named Astoria, at the mouth of the Columbia. Fearing that the post and stores might be captured by the British, they sold out, in October 1813, to the North West Company of Montreal. Two months later the commander of the British sloop of war the *Raccoon* took formal possession of the fort and surrounding country in the name of the British King and renamed the post Fort George.[31]

The injection of military conquest into what had hitherto been a commercial transaction gave the United States ground for claiming that Astoria should be restored to the United States under the terms of the Treaty of Ghent. The British government did not contest the claim, and, on October 6, 1818, the British flag was lowered and the stars and stripes raised over Fort George. The British foreign secretary, Lord Castlereagh, emphasized that he was not recognizing the American claim to sovereignty at the mouth of the Columbia; he was merely acknowledging that that claim had as much, or as little, force in 1818 as it had had in 1813. It became apparent, however, that the British were willing to concede priority of rights south of the Columbia. Just two weeks after the "restoration" of Astoria, Richard Rush and Albert Gallatin, American commissioners in London, signed a treaty fixing the boundary line along the 49th parallel, from the Lake of the Woods to the Rockies and establishing a temporary *modus vivendi* for the Oregon country.[32] When the

Americans proposed extending the same line to the Pacific, the British offered instead the Columbia River from its mouth to its intersection with the 49th parallel, with the river and the harbor at its mouth open to both British and American shipping. When negotiations stalemated, it was agreed that all territory on the northwest coast claimed by either Great Britain or the United States should be equally open during a 10-year period to the two powers' vessels, citizens, and subjects, without prejudice to the claims of Spain and Russia. This arrangement—the so-called joint occupation—was embodied, with the boundary east of the Rocky Mountains, in the treaty signed on October 20, 1818.

The Convention of 1818 settled another question of considerable importance, especially to New England. The treaty of 1783 had granted to Americans the "liberty" of inshore fishing along the coasts of British North America, but British officials claimed the War of 1812 canceled this "liberty." In return for the perpetual "liberty" to take fish inside the three-mile limit on the west coast and part of the south coast of Newfoundland, on the coast of Labrador, and in the waters about the Magdalen Islands, the United States renounced its claim to the inshore fisheries along all other parts of the coasts. American fishermen were allowed to land and cure their fish in the unsettled bays and harbors of Labrador and that portion of the south coast of Newfoundland where inshore fishing was permitted. With the signing of the Convention of 1818 and the creation of Ghent's arbitration commissions, there was an easing in Anglo-American tensions. But the West Indies trade problem had not been solved, the Oregon controversy had been merely postponed, and two questions that had been submitted to the arbitral process—the northeast boundary and the Lake Superior-Lake of the Woods boundary questions—had proved intractable.

The Transcontinental Treaty with Spain

While in London, Gallatin and Rush were fixing the northern boundary of Louisiana and sparring with the British over Oregon, and in Washington, John Quincy Adams was settling long-standing controversies with Spain. Spain had never accepted the American claim to the Perdido River as the eastern boundary of Louisiana, and American occupation of this area during the War of 1812 had been without Spain's consent. The United States desired an acknowledgment of its title to this area; it wished also to acquire Florida east of the Perdido. The western boundary of Louisiana had never been defined; nevertheless, with little justification, Washington claimed all land to the Rio Grande. Spain placed the boundary well to the eastward of the Sabine, leaving Texas and part of the state of Louisiana in dispute. Added to the boundary controversies were certain damage claims that each country held against the other. The United States claimed compensation for allegedly unneutral conduct by Spain during American hostilities with France, in 1798–1800, and for damages suffered by American commerce from the withdrawal of the right of deposit at New Orleans in 1802. Spain claimed damages for American incursions into Florida before and during the War of 1812 and for hospitality accorded in United States ports to privateers sailing under the flags of Spain's revolting colonies. The United States ignored Spain's damage claims and wanted all of Florida, East and West, to satisfy its own. Adams and Spanish minister Don Luis de Onis's discussions about the boundary and damage claims in the spring of 1818 were interrupted by warlike noises from Spanish Florida.

Florida, after the War of 1812, was in a state of near anarchy, with Spanish governors at St. Augustine and Pensacola powerless. Amelia Island, on the Atlantic coast just south of the U.S. border, became a haven for freebooters who claimed to operate under letters of marquee from one or another of Spain's revolting colonies. When one of them claimed East Florida as part of Mexico, President Monroe sent U.S. troops to take possession. Farther west, Creek warriors, fugitives from Jackson's campaign of 1814, had taken refuge with the Florida Seminoles abetted by several British adventurers. When the Creeks forcibly interfered with the surveying and settling of their former lands in Georgia and Mississippi Territory, Washington officials resolved to subdue them, even if that meant pursuing them across the border into Florida—a right the United States claimed under its 1795 treaty with Spain. This task was handed to General Andrew Jackson, commanding a small army of regulars and militia.

Jackson set out not only to chastise the Indians but also to take possession of Florida for the United States. He later claimed to have received a letter of authority from Monroe, through an intermediary; however, Monroe denied this.[33] Jackson seized and occupied the Spanish town and fort of St. Marks, and after burning a hostile Indian town from which the warriors escaped, turned his attention to Pensacola. On the pretext that the Spanish were harboring hostile savages, Jackson took possession of the town and fortifications, deposed the governor, seized the archives, appointed one of his officers as civil and military governor of West Florida, and directed him to enforce the revenue laws of the United States at the port of Pensacola. He also executed—after court-martial— two British subjects, whom he charged with being in conspiracy with the hostile Indians. Reports of Jackson's aggressive actions in Florida, accompanied by strong protests from the Spanish minister Onis, created consternation in the capital. Fortunately, for Jackson, he found a warm supporter in Adams, who wrote to the Minister to Spain George Erving, in November 1818, defending Jackson's actions.[34] Adams, insisting that Jackson's acts must be sustained, justified those actions as necessitated by self-defense. He denounced the unfriendly conduct of West Florida's governor and St. Marks commandant and demanded that those officials instead of Jackson be punished. Pensacola, he said, would be turned over to a proper Spanish official; St. Marks, to a force competent to hold it against Indian attack. In a later note, Adams presented Spain with an ultimatum: either place in Florida a force sufficient for the maintenance of order and the fulfillment of its obligations, or cede the province to the United States.

The Spanish government already had decided to make concessions necessary to reach an understanding with the United States. Failure to gain assurances of support from England, France, or Russia with regard to its troubles in the United States or South America, combined with American threats to recognize South American independence, induced Madrid to give in.[35] In October 1818, the Spanish were willing to cede the Floridas if the United States would agree to a satisfactory western boundary for Louisiana. This was achieved, after months of negotiation, in an agreement by which the United States surrendered whatever claim it had to Texas in exchange for Spanish claims on the Pacific coast, north of California. The "transcontinental treaty," as it has been called, was signed on February 22, 1819. By its terms, the King of Spain ceded to the United States "all the territories which belong to him, situated to the eastward of the Mississippi, known by the name of East and West Florida."[36] Each government renounced its damage claims and those of its citizens or subjects against the other, and the United States agreed to satisfy the claims of its citizens against Spain to an amount not to exceed $5 million.

On the west, the international boundary followed the western bank of the Sabine from the Gulf to the 32nd parallel; thence it ran due north to the southern bank of the Red River, which it followed to the meridian of 100° west longitude, thence to the south bank of the Arkansas and the source of the river; from the source of the Arkansas it ran north to the 42nd parallel, which it followed to the Pacific. Despite the surrender of Texas, the Senate unanimously approved the treaty, and Monroe ratified it on February 25. The Spanish King, Ferdinand VII, however, delayed ratification as a dispute had arisen over the validity of certain Spanish land grants in Florida that, if recognized, would have absorbed all the vacant land in the ceded territory. This difficulty was settled to the satisfaction of the United States, but only over the resistance of influential individuals at the Spanish court. Spain also attempted unsuccessfully to exact from the United States a promise not to recognize the independence of Spain's revolting colonies. Finally, in October 1820, the King ratified the treaty, the Senate again consented, and ratifications were exchanged in Washington on February 22, 1821, two years from the date of signature.[37]

CHAPTER 4

The Monroe Doctrine and Latin American Independence

Wherever the standard of freedom and Independence has been or shall be unfurled, there will her heart, her benedictions and her prayers be. But she [the United States] goes not abroad, in search of monsters to destroy. She is the well-wisher to the freedom and independence of all. She is the champion and vindicator only of her own.... She well knows that by once enlisting under other banners than her own, were they even the banners of foreign independence, she would involve herself beyond the power of extrication, in all the wars of interest and intrigue, of individual avarice, envy, and ambition, which assume the colors and usurp the standard of freedom.
—John Quincy Adams, Speech to House
of Representatives, July 4, 1821

In the wars of the European powers in matters relating to themselves we have never taken any part, nor does it comport with our policy so to do. It is only when our rights are invaded or seriously menaced that we resent injuries or make preparation for our defense.
—President James Monroe, Message
to Congress, December 2, 1823

James Monroe alone has the honor of having his name attached to a sacred national dogma—the Monroe Doctrine. This doctrine stands apart, with few Americans leaders having questioned it, and several having invoked it.[1] In the famous fight over American participation in the League of Nations, for example, opponents denounced such participation as contrary to the Monroe Doctrine, while Woodrow Wilson praised the league as representing a kind of worldwide adoption of the doctrine.[2] The

Monroe Doctrine owes its longtime popularity to the fact that it was the first official pronouncement of a deep-seated American belief—that the Atlantic and Pacific Oceans divide the world such that nations in the New World should be able to insulate themselves from the quarrels, the interferences, and the colonizing ambitions of Old World powers. On the one hand, this belief spelled American neutrality and abstention from European quarrels, while on the other, it spelled exclusion from the Americas of the political interference and the colonizing activity of Europe. The former idea was a cardinal principal of American foreign policy from the outset.[3] The latter idea was set forth in President Monroe's message to Congress of December 2, 1823. The "doctrine" expounded by Monroe was not a spontaneous invention. President Washington had declared in his 1796 Farewell Address: "Europe has a set of primary interests, which to us have none or a very remote relation."[4] Thomas Jefferson, writing in 1813 of the independence movement in Spain's American colonies, observed: "But in whatever government they end, they will be American governments, no longer to be involved in the never-ceasing broils of Europe. The European nations constitute a separate division of the globe: their localities make them a part of a distinct system; they have a set of interests of their own in which it is our business never to engage ourselves. America has a hemisphere to itself. It must have its separate system of interests: which must not be subordinated to those of Europe..."[5]

President Monroe's ideas were similar to those of Washington and Jefferson. He was led to state them by specific situations that confronted the United States in 1823.

After describing recent negotiations with Russia concerning its claims to territory on the Pacific coast of North America, the president said: "In the discussions to which this interest has given rise... the occasion has been judged proper for asserting, as a principle in which the rights and interests of the United States are involved, that the American continents, by the free and independent condition which they have assumed and maintain, are henceforth not to be considered as subjects for future colonization by any European powers."

This statement embodies what is generally called the "noncolonization" principle. Later in the message, after alluding to the recent suppression of liberal movements in Spain and Italy, Monroe stated what has since been called the "noninterference" principle:

> Of events in that quarter of the globe, with which we have so much intercourse and from which we derive our origin, we have always been anxious and interested spectators.... In the wars of the

European powers in matters relating to themselves we have never taken any part, nor does it comport with our policy so to do. It is only when our rights are invaded or seriously menaced that we resent injuries or make preparation for our defense.... *We owe it, therefore, to candor and to the amicable relations existing between the United States and those powers to declare that we should consider any attempt on their part to extend their system to any portion of this hemisphere as dangerous to our peace and safety.* With the existing colonies or dependencies of any European power we have not interfered and shall not interfere.

He went on to warn European nations that the United States supported colonies that had declared their independence and that "we could not view any interposition for the purpose of oppressing them, or controlling in any other manner their destiny." The United States would remain neutral in hostilities between Spain and its rebellious colonies, "provided no change shall occur which, in the judgment of the competent authorities of this Government, shall make a corresponding change on the part of the United States indispensable to their security."[6]

The Origin of Noncolonization

The noncolonization principle was the brainchild of John Quincy Adams, Monroe's secretary of state. Adams distrusted European colonial establishments in the strategic neighborhood of the United States. He disliked the commercial exclusiveness with which colonizing powers surrounded their dependencies, distrusted monarchical neighbors, and desired, according to one authority, to "keep North America open as a preserve for the republic of the United States to expand over at leisure." Thus, noncolonization was "a principle of territorial containment."[7] The timing for declaring the noncolonization principle stemmed from Russian claims on North America's Pacific coast. Russian traders had visited the northwest coast since 1727, but not until 1799 was the Russian American Company chartered, with exclusive trading rights and jurisdiction along the coast as far south as 55° north latitude. The company planted settlements north of that line and, in 1812, established Fort Ross at Bodega Bay a few miles north of San Francisco Bay. The American government was more alarmed by an imperial ukase of September 1821, by which Russia extended its exclusive claims down the coast to 51° and forbade all non-Russian ships to come within 100 miles of the American coast north of that latitude.[8] In discussions with Baron Tuyll, the Russian minister in Washington, Adams stated "agents for seamen and commerce" were sent to the new countries to protect American interests. When the European war ended and Spain sought to recover control of its America colonies, Washington adopted a position of neutrality, allowing colonial vessels to frequent U.S. ports to procure arms and other supplies. Henry Clay, Speaker of the House of Representatives, championed immediate recognition of the new governments. "Let us become real and true Americans, and place ourselves at the head of the American System," he urged and criticized Monroe and Adams for their timidity and subservience in postponing recognition.[13] The president and secretary of state had good reason for hesitation, for the recognition of rebellious subjects often had been a prelude to war. After all, France had recognized America's independence only when ready to go to war with England, and the British government later had seized on an unauthorized draft treaty with the United States as an excuse for attacking the Netherlands. Since Madrid, following the British precedent, might regard recognition as an act of war, the United States had no desire to be dragged into a war with Spain, and possibly the Quadruple Alliance, on behalf of the breakaway colonies.

Under what conditions, then, could recognition be granted to a state that had established itself by revolution without giving just offense to the parent state? As International law had as yet no clear answer to that question; officials in Washington had to devise their own formula. Jefferson had argued the thesis in 1792, during the French Revolution, that "It accords with our principles to acknolege [sic] any government to be rightful which is formed by the will of the nation substantially declared."[14] On another occasion he declared: "The only thing essential is the will of the nation."[15] But how was "the will of the nation" to be ascertained? Henry Clay, in 1818, offered a more practical test for recognition. "We have constantly proceeded on the principle," he said, "that the government de facto is that which we could alone notice.... But as soon as stability and order were maintained, no matter by whom, we always had considered and ought to consider the actual as the true government."[16] If Clay came close to stating what would become the standard American doctrine of recognition, Adams added important qualifications. The government of a state or a colony in rebellion might properly be recognized, he said, "when independence is established as a matter of fact so as to leave the chance of the opposite party to recover their dominion utterly desperate."[17] He also insisted on certain standards of behavior by the new authorities: they must carry out their responsibilities and duties as members of the international community. Complaining of the lawless acts by privateers carrying letters of marque from the unrecognized Latin American governments, Adams wrote that they "cannot

European powers in matters relating to themselves we have never taken any part, nor does it comport with our policy so to do. It is only when our rights are invaded or seriously menaced that we resent injuries or make preparation for our defense.... *We owe it, therefore, to candor and to the amicable relations existing between the United States and those powers to declare that we should consider any attempt on their part to extend their system to any portion of this hemisphere as dangerous to our peace and safety.* With the existing colonies or dependencies of any European power we have not interfered and shall not interfere.

He went on to warn European nations that the United States supported colonies that had declared their independence and that "we could not view any interposition for the purpose of oppressing them, or controlling in any other manner their destiny." The United States would remain neutral in hostilities between Spain and its rebellious colonies, "provided no change shall occur which, in the judgment of the competent authorities of this Government, shall make a corresponding change on the part of the United States indispensable to their security."[6]

The Origin of Noncolonization

The noncolonization principle was the brainchild of John Quincy Adams, Monroe's secretary of state. Adams distrusted European colonial establishments in the strategic neighborhood of the United States. He disliked the commercial exclusiveness with which colonizing powers surrounded their dependencies, distrusted monarchical neighbors, and desired, according to one authority, to "keep North America open as a preserve for the republic of the United States to expand over at leisure." Thus, noncolonization was "a principle of territorial containment."[7] The timing for declaring the noncolonization principle stemmed from Russian claims on North America's Pacific coast. Russian traders had visited the northwest coast since 1727, but not until 1799 was the Russian American Company chartered, with exclusive trading rights and jurisdiction along the coast as far south as 55° north latitude. The company planted settlements north of that line and, in 1812, established Fort Ross at Bodega Bay a few miles north of San Francisco Bay. The American government was more alarmed by an imperial ukase of September 1821, by which Russia extended its exclusive claims down the coast to 51° and forbade all non-Russian ships to come within 100 miles of the American coast north of that latitude.[8] In discussions with Baron Tuyll, the Russian minister in Washington, Adams stated the idea that he had been considering for several years. The United States, he told Tuyll in July 1823, would not only "contest the right of Russia to any territorial establishment on this continent," but would "assume distinctly the principle that the American continents are no longer subjects for any new European colonial establishments."[9] A few days later he embodied the idea in instructions sent to U.S. ministers Richard Rush in London and Henry Middleton in St. Petersburg. Adams supplied Monroe with virtually the exact language as his statement to Tuyll, and it became an integral part of the Monroe Doctrine.

The declaration of the noncolonization principle was likely aimed less at Russia than Great Britain, whose rivalry in territorial expansion Adams feared more.[10] An active candidate for the presidency in 1824, Adams may have been twisting the British lion's tail for political purposes. Political enemies were charging him with having betrayed American, and particularly western interests to Great Britain and Spain in the treaties of 1818 and 1819. A forthright statement forbidding further European colonization in "the American continents" would perhaps silence such criticism.

Actually, neither Adams nor the United States had any right to veto further colonial enterprises in unoccupied and unexplored territories. Two years earlier, he had told the British minister that Great Britain had no right to the northwest coast, and his cabinet colleagues restrained him from telling Tuyll that Russia had no right to any territory in North America. Yet in the treaty of 1818, he had essentially acknowledged British equality with American rights in the Oregon country; he was willing in 1824 and later to divide that region with the British at the 49th parallel. In 1824 he would accept the Russian claim to exclusive sovereignty north of 54°40'. Thus, Adams did not feel bound by the noncolonization principle, and no European government ever recognized it. "There is room to doubt its wisdom as a diplomatic move," noted Dexter Perkins, "and a harsh critic might even go so far as to describe it as a barren gesture."[11]

The Origin of Noninterference

The second fundamental principle of the doctrine—U.S. opposition to European interference with the independent nations of the New World—has a more complicated origin. At the time, it was America's answer to a British proposal for a joint Anglo-American declaration of noninterference. The circumstances that produced the British proposal resulted from two different series of events, in Europe and in America. After the overthrow of Napoleon in 1815, Europe was guided for years by an alliance of

Russia, Prussia, Austria, and Great Britain. At Vienna in 1815, the four jointly agreed to prevent France from again promoting "revolutionary principles" and to consider measures that might prove "most salutary for the repose and prosperity of Nations and for the maintenance of the Peace of Europe." Members of the Quadruple Alliance found the liberal spirit, suppressed by the Vienna settlement, revived in revolutions involving the kingdoms of Naples, Piedmont, and Spain that compelled their sovereigns to accept constitutions limiting their prerogatives. In 1820 and 1821, the Quadruple Alliance, under the leadership of Prince Metternich, Austrian foreign minister and chancellor, commissioned Austria to send troops into Italy to suppress the uprisings there. In 1822, the alliance sent French armies into Spain to overturn the 1820 liberal constitution and restore Ferdinand VII as an absolute monarch. During these actions, the composition of the Quadruple Alliance underwent change. If France's restored Bourbon sovereign, Louis XVIII, had employed its armies to enforce the alliance's aims, the conservative British government had objected repeatedly to the armed interventions in Italy and Spain. Having restored Ferdinand to power in Spain, continental statesmen also talked of restoring his authority in Spain's former American colonies. England again objected and sought U.S. cooperation.[12]

The Spanish colonies that Ferdinand would like to have recovered had been establishing their independence since 1810, as Napoleon's attempt in 1808 to put a French king on the Spanish throne had absolved them of allegiance to the monarchy. Ferdinand's restoration failed to tempt them back, and, by 1822, Spanish rule had been effectively overthrown in all the mainland colonies from Mexico to Argentina and Chile. The elimination of Spain's trade monopoly with new states had been economically beneficial to Britain and, to a minor extent, to the United States. Neither wished to see Spanish rule restored, and both frowned on the intervention rumor. Also, Britain feared that because of Spain's weakness, France might appropriate some of the colonies for itself, while Americans felt a natural sympathy for colonial populations who had won their independence and resented any attempt to restore the despotic rule of Spain.

Recognizing Spain's Rebellious Colonies

The United States recognized the independence of Colombia, Mexico, the United Provinces of Rio de la Plata (Argentina), and Chile, and other recognitions followed in due course. Recognition, however, had come only after a period of watchful waiting. At first, emissaries of the new governments were cordially, though unofficially, received in Washington, and "agents for seamen and commerce" were sent to the new countries to protect American interests. When the European war ended and Spain sought to recover control of its America colonies, Washington adopted a position of neutrality, allowing colonial vessels to frequent U.S. ports to procure arms and other supplies. Henry Clay, Speaker of the House of Representatives, championed immediate recognition of the new governments. "Let us become real and true Americans, and place ourselves at the head of the American System," he urged and criticized Monroe and Adams for their timidity and subservience in postponing recognition.[13] The president and secretary of state had good reason for hesitation, for the recognition of rebellious subjects often had been a prelude to war. After all, France had recognized America's independence only when ready to go to war with England, and the British government later had seized on an unauthorized draft treaty with the United States as an excuse for attacking the Netherlands. Since Madrid, following the British precedent, might regard recognition as an act of war, the United States had no desire to be dragged into a war with Spain, and possibly the Quadruple Alliance, on behalf of the breakaway colonies.

Under what conditions, then, could recognition be granted to a state that had established itself by revolution without giving just offense to the parent state? As International law had as yet no clear answer to that question; officials in Washington had to devise their own formula. Jefferson had argued the thesis in 1792, during the French Revolution, that "It accords with our principles to acknolege [sic] any government to be rightful which is formed by the will of the nation substantially declared."[14] On another occasion he declared: "The only thing essential is the will of the nation."[15] But how was "the will of the nation" to be ascertained? Henry Clay, in 1818, offered a more practical test for recognition. "We have constantly proceeded on the principle," he said, "that the government de facto is that which we could alone notice.... But as soon as stability and order were maintained, no matter by whom, we always had considered and ought to consider the actual as the true government."[16] If Clay came close to stating what would become the standard American doctrine of recognition, Adams added important qualifications. The government of a state or a colony in rebellion might properly be recognized, he said, "when independence is established as a matter of fact so as to leave the chance of the opposite party to recover their dominion utterly desperate."[17] He also insisted on certain standards of behavior by the new authorities: they must carry out their responsibilities and duties as members of the international community. Complaining of the lawless acts by privateers carrying letters of marque from the unrecognized Latin American governments, Adams wrote that they "cannot claim the rights & prerogatives of independent States, without conforming to the duties by which independent States are bound."[18]

In these discussions, brought on by the Latin American wars of independence, can be found the principles of the basic U.S. recognition policy. A government that has come to power by revolution (whether in an old or a new state) may properly be recognized when it: (1) is effectively exercising the powers of government; (2) shows promise of stability; and (3) shows willingness and ability to carry out its international obligations. The problem for Monroe and Adams was to ascertain, first, whether these requirements were met by the new Latin American governments and, second, whether Spain and its European allies would take an act of recognition as an excuse for hostile action against the United States. In 1817, when Clay began his campaign for recognition, victory for the revolutionists was still uncertain, and the quality of the new governments was open to doubt. Commissioners sent by President Monroe to Buenos Aires and elsewhere in South America disagreed as to whether the current status of various governments justified recognition. When Adams asked Britain, France, and Russia whether they would join the United States in recognizing the new governments, their responses were negative. In Washington, officials thought it best to postpone action until the new governments could provide better evidence of permanence and stability.

By 1822, victories over Spanish forces in South America had made it obvious that Spain, unaided, could never restore its rule. The emancipated colonies were making encouraging progress toward orderly government, and it seemed unlikely that recognition would lead to war. Monroe and Adams thought it appropriate to recognize the new governments to the south without approval of the European powers. A special message of March 8, 1822, conveyed that opinion to Congress, which authorized and funded diplomatic missions to such of the American nations as the president might deem proper. By the end of January 1823, accordingly, the United States had entered into formal diplomatic relations with Colombia (including also Ecuador and Venezuela), Mexico, Chile, and the United Provinces of Rio de la Plata.

Canning and Monroe Warn the European Allies

Meanwhile, in August 1823, reports reached George Canning, the British foreign secretary, that when France had completed its intervention in Spain, the alliance would probably discuss how to deal with the question of rebellious Spanish America. Canning had already, in the preceding March, warned France that Britain would oppose any attempt to appropriate any of the Spanish colonies. He now suggested to Richard Rush, the American minister in London, that the British and American governments signify—either by signing a convention or by an exchange of notes—their disapproval of any attempt by the European powers to restore the rule of Spain to its lost colonies. Great Britain, he said, subscribed to the following principles, which he believed to be also accepted by the United States:

1. We conceive the recovery of the Colonies by Spain to be hopeless.
2. We conceive the question of the recognition of them, as Independent States, to be one of time and circumstances.
3. We are, however, by no means disposed to throw any impediment in the way of an arrangement between them, and the mother country by amicable negotiations.
4. We aim not at the possession of any portion of them ourselves.
5. We could not see any portion of them transferred to any other Power, with indifference.

If any European power, Canning added, contemplated the forcible subjugation of the former colonies on behalf of Spain or the acquisition of any of them for itself, a joint declaration by Great Britain and the United States of the principles indicated "would be at once the most effectual and the least offensive mode of intimating our joint disapprobation of such projects."[19] Since Britain, with its unchallenged control of the seas, would have been able to prevent any attempt by the continental powers to restore Spanish rule in America, why should Canning have sought the cooperation of the United States? Scholars have suggested several reasons for Canning's proposal. The United States' acceptance of Canning's fourth principle would be viewed in London as a disclaimer of any American intent to acquire Cuba. It also has been conjectured that Canning hoped, through courting American cooperation, to secure a continuance of a tariff-free American market for British textiles and ironware—a hope, however, that was rebuffed in protectionist proposals contained in Monroe's famous message.[20]

Rush had no instructions that would have empowered him to join with Canning in any such proposal. He was, nevertheless, greatly attracted by it. If he could have secured from Canning an immediate recognition of the independence of the Spanish American states, he was prepared to state on behalf of the United States that it would "not remain inactive under an attack upon the independence of those states by the Holy [Quadruple] Alliance,"[21] leaving it for Washington to disavow his action if it saw fit.

Canning, backed by the prime minister, Lord Liverpool, but opposed by other cabinet members and the king, was not ready to risk recognition.[22] Nor was Rush willing to accept a mere promise of future recognition; therefore, he could only report the discussions to Washington and await instructions.

Adams was at home in Quincy, Massachusetts, when Rush's account of his discussions with Canning reached Washington. Monroe sought the advice of the two living ex-presidents, Jefferson and Madison. Should the United States join with Great Britain in the proposed declaration? Both elder statesmen answered affirmatively. Madison even proposed that the "avowed disapprobation" be extended to cover the French intervention in Spain and that the two governments issue also a declaration in behalf of the Greeks, then engaged in their war for independence against Turkey.

But in November, when Monroe's cabinet discussed Canning's proposal, Adams now opposed joint action with Great Britain. "It would be more candid, as well as more dignified," he argued, "to avow our principles explicitly to Russia and France, than to come in as a cock-boat in the wake of the British man-of-war."[23] Adams prevailed and Rush was instructed to decline Canning's proposal for a joint declaration, though at the same time assuring the foreign secretary that the United States accepted all of his stated principles except the second, which left the question of recognition to "time and circumstances." On this point, Adams said, "we considered that the people of these emancipated Colonies, were, of right independent of all other nations, and that it was our duty so to acknowledge them." He added, on behalf of the United States, "that we could not see with indifference, any attempt by one or more powers of Europe to restore those new states to the crown of Spain, or to deprive them, in any manner, whatever of the freedom and independence which they have acquired."[24]

The note did not close the door to the possibility of a joint declaration,[25] should an emergency make it expedient, but the decision on such a declaration was reserved to the Washington authorities. They would, said Adams, "according to the principles of our Government, and in the forms prescribed by our Constitution, cheerfully join in any act by which we may contribute to support the cause of human freedom, and the Independence of the South American Nations."

It was President Monroe who proposed that the American position be announced to the whole world through a presidential message instead of being buried in diplomatic correspondence. The notes for his annual message, which he read to his cabinet, included not only a vigorous statement of the noninterference principle, they also expressed disapproval of the French intervention in Spain and sympathy with the Greek revolt. To these latter expressions Adams objected. "The ground I wish to take," he said, "is that of earnest remonstrance against the interference of European powers by force in South America, but to disclaim all interference on our part in Europe; to make an American cause, and adhere inflexibly to that."[26] The president yielded. The message, while branding European intervention in the New World as "dangerous to our peace and safety" and as "the manifestation of an unfriendly disposition toward the United States," likewise the United States disclaimed taking of any part "in the wars of the European powers in matters relating to themselves." This last phrase left the door open for American participation in the wars of Europe, should such wars seriously menace American rights or American security. When this passage was written, the Treaty of Ghent was less than eight years old. Monroe, who had been secretary of state and, for a short time, secretary of war during the War of 1812, had not forgotten that European powers engaged in conflicts that were not always concerned solely with "matters relating to themselves."

Reception of the Doctrine

To James Monroe and the members of his cabinet, who concurred in the content and phraseology of his message to Congress of December 2, 1823, the threat of European intervention in America was real—to all, that is, except Adams, who remained unpersuaded. The British warnings had been reinforced by a communication from the Russian foreign office, exulting over the successes of the Quadruple Alliance in Europe and declaring it to be the czar's policy to guarantee "the tranquility of all the states of which the civilized world is composed." This expression, the Russian minister informed Adams, related to "the supremacy of Spain over the revolted colonies." The warning against intervention was therefore appropriate. For a young and weak nation to challenge four major powers of continental Europe appeared audacious, but Monroe was not bluffing; he had an ace in the hole, the British navy. For while there was no agreement, not even an "understanding," with Britain, Canning had revealed enough to Rush to assure Monroe that London also would oppose armed intervention in the Americas.

What neither Monroe nor Adams knew was that Canning had already served an ultimatum on France and received a satisfactory response. Discouraged by Rush's insistence on conditions that he was unwilling to meet, Canning had approached the Prince de Polignac, the French ambassador in London, and in a series of discussions during October had received assurances that France had no intention or desire to appropriate any of the Spanish possessions in America, nor "any design of acting against the Colonies by force of arms."[27] With the substance of these assurances embodied in a memorandum, Canning had lost interest in obtaining cooperation from the United States. He no longer needed it to secure British objectives, but he dropped the matter with an abruptness that shook American confidence in his good faith. After the secret Canning-Polignac conversations, there was no danger that the Quadruple Alliance powers would intervene by force in Latin America, if, indeed, any such danger had ever existed. None of the four governments involved—French, Russian, Austrian, and Prussian—had any real plan for the use of force against Spain's former colonies, and Prince Metternich, most influential of Quadruple Alliance statesmen, was realist enough to know that the restoration of Spain's rule in the New World was impossible.[28] Under these circumstances, it was unlikely that the alliance could have agreed on a military intervention in America.

A practically nonexistent danger had been completely dissipated by Canning's warning to Polignac nearly two months before Monroe's message went to Congress. His message, consequently, had little or no practical effect on the course of events in Europe. From the courts of the continental powers, the message elicited considerable unofficial abuse—it was described as "blustering," "monstrous," "arrogant," "haughty," and "peremptory"—but no official protests. The United States was still a small power, and its attitude on international questions was of minor significance. Continental reaction to Monroe's message may be summarized as holding that his declaration was impertinent but unimportant. George Canning, whose proposals had led to the inclusion of the noninterference principle in Monroe's message, was understandably annoyed at Monroe's independent pronouncement. Monroe, he felt, had stolen a march on him and was courting the favor of the Latin American republics as the principal protector of their independence. To establish British priority in that role, Canning published the Polignac memorandum of October 1823, which showed that the British government had anticipated the United States in warning the continental powers against intervention. Later, after Great Britain had extended recognition to the new governments in December 1824, Canning boasted, "I called the New World into existence to redress the balance of the Old."[29] By such claims, and in more direct ways, he sought to undermine the prestige of the United States with the Latin American governments and to establish England as their first and most powerful friend.

The other basic theme of Monroe's message, the noncolonization principle, contributed further to Canning's pique at the United States. With vast portions of North America still unoccupied, Great Britain could not assent to the right of the United States to veto all further colonizing enterprises in that area. For this reason, then, Canning refused to join the United States in tripartite negotiations with Russia over claims on the northwest coast and took an unyielding stand toward the United States on the Oregon boundary question. In due course, Great Britain and the United States would come to see mutual advances in the Monroe Doctrine, but the initial effect of Monroe's message on Anglo-American relations was doubtless more irritating than soothing. As for Russia, against whose expanded territorial claims the noncolonization principle had been ostensibly directed, it readily consented, in separate treaties with the United States (1824) and Great Britain (1825), to limit its territorial claims in North America to the area north of latitude 54° 40'. This Russia probably would have done even had it never been confronted with John Quincy Adams's sweeping declaration.

Monroe's message was received with some enthusiasm by the American press, while in Congress it earned both praise and criticism. A resolution of endorsement, introduced by Henry Clay in the House of Representatives, never came to a vote. The principles of the message remained, therefore, a simple pronouncement of the president of the United States, without legal standing at home or in the international community. In the Latin American capitals, supposedly the beneficiaries of the message, liberal and republican elements applauded the president's declaration, but they soon discovered that the United States was unwilling to back up its words with action. Five of the new governments, Argentina, Brazil, Chile, Colombia, and Mexico, applied to authorities in Washington for either treaties of alliance or promises of assistance against possible European intervention. All received negative replies. Of special interest was John Quincy Adams's August 6, 1824, reply to the Colombian minister in Washington, since it plainly indicated that without the support of Great Britain, the United States could not undertake to defend the Americas against the Quadruple Alliance. Thus, Latin American liberals learned what their conservative and monarchist rivals had known from the beginning: that the British navy was the chief protector of their newly won independence.

CHAPTER 5

Manifest Destiny Triumphant: Oregon, Texas, and California

[While] present interests may restrain us within our own limits, [it is] impossible not to look forward to distant times, when our rapid multiplication will expand itself beyond those limits, and cover the whole northern, if not the southern continent, with a people speaking the same language, governed in similar forms, and by similar laws.
—Thomas Jefferson to James Monroe, November 24, 1801

The great results which have been developed and brought to light by this war will be of immeasurable importance in the future progress of our country. They will tend powerfully to preserve us from foreign collisions, and to enable us to pursue uninterruptedly our cherished policy of "peace with all nations, entangling alliances with none."
—President James Polk on the war with Mexico, State of the Union Address, December 1848

While not quite fulfilling Jefferson's grand vision, the decade of the 1840s witnessed a period of dramatic territorial expansion.[1] Within three short years, between 1845 and 1848, the United States expanded its size by two-thirds, pushing the nation's boundaries westward to the Pacific and southward to the Rio Grande. Territorial expansion provided land for new settlers, exacerbated politics over the issue of slavery, and improved American security against external threats. Thus, it intensified internal perils, moving the nation further and further down the road toward sectionalism and, ultimately, Civil War.

Festering Oregon Question

The Oregon territory was, by the treaty of 1818, open to the use and occupation of both British subjects and American citizens. For many years, the British, who were on the ground, with organization and experience, exploited the country. The Hudson's Bay Company tightened its monopoly of the Oregon fur trade until there were few areas west of the Rockies in which traders from the United States dared compete with the great corporation. With the fur trade effectually closed to Americans, Oregon seemed to have little else to offer. Nevertheless, a few men in Congress, notably Senator Thomas Hart Benton of Missouri, viewed it as a route to the commerce of the Orient. In diplomatic negotiations during the 1820s, the United States, while claiming the entire area, offered to accept the 49th parallel as the boundary, while the British insisted on the Columbia River, from its mouth to its intersection with the 49th parallel, as the dividing line. With neither government willing to back down, and with the 10-year period of joint occupation due to terminate in 1828, the negotiators agreed to extend that arrangement indefinitely.

Not until the early 1840s did American migration to Oregon reach significant proportions. A census in 1845 showed 2,109 persons in Oregon, and the migration of that year brought nearly 3,000 more, posing the need for some regular form of government and for settlers to secure titles to the land they occupied. Following several petitions to Congress, asking that Washington to assume control of the area, the settlers, in July 1843, established the Oregon Provisional Government. In amending their organic act two years later, they stated that its provisions applied only "until such time as the United States of America extend their jurisdiction over us." The next move was up to the Congress and the diplomats.[2]

While Oregon was never formally considered, informal discussions during the Webster-Ashburton negotiations of 1842 revealed that Great Britain was still unwilling to concede the territory between the Columbia River and the 49th parallel. President John Tyler suggested, unsuccessfully, that if Great Britain induced Mexico to recognize Texas's independence and cede Upper California to the United States, he would accept the Columbia River as a northern boundary. U.S. naval officers discouraged surrendering the region north of the Columbia, however, because of the formidable bar at the mouth of the Columbia and excellent harbors on Puget Sound. Rumors of an offer to surrender northern Oregon in exchange for California created uproar in the western states that climaxed, in July 1843, when some 120 delegates from six states met in Cincinnati. Claiming the whole of Oregon from 42° to 54°40' north latitude was "unquestionable," the delegates asserted it to be "the imperative duty of the General Government forthwith to extend the laws of the United States over said territory."[3]

On the eve of a presidential campaign in which the annexation of Texas was certain to be a major issue, the Democratic Party decided it was expedient to link the two expansionist issues, Texas and Oregon, so that western votes for Texas might be obtained in return for southern votes for Oregon. After nominating James K. Polk, an advocate of possessing Oregon, the Democratic National Convention declared: "*Resolved*, That our title to the whole of the territory of Oregon is clear and unquestionable; that no portion of the same ought to be ceded to England or any other power; and that the re-occupation of Oregon and the re-annexation of Texas at the earliest practicable period are great American measures, which this convention recommends to the cordial support of the Democracy of the Union."[4] The syllable "re" prefixed to "occupation" and "annexation," suggested that the nation was merely about to resume possession of what had once been American.

Polk: "Fifty-four Forty or Fight"

Texas figured more significantly in the campaign than Oregon—the phrase "Fifty-four forty or fight" actually was coined after the campaign.[5] Since there was no serious Whig opposition to the Democratic pronouncement on Oregon, President Polk could interpret his electoral victory as a popular verdict favoring a vigorous Oregon policy. In his inaugural address, Polk asserted that the American title to all of Oregon was "clear and unquestionable."[6] Yet, since his predecessors had offered to settle for the 49th parallel, he instructed Secretary of State James Buchanan to repeat the offer. When the British minister rejected the proposal without even referring it to London, Polk withdraw it, intimating that the United States would assert its claim to the whole of Oregon. On December 2, 1845, Polk informed Congress that he was persuaded "that the British pretensions of title could not be maintained to any portion of the Oregon territory upon any principle of public law recognized by nations." His offer of compromise, on being refused, had been withdrawn, "and our title to the whole Oregon territory asserted, and, as is believed, maintained by irrefragable facts and arguments." He asked Congress to authorize the required one year's notice of termination of joint occupation, to extend the laws and jurisdiction of the United States over American citizens in Oregon, to likewise extend to Oregon the laws regulating trade with the Indians, and to provide for a line of fortified posts from the Missouri to the Rockies and the establishment of an overland mail route to the Columbia.

> At the end of the year's notice [said Polk], ... we shall have reached a period when the national rights in Oregon must either be abandoned or firmly maintained. That they cannot be abandoned without a sacrifice of both national honor and interest, is too clear to admit of doubt.
>
> Oregon is a part of the North American continent, to which, it is confidently affirmed, the title of the United States is the best now in existence.... The British proposition of compromise... can never for a moment, be entertained by the United States without an abandonment of their just and clear territorial rights, their own self-respect, and the national honor.[7]

Polk appeared to have closed the door to compromise, and this was heightened when Buchanan declined two British offers of arbitration. To one Congressman, who feared Polk's bold stand might lead to war with Britain, the president replied: "the only way to treat John Bull was to look him straight in the eye; ... if Congress faultered [sic] or hesitated in their course, John Bull would immediately become arrogant and more grasping in his demands."[8]

In reality, Polk was much less firm. He indicated a willingness to submit to the Senate any reasonable proposal that London might make. Lord Aberdeen, British foreign secretary, was informed that although the president "would accept nothing less than the whole territory unless the Senate should otherwise determine," he might submit to the Senate a British proposal for a division at the 49th parallel. The foreign secretary, meanwhile, had expressed his opinion that Polk was no longer interested in compromise, and thus it was his duty to withdraw his opposition to "the adoption of measures, founded upon the contingency of war with the United States, and to offer no obstacle in [the] future to preparations which might be deemed necessary, not only for the defence and protection of the Canadas, but for offensive operations." Such measures would include "the immediate equipment of thirty sail of the line, besides steamers and other vessels of war."[9] Polk, perhaps, had carried his game of bluff too far. Though publicly preserving a bold front, he permitted Buchanan to make a further bid for a compromise settlement. The president, he said, had always been ready "to receive and to treat with the utmost respect" any compromise proposal from the British government. The U.S. minister at London thought that he could secure an offer of settlement at the 49th parallel with one of several alternative modifications. Such an offer, Buchanan assured him, the president would send to the Senate. He added in a private note that the Senate would certainly approve it.[10]

Polk had, in effect, abandoned the claim to 54°40' and secretly reverted to the repeatedly proposed 49th parallel boundary. The Oregon debate in both houses was notable for two things: the popularization of the phrase "manifest destiny" and a dispute between spokesmen of the Northwest and those of the South over the proposed compromise on the boundary question. The phrase "manifest destiny" had apparently been coined by John L. O'Sullivan and was first used in an editorial on the Texas question printed in the *Democratic Review* of July and August 1845. It appeared again in the *New York Morning News* (also edited by O'Sullivan) of December 27, 1845, in an editorial setting forth "the true title" to Oregon. The "true title," was not to be found in rights of discovery, exploration, settlement, and contiguity—strong though the American case was on these grounds—but rather in "the right to our manifest destiny to overspread and to possess the whole of the continent which Providence has given us for the development of the great experiment of liberty and federated self-government entrusted to us.... The God of nature and of nations has marked it for our own; and with His blessing we will firmly maintain the incontestable rights He has given, and fearlessly perform the high duties he has imposed."

Within a few days the phrase "manifest destiny" was quoted in Congress by opponents, as well as advocates, of terminating joint occupation.[11]

The sectional controversy arose from the fact that southern leaders like John C. Calhoun, having secured Texas, now favored compromise with Great Britain on Oregon. Northwestern expansionists took literally the slogan "Fifty-four forty or fight," though professing to believe that England would not fight if the United States stood firm. The South was charged with "Punic faith" in deserting the West after realizing its own objectives. Southern Democratic senators joined with Whigs to pave the way for compromise. Whig senators shared the alarm of business and commercial groups at the possibility of a costly war with England. An anonymous pamphlet declared that "monied men, for the most part, think very unfavorably of belligerent measures for the acquisition of Oregon" and claimed that such men would not invest money in government bonds "issued for the purpose of asserting a claim to worse than useless territory on the coast of the Pacific."[12] Under such influences, the curt resolution finally passed by both houses on April 23, 1846, authorizing the president to give the year's notice. It also expressed a hope for "a speedy and amicable adjustment" of "the respective claims of the United States and Great Britain."

Controversy Settled

Buchanan forwarded the formal notice to the British government, but reiterated the president's willingness to consider any suitable British proposal. Lord Aberdeen, personally, had long been ready to accept the 49th parallel as a boundary. He attached little value to the disputed territory, and to the whole of Oregon for that matter, but he resented Polk's declaration that the American title to Oregon was "clear and unquestionable."[13] Aberdeen's problem, in abandoning the British claim to the Columbia boundary, was mainly to reconcile British opinion. He needed to convince the British public that no vital British interests were being surrendered, and guard the cabinet's slender majority in Parliament. Because of the decline of the fur trade and friction between the company's establishment at Fort Vancouver and the American settlers south of the river, the company had moved to Vancouver Island, thus abandoning the river. Now Lord Aberdeen could argue that the Columbia River boundary was not worth contending for.[14]

Aberdeen's offer, in the form of a treaty, proposed to draw the boundary line along the 49th parallel from the Rocky Mountains to the channel separating Vancouver Island from the mainland and thence through the channel around the south end of the island, leaving the entire island to the British. Polk objected to a provision that navigation of the Columbia from the boundary line to its mouth should be "free and open to the Hudson's Bay Company, and to all British subjects trading with the same." But the situation did not admit of delay. War with Mexico had begun, making a settlement with England imperative. Polk therefore sent the treaty to the Senate as it stood. The Senate advised acceptance of the British proposal without change, and the treaty was signed on June 15, and on June 18 the Senate gave its advice and consent for ratification by a vote of 41 to 14. The treaty was proclaimed on August 5, 1846. The long controversy was settled to the satisfaction of nearly everyone.[15]

Annexation of Texas

Mexico's resentment over the annexation of Texas proved an insuperable obstacle to amicable negotiation over claims and boundary. President James K. Polk's desire to gain California—for its shining harbors, not its still unknown golden treasure—probably made him less forbearing toward Mexico than he might have been otherwise. The war with Mexico, consequently, stemmed from four broad issues that interacted with one another in an adverse manner: (1) Mexico's resentment over the American annexation of Texas; (2) a dispute over what constituted the southwestern boundary of Texas; (3) the failure of Mexico to pay certain damage claims of citizens of the United States; and (4) President Polk's anxiety to acquire California for the United States.[16]

When the Tyler administration first contemplated the annexation of Texas, Mexico served notice that it would regard such action on the part of the United States as a *casus belli*. Repeated warnings had been delivered in the summer of 1843 and the spring of 1844. In March 1845, when Congress passed the joint resolution of annexation and President Tyler signed it, the Mexican government terminated relations with the United States, and all formal diplomatic intercourse ceased. Mexico, however, fresh from one revolution and with another on the horizon, was in no condition to go to war with the United States. The dispute over annexation was further embittered by a controversy over just what Texas territory had been annexed. The United States adopted the Texan claim that its boundary was the Rio Grande River; while Mexico insisted that historically Texas had never extended west or south of the River Nueces. Texas's claim to the Rio Grande boundary rested on an early act of the Texas Congress and the fact that Santa Anna's armies had retired beyond the Rio Grande. Thereafter the area between the rivers had not been effectively occupied or controlled by either party. Texas had done little or nothing through de facto occupation to counter Mexico's historic claim. The joint resolution of annexation had merely provided that the boundaries of Texas should be subject to the adjustment. American diplomats sought to revive the claim that the Rio Grande had been the ancient boundary of Louisiana, but the United States had given up that claim by the treaty of 1819.

President Polk was determined to uphold the claim to the Rio Grande boundary. He was willing to recognize merit in Mexico's position to the extent of canceling several millions of dollars of damage claims against Mexico if it would accept the Rio Grande boundary. Polk was not willing, in the meantime, to forgo occupation of the disputed territory. In July 1845, as soon as the Texas legislature agreed to annexation, he ordered Brigadier General Zachary Taylor, with some 3,900 U.S. troops, to Texas for defense against an anticipated Mexican invasion. Taylor was instructed to take up a position south of the Nueces and as near the Rio Grande "as prudence will dictate," but not to disturb any posts occupied by Mexican troops or Mexican settlements not under Texan jurisdiction.[17] The intent of these instructions was, while asserting title to the disputed territory, to avoid the initiative in any clash with Mexican forces. Exercising the discretion allowed him, Taylor, in August, stationed his army at Corpus Christi at the mouth of the Nueces, at a prudent distance from the Rio Grande, where he remained until March 1846.

A third dispute with Mexico regarded its failure to settle claims of American citizens, in the amount of several million dollars, that had originated from unpaid supplies purchased by the Mexican government, and in damages to U.S. persons and property suffered during revolutionary disorders. A 1839 treaty established a mixed claims commission that considered claims of over $8 million and granted awards of slightly over $2 million. Additional claims of over $3 million had been submitted too late for adjudication. Mexico agreed to pay the $2 million in 20 installments over five years, but paid only 3 installments, together with arrears to April 30, 1843, before suspending payments. Since the Mexican treasury was chronically empty, there was little hope that cash payments would be resumed. Following the precedents set by the Louisiana and Florida transactions, Polk proposed a boundary settlement in lieu of money. If Mexico would recognize the annexation of Texas with the Rio Grande boundary, Polk would release Mexico from all monetary claims of American citizens, which would paid by the U.S. Treasury. But Polk wished to carry the settlement still further. If Mexico would yield additional territory, coveted by Polk, the president was prepared to fill the empty Mexican treasury with American dollars.

Polk's California Policy

Soon after taking office, Polk remarked that two of the "great measures" of his administration would be "the settlement of the Oregon boundary question" and "the acquisition of California."[18] He successfully settled the Oregon question, and the acquisition of California would be accomplished, but not without bloodshed. Spanish and later Mexican control of California—its first Spanish settlers arriving during the American Revolution—never extended farther north than San Francisco Bay or farther inland than the coastal area. Aside from the presidios and Franciscan missions, Spanish activities consisted principally of sheep and cattle ranching. As late as 1846, the entire population of Spanish descent probably did not exceed 7,000 persons. The first American visitors to California came by sea, but in the 1820s, fur traders were beginning to make their way overland. Reports of official explorations by Lieutenant Charles Wilkes and

John C. Frémont, published in 1845, contributed to a growing interest in California. Thomas O. Larkin, first U.S. consul in Monterey, estimated that by 1846 there were some 900 Americans in California. The American contingent was rapidly growing and with it the prediction that the Americans would soon be "sufficiently numerous to play the Texas game."[19] The danger of a "Texas game" in California was apparent to authorities in Mexico City, but local Mexican officials disregarded orders to halt American immigration or expel Americans, having neither the will nor the power to enforce them. Mexico's hold on California grew steadily weaker, arousing suspicions in Washington that London would oppose the American acquisition of California. Rumors had it that Mexico would mortgage California to Britain as security for the large Mexican debt held by British subjects. No such plan existed, but if London officials were displeased with thought of U.S. occupation of California, they were not prepared to oppose American policy there at the risk of war.

Polk knew not the exact nature of British policy in California, but he was aware of London's attempt to thwart American policy in Texas, and the persistent rumors of British designs on California must have seemed credible to him. Polk saw two possible methods of acquiring California: by purchase which the president was determined to try; and, if Mexico refused to negotiate, the Californians might be induced to join the United States. Polk's reliance here was on bona fide Spanish Californians. He understood the shaky hold of Mexico City on California and the impatience many native Californians had with the ineptitude and inefficiency of Mexican rule. These individuals might be persuaded to sever their ties with Mexico and join the United States, with the idea of eventual statehood. Larkin became a confidential agent on October 17, 1845, with new duties. He was directed to win the friendship of the Californians and to assure them that if California should declare its independence, "we shall render her all the kind offices in our power as a sister republic." The United States, they were to be told, did not desire to extend its boundaries "unless by the free and spontaneous wish of all the independent people of adjoining territories." But, the instructions continued: "Whilst the President will make no effort and use no influence to induce California to become one of the free and independent States of this Union, yet if the people should desire to unite their destiny with ours, they would be received as brethren, whenever this can be done without affording Mexico just cause of complaint."[20] These instructions, which could easily be interpreted as an invitation to the Californians to revolt from Mexico and join the United States, reached Larkin on April 17, 1846.

Earlier Polk used his annual message on December 2, 1845, to remind Europe, in general, and Britain, in particular, of Monroe's noncolonization principle, becoming the first president since Monroe to refer to the Monroe Doctrine as a statement of official American policy.[21] Polk laid down another principle, sometimes called the "Polk corollary," stating: "We must ever maintain the principle that the people of this continent alone have the right to decide their own destiny. Should any portion of them, constituting an independent state, propose to unite themselves with our Confederacy, this will be a question for them and us to determine without any foreign interposition."[22] This declaration rebuked the British government for its efforts to prevent the annexation of Texas. It also rebuked the French premier, who had declared that there ought to be a "balance of power" in the Americas—a Latin counterweight to the United States. In this same message, Polk also asserted America's claim to all of Oregon, a most aggressive document.

Polk Ponders War

Meanwhile, Polk attempted a restoration of diplomatic relations with Mexico not only to purchase California but also to effect a peaceful settlement of all disputed questions. Peña y Peña, the Mexican foreign minister, wrote on October 15, 1845, that President Herrera was "disposed to receive the commissioner [*comisionado*] of the United States, who may come to this capital with full powers from his government to settle the present dispute in a peaceable, reasonable, and honorable manner."[23] Polk dispatched John Slidell to Mexico bearing a commission as envoy extraordinary and U.S. minister plenipotentiary. Polk and his cabinet had previously agreed to propose a boundary line following the Rio Grande from its mouth to El Paso in latitude 32° north or thereabouts, and thence directly westward to the Pacific—thus gaining New Mexico and Upper California as well as the Rio Grande boundary. Polk believed such a line might be obtained for $15 or $20 million, but he was willing to pay as much as $40 million.[24]

When Slidell arrived in Mexico City, President Herrera faced imminent overthrow and dared not antagonize public opinion by an appearance of concessions to the United States. Peña y Peña complained that Washington had sent an envoy extraordinary and minister plenipotentiary, implying a full restoration of diplomatic relations. In that capacity, he said, Slidell could not be received. While Slidell waited, on January 2, 1846, General Paredes assumed presidential authority but was in no position to be conciliatory. "Be assured," Slidell wrote as he prepared to leave, "that nothing is to be done with these people, until they shall have been chastised."[25] Polk's attitude toward Mexico combined simultaneous gestures with the sword and the olive branch. Willing to settle with Mexico, he was determined to have as a minimum the Rio Grande boundary as compensation for the American claims. Polk was hopeful that Slidell's mission would result in such a settlement, but if Mexico declined, the sword was ready. Thus, on January 13, 1846, on learning of Herrera's refusal to negotiate, he ordered General Taylor to take up a position on the Rio Grande.

A month later, Polk was visited by one Colonel A. J. Atocha, a friend of Santa Anna then in exile at Havana, who assured Polk that should Santa Anna again gain power, he would gladly negotiate the territorial settlement Polk desired. To reconcile Mexican public opinion to a cession of territory, the United States would have to take stronger measures—perhaps deliver an ultimatum supported by warships. Polk, favorably impressed by Atocha's suggestions, now proposed to his cabinet that Congress be requested to authorize the president, first, to present Mexico with an ultimatum, and second, if Mexico rejected his terms, "to take redress into our own hands by aggressive measures."[26] However, with the Oregon controversy approaching a crisis, Polk accepted the advice of Secretary of State James Buchanan not to precipitate war with Mexico till he was sure of peace with England. Later on May 9, Polk proposed to send to Congress a message recommending a declaration of war against Mexico. George Bancroft, secretary of the navy, "dissented but said if any act of hostility should be committed by the Mexican forces he was then in favour of immediate war."[27] On that very evening came tidings that such an "act of hostility" had occurred.

The Clash of Arms

General Zachary Taylor, under his orders of January 13, moved his army early in March from Corpus Christi to the Rio Grande, reaching the river without meeting resistance, and then occupied and fortified the east bank at the present site of Brownsville, Texas, opposite the Mexican town of Matamoros. Taylor's advance brought Mexican General Ampudia to Matamoros, when on April 12 he warned Taylor, on pain of hostilities, to withdraw his army beyond the Nueces. In reply, Taylor cited his orders from the secretary of war as authority for his advance. Furthermore, in retaliation for the Mexican refusal to permit him to use the river as a supply line, he instituted a blockade at its mouth, thereby denying its use to the Mexicans at Matamoros. This measure Taylor characterized as "a simply defensive precaution." It was, in reality, an act of war.

Learning of Taylor's blockade, President Paredes, on April 23, proclaimed the existence of a "defensive war" against the United States. Next day, unaware as yet of Paredes's proclamation, a Mexican force crossed the river above Taylor's position, and on the 25th, Mexican cavalry attacked a company American dragoons, killing or wounding 16, and captured the remainder. This was the news that reached President Polk on May 9, 1846, and two days later a "war message" went to Congress. The bulk of the message summarized Mexican offenses against the United States, with emphasis on its "breach of faith" in refusing to receive Slidell. Finally, Polk added a paragraph calculated to fire the patriot heart: "The cup of forbearance had been exhausted even before the recent information from the frontier of the Del Norte. But now, after reiterated menaces, Mexico has passed the boundary of the United States, has invaded our territory and shed American blood upon American soil. She has proclaimed that hostilities have commenced, and that the two nations are now at war."[28]

The shedding of American blood on "American soil" supplied the necessary emotional element to give Polk the war he wanted.[29] Within two days, Congress, by a vote of 173 to 14 in the House and 42 to 2 in the Senate, declared that a state of war existed "by the act of the Republic of Mexico," authorized the president to call out 50,000 volunteers, and appropriated $10 million for military and naval expenditures.[30] Thanks to Polk's diary, it is clear that he and his advisers, with a single dissenting vote, had chosen war before they knew of the attack.

Seeking Territory and Peace

Immediately, steps were taken seeking peace with the expectation that it would be a short and easy war. In Havana, Santa Anna expressed a desire to return to Mexico and "govern in the interest of the masses, instead of parties, and classes."[31] In expectation of Santa Anna's return to power, Secretary of State Buchanan on July 27 proposed negotiations to the Mexican foreign minister for "a peace just and honorable for both parties." Earlier, Santa Anna had returned to Mexico, assumed command of the "Liberating Army," and now proposed postponing consideration of a peace offer until a new Mexican congress met in December. Buchanan replied that no choice remained for the United States "but to prosecute the war with vigor," until Mexico exhibited a desire for peace.[32] Before hopes of an early peace faded, Polk's cabinet had discussed the war's objectives. Acquisition of territory was not the war's aim, Polk noted, but the United States should take California for indemnification. He would "meet war with either England or France or all the Powers of Christendom" rather than disclaiming any intention of dismembering Mexico or acquiring New Mexico or California.[33] Weeks later, a general agreement was reached that as a minimum the United States must secure the Rio Grande line, New Mexico, and Upper California—the maximum John Slidell sought. General Taylor, already on the Rio Grande, would advance "toward the heart of the enemy's country" to bring Santa Anna to terms, while another expedition, setting out from Fort Leavenworth, Kansas, would proceed to Santa Fe and occupy both New Mexico and California.

Taylor's army captured Monterey in September, and before the close of 1846 the capitals of three Mexican states, Nueve Leon, Coahuila, and Tamaulipas, were in American hands. After taking Santa Fe, Brigadier General Stephen W. Kearny's forces headed for California. The United States gained California, but not through a peaceful agreement with the Spanish Californians. Larkin began conversations, as directed, with some of the leading Californians, but his efforts to win their loyalty were interrupted by the strange behavior of Captain John C. Frémont. This young Army officer, already a noted explorer, had set out in the spring of 1845 for California, where he spent the winter. The Mexican commandant at Monterey ordered the Americans to leave the province, whereupon Frémont led his men up the Sacramento Valley and north into Oregon, where, in May 1846, he was overtaken by Lieutenant Gillespie, bringing instructions to Larkin and letters to Frémont. What the letters contained, or what verbal messages Gillespie may have brought, is debated; what happened next is not. Frémont returned to California and to the vicinity of San Francisco Bay, where he assisted a group of American frontiersmen in an unprovoked rebellion against the Mexican authorities—the so-called Bear Flag revolt—bringing him into direct conflict with the very Spanish Californians whom Polk had wished to conciliate.[34]

Frémont learned unofficially of the war early in July and cooperated with Commodore John D. Sloat, and later Captain Robert F. Stockton, to occupy all of California, but his erratic behavior had dampened the chances of gaining the Californians' good will. Before the end of July, the U.S. flag was flying over all the settlements north of Monterey when Stockton and Frémont took their commands by sea to southern California. In August they took possession of San Diego, San Pedro, and Los Angeles without armed resistance. With the first official news of the declaration of war, Stockton proclaimed the United States' annexation of California. At every point, American arms had occupied all the territory that the administration desired to wrest from Mexico. Now it was time to terminate the war with a treaty by which Mexico would confirm the annexations. Santa Anna, however, as yet showed no inclination to discuss peace terms. What, then, was to be done? Polk finally resolved to dispatch an expedition to seize Vera Cruz and then advance against Mexico City. The expedition's commander was Major General Winfield Scott, a capable officer and a Whig. Scott's army of some 10,000 men was put ashore south of Vera Cruz early in March 1847, and on March 29 received the city's surrender. General Santa Anna's Mexican forces were routed by Scott at Puebla, Mexico's second city, surrendered without opposition on May 15. The road to Mexico City lay open, but at Puebla, Scott had to await replacements for his one-year volunteers.

While Scott and his army rested at Puebla, a new attempt was made to bring the slippery Santa Anna to terms, but he refused to negotiate. But with American victories at Buena Vista and Vera Cruz, Washington saw new opportunities for negotiation. Polk decided to send Nicholas P. Trist, formerly consul in Havana with knowledge of the Spanish language, to Scott's headquarters, empowered to negotiate a treaty. Trist's instructions directed him to insist on the Rio Grande boundary and the cession of New Mexico and Upper California. In compensation, the United States would assume the claims against Mexico and pay, in addition, as much as $20 million. He was authorized, moreover, to pay an additional $5 million for Lower California and a similar sum for the right of transit across the Isthmus of Tehuantepec. Trist arrived at Vera Cruz on May 6, when almost at once he and Scott engaged in an epistolary duel that did neither credit. Fortunately, the antagonists reconciled and the two worked in friendship and harmony.[35] With reinforcements in place but no diplomatic progress, General Scott advanced on the Mexican capital. Scott's fair and generous dealing with the Mexican people along the route of his invasion had won their friendship and removed the menace of a hostile population to his long line of communications. Following hard-fought victories, Scott occupied Mexico City, and Santa Anna resigned the presidency. A new government, headed provisionally by Peña y Peña, was set up at Querétaro.

Exasperated by Mexico's refusal to accept what he considered generous terms of peace, Polk and his cabinet talked of exacting from the defeated enemy much more than initially contemplated. Two members of the cabinet, Buchanan and Secretary of the Treasury Robert J. Walker, considered conquering and absorbing all of Mexico, and wished the president to intimate as much in his annual message. Buchanan suggested a statement that "we must fulfill that destiny which Providence may have in store for both countries." Polk chose to say that we should "take the measure of our indemnity into our own hands." Walker and Buchanan, however, were expressing the thoughts of a vocal group of politicians and journalists. These "Continental Democrats" urged the annexation of Mexico. The long-prevalent view of this movement, like that of the war itself, ascribed the annexationist sentiment to southern cupidity for more slave territory and states. In reality, there was nothing peculiarly southern about either the promotion of the war or the talk of larger annexations of Mexican territory. Southern Whigs almost unanimously, and Calhoun and many southern Democrats, condemned the war and deplored acquisitions of new territory. The passage several times of the Wilmot Proviso by the House of Representatives, prohibiting slavery or involuntary servitude in any territory to be acquired from Mexico, had warned southerners that any attempt to extend slavery into new territory would be met with determined Northern opposition.

The "all-Mexico" movement was neither proslavery nor antislavery. Its greatest vocal support was in New York and in the western states, from Ohio to Texas. Its adherents were Democrats, and the arguments used in its behalf were those of Manifest Destiny. The *Democratic Review*, original propagator of that phrase, declared in October 1847: "This occupation of territory by the people, is the great movement of the age, and until every acre of the North American continent is occupied by citizens of the United States, the foundations of the future empire will not have been laid."[36] The *New York Herald* and *Sun* expressed similar ideas, and the same sentiments were common in Congress. President Polk had not aligned himself with this faction, but his December message stated that if Mexico rejected peace offers, we "must continue to occupy her country with our troops, taking the full measure of indemnity into our own hands."[37] Then, quite unexpectedly, a messenger arrived in Washington bearing a peace treaty that Trist, ignoring his recall as commissioner, had negotiated with the provisional government of Mexico.

Trist's Treaty

Not until November 16 had Trist received Buchanan's letter recalling him to Washington for allegedly disregarding his instructions. Trist, meanwhile, had contacted the newly formed Mexican government at Querétaro and had been informed that the government was anxious for peace. He notified the Mexican government of his recall and asked for peace proposals to take to Washington. The Mexican authorities (and General Scott) urged Trist to remain for negotiations, and on December 3, he informed the Mexican commissioners that he would proceed to negotiate if assured that Mexico would accept the United States' minimum territorial demands. Trist's unprecedented act of insubordination was to his credit. He knew that the party in power, the *Moderado* or Moderate Party, was the only group in Mexico with which there was any hope of making a treaty to Polk's satisfaction. Given the "all-Mexico" movement in the United States and suspecting that Polk favored it, Trist saw that the choice lay between a peace made at once with the Moderates on the basis of his original instructions and a protracted military occupation of Mexico, complicated by guerrilla warfare, possibly ending in annexation of the whole country. The latter course he believed would be a major calamity for the United States.

Since the negotiations moved slowly, it was not until February 2, 1848, that the treaty was signed at Guadalupe Hidalgo, a suburb of Mexico City. The treaty embodied the minimum territorial demands and the minimum monetary compensation proposed in Trist's instructions of April 15, 1847. The United States secured the Rio Grande boundary and retained New Mexico and Upper California, both of which were already occupied. The United States would release Mexico from existing claims and pay to Mexico $15 million. The arrival of the treaty placed Polk in a serious dilemma. He was indignant at Trist, not only for disregarding his recall but also because his recent communications had been critical of the president. Yet Trist's treaty conformed to his official instructions and to Polk's public professed war aims. If he rejected it and chose to carry on the war, the president knew he would meet with intensified opposition in Congress. Thus, with a cautious statement of approval, Polk sent it to the Senate.

The treaty was opposed in the Senate by a strange alliance of those who wanted less territory than it secured and those who wanted more. The former were Whigs, the latter, expansionist Democrats. Daniel Webster declared that New Mexico and California together were "not worth a dollar."[38] But the two groups of malcontents faltered in the final vote, and the treaty was approved on March 10, 1848 by a majority of 38 to 14. On May 19, 1848, the Mexican Congress approved the amended treaty, and on the thirtieth, ratifications were exchanged. The war was over, and by July 30 the last American soldiers had embarked from Vera Cruz for home.

* * *

Polk, a firm believer in territorial expansion, in three and a quarter years had completed the annexation of Texas, acquired the more valuable portion of Oregon, and, by a short, sharp war, secured the Rio Grande boundary, New Mexico, and the still unrealized wealth of California. The United States had become a Pacific power with a coastline stretching from San Diego to Puget Sound. Polk had taken serious chances, risking both a war with England and a prolonged, costly occupation of Mexico. If he owed his successes as much to good luck as to good management, the successes were nevertheless impressive.

CHAPTER 6

A House Divided: Diplomacy during the Civil War

I have understood well that duty of self-preservation rests solely with the American people. But I have at the same time been aware that favor or disfavor of foreign nations might have a material influence in enlarging and prolonging the struggle with disloyal men in which the country is engaged. A fair examination of history has seemed to authorize a belief that the past action and influences of the United States were generally regarded as having been beneficent towards mankind. I have therefore reckoned upon the forbearance of nations.

—Abraham Lincoln, Reply to the Workingmen of Manchester, England, January 19, 1863

Her Majesty's Government have felt that it was its duty to use every possible means to avoid taking any part in the lamentable contest now raging in the American States, and nothing but the imperative duty of watching British interests in case we should be attacked, justifies our interfering. We have not been involved in that contest by any act of giving advice in the matter, and for God's sake, let us, if possible, keep out of it.

—Foreign Secretary Lord John Russell, in the House of Commons, May 2, 1861

The four-year struggle of the American Civil War opened with the Southern Confederacy's attack on Fort Sumter on April 12, 1861. Seven states of the lower South had seceded following the election of Lincoln, and, at Montgomery, Alabama, had organized the Confederate States of America. After the firing on Fort Sumter and Lincoln's call on the states for troops to suppress the insurrection, four additional states, Virginia, North Carolina, Tennessee, and Arkansas, joined the Confederacy. With the Atlantic and Gulf coasts from Chesapeake Bay to the Rio Grande lying within the Confederacy, it was certain that the war would be fought on sea as well as land. Naval issues would inevitably raise troublesome questions similar to belligerents and neutrals during the Napoleonic Wars.

The United States found itself in an unaccustomed role—that of a belligerent in a war in which European powers were neutral. While Washington, generally speaking, held to the principles for which it had earlier contended, with a different emphasis, it now focused on the *rights* of belligerents rather than their obligations, and on the *obligations* of neutrals rather than their rights, resulting in an enlargement of belligerent rights and a more precise definition of neutral duties. After the outbreak of hostilities, however, the most serious question confronting the Lincoln administration was whether Europe, especially England and France, would remain neutral. Confederate leaders hoped in 1861 that intervention by one or more of the European powers would insure the independence of the South. While Secretary of State William H. Seward suggested in April 1861 that the internal crisis might be solved through the creation of an external one, raising the possibility of war with Spain and France simultaneously, it is clear that the avoidance of European intervention was vital to the triumph of the North.[1]

Formal recognition of the Confederacy as an independent state would be the necessary first step in any external intervention on behalf of the South, and Confederate agents in England and France worked unceasingly toward this end. The French Emperor, Napoleon III, favored the Confederacy, and was willing to consider recognition and intervention at any time the British government would join him. All depended, therefore, on London's attitude. The South looked to the power of "King Cotton" to compel European intervention, thinking that Europe, especially England, would intervene to ensure uninterrupted access to the white staple. The perceived significance of cotton was certainly not lost on the British, as eloquently captured in a poem in *Punch* in March 1861:

> Though with the North we sympathize
> It must not be forgotten
> That with the South we've stronger ties
> Which are composed of cotton[2]

The South's reliance on the power of King Cotton failed to take into account the large surpluses of cotton and cotton goods in European warehouses. To the owners of these stocks, the cutting off of further supplies was a boon. By the time the surpluses were exhausted, alternative sources were under cultivation in Egypt and India; thus, British economic considerations proved to be more conducive to nonintervention than to intervention. The war was profitable to British interests, not only in the enhanced prices of textiles, but in the sale of war supplies to both sides and in the prospects for harassment of northern shipping—England's chief maritime competitor—by Confederate cruisers.[3] Furthermore, a break with the North would entail serious risks for Britain since the North held Canada and the British merchant marine hostage for London's good behavior.

Recent scholarship has challenged the notion that British sympathies toward the belligerents divided neatly along class lines. Now a much more complex story has emerged, revealing wider support for the Confederacy, even among the labor movement.[4] The aristocracy, at that time still largely the governing class, would welcome the breakup of the Union as an object lesson in the failure of democracy. British liberals like John Bright, however, looked on the war as a test of democracy and hoped for a northern victory and preservation of the Union. Viscount Palmerston and Earl Russell, prime minister and foreign secretary, respectively, shared the sympathies of the British upper classes, but if their official policy could be called pro-southern, it was the result of a conviction that southern victory was inevitable and hence the prolongation of the war meant useless bloodshed and destruction of property. This conviction, combined with the growing impact of the war on British textile workers, led Britain to the verge of intervention in October 1862. News of the southern defeat at Antietam, arriving at an opportune moment, made a southern victory less certain and strengthened the opponents of intervention. In November, the government rejected French proposals for joint intervention. Never again did Palmerston and Russell approach so close to recognition of the Confederacy.

The War and Belligerent Rights

Although the Confederacy never secured recognition of its independence, the British government did promptly grant it belligerent rights. Such a course was not only in accord with American practice, it was rendered unavoidable by the Federal government's military preparations and by its blockade of southern ports—clearly an act of one belligerent against another. London's recognition of Confederate belligerency on May 13, 1861, was promptly imitated by the other major European governments. This meant that Confederate naval vessels or privateers would be treated as legitimate ships of war, not as pirates. Though Lincoln and William H. Seward, his secretary of state, resented the British proclamation as unfriendly or at least premature, they also found it necessary to treat the Confederacy as a belligerent, rather than a domestic insurrection.

The Declaration of Paris had answered, for Europe at any rate, many of the old questions concerning the rights and duties of belligerents and neutrals. Adopted on April 16, 1856, at the close of the Crimean War, Austria, France, Great Britain, Prussia, Russia, Sardinia, and Turkey insisted the following principles be recognized:

1. Privateering is, and remains, abolished;
2. The neutral flag covers enemy's goods, with the exception of contraband of war;
3. Neutral goods, with the exception of contraband of war, are not liable to capture under the enemy's flag;
4. Blockades, in order to be binding, must be effective; that is to say, maintained by a force sufficient to prevent access to the coast of the enemy.

The United States was invited to adhere to the Convention, but its second, third, and fourth articles were principles that Americans had long sought, and which they rejoiced when the great powers formally accepted, Washington was not then ready to abolish privateering. The United States had a large merchant marine, but its navy was far inferior to those of several European states. If it were unable, in a war with a European power, to supplement its small navy with privateers, it would be at a serious disadvantage. Its own merchant marine could be driven from the seas by the British navy, for example, while the American navy could inflict only trifling losses on British commerce. Only on one condition would the United States consent to end privateering—if the other powers would agree to the immunity of all noncontraband belligerent property at sea. Secretary of State Marcy unsuccessfully offered American adherence to the declaration if it were amended to include this principle.[5]

Since now privateering might work to the advantage of the Confederacy and to the detriment of the United States, Lincoln and Seward had reason to regret that their predecessors had not subscribed to the Declaration of Paris. Seward, in fact, proposed to Great Britain and other signatories that they accept U.S. adherence to the declaration without its previous amendment. Earl Russell offered to accept the adherence of the United States, but only with the understanding that such acceptance should not "have any bearing... on the internal differences now prevailing in the United States."[6] The qualification meant, of course, that Britain would not regard a ban on privateering as applicable in the current conflict. Seward declined the qualified offer but made it plain to the British Foreign Office that the United States proposed to adhere to the second, third, and fourth articles of the declaration.[7]

Observance of the fourth principle of the Declaration of Paris—that "blockades, in order to be binding, must be effective"—presented serious problems in Washington. In a proclamation of April 19, 1861, Lincoln announced the government's intention to blockade the ports of the seceded states, which were scattered along 3,000 miles of coastline, stretching from Chesapeake Bay to the Rio Grande. The navy, which bore responsibility for closing some 185 ports or openings in this extensive coastline, initially comprised about 100 vessels, of which two-thirds were antiquated sailing vessels. These were supplemented as rapidly as possible by the purchase of vessels of the most diverse types—steamers, tugs, ferry–boats, even sailing vessels—since any craft that could carry a few guns and remain at sea could be utilized for blockade purposes. Over 400 vessels were thus acquired during the war.[8]

Whether its blockade was technically effective has been questioned. If there were a great many violations—just how many is unknown—the United States captured or destroyed over 1,500 ships attempting to run the blockade. Also, before the end of the war, the principal Confederate ports were in Union hands. The British, nevertheless, accepted the blockade as effective and as binding under international law. Legality did not require, Earl Russell wrote, that a blockade make access to a port impossible; it needed only to create "an evident danger on entering or leaving it."[9] There is good reason to suppose London was delighted to see Washington, hitherto the champion of neutral rights, extending belligerents rights and establishing precedents useful to England in the future.[10] One such precedent of future value was Washington's acceptance of the doctrine of continuous voyage. As discussed previously, British courts first announced this doctrine in the *Essex* case in 1805, in connection with the Rule of 1756. American courts adopted it in the enforcement of the Civil War blockade.

Specially adapted steamers, carrying cargoes from Bermuda, Nassau, or Havana to Confederate ports, were most successful in running the blockade.[11] It was much easier to catch conventional ships bringing goods from Europe to the intermediate neutral ports. The U.S. Supreme

Court held that a voyage from Liverpool to Nassau could be interrupted if the ultimate destination of the cargo was a blockaded port. If the ship's papers or the character of the cargo showed conclusively that its real destination was a blockaded port, that the neutral destination was a subterfuge, then the voyage was *continuous*—even if in different ships—from origin to ultimate destination. The cargo, whether contraband or not, was liable to confiscation for breach of blockade. If ship owners were aware of the ultimate destination of the cargo, the ship was also subject to confiscation.

In the cases of the *Bermuda* and the *Springbok*, the Supreme Court affirmed the doctrine of continuous voyage. In the case of the *Peterhoff*, intercepted en route to Matamoros, Mexico, with a cargo destined for the Confederacy but not through a port actually blockaded, the court held that no breach of blockade was involved and that only seizing the contraband goods in the cargo was lawful.[12] Although continental jurists—French, German, and Dutch—vigorously criticized the Supreme Court's application of the doctrine of continuous voyage, the British government did not protest, although British subjects owned the condemned property. Apparently, London was content to see the United States adopt, adapt, and improve on, a concept useful to a belligerent controlling the sea lanes.

The *Trent* Affair

There were limits, however, to London's acquiescence in the United States' stretching of law and precedent. In November 1861, Captain Charles Wilkes, in the U.S. cruiser *San Jacinto*, took Confederate agents James M. Mason and John Slidell and their secretaries from the British mail steamer *Trent*. Mason and Slidell, en route to represent the Confederacy in England and France respectively, had slipped through the blockade to Havana and had taken passage on the *Trent* to St. Thomas, Danish West Indies, on their way to Europe. Wilkes, learning of their presence, halted the ship on his own responsibility and, over the protest of the *Trent* British commander, removed the men and landed them at Fortress Monroe, Virginia. In the United States, Wilkes's bold action provided a much-needed boost to Union morale, and he was praised by the press and congratulated by the secretary of the navy. A House of Representatives resolution unanimously applauded his "brave, adroit and patriotic conduct in the arrest and detention of the traitors, James M. Mason and John Slidell."[13] Wilkes's action caught the Confederacy unprepared and pointed to the ineptness of Confederate diplomacy.[14]

In London, Earl Russell instructed Lord Lyons, British minister in Washington, to demand the release of the envoys and an apology. If these demands were not granted after seven days, he was to close the legation and leave Washington. Seward was suspected of desiring to provoke a war with Britain, and it was widely assumed that Wilkes had acted under his instructions. With the prospect of war looming, British troops were ordered to Canada, and the Royal Navy was made ready.[15] Yet neither the British public nor the British government wished for war as the United States could threaten Canada, endanger the British merchant marine, and align antislavery crusading Britain with the slaveholding South. Lyons's instructions had been softened, at the instance of Albert, the Prince Consort—the minister was not to "menace" the United States or to inform Seward of the seven-day time limit.[16] Later, he was told that an explanation would be accepted instead of an apology.

Seward faced a serious dilemma. He knew that Wilkes's action had been irregular, that it would be difficult to defend, that European opinion solidly supported England, and that refusing the release of Mason and Slidell could mean war with England and the Confederacy's almost certain victory. Seward, who had long since discarded his "foreign war panacea," wanted none of this. Yet to surrender the Confederate agents would flout American public opinion and could be politically disastrous to the administration. In two long meetings, December 25 and 26, 1861, he gained Lincoln and the cabinet's support of his plan. Seward promised the British minister that Mason and Slidell would be released, but extended the promise in a document, at once made public, in which it appeared that in releasing them, he was vindicating a principle that America had long cherished and England had flouted. Reviewing Wilkes's conduct, he argued that the officer had followed correct procedures in stopping and searching the *Trent* and that Mason and Slidell were properly liable for capture since—and here Seward advanced a novel doctrine—"persons, as well as property, may become contraband." Wilkes's singular error had been in removing the envoys on his own responsibility instead of bringing the *Trent* before a prize court where their status could be determined by proper judicial authority. Wilkes was guilty, Seward said, of the very practice that the United States had bitterly complained of when it was followed by Britain—naval officers' arbitrary action in assuming the right to remove persons from neutral ships. What was this but impressment? Seward continued: "If I decide this case in favor of my own government, I must disavow its most cherished principles, and reverse and forever abandon its essential policy. The country cannot afford the sacrifice. If I maintain those principles, and adhere to that policy, I must surrender the case itself.... We are asked to do to the British nation just what we have always insisted all nations ought to do to us." By the proposed adjustment of the present case, Seward declared, a question that had alienated the two countries for more than half a century would be "finally and rightly settled between them."[17]

Seward could not resist criticizing the two southern envoys, whose "comparative unimportance," he remarked, together with the "waning proportions of the existing insurrection," made it unnecessary for him to detain them on grounds of national security.[18] Their self-esteem received a further blow when, on reaching Europe, they not only met with a cool reception and no encouragement with regard to recognition, but were informed editorially by the London *Times* that: "They must not suppose, because we have gone to the very verge of a great war to rescue them, that therefore they are precious in our eyes. We should have done just as much to rescue two of their own Negroes."[19] Seward's surrender on these terms was well received at home and gladly accepted in England, though Earl Russell made it plain that he did not accept all of Seward's reasoning. Only the southern agents and their sympathizers were disappointed. They found that the crisis and its settlement had favored the North. U.S. minister Charles Francis Adams reported to Seward that the *Trent* affair, "with just the issue that it had, was rather opportune than otherwise." Henry Hotze, a Confederate agent, complained that "the *Trent* affair has done us incalculable injury" and that Earl Russell was now "an avowed enemy of our nationality."[20]

Defining Neutral Obligations

Except for the *Trent* affair and the possibility of British recognition of the Confederacy in the fall of 1862, the only misunderstanding with England that reached crisis proportions concerned the British building of ships for the Confederate navy and subsequent hospitality given such ships in British Empire ports. These activities were made possible, as Americans saw it, by the inadequacy of the British neutrality laws and their lax enforcement. The British statute on neutral conduct, the Foreign Enlistment Act of 1819, forbade the equipping, furnishing, fitting out, or arming within British jurisdiction of vessels for the purpose of attacking the commerce of friendly powers, or the augmentation of "the warlike force" of such vessels; but did not prohibit the building of such ships. Taking advantage of this loophole, Captain James D. Bulloch, a Confederate agent, arranged with English shipbuilding firms for the construction of the ships which became famous as the Confederate cruisers

Florida and *Alabama*. In each case the ship was built, but not "equipped, fitted out, or armed," in a British shipyard. Each put to sea without equipment, and in a remote and unpoliced sanctuary—the *Florida* in the Bahamas, the *Alabama* in the Azores—met steamers bringing armament, officers, and crew. Each was then duly commissioned as a ship of the Confederate navy and began its career as a commerce destroyer. The *Florida* collected some 40 prizes before it was captured by the U.S.S. *Wachusett*—in a neutrality violation at the port of Bahia, Brazil. The *Alabama* destroyed 57 prizes and released many more on bond before it was sunk in a duel with the U.S.S. *Kearsarge* off the port of Cherbourg, France. Following these two in destructiveness and notoriety was the *Shenandoah*, purchased for the Confederacy from its English owners and armed and manned at sea. Beginning its career late and cruising in the Pacific, it destroyed a large part of the New England whaling fleet at a time when, unknown to its officers or their victims, the Confederacy had ceased to exist.[21]

In the cases of the *Florida* and *Alabama*, Charles Francis Adams, the U.S. minister to the Court of St. James, placed before the British government evidence that the ships were being prepared for the service of the Confederacy. The evidence against the *Alabama* was so strong that at the last moment Earl Russell ordered the ship held, but the order came too late. The *Alabama* had steamed out of the Mersey River on a "trial trip" from which it never returned. The United States held Great Britain guilty of breaches of neutrality, both in permitting its escape and in the construction of the *Florida*. The United States held also that Britain had violated the principles of neutrality in permitting Confederate cruisers to augment their strength in ports of the British Empire. The *Shenandoah*, for example, had put in at Melbourne, Australia, where, in spite of protests from the U.S. consul, it was allowed to make repairs, take on a supply of coal, and recruit additions to its crew. In addition to the actual destruction wrought by the *Alabama*, *Florida*, *Shenandoah*, and less celebrated raiders, their depredations had caused insurance rates to skyrocket, kept ships idle in port, and driven many northern ship owners to sell their vessels or transfer them to foreign registry. For all these losses, British negligence or partiality was held responsible.

The *Alabama* began its career in August 1862. Even before its escape, Captain Bulloch signed a contract with its builders, Laird Brothers, of Birkenhead, for the construction of two armored steamers, each to be equipped with four rifled guns mounted in turrets and armed with a ram at the bow—ships more powerful than any in the U.S. Navy. It was reported that the "Laird rams," as the vessels were called, were being built for France or for the viceroy of Egypt, but common knowledge held that the Confederacy was their real destination and their possession could imperil the blockade, perhaps, deciding the outcome of the war. Adams bombarded Earl Russell with evidence of the true character and destination of the rams, most of it gathered by the efficient American consul at Liverpool. Adams's protests reached a climax with the warning, September 5, 1863, that should the rams be allowed to depart: "It would be superfluous in me to point out to your lordship that this is war."[22] Before receiving Adams's threat, Russell had ordered the rams detained and made sure there was no danger the rams would escape. Months earlier, London had decided not to risk serious trouble with the Washington by permitting repetitions of the *Alabama* episode. In April, it had proceeded against the *Alexandra*, whose case resembled the *Alabama*'s, and in September it detained the Laird rams. There were no further such incidents.[23]

The suppression of Confederate transactions in English shipyards, together with England's continued refusal to recognize the Confederacy, made it clear to Richmond officials and their agents in Europe that British policy was actually beneficial to the North rather than the South. Mason withdrew from England under instructions in 1863, and in the same year, British consuls in the South were expelled. While nonexistent diplomatic relations could technically not be broken, these Confederate gestures were an equivalent manifestation of displeasure.

The British government's action against the *Alexandra* and the rams, although gratifying, did not atone for its earlier laxness, which facilitated the destructive careers of *Alabama* and *Florida* and the *Shenandoah*. The war's end, therefore, left the United States with a sense of grievance and a determination to insist on compensation for damages resulting from Great Britain's too casual observance of neutral obligations. An American proposal that Great Britain's responsibility for the depredations of the Confederate cruisers be submitted to arbitration was at first rejected by the British government. By 1869, however, London had concluded that the precedents set by the *Alabama* and its fellows could be injurious to British interests. In the event of an Anglo-Russian war, which seemed not unlikely, American shipyards might build cruisers for the czar's navy, with disastrous consequences for the British merchant marine. This danger was emphasized when the House of Representatives, in July 1866, voted to repeal those clauses of U.S. neutrality laws that forbade the sale of ships to belligerents.

Fear of such developments was one of the influences that led a new British ministry to agree, in 1869, to the Johnson-Clarendon convention, which provided for arbitration of all claims on either side that had arisen since the last general settlement in 1853. The "*Alabama* claims," as they were now called, were mentioned, but without special emphasis. With no expression of regret or apology for British delinquencies and leaving to be chosen by lot the neutral member of the proposed court of arbitration, help to explain its rejection by the Senate. Charles Sumner, chairman of the Foreign Relations Committee, in a celebrated speech, complained that the proposed convention took account of only a small fraction of England's debt to the United States. England should pay, he argued, not only for the value of the ships and cargoes destroyed by the English-built cruisers, estimated at $15 million, but also for the losses resulting from increased insurance rates and commerce driven from the sea or to the coverage of neutral flags. These items he put at $110 million. Only British encouragement, Sumner argued, had kept the Confederacy fighting after the battle of Gettysburg in July 1863. Britain ought, therefore, to pay half the cost of the war to the North, or $2 billion. The total bill of $2.125 billion, Sumner let it be known, could be paid only by ceding Canada and Britain's other American possessions to the United States.[24]

Sumner's speech, and the Senate's endorsement by a 54 to 1 vote against the Johnson-Clarendon convention, placed an obstacle in the path of any settlement of the claims. No British government could agree to the "indirect claims," as Sumner's second and third categories were called. British spokesmen in Washington also pointed out that Canada could not be ceded contrary to its own wishes, and few Canadians wished for annexation by the United States. Hamilton Fish, secretary of state under President Ulysses S. Grant, was anxious for a friendly settlement with Great Britain. He did not take Sumner's indirect claims seriously but did believe that they should be put forward, if only to be set aside by an authoritative arbitral body. With the concurrence of Grant (who had at first been disposed to back Sumner's position), he brought this matter and others before a joint high commission (five Americans, four British, and one Canadian), which met at Washington in the spring of 1871. The resulting Treaty of Washington, signed May 8, 1871, provided, among other things, for the arbitration of the *Alabama* claims. The treaty featured an unqualified expression of "the regret felt by Her Majesty's Government for the escape, under whatever circumstances, of the *Alabama* and other vessels from British ports, and for the depredations committed by those vessels."[25] Although not exactly an apology or an admission of wrongdoing, this statement went far enough to satisfy most Americans. The treaty then provided for a tribunal of arbitration of five persons, one each to be named by the president of the United States, the queen of Great Britain, the president of the Swiss Confederation, the king of Italy, and the emperor of Brazil. To this body were to be submitted all claims growing out of the acts committed by the *Alabama* and other vessels, "generically known as the 'Alabama Claims.'" "In reaching decisions, the arbitrators were to be governed by three rules, in addition to such principles of international law they might consider applicable.

The three rules were crucial. Of special importance was the first, which filled the gap in the foreign enlistment act by making it the duty of a neutral government to use due diligence to prevent the departure from its jurisdiction of any vessel intended to carry on war against a friendly power—"such vessels having been specially adapted, in whole or in part, within such jurisdiction, to warlike use." Since there could be little doubt that the *Alabama* and *Florida* had been so adapted within British jurisdiction, acceptance of these rules by the British government came close to being a surrender of its case. But when all seemed set for an ending to the controversy, a new crisis arose. When the court of arbitration convened in Geneva in December 1871, the case presented by the United States included the indirect claims, much as had been drawn up by Charles Sumner. This course was adopted not with any expectation that the judges would accept them, but to satisfy the Senate and public opinion in the United States and, as Secretary Fish viewed the matter, to have the claims judicially disposed of, once and for all. Under the impression that the United States had tacitly abandoned the indirect claims, the British charged bad faith and refused consideration of these claims by the court. It appeared that the court might have to adjourn with nothing accomplished, but a way was finally found around the obstacle. The court delivered an extrajudicial statement to the effect that the indirect claims were inadmissible. British and American governments promptly accepted the opinion, and the arbitration tribunal proceeded to consider the direct claims.

The tribunal's decision was made public on September 14, 1872. On British responsibility for the depredations of the *Alabama*, the judges were unanimous. The court also held the British government responsible for the careers of the *Florida* and the *Shenandoah*. Claims based on the careers of other cruisers were unanimously rejected. For the destruction wrought by the *Alabama*, *Florida*, and *Shenandoah*, the court awarded damages of $15.5 million to the United States. Sir Alexander Cockburn, the British member of the tribunal, declined to sign the award, but London promptly paid the bill. A troublesome controversy was settled, Anglo-American relations were restored to a cordial footing, and the obligations of neutrals were established with new precision.[26]

CHAPTER 7

Territorial and Commercial Expansionism: Alaska, the Caribbean, and the Far East

[The United States] is now beginning to loom far above all other countries, modern or ancient. What a spectacle it will be to see a country able to put down a rebellion able to put half a Million of soldiers in the field, at one time, and to maintain them! That will be done and is almost done already. That Nation, united, will have strength which will enable it to dictate to all others, conform to justice and right.
—Ulysses S. Grant, Letter, April 21, 1865

Nobody doubts any more that the Union is a power of the first class, a nation which it is very dangerous to offend and almost impossible to attack.
—The *Spectator*, February 17, 1866

Manifest Destiny defined U.S. foreign policy during the 1840s, despite sectionalism having reared its ugly head during the period. In the 1850s, bitter domestic divisions over the issue of slavery and its extension into new territories produced an erratic and disjointed record. In the face of the growing economic and political power of the North, Southerners believed their system's survival required acquisition of new territories, perhaps Cuba and in Latin America. Northerners, however, were determined to block the expansion of slavery and the South's increased power. Several of the motives for expansion operative in the 1850s also had dissipated in whole or in part. The need for an isthmian route to the Pacific became less urgent with the construction of the first transcontinental railroad—the Union Pacific—authorized in 1862 and completed in 1869. The menace of European intervention in the

Caribbean region disappeared as Spain, which had reannexed Santo Domingo in 1861, withdrew four years later, and France, in 1867, abandoned support of Maximilian's Mexican empire. The years following the Civil War, however, witnessed a return to expansionist projects. Congress, however, did not always cooperate with these schemes. The Democratic Party, formerly the party of Manifest Destiny, went into a long political eclipse while a few prominent individuals in the dominant Republican Party—notably William H. Seward—became devotees of that doctrine.[1]

The experiences of the U.S. Navy prior to and during the Civil War revealed a desire for insular naval bases in the Caribbean and the Pacific. Seward, secretary of state from 1861 to 1869, sought to meet this desire, as did President Ulysses S. Grant after 1869. In 1867, Seward negotiated a treaty with Denmark for the purchase of the Virgin Islands, with the fine harbor of Charlotte Amalie in St. Thomas. The price, $7.5 million, seemed excessive to the American Congress, especially since an earthquake, a tidal wave, and a tropical hurricane had devastated the islands. The House of Representatives warned that it would not feel bound to appropriate the money, and the Senate failed to ratify the treaty.[2] Seward then bargained for the purchase or lease of Samaná Bay, a spacious harbor at the northeastern corner of the island. President Andrew Johnson declared, in his annual message of December 9, 1868, that he was "satisfied that the time has arrived when even so direct a proceeding as a proposition for an annexation of the two Republics of the island of St. Domingo would not only receive the consent of the people interested, but would also give satisfaction to all other foreign nations."[3] Congress also rejected this proposal, and soon thereafter Seward left office.

President Grant took up the Santo Domingo project. Influenced by a pair of American speculators and against the advice of his able secretary of state, Hamilton Fish, he sponsored the annexation of Santo Domingo by the United States and tried to force it through the Senate, but found the body inhospitable. Carl Schurz of Missouri feared the nation was being seduced "by the deceptive allurements of tropical splendor." More pointedly, Thomas Bayard of Delaware warned that Grant's scheme would "embark the Government of the United States upon the vast and trackless sea of imperialism," and he warned, "the fiat of nature has declared that we are unable to elevate such a race as inhabit that island to the level of our own." The Senate rejected Grant's treaty by a vote of 28 to 28.[4]

If the postwar revival of Manifest Destiny lost some of its fascination, commercial expansion was another matter since American factories and farms were producing more than the home market could absorb. Every administration from Ulysses S. Grant to William McKinley, therefore, sought to expand the country's foreign markets. Quite distinct from the desire for further territorial acquisitions, it nevertheless provided a motive for some acquisitions. It helped to account for an American interest in Alaska, Midway Island, the isthmian region, Hawaii, the remote Samoan Islands, and, particularly, a continuing "open door" in the Far East.

From Alaska to Samoa

Alaska and Midway Island were to be the only new possessions acquired in the immediate postwar period. Seward was more successful in his desire to make the United States a Pacific power. He acquired Russian America, to be known as Alaska, in March 30, 1867.[5] A number of factors were behind the czar's decision to sell the land, including the perceived inevitability of American designs on Alaska, the need to replenish a treasury depleted by the Crimean War and Russian railroad enterprises, and a desire to free Russia of the unprofitable colony and concentrate on designs in the Far East, Siberia, and Central Asia. The czar's desire to sell was suggested by the Russian minister, Baron Stoeckel, when he returned from a visit to St. Petersburg and the two diplomats quickly agreed on a price of $7.2 million. The Senate promptly approved the treaty, as Charles Sumner, chairman of the Committee on Foreign Relations, emphasized the importance of cultivating friendship with Russia, the only major power that indicated sympathy for the North in the recent war. He and other legislators argued the acquisition of Alaska was another step in ousting the European monarchies from the continent and suggested it was Britain's turn to go next—in harmony with popular schemes for the annexation of Canada. Congressman William Munger of Ohio, declaring that "England's star had passed its zenith," predicted: "Russia will one day, and that at no distant period, control England's Asiatic possessions. When that happens, as a natural consequence the United States will take possession of the Bahamas and all the British West Indies islands; and Canada will fall into our lap like a ripe apple." He anticipated the day, much ahead of his time, that "the two great Powers on earth will be Russia and the United States."[6]

The purchase of Alaska was the United States' final acquisition of continental territory. Although popularly dismissed initially as "Seward's folly" or "Seward's icebox," it was a significant territorial addition, containing mineral, forest, and animal resources. In another respect the Alaska purchase was a turning point in the history of American expansion. Earlier acquisitions of territory by treaty—Louisiana, Florida, the Mexican cession, the Gadsden purchase—had stipulated, not only that the might divert their trade and political attachment to Britain, secured U.S. consent to a treaty. American exports to Hawaii expanded substantially under the free market, but these exports were considerably less than the U.S. Treasury's loss of revenue from the free admission of sugar and other Hawaiian products. The arrangement's value to America was political and strategic, not economic, since holding Hawaii in the American economic sphere also kept it in the United States' political sphere.[13]

Before the Senate approved renewal of the 1884 reciprocity treaty, it was amended, in 1887, to provide the United States with the exclusive use of Pearl Harbor in the island of Oahu—a privilege of which it made no immediate use. Hawaiian sugar production, which multiplied tenfold in the next 20 years, tied Hawaiian prosperity closely to the American market. An 1890 change in American tariff policy, admitting all foreign sugar on equal terms and providing a subsidy to domestic producers, brought about an economic crisis that contributed to a Hawaiian political crisis. The existence side by side of a modern system of economy and a monarchical government reflected a growing divergence between economic and political power. The propertied class, primarily composed of Americans, Hawaiian Americans, and British, supported an increasingly extravagant and corrupt government dominated by native Hawaiians. In a bloodless 1887 coup, the white business community forced on King Kalakaua a new constitution that effectively reduced his authority and created a legislature controlled by the propertied classes.[14]

Kalakaua was succeeded in 1891 by his sister, Liliuokalani, who attempted to recover the monarchy's prerogatives; however, she underestimated the determination of the white elite. Given the political apprehension and an economic depression induced by America's tariff policy, local white businessmen and lawyers looked on U.S. annexation to guarantee a stable government and economic prosperity. They planned to persuade or compel Liliuokalani to abdicate and then to offer the islands to the United States. In the spring of 1892, President Benjamin Harrison's cabinet and Congressional leaders secretly offered encouragement. When, in early 1893, the Queen announced plans to proclaim a new constitution, the annexationists immediately formed a committee of safety, set up a provisional government, and demanded the Queen's abdication. The U.S. minister John L. Stevens landed troops from the cruiser *Boston* and granted a precipitate de facto recognition. The queen yielded her authority "to the superior force of the United States of America" until the United States should "undo the action of its representative" and reinstate her "as the constitutional sovereign of the Hawaiian Islands." Stevens shortly advised the State Department that the "Hawaiian pear is now fully ripe, and this is the golden hour for the United States to pluck it," and warned that if annexation did not take place promptly, "these people, by their necessities, might be forced towards becoming a British colony."[15]

The provisional government dispatched a commission to Washington to negotiate a treaty of annexation. The commissioners met with no serious difficulty, and on February 15, President Harrison sent to the Senate a treaty providing for the annexation of the Hawaiian Islands as "an integral part of the territory of the United States" and for the payment to the deposed queen of a life annuity of $20,000. One of Grover Cleveland's first acts as president was to withdraw the Hawaiian treaty "for the purpose of reexamination." A few days later he sent a special commissioner to the Hawaiian Islands to investigate the character of the annexation movement. The report convinced the president that the revolution would not have been attempted and could not have been carried out without the encouragement and support of Minister Stevens, and that the great majority of the native people supported the queen and opposed annexation. Cleveland, therefore, not only buried the annexation treaty, but concluded that he was under a moral obligation to undo "the great wrong done to a feeble but independent State" by restoring the queen to her throne. Cleveland's new minister, Albert S. Willis, secured from a reluctant Liliuokalani a promise of amnesty for the revolutionists, but the provisional government refused to step down and restore the ex-queen. Only the superior armed force of the United States, said Hawaiian president Sanford B. Dole, could compel the provisional government to give up its authority.[16]

Cleveland referred the matter to Congress, which resolved that nothing be done. In Hawaii a constitutional convention, held in 1894, provided a republican constitution that perpetuated the power of the white minority. The new government suppressed a small royalist uprising in 1895 while the 1894 U.S. tariff restored Hawaiian sugar to its favored position in the American market. The Hawaiian republic enjoyed several years of peace and prosperity, but its leaders never lost sight of their chief desire, annexation by the United States.

The Venezuelan Crisis

The United States' unilateral assertion of the Monroe Doctrine, as a policy it alone interpreted and maintained, reached a climax in 1895 with a boundary controversy between Venezuela and the adjoining British Guiana. Venezuela's independence had been recognized by the United States in 1822; the country was then a portion of Colombia. The neighboring western portion of Guiana had been ceded to Great Britain by the Netherlands in 1814 without an agreed-on boundary line. In 1840, the British explorer Sir Robert Schomburgk drew a line that the British accepted but the Venezuelans rejected. When gold deposits were discovered in the interior, the boundary gained increased importance. Great Britain offered to arbitrate its claims west of the Schomburgk line but not east of it, where British settlers had for years occupied areas now contested. Venezuela insisted on arbitration without such limitations and appealed to the United States for support. The United States recommended arbitration to Great Britain from time to time, but not until 1895 did its recommendation assume the nature of an ultimatum.[17]

The new urgency that marked U.S. diplomacy in 1895 may be attributed in part to the economic depression that followed the panic of 1893. With railroad strikes and armies of the unemployed marching on Washington, the depression seemed to threaten the nation's very social fabric. Foreign markets appeared essential to reviving the economy and achieving social stability, and American businessmen jealously eyed European competition for South America markets. As the *British Trade Journal* commented in the fall of 1895, there was "an unwritten Monroeism working like yeast in the commercial world of America." Propaganda also played a role. The previous year, William L. Scruggs, an American paid agent of the Venezuelan government, had published a pamphlet entitled *British Aggressions in Venezuela, or the Monroe Doctrine on Trial* that stressed the Venezuelan side of the case. He advanced the proposition that the upper waters of the Orinoco River interlocked with those of the Amazon and the La Plata; hence, if the British claimed the southern shore of the Orinoco at its mouth, they also held "the key to more than a quarter of the whole continent."[18] Scruggs's lobbying aided in Congress unanimously endorsing a joint resolution early in 1895 that requested the president "most urgently" recommend to Great Britain and Venezuela they arbitrate their dispute.

Upon the death of Cleveland's secretary of state, Walter Q. Gresham in May 1895, preparation of a note to Great Britain was taken over by the vigorous Boston lawyer Richard Olney. Olney chose to rest his case on the "noninterference" principle of the Monroe Doctrine, which he contended Great Britain would violate if it took any territory claimed by Venezuela without submitting the issue of ownership to impartial adjudication. To demonstrate the United States' legitimate interest in the controversy, Olney argued that if Britain succeeded in appropriating Venezuelan territory, then other European powers would follow. European nations would be "permanently encamped on American soil" and the United

States no longer would be "practically sovereign on this continent, and its fiat is law upon the subjects to which it confines its interposition." Olney ended by requesting a reply by early December. The entire note smacked of an ultimatum.[19] Lord Salisbury, British foreign secretary, replied quite simply: first, the Monroe Doctrine was not binding on Britain, which refused to recognize special U.S. rights in the Western Hemisphere; and second, even if the Monroe Doctrine were recognized as valid international law, it would have no bearing on a boundary dispute between an American state and a British possession. The British insisted they would arbitrate claims beyond the Schomburgk line, but not within it.

It was difficult to refute the British argument. There were growing concerns in the United States about the threat posed to American economic and strategic interests by British moves in Brazil, Nicaragua, Trinidad, and Venezuela, as well as equally ominous French and German designs in Brazil and the Caribbean. Such concerns, and domestic political responses, influenced Cleveland's actions. Cleveland's foreign policy was denounced as weak for failing to prevent the British occupation in 1895 of the Nicaraguan port of Corinto to enforce payment of claims and for rejecting the annexation of Hawaii. Cleveland, a stubborn man, was in no mood to accept Salisbury's rebuff complacently, therefore, on December 17, 1895, he submitted the British correspondence to Congress. Since Britain had declined arbitration, Cleveland proposed that Congress authorize a commission to determine where the boundary ought to be, and that when the commission had reported, the United States assume responsibility for enforcing its decision. It was, he observed, "a grievous thing to contemplate the two great English-speaking peoples of the world as being otherwise than friendly competitors in the onward march of civilization," but even war, he implied, would be preferable to "a supine submission to wrong and injustice and the consequent loss of national self respect and honor."[20]

Thus, Cleveland, like his predecessor, James K. Polk, looked John Bull "straight in the eye." At home the message received enthusiastic support, and Congress promptly gave the president the authority he had asked for. Despite the bold language, however, there was little risk of war. Olney's message was a most skillful piece of work, satisfying even the wildest jingoes without, in fact, involving the United States in any real danger of conflict. If American opinion was chauvinistic, prevailing British opinion was quite the reverse as it expressed friendship for the United States. The German kaiser diverted British irritation from Washington to Berlin by congratulating President Paul Kruger of the Transvaal on repulsing an English raid at Jameson. Lord Salisbury, underrating American determination, sought a formula that would provide arbitration and yet save British face. Great Britain, protected against loss of territory long settled or held by British subjects, agreed to an arbitration court composed of two U.S. Supreme Court justices, two Englishmen, and a Russian jurist. It rendered a decision in October 1899 that agreed on a line differing from the Schomburgk line in assigning Venezuela the south bank of the Orinoco River at its mouth and another bit of territory in the interior.[21]

In France, Germany, Austria-Hungary, Italy, Spain, Holland, and Russia, official and newspaper opinion were hostile to the United States' assumption of the predominant position in the Western Hemisphere. Nor were Latin Americans appreciative of Uncle Sam's assuming the role of their protector or his pretensions as the "Colossus of the North." Yet the Monroe Doctrine had scored a notable victory, for Lord Salisbury, although denying it on principle, conformed to it in practice. The controversy marked a turning point in Anglo-American relations.[22] Within the next dozen years, all significant Anglo-American misunderstandings were amicably adjusted. An ancient dispute over inshore fishing rights along the coasts of British North America flared up with new heat in the 1880s along with a misunderstanding over the American claim of an exclusive right to regulate the taking of fur seals in the Bering Sea. Both controversies were eventually settled by arbitration; the fur seal dispute in 1893, the northeast fisheries question not until 1910.

Early U.S. Commercial Agents in Asia

The search for new markets, so keenly pressed after the Revolution, led American merchants into distant seas, where as colonials they had never ventured. As British subjects, they had been excluded from the trade of the Far East by the British East India Company's monopoly. The Jay Treaty admitted American ships to the trade with the British East Indies, and in other Far Eastern lands they needed only to secure the permission of the governments concerned. Ships from New York and New England soon made the U.S. flag a familiar sight from the shores of California and Oregon to those of China and Southeast Asia. Yankee skippers were trading with Oman on the Indian Ocean, with Batavia in the Dutch East Indies, with Manila in the Spanish Philippines, with the kingdom of Siam, with Botany Bay in Australia, but above all, with the Chinese port of Canton.

The Chinese Empire looked on itself as the possessor of the world's only true civilization, and all others were "barbarians" or "foreign devils," with whom the Chinese desired no intercourse. As a favor, foreign ships were admitted to the single port of Canton in south China, and at the same port foreign merchants were allowed to live in "factories" outside the city walls. China had no regular diplomatic relations with the outside world—no ambassadors or ministers abroad or recognized consulates in China. Since the emperor of the Middle Kingdom recognized no equals, foreign ambassadors were received at Beijing only as tribute-bearers from inferior states.[23]

China's neighbors, Japan and Korea, were even more isolated. Korea acknowledged the authority of China and traded almost exclusively with that country. The Japanese had once been an active seafaring people, their ports open to foreign traders and to Christian missionaries, who made many native converts. But early in the seventeenth century, Japan closed its doors, forbade Japanese to go abroad, expelled the missionaries, and outlawed native Christianity. Only the Dutch kept a trading post on Deshima Island in the harbor of Nagasaki, to which they could bring one ship a year. Some trade with China was also allowed through Nagasaki, but otherwise Japanese authorities shielded its people from all outside contacts.

The Americans sometimes followed, sometimes preceded, the European countries in opening commercial and diplomatic relations with the Far East. In its Chinese policy, it at first followed England, while in its Japanese policy, it led and Europe followed. European and American policies developed in different directions, since American aims were purely commercial and, as yet, projecting no colonial ambitions. For commerce, the United States desired most-favored-nation treatment, equality, or the "open door." Threats to the open door came from European powers, seeking colonies, spheres of interest, and special favors. China was torn by internal strains and encroachments of foreign powers; thus, America's policy sought to maintain China's independence and "territorial integrity." Japan, after opening its doors to western influences, speedily modernized. The United States, however, abstained from the use of force in pursuing its objectives. If other nations, particularly the British and French, used force to gain commercial advantages, the United States gained too through the most-favored-nation clauses.

The "Old China Trade"

The first American ship to visit Canton, the *Empress of China*, left New York in February 1784 and returned in May 1785. Ships from New York, Boston, and other Atlantic ports quickly followed to bring back Chinese products—tea, spices, silk and cotton fabrics, chinaware—but were hard put to find American commodities for the China market. Ginseng, a root plentiful in the United States and esteemed in China for its supposed medicinal properties, and sea otter furs from the northwest coast or seal fur from the South Pacific brought good prices in Canton. "After 1840," writes Tyler Dennett, "American policy in Asia was always directed with an eye to the future—to the day when Americans would supply the seemingly limitless markets of the East."[24]

The first effective blow against the Chinese policy of exclusion was struck by the British in the Opium War of 1839–1842, in which Chinese armies, fleets, and fortifications proved ineffectual against European armaments. By the Treaty of Nanking, August 29, 1842, China ceded to Britain the island of Hong Kong, opened four new ports for trade, and agreed to pay an indemnity of $21 million for confiscated opium, the cost of the war, and debts owing to British merchants. British traders might do business with any Chinese in the open ports.[25] Caleb Cushing, from Massachusetts, was sent to China by President Tyler to ensure that American ships and trade enjoyed privileges at least equal to those granted the British. On July 3, 1844, Cushing and a Chinese commissioner signed the Treaty of Wanghia that opened the five ports of Canton, Amoy, Foochow, Ningpo, and Shanghai to American ships and trade and authorized U.S. consular officers at these ports. It permitted American citizens to reside in the open ports with their families; to acquire sites for houses, places of business, hospitals, churches, and cemeteries; to purchase books; and to employ scholars to teach the Chinese language. It also gave Americans residing in China the right of extraterritoriality—the right, when accused of a crime, to be tried before an American official and according to American law. It fixed a low tariff, paid by Americans, on imports and exports. Finally, it contained a most-favored-nation article, assuring to the United States any additional rights or privileges that might be gained by another power.[26] Because of the inclusion of extraterritoriality and tariff limitation in the Chinese treaties with the United States and other European powers, these documents came to be referred to as the "unequal treaties." While they became a regular Chinese grievance against the West, not until China became an ally in World War II were the last of these unequal provisions abrogated.

The United States "Opens" Japan

Prior to 1853, British, Russians, and Americans had tried in vain to open diplomatic and trade relations with the island empire. In the meantime, the settling of the Oregon question in 1846 and the acquisition of

California in 1848 gave the United States the magnificent harbors in San Francisco Bay and Puget Sound. Forward-looking Americans saw the dawn of a great commercial era on the Pacific, and American foreign policy in the 1850s sought to open Japanese ports to trade, gain access to Japanese coal, and insure humane treatment for American sailors shipwrecked on Japanese shores. The key agents in attaining these were Commodore Matthew Galbraith Perry and diplomat Townsend Harris.[27]

Perry was, if possible, to deliver a letter from the president (Franklin Pierce replaced Millard Fillmore in 1853) to the emperor. He was to seek permission for American vessels to enter one or more of the Japanese ports for trading purposes, to establish a coal depot, and gain protection of shipwrecked American seamen. His instructions stated that if, "after having exhausted every argument and every means of persuasion, the commodore should fail to obtain from the government any relaxation of their system of exclusion, or even any assurance of humane treatment of our shipwrecked seamen, he will then change his tone," with that new tone coming in the form of a warning that "if any acts of cruelty should hereafter be practiced on citizens of this country, whether by the government or by the inhabitants of Japan, they will be severely chastised."[28]

Perry paid two visits to Tokyo Bay, in July 1853, and February 1854. The Japanese people had never seen steam powered ships, and some wondered if the "ugly barbarians" had "succeeded in floating volcanoes." The Japanese leadership, however, was aware of the power of western naval armament and knew that both Britain and Russia were planning similar demonstrations. Moderate concessions to Perry might shield them from immoderate demands of other powers. On his first visit, Perry was able to deliver the president's letter to a representative of the Shogun, at this time the head of the Japanese government. When he returned seven months later, he found the Shogun's government ready to sign the Treaty of Kanagawa on March 31, 1854. Japan agreed to give proper treatment to shipwrecked American sailors and a most-favored-nation clause. While American ships might enter two Japanese ports to procure supplies, these ports were isolated—Shimoda, southwest of Tokyo Bay, and Hakodate, on the northern island of Hokkaido—and all business was to be transacted through Japanese officials. There was no mention of a coal depot, but a United States consul could reside at Shimoda.[29]

Perry's treaty was accepted as the pattern, and Japan signed similar treaties with Britain, Russia, and the Netherlands. Both China and Japan had made their first treaties under duress—China as a result of defeat in war, Japan under threat of unpleasant consequences if it refused. Neither nation intended to go further than it was compelled to go in carrying out the spirit or the letter of its new obligations. The western powers, on the other hand, including the United States, were determined not only to enjoy the rights they had secured by the treaties but also to gain additional rights as soon as possible. Both Perry and Parker, who became U.S. commissioner to China in 1855, advocated an aggressive policy. When London obtained a base at Hong Kong, they encouraged Washington to secure bases in Far Eastern waters from which it might promote its interests. Perry occupied the Bonin Islands, arranged for a supply depot on Okinawa in the Ryukyus, and suggested a protectorate over Formosa. Parker also had schemes for making Formosa a protectorate. But in Washington, officials turned a deaf ear to their projects and announced that the only interests of the United States in China were in "lawful commerce" and "the protection of the lives and property of its citizens." The United States had no motive "for territorial aggrandizement or the acquisition of political power in that distant region."[30]

The Tientsin Treaties

The United States in the 1850s had no wish for territorial conquest in the Far East, nor would it, with a couple of minor exceptions, use armed force to advance its interests there.[31] It relied on the good faith of the Chinese and Japanese governments, on the persuasiveness of its diplomats, and, in China especially, on the operation of the most-favored nation article in its treaty with that country. In 1857, the French and British battled China to enforce their earlier rights and to gain further privileges. The United States and Russia remained neutral but sent their diplomats to cooperate in the negotiation of new treaties with China—which all four powers signed at Tientsin in 1858. The United States gained access to 11 additional ports on the coast and on the Yangtze River, the right to navigate the Yangtze as far as Hankow and to travel in the interior, and toleration for the Christian religion. Neutral Russia was the chief beneficiary from the hostilities of 1857–1860, for by the Treaty of Aigun (1858), China ceded the northern watershed of the Amur River. The Russian representative, mediator between China and the allies during ratification, was rewarded with the Maritime Province and immediately established a base at Vladivostok.

By gaining a new most-favored-nation article, the United States maintained the principle of equality of treatment, or the open door. In the 1850s and 1860s, it would also take a stand on behalf of the preservation of China's territorial integrity. When the Taiping Rebellion (1851–1865) threatened to divide the empire, the American commissioner at Canton sympathized with the imperial government's struggle to hold China together. Anson Burlingame, U.S. minister to China from 1861 to 1867, found the representatives of Great Britain, France, and Russia ostensibly willing to drop claims for special privileges and demands for further territory. His agreement with them, he reported, "is a guarantee of the territorial integrity of the Chinese Empire."[32]

Townsend Harris Ends Japan's Isolation

The first American consul at Shimoda, appointed in accordance with Perry's treaty, was Townsend Harris, a New York businessman with years of experience in the Far East. After Harris reached Shimoda in August 1856, the Japanese made his stay as uncomfortable and as dreary as possible hoping that he would leave. Harris, however, was a man of persistence, patience, and tact, and within a year, he had persuaded Japanese officials to sign a convention materially enlarging American privileges in Japan. Later that year he was permitted to travel in state to the seat of the Shogun's government and on July 29, 1858, secured the first full-fledged commercial treaty. In obtaining Japan's signature, Harris was aided by contemporary events in China, where the Chinese had to sign the treaties of Tientsin. The American treaty became the model for those soon after made with the Netherlands, Russia, Great Britain, and France.[33]

The convention of 1857 and the treaty of 1858 opened four new ports to American ships, authorized the appointment of consuls at all the open ports, permitted trade with private parties, gave to Americans the right to reside in the open ports, and there to hold property, build churches, and practice their religion. The treaty permitted each government to appoint a diplomatic representative to reside at the capital of the other. Like the Chinese treaties, it gave extraterritorial status to Americans and fixed upper limits for duties on imports and exports. Neither Perry nor Harris approved of extraterritoriality, but since the British, Dutch, and Russians had inserted it in their treaties, Harris could not forgo securing for the United States the same privilege. Japan, like China, became a victim of "unequal treaties." The treaties of 1858 were followed by a period of internal discord and strife in Japan. An imperial decree ordered all foreigners out of the empire by June 25, 1863, and while no serious effort was made to enforce this edict, foreigners were attacked and even murdered from time to time. During this difficult period, the United States cooperated closely with the other powers in Japan. American naval forces joined in a punitive expedition against rebellious clans in southwestern Japan, and the American minister was aboard a British warship at a joint naval demonstration at Osaka, in 1865, which persuaded the emperor to give his approval to the treaties signed seven years before. The period ended with the "restoration" of the emperor to sovereign power. After the "Meiji Restoration" of 1868, the imperial court, its seat removed to Edo, now rechristened Tokyo, quickly saw the advantages of Western ideas and technology. Relations with Japan after the Meiji Restoration of 1868 were, for many years, uneventful and generally cordial.

Again China, Korea, and Japan

American interest in the Far East after the Civil War was kept alive by a slow growth of trade and continuing American missionary activity, although the nation's relations with China suffered some deterioration. On July 28, 1868, Secretary Seward signed a treaty assuring most-favored-nation treatment to Chinese visiting or residing in the United States and reciprocally to Americans in China.[34] Cheap labor was in much demand on the Pacific coast, and Chinese workers were imported to build the Central Pacific railroad, but its completion in 1869 threw thousands of laborers out of work and generally depressed wages. The panic of 1873, followed by a long economic depression, found white workers on the Pacific coast and their spokesmen in politics complaining about the Chinese willing to work for a fraction of the wage they considered adequate. Anti-Chinese riots in California and insistent demands for prohibition or limitation of Chinese immigration prompted Congress in 1879 to pass such a limitation bill, which President Hayes vetoed for violating the 1868 treaty. China subsequently agreed that the United States might "regulate, limit, or suspend, but not absolutely prohibit" immigration of Chinese laborers. In 1904, without China's consent, the exclusion of working-class Chinese was made permanent.[35] Such racial discrimination produced resentment in China. At the same time, the occasional mistreatment of American missionaries in China fed anti-Chinese feeling in the United States. Hence as China and Japan drifted toward war over their conflicting interests in Korea, American sentiment tended to favor Japan rather than China.

Korea, the "hermit kingdom," had long paid tribute to China and, until 1832, to Japan also. Such submission, however, was ceremonial rather than political. In 1876, Japan, imitating Perry's technique, entered Korean waters and secured a treaty repudiating any Korean allegiance to China and opening the way for Japanese penetration. The Chinese government had often denied any responsibility for the treatment of foreigners in Korea, but now the Chinese began to assert their claims to suzerainty. Thus when the U.S. Navy sent Commodore Robert Shufeldt to make a treaty with Korea, the Chinese viceroy at Tientsin insisted the proper approach to Korea was through China. Commodore Shufeldt and Li Hung-chang negotiated a treaty at Tientsin, and it was signed in Korea on May 22, 1882, establishing American trade rights, permitting residence of Americans at the open ports, fixing import and export duties, and providing temporary rights of extraterritoriality.[36]

China and Japan, with Russia, now a neighbor of Korea on the north, schemed for hegemony in Korea. While the Russians withdrew, Chinese and Japanese troops entered the peninsula following assassinations, kidnappings, deportations, and an antiforeign uprising. Neither was willing to withdraw, and in August 1894, Japan declared war on China. Washington was officially neutral, but its attitude tended to favor Japan. The Japanese achieved a surprisingly easy victory on both land and sea over their much larger foe. The American legations in Tokyo and Beijing were useful in initiating peace negotiations. In the Treaty of Shimonoseki of April 17, 1895, Japan unwisely extracted harsh terms from China: recognition of Korean independence meaning a free hand for Japan there; the cession of Formosa, the Pescadores Islands, and the Liaotung peninsula on the mainland of southern Manchuria; new commercial privileges; and a large war indemnity. Outside intervention, of which Washington had earlier warned Tokyo, appeared when Russia, France, and Germany notified Japan that the three powers, "in the interest of the peace of the Far East," could not consent to Japanese acquisition of mainland territory. Japan was forced to return to China the Liaotung peninsula, receiving instead an increased war indemnity. The part played by Russia in this diplomatic maneuver marked it as Japan's rival.[37]

If the United States showed no great interest in the outcome of the Sino-Japanese war, it became deeply concerned over the events that quickly followed. The three powers that had vetoed Japan's acquisition of the Liaotung peninsula soon showed that they had no qualms about taking Chinese territory for themselves. Early in November 1897, two German missionaries were murdered in Shantung province; within two weeks German armed forces took possession of Tsing-tau on Kiaochow Bay on the Shantung peninsula. Berlin also demanded Chinese consent to the establishment of a German coaling and naval station in Kiaochow Bay and exclusive mining and railroad rights in the Shantung province. The Chinese government, having no means of resistance, bowed to the German demands and on March 6, 1898, granted them in full. Russian warships appeared at Port Arthur on the Liaotung peninsula, and Russia exacted a 25-year lease of Port Arthur as a naval base, of the neighboring port of Dairen, and of additional portions of the peninsula. With these virtual cessions, Russia secured exclusive railway and other economic rights in Manchuria, with policing and administration privileges. France had already annexed Cochin China and established a protectorate over the remainder of the Indo-Chinese peninsula, at the expense of Chinese claims to suzerainty. Now it obtained the lease of Kwangchow Bay on the south China coast and special mining and railroad rights for French citizens in China's three southern provinces. Britain's interests would have been best served by preserving China's territorial integrity, but after trying in vain to dissuade Germany, Russia, and France from their territorial demands, it joined in. London obtained a lease for the port of Weihaiwei, facing Port Arthur, for as long as Russia should hold Port Arthur; increased Russia's leased territory at Kowloon adjoining Hong Kong; and recognized Russia's economic interests in the Yangtze Valley.

Toward Commercial Reciprocity

If this process continued, Washington worried that China would soon be carved up into colonies and spheres of influence by competing European states. American policy since 1844 had been to insist on equality of opportunity—the open door—for American trade with China. To keep the door open, it had fostered the preservation of China's territorial integrity. The prospect of being excluded from the Chinese trade was particularly alarming to American interests in the 1890s, for they long envisioned a growing Chinese market for America's increasing surpluses. Secretary of State James G. Blaine succeed in amending McKinley's 1890 tariff to empower the president to impose higher rates on commodities imported from countries that imposed duties he deemed "reciprocally unequal and unreasonable" on U.S. products.

Armed with this bargaining weapon, Secretary Blaine succeeded in negotiating executive agreements with 10 countries by which they reduced or abolished import duties on various American agricultural and manufactured products. There was also an informal commercial arrangement with France, by which Paris agreed to apply minimum tariff rates to a small number of American products. The Wilson-Gorman tariff of 1894 abruptly terminated reciprocity, arousing resentment in participating American and European nations. The Dingley tariff of 1897 raised American duties to higher levels, increasing European antagonism since low-cost American products were successfully competing with European industry. The Austria-Hungarian foreign minister, Count Goluchowski, in late 1897 complained of the "destructive competition with transoceanic countries," warning that Europeans "must fight shoulder to shoulder against the common danger" and "must close their ranks in order successfully to defend their existence"[38]

Advocates of reciprocity, anticipating resentment abroad, succeeded in incorporating certain mild reciprocity provisions in the Dingley tariff act of 1897. One of these provisions empowered the president to lower the American rates on brandies, wines, paintings, and statuary imported from countries that agreed to equivalent reductions on U.S. products. A second provision directed the president to impose specified duties on coffee, tea, tonka beans, and vanilla beans—articles otherwise on the free list—when imported from any country whose duties on American products the president should deem to be "reciprocally unequal and unreasonable." A third provision empowered the president to negotiate reciprocal trade treaties with other governments, with the unrealistic condition that the Senate and House of Representatives must approve such treaties. The result of these cautious gestures toward reciprocity in an act that erected new tariff barriers had little effect on American trade.[39]

* * *

The prospect, though largely unfulfilled, of reciprocity treaties offered by the provisions of the 1897 act alleviated the danger of European discrimination against American industry—the threat that Count Goluchowski had voiced so dramatically. The threat itself, however, had the effect of turning American eyes afresh to the Far East, especially to China. China had been to some extent a market for American goods for a century. If Europe should close its markets to American exports, there was still China, where the stirrings of a modernization movement seemed to promise "four hundred million customers" for the products of the West. It was for these reasons that threats to the open door in China were so alarming to some Americans in 1898.

CHAPTER 8

War with Spain and the New Manifest Destiny

We are no longer a squalid Democracy, secure chiefly by reason of our isolation... We are a Nation—with the biggest kind of N, a great imperial Republic destined to exercise a controlling influence upon the actions of mankind and to affect the future of the world as the world was never affected, even by the Roman Empire.
—"Marse" Henry Watterson, *Louisville Courier-Journal*, 1896

A new consciousness seems to have come upon us-the consciousness of strength-and with it a new appetite, the yearning to show our strength.... Ambition, interest, land hunger, pride, the mere joy of fighting, whatever it may be, we are animated by a new sensation. We are face to face with a strange destiny. The taste of Empire is in the mouth of the people even as the taste of blood in the jungle.
—*Washington Post*, June 2, 1898

The United States was by the 1890s, as the naval historian Captain Alfred Thayer Mahan expressed it, again, "looking outward." The Republicans revived the phrase Manifest Destiny in 1892 and four years later wrote into their party platform an ambitious expansionist program. They called for a foreign policy that was "firm, vigorous, and dignified," for "a naval power commensurate with the nation's position and responsibility," for control of the Hawaiian Islands, for a Nicaraguan canal "built, owned and operated by the United States," and for "a proper and much-needed naval station in the West Indies." The Republican victory in 1896 was followed by war with Spain, the acquisition of a colonial empire in the Caribbean and the Pacific, and defense of the open door in

China and China's territory integrity. The party that had launched this program won easily at the polls in 1900.

The New Manifest Destiny

Captain (later Rear Admiral) Alfred Thayer Mahan in 1890 contributed to this revival with his masterpiece, *The Influence of Sea Power upon History, 1660–1783*. The work's simple thesis was that a powerful navy had raised England from a second-rate power to the world's most powerful state; thus, without sea power no nation could attain a foremost international position. In other publications throughout the 1890s,[1] he urged his fellow countrymen to profit by the British example. Respected at home and abroad, friend and confidant of Theodore Roosevelt and Senator Henry Cabot Lodge, Mahan exerted a significant influence on public affairs.

Mahan defined "sea power" broadly as "all that tends to make a people great upon the sea or by the sea," thus including commerce, merchant marine, navy, naval bases at strategic points, and overseas colonies. All of these England had in abundance. Although the United States had a growing overseas commerce, when Mahan first wrote it possessed only the rudimentary beginnings of a modern navy, no colonies, nor outlying naval bases. Without colonies and bases, American warships would "be like land birds, unable to fly far from their own shores. To provide resting-places for them, where they can coal and repair, would be one of the first duties of a government proposing to itself the development of the power of the nation at sea."[2]

Specifically, in addition to more warships, Mahan urged the acquisition of Caribbean and Pacific bases. Others piercing the isthmus with a canal would be "nothing but a disaster to the United States." The United States must not obtain Caribbean bases "by means other than righteous; but," he declared, referring to the rejection of Seward and Grant's annexation projects, "a distinct advance will have been made when public opinion is convinced that we need them, and should not exert our utmost ingenuity to dodge them when flung at our head."[3]

Like Seward, Mahan foresaw a great commercial future in the Pacific. Moreover, he prophesied that this ocean would witness a gigantic struggle between Western and Oriental civilizations—with the United States in a front-line position. Outposts in the Pacific, therefore, were of crucial importance; indeed, the issue might be determined by "a firm hold of the Sandwich [Hawaiian] Islands by a great, civilized, maritime power," and the United States was "naturally indicated as the proper guardian for this most important position."

At the root of sea power, according to Mahan, was trade—the source of national wealth and power. Without trade, a nation might require a navy for coastal defense, but other elements of sea power—colonies, bases, and merchant marine—would lose their significance. As Secretary of State James G. Blaine put it, the United States preferred the "annexation of trade" to the "annexation of territory."[4] The intensified quest for markets was partly a consequence of the 1890s economic depression. The depression, together with the revelation of the end of the American frontier in 1893, in Frederick Jackson Turner's famous essay "The Significance of the Frontier in American History" fostered widespread frustration. This feeling was expressed, historian Richard Hofstadter wrote, in both "an intensification of protest and humanitarian reform" and in a mood "of national self-assertion, aggression, expansion." The war with Spain fit this mood exactly, serving "as an outlet for expressing aggressive impulses while presenting itself, quite truthfully, as an idealistic and humanitarian crusade."[5]

The intellectual atmosphere and the psychological mood help to explain why American public opinion was more receptive to overseas expansion in the 1890s than in Seward's day. European neo-imperialism, from the 1870s onward, found those powers engaged in a race across Asia, Africa, and the Pacific islands for colonial possessions—a race brought home to Americans by the triangular quarrel over Samoa. "The great nations," Henry Cabot Lodge wrote in 1895, "are rapidly absorbing for their future expansion and their present defense all the waste places of the earth. It is a movement which makes for civilization and the advancement of the race. As one of the great nations of the world, the United States must not fall out of the line of march."[6] Despite the growing importance of foreign markets for the surplus of America's industrial production, however, the business community remained unconvinced of the need for colonies. Colonies, in their eyes, were not only difficult and expensive to administer but also meant foreign complications, perhaps even war. Rather than risky colonial ventures, business preferred to rely on the high quality and low prices of American products, backed by government-sponsored favorable treaties to insure their entry into the world's markets. Not until the spring and summer of 1898 did international affairs persuade American business that colonial possessions might be economically advantageous; and even then, the possessions that caught their eye—the Philippines, primarily—were valued more for their supposed entry to the China markets.

Benjamin Harrison's administration (1889–1893), led by Secretary of the Navy Benjamin F. Tracy, was the first since the Civil War to propose building an up-to-date fleet. His Annual Report of 1889 called for

20 battleships, 12 for the Atlantic and 8 for the Pacific, equal to the best in armor, armament, and speed. The next year Congress authorized the building of three first-class battleships, the *Indiana*, *Massachusetts*, and *Oregon*, which, with the *Iowa*, formed the backbone of the fleet in 1898.[7] Harrison's first secretary of state unsuccessfully attempted to secure naval bases in Santo Domingo and Haiti. Harrison repeatedly urged Congress, also unsuccessfully, to assist in building a Nicaragua canal. Harrison, Tracy, and Secretary of State John W. Foster were sympathetic to the annexation of Hawaii and might have succeeded if the opportunity had occurred before the Democratic victory of November 1892.

William McKinley, the successful Republican candidate in the 1896 presidential battle, indicated no aggressive intentions in the international sphere. Taking office in the midst of the depression, he did not consider foreign entanglements. He assured antiexpansionist Carl Schurz that his administration would entertain "no jingo nonsense," no scheming for annexation of Hawaii. The aging John Sherman, his first secretary of state, was of like mind—"opposed to all acquisitions of territory not on the mainland."[8]

The Crisis in Cuba

The war with Spain was not simply the product of the United States' expansionist urge. The "essential ingredient," as historian John Offner has put it, "was the deplorable condition of Cuba."[9] Spain's misgovernment of its Cuban colony, notorious for decades, had fostered periodic Cuban insurrections demanding independence or autonomy. The Spanish government's promised reforms at the close of the Ten Years' War (1868–1878) terminated slavery but otherwise had brought the Cuban people little relief. Ninety percent of the revenues collected in Cuba went either to service the cost of the war or into the pockets of the island's Spanish officialdom and military. Economic distress, made worse in 1893 by the worldwide depression and by the U.S. tariff of 1894, which reimposed a duty on raw sugar, combined with political discontent to produce, in February 1895, an armed revolt against Spanish rule.

An insurgent government in eastern Cuba and a Cuban junta in New York dispensed propaganda and desperately sought money and arms from sympathetic Americans. The insurgents destroyed cane fields, sugar mills, and other property to render the island valueless to Spain; while in February 1896, the newly appointed captain general, Valeriano Weyler, responded with a "reconcentration" policy. Weyler ordered the people of central and western Cuba into camps, surrounded by trenches, fortified with barbed wire, and guarded by blockhouses. Cubans who disobeyed his order were regarded as insurgents and shot on sight. For the thousands of women, children, and old men in the camps, there was no provision of adequate shelter, food, or sanitation. Famine and disease were rife, and by the spring of 1898 it was estimated that over 200,000 of the *reconcentrados* had died.

The Cuban conflict affected both American economic interests and humanitarian sensibilities. American capital invested in Cuban sugar and tobacco plantations, sugar mills, manganese and iron mines, and other properties amounted to $40 to $50 million. Trade with Cuba, in good years, amounted to as much as $100 million.[10] American businessmen with investments in Cuba or who traded with Cuba obviously desired to end the hostilities. Perhaps more important was American humanitarian and religious outrage at the suffering and death inflicted on innocent noncombatants in the concentration camps. The American public received vivid and frequently exaggerated accounts in the "yellow press," so named because of the garish color of its ink. William R. Hearst's *New York Journal*, Joseph Pulitzer's *New York World*, and other papers sent talented reporters and artists to Cuba, and their descriptions of conditions in the island were widely published. Their sensational reports, while not solely responsible for American involvement in the war, did undeniably create a wave of sympathy for the *reconcentrados*.

Gradually, the Protestant religious press and numerous daily newspapers, both Democratic and Republicans, clamored for intervention on behalf of the Cubans, as trade journals, boards of trade, and chambers of commerce generally advocated a hands-off policy.[11] American business, rapidly recovering by the fall of 1897 from the prolonged economic depression, feared that a war with Spain would interrupt its growing prosperity. Fear of inflation, caused by Spanish-inflicted losses on American commerce, joined with fear about war expenditures. Americans with investments in Cuba explicitly warned the State Department that they would suffer more heavily from a war between Spain and the United States than from the existing civil conflict.

Notably, the advocates of intervention usually did not ask to annex Cuba; if they mentioned that possibility, they did so only to disclaim it. Senator Lodge, who in 1895 had spoken of Cuba as a "necessity" to the United States, indicated a year later that he would be satisfied if it were "in friendly hands, in the hands of its own people." Other senators, speaking for intervention, either opposed annexation or professed a willingness to wait until the Cuban people should bring about union in the future. Although the *New York Tribune* preferred to leave the question open, the *Journal*, *World*, *Sun*, *Herald*, *Times*, and *Journal of Commerce*, of the same city, denounced any suggestion of annexation. The American public indicated that intervention, if it came, should be intervention for a free and independent Cuba.

American Intervention in Cuba

In Washington, officials could not ignore the situation in Cuba. American citizens, usually naturalized Cubans, arrested by the Spanish authorities required official action to secure their release. It was also necessary to patrol the coasts of the United States to prevent or break up attempts at "gun-running" by Cuban sympathizers. In the spring of 1896, Congress passed a concurrent resolution declaring that belligerent rights should be accorded the insurgents, but President Cleveland and Secretary of State Richard Olney ignored this suggestion. Both Cleveland and William McKinley, who succeeded him on March 4, 1897, hoped to avoid intervention. Cleveland intimated in his last message to Congress that the United States could not indefinitely stand aside and watch the cruel struggle continue, while McKinley made this position still clearer in instructions to the new minister to Spain in July 1897. Prospects for a settlement brightened in September when the assassination of the Spanish prime minister brought in a Liberal ministry, which had pledged a more generous and humane colonial policy. The new ministry recalled General Weyler, abandoned the reconcentration policy, and promised limited autonomy to the Cuban people through the election of their own legislature.

President McKinley welcomed the reform program in his annual message of December 6, 1897, and hoped Spain would carry it out, but warned again that if the new policy failed to pacify the island, "our obligations to ourselves, to civilization and humanity" might require intervention.[12] Limited autonomy was not acceptable to insurgent leaders, who would accept only complete independence; nor was it acceptable to Spaniards in Cuba, who resented the prospect of being ruled by a native Cuban legislature. On February 9, 1898, the *New York Journal* printed a private letter of Dupuy de Lome, the Spanish minister in Washington, which described McKinley as "weak and a popularity-hunter." The stolen letter also raised doubts about Spain's good faith in carrying out the reform program and in current trade negotiations with the United States. De Lome's immediate resignation and an apology from the Spanish government ended the episode but left an increment of ill will and distrust.[13]

Six days later, the U.S. battleship *Maine*, on a "courtesy call" to Havana following rioting in early January, was sunk at anchorage in the harbor, costing 266 American seamen their lives. The cause of the catastrophe has never been conclusively determined, although an internal coalbunker fire near the *Maine*'s forward ammunition magazines has been blamed.[14] At the time, however, American naval officers examining the wreck with divers, found evidence that the initial explosion had been caused by an underwater mine that set off the magazines. The Navy's report was not made public until March 28; meanwhile, many Americans, guided by sensational newspaper accounts, had concluded Spain was guilty of the act. "The readers of *The Journal*," boasted the New York newspaper in March, "knew immediately after the destruction of the *Maine* that she had been blown up by a Spanish mine."[15] "Remember the Maine!" became the popular watchword.

While Congress generally refrained from recriminations over the *Maine* tragedy until after the Navy's report, there was an intensified denunciation in the Senate of Spanish atrocities in Cuba. On March 17, Senator Redfield Proctor of Vermont described to the Senate his recent unofficial visit to Cuba. Outside of Havana the situation, he said, "is not peace, nor is it war. It is desolation and distress, misery and starvation." Of the 400,000 persons in concentration camps, "one-half have died and one-quarter of the living are so diseased that they can not be saved."[16] Outside the camps there was only desolation—no crops, no domestic animals; everything of value was destroyed. He described Captain General Blanco, Weyler's successor, as an "amiable gentleman," with good intentions, but utterly unable to relieve the situation or put down the rebellion. The speech persuaded many skeptics of the yellow press's revelations; even business interests, hitherto opposed to intervention, conceded that something had to be done. The *Wall Street Journal* reported on March 19 that the speech had "converted a great many people in Wall Street." Senator Proctor's statements, "as many of them expressed it ... made the blood boil."[17]

McKinley was under heavy pressure from the public, the press, and from virtually all Democrats and many Republicans, in the House and Senate, to take vigorous action against Spain. He reacted by following up the policy stated in his annual message—unless Spain could bring peace to Cuba, the United States would intervene. Spain not only failed to pacify Cuba, but also it was held responsible for the loss of the *Maine*. McKinley gave the Spanish government one more chance when, on March 27, he demanded Madrid finally abandon the reconcentration policy, grant an armistice until October 1, and enter, through McKinley, into peace negotiations with the insurgents. The president indicated Cuban independence was the only satisfactory outcome of the proposed peace negotiations. In Madrid, officials were caught on the horns of a dilemma: if they refused McKinley's demands, a disastrous war with the United States appeared certain; if they accepted his demands, popular indignation in Spain might overthrow the government. The Spanish government, seeking support from the European powers, received expressions of willingness to participate in a joint demonstration against the United States—if someone would take the lead. None, however, was willing to assume leadership. In England, Queen Victoria was sympathetic to the Spanish Queen Regent, but British public opinion was overwhelmingly pro–United States. On April 6, 1898, the British informed Washington that on Cuban matters they would be "guided by the wishes of the president."[18]

The Decision for War

Without hope, then, of substantial support from Europe, the Spanish government replied on March 31 that reconcentration was being abandoned and that if the insurgents asked for an armistice it would be granted. Rejecting McKinley's proposal of mediation, it stated that the Cuban parliament meeting in May should be the instrument of pacification, evidently rejecting the demand for independence. Spain was willing to submit to arbitration the question of responsibility for the destruction of the *Maine*. A few days later, April 9, the Spanish government declared a suspension of hostilities on its own initiative, and on the following day U.S. minister Stewart L. Woodford cabled from Madrid that he believed a solution satisfactory to all parties was obtainable.[19]

Paying slight heed to these last-minute concessions and assurances, McKinley sent to a war-minded Congress on April 11 a message describing the recent negotiations as unsatisfactory and declared that: "In the name of humanity, in the name of civilization, in behalf of endangered American interests which give us the right and the duty to speak and to act, the war in Cuba must stop." He asked for authority to use the military and naval forces of the United States "to secure a full and final termination of hostilities between the Government of Spain and the people of Cuba."[20] Congress eagerly seized on the president's message, but debated for a week whether it should recognize the independence of the Cuban people or whether it should also recognize the existing, but insubstantial, republican government of Cuba. The administration opposed recognition of the existing regime, which it did not believe could meet Cuba's needs.

The three resolutions Congress adopted, by a vote of 42 to 35 in the Senate, 311 to 6 in the House, and the president approved on April 20, declared that "the people of Cuba are, and of right ought to be, free and independent" and demanded that Spain "at once relinquish its authority and government in the Island of Cuba and withdraw its land and naval forces from Cuba and Cuban waters." The president was empowered to use the U.S. armed forces to enforce this demand. Without a record vote, the Senate adopted, and the House accepted, a fourth resolution prepared by Senator Henry M. Teller of Colorado, declaring: "That the United States hereby disclaims any disposition or intention to exercise sovereignty, jurisdiction, or control over said Island except for the pacification thereof, and asserts its determination, when that is accomplished, to leave the government and control of the Island to its people." The Colorado senator remarked that he wished to make it impossible for any European government to say, "when we go out to make battle for the liberty and freedom of Cuban patriots, that we are doing it for the purpose of aggrandizement for ourselves or the increasing of our territorial holdings." He wished this point made clear in regard to Cuba, "whatever," he added, "we may do as to some other islands." Thus, with a specific renunciation of annexationist designs in Cuba but with freedom of action with respect to Spain's other colonies—Puerto Rico, the Philippines, the Carolines and Marianas—the United States entered the conflict with Spain. Madrid at once severed diplomatic relations, and on April 24 declared war. Congress responded with a declaration of war the next day, making it retroactive to April 21.

The war would have momentous consequences for both Spain and the United States. For Spain, it meant the loss of the last remnants of its once great colonial empire. To the United States, it brought the sudden assumption of unprecedented imperial responsibilities and elevation to the status of a "world power." All of which was accomplished by a short and inexpensive war.

The Creation of an Empire

The conflict was one-sided from the beginning. The Spanish navy, on paper perhaps the equivalent of the American fleet, had nothing to match the *Massachusetts*, *Indiana*, *Iowa*, and *Oregon*. Spanish ships and crews, moreover, were in a wretched state and the officers imbued with a defeatist spirit, while the U.S. Navy was well prepared and spoiling for a fight. The Spanish army in Cuba outnumbered the American expeditionary forces, but, though Spanish soldiers fought bravely and stubbornly, they were ill equipped and supplied.

The first important battle took place in the Far East. Months before the war, Assistant Secretary of the Navy Theodore Roosevelt had submitted a memorandum suggesting that in the event of hostilities with Spain, the Asiatic squadron "should blockade, and if possible take Manila."[21] Even earlier, in June 1896, Lieutenant William W. Kimball had prepared a contingency plan for such an operation.[22] Roosevelt, on February 25, 1898, cabled Commodore George Dewey, at Hong Kong, to "begin offensive operations in the Philippines" as soon as he should be informed of a declaration of war. Although other drastic orders issued by the impatient Roosevelt, as acting secretary, were countermanded, the orders to Dewey were allowed to stand.

Dewey, on receiving the news of war, steamed south to the Philippines and on May 1 led his squadron of light cruisers past the forts and through the rumored minefields that guarded the entrance to Manila Bay. At dawn he spied the Spanish ships, equal in number to his own but hopelessly antiquated. The American cruisers fired so effectively that before noon the entire Spanish naval force lay sunk or burning, while the American casualties consisted of eight slightly wounded men. Dewey occupied Cavite and controlled Manila Bay, while on August 13 some 11,000 U.S. troops entered Manila against only token Spanish resistance. As an incident of their expedition to the Orient, the American forces occupied the island of Guam in the Spanish Marianas.

Meanwhile, the main Spanish fleet, four armored cruisers, and three destroyers had left the Azores and slipped into Santiago harbor on the south coast of Cuba. The Atlantic Fleet, under Commodores William T. Sampson and Winfield Scott Schley, closed in around the narrow entrance to Santiago Bay, while an army of 16,000 regulars and volunteers, commanded by Major General W. R. Shafter, landed on the Cuban coast a few miles east of Santiago and fought its way toward that city. On July 1, the Americans pierced the outer defenses of Santiago and were able to look down on the harbor. Caught between the U.S. Army and Navy, the Spanish squadron left the harbor on the morning of July 3 and in a running fight all its ships were sunk or run ashore. American losses were one man killed and one wounded. On July 16, the city of Santiago surrendered. Meanwhile, another American expeditionary force landed in Puerto Rico and prevailed, against feeble Spanish resistance, to take possession of that island. On July 18, the Spanish government requested France to arrange for a termination of hostilities.[23]

With Madrid's request for peace terms before them, President McKinley and his advisers confronted difficult decisions. What of Spain's other islands—Puerto Rico, Guam, and above all the Philippines, an extensive and populous area where Spanish misrule had brought about native rebellion only less formidable than that in Cuba? The Teller Amendment said nothing of these, and its author had expressly excluded "some other islands" from his ban on the annexation of Cuba. On the day after Dewey's victory, and before its completeness was known in Washington, the president had approved a State Department proposal for a "coaling station" in the Philippines, presumably Manila. McKinley was well aware of the Philippines' significance and was determined to acquire a base within 500 miles of the coast of China. Decisions to push the annexation of Hawaii and to occupy Guam between Hawaii and the Philippines were clearly part of the same pattern.

McKinley seems to have needed little prodding from the Republicans in Washington who had been urging expansion ever since Hawaii had invited annexation five years earlier.[24] Before going to Cuba as lieutenant colonel of the "Rough Riders" regiment, Roosevelt wrote of the importance of securing possession of the Philippines, as well as Puerto Rico. Three days after Dewey's victory, Senator Henry Cabot Lodge wrote: "We hold the other side of the Pacific, and the value to this country is almost beyond recognition." On no account, he added, must we "let the islands go... they must be ours under the treaty of peace." He assured Roosevelt: "Unless I am utterly and profoundly mistaken the Administration is now fully committed to the large policy that we both desire."[25]

American businessmen generally opposed to intervention in Cuba and obtaining colonies in the spring of 1898 underwent a sudden conversion. They were increasingly alarmed at the aggressive behavior of the great powers in China. In February and March, chambers of commerce and boards of trade on both the East and West Coasts urged the State Department to take energetic measures for the protection of American interests. An American Asiatic Association was formed in New York to lobby for the preservation of American rights and interests in the Orient. The *New York Journal of Commerce*, which had hitherto scoffed at colonies, isthmian canal schemes, and big-navy programs, now declared itself in favor of an isthmian canal, the annexation of Hawaii, and an increased navy—all for the purpose of strengthening the United States in the Pacific and safeguarding its rights in China.

Dewey's victory at Manila seemed to offer an effective remedy. With naval bases in the Philippines, Hawaii, and perhaps Guam, might not the United States become a great Pacific power, capable of defending its own interests in the Orient? Many trade journals agreed with the *New York Journal of Commerce*, which declared that to give up those islands now "would be an act of inconceivable folly in the face of our imperative future necessities for a basis of naval and military force on the Western shores of the Pacific."[26] Converted to colonialism by the situation in the

Far East, American business easily applied the same reasoning to the Caribbean. The erstwhile anti-imperialist *Journal of Commerce* now insisted that Puerto Rico be retained and suggested that it might be necessary to control Cuba in spite of the Teller Amendment. The former Spanish islands might furnish not only outlets for trade but also profitable fields for investment. The war for humanity might be made to pay dividends. Protestant opinion, while split, was similarly influenced by American victories.[27] The churches began laying plans for new missionary enterprises, for they were about to enter what one religious writer labeled "the imperialism of righteousness." McKinley had been committed to retaining a secure naval base in the islands since the first week of the war, but the churches wanted an opportunity to practice their benevolence among the 7 million Filipinos. Their zeal may ultimately have influenced the president's decision to demand cession of the entire archipelago.

Washington's reply to the Spanish request for peace terms offered an immediate cessation of hostilities on condition that Spain relinquish all authority over Cuba, cede to the United States Puerto Rico and an island in the Ladrones (Marianas), and consent to American occupation of Manila, pending a definitive peace treaty to determine the future of the Philippines. On this basis an armistice protocol was signed on August 12, with American and Spanish peace commissioners scheduled to meet in Paris not later than October 1. Thus, several months were allowed for discussion and testing of public opinion before the final decision on the Philippines needed to be made. By this time American business and religious leaders would be heard, and McKinley would also have received from abroad significant hints that he would do well to retain the Philippines. London indicated it would be glad to see the United States keep the islands. Tokyo expressed a similar preference, though it added that Japan would be willing to join with the United States and a third power in a joint administration. These friendly gestures were presumably designed to prevent the Philippines from falling into Germany's possession. After Dewey's victory, the Germans had sent a naval squadron to Manila, where its commander made things difficult for Dewey by disregarding the latter's rules of blockade. Should the United States abandon the Philippines, the Germans were available to promote their own interests.[28]

The American commissioners were instructed on September 16 that the United States demanded full sovereignty over the principal island of Luzon, but in Paris they were advised that the archipelago formed an economic unit with Manila as its commercial center. The commissioners cabled the president a strongly worded argument for the retention of the entire group. McKinley, who had sounded public opinion in the

Midwest, had apparently reached a similar conclusion. On October 26, Secretary Hay informed the commissioners that the United States must retain all the Philippines. Little heed was paid to Filipino insurgents, led by Emilio Aguinaldo, who demanded independence and had set up a government of their own near Manila. It was generally agreed, by whites who knew the Philippines, that the natives were not prepared for self-government. Independence under these conditions might breed anarchy, and anarchy would invite foreign—quite possibly German—intervention. Spain, reluctant to surrender the remaining remnants of its colonial empire, could do nothing but accept the American terms. The blow was softened by an agreement to pay Madrid $20 million for the islands' public works and improvements. By the treaty of December 10, 1898, Spain relinquished "all claim of sovereignty over and title to Cuba," ceded to the United States the Philippine Islands, Guam in the Marianas or Ladrones, Puerto Rico, "and other islands now under Spanish sovereignty in the West Indies."[29] The inhabitants of the ceded territories were promised "the free exercise of their religion," but it was stipulated that their "civil rights and political status" should "be determined by the Congress." For the first time, a treaty acquiring territory made no promise of citizenship and no promise, actual or implied, of statehood. The United States thereby acquired not "territories" but possessions or "dependencies" and became, by definition, a "colonial" power.

The Senate Debates Imperialism

The peace treaty, however, still had to meet the Senate's approval and there it encountered determined opposition. Few senators appear to have objected seriously to the annexation of tiny Guam or of Puerto Rico, which was nearby and peopled chiefly by the white race, though of alien tongue. But annexation of the Philippines was a much greater break with American tradition. Their distance, 6,000 miles from San Francisco; their population of 7 million Malays, including a minority of pagans and Moslems; the existence of a vigorous independence movement whose leaders were as hostile to American as to Spanish sovereignty—all these factors made their acquisition seem to many, in and out of the Senate, a dangerous venture in imperialism and a violation of time-honored American principles. An Anti-Imperialist League was organized to combat annexation, while in the Senate many Democrats and a few Republicans proposed to vote against ratification.

Debate on the treaty was in executive session, but weeks before it reached the Senate, members publically expressed their views in debating a number of resolutions dealing with the acquisition of colonial territory. The most important of these, introduced by Senator Vest of Missouri, declared: "That under the Constitution of the United States no power is given to the Federal Government to acquire territory to be held and governed permanently as colonies."

Democratic senators, ably supported by Republican George F. Hoar of Massachusetts, argued that under the Constitution there was no place for a colonial system based "upon the fundamental idea that the people of immense areas of territory can be held as subjects, never to become citizens." It was against that very system that Americans had rebelled in 1776; thus, if the United States took the Philippine Islands, their inhabitants must have all the rights of citizens. They could not be governed as subjects, nor could they and their products be excluded from the United States. American agriculture and American labor could be subjected to unchecked competition from the Filipinos. It was foolish to believe, furthermore, that American institutions would operate successfully among a people so widely different in race, language, religion, and customs.[30] Even if the United States might constitutionally annex the Philippines and govern them as a colony, was it expedient to do so? No, responded opponents: departure from the spirit of republican institutions in governing the colonies could destroy those institutions at home. Possession of the Philippines, moreover, might embroil the United States in the international politics of the Far East and endanger the Monroe Doctrine. How could America forbid Europe to interfere in the Western Hemisphere when they were interfering in the Eastern? "The Monroe Doctrine is gone!" lamented Senator Hoar. Opposition senators also minimized the trade advantages to be expected from annexation and ridiculed the religious argument. "In order to Christianize these savage people," one senator remarked, "we must put the yoke of despotism upon their necks;... Christianity can not be advanced by force."

Supporters of the treaty answered all these arguments. The constitutional argument advanced by Senator Orville H. Platt of Connecticut, in fact, anticipated subsequent Supreme Court decisions.[31] The right to acquire and the right to govern territory, said Platt, were sovereign rights that the United States enjoyed in common with other sovereign nations, and the right to govern implied the right to establish whatever form of government was suitable to the condition of the territory and the character of its inhabitants—be they savages, barbarians, or civilized folk. Platt denied that there would be any obligation to admit the Philippines as a state or to confer citizenship on Filipinos. He denied that either the people or the products of the islands could be admitted to the United States without the consent of Congress. The senator affirmed, in brief, precisely what his opponents denied. The debate continued from early December until February 6, 1899. William Jennings Bryan, titular head of the Democratic Party, came to Washington to urge Democratic support of the treaty, arguing that peace should be made as soon as possible and that the question of freeing the Philippines could be disposed of later.[32] The Senate approved the treaty 57 to 27—a single vote above the necessary two-thirds majority.

Meanwhile, on February 4, two days before the Senate approved the treaty, hostilities had broken out between American troops in Manila and Filipino insurgents, led by Aguinaldo. In annexing an empire the United States also annexed a war, which was to prove much longer and more troublesome than that with Spain. Not until July 1902, with substantial casualties on both sides, was armed resistance in the Philippines effectually subdued.

Hawaii, Wake, and Samoa

The War with Spain, which gave the United States Puerto Rico, the Philippines, and Guam, also furnished the impetus necessary to effect the long-delayed annexation of Hawaii. It was followed within a year by the partition of the Samoan group, in which the United States received the island of Tutuila, where since 1878 it had possessed rights for a coaling station in Pago Pago harbor.

Advocates of Hawaiian annexation, in March 1898, had all but abandoned hope of accomplishing their object by treaty and brought into the Senate a joint resolution of annexation. The resolution, however, made no headway until Dewey's victory at Manila turned American eyes to the Pacific.[33] If the American flag were to remain in the Philippines—if from a Philippine base, the United States was to defend its rights in China—Hawaii, it was argued, provided an essential naval base and coaling station en route to the Far East. The Hawaiian government, during the hostilities, had placed Honolulu harbor at the United States' disposal and offered an alliance. The friendly attitude of Hawaii and that it was subjecting itself to possible Spanish reprisals enabled the annexationists to argue that Hawaii should be brought under the American flag for its own protection. The war thereby strengthened the case for annexation. Much was also said of the "yellow peril" in Hawaii—the rapid growth of its Japanese population and the danger that Hawaii might be absorbed in Japan's growing empire. A new joint resolution was introduced in the House of Representatives three days after the Manila Bay battle and passed on June 15 by a large majority. Senate opponents could delay but not defeat the measure, which passed on July 6, 1898, and promptly received the president's signature. On the following August 12, Hawaii formally came under the jurisdiction of the United States.

The Hawaiian Islands; their outpost Midway, acquired in 1867; and Guam secured the route to the Philippines and the Far East. The wide gap between Midway and Guam was soon filled in by the annexation of Wake Island. The naval explorer, Commander Charles Wilkes, had asserted title to Wake for the United States in 1841, but it was not until January 17, 1899, that the United States took formal possession.[34] The year of the Spanish-American War witnessed a new outbreak of native trouble and international friction in Samoa, which was resolved the following year by a partition of the islands, the United States receiving Tutuila, while Upolu and Savaii passed to Germany. A treaty of partition was signed in Washington on December 2, 1899. From the treaty, the United States obtained no title to Tutuila (subsequently, with the small neighboring islands, known as American Samoa), merely German and British renunciation of their claims. The native chiefs of Tutuila, however, formally ceded their island to the United States in 1900, and those of the nearby Manu'a group followed suit in 1904. President Theodore Roosevelt accepted these cessions without submission to the Senate. The American title was never questioned, but to remove any doubt, Congress, by a joint resolution of February 20, 1929, accepted, ratified, and confirmed these cessions.

A Popular Verdict on Empire

The expansionist policies growing out of the war with Spain had, in general, been sponsored by Republicans and opposed by Democrats. It was perhaps inevitable that "imperialism" should become an issue in the presidential campaign of 1900. The Democrats criticized opponents for holding the Philippines by armed force against the will, and despite the resistance, of the most vocal native faction. While the Republican platform justified the establishment of American sovereignty in the Philippines as a result of the breakdown of Spanish rule, and promised to confer on the Filipinos "the largest measure of self-government consistent with their welfare and our duties," the Democrats officially denounced "the Philippine policy of the present Administration" and "the greedy commercialism" that had dictated it. "We are unalterably opposed," said the Democratic platform, "to the seizing or purchasing of distant islands to be governed outside the Constitution and whose people can never become citizens." "Imperialism," said the Democrats, "is the paramount issue" in the campaign.

Bryan, the Democratic candidate, fully endorsed—and probably dictated—the party's platform declarations with regard to the Philippines. The attack on imperialism, however, was not confined to the Democrats. Many prominent Americans of both parties joined the Anti-Imperialist League, which conducted a vigorous campaign based on the principle of "government by the consent of the governed."[35] Opposed from the beginning to annexation of the Philippines, the league joined the Democratic Party in denouncing the war of subjugation against the Filipino insurgents and in demanding that they be given independence. On the surface, the political issue for 1900 seemed clear-cut, but as usual in presidential campaigns, the "paramount issue" does not stand alone.[36] Bryan also had insisted on incorporating a "free-silver" plank in the Democratic platform. "Bryan would rather be wrong than President," quipped Thomas B. Reed, Republican Speaker of the House, for many Republican anti-imperialists discovered that they preferred McKinley, with the gold standard and a little imperialism, to Bryan and free silver. Bryan, as the campaign progressed, found that his diatribes against imperialism excited little popular enthusiasm and shifted his emphasis to an attack on the trusts, the plutocracy, and special privilege. But even if attention had been concentrated on the Philippines, there was no stark difference between the Democratic and Republican positions. Republicans promised "self-government" and never expressed a desire to hold the Philippines permanently. The Democrats, not proposing to surrender to Aguinaldo and his insurgents, promised to "give" the Filipinos "a stable form of government" and independence, but under "protection from outside interference"—a "protectorate" of undefined duration.

When American voters went to the polls in November 1900 to cast their ballots for McKinley or Bryan, it is none too clear what their votes actually meant with respect to policy regarding the Philippines or, for that matter, colonial expansion. Certainly those who wished to vote for McKinley and the gold standard, or for McKinley and the continuation of prosperity under his administration, could persuade themselves that they were voting for little more "imperialism" than was implicit in the Democratic proposals. But there must have been many, influenced by business and the churches, who were anxious to vote for a profitable imperialism that was also an "imperialism of righteousness." At any rate, when McKinley and Theodore Roosevelt won the election by a handy popular plurality of nearly 900,000 votes, the Republicans could be pardoned for assuming that the nation had accepted and approved of their territorial expansion.

CHAPTER 9

The United States Adjusts to Its New Status

Chronic wrongdoing, or an impotence which results in a general loosening of the ties of civilized society, may in America, as elsewhere, ultimately require intervention by some civilized nation, and in the Western Hemisphere the adherence of the United States to the Monroe Doctrine may force the United States, however reluctantly, in flagrant cases of such wrongdoing or impotence, to the exercise of an international police power.
—President Theodore Roosevelt, State of the Union Address, December 6, 1904

As near as I can make out the Constitution follows the flag—but doesn't quite catch up with it.
—Elihu Root, Secretary of War, 1901

After 1898, American power and influence were demonstrated through U.S. dominance in the Caribbean, leadership in the Far East, and participation in European affairs. The nation had acquired Puerto Rico, Hawaii, and the Philippines, ceasing to be land-bound and inward-looking. These acquisitions did not themselves cause the assumption of worldwide responsibilities, but rather were a result and a symbol of a new attitude toward the world. Theodore Roosevelt, entering the White House in September 1901, found a navy already comprised of 17 battleships, and under his leadership, it grew steadily. The United States in 1890 had been a relatively negligible naval power; in 1904, its naval strength stood in fifth place; and by 1907, in second place. When war began in 1914, the U.S. fleet in battleship strength was easily one of the three foremost powers.[1] Outlying naval bases had been developed at

Guantanamo Bay in Cuba and at Pearl Harbor in Hawaii. In the meantime, the United States had built an isthmian canal at Panama, and, to safeguard that vital defense link against European interference, had ringed the Caribbean Sea with protectorates whose governments were friendly and dependable.

American supremacy in the Western Hemisphere was facilitated by British accommodation. Great Britain's retreat in the Venezuela controversy and its friendliness during the Spanish-American War were early steps in what historian Bradford Perkins labeled "the great rapprochement."[2] Alarmed by the threat of rising German commercial and naval rivalry, Britain closed or deactivated its naval bases at Halifax and on Puget Sound, concentrated its naval power in European waters, and conceded naval supremacy on American coasts and in the Caribbean to the United States. In the same spirit, it yielded to American desires regarding the isthmian canal and the boundary of Alaska, approved of American protectorates in the Caribbean, arbitrated a long-standing dispute over fishing rights, and accepted an American policy for Mexico. A traditional opponent had become a cooperative friend.

The Canal and Caribbean Protectorates

America's primary interest in the Caribbean focused on an isthmian canal—in Nicaragua or Panama. The war with Spain and the acquisition of new possessions and interests in the Pacific had emphasized the importance of American control of any canal as a means of moving its fleet from one ocean to the other. President McKinley declared on December 5, 1898, "the construction of such a maritime highway is now more than ever indispensable" and "our national policy now more imperatively than ever calls for its control by this Government."[3] The situation seemed favorable as the financially troubled Panama Canal Company, successor to the original French company, was willing to dispose of its rights, if the consent of Colombia could be obtained, and the failing Maritime Canal Company in Nicaragua had forfeited its concession. The governments of Nicaragua and Costa Rica were willing to discuss the rights necessary for the construction of a canal by that route.[4] Finally, London signed a new treaty in November 1901 abrogating the Clayton-Bulwer Treaty, thus freeing the United States to construct, manage, and police its own canal. The only U.S. obligation was a guarantee that the canal would be open to the vessels of commerce and war of all nations "on terms of entire equality."[5]

Congress had long supported Nicaragua as the favorite location of a canal route, but Panama now had persuasive advocates, notably the

New York law firm of Sullivan and Cromwell, and the Frenchman Philippe Bunau-Varilla. Both represented the interests of the New Panama Canal Company that hoped the United States would salvage its enterprise. A commission of engineers reported first in favor of Nicaragua, then switched to Panama when the company lowered the price for its rights to $40 million, a figure the commission thought reasonable. A House of Representatives bill supported a Nicaraguan canal, but the Senate amended it to favor Panama. An earthquake in Nicaragua pointed to danger of a canal in that volcanic-prone country.[6] President Theodore Roosevelt signed the Isthmian Canal Act on June 28, 1902, making the Panama route the first choice.

The United States needed the consent of Colombia to the transfer of rights from the New Panama Canal Company and its consent for the United States to the exercise in the proposed Canal Zone the authority necessary to operate and protect the canal. The consent was arranged in a treaty signed in January 1903; however, the Colombian Senate rejected it, holding that the price ($10 million) was too low and the impairment of Colombian sovereignty too sweeping.[7] When the Department of Panama then revolted, the United States promptly recognized its independence and shielded it from Colombian vengeance. A few days later, November 18, 1903, the United States received in perpetuity the use of a zone across the isthmus, 10 miles wide, where it exercised sovereign rights and authority. It could ensure sanitation and maintain public order in the cities of Colon and Panama, and fortify the canal. The United States, in turn, would pay to Panama $10 million at once and $250,000 annually beginning after nine years. In addition, the United States promised to maintain "the independence of the Republic of Panama."

The treaty was signed for Panama by Philippe Bunau-Varilla, who had promoted and helped to finance the revolution and, in return, had been named the first minister of Panama to Washington.[8] The circumstances of the Panamanian revolution—the appearance of U.S. collusion, the prevention of Colombian attempts to suppress the uprising, the unusual haste with granting recognition, and the resulting advantageous treaty—created bitter resentment in Colombia and divided opinion in the United States. Roosevelt, however, energetically defended his handling of the Panama crisis. He labeled it "by far the most important action I took in foreign affairs" in his *Autobiography*, and in 1911 supposedly boasted: "I took the Isthmus, started the canal, and then left Congress—not to debate the canal, but to debate me."[9] Washington consistently refused to submit the propriety of its conduct to arbitration. Finally, in 1921, the United States, without admission of wrongdoing, paid Colombia

$25 million in restitution—a tacit admission of U.S. wrongdoing. Senatorial approval of the payment was further eased by pressure from American financiers who were rewarded for the settlement with Colombian oil concessions.[10] Construction of the canal, though attended with some misfortune at the outset, went forward rapidly, and on August 15, 1914, the Panama Canal was opened to traffic.

U.S. possessions in the Caribbean consisted of Puerto Rico, acquired from Spain in 1898; the Virgin Islands, purchased from Denmark in 1916;[11] and on perpetual leases, almost the equivalent of annexation, as in the Panama Canal Zone. Between 1901 and 1917, the United States instituted a system of unofficial "protectorates," by which small Caribbean republics were bound to an American "sphere of influence." The principal recipients of American "protection" were Cuba, Panama, the Dominican Republic, Nicaragua, and Haiti. The special relations with these republics were embodied in treaties, no two of which were alike; but only the Republic of Panama received a U.S. promise of "protection."[12] Other treaties, as with Cuba and Haiti, contained engagements by the "protected" states not to impair their independence or cede any of their territory to a third party. Since careless public finance could lead to foreign intervention and possible loss of independence, the treaties with Cuba, Haiti, and the Dominican Republic contained restrictions on, or gave the United States supervision over, their financial policies. Treaties with Cuba and Nicaragua provided the United States the use of naval bases within their territorial limits and exclusive canal rights through Nicaraguan territory.

American investments in these Caribbean protectorates benefited from the increased stability and financial responsibility where, for example, in the Dominican Republic, Haiti, and Nicaragua this resulted in a transfer of government obligations from European to American bankers. Yet, in none of the five republics, save Cuba, were American financial interests significant, and the primary motives behind American policy were clearly political and strategic. The Panama Canal made the isthmian area vital to the American defense system; consequently, Washington sought to prevent rival nations from obtaining a foothold in the vicinity of the canal or on the approaches to it. Hence, the United States secured base rights in Cuba and Nicaragua, exacted nonalienation agreements from Cuba and Haiti, and controlled the public finance of these and other Caribbean republics. The protectorates became part of "preventive intervention," which Theodore Roosevelt, in his "corollary" message of December 1904, sought to justify as an application of the Monroe Doctrine. Beyond strategic concerns, different administrations were, to varying degrees, also motivated by genuine desires to substitute orderly democratic processes for the frequent revolutions that afflicted the region.

Roosevelt and the Platt Amendment

As the war with Spain ended, U.S. armed forces occupied Cuba. Spain had relinquished sovereignty over the island, and the United States had renounced any thought of annexing it; but Washington was not absolved, in its own eyes, from responsibility for Cuba's future. President McKinley noted on December 5, 1899, that the United States had assumed "a grave responsibility for the future good government of Cuba." The island, he continued, "must need be bound to us by ties of singular intimacy and strength if its enduring welfare is to be assured." Secretary of War Elihu Root and General Leonard Wood defined those initial ties.[13] Wood convened a constitutional convention at Havana from November 1900 to February 1901 that wrote a constitution for an independent Cuba, but failed to define the relations between the Cuban government and the U.S. government. Secretary Root outlined his concept of what those relations should be, and Orville H. Platt of Connecticut introduced in the Senate what became known as the Platt Amendment. Actually an amendment to the Army Appropriation Bill of March 2, 1901, provided, among other things, that Cuba should never permit any "foreign power" to gain a foothold in its territory or contract any debt beyond the capacity of its ordinary revenues to pay; that Cuba consent that the United States could intervene for the preservation of Cuba's independence or "the maintenance of a government adequate for the protection of life, property, and individual liberty"; and that Cuba should lease or sell to the United States land necessary for coaling or naval stations.[14]

The Cuban Convention at first rejected the Platt Amendment's terms but later accepted them after receiving Root's assurances that the United States would intervene only in the event of foreign threat or serious domestic disturbance, not in a spirit of "intermeddling or interference with the affairs of the Cuban government." The new Cuban government was inaugurated on May 20, 1902, while the Platt Amendment became an Annex to the Cuban Constitution. The Amendment, embodied in a 1903 treaty remained in force until 1934, when all of the treaty was abrogated except an article that allowed the United States the use of Guantanamo Bay, on the south coast, as a naval station. Washington had intervened in subsequent years, notably in 1906–1909, so frequently as to constitute, in the opinion of many, "intermeddling or interference."[15] Such intervention ceased after 1934, but the United States kept its naval base at Guantanamo and also the assurance that no rival power would secure a foothold in Cuba.

The Platt Amendment's restricting of the debt-contracting power of Cuba and permitting the United States to intervene to preserve an orderly government hinted that enforcing the Monroe Doctrine involved certain policing responsibilities. A more concrete declaration of such a principle came with the Venezuelan crisis in 1902–1903. In 1901, when the German and British governments contemplated using force to collect debts from the Venezuelan dictator Cipriano Castro, Roosevelt (as yet only vice president) wrote to a German friend: "If any South American country misbehaves toward any European country, let the European country spank it"; and a few months later, as president he stated that the Monroe Doctrine did not guarantee any American state against punishment for misconduct, provided that punishment did not result in acquisition of territory. However, in the winter of 1902–1903, when Germans and British actually imposed a "pacific blockade," anti-German sentiment flared in the United States, and Roosevelt worried that such a situation could ignite a crisis between the United States and some European power. The Venezuelan episode was resolved when Castro agreed to submit the dispute to arbitration. But when might Venezuela or one of its neighbors present a new invitation to coercion? Roosevelt provided a formula that removed all excuses for European intervention in the New World.

Roosevelt announced his formula in his annual message of December 6, 1904. Any country that conducts itself well could count on the United States' friendship. If it acts "with reasonable efficiency and decency in social and political matters, if it keeps order and pays its obligations, it need fear no interference from the United States." But "Chronic wrongdoing, or an impotence which results in a general loosening of the ties of civilized society, may in America, as elsewhere, ultimately require intervention of some civilized nation, and in the Western Hemisphere, the adherence of the United States to the Monroe Doctrine may force the United States, however reluctantly, in flagrant cases of such wrongdoing or impotence, to the exercise of an international police power."

The "Roosevelt Corollary of the Monroe Doctrine" transformed Monroe's defensive dictum into a more aggressive policy, with Uncle Sam assuming the role of hemispheric policeman—kindly to the law-abiding, but apt to lay a stern hand on those that fell into disorder or defaulted on their obligations. Perhaps his Corollary could be better characterized as a new principle epitomizing Roosevelt's "big stick" view of foreign relations.[16]

Intervention and Dollar Diplomacy

The Roosevelt Corollary, providing the foundation for establishment of Caribbean protectorates, found its first application coming in the Dominican Republic. Indeed, the disturbing situation there was largely behind Roosevelt's pronouncement. The government of the Dominican Republic, or Santo Domingo since it became independent of Haiti in 1844, had been a dictatorship tempered by revolution. Revolutions are costly, and by 1904 the Dominican debt—some $32 million—reached the point where national revenues administered by native taxes collectors were incapable of servicing it. The largest single creditor, representing both American and British capital, was the San Domingo Improvement Company of New York, which played a central role in leading to U.S. intervention.[17] The Dominican government had pledged the customs duties at various ports as security for its debts, but the pledges sometimes conflicted. Intervention in 1903 and 1904 by the United States on behalf of the Improvement Company resulted in that company collecting customs at Puerto Plata and Monte Cristi, bringing protests from the European creditors claiming these revenues had previously been pledged to them. An international scramble for control of the Dominican customhouses threatened.

Encouraged by Thomas C. Dawson, U.S. minister to the Dominican Republic, President Morales invited Washington to take charge of the nation's customhouses and administer the collection of import duties in order to satisfy the republic's creditors and provide its government with revenue. Roosevelt attempted to bypass the Senate with an executive agreement to this effect in January 1905, but his action aroused so much criticism that Dawson had to put the terms in a formal treaty, subject to Senate ratification. The treaty was duly signed, but Democratic opposition prevented action on it; however, Roosevelt salvaged the essence of the arrangement in a new executive agreement (a *modus vivendi*) signed in April 1905. The Dominican government agreed that the customs agent would be a U.S. citizen nominated by the American president. Forty-five percent of the receipts were to go to the Dominican government; the remainder, less collection costs, was to be deposited in a New York bank and apportioned among the republic's creditors if the Senate approved the treaty, or returned to the Dominican government if the treaty was finally rejected.[18] The *modus vivendi* remained operative for over two years. Meanwhile, the Dominican government's creditors readjusted the debt from over $30 million to $17 million. A new $20 million bond issue, floated in the United States, was applied to the adjusted debt and to the island's needed public works. In February 1907, a new treaty was signed, which the Senate promptly approved, essentially perpetuating the *modus vivendi* arrangement. The Dominican receivership produced gratifying short-term results, with the republic experiencing financial solvency and political stability. Then there began a new series of revolutionary disturbances that led to a more drastic form of intervention by the United States.

The intervention in the Dominican Republic became the model for the "dollar diplomacy" of the William H. Taft administration. On one side, dollar diplomacy was used to advance and protect American business abroad; on the other, it was the use of dollars abroad to promote political and economic stability, often requirements of American diplomacy. In the first sense, it was practiced by many administrations before Taft and since. The employment of American dollars to diplomatically advance political and strategic aims was a less familiar technique. It was visible in the re-funding of the Dominican debt and instituting of the receivership under Theodore Roosevelt. Invoking, as Roosevelt had done, the Monroe Doctrine as their justification, Taft and his secretary of state, Philander C. Knox, made a similar arrangement with Nicaragua and sought unsuccessfully to do the same with Honduras and Guatemala.

Establishment of the Nicaraguan customs receivership came at the conclusion of years of turmoil in Central America, largely the work of the Nicaraguan dictator, Jose Santos Zelaya. Having supported the ousting of Zelaya, Taft and Knox were anxious to bring peace and order to Central America by applying there the same remedy that had achieved some success for the Dominican Republic. They found a cooperative leader in Nicaragua, Adolfo Dias, who despised militarism and craved order and good government. Dias willingly compromised his country's independence by granting to the United States broad powers of intervention. When faced with insurrection, the United States, at his request, landed over 2,000 marines, suppressed the rebellion, deported its leaders, and left at the capital, Managua, a "legation guard" of marines that from 1912 to 1925 "stabilized" the Nicaraguan government under Dias and his successors.[19] Knox's attempt, with the aid of Dias, to set up a customs receivership in Nicaragua by treaty was blocked in the Senate, but a receivership was established nevertheless among Nicaragua, certain American banks, and the State Department. One mixed claims commission reduced the claims against Nicaragua from $13.75 million to $1.74 million, as another gained limited control over Nicaragua's spending policy. President Woodrow Wilson and his first secretary of state, William Jennings Bryan, continued the Taft administration's program. To meet Nicaragua's urgent need for funds, and at the same time to provide for the United States' possible future canal need, the Bryan-Chamorro Treaty signed August 5, 1914, provided for a payment of $3 million to Nicaragua in return for certain concessions. These included the exclusive right to construct a canal through Nicaragua and, for 99 years, the right to establish naval bases at either end of the route.

Two of Nicaragua's neighbors, Costa Rica and El Salvador, contested Nicaragua's right to grant these concessions, claiming they infringed on their sovereignty.[20] The two submitted their case to the Central American Court of Justice, where they won a verdict against Nicaragua. Neither Nicaragua nor the United States accepted the decision, and the court closed in 1918. The United States succeeded, not by treaty but by informal agreement with Nicaragua and the bankers, in reducing the Nicaraguan debt and in creating a customs receivership that would apply a suitable portion of the national revenue to the debt. Application of the Roosevelt Corollary, implemented by dollar diplomacy and the landing of a few marines, had made Nicaragua secure against any infringement of the Monroe Doctrine.

Wilson's Latin American Interventionism

The anti-imperialist Wilson administration (1913–1921), with first Bryan and later Robert Lansing as secretary of state, although promoting independence for the Philippines and self-government for Puerto Rico, imposed on Haiti a protectorate treaty of unprecedented severity and established a military regime in the Dominican Republic. Wilson indicated initially he would frown on revolutions in the neighboring republics: "I am going to teach the South American republics to elect good men!"[21] This remark foreshadowed an addition to American interventionist policy—promotion of democracy became an objective along with preservation of the Monroe Doctrine and protection of the United States' economic and strategic interests. Unfortunately, although the new measures were effective in restoring order and preventing violent revolutions, they did little toward providing free and fair elections.

The Republic of Haiti, unlike the Dominican Republic, had maintained its independence continuously since the time of Toussaint L'Ouverture and had been reasonably successful in meeting the interest payments on its substantial foreign debt. In the early twentieth century, however, corruption grew more flagrant, revolution more frequent, and bankruptcy, default, and the threat of European intervention loomed. Consequently, Bryan asked for the right to appoint a customs receiver, as in Santo Domingo, and a financial adviser. He also asked the right to supervise

Haitian elections and a nonalienation pledge to Mole St. Nicolas, a potential naval base at the northwest corner of the island. Negotiations along these lines proceeded, but so kaleidoscopic were the changes in Haitian administrations that no results had been achieved by July 1915. On July 28, the U.S.S. *Washington* dropped anchor at Port au Prince Harbor, and before nightfall, the marines had occupied the town.[22] Exasperated at the long reign of anarchy in Haiti, Washington resolved to enforce its demands on the Haitian government. By seizing the customhouses and impounding the revenue, and by the threat of continued military control, the United States dictated the choice of a new president and prevailed on him and the National Assembly to accept a treaty embodying the American demands.

The Treaty of 1915 with Haiti went further in establishing American control and supervision than the Cuban or Dominican treaties. It provided that the president of Haiti, on nomination by the president of the United States, appoint a general receiver of customs, a financial adviser, an engineer or engineers to supervise sanitation and public works, and officers of the newly organized native constabulary. All Haitian governmental debts were to be classified, arranged, and serviced from funds collected by the general receiver, Haiti could not borrow without U.S. consent, and Haiti agreed to do nothing to impair its independence. Finally, as in Cuba, Washington might take any necessary measures to preserve Haitian independence or to maintain "a government adequate for the protection of life, property, and individual liberty." The treaty was for 10 years but permitted extension for another 10-year period—which the United States invoked in 1917. Aside from the immediate restoration of order and elimination of all excuse for European intervention, it was presumed that controlling the revenues and organizing an efficient constabulary would remove the chief motive for revolution. Neither at this time nor in the new Haitian constitution, drafted with American aid in 1918, were steps taken to complement these reforms with the introduction of democratic political processes. The result was a reasonably efficient dictatorship dominated by U.S. treaty officials and supported by its armed forces.

Interest in the Caribbean now shifted to the Dominican Republic, where until 1911, the customs receivership of 1905 and 1907 had worked admirably. Under Ramon Caceres (1906–1911), stable government and orderly finances had been the rule; constitutional reforms adopted, and surplus revenues applied to port improvements, highway and railroad construction, and education. Such a novel government employment of its powers and resources displaced many Dominican politicians, and on November 19,

1911, Caceres was assassinated. The republic reverted to its normal factional turmoil and civil war, and the need to suppress revolutions resulted in a large debt, contrary to the spirit, if not the letter, of the 1907 treaty with the United States. Thus, the Wilson administration found in the Dominican Republic a situation as difficult as that in Haiti. Under a plan drafted by Wilson and accepted by the Dominican leaders, the United States supervised its 1914 elections. Washington now demanded a treaty providing for the appointment of a financial adviser to oversee disbursements, for a general receiver to control internal revenue as well as customs, and for the organization of a constabulary. These demands were rejected as violating Dominican sovereignty, and in the spring of 1916 the situation worsened when new revolutionaries seized Santo Domingo. On May 15, U.S. Marines landed at Santo Domingo and gradually occupied other ports and the island's interior. Since Dominican officials refused to accept the proposed treaty, President Wilson placed the Republic under military government.

Accordingly, on November 29, 1916, the commanding naval officer at the capital proclaimed a military government with Marine Corps officers assuming the cabinet posts and the legislature suspended. For the next six years the Dominican Republic was administered by the U.S. Navy Department. The situation differed from Haiti as the Haitian government consented to the United States' protectorate treaty and had preserved some vestiges of its independence, whereas the Dominican government's refusal of less drastic demands had seen its functions taken over by officers of a foreign power. In both republics, though in slightly different ways, the Wilson administration carried to its logical conclusion the "international police power" doctrine of Theodore Roosevelt.

Wilson confronted a more serious crisis with Mexico. Porfirio Diaz, who had governed Mexico since 1877, was briefly succeeded in 1911 by Francisco I. Madero, who attempted to create a democratic government and to provide for small farmers and landless workers. Powerful interests, foreign as well as Mexican, opposed his program and in February 1913 replaced him with General Victoriano Huerta. Huerta betrayed Madero and, after compelling him to resign, had him shot. Huerta, who assumed the Mexican presidency, was initially welcomed by foreign interests and the American ambassador, Henry Lane Wilson. They had had little patience with Madero's attempted reforms and felt Huerta would continue Diaz's considerate treatment of foreign capital.[23] Huerta's government, facing armed opposition from Madero's former followers, was recognized by European powers and Japan. Shocked by the assassination of Madero, Wilson looked on the Huerta regime as "a government of butchers," unworthy of recognition.[24] On March 11, 1913, he announced that friendship and cooperation with the "sister republics" of Latin America would be possible "only when supported at every turn by the orderly processes of just government based upon law, not upon arbitrary or irregular force.... We can have no sympathy with those who seek to seize the power of government to advance their own personal interests or ambition."

Although prompted by rumors of revolutionary plots in Nicaragua, this statement was applicable also to Mexico. It hinted at what would become a feature of Wilson's foreign policy vis-à-vis Latin America: refusal to recognize governments that had attained power by force and violence. This deviated from the traditional practice, followed since Jefferson's day, of recognizing a government firmly seated and capable of performing its duties, internally and externally.

Unfavorable reports of Huerta's regime confirmed the president's conclusions. He had come, Wilson said, to feel a "passion ... for the submerged eighty-five percent of the people of that Republic who are now struggling toward liberty."[25] Since Huerta was unlikely to serve the interests of "the submerged eighty-five percent," Wilson would recognize Huerta only if he would agree to hold a fair election in which he was candidate. When Huerta, on the eve of the election, arrested 110 opposition members of the Mexican Congress, Wilson decided the dictator must go. Wilson was prepared to intervene in Mexico's domestic politics, because it was in the interest of the Mexican people. As he later told a group of Mexican editors, "our sincere desire was nothing else than to assist you to get rid of a man who was making the settlement of your affairs for the time being impossible."[26] Wilson then permitted Huerta's opponents to secure arms in the United States, persuaded London to remove its minister from Mexico who was antagonistic to American policy, and occupied the city of Veracruz on April 21, 1914. In July, Wilson's campaign against Huerta achieved its objective: the latter resigned and fled to Europe. The occupation of Veracruz, accomplished after considerable fighting, was ostensibly to secure an apology for a minor indignity to the U.S. flag. Its main objective was ousting Huerta by depriving him of the port's revenues and cutting off European arms shipments. It was, of course, an act of war; but Wilson insisted that he was taking action only against Huerta and his supporters.

Huerta's leading opponent and probable successor Venustiano Carranza, a former follower of Madero and governor of Coahuila, had taken up arms after Madero's death. Carranza and his forces, the Constitutionalists, occupied Mexico City in August 1914, but peace did not come to Mexico or harmony in U.S.-Mexican relations. Carranza's rule was contested by Emiliano Zapata in the south and by Francisco Villa in the north with considerable loss of life and property. Lansing, now secretary of state, called together representatives from Argentina, Brazil, and Chile, together with those of Uruguay, Bolivia, and Guatemala, who recommended recognition of Carranza as head of a de facto Mexican government. Washington took this step in October 1915. Carranza's enemies continued their resistance. Villa's guerrilla forces, in January 1916, held up a train carrying 17 American mining engineers and shot all but one, and on March 9 shot up Columbus, New Mexico. A punitive expedition under Brigadier General John J. Pershing followed Villa into Mexico but failed to catch him. The presence of American troops on Mexican soil rallied Mexicans to Carranza's banner and helped consolidate his power.[27] Although Carranza grudgingly consented to the pursuit of Villa, he resented the presence of U.S. troops in Mexico, and on June 21, 1916, in a clash with Mexican government forces at Carrizal, 12 U.S. soldiers were killed and 23 captured. With Wilson ordering the National Guard to the border and the two nations close to war, at Carranza's suggestion a joint commission was created to study the entire situation. The commission found no solution acceptable to both governments, but the U.S. members finally advised withdrawal of troops from Mexico and the granting of full diplomatic recognition to the Carranza government.

Accordingly, General Pershing and the last of his troops left Mexican soil on February 5, 1917, and on March 3, Henry P. Fletcher presented his credentials as ambassador of the United States. Within a few weeks thereafter the United States entered the war against Germany. Throughout the period of that conflict, relations with Mexico continued to be marked by bickering—over border disturbances, over threatened expropriations of American property under the new Mexican constitution—but there was no further danger that the United States might have to fight a war in its backyard.

The "Open Door" Policy

On the eve of the Spanish-American War, Germany, Russia, France, and Great Britain had seized harbors suitable for naval bases on the coast of China and had exacted from the Chinese government long-time leases and economic concessions in the neighboring areas, establishing individual "spheres of interest." The United States had a small but growing trade with China and was looking to China as a market for the surplus products of its industry that European states were threatening to exclude.

Since signing its first treaty with China in 1844, America had been assured of most-favored-nation treatment or an "open door" for its trade. The open door was threatened by the spheres of interest with discriminatory trade policies. An invitation from London to join in defending the open door in China was rejected by Washington in March 1898. Admittedly an Anglophile, Secretary of State John Hay welcomed closer cooperation with Great Britain in the Far East, but public and senatorial opinion would reject any alliance. Hay could only invite powers chiefly concerned with China to respect the open door principle, hoping, as Monroe and Adams had hoped in 1823, that Great Britain would back the American position.

A suitable occasion for such an invitation was offered by a Russian imperial ukase in mid-August 1899, providing assurance that Russia would not interfere with or control the collection of Chinese customs or place any restrictions on "foreign commerce and trade" in its sphere of interest. Sensing opportunity to get general assent to preservation of the open door principle, Hay received a memorandum from his chief adviser on Far Eastern matters, W. W. Rockhill, proposing such a course.[28] Similar diplomatic notes were presented to Great Britain, Germany, Russia, France, Italy, and Japan on September 6, 1899.[29] The note to the U.S. ambassador in Berlin stated that

> the Government of the United States would be pleased to see His German Majesty's Government give formal assurances, and lend its cooperation in securing like assurances from the other interested powers, that each, within its respective sphere of whatever influence—
>
> *First.* Will in no way interfere with any treaty port or any vested interest within any so-called "sphere of interest" or leased territory it may have in China.
>
> *Second.* That the Chinese treaty tariff of the time being shall apply to all merchandise landed or shipped to all such ports as are within said "sphere of interest" (unless they be "free ports"), no matter to what nationality it may belong, and that duties so leviable shall be collected by the Chinese Government.
>
> *Third.* That it will levy no higher harbor dues on vessels of another nationality frequenting any port in such "sphere" than shall be levied on vessels of its own nationality, and no higher railroad charges over lines built, controlled, or operated within its "sphere" on merchandise belonging to citizens or subjects of other nationalities transported through such "sphere" than shall be levied on

similar merchandise belonging to its own nationals transported over equal distances.

The notes did not propose the abrogation of spheres of interest. Rather, they asked assurance that within those spheres that the regular Chinese tariff should continue to be collected and that the trade of all nations should be treated without discrimination as to tariffs, railroad rates, and harbor dues. They asked, essentially, that American trade have an opportunity to expand in China without the burdens of colonial responsibilities or the obligations of protectorates. Five of the six governments addressed replied that they were willing, in their spheres of interest, to abide by Secretary Hay's principles if the other governments agreed to do the same. The Russian reply was less forthright, dealing specifically only with the question of tariffs; but its Foreign Office, nevertheless, authorized Hay to treat the reply as favorable. On March 20, 1900, he notified the six governments that the United States regarded acceptance by all as creating a binding agreement. Thus, as Hay's biographer writes, "What began as straightforward diplomacy... ended in diplomatic prestidigitation."[30]

John Hay and the Boxer Rebellion

While the diplomats were still debating the significance of the open door notes, events occurred in China that threatened to provide an pretext for a further partitioning of the empire—perhaps even for the final extinction of its independence. Chinese leaders at the turn of the century were of two minds. A reform party, headed by the well-meaning but weak emperor, Kuang Hsu, wished to westernize and modernize China in emulation of Japan. A reactionary party, which secured the support of the dowager empress, Tzu His ("Old Buddha" foreigners called her), advocated expulsion of the "foreign devils" and destruction of their influence. The spearhead of the reactionaries was the secret society known to the West as "Boxers," from the emblem of a clenched fist. When the emperor attempted to institute a reform program, "Old Buddha" came out of retirement and seized the reins of government. With China's secret connivance, the Boxers began a campaign of violence, at first directed against foreign missionaries and their Chinese converts in Shantung province, but soon broadened to eliminate all foreign influence from China. From Shantung the Boxers advanced to seize possession of Beijing, murdered the German minister in the streets, and laid siege to the legation quarter, where foreign diplomats and other foreign residents established precarious defenses.

For weeks in the summer of 1900 the foreigners in Peking were cut off from all communication with the outside world, where it was feared that all might have perished. The long-term danger was not that Western influence in China would be destroyed, but rather that the injured powers would seize on the Boxer outrages as a pretext for partitioning China among them. If China's independence and territorial integrity were thus violated, few predicted a long life for the open door. It became U.S. policy, as stated by John Hay, to liquidate the Boxer outbreak so there would be no further seizures of territory by foreign nations.

While preparations were underway for an international army to relieve the legations in Peking, Hay insisted that the powers were not at war with China but only with a rebellious faction within the empire. He succeeded in reopening communications with the American minister in Beijing, learning that the legations were still holding out. Most celebrated of Hay's measures was his circular note to the powers of July 3, 1900, setting forth America's objectives. The president, he said, was acting concurrently with the other powers to protect American lives, property, and legitimate interests wherever they might be imperiled. At the same time, Hay continued, "the policy of the Government of the United States is to seek a solution which may bring about permanent safety and peace to China, preserve Chinese territorial and administrative entity, protect all rights guaranteed to friendly powers by treaty and international law, and safeguard for the world the principle of equal and impartial trade with all parts of the Chinese Empire." Hay recognized the relationship between the preservation of China's territorial integrity ("entity") and the maintenance of the open door in China. It was the policy of the United States, he said, to "seek a solution" that would preserve both. Orally or in writing, France, Great Britain, Germany, Russia, and Italy agreed with Hay's statement, and, on October 29, 1900, Hay stated that the United States was gratified to learn that "all the powers held similar views."[31]

Meanwhile, an international army of 19,000, chiefly Japanese and Russian but including 2,500 American troops from the Philippines, set out from the coast for Beijing. The empress fled, resistance collapsed, and on August 14, the expeditionary force entered the Chinese capital, relieved the besieged foreigners, among them Herbert Hoover. The antiforeign movement disintegrated, and the Chinese government agreed to pay off an indemnity for foreign lives lost and property destroyed. The various governments concerned did not ask additional cessions or leases of territory, but foreign powers were permitted to police the railroad line connecting Beijing with the coast near Tientsin. An indemnity of

$333 million was agreed on, with slightly less than $25 million assigned to the United States; when American losses totaled little more than half of this sum, Washington voluntarily remitted the balance. China put the remitted portion into a fund for the education of young Chinese in American universities.[32]

Through it all, the United States never lost sight of its main objective, the China market. In tariff negotiations that accompanied those on indemnities, the United States joined the other powers in withholding tariff autonomy from China, and the rates were so adjusted as to discourage China from developing "a more balanced, advanced, and sophisticated economy." China must still look to the West for all but the simplest products of the machine age.[33]

The Russo-Japanese War

While the United States relied largely on words, England and Japan looked about for more substantial means of defending their interests in Asia. The British turned first to Germany and in October 1900 concluded an agreement that respected the integrity of China and the open door, unless aggressions by a third power should compel them to reconsider their decision. This document was so phrased as not to apply to Manchuria, where Germany desired Russia to have a free hand. Since Russia was England's chief rival in Persia and Afghanistan and also Japan's in the Far East, London and Tokyo developed an alliance designed to check Russia. The 1902 Anglo-Japanese alliance acknowledged the territorial integrity and the open door in China and Korea, and recognized each other's special interests in China. Britain also recognized Japan's special interests, "politically as well as commercially and industrially," in Korea. Each promised to remain neutral if the other became involved in war with a third power and to support the other should it be attacked by two or more enemies.[34]

Within two years the chief purpose of the treaty was revealed—the protection of Japan from attack by other powers while it expelled Russia from southern Manchuria. Since the Sino-Japanese war of 1894–1895, Russia posed as a friend of China, taking the lead in forcing Japan to restore the Liaotung peninsula to China, and was rewarded with permission to extend the Trans-Siberian Railway across northern Manchuria to Vladivostok. In 1898, Russia exacted from China a 25-year lease of the same Liaotung peninsula with the right to build and police the South Manchuria Railway. Russia proceeded at Port Arthur to build a naval base, and the Boxer outbreak provided an excuse for them moving troops into Manchuria; they obviously desired to turn Manchuria into a Russian colony. More alarming to Tokyo were Russia's encroachments in Korea, the nominally independent kingdom that since 1895 had come under Japanese influence. Korea was, in the words of an old saying, "a dagger pointed at the heart of Japan." Japan and Russia in 1903 sought to settle both questions, but neither party would meet the demands of the other.

In February 1904, Japan broke off the negotiations and launched a surprise attack on the Russian fleet at Port Arthur. The Russo-Japanese war lasted for a year and a half and ended in a complete victory for Japan. Russia's Far Eastern fleet, divided between Port Arthur and Vladivostok, was destroyed piecemeal. Its Baltic fleet, after a long voyage from European waters, was annihilated in a one-sided battle in Tsushima straits in May 1905. Meanwhile, Port Arthur surrendered in January 1905 after a long siege, and the main Russian army was defeated in the battle of Mukden, February-March 1905.

Roosevelt the Peacemaker

Although President Roosevelt admired the Japanese and had only contempt for Russian officialdom, Washington adopted a neutral attitude and assisted in persuading the belligerents to respect the neutrality of China. He assured Japan that American neutrality would be "benevolent" and warned Germany and France, so he reported later, that he would intervene if necessary to protect Japan from being robbed of the fruits of a successful war, as she had been in 1895 after defeating China.[35] If Roosevelt's preferences were partly sentimental, they were also based on his conception of the Far Eastern balance of power. Since Russia presented the major threat to that balance and also to China's territorial integrity and the open door, Roosevelt backed Japan against Russia. But with Japanese victories, he became apprehensive lest the power pendulum swing too far in Japan's direction. The prospect that, if war continued, Japan might take and hold all of Eastern Siberia he viewed with some alarm.[36] It was partly for this reason that he welcomed the opportunity to assist in making peace.

Japan, though everywhere victorious, had drained its resources and wanted to end the war. Tokyo confidentially asked Roosevelt in the spring of 1905, "on his own initiative," to propose a peace conference. This he did, and in August 1905 Russian and Japanese delegates met at Portsmouth, New Hampshire. The principal obstacle was Japan's demand for a large money indemnity, $600 million or more, to cover the cost of the war. This Russia resolutely refused, and the conference came close to ending in failure. President Roosevelt, however, persuaded Japan to drop the indemnity from its list of demands, and a treaty was signed, September 5, 1905. The signing took place in such an atmosphere of amity and goodwill that Russia's Baron Rosen declared that "in negotiating with our hitherto adversaries we have been dealing with true and thorough gentlemen to whom we are happy to express our high esteem and personal regard."[37]

By the treaty of Portsmouth, Russia recognized Tokyo's paramount interest in Korea and ceded to Japan the southern half of the island of Sakhalin, all Russian rights in the Liaotung peninsula, and the South Manchuria Railway extending from Port Arthur and Dairen to Changchun. Both powers withdrew their troops from Manchuria other than railway guards and agreed to restore the province to Chinese civil administration. In July 1905, before the delegates gathered at Portsmouth, Secretary of War William H. Taft had visited Tokyo. Taft received assurances from Japanese premier Count Katsura that Japan would respect United States sovereignty in the Philippines, and in return, Taft promised American approval if Japan should assume control of Korea. Roosevelt endorsed the understanding, and the following November, when Tokyo took charge of Korea's foreign relations, Washington immediately approved and closed its Korean legation. Nor did the United States protest when, five years later, Japan assumed complete sovereignty over Korea. At the close of the Russo-Japanese war, the Japanese and American governments enjoyed a mutual friendliness and cordiality. The American people, too, had shown overwhelming sympathy for Japan—little David in a struggle with giant Goliath.

The terms of peace bitterly disappointed the Japanese public, who had been led to expect much more—a huge money indemnity and cession of all Sakhalin, perhaps even Vladivostok and Russia's maritime province. For what they considered the meagerness of the peace terms, the Japanese press and public blamed partly their own government, partly the United States and President Roosevelt. When the terms were announced, angry mobs rioted in Tokyo and other cities, attacking government buildings and the progovernment press, threatening foreigners, and burning Christian churches, most of them American. A regime of martial law put an end to the disorders, but the popular attitude boded ill for the future of Japanese-U.S. relations.

CHAPTER 10

Woodrow Wilson and a World at War

The world must be made safe for democracy.
—Woodrow Wilson, war message to Congress, April 2, 1945

War ought to have been, and could have been avoided.
—David Lloyd George, former British prime minister, 1937

Though informed Americans had been aware of the growing tensions in Europe, the actual outbreak of war took the American public and government by surprise. The assassination of Archduke Francis Ferdinand, heir to the Austro-Hungarian throne, at Sarajevo, June 28, 1914, by Gavrilo Princip, a young, ardent Serbia nationalist and member of the terrorist group the Black Hand, activated the complex alliance system that was supposed to guarantee European stability. For over three weeks, there were few hints of serious trouble brewing. Then on July 23, Austria-Hungary presented to Serbia a 48-hour ultimatum whose terms, if accepted, would have largely extinguished Serbian sovereignty. Rejecting Serbia's partial acceptance as unsatisfactory, Austria-Hungary on July 28 declared war. Two days later, Russia mobilized, determined to defend its small protégé. On August 1, Germany declared war against Russia; on August 3 against France, Russia's ally, which had refused to give assurance of remaining neutral; and on August 4 against Belgium, which had denied passage to German armies en route to France. On August 4, Great Britain also declared war on Germany—ostensibly as a joint guarantor of Belgian neutrality; more realistically, because of moral commitments to France and Russia and unwillingness to acquiesce in Germany's domination of Western Europe. Subsequently, Turkey and Bulgaria entered the war as allies of Germany and Austria-Hungary—the "Central Powers";

while Italy and Rumania eventually joined the Triple Entente powers—the "Allies." Meanwhile, Japan had declared war on Germany on August 23, 1914, and seized German holdings in China's Shantung peninsula and the German islands in the North Pacific. Eventually no less than 32 nations—including the British Dominions and India—were involved in the war against Germany.

To most Americans the war in Europe seemed remote—a deplorable tragedy that might only inconvenience trade or travel. But some Americans saw the struggle much differently, one that held a deep ideological significance for the United States. Elihu Root wrote to an English friend: "Underlying all the particular reasons and occasions for the war, the principle of Anglo-Saxon liberty seems to have met the irreconcilable conception of the German State, and the two ideas are battling for control of the world."[1] Robert Lansing, who in July 1915 became Wilson's secretary of state, took a view similar to Root's and drew from it a practical conclusion: "Germany must not be permitted to win this war or to break even, though to prevent it this country is forced to take an active part. . . . American public opinion must be prepared for the time, which may come, when we will have to cast aside our neutrality and become one of the champions of democracy."[2]

Still other Americans foresaw a danger to the United States in Germany's upsetting the European balance of power. Great Britain and France were "satisfied" powers; so long as they dominated the eastern Atlantic, the United States had nothing to fear. But should their place be taken by imperial Germany, "unsatisfied" and hungry for colonies and colonial markets, Americans might have to surrender the Monroe Doctrine or fight to defend it.[3] But these were the opinions of a select few. Although Americans might sympathize with one side or the other, the war was a European affair. German submarine attacks on American ships with the loss of American lives—inhumane and illegal in American eyes—finally persuaded the United States to intervene.

President Wilson issued a formal proclamation of neutrality on August 4, 1914. Fifteen days later, reminiscent of Washington's Farewell Address, Wilson appealed to his countrymen to avoid taking sides in the European struggle. Otherwise, he warned, Americans might "be divided in camps of hostile opinion, hot against each other, involved in the war itself in impulse and opinion if not in action." He attempted, during the next two and a half years, to keep the United States "neutral in fact as well as in name," though consciously or unconsciously American interpretations of international law consistently favored the Allies. The American people could not really be persuaded to be "impartial in thought," nor was the president's official family impartial. If William Jennings Bryan, secretary of state until July 1915, saw little to commend the British case over the German, Robert Lansing, his successor, believed that the United States must enter the war if necessary to prevent a German victory. Walter H. Page, ambassador to Great Britain, saw the war as a crusade, and Edward M. House, Wilson's close unofficial adviser, was almost as pro-Ally. Wilson, impartial at first, had come by May 1915 to believe that "England is fighting our fight," yet a year later certain British practices drove him back to a relatively impartial attitude.

Public opinion from the beginning tended to be pro-Ally. Americans had ties of race, language, culture, and political ideals with England and bonds of ancient friendship with France, which had no substantial counterpart in their relations with Germany. In communities where the German or Irish heritage was strong, there was likely to be a pro-German (or anti-British) sentiment. Both sides in the war made their propaganda appeals to American public opinion. The British had the advantage of controlling the cables and thus of shaping news about the war. German "atrocities" were magnified, even invented, and often accepted as sober truth. German propaganda, on the other hand, was more often spotted as such and discounted accordingly.

The American Economy and the War

The war would bind the United States to France and Great Britain. The initial effect on the American economy was disastrous as the British navy cut off German markets while Allied ships were often away from their customary routes. American business, already floundering in minor cyclical depression, was further depressed by these disruptions. Relief soon came, however, with large munitions orders from the Allies; by the end of 1915, America was enjoying a war-born prosperity. The sale of munitions to the Allies raised questions of neutral obligations. German sympathizers complained that such sales, being made exclusively to the Allied side, were not neutral. To such critics Lansing answered: "If one belligerent has by good fortune a superiority in the matter of geographical location or of military or naval power, the rules of neutral conduct cannot be varied so as to favor the less fortunate combatant." Law and precedent held that the sale of war matériel to England and France did not violate America's neutrality. The sale of munitions and other supplies continued at an increasing rate—$6 million in 1914, jumping to $467 million in 1916.

It became readily apparent that the Allies, if their purchases were to continue over a long period of time, would need to finance them in the

American money market. In August 1914, the New York firm of J. P. Morgan inquired of Secretary Bryan the government's position regarding such transactions. Bryan replied that loans by bankers to belligerent governments were "inconsistent with the true spirit of neutrality." Whatever the ethics of Bryan's position, it had no legal standing. Both North and South had borrowed in Europe to finance the American Civil War. Japan had borrowed extensively in England and the United States to pay for its recent war with Russia, and Russia had fought with money borrowed in France. Bryan retreated from his untenable position by distinguishing between loans and "credits." In October 1914, Morgan granted the first "credit" to the French and other credits followed.[4] "Loans" were still banned when Bryan resigned, but in late 1915, Secretary of State Lansing and Secretary of Treasury William G. McAdoo changed Wilson's position, arguing Allied purchasing would taper off without large-scale loans and the United States would face a depression. Before American entry into the war, in 1917, the Allies had borrowed over $2.25 billion in the United States—London requiring $1.5 billion.

German Submarines Raise New Problems

British maritime practices, which drew an occasional U.S. protest, violated only property rights, endangering no lives. Germany's use of submarines to disrupt commerce differed radically—the major American grievance. On September 2, 1916, Wilson clarified the different grievances, stating that when American rights became involved our guiding principle was that "property rights can be vindicated by claims for damages when the war is over, and no modern nation can decline to arbitrate such claims; but the fundamental rights of humanity cannot be. The loss of life is irreparable."[5] German submarines violated "the fundamental rights of humanity." On February 4, 1915, Berlin declared the waters around the British Isles to be a "war zone" in which German submarines would sink enemy merchant vessels on sight. Since the British ships frequently flew neutral flags, Germany could not guarantee the safety of neutral vessels in the war zone.[6] Washington promptly replied that Berlin would be held to a "strict accountability" for any loss of American ships or lives "due to the new policy." So began the controversy that would involve the United States in the war.

Submarines could not easily conform to traditional maritime rules. Recognized practice called for the enemy warship to visit and search a commercial vessel and, if possible, bring the suspected ship into a home port of the captor for adjudication by a prize court. If this procedure was impossible, international law permitted destruction of the prize at sea, but only if adequate provision was made for safety of crew and passengers. A fragile submarine, however, was vulnerable when surfaced to challenge a resisting merchant ship. The State Department wondered how to meet the new German policy. Bryan, fearing that challenging Germany on this issue might lead to war, would warn American citizens that they traveled on belligerent ships at their own risk. His deputy, Lansing, argued that American citizens had a right to travel even on armed British ships and that the United States must defend these citizens. Lansing erred on two counts: (1) persons of whatever nationality on a British ship could expect only the British government's protection; and (2) an armed merchant vessel, even with defensive armament, forfeited its immunity from armed attack.[7] Wilson, nevertheless, accepted Lansing's position. Two compromises were offered. Initially, Washington proposed that German submarines legally visit and search merchant vessels, in return for a relaxation of the British food blockade and a British promise to stop using neutral flags. This attempt failed when Berlin demanded free access to raw industrial materials as well as food. Then in early 1916, Lansing proposed the British halt arming their merchant ships in return for a German agreement that submarines would not attack unarmed ships without warning, taking precautions for the safety of those aboard. London and Paris rejected this proposal. Wilson blocked a Congressional effort to warn American citizens against travel in armed belligerent ships, insisting that he could not "consent to any abridgment of the rights of American citizens in any respect."

Long before this second proposal, German-American relations confronted their first serious crisis, brought on by the torpedoing of the British liner *Lusitania* off the Irish coast on May 7, 1915, with 1,198 persons losing their lives, including 128 American citizens. Despite the German embassy's published warnings for Americans to avoid the *Lusitania*, there was no deliberate German plot to "get" that particular ship. The big liner was sighted, steaming with culpable disregard of the British Admiralty's prescribed precautions. Lansing and some others wished for a declaration of war against Germany but could not arouse public support. Despite Bryan's resignation, the president demanded Berlin officials disavow the sinking, provide reparations, and take "immediate steps to prevent the recurrence" of such acts. The German government, unwilling to publicly surrender but not ready to break with Washington, secretly ordered submarine commanders not to attack passenger ships without warning. In Washington, the German ambassador Count von Bernstorff offered the assurance that: "Liners will not be sunk by our submarines without warning and without safety of the lives of non-combatants, provided that the liners do not try to escape or offer resistance." Later, Berlin conceded its "liability" for the sinking of the *Lusitania*.[8]

Another crisis arose, in March 1916, when the unarmed French passenger steamer *Sussex* was torpedoed in the English Channel. The *Sussex* made port and no American passengers were lost, though some were injured. Although the submarine commander mistook the Sussex for a British mine-layer that it closely resembled in silhouette,[9] to Washington it appeared a deliberate violation of recent assurances. Lansing and House advised breaking off diplomatic relations with Germany, but Wilson hesitated. "Unless the Imperial Government," the president told Berlin, "should now immediately declare and effect an abandonment of its present methods of submarine warfare against passenger and freight-carrying vessels, the Government of the United States can have no choice but to sever diplomatic relations with the German Empire altogether."

Again, the German government yielded, with assurances on May 4, 1916, that merchant vessels would "not be sunk without warning and without saving human lives, unless these ships attempt to escape or offer resistance." Berlin, in return, expected that the United States insist England abandon its allegedly illegal practices; should London refuse, "the German Government would then be facing a new situation, in which it must reserve [to] itself complete liberty of action."

The British Try Wilson's Patience

During the following eight months, German submarines challenged Allied commerce but acted within international maritime rules. Yet the British were uncooperative when early in 1916, Wilson permitted Colonel House to seek an end to the war. Wilson proposed to invite the belligerents to a peace conference; if the Allies were to accept, but if Germany declined, as expected, or if, after accepting, refused a peace on "reasonable" terms (already agreed on by Wilson and the Allies), the United States would enter the war against Germany. The plan, accepted by House and Britain's Sir Edward Grey, was cabled to Wilson. The president, constitutionally unable to promise a declaration of war, inserted "probably" in the clause predicting American action. Whether because of this uncertainty or because they hoped for victory, the Allies never signified their readiness for the president's proposed invitation. Wilson, like House, was chagrined at this cool treatment and intensely annoyed at the British government's July 1916 blacklisting of nearly 100 American firms or individuals for supposed German connections. The blacklist, coupled with the British government's ruthless suppression of an Irish rebellion, in

April 1916, aroused anti-British feelings. "I am... about at the end of my patience with Great Britain and the Allies," Wilson wrote House. "This blacklist is the last straw." Wilson also noted that earlier public sympathy for England and the Allies "had greatly changed."[10] The president found himself not loving Germany more but Britain less. His supporters campaigned for his reelection with the slogan "He kept us out of war," implying he would continue to do so. Yet he endorsed U.S. military preparedness—a strengthening the army and greatly increasing the navy. Bowing to the naval chiefs, the increases were for battleships that might challenge the British Grand Fleet.

Had Berlin acted with a modicum of wisdom and moderation, it might have ensured the continued neutrality of the United States. Chancellor von Bethmann-Hollweg and other civilian officials desired to continue appeasing the United States, but they faced mounting pressure from the military and naval leaders, desiring either immediate peace on their terms or else a submarine fleet capable of starving Britain into surrender. Victorious against Russia and Rumania, and holding their own on the western front in France and Belgium, Germany and its allies urged Wilson to invite the belligerents to a peace conference. When he procrastinated, on December 12, 1916 Germany announced that it was ready for peace negotiations. In London, the new prime minister, David Lloyd George, responded that only Germany's defeat could ensure a lasting peace. If the Allies rejected the German invitation, Wilson, still seeking a compromise, asked both sides to state their peace terms. The Central Powers stated a conference was the proper place for announcing terms, while the Allies named extravagant terms.[11] Realizing failure of these efforts met unrestricted submarine warfare, undoubtedly a prelude to hostilities, Wilson made one last effort at peace. For months he had been considering a league of nations that would guarantee world peace from future wars.[12] Addressing the Senate on January 22, 1917, Wilson stated the conditions under which the United States "would feel justified in asking our people to approve its formal and solemn adherence to a League for Peace." His conditions included: "a peace without victory" based on the equality of rights of all nations, the principle of government by the consent of the governed, the access to the sea for "every great people," the freedom of the seas, and a general reduction of armaments. Wilson's proposal came too late to be useful.

The Germans Abandon Moderation

Three days earlier, the German government had decided to resume unrestricted submarine warfare on February 1. Ambassador Von Bernstorff urged them to reconsider their decision. Wilson had promised, he reported, that if Germany adhered to the *Sussex* pledge and offered reasonable peace terms, the president would bring the Allies into line. His plea unheeded, the ambassador informed Lansing on January 31 that because Great Britain continued its illegal practices, Germany would resume the "freedom of action" reserved in the *Sussex* note and, beginning the next day, would sink all vessels encountered in the seas adjacent to the British Isles and the coasts of France and Italy. Neutral ships at sea prior to the notification would be spared, and one American steamer weekly, carrying no contraband and painted with red and white stripes, might proceed unmolested from New York to Falmouth, England.

On February 3, 1917, von Bernstorff was given his passport and Ambassador Gerard was recalled from Berlin, diplomatic actions Wilson hoped might deter Germany from carrying out its threat.[13] But Germany's military leaders expected a submarine blockade to crush England before America took a significant role in the war. Meanwhile on February 24, the State Department had received from London an intercepted note from German foreign minister Arthur Zimmermann to the German minister in Mexico, proposing if the United States entered the war, Mexico should ally itself with Germany and persuade Japan, Great Britain's ally, to do the same. For its cooperation, Mexico would regain its "lost provinces" of Texas, New Mexico, and Arizona. Publication of Zimmermann's absurd proposal on March 1 outraged Americans, particularly in the Southwest.[14] Meanwhile, two American women died when a German submarine sank the Cunard liner *Laconia* on February 25.[15] With the *Laconia*'s sinking along with the March 18 torpedoing of three American merchant ships, the German submarine campaign was obviously underway, and American lives and ships were endangered. Addressing a special session of Congress on April 2, 1917, Wilson reviewed the history of the submarine controversy, denounced the current submarine campaign as "warfare against mankind" and "war against all nations," and advised Congress to "accept the status of belligerent which has thus been thrust upon it." He also declared that the United States' goal was "to vindicate the principles of peace and justice." In his final paragraph, he declared: "We shall fight for the things which we have always carried nearest our hearts—for democracy, for the right of those who submit to authority to have a voice in their own Government, for the rights and liberties of small nations, for a universal dominion of right by such a concert of free peoples as shall bring peace and safety to all nations and make the world itself at last free."

Four days later, Congress resolved: "That the state of war between the United States and the Imperial German Government which has been thrust on the United States is hereby formally declared." The vote was 373 to 50 in the House, 82 to 6 in the Senate.[16] Following the United States' declaration of war, Austria-Hungary and Turkey broke off diplomatic relations. Bulgaria did not do so, nor did the United States sever relations with Bulgaria or declare war against Turkey. On December 7, 1917, after the Italian army's disaster at Caporetto, Congress declared war against Austria-Hungary to bolster Italian morale. With the British and French and their various allies, the United States became an "associated power"—merely a gesture respecting American's tradition against "entangling alliances."

The United States, in the spring of 1918, accepted French general Foch as supreme commander of all armies on the western front. General John J. Pershing, commander of the American Expeditionary Force, successfully resisted the Allied demand that American troops be merged with British and French, insisting they be deployed as a distinct U.S. Army. The withdrawal of Russia from the war after the Bolshevik revolution of November 1917[17] enabled Germany to shift large forces from the eastern to the western front and to launch a succession of formidable offensives in the spring of 1918. With France and England near exhaustion, the timely arrival of American forces prevented a German victory. The German drives were halted, and after the last one, launched in July, failed, the German armies were pushed back. Its allies succumbed one by one. Bulgaria surrendered September 29; Turkey, a month later. An Austrian proposal of September 16 for a peace conference was rejected. Finally, on October 6 and 7, Germany and Austria-Hungary offered to accept the terms previously set forth by Wilson.

The Fourteen Points

Shortly after the United States entered the war, Wilson felt that an explicit statement of war aims was desirable. Such a statement might commit the Allied governments to a peace of justice rather than a peace of vengeance. Immediately after seizing power on November 7, 1917, the Bolshevik leaders exposed the Allies' secret treaties and appealed to all the belligerents to make peace based on universal self-determination, a peace without annexations or indemnities. Only Germany and its allies responded favorably to this proposal, offering the prospect of a separate Russian-German peace. Colonel House urged Allied leaders to meet the Soviets' declaration of war aims, hoping to induce the Russians to stay in the war. When French and Italian premiers refused to disavow their nationalistic objectives, Wilson addressed Congress on January 8, 1918, outlining U.S. peace terms in his famous Fourteen Points.

The address referred particularly to Russia. The president discussed current negotiations between the new Soviet government and the Central Powers, and assured the Russian people of the United States' sympathy. "It is our heartfelt desire and hope," he declared, "that some way may be opened whereby we may be privileged to assist the People of Russia to attain their utmost hope of liberty and ordered peace." Wilson then stated American war aims, the object of which was "that the world be made fit and safe to live in; and particularly that it be made safe for every peace loving nation." The Fourteen Points, briefly summarized, comprised: "open covenants of peace, openly arrived at"; freedom of the seas; removal of economic barriers; limitation of armaments; recognition of the interests of native populations in the adjustment of colonial claims; evacuation and restoration of Allied territory invaded by the Central Powers; readjustment of the boundaries of Italy, the Balkan States, and Turkey on lines of nationality; an independent Poland; opportunity for autonomous development for the peoples of Austria-Hungary; and the creation of "a general association of nations."

Point 6 called for the evacuation of all occupied Russian territory and a sincere welcome of Russia "into the society of free nations under institutions of her own choosing;... The treatment accorded Russia by her sister nations in the months to come," the president continued, "will be the acid test of their good will, of their comprehension of her needs as distinguished from their own interests, and of their intelligent and unselfish sympathy." Wilson appealed directly to the Russian people to continue fighting, but to no effect. In the harsh Treaty of Brest-Litovsk, March 3, 1918, the Soviets surrendered title to Finland, the Baltic provinces, Lithuania, Russian Poland, and the Ukraine and withdrew from the war. Although Wilson's Fourteen Points failed to keep Russia in the war, they did offer an idealistic peace program that gained a popular worldwide hearing. Because the Allies did not at the time take exception to them, the Fourteen Points were accepted as a statement of the war aims of the Allies and became the basis on which Germany offered to make peace.[18]

Allied Intervention in Russia

Conservative leaders in the Allied ranks, including President Wilson and Secretary Lansing, strongly disapproved of the new Bolshevik government of Russia because of the vast ideological differences. When the Bolsheviks repudiated all previously accumulated debts, Wilson insisted these obligations be met before the United States would recognize the new government—a policy that continued until November 1933. During the spring of 1918, officials in London and Paris sought a way to intervene in Russian affairs and, as they informed Wilson, to maintain an eastern front. Lacking the troops to intervene, they turned to the United States and Japan. Initially, he was not convinced an Allied intervention in Russia was justified, but in July, Wilson changed his mind and sent 7,000 American troops to Northern Russia and 9,000 to assist the Japanese in Siberia. Czechoslovakia's leader Thomás Masaryk convinced Wilson that the marooned Czech Legion in Siberia required U.S. assistance, while the decision to send forces to Murmansk was to secure 160,000 tons of military supplies. If the president did not believe the intervention was to topple the Russian government or gain territorial concessions, the British, French, and Japanese saw the episode differently.

U.S. troops joined British and French forces at outposts around Archangel and Murmansk, but because freezing weather closed the ports they had to wait seven months after the armistice to withdraw in June 1919. The French, instructed by Premier Georges Clemenceau to eliminate Russian Bolshevism, also intervened at Odessa in the Ukraine, joining former czarist and local nationalist forces. In April 1919, however, domestic politics led Clemenceau to bring French forces home without accomplishing their mission. This venture was the clearest example of Allied efforts to overthrow the Bolsheviks. Tokyo sent some 72,000 troops to seize the Trans-Siberian Railway inland as far as Irkutsk, where they met the Czech forces and secured positions in Manchuria and eastern Siberia. U.S. forces, after limiting the impact of Japanese presence, left in April 1920 with the Czech units, while the Japanese reluctantly departed in October 1922.

The Bolshevik revolution and Allied intervention long influenced Soviet and American attitudes. In the United States, Bolshevik successes aroused absurd fears of communist agitation that with official approval launched the nation's first Red Scare from 1919 to 1920. In the Soviet Union, the interventions heightened suspicions of the West's policies during and after the Second World War.

The Armistice

President Wilson acted as spokesman for "the principal Allied and Associated Powers" in answering the Austrian and German peace overtures. As far as Austria was concerned, the president replied that

Point 10, calling for the autonomous development of the peoples of Austria-Hungary, was no longer wholly applicable. Since the United States had recognized the Czechoslovak National Council, it was for the other nationalities to determine what concessions would satisfy them. To Germany, Wilson specified five conditions: acceptance of the Wilsonian terms; evacuation of Allied territory; abandonment of illegal practices on sea and land; assurance that the German officials conducting the negotiations represented the people; and the abdication of the kaiser. The kaiser left on November 9, 1918, and there was organized the same day a provisional German People's Government. Germany meanwhile had accepted Wilson's other conditions. It soon became apparent that Wilson's idealism had outdistanced the interests of his European allies; for only after a protracted argument, and even a threat of a separate peace, did Colonel House secure England, France, and Italy's acceptance of the Fourteen Points, with two reservations. On Wilson's second point, "freedom of the seas," a phrase open to varied interpretations, they reserved complete freedom of decision. Wilson's statement that territory occupied by the enemy should be "restored" as well as freed was construed as meaning that Germany must pay compensation. Wilson accepted this second reservation, which would serve as the basis of the large reparations bill presented to Germany. The Germans were also informed that Marshal Foch would formulate the military terms of an armistice that would render Germany incapable of renewing the struggle.

German armies were still intact and on foreign soil, but morale in both the civilian population and the armed forces had nearly collapsed. Since the high command feared to continue the war, the German government accepted Marshal Foch's terms. In a railway car near Compiegne, the German commissioners signed the armistice on November 11, 1918. Austria and Italy agreed to an armistice on November 3.

Wilson Goes to Paris

Wilson decided to participate in the peace negotiations. His objectives at Paris were twofold: (1) a just peace based, with respect to territorial adjustments, on the principle of self-determination—a settlement eliminating centers of infection productive of future wars; and (2) the creation of a league of nations to ensure preservation of peace. Adherence to the principles of the Fourteen Points, Wilson believed, would accomplish these objectives, but he faced serious obstacles. His eloquent statements of idealistic war aims had led war-weary or oppressed populations throughout the world to hail him as their deliverer. This moral leadership faded as ideals clashed with practical considerations and as incompatible aspirations. One obstacle was the secret agreements that the Allies had arranged among themselves before the United States entered the war. Thus France had been promised by Russia, although not by Great Britain, not only the return of Alsace-Lorraine, but also possession of the Saar Valley and the conversion of German territory west of the Rhine into an independent "buffer state." Italy had been assured of large accessions of Austrian territory in the Trentino or southern Tyrol and about the head of the Adriatic, and Japan had been promised the German islands in the North Pacific and the inheritance of German rights in Shantung, China. Russia had been promised Constantinople and other Turkish territory, and still other portions of the Ottoman Empire had been apportioned prospectively among France, Great Britain, Italy, and Greece. The Bolsheviks renounced Russian claims, but other Allies pushed their claims. The French and Italian claims in Europe and Japan's claim to Shantung were destined to be Wilson's major dilemmas. The secret claims conflicted with the principle of self-determination and, specifically, with Wilson's declaration that "peoples and provinces are not to be bartered about from sovereignty to sovereignty as if they were mere chattels and pawns in a game."[19]

Wilson had made no effort to have the secret treaties set aside and rejected a French proposal that they be suspended. In the end, the principle of self-determination was often sacrificed to claims based on these treaties. His second obstacle was the vindictive attitude prevalent among the Allied publics, not excluding the United States. Britain's Lloyd George, France's Clemenceau, and Italy's Vittorio Orlando had promised that Germany would pay for the war, the kaiser hanged, and so forth. Now, often against their better judgment, they felt public pressure to make good on these promises. A third obstacle to Wilson's planned objectives was the other negotiators' awareness that his domestic popularity had slipped. When a recent midterm election gave majorities in both houses to the Republicans, Theodore Roosevelt exulted in a public statement that "Mr. Wilson has no authority whatever to speak for the American people at this time." The electorate's decision inevitably lessened his bargaining power.

Treaty of Versailles

Wilson arrived in Paris on December 13, 1918, but not until the following January 12 did the representatives of the great powers hold their first formal meeting. Since November 1917, the British, French, and Italian prime ministers, with the occasional attendance of Colonel House representing the president, had exercised direction of the war as the Supreme War Council. Now the three—Lloyd George, Clemenceau, and Orlando—along with President Wilson and the ranking Japanese delegate, representing the "Big Five" powers, dominated the conference, attended by 27 victorious nations and their 70 delegates, and made all crucial decisions. Neither Germany nor its wartime allies were represented since they were expected to merely sign arrived-at agreements. Nor were the Soviets invited to join the conference. If disarming Germany and creating the League of Nations were major concerns, Allied leaders also worried about the influence of indigenous communists amidst the chaos and uprisings in Germany and central Europe. Thus, fear of the Bolsheviks disrupted some treaty negotiations and often subtly influenced decisions.

Wilson's greatest success at the conference was adoption of the Covenant of the League of Nations and the decision it should be an integral part of each peace treaty. Wilson was chairman of the commission that drafted the covenant. On February 14, it was presented to the conference, where, with a few changes, it became the Covenant of the League. His desire to gain support for the league, however, forced him to allow France to draft terms of a peace treaty punishing Germany. With his initial triumph, Wilson boarded the steamer *George Washington* to return to the United States, to find supporters and opponents of the League of Nations idea were already busy. With partisan opponents organizing in the Senate, Wilson must now attempt to convince his own countrymen of the league's value. Wilson had invited the members of the Senate Foreign Relations and House Foreign Affairs committees to the White House on February 26 to discuss of the League Covenant, but won no converts. A few hours before Congress adjourned, Senator Henry Cabot Lodge read a statement signed by 37 Republican senators or senators-elect, declaring that "the constitution of the league of nations in the form now proposed ...should not be accepted by the United States" and that peace with Germany should be made as soon as possible after which "the proposal for a league of nations to insure the permanent peace of the world should then be taken up for careful and serious consideration."[20]

In a speech at New York City, before returning to Paris, Wilson told his opponents that when his work was done, the treaty of peace would be tied with so many threads to the League Covenant that it would be impossible to separate them. It did not occur to him, apparently, that such organic union might result not in acceptance of the covenant, but in rejection of the treaty. On the advice of Democratic and Republican friends of the league who warned that without some changes the covenant would never receive Senate approval, Wilson reconvened the League of Nations Commission and asked that the covenant be amended. The changes deemed essential to insure Senate approval were four: (1) recognition of the right of members to withdraw from the league; (2) exemption of domestic questions (such as tariff and immigration) from league jurisdiction; (3) a statement that no member would be required, against its will, to accept a mandate over a former enemy colony; and (4) a declaration safeguarding the Monroe Doctrine. France, Great Britain, Italy, and Japan all tried to exact a quid pro quo for their consent to the American amendments. France requested an international general staff to direct action against new aggressions. Great Britain demanded that the United States give up its ambitious naval building program. Italy insisted that its new boundaries include Fiume, a city and port on the Adriatic. Japan revived a proposal for recognition of racial equality in the Preamble of the Covenant. Wilson ultimately secured the desired amendments, adopted by the conference on April 28, without accepting the changes in the covenant proposed by others.

Subsequent events suggest that Wilson's most serious failure at Paris was his consent to the reparations clauses in the German treaty. Although they brought little benefit to the victors, and in the end were largely nullified, they imbued Germans with a feeling of grave injustice, a grievance that bode ill for the future. The president had declared earlier that there should be "no contributions, no punitive damages,"[21] which along with the Fourteen Points comprised the basis of Germany's surrender. The Allied reservation to this stipulation was Germany's obligation to "restore" occupied territory while embracing payment "for all damages done to the civilian population of the Allies and their property by the aggression of Germany by land, by sea and from the air." This phrasing would seem to have precluded placing the entire cost of the war on Germany, but Allied statesmen, particularly the British in the parliamentary election campaign of December 1918, had promised to do just that. Lloyd George brought forward the specious contention that pensions and separation allowances paid to Allied soldiers and their dependents could properly be classified as "damages done to the civilian population"—a contention that doubled the aggregate reparations bill, substantially increasing Britain's share. Wilson allowed himself to be persuaded by the British argument, apparently under the impression that the increased British share was taken from a fixed sum based on Germany's capacity to pay.

The claim based on pensions and separation allowances was added to claims for other losses, increasing the total reparations bill to a sum far exceeding Germany's capacity to pay, particularly when the treaty also reduced its resources. These included its colonies, merchant marine,

German-owned property in Allied countries, the coal of the Saar, the iron ore of Lorraine, and a substantial fraction of its industrial and agricultural capacity. A Reparations Commission eventually set the reparations figure at $33 billion. Though only a small part of it was ever paid, the enormous bill left Germany with a sense of having been double-crossed. This feeling was aggravated by the imposition of the "war guilt" clause (Article 231) of the treaty by which Germany was required to accept moral and legal responsibility "for causing all the loss and damage" that the Allies and their nationals had suffered "as a consequence of the war imposed upon them by the aggression of Germany and her allies." Those who wrote the treaty may have believed this thesis, but Germans accepted it only under duress.

Germany Accepts

The Germans were summoned to Paris—not to discuss the treaty, but to receive and to sign it. On May 7, 1919, Premier Clemenceau, as president of the conference, handed the lengthy document of 440 articles to the German delegation. The Germans received the treaty with a display of sullenness and discourtesy and made their reply on May 29 in a similar spirit. Thereby they had injured their own case. Many in the Allied delegations, having at last seen the treaty as a whole, were appalled at its severity. Dissatisfaction with the treaty was especially strong among members of the British delegation. Had the Germans been so inclined, they might have divided their opponents and won concessions; however, by their resentful attitude and attacking all major features of the treaty, they helped consolidate Allied delegations around the rigid Clemenceau. A few concessions were granted—slight modifications of the boundaries between Germany and Poland and Denmark, agreement that the disposition of a part of Upper Silesia should be decided by plebiscite instead of by outright cession to Poland, better German representation on the commissions that were to control German rivers, and assurance that the limitations of armaments imposed on Germany was "also the first step towards that general reduction and limitation of armaments... which it will be one of the first duties of the League of Nations to promote." With such changes and assurances as these, the Germans had to be content.[22] On June 23, 1919, they accepted the treaty.[23]

The League of Nations and the Senate

Wilson presented the treaty to the Senate on July 10, 1919. Weeks earlier, however, Senator William E. Borah of Idaho, a leading opponent of the league, had procured a copy and read the long text verbatim into the *Congressional Record*. Now, members of Congress and any citizen might peruse it. The League of Nations Covenant had been known since February and had been debated by both friends and foes alike. The amendments subsequently added to the covenant had also been published, and Senator Lodge had indicated that Wilson's changes did not satisfy him. From the time that the Senate met in special session in May, Republican opponents of the treaty had been planning a strategy. Senator Lodge, who desired to see the treaty defeated despite protestations to the contrary,[24] believed that sentiment for the league was so strong that the treaty could not be defeated by direct attack. The course adopted was: first, to delay action by prolonged hearings and debate, giving pro-League enthusiasm time to cool; and second, to load the treaty with amendments or reservations and count on Wilson and the Democrats to kill it.[25]

Opposition to the treaty stemmed from varied motives. Some feared the league as a "super-state," which would destroy American independence and drag the United States into endless international quarrels. A resurgent nationalism saw treason in an attempt to subject the will of the American people to any form or degree of international control. The league, Senator Borah said, was "the first step in internationalism and the sterilization of nationalism" that was designed by Wall Street bankers and big business. Others, former supporters of Wilson, charged him with surrendering his principles and selling out to British, French, and Japanese "imperialists." Socialists of nearly all varieties would have none of the league because, as they charged, it enthroned capitalism.[26] While liberals and radicals were damning the league as an invention of big business, other opponents obtained funds from millionaires Andrew W. Mellon and Henry Clay Frick to fight the treaty. The battle made strange bedfellows.

Partisanship and personal feuds also contributed to the opposition. Republicans, with an eye on the 1920 campaign and suspecting Wilson might run for a third term, were reluctant to place such an impressive achievement as the league in Democratic hands. Senatorial jealousy of the executive and personal dislike for Wilson certainly stimulated the fight against the League Covenant and the treaty. Leader and organizer of the Senate opposition, Lodge was chairman of the Committee on Foreign Relations in the Senate, where the Republicans held the slender majority of 49 to 47. Of the 49 Republicans, 15 were determined opponents of the league—"irreconcilables" who would support any reservations Lodge proposed and, at the end, would still vote against the treaty. Thirty-four would vote for reservations and the treaty with reservations that suited them. The Senate Democrats, too, were divided. A few would support the treaty only with strong reservations; others, pro-league but not 100 percent behind Wilson's covenant, would support Lodge at least part of the way. The remaining Democrats were divided about equally between those who insisted on the covenant as it was and those who would take it either with or without reservations.

Lodge had seen to it that the Senate Committee on Foreign Relations was "packed" with senators unfriendly to the league.[27] Officially printed copies of the treaty reached the committee on July 14; however, hearings were delayed until July 31. Wilson was heard—the committee meeting with him at the White House on August 19. William C. Bullitt, who resigned in a huff, at Paris, now bared the rift in the American delegation. He revealed a confidential conversation with Lansing, in which the secretary reportedly described the League of Nations as "entirely useless" and added that "if the Senate could only understand what this Treaty means, ... it would unquestionably be defeated." Though Lansing claimed that his language had been distorted, Bullitt's testimony was damaging. So also was much of the other testimony, for the committee heard largely unfriendly witnesses.

An Appeal to the People

It now appeared that the committee, and perhaps the Senate, would insist on more interpretative reservations that Wilson was willing to accept. The president, consequently, resolved to appeal to the country. His tour was routed through the Old Northwest, the Upper Mississippi Valley, and the Far West—the sections that furnished much of the opposition to the treaty. Despite the rather academic style of his addresses, Wilson roused much popular enthusiasm for a league that should make unnecessary a repetition of recent sacrifices and future U.S. interventions. Although Wilson had captivated popular audiences, he had no success in winning the needed senatorial support. His references to his opponents were tactless and occasionally offensive. He offered no compromise; the Senate, he said, must take the treaty as it was or have no treaty at all. Senators who withheld U.S. support from the peace organization would be, he said, "absolute, contemptible quitters." Isolationist senators trailed his footsteps, giving their side of the argument to the same public.

The trip was a political failure, ending in personal tragedy. The strain of 36 formal addresses, numerous "whistle-stop" back-platform speeches, the intense heat, and unrelenting personal interviews and press conferences was too much for Wilson's health. After the speech at Pueblo, Colorado, on September 29, he was rushed back to Washington, a very ill man.

A few days later came the paralytic stroke that made him an almost helpless invalid and from which he never fully recovered. Secluded from friends and shielded from sound advice by his solicitous wife, the sick man in the White House clung to his conviction that the treaty must be approved as he had written it or not at all.[28]

Meanwhile, the Foreign Relations Committee had completed hearings on the treaty, and on September 10, the majority report proposed 45 amendments and four reservations. This action was too drastic even for many Republicans, and the idea of amending it was given up. On November 6, Lodge proposed a resolution of advice and consent to ratification subject to 14 reservations.[29] Wilson was not opposed to all compromise. Before setting out on his speaking tour, he had handed to Senate minority leader Gilbert M. Hitchcock four reservations that he would accept if necessary to get the treaty approved. These dealt with withdrawal from the league, Article 10, the Monroe Doctrine, and domestic questions, and differed from Lodge's reservations on the same points more in wording than in substance. They were so similar to proposals made by Republican mild reservationists as to suggest that they and the Democrats could have reached a compromise with Wilson's encouragement. But when, in November, Hitchcock introduced the substance of the Wilson reservations, adding a fifth on the British Empire's six votes,[30] the moderate Republicans had committed themselves to the Lodge program and complained with reason that Hitchcock came too late.

Wilson denounced Lodge's reservation on Article 10 as "a rejection of the covenant." As the day approached for the vote on the treaty with the 14 reservations, he wrote Senator Hitchcock that: "I trust that all true friends of the treaty will refuse to support the Lodge resolution." Hitchcock and the Democrats heeded the word of their stricken leader, and so on November 19, 1919, all but four of the Democrats joined the Republican irreconcilables to defeat the treaty with reservations. Neither with the Lodge reservations, nor without any, could the treaty command a bare majority of the Senate, not to mention the required two-thirds. The Senate adjourned.

The Last Chance

Not all "true friends of the treaty" favored Wilson's uncompromising position. House, no longer in the president's good graces, had urged compromise. Herbert Hoover had urged acceptance of the Lodge reservations, as had former president, William H. Taft. When the next session of Congress convened in December, new hope for compromise arose. At the Jackson Day dinner in January 1920, William Jennings Bryan told fellow Democrats that democracy required that the president bow to a majority of the Senate. London indicated that it would welcome American ratification, with or without the Lodge reservations. But Wilson stood firm. Nevertheless, during the same month, Republican and Democratic senators, including Lodge and Hitchcock, met informally seeking common ground in a modified set of reservations. Lodge, however, reassured a delegation of alarmed, irreconcilable senators, "that there was not the slightest danger of our conceding anything that was essential or that was anything more than a change in wording."[31] Agreement was reached on minor points but not on the crucial questions of Article 10 and the Monroe Doctrine.

On February 10, 1920, Lodge again reported the treaty to the Senate, with a few recent changes in the November reservations; and the Senate went over the old ground, readopting the Lodge-changed reservations. The resolution of ratification did provide, as Lloyd George had suggested, that failure of the allied and associated powers to object to the reservations should be counted as acceptance. But even this was balanced by giving the right of objection to all or any of the allied and associated powers, rather than only to the Big Four. Yet nothing changed that could have made the reservations more palatable to Wilson. Again, on March 8, he urged supporters to defeat ratification on Lodge's terms. In the final vote on March 19, 1920, the tally for the treaty, with the reservations, fell seven short (49 ayes, 35 nays) of the necessary two-thirds for approval.[32] The treaty, together with Wilson's vision of the great departure for America, was dead.

CHAPTER 11

The Slow Death of Versailles

All the problems which are causing such unrest today lie in the deficiencies of the Treaty of Peace which did not succeed in solving in a clear and reasonable way the questions of the most decisive importance for the future.
—Adolf Hitler, Speech in the Reichstag, May 17, 1933

European history know no more tragic day than that of Munich.
—George F. Kennan, American Diplomat

While the United States slid deeper and deeper into the Great Depression, the blight spread abroad, inflicting paralysis and despair in Europe and Asia, with only the rigidly controlled state economy of the Soviet Union remaining relatively immune. The Depression not only visited incalculable misery on millions of people, it wrecked the postwar system established at Versailles in 1919. As America tried to pull itself out of the Great Depression, its attention was increasingly diverted to Europe and Asia, where the rise of Adolf Hitler in Germany, Benito Mussolini in Italy, Josef Stalin in the U.S.S.R., and ultraconservative militarists in Japan, were clearly at odds with American national interests. The 1930s proved that America could not be protected by any self-imposed isolation and remain oblivious to what was happening abroad. Thus, despite America's concentration on domestic efforts to end the Great Depression, the slow death of Versailles increasingly demanded Washington's attention. The international economic system's collapse seemed to result in irrationalism, violence, and war. Germany's democratic Weimar Republic crumbled as Hitler seized power; Italy already had succumbed to the Fascist dictator Mussolini; totalitarian parties on the left and right proliferated throughout Europe, even afflicting the old democracies of Britain and France. In China, warlords, nationalists, and communists battled for control, while in Japan nationalist and military groups chose to solve the nation's problems through imperialism and conquest.

At the same time, the Great Depression profoundly impacted the conduct of American diplomacy. As one observer put it, "It palsied the hands of American statesmen and sent them searching for formulas and phrases in which to settle, so they hoped, the difficulty of the moment."[1] Desperate to achieve domestic recovery and fearful of wars in Asia and Europe, most Americans seemed determined not to become entangled in the outside world's political problems. The mid-1930s neutrality laws were indicative of that determination. A paralysis of will afflicted not only the United States but also Britain and France, who helplessly observed the dictators that were contemptuous of democracy and rarely hid their plans to "rectify" the Versailles settlement. Only belatedly did the Western democracies, America most tardily of all, recognize the peril and act to meet it.

Hoover and the Far East

East Asia had seemed to promise a new era of progress and stability during the twenties. The great powers had curbed the naval arms race and agreed to preserve the territorial status quo in the Pacific at the Washington Conference. In Japan, moderates pursued a policy of conciliation toward China, cooperated with the Western powers, curbed military expenditures, and undertook social reforms at home. Even China seemed to make progress toward stability, as the Nationalist Party leader, Jiang Jieshi (Chiang Kai-shek), had succeeded by 1929, at least outwardly, in unifying his country. By the early 1930s, however, the region seethed with discontent and conflict. Once again, the U.S.S.R., China, and Japan became embroiled in a conflict over Manchuria, a fertile and strategically important frontier area.[2] By 1937, Japan, now governed by anti-Western supernationalists, had driven back Chinese troops in Manchuria, pulled out of the League of Nations (1933), embarked on a naval building program that reached the limits of the 1920s and 1930s naval limitation treaties, and disregarded the territorial agreements of the Washington Conference. It presented the United States and other major powers with interests in the region with a serious challenge.[3]

President Herbert Hoover differed rather sharply with his secretary of state, Henry L. Stimson, over Far Eastern policy.[4] Hoover was determined to limit America's foreign commitments, reduce naval expenditures, and keep the nation at peace. Stimson, confident, moralistic, and with a Roman sense of duty, believed world relations to be governed by standards of moral principles and mutual respect. He sympathized with China, but, more importantly, considered Tokyo's activities a threat to the Versailles system and on which, he was convinced, rested world peace. Stimson was at first inclined to trust the Japanese civilian leaders to restrain their military, but like many observers, he underestimated the determination of the Japanese military.

The United States, which failed to build up its fleet to authorized treaty limits, lacked sufficient naval power to impress Japanese militarists. Moreover, Washington's policies affronted one of its best customers—America's China trade, despite the old illusion of a vast market, proved quite small, while Japan was the third-largest purchaser of American exports. While Washington displayed moral outrage and traditional missionary-nourished sympathy with China over Japan's aggression in Manchuria, many Japanese regarded Western condemnation as hypocritical. Yosuke Matsuoka, later Japan's foreign minister, observed: "The Western Powers taught Japan the game of poker but after acquiring most of the chips they pronounced the game immoral and took up contract bridge." There was a realistic element also—Stimson feared that Japan had undermined the postwar settlement and if unchecked would stimulate aggression elsewhere.

Roosevelt Approach to Foreign Policy

President Franklin D. Roosevelt's early foreign policy at least through 1936 essentially adhered to that of Hoover.[5] His private correspondence reveals a great interest in international affairs and reflects his earlier "education" in the Wilson administration. Domestic issues of recovery and reform absorbed most of his administration's early energies. A practical politician, Roosevelt understood the need for caution in foreign affairs in order to obtain the support of powerful liberal isolationists in Congress for his domestic legislation. But despite his internationalist or Wilsonian orientation, Roosevelt could not be impervious to the current nonentanglement mood—which to some degree he shared.[6] Consequently, Roosevelt's first administration revealed drift and inconsistency, with isolationist and internationalist policies incongruously intermixed. His long-serving secretary of state, Cordell Hull, a Tennessee politician and dedicated Wilsonian, viewed world affairs as grounded in idealistic principles: "There should be no laxity on the part of this nation or any other nation in the observation of both the letter and spirit of treaties and international good faith."[7] His panacea for the world troubles required freer trade, revival of international moral behavior, and application of international law. Hull's absorbing interest was to remove or reduce barriers to international trade; in other areas, he offered few specific solutions. His most significant contributions to New Deal foreign policy were in trade reciprocity and the Good Neighbor policy; but his rejection of the role of power in international politics and faith in exhortations of basic principles failed to prepare him for the aggressions in Europe and the Fear East. Never close to Roosevelt, Hull nevertheless played an important foreign policy role until Pearl Harbor. Thereafter, he found himself increasingly bypassed.[8]

Roosevelt continued his predecessor's questionable policies toward the League of Nations and the war debts question. During the 1932 election, he pleased William Randolph Hearst and other isolationist die-hards when he stated that the present league had fallen away from Wilson's ideal and the United States had no place in it. He even left it to Secretary of Labor Francis Perkins to get the United States into the International Labor Organization. Hoover desired to scale down the war debts owed to America, but Roosevelt, recognizing this would be unpopular, continued to insist on full payment. When all European debtors except Finland defaulted in whole or in part, he signed the 1934 Johnson Act prohibiting private or governmental loans to foreign governments in default. Later, in 1940 and 1941, he regretted tying his hands when Britain and China needed loans to purchase arms.

The World Disarmament Conference, finally convened in 1932, still limped along when Roosevelt entered office.[9] France demanded security before arms reductions, and Germany insisted on equality with France. Hoover previously suggested abolition of all offensive weapons and, when that was dismissed, proposed one-third reduction in all armaments. Roosevelt offered a pledge of nonaggression, overall arms reductions, and an American promise in case of crisis to consult with other powers—if Washington agreed on the designation of an aggressor, it would not interfere with any sanctions the league might impose. Roosevelt apparently dared not go further toward collective security. In any case, the conference ended in failure when Hitler withdrew the German delegates from the league and announced Germany would rearm. Hull meanwhile finally obtained the Reciprocal Trade Agreement Act of 1934, regularly renewed in subsequent years, by which the executive could negotiate reductions in existing tariff rates by as much as 50 percent. The State Department completed 16 agreements within the first three years under the act, most of them with Latin America. By 1940, the number had increased to 22.[10] Apart from winning goodwill abroad and improvement of trade, especially in Latin America, the reciprocal trade approach had fallen short of Hull's vision.

Diplomacy and the Soviet Union

Roosevelt's Republican predecessors had continued Wilson's policy of nonrecognition that reflected disapproval of communist ideology, its methods of government, and the Soviets' repudiation of foreign debts. While most Americans approved nonrecognition, some had been inclined toward tolerance or even endorsement of the Soviet system. Many American businessmen believed that recognition would bring increased trade with Russia, since, after recognition, most European countries renewed economic ties. The Great Depression heightened the lure of trade, which Soviet authorities exploited to facilitate diplomatic recognitions.[11] The fascist threat in Europe and Japanese expansion in the Far East also made recognition attractive as it might provide some security. By 1933, American firms, such as General Electric, Ford, and International Harvester, had entered the Soviet market, as Josef Stalin's first Five Year Plan seemed to promise new opportunities. Disappointment grew, therefore, when Germany replaced the United States as the Soviets' foremost supplier. Business spokesmen and politicians such as Senators Hiram Johnson and William Borah, both dedicated opponents of foreign entanglement, argued that recognition would greatly increase American trade with Moscow. Many Americans still remained opposed to recognition on ideological and religious grounds. The American Legion, the Daughters of the American Revolution, members of Protestant and Roman Catholic churches, the AFL, and chambers of commerce provided the bulk of the opposition.

Roosevelt favored formal diplomatic relations, for, whatever one thought of it, the Soviet regime had existed for 16 years; moreover, an official relationship might bolster the status quo in East Asia and strengthen nonaggressive forces in Europe. After preliminary discussions, Soviet foreign commissar Maxim Litvinov arrived in Washington, making it clear that Moscow preferred unconditional recognition prior to negotiations on outstanding issues. The American authorities, however, insisted on negotiations first. With Roosevelt taking a direct part in the talks, recognition was completed on November 16, 1933. The arrangement established diplomatic relations, provided freedom of religious worship for Americans in the Soviet Union, and promised to halt Soviet propaganda and subversion in the United States. Roosevelt and his advisers insisted on the religious provision, because many American people had long condemned the Soviet regime as godless. Public opinion also required the promise that neither government would interfere "in any manner" in the internal affairs of the other. Litvinov dropped claims for compensation for damages during the American intervention in North Russia and Siberia and promised further negotiations on American claims, totaling over $630 million. In their "gentlemen's agreement," Litvinov mentioned a possible settlement for $75 million, while Roosevelt suggested $150 million.[12] Most Americans approved the establishment of formal relations. Litvinov was honored at a farewell luncheon at the Waldorf-Astoria Hotel, attended by representatives of major capitalistic firms. The president of International Business Machines even urged Americans to promote better relations in the future by refraining "from any criticism of the present form of Government adopted by Russia."

Unfortunately for enthusiasts, recognition of the Soviets proved a disappointment. Trade remained small, primarily because the Soviet Union lacked the necessary funds, and businessmen and financiers deemed private long-term credits too risky. Diplomatic benefits also proved illusory as the two powers failed to achieve any notable collaboration in regard to Japan or Europe prior to World War II. The debt negotiations also ended in deadlock. Moscow, in effect, refused to agree to any sum unless the United States provided long-term governmental loans or credits in double that amount—the State Department refused to increase Soviet indebtedness. The Soviets continued their propaganda and subversion. When Hull protested the continuation of worldwide revolutionary activities, trumpeted at the Seventh Congress of the Comintern at Moscow in 1935, Moscow disavowed the private and separate international communist apparatus that happened to be meeting on Soviet soil. The State Department lodged repeated protests, and a growing number of Americans came to regret recognition.

The Good Neighbor Policy

Much earlier, the Wilson administration and its Republican successors in the 1920s became aware of Latin American resentment of the "Colossus of the North" and tried to assuage it. Latin American critics cited a long list of Yankee "crimes" and blunders: the "rape of Panama"; armed interventions and military rule in the Caribbean; economic penetration and exploitation of Latin America; and U.S. refusal to subject its actions to international restraints. Above all, the Monroe Doctrine and its infamous Roosevelt Corollary—justifying intervention in the Caribbean—aroused hatred and fear among neighbors to the south. American businessmen, eager for new markets and investment opportunities, urged the State Department to take a more conciliatory course. So did other Americans, appalled at the accounts of the marines' harsh action in Haiti and the Dominican Republic. For these reasons, then, and because the United States no longer felt insecure about the Panama Canal, the government began to abandon its benevolent imperialism. Hoover's contributions to Pan-Americanism has prompted some historians to credit him with originating the Good Neighbor policy. While president-elect, Hoover undertook a goodwill tour of Latin America, in 1928, during which he tried to dispel distrust and several times used the phrase "good neighbor." In office he refused further armed interventions, despite disturbances in Panama; removed American troops from Nicaragua in 1933; and promised withdrawal from Haiti. He also abandoned Wilson's idealistic recognition policy—recognizing only an orderly, righteous government that represented its people—for a return to the traditional practice of recognizing de facto regimes regardless of how they came to power. Yet, like his predecessors, Hoover refused to give up the right of armed intervention.

In his inaugural address, President Roosevelt pledged a policy of the Good Neighbor toward the entire world, but the phrase was soon applied exclusively to Latin America. His Good Neighbor policy focused on nonintreventionism and the multilateralization of the Monroe Doctrine from a U.S. doctrine to a hemispheric responsibility. Further, it supplanted Republican protectionism with reciprocal trade agreements and sacrificed, when necessary, private American economic interests for the United States' national interests. Cordell Hull delighted Latin Americans at the Seventh Pan American Conference at Montevideo in 1933 when he voted for a resolution of nonintervention by armed force in the internal affairs of any Western Hemisphere state, except as sanctioned by international law. Latin Americans cheered this U.S. renunciation. A Mexican delegate at the Montevideo conference expressed the conviction that there is in the White House "an admirable, noble, and good man—a courageous man who knows the errors of the past but who feels that the errors really belong to the past." The marines left Haiti as Hoover had promised, and in 1934, the State Department agreed to terminate the so-called Platt Amendment with Cuba—that gave the United States the right to intervene in the island. The latter action came after Washington nearly intervened during the overthrow of the Gerardo Machado dictatorship and its successor. Sumner Welles, American ambassador to Cuba, had encouraged Machado's fall, but disturbed by the subsequent violence, threatened armed intervention. Roosevelt and Hull, perceiving the repercussions, rejected Welles's recommendation and willingly renounced the right to intervene in Cuba.

Alarmed at the threat of war in Europe and by fascist activities in Latin America, the United States sought to change the Monroe Doctrine from a unilateral U.S. policy to a collective defense system for the Western Hemisphere. Argentina, traditionally a rival of the United States for leadership in the Western Hemisphere and itself increasingly under strong fascist influences, repeatedly blocked Washington's proposals for a binding commitment to repel outside aggression. Hull finally obtained a vague declaration at the Eighth Pan American Conference, held at Lima in 1938, for consultation and cooperation against subversion or external threats to the peace of the hemisphere. Canada, a self-governing dominion within the British Commonwealth, remained apart from the Pan American movement in order to preserve its ties to Britain. In effect, however, Roosevelt brought Canada into the inter-American system when at Kingston, Ontario, in 1938, he declared that the United States could not see Canada threatened by conquest. After the outbreak of the Second World War, Canada and the United States concluded joint defensive arrangements. Roosevelt had prepared the means for close hemispheric collaboration during World War II and the creation of the Organization of American States after the war.

The Roosevelt administration during these years indicated that while it continued to be concerned with the legitimate economic interests of American citizens in Latin America, it was no longer a bond collector for Wall Street. When Bolivia expropriated Standard Oil Company holdings and Venezuela demanded increased royalties from American oil companies operating in that country, the State Department refrained from threats or retaliation and sought to arrange equitable settlements. Mexico proved more difficult, but there, too, the State Department successfully applied the new approach. President Lazaro Cardenas, a leftist reformer, expropriated foreign-owned lands and oil properties in 1938. Although an exasperated Hull inclined toward retaliation, Roosevelt arranged settlements that displeased American investors but avoided a serious crisis between the two countries. American oil companies had to accept compensation of $24 million for holdings they evaluated at half a billion dollars. A subsequent Import-Export Bank loan from the United States helped Cardenas's successor pay for even these reduced compensations.

Roosevelt's new policies contributed to hemispheric harmony and paid handsome dividends in promoting the security and unity of the Western Hemisphere as the danger of another world war loomed. Latin Americans hailed Roosevelt as "*el gran democrata*," and many viewed his New Deal as a model for their reforms. His accomplishments in Latin America, his role as leader of the Western world during the

Second World War, and his advocacy for the aspirations of the common man everywhere earned Roosevelt near deification in Latin America. Whatever the debate about the authorship of the Good Neighbor policy, Latin Americans almost unanimously gave the credit to Roosevelt.[13]

The First Neutrality Legislation

By the mid-1930s, economic distress at home, disillusionment with the 1917–18 Great Crusade, and war clouds abroad generated a growing popular conviction that America must avoid foreign entanglements that might lead to war. As Senator Borah said in 1934, America was not and would not be isolated economically; "But in all matters political, in all commitments or any nature or kind, which may encroach in the slightest upon the free and unembarrassed action of our people, or which circumscribe their discretion and judgment, we have been free, we have been independent, we have been isolationist." Political isolationism, particularly strong in the Midwest, was not limited to that region. The Midwestern reaction reflected the large number of German and Scandinavian Americans and geographical remoteness, and above all agrarian radicalism. Many agrarian radicals believed that big businessmen and financiers had brought about U.S. intervention in the recent world war, from which they had profited at the farmers' expense. Avoiding foreign entanglements obviously appealed to urban reformers and idealists, and crossed political lines. This isolationism gradually became more conservative as liberals swung toward internationalism in the last years of the decade.

Antiwar novels, articles, movies, and revisionist histories reflected and contributed to the popular mood of pacifism, disillusionment, and withdrawal. Peace movements proliferated and flourished, with college students demonstrating against war and demanding the expulsion of ROTC units from campuses. Erich Remarque—his novel *All Quiet on the Western Front* (1929) became a popular movie (1930)—and Ernest Hemingway along with John Dos Passos depicted war as senseless and barbaric. Muckraking books by Helmuth C. Englebrecht, *Merchants of Death*, and George Seldes, *Iron Blood and Profits* (1934), convinced many that the common man fought so that bankers and munitions manufacturers might prosper. Some historians revised the previously accepted version that Germany had been solely responsible for the war in 1914 and for American involvement in 1917. Revisionist scholars also sought to influence current public discussions on foreign policy and to prevent intervention in another war as injurious to liberal reform at home. Harry Elmer Barnes, an ardent supporter of Wilsonian internationalism until disillusioned by the postwar settlement, pioneered revisionist studies during the mid-1920s. His *Genesis of the World War* (1935) and C. C. Tansill, *America Goes to War* (1938) indicted the one-sided nature of American neutrality in 1914–1917. To a large degree, the revisionists persuaded the intellectual community and helped create that climate of public opinion that explains passage of the 1930s neutrality laws. A Gallup Poll in April 1937, for example, revealed that 64 percent of the public regarded American intervention in the First World War as a mistake.

The Nye Committee Hearings were symptomatic of the popular disillusionment. Responding to demands for federal regulation of the arms industry, the Senate in 1934 authorized a special inquiry into the munitions industry. The administration, caught off-guard, failed to block the selection of Republican Senator Gerald P. Nye of North Dakota, a rough-hewn arch-isolationist, to head the inquiry. The committee's sensational releases convinced many citizens that profit-hungry capitalists had dragged the United States into the world war. As Nye summed it up, "When Americans went into the fray, they little thought that they were there and fighting to save the skins of American bankers who... had two billions of dollars of loans to the Allies in jeopardy." The investigation seemed almost as much anti–big business as antiwar, and it reflected the widespread view that greedy bankers and industrialists encouraged international strife. As hostilities threatened between Italy and Ethiopia, Roosevelt suggested neutrality legislation to the Nye Committee in 1935, seeking to bar American citizens from traveling on belligerent ships. Roosevelt wanted to avoid being involved in issues of neutral rights so American policy, freed of the burden that had plagued Wilson, could be based on more fundamental national interests. He desired a ban against the arms trade that would permit him to discriminate between aggressive and defensive nations but, encountering a threatened filibuster in Congress, accepted a mandatory arms embargo. Upon a presidential proclamation of the existence of a foreign war, the sale or transportation of munitions to belligerent countries would be prohibited, and at the executive's discretion citizens could be warned not to take passage on belligerent vessels. Roosevelt, to Hull's disappointment, signed the measure because it was due to expire in six months and he hoped at that time to obtain a more satisfactory law.

When Congress passed the Neutrality Act, Europe seemed once more on the threshold of a major war. Led by Benito Mussolini, Italian Fascists achieved some worthwhile reforms and social stability but at the price of a totalitarian dictatorship. Mussolini, in general, remained pacific in foreign policy until the Great Depression and the rise of Adolf

Hitler in Germany began to undermine the Versailles settlement. Hitler adeptly exploited popular resentment of the Versailles Treaty, mass unemployment and economic distress, and the weaknesses of the postwar democracy in Germany. His National Socialist or Nazi Party espoused policies similar to Italian fascism and was elected to office in early 1933, only a few weeks before Roosevelt's inauguration. Hitler gradually assumed dictatorial powers, began rearming Germany, threatened to use force to rectify the 1919 settlement, and launched violently anti-Jewish persecutions within the Third Reich. The American ambassador, William E. Dodd, warned the president and the State Department about Hitler's plans, while the anti-Semitic Nuremberg Laws fully revealed the bestial nature of the Nazi regime. A growing exodus of German Jews fled to Britain, the United States and other refuges, among them the noted physicist Albert Einstein. Yet, until Mussolini's Ethiopian venture revealed Great Britain and France's cautious response, Hitler acted fairly cautiously in foreign affairs. When Mussolini invaded Ethiopia in the fall of 1935, the League Council condemned the attack and invoked economic sanctions prohibiting loans and the export of arms and war materials to Italy. The alarmed British and French governments, however, anxious not to drive Italy into Hitler's arms, carefully left oil, vital to Mussolini's war machine, off the list of sanctions. This appeasement also led to a stillborn compromise, the Hoare-Laval plan for giving Mussolini two-thirds of Ethiopia, but public wrath in Britain and France caused its repudiation. Meanwhile, Mussolini's legions, armed with advanced weapons and using poison gas, overran all of primitive Ethiopia.

Roosevelt and Hull, deeming it politically unwise to cooperate openly with league sanctions, invoked the Neutrality Laws even though Mussolini had not formally declared war. Contrary to their expectations, this action had little effect on Italy, which did not need to import arms, while injuring Ethiopia, which did. The administration then urged American firms to join a moral embargo of oil shipments to Italy, but found it difficult to enforce the embargo while its action failed to encourage the league to adopt sterner sanctions. Hitler meanwhile reoccupied and fortified the Rhineland, restored conscription, and launched a naval and military aviation program in defiance of the Versailles Treaty.

Second and Third Neutrality Acts

Conclusion of the Rome-Berlin Axis in 1936 solidified the new alignment of fascist powers against the Western democracies, supplemented in the same year by German and Italian anti-Comintern pacts with Japan.

Congress approved the second Neutrality Act in February 1936 that prohibited loans as well as sales of arms to belligerents and directed the president to extend the ban to new belligerents entering a war. The tenor of American sentiment and policy became clear when the Spanish Civil War broke out in the summer of 1936. Despite a nonintervention agreement among the major European powers, Germany and Italy actively supported the conservative and fascist-tinged rebel forces of General Francisco Franco against the Spanish republican armies. Many American liberals and intellectuals sympathized deeply with the legal republican government of Spain; and several thousand American volunteers fought for the Republic. Although the communists were active in organizing pro-Loyalist committees in America, most American sympathizers simply admired the heroic resistance of the Republicans and viewed the civil war as a crucial struggle between democracy and fascism. Conversely, a minority of American conservatives and Roman Catholic spokesmen saw conservative Franco as a bulwark against atheism, socialism, and communism in Spain. The majority of Americans, however, tended to be apathetic or neutral about the civil war. A poll classified 12 percent of the public pro-Franco, 22 percent pro-Loyalists, and the remainder either neutral or without an opinion.[14] The Roosevelt administration supported Anglo-French efforts to isolate the Spanish Civil War. Although normally a recognized government is permitted to import arms during an internal disturbance, Roosevelt and Hull treated the conflict as one between two sovereign states. They proclaimed a moral embargo against shipment of war matériel to either the rebels or the legal government in Spain. Subsequently, Congress formally extended the neutrality law to apply to the civil war. The Loyalists alone suffered from the Anglo-French and American attempts to isolate the conflict, for Germany and, especially Italy, cynically violated their non-intervention pledges to supply Franco with arms and "volunteer" troops. President Roosevelt contemplated raising the embargo against the Loyalists, but he desisted because of domestic opposition and the obvious hopelessness of the republican cause.

The third Neutrality Act, enacted in 1937, marked the final stage in the effort to protect America from war. Although Roosevelt desired more flexible provisions to permit him to discriminate between aggressors and their victims, he was deeply involved in a domestic squabble and left primarily responsibility to Senator Key Pittman of Nevada, chairman of the Senate Committee on Foreign Relations. Pittman repeatedly advised the administration to move cautiously in seeking modifications in the neutrality laws. The 1937 act renewed the ban on arms sales and loans to belligerents and prohibited travel on belligerent passenger and merchant vessels whenever the president should proclaim the existence of a foreign war. At the president's discretion, the exportation of nonmilitary goods to belligerents could also be prohibited during any war in the next two years unless done on a "cash and carry" basis. The new measure represented a compromise, benefiting the Axis powers in case of war with an arms embargo and yet offering the Western democracies that controlled the seas an opportunity to purchase vital raw materials for cash and to transport them in their own ships. "Cash and carry" also reflected an agrarian determination to keep open profitable markets for farm products in Europe.

The president's freedom of maneuver was sharply restricted. Arms and loan bans would have to be applied to aggressor and victim alike. Underlying this act and the earlier neutrality laws were highly questionable assumptions that no basic moral principles were involved in the struggles taking place abroad, that no fundamental American national interests were at stake, and that the nation could be secure in its hemisphere regardless of developments elsewhere. For the sake of avoiding political entanglements, Congress had abandoned the nation's traditional policy of defending neutral trading rights on the high seas. As several commentators quipped, the neutrality acts appeared to be an attempt by Congress to legislate the United States post facto out of World War I.

The United States and Japan's Invasion of China

Prior to 1937, Roosevelt and Hull had not followed a consistent foreign policy. Not only had the administration accepted crippling neutrality legislation without resistance, Roosevelt felt it occasionally necessary to take a public isolationist position. The Democratic platform in 1936 reassured the electorate that the country would not be pulled into war by political or commercial entanglements. During the campaign, Roosevelt declared his resolve to insulate America from foreign conflicts: "I hate war. I have passed unnumbered hours, I shall pass unnumbered hours, thinking and planning how war may be kept from the Nation." But the situation in China and the crises in Europe pressured Roosevelt to take a more internationalist course. He hoped to avoid a general war but, if that failed, to strengthen peace-loving states against their assailants. When Japan's armies advanced toward the heart of China in 1937, Roosevelt worried that the forces of stability everywhere stood on the defensive and Japan's aggression comprised only one aspect of this assault. He chose not invoke the neutrality laws in Japan's undeclared war, because he wanted to give China whatever aid possible.

In his "Quarantine Speech," at Chicago on October 5, 1937, the president tried to prepare the American people for a more responsible foreign policy. Speaking in the heartland of isolationist America, he pointed out that: "Innocent peoples and nations are being cruelly sacrificed to a greed for power and supremacy which is devoid of all sense of justice and humane considerations." If aggressor nations prevail, "Let no one imagine that America will escape, that America may expect mercy, that this hemisphere will not be attacked." After proclaiming the principle that international gangsters should be segregated as society quarantines the carriers of dangerous diseases, Roosevelt declared, "We are determined to stay out of war ... but we cannot *insure* ourselves against the disastrous effects of war and the danger of involvement; we cannot have complete protection in a world of disorder in which confidence and security have broken down." The address aroused favorable response across the country, but it also ignited isolationist criticism, charges of warmongering, and even muttered threats of impeachment. It soon became apparent, however, that the president had no clear policy changes in mind.[15] In subsequent remarks to reporters, he denied even the intention of condemning the aggressors. In retrospect, it seems clear that thereafter Roosevelt felt more apprehensive than he should have been about the antiwar spirit in America.

The League of Nations condemned Japan's action in China as violating the Kellogg-Briand and Nine Power Pacts and suggested a conference of signatories of the 1922 Nine Power Pact. Shortly before, the United States and the other signers, plus Russia, met at Brussels in November in 1937, where Roosevelt indicated he did not favor vigorous measures against Japan; apparently he saw the conference's role as simply to bring moral pressure to bear. Japan declined to attend, and only Russia advocated strong measures. Britain and France left the initiative to the United States, while Roosevelt and Hull recoiled from economic sanctions against Japan. Consequently, the conference achieved nothing beyond a pious reaffirmation of treaty principles. The Brussels Conference was not just a fiasco, it was a disaster. The fact that it met encouraged China to expect substantial assistance, while its failure emboldened Japan's leaders in their plans. The *Panay* incident in December 1937 further revealed the reluctance of Washington to risk conflict with Japan. Japanese warplanes deliberately attacked the American gunboat *Panay* and three Standard Oil Company tankers on the Yangtze River, strafing survivors in the water. Yet unlike the *Maine* incident in 1898, most Americans reacted mildly and wanted to withdraw all our ships and men from the area to avoid future incidents. The government accepted Japanese apologies and reparations. The incident also quickened Congressional support for the so-called

Ludlow Amendment to the Constitution, prohibiting war except in case of actual invasion or with majority approval in a national referendum. The administration exerted considerable pressure, including a letter from the president read in the House of Representatives, to block the bill from coming to the floor for formal debate and action.[16]

Encouraged by slowly increasing public support for stronger policies, the State Department began to deal more firmly with Japan. The Two-Ocean Naval Act of 1938 vastly increased naval construction—even isolationists accepted the need for greater hemispheric defense. Meanwhile Japan, heretofore apologetic for many of its acts, openly proclaimed in 1938 a "New Order" for East Asia. No longer would Tokyo even give lip service to the principles of China's Open Door. Hull strongly objected to the "New Order" and reasserted American rights in China and the Far East. The administration gave Jiang Jieshi a small loan in 1938 to bolster China's currency and its morale, and slapped a moral embargo against the sale and shipment of aircraft to Japan. Roosevelt ordered the Pacific Fleet moved temporarily to Pearl Harbor, a graphic reminder to Tokyo of American power and will to resist. Finally, the State Department opened the way for economic retaliation on July 26, 1939, when it gave notice terminating the Japanese-American commercial treaty of 1911. War between the two nations was not yet inevitable, although clearly they were following sharply diverging courses. From the standpoint of practical interests, American policy could be viewed as highly unrealistic, for its economic stake in China fell far short of its trade with Japan. Moreover, Japan clearly ranked as the strongest power in East Asia. Roosevelt and Hull, however, believed that aggression must be opposed lest it spread. In short, they saw Japan's attack on China as part of the general breakdown in world security and peace. Moreover, the American leaders thought that a greater display of firmness offered a chance of restraining Japan. Even after the European war erupted in 1939, Roosevelt and Hull continued to hope that hostilities could be avoided with Japan, while they concentrated American attention on Europe. Japan was not viewed as an immediate threat to American security until Tokyo concluded the Tripartite Alliance with the Axis powers in September 1940.

Public Opinion and the Prospect of War

Public opinion splintered under the impact of foreign events. Isolationists and noninterventionists feared involvement in war and were increasingly suspicious of Roosevelt's leadership, as the Ludlow Amendment indicated. The internationalists, however, felt a growing apprehension about the Axis threat in Europe and Japanese militarism in Asia and supported the administration's movement toward collective security. Many previously pacifist or isolationist liberals moved to the internationalist camp. Some professed to fear fascism at home, as anti-Semites rallied behind fascist organizations such as William Dudley Pelley's Silver Shirts, the German-American Bund, and the Christian Front, movements stimulated by the growing numbers of Jewish refugees fleeing Central Europe.[17] The formation of the House Committee on Un-American Activities, in 1938, also disturbed thoughtful citizens. Headed by Democratic Representative Martin Dies of Texas, the committee ignored right-wing activities and concentrated on ferreting out communist infiltration and front organizations. The Dies Committee permitted witnesses at its hearings to make unsubstantiated and reckless charges of communism against individuals who often had no opportunity for rebuttal. Some 640 organizations were denounced as controlled or infiltrated by the communists.

Yet communism became more respectable when the Soviet Union joined the Western democracies in opposition to fascist aggression. In the United States, Earl Browder, now general secretary of the American Communist Party, pursued a Popular Front strategy, omitting revolutionary jargon and urging a coalition of all democratic forces to oppose fascism. Browder boasted of his Revolutionary War ancestry and described communism as merely twentieth-century Americanism. The Communist Party successfully penetrated various peace and youth groups, made inroads in various labor unions—where they were often the most sincere organizers—and a few also found places in the executive government. Their importance usually has been grossly exaggerated.

The Prelude to War

During 1938, Adolf Hitler took the first two steps in his drive to the east, annexing Austria and the predominantly German sections of Czechoslovakia. British prime minister Neville Chamberlain paid two visits in mid-September 1938 to the German dictator to broker a peaceful settlement. His missions were in vain; the further Britain, France, and Czechoslovakia moved toward Hitler's demands, the more extreme Hitler's demands became. At the end of September, when Roosevelt entered the fray, the continent was on the brink of war. Roosevelt joined with Chamberlain and French premier Daladier in urging Mussolini to gain Hitler's acceptance a peaceful settlement that gave him substantially all he wanted. Hitler met with Mussolini and the French and British premiers at Munich, where on September 29 Hitler, Mussolini, Chamberlain, and Daladier agreed to a plan that the Czech government was forced to accept. It surrendered the German-speaking region of Czechoslovakia, after which Hitler indicated it was all he wanted. Thus, it was assumed, war had been averted. Chamberlain told the people of England that he had brought back "peace with honor. I believe," he added, "it is peace in our time."

Americans greeted the Munich settlement with profound relief that war had been avoided. Thus the American government and people at this time obviously favored appeasement of the Nazi dictator. As Hitler violated his pledges and anti-Jewish outrages multiplied in Germany, Roosevelt publicly voiced disapproval. After the violent *Kristallnacht* in Germany— a wave of anti-Jewish riots and stringent repressive measures that followed the assassination of a German diplomat in Paris by a Jew—Roosevelt recalled the American ambassador in Berlin, remarking that "I myself could scarcely believe that such things could occur in a twentieth century civilization."[18] Hitler fully reciprocated American dislike and recalled his ambassador. He viewed the United States as a racially mongrelized society that could not even cope with the economic depression. America need not be taken seriously, he told his intimates in 1938, because it was too impotent to fight and would not go beyond meaningless moral gestures in international affairs. The German military shared his opinion. The neutrality laws merely strengthened his contempt.[19] The Munich settlement proved to be but the prelude to the complete extinction of Czechoslovakia as an independent nation. Hungary and Poland at once demanded and received slices of territory where Magyars and Poles were numerous. Internal dissension between Czechs and Slovaks afforded Hitler in March 1939 an excuse for absorbing Bohemia-Moravia and Slovakia as German protectorates. Meanwhile, Mussolini seized the occasion to strengthen Italy's position in the Mediterranean. On April 7, 1939, Italian troops occupied independent Albania, which, a few days later, was added to the empire Mussolini ruled in the name of King Victor Emmanuel III.

Hitler had declared at Munich: "This [Sudetenland] is the last territorial claim which I have to make in Europe." His absorption of Czechoslovakia gave lie to that declaration, and by April 1939, he was pressing Poland for consent to annex the free city of Danzig and a German corridor across Poland to give Germany freer access to East Prussia. By this time Chamberlain, losing faith in Hitler's promises, abruptly abandoned appeasement and, with France, guaranteed assistance against aggression to Poland and later to Rumania and Greece—the latter threatened by Italy's occupation of Albania. Geography made it difficult to effectively implement these guarantees, but they served notice on the Axis powers that further aggression against their small neighbors would mean war. Political leaders in London and Paris owed their offices to publics still feeling the effects of the last war and dreading another one, mired in a corrosive depression, and resentful of expenditures for arms rather than relief. These officials found it much more difficult than have postwar analysts to know where and when to draw the line against the dictators. British and French officials had difficulty finding their vital interests at stake in Ethiopia, given concern for their possessions around the Mediterranean. Spain posed a different dilemma. Conservative leaders, especially in London, found little common interest with the radical, communist-supported, republican government in Madrid; indeed, many preferred either Hitler or Mussolini. In Hitler's violation of the Munich agreement, however, these leaders and their reluctant publics finally had evidence they confronted an aggressor that threatened the very existence of their nations. Perhaps they had been appeasers, but now, ill prepared militarily, they had drawn the line.

In Washington, the sympathies of the Roosevelt administration were unequivocally on the side of the European democracies and against the fascist dictatorships. In his message to Congress on January 4, 1939, Roosevelt remarked that although the United States had no intention of using other than peaceful methods to discourage aggressors, there were "many methods short of war, but stronger and more effective than mere words, of bringing home to aggressor governments the aggregate sentiments of our own people." But "methods short of war," if that phrase meant material aid, were barred by the neutrality laws, as the president complained in the same message, which "may actually give aid to an aggressor and deny it to the victim." Thus began a long campaign to have the neutrality laws repealed or revised. On April 15, 1939, a week after Italy seized Albania, Roosevelt addressed Hitler and Mussolini. Referring to the fear of war that hung over the world, he suggested that the two dictators could dispel it by giving a 10-year nonaggression guarantee to their neighbors in Europe and the Near East—31 nations in all. He would seek, in return, similar promises from their neighbors. If this were accomplished, the United States would gladly participate in discussions aimed at easing the burden of armaments and freeing the channels of international trade. Mussolini did not reply; but Hitler responded two weeks later claiming to have asked all the 31 governments Roosevelt named whether they feared German aggression and therefore felt the need of the president's proposed promises. In each case, he said, the answer had been negative. Any fear of German aggression, he implied, existed only in President Roosevelt's imagination.

As tension mounted in Europe over the Polish question, Roosevelt and Hull became increasingly persuaded that the neutrality laws, especially the arms embargo, only encouraged Hitler's aggression by assuring that in a general European war Great Britain and France could not purchase in the United States needed arms, ammunition or implements of war. Repeal of the arms embargo, the administration believed, would give Hitler reason to pause before inviting war with the democracies. During June and July, the administration's allies in Congress attempted to secure repeal of that provision while leaving the remainder of the law intact or slightly modified. The House passed a bill so mutilated as to be worthless. In a final effort, Roosevelt and Hull met with leading senators and sought to impress on them the danger of war in Europe and the perils that would confront the United States if the Axis won. The surest road to security for America, they argued, lay in taking action that would assure Great Britain and France of access to American materials and so deter Hitler from starting a war. Senator William Borah, always the isolationist, replied that he had sources of information in Europe more reliable than those of the State Department, and that his sources assured him that there would be no war. Congress adjourned without taking action.

While Roosevelt asked in vain for legislation to strengthen the democracies, the British and French sought the support of the Soviet Union as a means of making effective their guarantees to Poland and Rumania. Although Russia had been ignored at Munich, the Soviet dictator Josef Stalin, in April 1939, offered France and Great Britain a defensive alliance against further German aggression. Negotiations began in April and dragged on into August. The stumbling block was the refusal of Poland, Rumania, and the Baltic States to accept a Russian guarantee of their territory, which implied a right to enter it for protection against German aggression. To the Russians, this right was an essential element in their plans for defense, but to the small states lying between Germany and the Soviet Union, the eastern giant was at least as great a peril as the western. When the British and French refused to force Russia's attentions on its neighbors, Moscow secretly opened parallel negotiations with Germany. On May 3, Maxim Litvinov, a friend of the West, was replaced as foreign commissar by Vyacheslav M. Molotov. For three months Molotov shrewdly kept two paths open, one to Berlin, one to Paris and London. The first clue to the outcome was the August 20 announcement that Russia and Germany had signed a trade agreement. Immediately thereafter, Nazi foreign minister Joachim von Ribbentrop flew to Moscow and on August 23 signed a nonaggression pact that assured Hitler of Soviet neutrality if he invaded Poland. Accompanying it was a secret agreement for the partition of Poland between Germany and the U.S.S.R. and for delimitation of their spheres of influence in the Baltic States.

Hitler pressed his territorial demands on Poland, hoping to avoid war with Britain and France but willing to face it rather than retreat. Last-minute efforts at a settlement broke down, and on September 1, 1939, German armies crossed the Polish frontier and German airplanes bombed Polish cities. The expectation that the subjugation of Poland would provoke only formal protests from London and Paris was shattered by their declaration of war on Berlin on September 3. World War II had begun. But while desire to remain aloof from European affairs remained powerful in America, the shock of recent events had badly startled the country. Polls since 1937 indicated most Americans viewed Nazi Germany as morally wrong, and despite the neutrality laws, in case of a major war they favored supplying arms to the Western democracies. As war raged in Poland, another Gallup Poll indicated that 84 percent of the American people desired an Allied victory, and 76 percent, despite an overwhelming desire to remain at peace, expected America to become involved sooner or later. Although over two years would have elapsed before the United States entered the war, public opinion had begun to adjust to that prospect by the fall of 1939.

CHAPTER 12

World War II: The Grand Alliance

a decidedly unneutral act by the United States
—Winston Churchill, on the transfer of American destroyers to Great Britain, September 2, 1939

Unconditional surrender does not mean the extermination or enslavement of the Japanese people.
—President Harry S. Truman, in a message to Japan, May 8, 1945

President Roosevelt on September 5, 1939, after Britain and France had declared war on Hitler's Germany, issued the customary proclamation of American neutrality. With the principal belligerents formally declaring war, he had no choice but to invoke the arms embargo and other features of the neutrality act against both belligerent camps. There was, however, no pretense of impartiality on the part of the administration. Step-by-step, with the president at the helm, the United States would move away from neutrality and nearer to war with the Axis powers. The first step was modification of the neutrality law. Roosevelt called Congress to a special session on September 21 and asked for legislation to permit the sale of arms to the Allies. After six weeks of debate, Congress passed the Fourth Neutrality Law, effective November 4, 1939, which repealed the embargo on arms, ammunition, and implements of war and placed sales to belligerents of goods of all kinds on a cash-and-carry basis. It empowered the president to designate "combat areas," which American ships and American citizens would be prohibited from entering. Other restrictions of the earlier legislation were generally retained. The significance of the new law was availability of American war goods to the French and British, since they alone, of the European belligerents, could buy and carry away.

In Europe, a lightning German campaign against Poland was followed by months of comparative inactivity—the *Sitzkrieg* (sitting war) or "phony war." But in April 1940, the *Sitzkrieg* suddenly became a *Blitzkrieg* (lightning war). German airborne troops and motorized columns quickly overran Denmark, Norway, the Netherlands, and Belgium. The French armies were crushed, the Maginot Line taken from the rear. The British Expeditionary Force escaped from Dunkirk, but left all its heavy equipment and most of its small arms on the beaches. On June 10, Mussolini, who hitherto had preserved a nonbelligerent status in his partner's war, declared war on stricken France. On June 22 France surrendered. All of northern and western France became occupied territory; the south and east Hitler left to a government established by Marshal Petain at Vichy. President Roosevelt's response to these events was prompt and emphatic. Speaking at Charlottesville, Virginia, June 10, he declared: "In our American unity, we will pursue two obvious and simultaneous courses: we will extend to the opponents of force the material resources of this nation, and at the same time we will harness and speed up the use of those resources in order that we ourselves in the Americas may have equipment and training equal to the task of any emergency and every defense."

During the summer of 1940, Congress, at Roosevelt's request, took important steps toward strengthening the United States' armed forces and stepping up production of war material for the "opponents of force." The army was enlarged from an authorized strength of 280,000 men to 1,200,000 as soon as the men could be raised and trained, with other increments to follow. Army and Navy air strength was established at over 18,000 planes, and a production goal of 50,000 planes annually was set. Authorization of an unprecedented navy laid the basis for a "two-ocean Navy." The total defense appropriation of over $5 billion, more than the president had asked, broke all peacetime records, while authorizations for future construction contracts brought the total to some $16 billion. In September, Congress passed the first peacetime selective service act in American experience. Fear of Hitler had stimulated a tardy but impressive drive for rearmament.

From Neutrality to "Shooting War"

The surrender of France soon after the president's Charlottesville speech reduced the active "opponents of force" to Great Britain in the west and China in the east. Roosevelt's most immediate concern was with Britain, now assailed from the sea and air by Germany. Should Britain fall, or should its fleet be destroyed or pass into hostile hands, America would indeed face a dark future. Britain's most immediate need was for swift naval vessels for antisubmarine patrol and convoy duty. The United States had 50 overage destroyers, which the president felt better served America if put to active use by the British than laid up "in moth balls" in U.S. harbors. In September, Roosevelt turned the destroyers over to the British navy in return for the right, over 99 years, to maintain American military bases in eight British possessions stretching from Newfoundland to British Guiana. The naval and air bases covered the approaches to the United States' Atlantic coast and the Caribbean. In announcing the deal to Congress, the president claimed: "This is the most important action in the reinforcement of our national defense that has been taken since the Louisiana Purchase." Congress and public opinion, for the most part, acquiesced in Roosevelt's startling fait accompli. The transfer of the destroyers to Great Britain was, as Winston Churchill later wrote, "a decidedly unneutral act by the United States." That would, in his words, "according to all the standards of history, have justified the German Government in declaring war."[1]

In July, the Democratic Party broke precedent by nominating Roosevelt for a third term as president. The president's prior move of inviting two prominent Republicans into his cabinet, Henry L. Stimson as secretary of war and Frank Knox as secretary of the navy, failed to appease the Republican Party. The Republican candidate, Wendell L. Willkie, shared the president's belief in the importance of aiding Britain, and therefore, isolationism was not a campaign issue. Both party platforms and both candidates declared emphatically against participation in "any foreign war." The Republicans, however, painted Roosevelt as a war candidate, and the president found it expedient to reiterate the assurance: "Your boys are not going to be sent into any foreign wars." Roosevelt won the election easily. Now Prime Minister Churchill informed the president that Britain was able to pay for goods already ordered, but would need "ten times as much" for the extension of the war. Churchill hoped that Roosevelt would regard this as a statement of the minimum requirement necessary to achieve the common purpose. The problem, as Roosevelt saw it, was how to aid England in the common cause without incurring a war debt problem as occurred after World War I. During a Caribbean cruise on the U.S.S. *Tuscaloosa*, he formulated the concept of lending goods instead of money. He wanted, as he told the press, to get away from that "silly, foolish old dollar sign," and he compared his proposal to that of lending a neighbor a garden hose to put out a fire that might otherwise spread to one's own house.[2] In a "fireside chat" on December 29, 1940, he pictured America as the "arsenal of democracy," and in his message to Congress a few days later, he officially proposed the lend-lease legislation.

The Lend-Lease Act of March 11, 1941, empowered the president to make available to "the government of any country whose defense the president deems vital to the defense of the United States" any "defense article," any service, or any "defense information." Arms might be manufactured expressly for the government that was to receive them, or they might (after consulting with military and naval advisers) be taken from existing U.S. stocks. Launched on a modest scale, the lend-lease program eventually shipped goods and services valued at over $50 billion to American friends and allies in World War II, without the exasperating war debt problem of the 1920s. From January to March 1941, meanwhile, British and American military and naval officers held secret staff conferences in Washington to coordinate their efforts on: (1) distribution of lend-lease while the United States remained nonbelligerent; and (2) joint military and naval operations when and if America entered the war. The conferences decided that Germany was to be Enemy Number One, and its defeat, even if Japan entered the war, was to have priority.[3] Subsequently, American officers went to England to select sites for future naval and air force bases.

Washington also reached arrangements with belligerent Canada. A year before the outbreak of war, President Roosevelt and Prime Minister Mackenzie King had exchanged assurances of mutual assistance if needed, the president declaring that the United States would not "stand idly by if domination of Canadian soil is threatened by any other empire."[4] Meeting at Ogdensburg, New York, on August 17, 1940, the two statesmen established a Permanent Joint Board of Defense for mutual protection. After the passage of the Lend-Lease Act, they met again at Roosevelt's home at Hyde Park, in April 1941, to create a Joint Defense Production Committee for their own defense and that of Britain. Thus months before the United States became a belligerent, Washington was working closely with Canada for a common objective: defeat of Germany.

In August 1941, Churchill and Roosevelt met secretly for their first conference at Argentia, Newfoundland. Churchill believed, as he wrote afterwards, "a conference between us would proclaim the ever closer association of Britain and the United States, would cause our enemies concern, make Japan ponder, and cheer our friends."[5] The two statesmen discussed a variety of topics connected with the war, including means of deterring Japan from attacking the British or Dutch possessions in the Far East. But their most famous and important achievement was the document known as the Atlantic Charter.[6] This pronouncement, which came chiefly from Churchill's pen, roughly comparable to Wilson's Fourteen Points, set forth objectives that might appeal to people everywhere. That it brought the United States a step nearer to war was appreciated by Churchill, who wrote: "The fact alone of the United States, still technically neutral, joining with a belligerent Power in making such a declaration was astonishing. The inclusion in it of a reference to 'final destruction of the Nazi tyranny'... amounted to a challenge which in ordinary times would have implied warlike action."[7]

For the United States to convoy British shipping carrying lend-lease "defense articles" would have stretched nonbelligerency beyond what even Roosevelt thought expedient, but a substitute method was found. A Conference of American Foreign Ministers at Panama in September–October 1939 had proclaimed the neutrality of a wide belt of the western Atlantic and warned the belligerents against hostilities in these waters. Although neither London nor Berlin paid any heed to this declaration, Roosevelt decided in early 1941 to have the U.S. Navy "patrol" not only the defined neutral waters but the entire North Atlantic west of 26° west longitude and to "publish the position of possible aggressor ships or planes."[8] British convoys could be alerted to the location of Nazi submarines discovered by the U.S. Navy. American occupation of Greenland on July 7, 1941, agreed to by local authorities, facilitated the navy's patrolling and halted German aerial activity and its establishment of weather stations around the island. The United States now had a legitimate reason for convoying its supply ships to Iceland. Two days later, Admiral E. J. King, commanding the Atlantic Fleet, directed a naval task force to "escort convoys of United States and Iceland flag shipping, *including shipping of any nationality which may join such ... convoys, between United States ports and bases, and Iceland.*"[9] Thus the United States, in company with Canada, began escorting British lend-lease convoys as far as Iceland, where the British navy took over.

Such "nonbelligerent" activity ultimately resulted in clashes with German U-boats. On September 4, 1941, the destroyer *Greer*, while trailing a submarine and signaling its position to a British plane, became a target for two torpedoes from the U-boat, both of which missed their mark. A week later President Roosevelt, without describing the incident's circumstances, denounced the German attack as "piracy" and warned "German or Italian vessels of war" that they entered American waters at their own peril. Orders to "shoot on sight" such vessels, he said, had been issued. Other attacks continued: on October 17, the destroyer *Kearny*, bound for Iceland, was torpedoed with the loss of 11 men; and on October 31, the *Reuben James* lost 96 men in a similar attack. Ten days after the attack on the *Kearny*, the president informed the country: "We have wished to avoid shooting. But the shooting has started. And history has recorded who fired the first shot." On October 9, 1941, Roosevelt asked Congress to repeal the 1939 neutrality law's section forbidding the arming of merchant vessels. In spite of large anti-interventionist blocs in both houses, in spite of warnings that repeal meant war, Congress passed and the president signed, on November 17, 1941, a law that not only permitted arming American merchantmen, but also repealed the cash-and-carry and combat-area provisions. American merchant ships were now free to arm themselves and to sail anywhere, carrying, if their owners wished, arms, ammunition, and implements of war.[10] American destroyers and German submarines were already trading depth charges and torpedoes in the North Atlantic.

The Road to Pearl Harbor

While the United States drifted into an undeclared naval war in the Atlantic, it was approaching a deadly crisis in the Pacific. Japan followed up its announcement of the "New Order for East Asia" by seizing, in February 1939, Hainan, an island off the south China coast and, a month later, the Spratly Islands in the South China Sea. Hainan lay close to the British shipping lane between Singapore and Hong Kong, while the Spratly Islands were uncomfortably close to French Indochina and the American Philippines. Japan appeared to be moving southward, where its forces constituted a potential threat to the possessions of France, the United States, Great Britain, and the Netherlands. At the same time, Tokyo continued its policy of gradually closing the door of China to Western trade and culture. Ambassador Joseph C. Grew, at home from Tokyo, during the summer of 1939 found "an unmistakable hardening of the administration's attitude toward Japan and a marked disinclination to allow American interests to be crowded out of China."[11] This attitude took tangible form when, on July 26, 1939, Washington gave the required notice of the abrogation of its 1911 commercial treaty with Japan; thus, it would be free, early in 1940, to restrict Japan's trade with the United States.

The spring and summer of 1940 opened opportunities to the ambitious Japanese. First the Netherlands and then France succumbed to German forces; only the English Channel and the Royal Air Force and Navy barred Hitler from Britain, and how long those barriers would hold was difficult to tell. Meanwhile, the enlargement of Japan's prospective empire, also called the "Greater East Asia Co-prosperity Sphere" and chiefly the inspiration of the new foreign minister, Yosuke Matsuoka, was defined. His concept was defined by a Liaison Conference (cabinet and army and navy leaders) in Tokyo on September 19, 1940, as comprising the former German islands under mandate to Japan since 1920 (the Carolines, Marianas, and Marshalls), French Indochina and French islands in the Pacific, Thailand, British Malaya and Borneo, the Dutch East Indies, Burma, Australia, New Zealand, and India, "with Japan, Manchuria, and China as the backbone." The Philippines were conspicuously missing from this list. To take care of such omissions, Matsuoka noted, "this sphere could be automatically broadened in the course of time."[12]

In April, after the fall of Holland, Secretary Hull had warned that any alteration of the Netherlands East Indies by other than peaceful means "would be prejudicial to the cause of stability, peace, and security ... in the entire Pacific area." The Japanese temporarily proceeded with caution, but in August demanded French officials in Indochina grant them access to the ports, cities, and airfields in the northern region. These were important to the Japanese because they commanded a principal supply route to the Chinese at Chungking. Pressure by Hitler on the Vichy regime forced the French to give way. Representatives of Vichy continued in office, but on September 22, Japanese forces occupied key centers in the Tonkin area. They could now halt supplies to China via the railroad from Hanoi, and their planes could threaten traffic over the Burma Road. Then on September 27, 1940, representatives of Germany, Italy, and Japan signed a Tripartite Pact, comprising mutual recognition by the three partners of the "new orders" instituted by them in Europe and Greater East Asia, and also a defensive alliance. By the latter, Article 3, the three powers agreed "to assist one another with all political, economic and military means when one of the three contracting powers is attacked by a power at present not involved in the European war or in the Chinese-Japanese conflict." This article was obviously aimed at the United States, since another article excluded the Soviet Union, to deter America from entering the war against either Germany or Japan. With American interference fended off, Matsuoka believed, Japan could take possession of French, Dutch, and British colonies in Greater East Asia. He hoped, too, that the pact would enable Japan to improve its relations with the Soviet Union and, by isolating China, to compel Chiang Kai-shek to make a peace satisfactory to Japan.[13]

The United States Applies Pressure

Far from intimidating the United States, the Tripartite Pact further stiffened Washington's attitude toward the Axis. The threat of encirclement, in Roosevelt's mind, only strengthened his determination to aid Britain—hence the lend-lease program. In a letter to Ambassador Grew on January 21, 1941, he explained the "global strategy" that he thought imperative to American security: "Our strategy of giving them [the British] assistance toward ensuring our own security must envisage both sending supplies to England and helping to prevent a closing of channels of communication to and from various parts of the world, so that other important sources of supply will not be denied to the British and be added to the assets of the other side."[14] The president referred specifically to the Dutch East Indies and British Malaya, as sources of rubber, petroleum, and tin. A few weeks later, this idea was passed on to the Japanese vice minister for foreign affairs, who was also told that the United States had direct and indirect interests in the products of Malaya and the Dutch East Indies. Tokyo was bluntly informed, "a Japanese threat to occupy areas from which the United States procured essential primary commodities would not be tolerated."[15]

As the fateful year 1941 dawned, friction between the United States and Japan increased. Resentful of Japan's assault on China's independence and its violation of the open door, Washington also worried about Tokyo's affiliation with the European Axis and its threatened seizure of Southeast Asia's raw materials. During the previous year, consequently, the United States had begun exerting economic pressure. On July 25, 1940, under the pretext of needing these supplies at home, the president prohibited the export without license of petroleum, petroleum products, and scrap metal. Six days later, he embargoed the exporting of aviation gasoline to all countries outside the Western Hemisphere. As an answer to the movement of Japanese forces into Indochina and the advance news of the signing of the Tripartite Pact, Roosevelt on September 26 placed a similar embargo on exports of scrap iron and steel. Other gestures designed as warnings to Japan were a $25 million loan to China through the Export-Import Bank and a notice to all American citizens in the Far East urging that they return home.

Deadlocked Negotiations

Such economic measures, and the possibility of still more drastic ones, gave Tokyo pause, for its industry and ability to make war depended on the embargoed supplies. Japanese policy in early 1941 had a three-fold purpose: (1) to reach agreement with the United States if possible at not too great a cost; (2) to bring the Netherlands East Indies into the Co-prosperity Sphere, peaceably if possible, forcibly if necessary; and (3) to remove the Soviet threat if Japan's southward expansion should involve it in war with the United States or Great Britain. Serious negotiations began in April, following the arrival in Washington of a new Japanese ambassador, Admiral Kichisaburo Nomura. Nomura's negotiations with Hull were complicated by two Roman Catholic clerics who had returned from Japan bringing what they thought to be an offer from the Japanese government. Japan, they reported, was ready to recall Japanese troops from China and to nullify the Tripartite Pact insofar as it was a threat to the United States. Hull soon discovered that the offer misrepresented Japanese intentions.[16] As discussions with Nomura revealed, Tokyo desired Washington to press Chiang Kai-shek to accept Japan's terms—including merger of his government with the puppet regime at Nanking and retention of some Japanese troops in North China and Inner Mongolia. If he refused, the United States should deprive him of any further aid. The United States was also to restore trade with Japan, as needed articles were available, and to assist Japan in obtaining raw materials from Southeast Asia. In return, Tokyo would use only peaceful means in seeking its ends in Southeast Asia and would reserve the right to interpret its obligations under the Tripartite Pact; in other words, if the United States went to war with Germany, Tokyo would decide independently whether it would assist its Axis partner.

Washington, for its part, asked Japan's acceptance of four general principles set forth by Secretary Hull: (1) respect for the sovereignty and territorial integrity of all nations; (2) noninterference in the internal affairs of other countries; (3) the open door, or equality of commercial opportunity; and (4) no disturbance of the status quo in the Pacific except by peaceful means. Specifically this called on Japan to withdraw its armed forces from China and Indochina, accept Chiang Kai-shek as head of China's legitimate government, and disavow the Tripartite Pact as aimed at the United States. Each government was inflexible in its demands, and by June 1941, an impasse had been reached. Japan, moreover, had been rebuffed in its attempt to peacefully take control of the Netherlands East Indies when a Japanese mission, visiting Batavia in quest of concessions, returned home empty-handed in June 1941. With Moscow, Tokyo was more successful when on April 13, 1941, the two countries signed a five-year treaty of neutrality, pledging each party to remain neutral if the other should become involved in war. The Soviets agreed to respect the territorial integrity of Manchukuo, and Japan promised to respect Soviet influence in Outer Mongolia. Matsuoka, pleased with Moscow's pledge of neutrality, did not know, though he had just come from Berlin, that Hitler was preparing to attack the Soviet Union. When that occurred, on June 22, 1941, the neutrality pact was more valuable to Moscow than to Tokyo.

Japan Moves South

Matsuoka, as a matter of fact, wished to violate the pact that he had just made and join Germany in war against the Soviets, but he was overruled and later removed from office. The Japanese cabinet and top military men preferred a southward drive, combined with neutrality in the Russo-German war. (In a 1939 Mongolia-Manchuria border conflict, Soviet armored forces so decisively defeated Japan's Kwantung Army that Japanese generals feared a full-scale war with the Soviet Union.) An Imperial Conference, led by the emperor, on July 2 decided on advancing into southern Indochina and Thailand, even at the risk of war with the United States and Britain. From Indochina, attacks on Singapore and the Netherlands Indies would be launched. In late July, the Vichy government reluctantly permitted Japan to establish air and naval bases while Tokyo promised to respect French political and territorial rights. This preparatory move by Japan brought a quick response from the United States, Great Britain, and the Netherlands.[17] President Roosevelt responded to the Japanese excuse for its action—that the occupation was a defensive measure against British designs—by proposing that Indochina be neutralized, a suggestion that Tokyo refused. Washington, meanwhile, broke off discussions with Nomura and on July 25 froze all Japanese funds in the United States, a move followed by Britain and the Netherlands. This freezing of assets cut Japan off from it most important markets and sources of raw material.

Many officials in London and Washington believed that Tokyo would retreat before this united front. Winston Churchill, at the Atlantic Conference in August, urged Roosevelt to warn Japan that an attack on British or Dutch possessions in the Far East would compel the United States "to take counter-measures, even though these might lead to war between the United States and Japan." This harsh phrasing was toned down by the State Department, and the president warned the Japanese ambassador on August 17 that if his government continues its "policy or program of military domination by force or threat of force on neighboring countries," Washington "will be compelled to take immediately any and all steps" necessary to safeguard "the legitimate rights and interest of the United States and American nationals and toward insuring the safety and security of the United States." Accompanying the warning was an offer to reopen the interrupted negotiations and institute a helpful

Pacific economic program if Japan were willing "to suspend its expansionist activities...and to embark upon a peaceful program for the Pacific."[18] President Roosevelt was at first quite taken by a suggestion of senior leaders holding a Pacific Conference. Secretary Hull, however, rejected the idea because he feared the meeting would result in a fiasco, beneficial only for Japanese propaganda.

Final Negotiations

The discussions of a possible Pacific meeting were carried on simultaneously with Japanese planning for war if no agreement with America were reached. An Imperial Conference on September 6 had decided on war with the United States, Great Britain, and the Netherlands if negotiations by early October failed to promise a satisfactory outcome. The emperor encouraged this decision, and though the Supreme Command ("top brass" of the army and navy) had proposed it, some officers had misgivings. Early in October, General Hideki Tojo, minister of war, intimated that if the Navy would state explicitly its opposition to war with America, "the Army would have to reconsider its position." When the Navy refused to advertise its reluctance, Tojo suggested a new premier and cabinet take responsibility for reversing the decision of September 6.[19] As this proved unfeasible, on October 18, General Tojo became premier. Upon Tojo's assuming office, he announced that negotiations with the United States would continue. An Imperial Conference of November 5 resolved to send another ambassador, Saburo Kurusu, to assist Admiral Nomura in Washington. At the same time, the conference decided that preparations for war should be completed by early December.

During the next two weeks, Operation Magic—the decoding and translation by Naval Intelligence of intercepted Japanese messages—picked up a steady stream of messages passing between Tokyo and the Japanese embassy in Washington. It was known that the Japanese envoys had been given two sets of proposals to place before the American government, Plan A and Plan B, the latter to be presented if the former were rejected. Plan B represented the greatest concessions that Japan was willing to make. It was known, too, that Japan had set a deadline—first, November 25, later November 29—by which time the negotiations must be completed. "After that," ran one intercepted message, "things are automatically going to happen." Tokyo bluntly refused pleas from the ambassadors for more time and further concessions. Washington knew something was going to happen, but not what or where. Japanese concentrations of troops and transports pointed to attacks on British Malaya,

Thailand, the Dutch East Indies, or possibly the Philippines. It was assumed in Washington that an attack on British or Dutch possessions would, or at least ought to, bring the United States into the war. Such a course was in line with Roosevelt's "global strategy" and had been made plain to Japan. But neither the U.S. Army nor the Navy was prepared for a Pacific war; both desperately needed time. Secretary of War Stimson, in particular, believed that in three months he could build up a force of B-17s (Flying Fortresses) in the Philippines that could block Japan's southward expansion. As the army and navy pleaded for a postponement of the showdown, for three months at least, there was talk of a possible temporary *modus vivendi* if no permanent agreement could be reached.

Japanese Plan A having been presented piecemeal and rejected by Secretary Hull, the envoys introduced on November 20 their Plan B, which was described as a *modus vivendi*, or way of getting along at least temporarily. The proposals were as follows: (1) neither government send armed forces to the Southeast Asia or South Pacific, except Indochina; (2) the two governments cooperate to secure needed commodities from the Netherlands Indies; (3) commercial relations to be restored to their status before the freezing of funds, the United States to supply Japan with "the required quantity of oil"; (4) the United States would not "resort to measures and actions prejudicial ... for the restoration of general peace between Japan and China"; and (5) Japan to move its troops in southern Indochina into the northern portion on the conclusion of this agreement, and withdraw all troops from Indochina on the making of peace with China "or the establishment of an equitable peace in the Pacific area." In regard to Japan's relations with Germany, Kurusu had informed President Roosevelt on November 17 that Japan could not openly abandon the Tripartite Pact, but it "had no intention of becoming a tool of Germany nor did she mean to wait until the United States became deeply involved in the battle of the Atlantic and then stab her in the back."[20]

The United States rejected Plan B. Its acceptance, Hull wrote later, "would have placed her [Japan] in a commanding position later to acquire control of the entire western Pacific area.... It would have meant abject surrender of our position under intimidation." But since the army and navy were desperate for time, Hull prepared a *modus vivendi* that he thought of proposing to the Japanese as a basis for a three months' truce, during which either a permanent agreement might be reached or, if not, the armed forces would have had that time to prepare for war. The new proposals comprised mutual pledges of peaceful policies; promises that neither would advance further in the Pacific area by means of force or threat of force; withdrawal of Japanese forces from southern to northern Indochina and limitation of those in that area to 25,000; resumption of trade with Japan on a limited scale; sale of petroleum to Japan for civilian use only; and any settlement between Japan and China to be "based upon the principles of peace, law, order, and justice." The difference between these proposals and Japan's Plan B did not rule out possible agreement. But they provided so little to China that it, along with the British, the Netherlands, and Australia, protested bitterly. With British and Dutch opposed and since their publication at home was sure to bring charges of "appeasement," Hull, after consulting with Roosevelt, reluctantly decided to discard the *modus vivendi* entirely and instead submitted a 10-point program for a permanent settlement along strictly American lines. As this program called for withdrawal of all Japanese troops from China and Indochina and for a virtual disavowal of the Axis Pact, Hull surely knew when he presented it on November 26 that Japan would spurn it and that "things" would begin to happen. He made this clear next day by telling Stimson: "I have washed my hands of it, and it [the situation] is now in the hands of you and Knox, the Army and Navy."

The Japanese reply—an extended complaint against American policy in the Far East, ending with breaking off the negotiations—was presented to Hull on Sunday afternoon, December 7, 1941. The hour set for delivery had been one o'clock, a few minutes before the first bombs were to fall on Pearl Harbor, but delay in decoding postponed the envoys' visit. When they reached his office, Hull knew, as they did not, of the Japanese surprise attack. After glancing at the note, Hull castigated it as "crowded with infamous falsehoods and distortions." Later in the day word arrived that Japan had formally declared war, some two hours after the Pearl Harbor attack. Congress responded the next day with a declaration of war against Japan—the British government had done the same a few hours earlier. On December 11, Germany and Italy declared war and the United States responded, saving Roosevelt the task of explaining to the American people why the nation needed a two-front war.

The Grand Alliance

In World War II, although there was no formal treaty of alliance, the United States took the lead in drawing up and signing on January 1, 1942, the Declaration by United Nations. Other signatories were Great Britain, the Soviet Union, and China; the five nations of the British Commonwealth, the governments in exile of eight European countries overrun by the Axis powers; and nine states of Latin America that had followed the United States into the war. The signatory governments, endorsing the "program of purposes and principles embodied in the... Atlantic Charter," and avowing their conviction "that complete victory over their enemies is essential to defend life, liberty, independence, and religious freedom, and to preserve human rights and justice," declared:

1. Each Government pledges itself to employ its full resources, military or economic, against those members of the Tripartite Pact and its adherents with which such government is at war.
2. Each Government pledges itself to cooperate with the Governments signatory hereto and not to make a separate armistice or peace with the enemies.

In this declaration, President Roosevelt, as one authority has remarked, "virtually contracted an alliance, and this without the consent of any legislative body, and indeed almost without a voice raised in criticism."[21] The brunt of the fighting was borne by the "Big Three," the United States, the United Kingdom, and the Soviet Union, with China a poor fourth. The British Dominions, the Yugoslav guerrillas, and the Free French under General Charles de Gaulle did their share. All the allies that contributed to the war, and some that did not, received the benefits of the United States' lend-lease program.

The cooperation between the United States and the United Kingdom originated at the highest level. Within a few hours after receiving the news from Pearl Harbor, Winston Churchill was preparing to visit Washington. He spent several weeks at the White House in December and January (with excursions to Ottawa and Palm Beach). This conference (code-named "Arcadia") was the first of a notable series of meetings in which the president and the prime minister with their advisers reached decisions on high strategy, both political and military.[22] They did not always agree, but they always resolved their differences amicably. The president, commanding the greater resources in men and matériel, had his way most often. On one basic matter there was no difference of opinion: Hitler's Germany was their principal enemy. This decision had been reached in staff conferences nearly a year before the United States entered the war. Germany was viewed as the more dangerous foe, and its defeat must have priority. From the British point of view this was an obvious truth. It was less so to American commanders, like General Douglas MacArthur and Admiral Ernest King, who had the task of fighting Imperial Japan. Even General George Marshall, the chief of staff, and Roosevelt sometimes wavered. There were differences on some other important aspects of the war. Roosevelt, much more than Churchill, rated as high the importance of assisting China because he expected it to follow America's lead in postwar policy. This difference was not of too great practical importance, since the war against Japan would be won not on the Chinese mainland, but finally by sea and air attacks on the Japanese homeland.

In the strategy of the European war, the differences that arose were between the two men's military advisers as much as the leaders. The Americans, anxious to deliver a knockout blow to Germany at the earliest possible moment, urged a crossing of the English Channel by Anglo-American forces in the spring of 1943. The British, with memories of the tragic Dieppe Raid in August 1942, would not agree to such a crossing until assured of possessing overwhelming force and adequate landing equipment. Nineteen forty-three, they insisted, was too early. A compromise was found in Operation Torch, the North African landing, in November 1942, followed by the advance into Sicily and Italy in 1943, and Operation Overlord, the proposed Normandy landing, in June 1944. The dispute was over timing, not the final objective. A proposal of Churchill's in 1944 that troops in Italy, earmarked for southern France, be sent instead across the Adriatic into Yugoslavia and perhaps as far as Vienna and Hungary (where they might have anticipated the Russian armies) was vetoed by Roosevelt. Churchill, disturbed by the advance of the Red armies, was more concerned for the political future of Central Europe than were Roosevelt and his advisers, who focused largely on the military objectives.

There was, however, one real difference in outlook between the two men. Roosevelt had no enthusiasm for preserving or restoring French or British colonial holdings, and occasionally urged on Churchill the claims of India to independence and freeing other British possessions. Churchill, not unexpectedly, objected to such ideas. He proclaimed in the House of Commons, soon after the Anglo-American landing in North Africa: "I have not become the King's First Minister in order to preside over the liquidation of the British Empire."[23] The anticolonialism of Roosevelt and Cordell Hull was in line with Woodrow Wilson's principle of self-determination, but it also had an important economic significance. Colonial empires, even the liberal British Commonwealth, were associated with "imperial preference" that partially closed their economic systems. These were contrary to the nondiscriminatory, or "open door," principle that Hull promoted through the reciprocal trade treaties and the terms of lend-lease agreements. Here, as in other matters, American principles were in harmony with American economic interests.

Between conferences, Roosevelt and Churchill kept in touch through frequent letters, telegrams, and telephone conversations often bypassing regular diplomatic channels. As one consequence of the Arcadia

Conference, a Combined Chiefs of Staff was created in Washington during January 1942. This was made up of the Chiefs of Staff of the United States (the army, navy, and army air force, later on the chief of staff to the president) and deputies of the corresponding British Chiefs. This body was charged with making and executing plans for the strategic conduct of the war, for meeting war matériel requirements, and for allocating munitions and transportation facilities, under the general direction of the president and the prime minister.

Relations with the Soviet Union

With the Soviet Union, such close and mutually beneficial relations proved impossible. It would, indeed, have been remarkable if the new partnership in the war against Hitler had produced friendship and confidence where incompatible ideologies and national interests had long bred suspicion. If a lack of cordiality characterized Soviet-American relations until 1939, the events of that year and of 1940 turned American sentiment violently against the Soviets. Stalin's pact with Hitler was quickly followed by Soviet occupation of eastern Poland. The Baltic states of Lithuania, Latvia, and Estonia were first required to admit Russian troops for their "protection" and then quietly incorporated into the Soviet Union.[24] When Finland refused to grant the Kremlin's demand for bases on Finnish territory and was invaded, it put up a stout but hopeless fight, which won the sympathy of Americans. These acts largely alienated whatever sympathy American noncommunists may have felt for the Soviet Union.

When Hitler invaded the Soviet Union on June 22, 1941, however, this attitude changed dramatically. Washington joined London in welcoming Moscow into the struggle against totalitarianism. Secretary Hull, ill at home, phoned the president: "We must give Russia all aid to the hilt. We have repeatedly said we will give all the help we can to any nation resisting the Axis."[25] Roosevelt agreed. Convinced by Harry Hopkins's on-the-spot investigations and Averell Harriman, among others, that Russia could hold out if adequately supplied, the president informed Stalin on October 30 that military equipment and munitions to the value of $1 billion would be supplied under lend-lease. A week later he instructed the Lend-Lease administrator that he had "today found that the defense of the Union of Soviet Socialist Republics is vital to the defense of the United States," and that defense supplies were therefore to be transferred to the Soviets. This was the first installment of lend-lease goods supplied to the Soviet Union during the war, ultimately amounting to $11 billion. Shipments reached the Soviets via Murmansk, via Vladivostok (under the noses of the Japanese), and via the Persian Gulf and Iran. In return, the Red Army played the major role in defeating Nazi Germany.

The Soviet government, meanwhile, endorsed the liberal principles of the Atlantic Charter, with a qualification that "considering that the practical application of these principles will necessarily adapt itself to the circumstances, needs, and historic peculiarities of particular countries."[26] The Soviet Union was one of the original signers of the Declaration by United Nations, and, in May 1943, dissolved the Communist International, or Comintern, and all former supporters of the Comintern were called on "to concentrate their energies on the whole-hearted support of and active participation in the war of liberation of the peoples and the states of the anti-Hitlerite coalition."[27] Thus, seemingly putting aside the basic antagonism of Soviet communism for the capitalist world led many Americans to hope that the cooperation of wartime would survive the destruction of Hitler. Roosevelt and some advisers, civil and military, were not unaware of the problem that a powerful postwar Soviet Union might pose. Yet there was concern that Moscow might make a separate peace or that the Soviets would not aid in defeating Japan. Washington's basic problem, then, was to make sense of the Soviet Union's motives and intentions. The political interplay during World War II would find American officials, who understood that Nazi Germany could not be defeated without a huge assist from the Red armies, consistently urging a return to the prewar European status quo with democratic governments chosen by free elections. Meanwhile, the Kremlin continually pressed for a postwar realignment in Central and Eastern Europe that would install "friendly" governments along its borders and enhance the Soviet Union's security. When its proposals were rebuffed, Washington instituted a strategy of postponing decisions until Hitler was vanquished that at various conferences papered over the essential points of contention with Moscow.[28]

The Soviet Union, for its part, was not without grounds for suspicion of its Western allies, as many of their officials would have been pleased if the Nazis and Soviets destroyed each other. This suspicion surfaced when Stalin urged opening without delay of a second front in Europe to relieve the pressure on the Eastern Front armies. He was first assured of a second front in 1942, but, as mentioned earlier, the British objected for viable reasons. Churchill not surprisingly had difficulty in persuading Stalin that the landing in North Africa in November 1942 was the only offensive possible to the Western Allies at that time. Up to the Normandy landing in June 1944, there were periodic complaints from Moscow that the Anglo-American forces were dragging their feet. And as late as March 1945, Anglo-American negotiations looking to the surrender of German troops in northern Italy brought from Stalin angry accusations that his allies were planning a separate peace. In the meantime, there was endless friction in negotiation over other matters—over the use of bases in Soviet territory, over liberated prisoners of war, even over the details of lend-lease. When the president and his advisers met with their Soviet counterparts, as they did on several occasions, harmony that glossed over the most critical issues was generally achieved. Unfortunately, later this led to misinterpretations and mutual recriminations.

The Grand Alliance: Policies and Plans

In January 1943, two months after the successful landings in North Africa, Roosevelt and Churchill met at Casablanca, on the Atlantic coast of Morocco. Premier Stalin was invited to attend the meeting, but he declined as the military situation on the eastern front was uncertain. The principal business of the conference was the planning of campaigns to come in the Mediterranean theater and elsewhere, but in his remarks to the press at the close of the conference on January 26, 1943, the president used the phrase "unconditional surrender." Roosevelt informed the reporters: "The democracies' War plans were to compel the 'unconditional surrender' of the Axis." The use of this phrase, approved by Churchill and the British War Cabinet, was apparently designed to persuade Stalin that America and England were determined to fight the war to a finish. In the opinion of most analysts, however, it had the unintended effect of stiffening enemy resistance and postponing the surrender, certainly of Germany and Japan, perhaps of Italy.

Similarly unfortunate in its effect on German resistance was Roosevelt and Churchill's endorsement, in September 1944, of the so-called Morgenthau Plan, the work of Secretary of the Treasury Henry Morgenthau Jr. for the postwar treatment of Germany. In the words of the memorandum signed by the two heads of government at Quebec, September 16, 1944: "This programme for eliminating the war-making industries in the Ruhr and in the Saar is looking forward to converting Germany into a country primarily agricultural and pastoral in its character." Secretaries Hull and Stimson vigorously opposed the proposed plan. Churchill recalled that he had "at first ... violently opposed the idea, but the President, with Mr. Morgenthau—from whom we had much to ask—were so insistent that in the end we agreed to consider it." Roosevelt and Churchill soon understood that the program would have eliminated the most productive industrial workshop in Europe, leaving a void in the European economy and starving millions in western Germany. The plan was quietly shelved, but not before it had been "leaked." To Joseph Goebbels, minister of information in Berlin, it had obvious propaganda value.[29]

In October 1943, Secretary Hull, despite his 72 years and frail health, flew to Moscow to confer with Molotov and Anthony Eden. Italy had surrendered to Anglo-American forces in September, and the German divisions were being steadily pushed back. The Soviet armies, too, had taken the offensive. The tide of war had turned, and American internationalists wanted to consider postwar arrangements. At the close of the conference on October 30, the Big Three's foreign ministers indicated they had agreed on setting up in London a European Advisory Commission (EAC) to make recommendations on questions that might arise as the war developed. A declaration regarding Italy promised a government "made more democratic by the introduction of representatives of those sections of the Italian people who have always opposed Fascism." It also promised to the Italian people restoration of freedom of speech, the press, political belief, public meeting, and religious worship. Another declaration promised Austria liberation from German domination and recorded the desire "to see reestablished a free and independent Austria."

At the urging of Secretary Hull, China was invited to join in a Declaration of Four Nations on General Security. In this, the four governments pledged that the united action of wartime would be "continued for the organization and maintenance of peace and security" and recognized "the necessity of establishing at the earliest practicable date a general international organization" for that purpose. Here was the first definite international commitment to the idea of a postwar substitute for the League of Nations. In Secretary Hull's mind, the fact of having secured a Russian pledge to cooperate with the Western powers in a postwar security organization was an important achievement.

During the Moscow Conference, arrangements had been perfected for a meeting of Roosevelt, Churchill, and Stalin at Tehran, the capital of Iran. This was as far as Stalin could be induced to journey from his own borders. Chiang Kai-shek joined Roosevelt and Churchill as they stopped there en route to Tehran. From Cairo the three statesmen issued a declaration (released December 1, 1943) for the postwar Far East. Japan would "be stripped of all the islands in the Pacific which she has seized or occupied since ... 1914, and that all the territory Japan has stolen from the Chinese, such as Manchuria, Formosa and the Pescadores, shall be restored to the Republic of China." The three governments, "mindful of the enslavement of the people of Korea, are determined that in due course Korea shall become free and independent." Unmentioned was the fact that Chiang Kai-shek was expending more of his resources combating the Chinese communists than Japanese forces.

At Tehran, where the Big Three leaders and their advisers conferred from November 28 to December 1, 1943, was, in fact, a quite harmonious affair. Important military decisions were reached; notably that the cross-Channel invasion, known as Operation Overlord, should be launched in May or June 1944, with a supporting landing on the south coast of France and a simultaneous Russian offensive in the east. Stalin repeated the promise, made to Hull at Moscow, that as soon as Germany was defeated, Russia would enter the war against Japan. It was also agreed that in Yugoslavia all aid should be given to Tito and his partisans—a decision that insured communist, though not necessarily Soviet, domination of that country. On the political side, the most important questions debated were the boundaries of Poland and the future of Germany. The three leaders were in general agreement that Poland's eastern boundary should be the Curzon Line, a supposedly ethnographical demarcation proposed in 1919. Poland would thus lose some White Russian and Ukrainian areas that it had held from 1921 to 1939. For these losses in the east it was to be compensated in the West by accessions of German territory up to the Oder River. Roosevelt and Churchill agreed with Stalin that there should be no revival of German military power. Roosevelt proposed that Germany be partitioned into five independent states, excluding the Ruhr-Saar and Kiel areas, which should be internationally controlled. Churchill preferred to isolate Prussia on the one hand and, on the other, to construct a Danubian Confederation along lines resembling those of the former Austro-Hungarian Empire. Stalin preferred Roosevelt's solution to Churchill's. No decision was reached, but the discussions revealed again Stalin's determination to prevent hostile governments on the Soviet Union's borders.

Roosevelt and Stalin did not meet again until the Yalta Conference in February 1945. In the interval, Churchill visited Moscow, in October 1944 (code-named TOLSTOY) to seek an understanding on the affairs of Poland and the Balkan States. The latter problem proved the easier to solve because of the advance of the Russian armies into Rumania and Bulgaria and a threatened conflict between Russian and British interests, especially in Greece and Yugoslavia. President Roosevelt had agreed to a temporary arrangement the previous June that provided Moscow predominance for three months in Rumania and to Britain the same in Greece over objections of the State Department that wanted all such issues postponed to a general peace conference after the war. Understanding the political implications of military reality, Churchill proposed and Stalin accepted an extension of this arrangement on a mathematical formula. According to Churchill's notation, as amended, the Soviets should have 90 percent predominance in Rumania and Great Britain would have 90 percent in Greece. Soviet influence would predominate 20 to 80 percent in Bulgaria and Hungary, while in Yugoslavia the proportion was to be 50-50.[30] Perhaps this exercise in arithmetic had no binding force, particularly since Roosevelt had cautioned that he would not be bound by any agreement made in his absence, but it reflected a rapidly moving political situation.

At Churchill's urging, Stanislaw Mikolajczyk, head of the conservative, anticommunist Polish government in exile at London, joined the Moscow conference. There, he and several of colleagues met with representatives of a Soviet-sponsored Polish government established at Lublin. The two groups failed to agree as to their respective shares in a new government for Poland. Mikolajczyk finally consented to urge his London colleagues to accept the Curzon Line, but the outcome was in doubt.[31]

The Yalta Conference

Roosevelt joined Churchill and Stalin for their final meeting, this time at recently liberated Yalta in the Russian Crimea. Here the three statesmen, with their diplomatic and military staffs—700 British and Americans were flown in at night from Malta to Yalta—met from February 4 to 11, 1945. Four principal subjects occupied the conference: (1) details of the proposed United Nations Organization (discussed in the following chapter); (2) the treatment of defeated Germany; (3) occupation and restoration of governments in the eastern Europe countries, occupied in whole or in part by Soviet armies; and (4) the terms of the Soviet Union's entry into the war against Japan.

Germany would be occupied, divided, and disarmed. The United Kingdom, the United States, and the Soviet Union were to possess "supreme authority" to "take such steps, including the complete disarmament, demilitarization and dismemberment of Germany as they deem requisite for future peace and security." Study of dismemberment was referred to a committee consisting of the British foreign secretary and the American and Russian ambassadors in London, who might, at their discretion, bring in a French member. In the meantime, Germany was to be divided into four zones of military occupation, a French zone to be formed out of previously agreed-on American and British zones. Germany was to pay reparations in kind, initially to the nations that had borne the main burden of the war, suffered most heavily, and "organized victory over the enemy." Reparations were to be of three categories: (1) removal, over a two-year period, of capital goods located either within or without German territory, "chiefly for the purpose of destroying the war potential of Germany"; (2) "annual deliveries of goods from current production for a period to be fixed"; and (3) "use of German labor." A reparations commission representing the three governments was to be established in Moscow. The American and Soviet delegations agreed in recommending that the commission should take, "as a basis for discussion," a total reparations figure of $20 billion, half to go to the Soviet Union. The British delegation was opposed to naming any figure, pending consideration by the commission. The punishment of major war criminals was a question left to be resolved.

The conference agreed that a new Polish Provisional Government of National Unity should be established, constituted by including with the existing Communist Provisional Government at Lublin "democratic leaders from Poland itself and from Poles abroad." The new government should be "pledged to the holding of free and unfettered elections as soon as possible on the basis of universal suffrage and secret ballot." The "three heads of Government" considered that Poland's eastern boundary should be the Curzon Line, with some deviations in favor of Poland, and that Poland should receive undefined "substantial accessions of territory in the north and west." Roosevelt and Churchill fully grasped the delicate nature of the Polish political situation, since Stalin had made clear his determination to prevent a reactionary government in Warsaw such as existed in the 1920s and 1930s. How would the "democratic elements" be defined, how could free elections be held that would not be vetoed by the Kremlin (and the occupying Soviet army)? The same dilemma existed for other portions of liberated Europe and for former Axis satellites (such as Hungary, Rumania, and Bulgaria). The three statesmen promised these countries assistance in the establishment of internal peace, in relief of suffering, in the setting up of interim governments "broadly representative of all democratic elements," and in "the establishment through free elections of governments responsive to the will of the people."

Both the American and British governments had for some time considered Russian aid indispensable against Japan if the war in the Far East were to be brought to an early conclusion. Stalin had promised such aid to Hull in Moscow, to Roosevelt at Tehran, and to Churchill during his visit to Moscow in October 1944. Beyond specifying that he would need to stockpile over a million tons of lend-lease goods for the campaign in the Far East, Stalin had hinted in October 1944 that there were political questions that should be "clarified" before Russia entered the war. In an interview between Stalin and Ambassador Averell Harriman in December 1944, the Soviet questions were answered.[32] They were embodied almost word for word in the Yalta agreement. Stalin promised that the Soviet Union would enter the war against Japan "in two or three months" after the German surrender, on the following conditions:

1. Preservation of the status quo in Outer Mongolia; that is, continuance of the Soviet-sponsored Mongolian People's Republic in an area long claimed by China.
2. Restoration of "the former rights of Russia violated by the treacherous attack of Japan in 1904"; namely: (a) return to the Soviet Union of southern Sakhalin; (b) internationalizing of the port of Dairen, with safeguards for the "preeminent interests of the Soviet Union," and restoration to Russia of the lease of Port Arthur for a naval base; (c) the Chinese Eastern and South Manchurian Railroads to be operated by a joint Soviet-Chinese company, with safeguards for "the preeminent interests of the Soviet Union" and retention of Chinese sovereignty in Manchuria.
3. Cession of the Kurile Islands to the Soviet Union.

President Roosevelt obtained Chiang Kai-shek's concurrence in the provisions in regard to Outer Mongolia and the Manchuria ports and railroads. Stalin, for his part, expressed a readiness to conclude a treaty with Chiang's government for the purpose of aiding in "liberating China from the Japanese yoke."[33]

World War II Ends

Events moved swiftly after the Yalta Conference. As Allied armies were pouring into Germany from east and west, and the German front in Italy was collapsing, President Roosevelt died on April 12, 1945. On May 1, with Soviet forces entering Berlin, Hitler suicided in the Reichchancellery, and Admiral Karl Doenitz organized a short-lived provisional government. German army officers signed surrender terms at Reims, on May 7, and the following day President Harry Truman and Prime Minister Churchill proclaimed V-E (Victory in Europe) Day. On May 9, the formalities of surrender were completed in Berlin, and Stalin announced the end of the war to the Soviet people. Early in June an Allied Control Committee for Germany began functioning in Berlin.

The war in Europe was ended, but the Pacific War went on, although Japan's surrender was nearer than most Allied statesmen supposed. From the first Japanese naval reverses in the Coral Sea and at Midway in May and June 1942, Japan's defeat was inevitable. With U.S. air and naval forces roaming free over and around the Japanese islands, the islands were punished with bombs, and Tokyo was prevented from recalling its scattered armies. The cabinet headed by the octogenarian Admiral Suzuki found an obstacle to peace in the "unconditional surrender" formula. Loyalty to the emperor prescribed that the throne must be preserved.[34] Beginning in June, Japan made a series of attempts to secure Soviet mediation in obtaining a peace. In Washington, meanwhile, the War Department was planning an invasion of Japan's home islands, to begin November 1. President Truman, celebrating V-E Day, called on the "Japanese military and naval forces"—not the Japanese government—to "lay down their arms in unconditional surrender," adding the assurance: "Unconditional surrender does not mean the extermination or enslavement of the Japanese people."[35]

From Potsdam on July 26, 1945, over the signatures of Truman, Attlee (who had succeeded Churchill), and Chiang Kai-shek, came the Potsdam Declaration calling for the unconditional surrender of the Japanese armed forces, for the complete elimination of militarism and militarists, the setting up of "a new order of peace, security and justice," the removal of obstacles to democratic tendencies, the punishment of war criminals, and the carrying out of the terms of the Cairo Declaration. Allied forces would occupy designated points in Japanese territory until the objectives were accomplished and until there should have been "established in accordance with the freely expressed will of the Japanese people a peacefully inclined and responsible government."[36] Premier Suzuki told the press that Japan would "ignore" the declaration.[37]

This note of defiance led to the decision in Washington to drop the newly developed atomic bombs on Hiroshima (August 6) and Nagasaki (August 9).[38] The Soviet Union entered the war, as promised on August 8, sending armies into Manchuria and Korea. From Tokyo on August 10, by way of Switzerland, came an acceptance of the Potsdam terms, but with the understanding that the declaration "does not comprise any demand which prejudices the prerogatives of His Majesty as a Sovereign Ruler." To the request for an "explicit indication" that this understanding was warranted, James Byrnes, now secretary of state, replied that during the occupation the authority of the emperor would be subject to the Supreme Commander of the Allied Powers, and that the ultimate form of Japan's government should be determined "by the freely expressed will of the Japanese people." President Truman proclaimed Japan's surrender on August 14. The formal signing of surrender terms took place on the battleship *Missouri*, in Tokyo Bay on September 2, 1945. World War II had come to an end.

CHAPTER 13

A New Global Struggle: Founding of the UN to the Cold War

From Stettin in the Baltic to Trieste in the Adriatic, an iron curtain has descended across the Continent
—Winston Churchill's "Iron Curtain" speech at Fulton, Missouri, March 5, 1946

I believe it must be the policy of the United States to support free peoples who are resisting attempted subjugation by armed minorities or by outside pressure.
—The Truman Doctrine, March 15, 1947

The Japanese attack at Pearl Harbor, together with the global war that followed, silenced, if it did not end, isolationism in the United States. The elaborate neutrality legislation of the 1930s had failed to insulate the United States from war in Europe and Asia. To many Americans, it appeared that in the future the United States could hope to avoid war only by joining in a system of collective security capable of preventing war. To these citizens who enthusiastically embraced the idea, American membership in an improved and strengthened League of Nations seemed the only hope of peace—the United Nations. In spite of much planning and preparing the American people to accept a process of international cooperation, the United Nations would not be able to live up to its promise. Ideologies shaped national perceptions of their vital interests and, as much as anything, bred distrust and alienation between the victors.

For a small minority of U.S. officials and writers, well conditioned to distrust the Kremlin, the euphoria of victory and peace in 1945 evaporated quickly. If the Soviet Union's costly victory over Nazi military forces had been a vital contribution to V-E day, these Americans now feared that the historic European balance of power had been upset. The continued Soviet occupation of Eastern Europe enhanced that country's strategic position in the Balkans and rendered bordering regions vulnerable to further Soviet expansion.[1] It required only the Kremlin's postwar demands on Iran and Turkey to unleash visions of Soviet military expansion reminiscent of the Italian, German, and Japanese aggressions. Joseph and Stewart Alsop, writing in the May 20, 1946, issue of *Life*, defined the emerging Soviet threat in Hitlerian terms:

> Already Poland, the Baltic States, Rumania, Bulgaria, Yugoslavia and Albania are behind the Iron Curtain. Huge armies hold Hungary and half of Germany and Austria. Czechoslovakia and Greece are encircled.... In the Middle East, the Soviets are driving southward. Iran is in danger of being reduced to puppethood; Turkey and Iraq are threatened. Finally, in the Far East, the Kuriles has been stripped and left in condition to be transformed at will and half of Korea are occupied and Manchuria into another Azerbaijan. The process still goes on. One ... must also wonder whether they will ultimately be satisfied with less than dominion over Europe and Asia.[2]

Responding to Soviet pressures on Turkey for a new Straits settlement, in August 1946, a memorandum, signed by Acting Secretary of State Dean Acheson, Navy Secretary James Forrestal, and Secretary of War Robert Patterson, warned: "If the Soviet Union succeeds in its objective of obtaining control over Turkey, it will be extremely difficult, if not impossible, to prevent the Soviet Union from obtaining control over Greece and over the whole Near and Middle East ... (including) the territory lying between the Mediterranean and India. When the Soviet Union has once obtained full mastery of this territory ... it will be in a much stronger position to obtain its objectives in India and China."[3]

A new conflict loomed, a "cold war," driven by Washington's fear of Soviet expansionism with a domino effect.

Origins of the United Nations

Shortly after the outbreak of war in Europe, Secretary of State Cordell Hull and his State Department staff began planning for a new world organization, of which the United States should be a leading member. In January 1940, Hull announced the appointment of an Advisory Committee on Problems of Foreign Relations, with subcommittees to study political, economic, and security questions. Hull, a follower of Woodrow Wilson and advocate of the League of Nations, was acutely aware of Wilson's mistakes and determined to avoid them. In particular, he was careful to take Republicans as well as Democrats into his confidence to remove any tinge of partisanship. President Franklin Roosevelt, though he may have shared in the belief that the United States must lead in the preparation for a new League of Nations, reacted cautiously, worried about the political reaction to the idea. At the Atlantic Conference in August 1941, he rejected a declaration, proposed by Churchill, for a peace that would, "by effective international organization ... afford to all States and peoples the means of dwelling in security." Such an expression, he feared, would rouse the suspicion of the isolationists, in Congress and out. But he let himself be persuaded to accept the same idea worded differently. Paragraph 8 of the Atlantic Charter proposed the disarmament of aggressor nations, "pending the establishment of a wider and permanent system of general security."[4]

By the fall of 1943, the political hazards of advocating American participation in a collective security organization had largely been eliminated. By large majorities, the Senate and the House of Representatives had passed the Connally and Fulbright Resolutions, declaring that the United States, acting "through its constitutional processes," should participate in international machinery to prevent aggression and preserve the peace of the world. A Republican Post-War Advisory Council, meeting at Mackinac Island in September, adopted a similar resolution. In the spring of 1944, speeches by the secretary of state and by the president alerted the public that the State Department was planning a postwar international organization. They even sketched out its general lines: an assembly representing all members of the organization, a smaller body with power to act against aggression, and an international court of justice. The structural similarity to the League of Nations was obvious, but the planners sought to avoid its weaknesses: first, by including all the great powers in the membership; and, second, by creating a vigorous enforcement agency.

Hull emphasized the belief that "there was no hope of turning victory into enduring peace unless the United States, the British Commonwealth, the Soviet Union, and China agreed to act together."[5] The Four Nations' Declaration, issued at Moscow, October 30, 1943, appeared to be a good omen. To ensure a plan acceptable to these four powers, the United States invited delegations from the other three to Washington, in August 1944, to produce a tentative charter for a permanent United Nations Organization. The conference was held at Dumbarton Oaks (a Washington estate) from August 21 to October 7. The Soviet Union, still at peace with Japan, refused for that reason to confer with belligerent China. Hence, the conference had two phases: the United States, Great Britain, and Russia; and the United States, Great Britain, and China. For the most part, the Chinese delegation accepted the work already done by the other three. The Dumbarton Oaks Proposals, published October 9, 1944, contained many provisions that appeared in the United Nations Charter. They urged the creation of a permanent organization—the United Nations—open to "all peace-loving states" and based on the "sovereign equality" of such states. Its purpose was to be: (1) maintaining peace and security through collective measures; (2) developing friendly relations between states; (3) affecting cooperation in the solution of international economic, social, and humanitarian problems; and (4) affording a center for harmonizing the action of nations for their common ends. The principal organs included a General Assembly; a Security Council of 11 members (4 permanent, the others chosen for two-year terms); a Secretariat; an Economic and Social Council (subsidiary to the General Assembly); and an International Court of Justice. The architects of the plan hoped that the General Assembly and the Economic and Social Council would remove or at least alleviate causes of friction, the International Court would settle peaceably any disputes susceptible of judicial determination, and the Security Council would assist in the peaceful settlement of disputes and suppress any acts of aggression or breaches of the peace that might occur.

The Dumbarton Oaks delegates had failed to reach agreement on several questions. When and where should a general meeting be held to formalize the charter? What nations should be invited and thus become original members of the United Nations? What should be done with the former Japanese-mandated islands? Should the constituent republics of the Soviet Union or any of them have separate membership in the United Nations? Most crucial of all remained the question, Should each of the great powers, permanent members of the Security Council, have the right of veto? Roosevelt, Churchill, and Stalin addressed these questions when they met at Yalta in February 1945. They easily reached agreement on these questions. The conference on world organization would take place at San Francisco on April 25, 1945. The participating governments would be those already cooperating as the United Nations and such others as might declare war "on the common enemy" by March 1, 1945. Stalin had once intimated that all 16 republics of the Soviet Union should be separately represented—to which Roosevelt responded he would ask separate membership for all of the United States' 48 states. Stalin moderated his demands, now asking separate membership in San Francisco and in the proposed world organization only for the Ukraine and White Russia. When Roosevelt and Churchill agreed to support this request at San Francisco, Stalin offered to support Washington if it should ask for three votes in the General Assembly. In theory, at least, these proposed multiple votes were intended to balance the six votes of nations of the British Commonwealth.

It was tentatively agreed to replace the league's Mandate System with territorial trusteeships—much the same idea under a different name. It was to apply to (1) existing mandates of the League of Nations, (2) territories taken from the enemy in the current war, (3) any other territory that a sovereign power might voluntarily place under trusteeship. On the question of the right of veto in the Security Council, Secretary Hull understood that neither the Soviet Union nor the U.S. Senate would accept a charter that failed to vest the right of veto in the permanent members. The great-power veto was a practical necessity, though there were no illusions.[6] The State Department's formula, approved at Yalta and eventually adopted at San Francisco, permitted decision in procedural matters by the votes of any 7 of the 11 members of the Security Council. In all substantive matters, however, the seven affirmative votes must include the votes of all five permanent members—the United States, the U.S.S.R., Britain, France,[7] and China. The price of securing the adherence of the Soviet Union, and of ensuring a favorable vote by the U.S. Senate, was a veto provision that could paralyze the Security Council in any controversy between two or more of the Big Five powers.

The San Francisco Conference

President Roosevelt before his death named members to the American delegation to the San Francisco Conference—the United Nations Conference on International Organization, or UNCIO. Headed by the secretary of state, Edward R. Stettinius Jr., who had succeeded Cordell Hull, the delegation was bipartisan and contained members of both the Senate and House: the chairmen and ranking minority members of the Senate Committee on Foreign Relations and the House Committee on Foreign Affairs. Republican Senator Arthur Vandenberg of Michigan, a trusted leader and long an outspoken critic of Roosevelt, worked effectively at San Francisco and turned away Republican opposition when the charter came before the Senate. The U.S. delegation, as promised, helped to secure from the conference admission of delegates from the Ukraine and White Russia. The Latin American republics reluctantly consented to this action and, in return, asked for and obtained the admission of

Argentina, which had been slow to break with the Axis. Denmark, now liberated, was also admitted, raising to 50 the number of nations participating. These became "charter members" of the United Nations; later Poland, though not at the Conference, was considered an original member. In the future, membership in the organization was to be open to "all other peace-loving states" that would accept the obligations contained in the charter and be judged able and willing to carry them out. The conference labored from April 25 to June 26. The resulting charter followed closely the Dumbarton Oaks Proposals in general structure. To the four "principal organs" originally proposed—General Assembly, Security Council, Secretariat, and International Court of Justice—the conference added two: the Economic and Social Council (raised from subsidiary level) and a Trusteeship Council.

The action of the U.S. Senate on the UN Charter contrasted strikingly with the Senate's mutilation and final rejection of the Covenant of the League. The Senate approved the charter on July 28, 1945, by a vote of 89 to 2. Congress later provided that after contingents of American armed forces had been designated for use at the call of the Security Council, the president might use them at the Council's call without awaiting special permission by Congress. The Senate, which had originally rejected membership in the World Court, now, by a vote of 60 to 2, accepted compulsory jurisdiction of the International Court of Justice by approving the "optional clause" in the Statute of the Court.

The chief function of the Security Council was expected to be its policing function to prevent acts of aggression, whether by force or the threat of force. The council was empowered, if efforts at peaceful settlement of a controversy failed, to call on UN members to sever diplomatic relations with an offender and to apply economic sanctions. If such measures proved inadequate, the Security Council was to have at its disposal armed contingents made available in advance by the members. A Military Staff Committee, made up of the chiefs of staff of the Council's permanent members, would direct such forces. In reality, this enforcement machinery, impressive on paper, was paralyzed from the beginning by the rift between the Soviet Union and the West. No contingents of armed forces were made available to the Security Council, because the Military Staff Committee could not agree on their composition. The British and Americans would furnish the principal naval and air contingents and expected the Soviets, with their huge army, to provide most of the land forces. The Soviets, however, insisted on equal and similar contributions from all five of the major powers. This disagreement was never resolved, although the United Nations did eventually utilize "peacekeeping" forces.

The International Control of Atomic Energy

After August 1945, the specter of atomic war hung over the world. The United States, having at the time the atomic expertise and the atomic weapons, took the lead in proposing international controls. In January 1946, the UN Assembly established a United Nations Atomic Energy Commission. On June 14, 1946, the American member, Bernard Baruch, submitted a proposal to the commission thereafter generally referred to as the Baruch Plan. It called for the creation of an International Atomic Development Authority, to have complete control over the primary production of fissionable materials and all dangerous forms of atomic energy development, as well as licensing and inspection authority over nondangerous forms. The authority should have unrestricted rights of inspection. As soon as the proposed system of control and inspection was set up and functioning, the United States would dispose of its stockpile of atomic weapons, and the production of such weapons would thereafter be strictly prohibited. Any violation of this or other prohibitions would be subject to prompt and severe punishment; and here Baruch emphasized that no veto could stand in the way of punishment.[8] The Baruch Plan was rejected by the Soviet Union, for Moscow would neither accept national control of atomic activities, submit to effective inspection, nor waive the veto. The Soviets offered their own plan, without stringent inspection, that insisted that existing atomic bombs be at once destroyed and the manufacture and use of others be strictly prohibited.

Two weeks after Baruch presented his plan, the United States began testing atomic devices at Bikini Atoll—Operation Crossroads—ostensibly to determine their effect on naval vessels. Washington had announced the tests months earlier, prompting several scientists and senators to complain that the United States "would be accused of conducting atomic diplomacy; detonating weapons while simultaneously negotiating international agreements." Their concern proved valid, as the Soviets questioned the validity of American diplomacy. In Moscow, its principal newspaper, *Pravda*, declared that Washington was more interested in improving its atomic bomb to threaten others than in eliminating these weapons.

From the outset, American and Soviet diplomats had been at odds. The United States viewed the atomic bomb as an important source of its military power and insisted on extensive safeguards before destroying its atomic weapons or releasing information on their manufacture. The Soviets and others argued that the Americans were insincere since they would not relinquish their atomic arsenal, while expecting others to forgo developing their own atomic energy programs. And they were not far off target. "America can get what she wants if she insists on it," Baruch asserted in December 1946. "After all, we've got it and they haven't, and won't for a long time to come." Although he regarded his plan as a basis for discussion, its principles came to be the definitive statement of U.S. policy for many years. While some writers blame Washington for the failure of the negotiations, historian Barton Bernstein suggested a more realistic perspective: "Neither the United States nor the Soviet Union was prepared in 1945 or 1946 to take the risks that the other power required for agreement. In this sense, the stalemate on atomic energy was a symbol of the mutual distrust in Soviet-American relations."[9]

The impasse that developed, in 1946, had not been resolved in September 1949, when it was revealed that the Soviet Union had tested its own atomic weapon, nor in August 1953, when both the Americans and Soviets produced the still more potent hydrogen bomb. Not until the ill-fated UN discussions focusing on general and complete disarmament in the 1960s were such broad-gauged approaches again examined.

The United States and Ideological Origins of the Cold War

The rift in the United Nations between the Soviet Union, backed by its satellites, and the United States, generally supported by the other democracies, reflected a mounting antagonism between the two groups. At issue in America's growing fear and distrust of the U.S.S.R. was not the dislike of communism, for, to most of them, the ideological foundations of the Soviet state were not important. U.S. citizens, however, overwhelmingly opposed communism as inimical to Western principles of liberal democracy. The country's emerging anticommunist elite saw the real Soviet danger in the limitless promise of Soviet ideological expansion. Soviet rhetoric had long predicted communism's ultimate world conquest. For those Americans who took the Soviet rhetoric seriously, the U.S.S.R., as the self-assigned leader of world communism, possessed the power and will to incite or support communist-led revolutions everywhere, imposing on them its influence, if not its direct control. It mattered little whether Soviet troops or even Soviet officials were present, for ideological expansionism assured future Soviet triumphs without war. This alleged capacity to expand far beyond the reach of its armies seemed to transform the U.S.S.R. into an international phenomenon of unprecedented expansive power. The chaotic economic, social, and political conditions prevailing throughout most of postwar Eurasia presented an immediate danger to Western security and fertile soil for Soviet ideological exploitation.

Anticommunist writers and spokesmen, as early as 1946, detected few limits to the Kremlin's external needs and ambitions. In February, Soviet specialist and diplomat George F. Kennan's famed Long Telegram attributed to the Kremlin a paranoia that demanded America's destruction. "We have here," he warned, "a force committed fanatically to the belief that with the United States there can be no permanent *modus vivendi*, that it is desirable and necessary that the internal harmony of our society be disrupted, our traditional way of life destroyed, the international authority of our state broken, if Soviet power is to be secure."[10] Writing in *Life* magazine, foreign policy expert (and future secretary of state) John Foster Dulles warned in June that the Soviets intended "to have governments everywhere which accept the doctrine of the Soviet Communist Party." Should the Soviets achieve that goal, he acknowledged, they would gain world hegemony.[11] The report of Clark Clifford and George Elsey on the Soviet danger, presented to President Truman in September 1946, reflected the convictions of Washington insiders. "The key to understanding of current Soviet policy," the report concluded, "is the realization that Soviet leaders adhere to the Marxian theory of ultimate destruction of capitalist states by Communist states."[12]

Anticommunism's central assumption was the fearful threat of Soviet ideological expansionism; but ideology was no expansive force. Nationalism and each nation's pursuit of its self-interest would provide a universal defense against Soviet ideological expansionism. Individual indigenous communist struggles for power, lacking external military support, invariably succeeded or failed on their own. No communist regime would willingly compromise its country's sovereignty merely to serve the Kremlin's interests. Therefore, throughout the decades of Cold War, the Kremlin relied on generally risk-free policies, gaining nothing territorially, or even politically.

The United States found its own policies constrained by various limitations. Its anticommunism's boundless rhetorical fears, demands, and aspirations reduced Washington's time and, especially, its focus to fully comprehend the long-term consequences of decisions required for successful coexistence. Despite its rhetoric, Washington never pursued a genuine anticommunist program: it never seriously attempted to free Eastern Europe, China, the Soviet Union, or any other region of the globe, from communist control. Indeed, what made possible the decades of fortunate superpower coexistence was the decision of successive U.S. administrations to avoid the dictates of ideology and pursue the limited goals of containment; and, where dangerous, a studied avoidance of direct and unnecessary conflict with the Soviet Union.

Central and Eastern Europe

The decades-long superpower confrontation, dubbed the "Cold War," began with Washington's refusal to accept the Soviet Union's expansionism in Central and Eastern Europe. It began when the Red army overran this region in the final days of the war and then fostered postwar indigenous communist governments that relied on Moscow and, often, the Soviet military for survival. Washington desired a return to the prewar status quo in this region, with the re-creation of independent, freely elected, democratic governments as proclaimed at wartime conferences. The Kremlin insisted that governments in its new sphere of interest were independent and democratic. It could also have been pointed out that several of the prewar states were not democratic, nor were experienced in free elections.

As a matter of the first importance for the future European peace, the Allied governments undertook to determine the fate of Germany. At Yalta, no decision had been reached. To be sure, Germany would be de-Nazified and demilitarized, and forced to pay a large (as yet undetermined) amount of reparations. Wartime arrangements called for temporary military occupation by the victors. A European Advisory Commission drew the boundaries of the occupation zones, after Germany's surrender, by Russian, British, American, and later, French forces. The zone assigned to Russia—including Mecklenburg-Pomerania, Brandenburg, Saxony-Anhalt, Thuringia, and all to the eastward—contained 40 percent of the territory, 36 percent of the population, and 33 percent of the productive resources of pre-1937 Germany. This no doubt seemed a fair division at the time, but it had placed Berlin far within the Soviet zone, a hundred miles or more distant from the British zone. The consequence was that, except by air, American and British access to Berlin was at the option of the Russian occupiers.

The unexpectedly rapid advance of the Anglo-American armies brought them into the Soviet zones of Germany and Austria and also into western Czechoslovakia, which the Russians viewed as within their sphere. Prime Minister Churchill wished to take advantage of Western military success by seizing Berlin and holding all the territory occupied until Stalin could be induced to live up to the promises made at Yalta.[13] Otherwise, Churchill warned, an "iron curtain," which the Russians had already "drawn down upon their front," would descend over a much wider area, and "a broad band of many hundreds of miles of Russian-occupied territory will isolate us from Poland."[14] But Eisenhower, supported by Roosevelt and then by Truman, declined what he thought a useless advance to Berlin, and Truman refused to postpone the withdrawal of American troops from the Russian zone beyond July 1. The Russians took Berlin, Prague, and Vienna—the three great ancient capitals of Central Europe.

The Big Three heads of government held their last wartime meeting at Potsdam, just outside the ruins of Berlin, from July 17 to August 2, 1945. Truman had replaced Roosevelt, and midway through the conference the Labour Party's victory in the British elections removed Churchill and Eden and substituted Clement Attlee and Ernest Bevin as prime minister and foreign secretary, respectively. The atmosphere was friendly, and the discussions were generally good-tempered. Many controversial issues, however, were unresolved: the West complained of one-party domination in Bulgaria and Rumania, while the Soviets requested British and American recognition of these governments;[15] the Soviet desire for control of the Dardanelles and a trusteeship over former Italian possessions in the Mediterranean; and the American interest in the internationalization of such waterways as the Dardanelles and the Danube. On other important matters there was agreement. The task of drawing up treaties with Italy and with the Axis satellites Hungary, Bulgaria, Rumania and Finland[16] was assigned to a Council of Foreign Ministers, which was to meet in London.

The three leaders agreed that supreme authority in Germany should rest in the hands of the commanders of the four occupying armies, each in his own zone, and acting together in Berlin as a Control Council in matters affecting Germany as a whole. Germany was to be demilitarized, de-Nazified, and democratized. War criminals were to be punished. Local German governments were to be established, and certain central administrative departments were to be set up in such fields as finance, transport, communications, foreign trade, and industry. It was expected that Germany would be administered as an economic unit, with common policies in all major fields of economic activity. Production policies were to be adjusted to meet the needs of the occupying forces and displaced persons, and to maintain for the German population a certain, limited standard of living. The United States and Britain accepted the Polish occupation of German territory up to the Oder-Neisse line (except the Königsberg area of East Prussia, which was claimed by the Soviets) and the expulsion of the German population from that area, though nominally the fixing of Germany's eastern boundary was reserved for the future treaty of peace. For reparations, the Potsdam agreement authorized each occupying power to remove property from its own zone and to seize German assets abroad. In order to balance the predominance of industry in the Western zones against that of agriculture in the East, Russia was entitled to 10 percent of industrial equipment taken from the Western zones, plus another 15 percent that was to be exchanged for products of the East, chiefly coal, raw materials, and foodstuffs. What remained of the German merchant marine and navy was to be divided equally among the United States, the United Kingdom, and the Soviet Union.

The Satellite Treaties

The Council of Foreign Ministers met in London in September 1945, Moscow in December 1945, Paris in April-May and June-July 1946, and New York in November-December 1946 to work out treaties with the former so-called Axis satellites. The first meeting of the Council, to which Secretary of State James Byrnes went "with the atomic bomb in his pocket," produced nothing but an unseemly wrangle. Though the agenda was limited to Europe, Molotov complained repeatedly of the exclusion of the Soviets from a share in the control of Japan. Who controlled occupation decision-making was a persistent area of disagreement that began when Italy surrendered and the United States and Britain established and dominated the commission that controlled occupation decisions despite Soviet resentment at being excluded. Moscow, in turn, followed the same pattern when it occupied the countries in Eastern Europe, this time with the West complaining. At Moscow, three months later, the Soviet Union consented to the holding of a conference of the Big Five with the 16 other nations that had made more than nominal contributions to the war in Europe. This conference sat in Paris from July 29 to October 15, 1946. Agreement was finally reached in New York in December 1946, and the treaties were signed in Paris on February 10, 1947.

The treaties imposed monetary indemnities on all the former Axis satellites, Finland, Hungary, Rumania, and Bulgaria, as well as on Italy. They required Finland and Rumania to cede territory to the Soviet Union, and Italy to surrender its African conquests, and they imposed strict limits on their armed forces. Unable to agree on the disposition of Italy's former African possessions—although the Soviets dropped their demand for a Libyan trusteeship—the foreign ministers turned over the problem to the UN General Assembly, which put Libya and Italian Somaliland on the road to independence and federated Eritrea with Ethiopia. The most difficult problem the foreign ministers faced was the conflict between Yugoslavia and Italy over Trieste. The Yugoslav claim was backed by the Kremlin; the Italian claim, by the Western powers. Until 1954, the territory remained under military occupation, the city and northern portion (Zone A) by Anglo-American forces, the remainder (Zone B) by the Yugoslav army. By an agreement signed on October 5, 1954, Italy received Zone A, with slight adjustments in the boundary; Zone B was retained by Yugoslavia. The Soviet Union, more flexible since Stalin's death in 1953, announced that it approved the settlement. The United States was a party to, and in due time ratified, all these treaties except that with Finland. (The United States had never declared war on Finland, which fought with Germany against the Soviet Union.) The United States recognized the communist-dominated government of Bulgaria, as it had already done in the case of Rumania. At Moscow, in December 1945, Stalin had promised a relaxing of one-party control in Rumania and Bulgaria. The United States had recognized Rumania without waiting for the promise to be fulfilled, and Bulgaria, after waiting a year in vain.

Austria presented more complicated problems. At Moscow in 1943, the Big Three foreign ministers had promised that Austria, as "the first free country to fall a victim to Hitlerite aggression," should be "liberated from German domination" and reestablished as "free and independent"; and that the way should be opened for the Austrian people to find "political and economic security." At Potsdam, Austria was exempt from the payment of reparations. Yet it was subjected, like Germany, to a four-power occupation, with Vienna a divided city. In November 1945, the Austrians were permitted to elect their own Parliament, which was, and remained thereafter, overwhelmingly anticommunist and pro-Western. Negotiations for a treaty, which should liberate the country from military occupation, began in 1946, but not until the spring of 1955 were Soviet objections met. On May 15, 1955, a treaty was signed that ended the occupation and reestablished Austria as a free and independent state. Separate agreements with the Soviet Union and the Western powers guaranteed its neutralization.

Deadlock in Germany

The Four-Power Control Council, established in Berlin, soon reached a condition of chronic deadlock, resulting from the requirement that all decisions be by unanimous vote. The French, annoyed at their exclusion from Yalta and Potsdam, were guilty of some of the most flagrant obstructionist tactics in the early months of the occupation; but in the end it was the Soviets who sabotaged attempts at a common policy for the four zones by repudiating in practice the Potsdam agreement that Germany should be treated as an economic unit. The consequence was that each of the four powers applied its own ideas in its zone. The Americans undertook to build democracy, starting from the grass roots, combined with a system of free enterprise. The Soviets forced a union of communists and Social Democrats to form the Socialist Unity Party, which became their instrument of government. Large landed estates were broken up, and large industries were nationalized. The French and British were less zealous for democracy than the Americans, and the British, under a Labour government, talked little of free enterprise and much of nationalizing the giant Ruhr industries, located in their zone. But policies in the three Western zones were sufficiently alike to eventually make their economic and political union compatible.

The Soviets' independent course on reparations—taking from their zone whatever they wished in capital goods and current production— and their refusal to send food and raw materials to the Western zones led to an abandonment of the reparations policy in the latter in the spring of 1946 and, a few months later, to the economic union of the American and British zones. The Russians refused an invitation to merge their zone with the "Bizonia" thus formed, denouncing it as a step toward a permanent division of Germany. France also held aloof.

In order to prevent Germany's permanent division and lessen the Western powers' economic support, Secretary of State Byrnes, in a speech at Stuttgart, September 6, 1946, proposed that Germany be reunited, not only economically but politically, with a central government on a federal pattern. To quiet French or Russian fears of a revived and rearmed Germany, Byrnes repeated an earlier offer on the part of the United States, to sign a 25- or even 40-year four-power treaty to keep Germany disarmed and to leave American troops in Germany as long as any armed occupation should be necessary.[17] The Soviet government rejected this offer to guarantee German disarmament. It was rejected again in March 1947, when George Marshall, then secretary of state, went to Moscow for another meeting of the Council of Foreign Ministers. The West made another bid for German unification, economic and political— the failure of which led to the organization of West Germany as a separate entity. The Soviets would agree to economic union on two conditions: a share in control of the industry of the Ruhr and recognition by the West of Russia's claim to $10 billion in reparations. On neither point would the Western powers yield. The two camps were equally far apart on political organization, the Western allies proposing a rather loose federal system, the Russians insisting on a strongly centralized government. The former, it was believed, would be a barrier against communism; the latter might facilitate the communizing of the entire German state.[18]

Engaging the Containment Policy

A mutual antagonism had been building up since early 1946. Stalin, on February 9, began preparing Soviet citizens, who had suffered incredible wartime hardships, for the sacrifices required to rebuild the devastated countryside. Drawing on Marxist-Leninist predictions of an inevitable war between communism and capitalism, he called for three five-year plans to prepare the Soviet Union for the struggle. Stalin followed his speech with a tightening of the Kremlin's hold on the governments of Eastern Europe and a propaganda campaign directed against the West, especially the United States. A month later, Winston Churchill—not then a member of the British government—also employed the element of fear at Fulton, Missouri, in delivering his famous denunciation of the "iron curtain" and urged "a fraternal association of English-speaking peoples" to defend the free world. Standing beside Churchill and applauding, President Truman endorsed the growing political chasm.

Actions on both sides contributed to the growing tension: Washington's ignoring the Soviets' application for an American loan; Soviet rejection of Secretary Byrnes's Stuttgart offer; disruption of the reparations program; pressures of Soviet or Soviet satellites on Greece and Turkey; and replacement of negotiations by mutual propagandist oratory in the meetings of the Council of Foreign Ministers. Yet, to the end of 1946, hope of accommodation was not wholly ended. The satellite treaties were made and ratified. Soviet troops, whose presence in Iran delayed wartime promises, were finally withdrawn, and Stalin sometimes talked affably with visitors from the West of peaceful relations between the opposing systems. By the spring of 1947, with the failure of the Moscow Conference and the simultaneous announcement by the United States of the policy of "containment," the Cold War was underway. The new American policy was based on the thesis that the Soviet Union had a persistent tendency to expand the boundaries of its empire wherever possible but would not undertake to do so at the risk of major war. The United States, therefore, by exerting counter pressure could "contain" the U.S.S.R. and its communist satellites within their existing bounds, hoping that time and internal strains would eventually sap the strength of the Soviet empire.[19]

While the foreign ministers were wrangling in Moscow, President Truman went before Congress on March 12, 1947, to ask for $400 million in military and economic aid for Greece and Turkey. Since 1945, the royal government of Greece had been struggling against local communist forces, aided by assistance from Greece's three northern neighbors, satellites of the Soviet Union. Moscow, authorized by the 1936 Montreux Convention, requested a revision of Turkey's role in controlling the straits and the surrender of the districts of Kars and Ardahan at the eastern end of the Black Sea, which Russia had lost at the end of World War I. Great Britain, which had been aiding both Turkey and Greece, informed Washington in February 1947 that it would no longer be able to do so. Truman promptly asked authority and funds to assist Greece and Turkey, and in doing so, his announcement came to be referred to as the "Truman Doctrine." "I believe [the president said] that it must be the policy of the United States to support free peoples who are resisting attempted subjugation by armed minorities or by outside pressures..."

While Truman's proposal met a generally favorable response in the United States, some critics thought its scope too broad. It had shifted the narrow concept of assisting a state dealing with an external invasion to include the unlimited prospects of intervening in internal strife. Congress, after two months of debate, authorized on May 22, 1947, the expenditure of $100 million in military aid to Turkey and, for Greece, $300 million equally divided between military and economic assistance. The act also empowered the president to send military and civilian experts as advisers to the Greek and Turkish governments. The Truman administration moved quickly to assume even broader responsibilities.

In Western Europe, the danger from communism lay principally in the economic stagnation that had followed the war. By the spring of 1947, these countries were facing a potentially catastrophic situation after an exceptionally severe winter. Food and fuel were in short supply, and foreign exchange—notwithstanding the large dollar loan to England—would be exhausted by the end of the year. Large communist parties in France and Italy stood ready to profit from the impending economic collapse caused by unemployment, wartime devastation, and general human suffering. In Washington, the best chance of halting the spread of indigenous communism appeared to be economic recovery. Secretary of State George Marshall, speaking at the Harvard Commencement, June 5, 1947, offered American aid to those European nations that agreed to coordinate their efforts for recovery and present the United States with a program and specifications of their needs. Marshall drew no distinction between communist and noncommunist Europe, but the Soviet Union spurned the proposal as a new venture in "American imperialism." The satellite governments obeyed the dictum from Moscow, as did Finland and Czechoslovakia, which dared not offend the Soviet giant. They had been tempted, as had Poland, by Marshall's proposal, but all three declined with regret.

The other 16 nations of Europe (excluding Franco's Spain, which was not invited, and Germany, which as yet had no government) formed a "committee of European Economic Cooperation," which in September 1947 proposed to the United States the achievement by 1951 of a self-sufficient European economy, at an estimated cost of $19.3 billion. In December, President Truman laid the proposal before Congress with a request for $6.8 billion for the first 15 months of the program and $10.2 billion for the succeeding three years—a total of $17 billion. In explaining his request, the president said: "I am proposing that this Nation contribute to world peace and to its own security by assisting in the recovery of sixteen countries which, like the United States, are devoted to the preservation of free institutions and enduring peace among nations." Congress slashed the figure somewhat, but on April 3, 1948, established the Economic Cooperation Administration to handle the program and at the end of June appropriated an initial $4 billion for the program. (Almost all of the money was spent in the United States to purchase industrial equipment and supplies, thus stimulating the host country's economy.) The European Recovery Program, which continued for three years, ultimately cost the United States $13 billion. It contributed to an impressive European economic recovery.

The Marshall Plan was designed to aid in the recovery of nations with advanced economies that had been dislocated by the war. By increasing production and trade, by alleviating unemployment and poverty, its authors expected it to halt the growth of communism among the working classes of Europe. But Washington also worried about the threat of communism among the poverty-stricken masses in countries of Asia, Africa, and Latin America without a modern economy. The global "containment" of communism called for measures to raise the standard of living in these countries. President Truman, in an address on January 20, 1949, proposed a "Point Four," or Technical Assistance program: "we must embark on a bold new program for making the benefits of our scientific advances and industrial progress available for the improvement and growth of underdeveloped areas."[20] The Point Four program was launched in 1950 with a modest appropriation of $35 million, but authorized expenditures for 1951–1954 increased to nearly $400 million. In 1953, the program was placed, with other forms of foreign aid, under the Foreign Operations Administration (FOA).

The West German Republic

In the meantime, there had been important developments in Germany. Failure of the foreign ministers to reach agreement on Germany's future in 1947 led the Western powers to join their three zones and create a unified and self-governing West Germany. Consultations in London in the spring of 1948 by representatives of France, Great Britain, the United States, and the three Benelux countries (Belgium, the Netherlands, and Luxembourg) resulted in agreements, announced June 7, proposing the creation of a West German government. As a safeguard, an international authority representing the six states and West Germany would control the Ruhr industries. The Germans of the Western zones would elect members of a constituent assembly. This body would then draw up a constitution for a federal state, which might eventually include the Eastern zone. The new government would exercise sovereignty over its domestic affairs and limited control over foreign relations; but the ban on rearmament would remain, and the military occupation would continue "until the peace of Europe is secured."[21] The West German Constituent Assembly met at Bonn, on September 1, 1948, and proceeded to prepare a constitution. A German Federal Republic, comprising the three Western zones, was inaugurated at Bonn in September 1949. Military government ended, although occupation forces remained, with Allied authority exercised through a High Commission, to which the United States, France, and the United Kingdom each appointed one member. The Federal Republic was soon made eligible for Marshall Plan aid and was given a voice in the international control of the Ruhr. Under its first chancellor, Konrad Adenauer (1949–1963), it showed a spirit of willing cooperation with the West.

The Soviets criticized these Western moves. They interpreted the Marshall Plan as an aggressive U.S. scheme and worried about the ambitions of the new West German government. In response, they held a conference of nine East European states in Warsaw during September 1947, which resolved to do everything possible to defeat the program of "American imperialism." Communist-inspired strikes in France and Italy sought in vain to deter these countries from accepting Marshall Plan aid. The Communist Information Bureau (Cominform), a successor of the Comintern, was established at Belgrade. Defensive alliances linking the Soviet Union with Bulgaria, Finland, Hungary, and Rumania were added to treaties previously negotiated with Czechoslovakia, Poland, and Yugoslavia. As the West moved toward the unification of West Germany, Moscow tightened its grip on its satellite states. In February 1948, a communist coup overthrew the democratic government of Czechoslovakia and installed one firmly attached to Moscow. The Soviets encountered resistance when Yugoslavia, under Tito's leadership, broke with the Cominform and with Moscow. Tito's government remained firmly communist, but it ceased to take orders from the Kremlin and assumed a neutralist position in the Cold War.

When the six-power talks on Germany opened in London, the Soviets complained that the Western powers were destroying the four-power control of Germany agreed to three years earlier and, hence, that they must leave Berlin. The Western Allies, on the other hand, maintained that they were in Berlin by virtue of their role in the defeat of Germany. Stalin attempted to squeeze the Western forces out of Berlin, which lay well within the Soviet zone with no guaranteed connecting surface corridor. Restrictions on movement to and from the city were first imposed in April 1948, and by June all surface transportation between Berlin and the Western zones was halted. The Western powers faced either withdrawing their garrisons from Berlin or finding means of supplying them and the 2 million people of West Berlin. Rejecting advice that he "call the Russian bluff"—open the roads by military force—President Truman, and the British, resorted to air transport, authorized by signed agreements with the Soviets. The "airlift" started at once, and by September 1, American and British planes were flying into Berlin 4,000 tons of supplies daily. Soviet aircraft occasionally harassed the American and British cargo planes but were instructed not to attack. Allied persistence and patience eventually paid off. In May 1949, the Soviet Union ended the blockade.

In October 1949, after the inauguration of the German Federal Republic at Bonn, the People's Council in Berlin proclaimed a new government for the Soviet zone of Germany. The new German Democratic Republic, East Germany, rested on a constitution designed, like that at Bonn, to unite all of Germany. Two Germanys had come into being and would wait several decades for unification.

Collective Defense Agreements

The communist coup in Czechoslovakia and the Berlin blockade further alarmed the Western powers. Though the blockade had been ended, there was no guarantee that the Soviets might not make a new attempt to oust the West from Berlin or to prevent the formation of the German Federal Republic. The Soviets since 1945 had reduced their armed forces from 11.5 million men to fewer than 3 million,[22] but they still far outnumbered those available in the West. Their numerical superiority, it was feared, might tempt Moscow to commit some aggressive act. "Containment" of the Soviets had been dependent chiefly on economic and political means; now interest was aroused in developing military muscle. If the Soviet Union could be warned that an act of aggression against any one of the free nations of Western Europe would mean hostilities with the others and also with the United States, it might well be deterred. The United

Nations, because of the Soviet veto, could not supply such a deterrent, but Article 51 of the UN Charter legalized "collective self-defense" by groups within the United Nations, and the West turned now to agreements under Article 51. In the Americas, the Rio Pact of September 2, 1947, had already invoked Article 51 in a hemispheric collective security agreement. In Europe, a beginning was made in March 1948, when Great Britain, France, and the Benelux countries signed at Brussels a 50-year treaty of economic, social, and cultural collaboration and collective self-defense. But in order to bolster the treaty, it needed the backing of the United States.

President Truman, on March 17, 1948, proposed restoring the strength of the United States' military forces in an address to Congress. After warning of the Soviet danger, he urged the adoption of a universal military training program and temporary reenactment of selective service legislation. The United States had also greatly reduced its military after the war. The buildup of American armed strength began with the enactment by Congress of a new selective service, or draft, law in June 1948. With the draft and under the stimulus of war in Korea, which began in June 1950, the strength of the army, navy, and air force grew from 1,350,000 in 1948 to 3,630,000 in June 1952. For the first time in nearly a century and a half, the Vandenberg Resolution of June 11, 1948, agreed that the United States should, among other measures for promoting peace, associate itself, "by constitutional process, with such regional and other collective arrangements as are based on continuous and effective self-help and mutual aid, and as affect its national security." The United States ought also, the resolution declared, to make clear "its determination to exercise the right of individual or collective self-defense under article 51 should any armed attack occur affecting its national security."[23]

The Vandenberg Resolution was the prelude to the North Atlantic Treaty, an ambitious venture in search of collective security. The treaty—a pronounced departure from the principle of "no permanent alliances"—was signed April 4, 1949, by 12 nations of the North Atlantic and Western Europe. This number was increased to 15 by the accession of Greece and Turkey in 1952 and West Germany in 1955.[24] The parties agreed to settle peacefully all disputes between themselves and to develop their capacity to resist armed attack "by means of continuous and effective self-help and mutual aid." But the heart of the treaty was Article 5, which declared that an armed attack on any one of the members in Europe or North America would be considered an attack on all and pledged each member in case of such an attack to assist the party attacked "by such action as it deems necessary, including the use of armed force." Thus began the North Atlantic Treaty Organization, or NATO, with the North Atlantic Council, consisting of the foreign, defense, and finance ministers of the member states, as its directing body.

The United States took the lead in providing and organizing the military deterrent envisaged by the framers of the North Atlantic Treaty. The American position in the superpower struggle was aggressively defined in a top-secret document labeled NSC 68, prepared by the State and Defense Departments in the spring of 1950. NSC 68 started from a vastly overstated assumption as to Soviet intentions, which as Secretary of State Dean Acheson admitted, was opposed by some of the more prominent Soviet experts in the State Department. In this analysis, the Russian threat, in Acheson's words, "combined the ideology of communist doctrine and the power of the Russian state into an aggressive expansionist drive, which found its chief opponent, and, therefore, target in the antithetical ideas and power of our own country." The threat to Western Europe, he thought, seemed "singularly like that which Islam had posed centuries before, with its combination of ideological zeal and fighting power."[25] With such an extravagant perceived threat to Western Europe and ultimately to the United States, NSC 68 recommended that the United States "strike out on a bold and massive program of rebuilding the West's defensive potential to surpass that of the Soviet world, and of meeting each fresh challenge promptly and unequivocally." With the security of the free world at stake, costs of such a program were immaterial. The country could afford to spend, if necessary, 20 percent of its gross national product on defense. President Truman quietly approved NSC 68 in September 1950. This was the first of several U.S. government overstatements of Soviet goals issued during the ensuing decades, designed to arouse what was perceived as a flagging public to the need for more militant and expensive Cold War policies.

The assumption of NSC 68 as to Moscow's aggressive purposes seemed to Acheson and others to be borne out by events in the Far East and by the revelation, in August 1949, that the Soviet Union had successfully exploded its first atomic bomb. The Chinese Communists' conquest of the mainland was completed in the summer of 1949, and the government of the People's Republic of China was proclaimed at Beijing on October 1. The Chinese Communists were, incorrectly as it turned out, regarded as puppets of Moscow and their victory as a major triumph in the Kremlin's program of world revolution. Then, on June 25, 1950, several months before the approval of NSC 68, communist North Korea, with the approval of Stalin, forcefully attempted to unify the country. Korea, after the

Japanese left, had been divided into two zones, the North under the influence of the Soviet Union and the South occupied by the United States, until a peaceful unification could be negotiated. Due to ideological disagreements, these negotiations failed. In 1950, with the North's attack, Washington generally assumed that this was yet another Soviet attempt at enlarging its empire.[26] Here was a "fresh challenge" of the kind that NSC 68 had said should be met "promptly and unequivocally"; the U.S. military responded to the challenge. The North Korean attack made the task of "selling" NSC 68 to arouse the American public easier than had been anticipated. The Cold War climate hardened.

With the Korean War underway, the United States, working now through NATO, began building the military defenses in Western Europe against supposed Soviet plans for an attack. Early in 1951, the North Atlantic Council set up military headquarters near Paris, known as SHAPE (Supreme Headquarters, Allied Powers in Europe), with General Dwight Eisenhower as Supreme Commander. Its purpose was to build a defense force in Western Europe, not equal to the army maintained by the Soviet Union (175 Russian divisions and 60 or more divisions from the satellite states), but strong enough to hold the Soviet forces in check until the United States' strategic airpower could, with atomic bombs, destroy the centers of Soviet strength. Thus, American aid to Europe shifted from economic to military. The Mutual Security Agency in 1951 replaced the Economic Cooperation Administration and was in turn, in 1953, succeeded by the Foreign Operations Administration. From October 1949 to the end of 1953, the United States supplied nearly $6 billion worth of arms and military equipment to its European allies, as well as $1.7 billion worth to other countries. The United States also increased its divisions stationed in Germany and Austria from two to six, following a "great debate" in which the Senate approved this increase but advised against sending additional troops abroad without the consent of Congress. The European allies in the same period spent over $35 billion in building up their military forces and installations. The result was a substantial increase in the troops, planes, and airfields available for NATO service.

Throughout this period, the United States strongly urged the inclusion of West German units in the defense forces. The prospect of a rearmed and nationalistic Germany was almost as alarming to France and the Benelux countries as the Soviet danger. The French government proposed a European Defense Community (EDC) that would make it possible to use and yet control German troops by integrating them with those of France, Italy, and the Benelux states. In spite of urgent pleas by U.S. secretary of state John Foster Dulles, the French Assembly in August 1954 finally rejected it. A substitute was found in a set of treaties constituting Western European Union (WEU)—an alliance rather than the EDC's organic union—that became effective on May 6, 1955. Under this arrangement, Italy and the Federal Republic of (West) Germany were admitted to the Brussels Pact alliance of 1948 with Britain, France, and the three Benelux countries. West Germany recovered its sovereignty and was permitted to rearm, though pledging itself not to manufacture atomic, chemical, or bacteriological weapons. U.S., British, and French troops were to remain in West Germany for its defense and that of the North Atlantic area until the Bonn government could provide its own defense forces. Also, West Germany became a member of NATO, and the armed forces of the Western European Union, with certain exceptions, became subject to the NATO supreme command. To quiet French fears of a rearmed Germany, Great Britain and the United States agreed, in principle, to maintain substantial military forces on the continent.

The hopes of 1955 for a substantial NATO army were never realized. The gain in strength from the addition of the West German army to NATO forces was largely offset by losses elsewhere. The nationalist rebellion against the French in Algeria, which had begun in 1954, drew off the greater part of the French forces that had been committed to NATO. Pressure for economy, doubt as to the efficacy of conventional forces in an age of nuclear weapons and long-range ballistic missiles, and occasional relaxation in East-West tensions led to reductions in other national contingents. The goal of 96 divisions, set at the Lisbon meeting of the North Atlantic Council in 1952, was abandoned, and the "irreducible minimum" of 30 divisions, announced year after year by American Supreme Commanders at SHAPE, was never attained. Shortages of manpower, indeed, were compensated for by increases in firepower, as NATO troops in Europe were gradually equipped with tactical (low-yield) atomic weapons. These were supplied by the United States, and their atomic warheads were kept under American custody, as required by the U.S. Atomic Energy Act. Any satisfaction afforded by this modernization of weaponry was qualified, however, by the reflection that the Soviets would feel it necessary to make similar improvements.

The Kremlin had watched with misgivings the formation of NATO and the Western European Union, and especially the plans for rearming West Germany. It tried to halt the process by threats, persuasion, and offers of compromise, but was largely ignored. What the Soviets feared most was the rearming of West Germany, especially the possibility that German troops, as NATO forces, might acquire atomic weapons. Having failed in their attempts to block these measures of the West, they turned to countermeasures. At Warsaw on May 14, 1955, the Soviets negotiated an alliance of eight communist states—the Warsaw Pact—for defense against any aggressive intentions of NATO.

The Arms Race

The weapons picture was slowly changing since the end of the war. Then the United States held a monopoly of atomic weapons, and with its fleet of long-range bombers under the Strategic Air Command (SAC), gradually possessed a capability of destroying Soviet centers of population and industry. In 1949, however, the Soviet Union at considerable expense exploded its first atomic bomb to reestablish a balance of power. Four years later, it followed the United States by only a few months in setting off its first hydrogen, or thermonuclear, device, thus closing the gap between the nuclear-weapon capabilities of the two superpowers. The Soviet success in launching the rocket-propelled satellites Sputnik I and Sputnik II (October 4, November 3, 1957) and the Americans development of the Atlas and Titan missiles ushered in the age of the intercontinental ballistic missile (ICBM), with its no less potent relative the intermediate-range ballistic missile (IRBM) and the less vulnerable submarine-launched ballistic missiles (SLBMs). These missiles soon became the primary carriers of nuclear destruction, although the slower and more vulnerable bombers remained one leg of the U.S. nuclear triad. In the early 1960s, the Soviets lagged behind in numbers of ICBMs, but by the 1970s something like a parity had been reached between the Americans and Soviets in nuclear weaponry. Since each had achieved the unquestioned power to destroy the other, a nuclear war had become "unthinkable." Although terms such as the "balance of terror" or "mutual deterrence" described the relationship, each government continued to search for more powerful and reliable weapons. Initially, this search involved the decision to explode test nuclear devices in the atmosphere, with the resulting fallout of radioactive particles that created worldwide hazards to health. An unofficial moratorium on such tests was instituted in 1958, but the Eisenhower administration was unable, some officials even unwilling, to agree to a formula to terminate this hazard. In 1961, the testing resumed. Shortly after the nerve-racking "Cuban" missile crisis, the Kennedy administration, aided by the British prime minister and a co-operative leader, Nikita Khrushchev, temporarily resolved the issue. On August 5, 1963, the three powers signed the Limited Test Ban Treaty, by which they agreed to abstain from exploding nuclear devices in the atmosphere, in outer space, and underwater. Underground tests were not banned. The treaty was promptly ratified by the signers and adhered to by most of the governments, excluding France, Israel, communist China, and Cuba.[27] The quest for a comprehensive nuclear test ban, which many believed would reduce the proliferation of nuclear weapons, trudged on.

CHAPTER 14

Crises, Conflicts, and Coexistence

There is no substitute for victory.
—General Douglas MacArthur on the Korean War

Today, in the world of freedom, the proudest boast is "Ich bin ein Berliner."
—John F. Kennedy, West Berlin, June 26, 1963

The Cold War flourished in Asia and Europe from the 1950s to the 1970s. The United States' refusal of any Soviet participation in occupied Italy and Japan, its gradual ringing of the U.S.S.R. with U.S. military bases, and its encouragement of rearming Germany did little to ease the tensions. The Soviet Union responded in kind with the Warsaw Pact, encouraging the North Koreans' attack, and placing missiles in Cuba. The onset of the Korean War solidified the view of many in Washington that, indeed, the Kremlin's true object was a global empire. The Soviet misadventure that precipitated the missile crisis of 1962 brought home to virtually everyone the terrifying prospects of a nuclear holocaust. Subsequently, superpower nuclear parity did allow for the beginning of meaningful arms control activities and a temporary détente.

Occupying Japan

Japan escaped the divided control that frustrated unification in Germany, Austria, and Korea. The Foreign Ministers conference at Moscow in December 1945 agreed that a four-power Allied Council, representing the United States, the Soviet Union, the British Commonwealth, and China, established in Tokyo would advise the head of occupation forces in Japan. A Far Eastern Commission in Washington, speaking for the 11 powers that had fought against Japan, was to make policy for the occupation; in reality it acquiesced in General Douglas MacArthur's decisions. He received instructions from Washington, ignoring a Soviet request to share in the occupation. This refusal and the assumption by the United States of unilateral control over Japan doubtless offended the Soviets and contributed to their frequently uncooperative attitude in Europe and China.

Japan's once impressive empire was cut down to the four islands that had formed its domain at the time of Commodore Perry's visit in 1853. Its armed forces were abolished and war industries liquidated. In the new constitution, largely prepared by occupation authorities and put into effect on May 3, 1947, the Japanese people "forever renounce[d] war as a sovereign right of the nation" and agreed that "land, sea, and air forces, as well as other war potential, will never be maintained. The right of belligerency of the state will not be recognized." After the Hiroshima and Nagasaki atomic bombings, most Japanese enthusiastically endorsed this pledge. War criminals were punished; some, such as wartime premier General Tojo, with the death penalty. Political life was purged of those individuals who could be held most responsible for Japan's war policy. The new constitution, although retaining the monarchy, placed all power in the representatives of the people. These were to be chosen by democratic procedures, including female suffrage. The emperor, on January 1, 1946, repudiated "the false conception that the Emperor is divine and that the Japanese people are superior to other races and fated to rule the world." By dissolving the great industrial and commercial combines, the Zaibatsu, and by consigning all but the smallest landed estates to peasant proprietorship, the occupation also attempted to democratize economic life. Educational reform accompanied these political and economic transformations. The dissolution of the Zaibatsu did not long outlast military occupation: the other reforms promised to be more permanent.

Communist Chinese Gain Control

In 1945, Stalin suggested he wished to see China unified under Chiang Kai-shek, would not support the Chinese Communists, and would respect Chinese sovereignty in Manchuria and the open-door principle.[1] The Sino-Soviet treaty and agreements signed on August 14, 1945, were one of friendship and alliance against Japan. The Nationalist Chinese and Soviets promised to bring about Japan's defeat and to prevent a repetition of its aggression, respect for each other's sovereignty and territorial integrity, and noninterference in each other's internal affairs. Reassuring to Chiang Kai-shek was the Soviet Union's reaffirmation of respect for "China's full sovereignty" over Manchuria and, especially, a promise that support and assistance would "be entirely given to the National Government as the central government of China." The last promise, if observed, would have eliminated the danger of Soviet support for the Chinese Communists, against whom Chiang had been warring for over a decade.[2] Stalin had supported Chiang in the early years of fighting Japan; however, he did not have harmonious relations with Mao Tse-tung. With Sino-Soviet relations apparently harmonized, Washington could proceed to develop its policy for the creation of a "strong, united, and democratic China." American postwar policy toward China was based on the fallacious belief that communists and nationalists could work together. With Japan defeated, the United States worked for the peaceful unification of China. In the fall of 1945, communist leader Mao Tse-tung spent six weeks in negotiations with Chiang Kai-shek. The two parted on apparently friendly terms, announcing that they had reached agreement on the majority of points in dispute and were not too far apart on the remainder.

In the meantime, Chiang's Nationalist forces, with American arms and transportation, were replacing the Japanese along the coastal area of China and in most of its large cities. Communist armies continued to hold large areas of the interior in the Northwest and North and were filtering into Manchuria. Here, they took over arms and supplies from the surrendering Japanese and were soon receiving some assistance from the Kremlin. Armed clashes between the longtime foes, the nationalists and communists, occurred with increasing frequency. In November 1945, President Truman selected General George C. Marshall, who had just retired as Army Chief of Staff, to seek a truce in the fighting and political unification of nationalists, communists, and other groups. He had considerable discretion, but it was emphasized that the existing Nationalist government, "the only legal government in China," was to form the foundation of the new political structure. That government, Truman stated publicly, "is the proper instrument to achieve the objective of a unified China."[3] After Marshall's China mission, despite its promising beginning, during which the communists apparently agreed to accept a minority position in a unified government and a subordinate position in a unified army, the two factions fell to fighting again, and nothing that Marshall could do could halt the drift into full-scale civil war. Marshall's report, dated January 7, 1947, blamed the failure of his mission on "extremist elements against outside aggression."[7] The Acheson statement, though not a green light for aggression, did hold out the rather vague prospect of UN action instead of a warning that the United States would regard an attack on South Korea as a threat to its own security. With Stalin's blessing, the North Koreans, on June 25, 1950, launched a well-organized attack along the entire width of the 38th parallel.

President Truman immediately requested a meeting of the UN Security Council. On June 25, that body adopted a U.S. resolution declaring the North Korean action a "breach of the peace," demanding that the aggressors withdraw beyond the 38th parallel and calling on all members of the United Nations "to render every assistance to the United Nations in the execution of this resolution and to refrain from giving assistance to the North Korean authorities."[8] The resolution passed the Security Council by a vote of 9 to 0; the temporary relief from the council's chronic paralysis was due to the Russian delegate's absence. Until Soviet delegate Yakov A. Malik returned on August 1 to take his turn as chairman, the Security Council was able to act with vigor. Its resolution of June 27 recommended that UN members "furnish such assistance to the Republic of Korea as may be necessary to repel the armed attack and to restore international peace and security in the area." On July 7, the council requested Truman to name a commander for all UN forces serving in Korea. He named General MacArthur.

The president had acted promptly in throwing the weight of the United States into the struggle. On June 27, he announced that American air and sea forces were on their way "to give the Korean Government troops cover and support." Three days later, on the advice of General MacArthur, he authorized the use of U.S. ground troops in Korea, ordered a naval blockade of the Korean coast, and directed the air force to attack targets in North Korea "wherever militarily necessary." Truman also revealed another action that constituted a distinct change in U.S. policy, since it was evident, he said, "communism has passed beyond the use of subversion to conquer independent nations and will now use armed invasion and war." He, therefore, "ordered the Seventh Fleet to prevent any attack on Formosa" and called on the Chinese on Formosa to cease all attacks on the mainland—even instructing the Seventh Fleet to "see that this is done." He also accelerated military assistance to the Philippines and Indochina, the scenes of other armed conflicts with indigenous communist forces.

Such was the superiority of the North Korean troops in equipment and preparation that they were able to push back the South Koreans and the few UN troops at first available into the extreme southeast corner of of its aggression, respect for each other's sovereignty and territorial integrity, and noninterference in each other's internal affairs. Reassuring to Chiang Kai-shek was the Soviet Union's reaffirmation of respect for "China's full sovereignty" over Manchuria and, especially, a promise that support and assistance would "be entirely given to the National Government as the central government of China." The last promise, if observed, would have eliminated the danger of Soviet support for the Chinese Communists, against whom Chiang had been warring for over a decade.[2] Stalin had supported Chiang in the early years of fighting Japan; however, he did not have harmonious relations with Mao Tse-tung. With Sino-Soviet relations apparently harmonized, Washington could proceed to develop its policy for the creation of a "strong, united, and democratic China." American postwar policy toward China was based on the fallacious belief that communists and nationalists could work together. With Japan defeated, the United States worked for the peaceful unification of China. In the fall of 1945, communist leader Mao Tse-tung spent six weeks in negotiations with Chiang Kai-shek. The two parted on apparently friendly terms, announcing that they had reached agreement on the majority of points in dispute and were not too far apart on the remainder.

In the meantime, Chiang's Nationalist forces, with American arms and transportation, were replacing the Japanese along the coastal area of China and in most of its large cities. Communist armies continued to hold large areas of the interior in the Northwest and North and were filtering into Manchuria. Here, they took over arms and supplies from the surrendering Japanese and were soon receiving some assistance from the Kremlin. Armed clashes between the longtime foes, the nationalists and communists, occurred with increasing frequency. In November 1945, President Truman selected General George C. Marshall, who had just retired as Army Chief of Staff, to seek a truce in the fighting and political unification of nationalists, communists, and other groups. He had considerable discretion, but it was emphasized that the existing Nationalist government, "the only legal government in China," was to form the foundation of the new political structure. That government, Truman stated publicly, "is the proper instrument to achieve the objective of a unified China."[3] After Marshall's China mission, despite its promising beginning, during which the communists apparently agreed to accept a minority position in a unified government and a subordinate position in a unified army, the two factions fell to fighting again, and nothing that Marshall could do could halt the drift into full-scale civil war. Marshall's report, dated January 7, 1947, blamed the failure of his mission on "extremist elements on both sides." Between the communists, who "frankly state that they are Marxists," and the conservative Nationalist leaders, Marshall saw no hope of a compromise settlement.[4]

The end of Marshall's mission meant also the end American mediation of China's internal politics. The United States continued to recognize the government of Chiang Kai-shek as the legitimate government of China but was unwilling to give Chiang the massive military aid and cooperation that alone might have enabled him to survive.[5] Washington had simply lost faith in Chiang's ability to solve China's problems. It was now, furthermore, committed to fostering European recovery under the Marshall Plan and to succoring Greece and Turkey with both economic and military aid. Europe came first and China was relegated to a secondary position. The rapid deterioration of the Nationalist position and a series of victories by the communists gave them control of all mainland China by the end of 1949. In December, Chiang fled to Formosa (Taiwan), where he set up a new capital at Taipei. Incompetent military leadership, together with a collapse in morale, rather than lack of military supplies, accounted for the debacle.[6]

In September 1949, a Chinese People's Consultative Conference met at Beijing and produced a constitution for the People's Republic of China that closely followed the Soviet pattern. The new government was inaugurated October 1, with Mao Tse-tung holding the office equivalent to the presidency and Chou En-lai as premier and foreign minister. The Soviet Union and its satellites recognized the new government, and a new treaty, signed at Moscow on February 14, 1950, formed an alliance between the Soviet Union and communist China—a defensive alliance against aggression "by Japan or states allied with it."

The People's Republic of China was also recognized (after Chiang's flight from the mainland) by Great Britain and a number of other noncommunist governments in both Europe and Asia. Washington, for largely domestic political reasons, withheld recognition of Beijing and continued to regard the Nationalist government on Formosa as the government of China. Certainly, by the treatment of American Consular officers, businessmen, and missionaries, and Beijing's denunciation of "American imperialism," communist China did nothing to invite U.S. recognition or support for admission to the United Nations. To Congressional proposals that the United States should defend Formosa, President Truman stated on January 5, 1950, that the United States had no intention of establishing bases on Formosa or of providing "military aid or advice" to Chiang's forces. A week later, in a speech defining the U.S. "defensive perimeter" in the Far East, Secretary of State Dean Acheson omitted Formosa (as well as Korea) from the areas that the United States considered it necessary to defend. Within a few months, the political scene was greatly changed by the war in Korea.

The Korea Conflict

For the purpose of receiving the surrender of Japanese forces, Korea was divided temporarily at the 38th parallel into a Soviet and an American zone. The two parts of the country were complementary: the north supplied the electric power and most of the industry; the south was agricultural. North of the line, local government was organized on a communist basis; south of it, provisional organs of government had a strong rightist tinge. Following earlier failures to set up a government for a united Korea, Washington placed the issue before the UN General Assembly that, in November 1947, appointed a Temporary Commission on Korea and directed it to hold elections for a constituent assembly. Excluded from the Soviet zone, the commission held elections in southern Korea, and the assembly drew up a constitution for the Republic of Korea, which was inaugurated at the old capital of Seoul in August 1948. Dr. Syngman Rhee, who had been educated and had long resided in the United States, became president. North of the 38th parallel, the Soviets organized a Democratic People's Republic of Korea, with the seat of government at Pyongyang and Kim Il Sung as president. Thus, there were two Korean governments, each of which aspired to extend its rule over the entire peninsula. Each had its army, that in the north trained and supplied by the Soviets, that in the south by the Americans. The Soviets had equipped the northern army with tanks and heavy artillery; but the Americans—largely because of Syngman Rhee's unconcealed ambition to conquer the north—had provided mostly small arms and light artillery.

The withdrawal from Korea of U.S. armed forces (with the exception of a military advisory group of some 400) may have created the impression that the United States would not defend the Republic of Korea against attack from the north. Such an impression would have been strengthened by Secretary of State Acheson's statement that the U.S. "defensive perimeter" in the Pacific ran through the Aleutians, Japan, the Ryukyus, and the Philippines. Areas beyond that line, he said, could not be guaranteed against military attack. Should an attack occur in such an area (for example, Korea), "the initial reliance must be on the people attacked to resist it and then upon the commitments of the entire civilized world under the Charter of the United Nations which so far has not proved a weak reed to lean on by any people who are determined to protect their independence against outside aggression."[7] The Acheson statement, though not a green light for aggression, did hold out the rather vague prospect of UN action instead of a warning that the United States would regard an attack on South Korea as a threat to its own security. With Stalin's blessing, the North Koreans, on June 25, 1950, launched a well-organized attack along the entire width of the 38th parallel.

President Truman immediately requested a meeting of the UN Security Council. On June 25, that body adopted a U.S. resolution declaring the North Korean action a "breach of the peace," demanding that the aggressors withdraw beyond the 38th parallel and calling on all members of the United Nations "to render every assistance to the United Nations in the execution of this resolution and to refrain from giving assistance to the North Korean authorities."[8] The resolution passed the Security Council by a vote of 9 to 0; the temporary relief from the council's chronic paralysis was due to the Russian delegate's absence. Until Soviet delegate Yakov A. Malik returned on August 1 to take his turn as chairman, the Security Council was able to act with vigor. Its resolution of June 27 recommended that UN members "furnish such assistance to the Republic of Korea as may be necessary to repel the armed attack and to restore international peace and security in the area." On July 7, the council requested Truman to name a commander for all UN forces serving in Korea. He named General MacArthur.

The president had acted promptly in throwing the weight of the United States into the struggle. On June 27, he announced that American air and sea forces were on their way "to give the Korean Government troops cover and support." Three days later, on the advice of General MacArthur, he authorized the use of U.S. ground troops in Korea, ordered a naval blockade of the Korean coast, and directed the air force to attack targets in North Korea "wherever militarily necessary." Truman also revealed another action that constituted a distinct change in U.S. policy, since it was evident, he said, "communism has passed beyond the use of subversion to conquer independent nations and will now use armed invasion and war." He, therefore, "ordered the Seventh Fleet to prevent any attack on Formosa" and called on the Chinese on Formosa to cease all attacks on the mainland—even instructing the Seventh Fleet to "see that this is done." He also accelerated military assistance to the Philippines and Indochina, the scenes of other armed conflicts with indigenous communist forces.

Such was the superiority of the North Korean troops in equipment and preparation that they were able to push back the South Koreans and the few UN troops at first available into the extreme southeast corner of

Korea, an area that included the port of Pusan. The tide turned on September 15, when General MacArthur in a risky maneuver landed UN forces at Inchon, far behind the North Korean lines. Large elements of the North Korean army were destroyed or captured, and the remainder driven beyond the 38th parallel. Backed by a General Assembly resolution reiterating the objective of "a unified, independent and democratic Korea," MacArthur's forces crossed the 38th parallel on October 8 (U.S. time) and pushed on toward the Yalu River, Korea's northern boundary. Too little heed had been given to warnings over the Beijing radio and through the Indian delegate in the UN Assembly that communist China might feel called on to prevent the extinction of the Korean People's Republic. After a skillful buildup, Chinese armies, late in November, launched a massive surprise attack that in a few weeks threw the Allied armies back below the 38th parallel and recaptured Seoul.[9] By mid-January 1951, however, the line had been stabilized and the UN forces were ready for a counterattack, which eventually pushed Chinese and North Koreans again beyond the 38th parallel.

In November, the UN General Assembly adopted the "United Action for Peace" plan, proposed by Secretary of State Acheson. At the urging of the United States, the Assembly on February 1, 1951, adopted a resolution declaring the People's Republic of China (PRC) an aggressor and appointing two committees: one to consider additional measures to be used against the aggressors, the other to continue efforts for a peaceful settlement. On the advice of the former, the assembly on May 18, 1951, recommended that member states prohibit the shipment to communist China and North Korea of "arms, ammunition, and implements of war, atomic energy materials, petroleum, transportation materials of strategic value, and items useful in the production of arms, ammunition, and implements of war." These actions by the assembly were taken, over the opposition of the Soviet bloc and with abstentions that showed considerable dislike of American policy, particularly on the part of the Asian and Arab members.

On April 11, 1951, President Truman relieved General Douglas MacArthur of his dual position as commander of UN forces in Korea and of the occupation forces of the United States in Japan. Growing friction between the general and the administration had resulted from MacArthur's impatience at the restraints placed on his military activities and his habit of publicly voicing his disagreements with administration and UN policy. In particular, MacArthur had complained at the prohibition on bombing enemy sources of supply and communications in what he termed the "privileged sanctuary" of Manchuria. His recall set off a heated but relatively short-lived debate in the United States. The issue was whether to limit the war to Korea or to go all out for victory against communist China at the risk of bringing in the Soviet Union. The arguments were epitomized in General MacArthur's assertion, "There is no substitute for victory," and the warning of General Omar N. Bradley, chairman of the Joint Chiefs of Staff, that a full-scale war against Beijing would be "the wrong war at the wrong place, at the wrong time and with the wrong enemy." The administration's instinct for Europe first and its deference to Allied opinion proved vital, while MacArthur believed Asia to be the decisive theater in the struggle with Communism and would have the United States "go it alone if necessary." Consequently, the administration adhered to its policy of limited war.[10]

On June 23, 1951, in New York, Yakov A. Malik, head of the Soviet delegation at the United Nations, instigated the opening of armistice negotiations on July 10, 1951, at Kaesong, just north of the 38th parallel. There, and later at Panmunjom, the negotiations proceeded with several interruptions until July 27, 1953. The Chinese dropped their earlier demands in regard to Formosa, admission to the United Nations, and withdrawal of foreign troops as indispensable conditions. The questions that proved most troublesome were the location of the cease-fire line, machinery for enforcing the armistice terms, and repatriation of prisoners. By the spring of 1952, agreement had been reached on all points but the last. The communists demanded that all prisoners of war be repatriated. The United Nations would not agree to compulsory repatriation of Chinese and North Korean prisoners unwilling to return home. President-elect General Eisenhower, after a visit to the Korean front in December, let it be known that he supported the United Nations stand on prisoners of war. He was determined to bring the war to an end and to remove President Truman's ban on operations from Taiwan against the Chinese mainland.[11] In April 1953, armistice negotiations resumed and found the communist delegates ready to make concessions on the prisoners of war issue, and in spite of the violent opposition of President Syngman Rhee, an armistice agreement was signed at Panmunjom on July 27, 1953.

The agreement provided for a cease-fire and withdrawal of the armies two kilometers from the existing battle line that ran northeasterly from a point just below the 38th parallel on the west coast to a point some 30 miles above it on the east. A neutral commission (Sweden, Switzerland, Czechoslovakia, and Poland) would supervise enforcement of the armistice terms. Willing prisoners were to be exchanged and repatriated within 60 days. Disposition of others who still remained unwilling was to be

Crises, Conflicts, and Coexistence 245

settled by a political conference, but this fell through when the UN, on January 24, 1954, began releasing the 22,000 Chinese and North Korean prisoners who had refused repatriation. Most of the Chinese were transported to Formosa. Three hundred fifty UN prisoners, including 21 Americans, refused repatriation. In all, 15 nations, other than the United States and South Korea, had sent armed forces to participate in the fighting. As of February 1951, the United States supplied 48 percent of the manpower and the Republic of Korea 43 percent. Overall troop contributions for the period of the war were: Republic of Korea, 500,000; United States, 300,000; others, 40,000. Of 411,000 casualties (killed, wounded, captured, missing), the Republic of Korea suffered 63 percent, the United States 33 percent, others 4 percent. The Chinese and North Korean losses, unreported, were quite substantial.

No War, No Peace, in Korea

The United Nations had tired of Syngman Rhee's demand that Korea be unified by force, and armistice conditions—neither peace nor war—continued to prevail. The United States and the Republic of Korea agreed to a treaty of mutual defense, similar to others being negotiated in the Pacific area, on October 1, 1953. Korea consented to the stationing of UN armed forces "in and about" its territory. Two American army divisions remained in Korea, nominally as part of a UN force, and the United States continued to provide the Republic of Korea with economic and military aid.[12] Relations between South Korea and the U.S.-UN military command and North Korea remained uneasy after the armistice in 1953, with both parties guarding their respective sides of the demilitarized zone (DMZ) that straddled the cease-fire line. The neutral commission charged with supervising the armistice's enforcement failed to function, and a military buildup with modernization of equipment, contrary to armistice terms, proceeded apace on both sides. Spokesmen of the two military commands, U.S.-UN and North Korean, constituting the Military Armistice Commission, met from time to time in Panmunjom on the armistice line.

Each Korean government has aspired to unite the country, but on its own terms. South Korea's endeavors to that end were limited, by UN resolution and by its dependence on the United States, to peaceful means. When the United States became deeply involved in the Vietnam War, Premier Kim Il Sung apparently saw an opportunity to move toward his goal by force, by stirring up in South Korea the kind of guerrilla warfare that the United States found so difficult in South Vietnam. Beginning late in 1966, there was a sharp increase of infiltrations through the DMZ and around it by water, culminating in a series of dramatic incidents in 1968–1969, which could easily have brought renewal of the war. On January 21, 1968, a suicide squad of 31 North Korean terrorists penetrated the DMZ and reached Seoul, with the mission of assassinating President Park. Their leaders were captured less than a mile from the presidential palace. Two days later, the U.S. naval intelligence ship *Pueblo* was attacked and captured with its officers and crew. After 11 months of negotiations, the 82 officers and men of the *Pueblo* (and the body of one killed at the time of the capture) were released.[13] Before President Richard Nixon had been in office three months, there was another crisis. On April 14, 1969, an unarmed U.S. naval intelligence plane with a crew of 31 was shot down by North Korean planes over the Sea of Japan, at an estimated distance of 90 miles from the Korean coast. Nixon confined his response to a strong protest to the commission at Panmunjom and, briefly, the dispatch of a large naval task force into the Sea of Japan. There was no repetition of the incident.

There was, furthermore, a distinct tapering off of communist infiltration and other encounters along the DMZ. And though talk of war was still in the air, there were indications that Premier Kim Il Sung had adopted a new approach, although his basic objective of unification remained the same. In 1972, the North Korean leader opened negotiations with the South aimed at a peaceful political reunification and began bargaining about the reuniting of families. Unfortunately, as American operations receded in Vietnam, North Korean tactics changed. American personnel were set upon, elaborate tunnels were dug below the DMZ presumably for invasion purposes, commando raids were initiated, and Kim Il Sung traveled to Beijing to secure military assistance. The North Koreans, in August 1976, dismissed Secretary of State Henry Kissinger's invitation a year earlier to discuss reducing tensions. At the same time, the North Korean leadership intensified its effort to force the withdrawal of the United States by depicting the presence of American forces as a source of tension to the stability of the peninsula. Thus, the stage was set for one of the more bizarre incidents of the Cold War. On August 18, 1976, a UN work crew of five Korean laborers accompanied by three UN Command officers (two Americans and one South Korean) and a seven-man security force entered a joint area at Panmunjom to prune a tree obstructing the line of sight between two UN Command guard posts. Shortly after the party began work, North Korean demanded the work stop. The UN work crew refused, the North Koreans called for reinforcements, and 30 North Koreans attacked the UN party with axes and metal pikes in an incident, lasting less than five minutes, that caused American casualties, including the deaths of two U.S. Army officers. The United States' response was swift and unequivocal. President Ford ordered the deployment of the F-4 aircraft from Okinawa, and the F-lll's from Idaho, to Korea; dispatched the Midway task force to the region; raised the nation's alert status; and initiated daily B-52 flights from Guam to Korea. Moreover, and in spite of Kim II Sung's decision to put the forces at his disposal on a state of combat readiness, President Ford, who was fighting for his political life at the Republican nominating convention in Kansas City, ordered that the tree in question be cut down on August 21. Impressed with the American show of force, North Korea's leader conveyed his regrets to the UN command several days later, and the crisis was weathered.[14]

From Peaceful Coexistence to Détente

The death in March 1953 of Marshal Josef Stalin was the prelude to the rise to power in Moscow of more flexible leadership, especially Nikita S. Khrushchev. In March 1958, he took over the premiership from Nikolai A. Bulganin. At the Twentieth Congress of the Communist Party of the Soviet Union meeting in Moscow, during February 1956, Khrushchev secretly and roundly condemned Stalin's bloodthirsty methods and outdated policies. He enunciated a policy of "peaceful coexistence," repudiating the Leninist doctrine of inevitable war between the communist and capitalist societies, declaring that communism could achieve its victory by peacefully demonstrating its superiority. The Soviet government, meanwhile, having negotiated the Warsaw Pact in response to NATO, signed the treaty on May 15, 1955, ending the occupation of Austria and accepting on the same day an invitation from the United States, Great Britain, and France for a summit meeting of the Big Four heads of government at Geneva in July.

At Geneva, July 18 to 23, 1955, President Eisenhower, Prime Minister Anthony Eden (who had recently succeeded Winston Churchill), French premier Edgar Faure, Soviet premier Bulganin, their foreign ministers, and other dignitaries (including, of course, Party Secretary Khrushchev) met face to face in an effort to resolve critical East-West difficulties. The meeting had been heralded from Moscow and Washington as promising agreement, and its sessions were conducted in a tone of cordiality. On substantive matters, however, no agreement was achieved, as neither side was ready to offer concessions. On disarmament, the West considered effective inspection essential; the Soviets held it inadmissible, often because they did not wish to expose their weaknesses. President Eisenhower's proposal that East and West exchange "blueprints" of their armed forces and permit mutual "open skies" aerial inspection of their territory was rejected as being a form of espionage. (No similar objection was raised when orbital "spy" satellites were introduced.) Only on such minor matters as freer cultural exchanges was there any meeting of minds. An important characteristic of Soviet policy after Stalin was a relaxation of Moscow's control of communist parties and governments in neighboring states. The dissident Marshal Tito of Yugoslavia, after playing host to Khrushchev, was welcomed on a visit to Moscow and assured that the Kremlin accepted the principle of "national Communism," which he espoused. Encouraged by this display of conciliation toward Yugoslavia, the Polish Communists installed a pronounced anti-Stalinist, Wladyslaw Gomulka, as Party secretary and dissuaded Khrushchev from interfering. Still communist and continuing to adhere to the Warsaw Alliance, the Polish regime had successfully defied the dictatorship of the Kremlin.

From 1955 to 1963, relations of the United States and its NATO allies with the Soviet bloc, so far as Europe was concerned, involved a series of alternating crises. The first serious crisis after the Geneva summit meeting of 1955 was a dual one produced by Soviet suppression of Hungary's attempted anticommunist revolution and by Israel, France, and Great Britain's attack on Egypt. In Hungary, anti-Soviet and antigovernment riots in Budapest led to the formation of a new government on October 24, 1956, headed by Imre Nagy. A few days later, Nagy, though a communist, admitted noncommunists to his government. On November 1, the government repudiated the Warsaw Alliance, declared Hungary a neutral state, and appealed to the United Nations for assistance. Moscow reacted violently to Hungary's secession from the communist bloc. After temporarily withdrawing its tanks and troops from Budapest, it sent them back in force, suppressed the popular uprising in the city, and installed a new communist government headed by Janos Kadar that invited Russian assistance. Nagy, initially taking refuge in the Yugoslav embassy, was enticed out by hints of office in the new government, seized, abducted to Rumania, and later executed. Weeks of fighting followed, but a virtually unarmed populace was no match for Soviet tanks. No aid came from the West, for the cost of doing so would likely be considered by Moscow as an act of war. The collapse of the insurrection was inevitable.

In Washington, President Dwight D. Eisenhower had been elected in 1952 after a campaign in which the Republican Party had condemned the "containment" policy of the Democrats as "negative, futile, and immoral" and promised to "again make liberty into a beacon light of hope that will penetrate the dark places." "Liberation" of peoples under the communist yoke was to replace "containment" of communism. Whether the Hungarians had been encouraged to hope for aid by these campaign declarations and by official Voice of America and unofficial Radio Free Europe broadcasts is impossible to say. Neither President Eisenhower nor Secretary of State John Foster Dulles intended to encourage a popular rebellion against impossible odds or to assist such a rebellion at the risk of war with the Soviet Union. Action by Washington was limited to the expression of sympathy for the Hungarian people and the offering of asylum in the United States to Hungarian refugees.

The next serious crisis concerned Berlin. In a speech of November 10, 1958, and in notes to the United States, Great Britain, and France on the 27th, Khrushchev demanded an end to the occupation of West Berlin by the three Western powers. He insisted on a solution within six months, threatening otherwise to make a separate peace treaty with East Germany and leave the Allies to negotiate their rights in Berlin with, and their access to, an East German government they did not recognize. Any attempt to maintain their position by force, Khrushchev warned, would be met by the full power of the Warsaw Alliance. The Soviet ultimatum received a unified response from the Western powers. In Paris, December 14, the foreign ministers of the United States, Great Britain, France, and West Germany joined in an unqualified rejection of the Soviet ultimatum, and the NATO Council endorsed their position two days later. Briefly stated, the Western argument was that the Soviet Union had no right by unilateral action to cancel the rights of the Western Allies in West Berlin, which were theirs by virtue of the common victory over Germany. The Allies also emphasized their obligation to maintain the freedom of the more than two million people of West Berlin. They expressed their desire to see the Berlin question settled as a part of the German question as a whole and repeated their proposal that Germany be unified through the holding of free elections in both parts of the divided country.

Faced with determined and united Western opposition, Khrushchev first withdrew his time limit. From May 11 to June 30 and again from July 13 to August 5, 1959, the foreign ministers met at Geneva, but reached no agreement on this or on any of the other major issues. President Eisenhower, who had at first made some preliminary agreement a prerequisite of another summit meeting, now waived that requirement. He invited Nikita Khrushchev—now chairman of the Council of Ministers of the U.S.S.R., or premier—to visit him at Camp David, the presidential retreat in Maryland. The Camp David meeting, from September 25 to 27, 1959, climaxed 10 days in which Khrushchev toured the United States and proposed to the United Nations General Assembly a plan for general and complete disarmament. His conversations with Eisenhower were marked by cordiality. Their joint *communiqué* stated that the talks had been useful in mutually clarifying the positions of the two leaders and should thus contribute "to the achievement of a just and lasting peace." The two had agreed that the question of general disarmament was "the most important one facing the world today." On the Berlin question they had agreed that, subject to the approval of the other parties concerned, negotiations should be reopened in the hope of reaching a satisfactory solution. It was also agreed, Eisenhower told a news conference, and Khrushchev concurred, "that these negotiations should not be prolonged indefinitely but there could be no fixed time limit on them." The leaders rejected the use of force in settling "outstanding international questions."

In December, after the Camp David meeting, Great Britain and France joined the United States in proposing a summit meeting of the Big Four. The Russians accepted, and they would meet on May 16, 1960, at Paris. In the months prior to the Paris meeting, the "spirit of Camp David" was clearly deteriorating. There were renewed threats from Khrushchev of drastic action if the Berlin question were not soon settled, and equal assurances from Washington that the United States would never desert the people of West Berlin. Prospects of agreement, growing dim already, were completely destroyed by the U-2 incident early in May. On May 1, a high-flying U.S. reconnaissance airplane, a U-2, was shot down while on a flight across Russia and the pilot, Francis Gary Powers, was captured unharmed, along with his photographic and other equipment. Khrushchev adroitly held back details while the State Department tried to explain the presence of the U-2 over Soviet territory result from a navigational error. Finally, Secretary of State Christian A. Herter admitted that the U-2 flight was but one of a number of such flights, conducted to photograph Soviet installations. The president confirmed Herter's admission, and both men defended this type of espionage as a means of guarding against surprise attack, necessitated by Soviet secretiveness. Khrushchev arrived at Paris and refused to negotiate unless President Eisenhower apologized for the U-2 flight and agreed to punish those responsible for it. He was not mollified by the president's assurance that there would be no more U-2 flights during his term of office or by the conciliatory efforts of President de Gaulle and Prime Minister Macmillan. Eisenhower walked out and the summit abruptly ended on May 17, one day after its opening.[15]

Chairman Khrushchev temporarily put aside his threat to conclude a separate peace treaty with the East German regime, hoping to find Eisenhower's successor more yielding. In June 1961, Khrushchev and President John F. Kennedy met for a two-day conference at Vienna that the American found traumatic. The Soviet chairman lectured the young president on the German situation, repeating his earlier ultimatum with the six months' time limit. Unless within that time the four governments could agree on a peace treaty or treaties with Germany, united or divided, the Soviets would conclude a separate treaty with the German Democratic Republic, and occupation rights in West Berlin would end. West Berlin might continue as a "free city," and either neutral UN troops or "token forces" of the three Western powers and the Soviet Union might be stationed there, but it seemed clear that the city's contacts with the West would be at the mercy of the East German authorities.[16] Kennedy replied, as had the Eisenhower administration, that the United States had, together with its British and French Allies, "a fundamental political and moral obligation" to "maintain the freedom of over two million people in West Berlin." Any attempt to hinder the fulfillment of that obligation "would have the gravest effects upon international peace and security and endanger the lives and well-being of millions of people."

In a nationwide broadcast on July 25, Kennedy told the country: "We cannot and will not permit the Communists to drive us out of Berlin, either gradually or by force." Although, he concluded, "we do not want to fight ... we have fought before." Kennedy announced that he would ask Congress for a $3.25 billion increase in the defense budget for army, navy, and air force manpower, and for authority to call various reserve units to active duty. By increasing the conventional forces at home and in Europe, the president intended "to have a wider choice than humiliation or all-out nuclear action."[17] Congress gave Kennedy what he asked for, and an additional force of 45,000 troops was sent to Europe. France and West Germany also strengthened their NATO forces. Whether or not he expected these warlike gestures, Khrushchev again dropped the time limit for a Berlin settlement. On August 13, 1961, the East German regime began construction of the wall separating East from West Berlin, thus effectively putting an end to West Berlin's important role as an "escape hatch" from communist East Germany. The United States protested, but did not press the issue. At the end of August, since the Eisenhower administration could not find a formula to end nuclear testing, Khrushchev announced a new series of atmospheric nuclear tests, ending an informal moratorium begun in 1958. The United States and Great Britain hesitated little in conducting its own tests.

The United States and Central and Latin America

President Kennedy on March 13, 1961, proposed his Alliance for Progress to Latin American ambassadors assembled at the White House.

This program implemented the Act of Bogota, signed by 19 nations in September 1960, which established a cooperative program—including a 10-year American pledge of $20 billion—for Latin American economic development. Thus by 1970, "the need for massive outside help will have passed" and each American state would be "the master of its own revolution of hope and progress." The Alliance for Progress, like the Act of Bogota, attached to the promise of aid the requirement for Latin American economic and political reform. What troubled the alliance was its lack of a standard to determine when recipient countries had taken adequate steps toward reform. Moreover, U.S. special interests placed a variety of obstacles before Latin American nations' exports and imports. These roadblocks, combined with the unwillingness of established Latin American elites to give up their privileged positions, doomed the program from the outset. Despite American efforts to establish task forces on education, land and tax reform, and low-cost housing—the essential ingredients in social progress—the alliance produced little social change and less democracy. Military coups in Brazil, Argentina, and Peru during the first year further eroded the impact of the alliance. On October 6, 1963, Edwin A. Martin, assistant secretary of state for Latin American Affairs, regretfully reported that the fundamental principle of the alliance was beyond attainment and acknowledged that military coups were a traditional part of Latin American politics. Latin Americans understood that the alliance came in response to the administration's fear of Cuban-based communism. They soon discovered that such economic and technical assistance programs as the Peace Corps and the alliance for Progress, despite their humanitarian overtones, embraced Cold War objectives by seeking to render the hemisphere more resistant to revolutionary pressures.[18]

Fidel Castro's dictatorial methods, his nationalization program, his ties to the Soviet bloc, his support of revolutionary movements in Latin America, and his intemperate denunciations of U.S. "imperialism" brought Cuban-American relations to the breaking point in April 1961. The Eisenhower administration in 1960 had ended diplomatic relations with Cuba and handed Kennedy a poorly planned counterrevolutionary movement, designed to overthrow the Castro regime in the spring of 1961. At the time of Kennedy's inauguration, some 2,000 to 3,000 rebel Cuban refugees were training in the United States and Guatemala for an invasion of the island.[19] With the Cuban people living under the duress of communism domination, the guerrilla invasion would assuredly ignite a revolution and free the country. Several American officials had doubts about the CIA's plan. General Edward Lansdale, the government's leading expert on counterinsurgency, told an uneasy Paul Nitze, now the assistant secretary of defense for International Security Affairs, that the operation was too poorly managed to succeed. Yet Nitze supported the project, as he explained in his memoirs: "The Soviet Union had inserted itself in our backyard... in the form of the Castro regime in Cuba. Like a spreading cancer, it should, if possible, be excised from the Americas."[20] Kennedy doubted the wisdom of the invasion, but grudgingly consented after insisting that he would never commit American forces to the assault.[21] On April 17, 1961, the Cuban refugee assault brigade struck the Cienaja de Zapata swamps of Las Villas Province (Bay of Pigs) on the south coast of Cuba. There was no popular uprising. Kennedy's refusal to back the invasion with U.S. airpower assured Castro's control of the skies. Cuban regulars quickly defeated the vastly outnumbered invading forces—the brigade's losses were 114 men dead and 1,189 captured. The Castro regime was more solidly in power than ever before.[22]

The president accepted blame for the fiasco, but lamented to his special counsel, Theodore C. Sorensen, "How could I have been so stupid to let them go ahead."[23] Yet so favorable was the public response to such Executive candor that Kennedy's popularity soared. Upon reflection, Kennedy believed that any unilateral aggression "would have been contrary to our traditions and to our international obligations." However, "should it ever appear that the inter-American doctrine of non-interference merely conceals or excuses a policy of nonaction... then I want it clearly understood that this Government will not hesitate in meeting its primary obligations which are to the security of our Nation!"[24]

Whether Cuba, despite its ties to Moscow, merited Washington's concern was questionable, for as a threat to hemispheric stability, Cuba was no match for the 200 million Latin Americans who lived in misery—the real source of revolutionary pressures. During 1962, nonetheless, the Kennedy administration embarked on a variety of maneuvers to weaken the Castro regime.[25] The administration sent sabotage units of Cuban émigrés into Cuba under a covert action plan called Operation Mongoose. After the necessary internal preparations, guerrilla operations would begin in August and September 1962; during October, an open revolt would establish the new government. Attorney General Robert Kennedy, determined to remove Castro after the Bay of Pigs, was Mongoose's driving force.[26] The Kennedy administration never accepted Senator J. William Fulbright's assessment of the Cuban threat. Earlier, having learned of the impending ill-fated Bay of Pigs invasion, Fulbright urged the president to "Remember always the Castro regime is a thorn in the flesh, but it is not a dagger in the heart."[27]

Kennedy's assassination was a devastating blow to many people throughout Latin America. "The young, dashing president with... the beautiful wife who spoke Spanish... during their visits to countries in the region," as a noted historian has written, "had captured the imagination and the heart of people rich and poor, old and young, from Mexico to the Southern Cone." Kennedy's Alliance for Progress program, which was greeted passively by the American public, had created widespread anticipation among those who hoped it marked a shift from authoritarian to democratic governments.[28]

The Lyndon Johnson administration took a more pragmatic and technical view of the Alliance for Progress. The new assistant secretary for Inter-American Affairs, Thomas C. Mann, insisted progress toward social and political democracy had to be evolutionary, not revolutionary. He assumed that Castro was linked to any Latin American political disturbance and, in March 1964, redefined the alliance's essential objectives to: "(1) foster economic growth and be neutral on internal social reforms; (2) protect U.S. private investments in the hemisphere; (3) show no preference, through aid or otherwise, for representative democratic institutions; and (4) oppose communism." Cooperation with authoritarian or military governments was fine as long they were not communist-controlled. In a December 30, 1964, *U.S. News and World Report* article, Mann emphasized the administration's anti-Castro line by calling Cuba a "cancer" that the United States "needed to isolate," while warning that some social reforms had frightened private investment.[29]

Both the Kennedy and Johnson administrations worried about possible communist influence or domination of other Latin American governments. In January 1963, the Standing Group on Cuba within Kennedy's National Security Council concluded that the alliance was "not strong enough to serve as the first line of defense against subversion" by radicals. Johnson and his advisers were constantly concerned about political instability in what they referred to as the Caribbean Danger Zone.[30] The 1964 Panamanian incident, which erupted in January between Panamanian nationals and Canal Zone residents over flying the Panama flag, demonstrated the administration's new rigidity. When President Roberto Chiari insisted that the original treaties governing the canal must be renegotiated, Johnson refused. Mann was told that under no circumstances would Washington be pressured to negotiate, for as presidential adviser McGeorge Bundy put it, "we cannot let our foreign policy be governed by Molotov cocktails." The State Department drafted an agreement that provided for negotiation of new terms, recognized Panamanian sovereignty, and stipulated a termination date. Discussions over the new treaties remained in limbo for a decade until President Jimmy Carter acted on them.[31]

Santo Domingo presented the ultimate test of the Johnson administration's anti-Castro policy. That Caribbean country's immediate troubles began in December 1962 when Juan Bosch, a reformist intellectual, overwhelmingly won election as president. American officials were not impressed with him. Predictably, in September 1963, a military coup overthrew and exiled Bosch, but was scarcely more effective. On April 24, 1965, a few Dominican army units favoring Bosch initiated an armed uprising, with communists and other radicals entering the chaotic fray.[32] President Johnson, on April 28, landed marines and naval personnel ostensibly to protect American lives and restore order, but actually to quash the communists and Bosch supporters. Mann had concluded that the rebel cause was communist-dominated; only its defeat, he warned, would prevent another communist encroachment in the Caribbean.[33] The administration did not want "another Cuba." On May 3, the president commented that he "didn't propose to sit here" in his rocking chair and "let the Communists set up any government in the Western Hemisphere." This bald declaration of Latin America as the United States' dominant sphere of interest has been referred to as Johnson's "rocking chair doctrine." Shortly, however, the administration's hemispheric anticommunist program began to unravel as the U.S. embassy's lists of alleged communists proved largely incorrect. The president dispatched Ellsworth Bunker, ambassador to the Organization of American States (OAS), to the Dominican Republic, where, with infinite patience, skill, and OAS support, he negotiated an interim government.[34]

By the end of the decade, the ongoing contributions of the Agency for International Development and the expansion of the Inter-American Development Bank allowed the Alliance for Progress to leave a permanent legacy; but hemispheric relations continued to be diminished by the fear of Cuban subversion. The persistent, knee-jerk rejection of all Cuban proposals, often for domestic political reasons, carried a penalty. It was the ultimate irony that the United States came to be an almost compulsive opponent to reform-minded governments, with a poorly managed endorsement of authoritarian and military ones "whose only claim to legitimacy was fervent anticommunism and the violent suppression of dissidents."[35]

The Missile Crisis of 1962

The following year, as the second Berlin crisis was fading into history, 1962, marked the most dangerous confrontation of the Cold War when

Khrushchev sent missiles to Cuba in early September, where they were undetected for a month. Among the factors governing his decision to send intermediate- and short-range missiles to Cuba was the desire to establish a superpower strategic nuclear balance prior to the fielding of Soviet intercontinental ballistic missiles. Khrushchev was also motivated in his decision to send missiles to Cuba by several other factors such as dissatisfaction with Berlin's divided status, U.S. missiles based in Turkey across the Black Sea from Khrushchev's summer residence, and the Sino-Soviet contest for leadership of the worldwide communist movement. Later, it was suggested that the Soviet missile deployment in Cuba was designed primarily to defend Cuba and, secondarily, to correct the balance of power. Few Cubans knew of the formal arrangements; however, Castro found it difficult to refrain from boasting about his new military strength. There were, meanwhile, plenty of public hints of the new missile arrangement, but the CIA did not take them seriously.

Explaining to his contemporaries why he sent missiles to defend Cuba after the ill-fated Bay of Pigs episode, Khrushchev elaborated: "We didn't want to unleash a war, we just wanted to frighten them, to restrain the United States in regard to Cuba." When the Americans finally discovered the missiles, he could not comprehend why Washington became so upset, because the United States had military bases next door to the Soviet Union. If the Americans attempted to invade Cuba to destroy the missile sites, he explained to his colleagues, they would be met with dozens of short-range, nuclear-armed missiles capable of annihilating an invading force. "The tragic thing is that they can attack us, and we will respond," he worried. "This could all end up in a big war." Khrushchev had worried that some American leader "might think" that given "a seventeen-to-one superiority" in intercontinental ballistic missiles (ICBMs), a "first strike was possible." To Moscow, this was an "impossible" situation. American commentators have viewed the episode differently. "I do not know what insanity caused the Soviets to send missiles to Cuba," one later wrote, "after showing commendable caution about the deployment of this gadgetry in far less dangerous locations." But he neglected to point out that such caution was "not paralleled" by Washington and NATO when they located tactical nuclear weapons in Europe and Jupiter missiles on Turkish soil across the Black Sea from the Soviet Union. Kennedy's advisers promoted the thesis that Khrushchev was testing Kennedy and America's willingness to respond to an aggressive Soviet move. Much later a Khrushchev aide acknowledged that Kennedy often was perceived as "weak."[36]

The president secretly called together a small group of high-level advisers, a group known as Ex Com, the Executive Committee of the National

Security Council. The Ex Com immediately rejected the notion that the Soviets merely meant to protect Cuba. Some concluded, logically enough, that Khrushchev mainly sought to redress the Soviet Union's exposed strategic inferiority. The Joint Chiefs accepted that judgment; but for them, the nearness of Cuba was sufficient to change the strategic balance. Other Ex Com members detected little increase in Soviet first strike or retaliatory capabilities from Cuban-based missiles, for as Secretary of Defense Robert McNamara declared, "a missile is a missile. It makes no difference whether you are killed by a missile fired from the Soviet Union or from Cuba." What was at stake, the Ex Com finally agreed, was the nation's will and credibility—a rationale that appeared frequently in Washington. Neither friends nor enemies, at home or abroad, it was argued, would take Washington's pledges seriously if the Soviets were permitted, uncontested, to place offensive missiles in Cuba. At first, several members of Ex Com—including bankers, lawyers, and diplomats—advocated an air strike to eliminate the missile bases or an actual invasion of the island. The Joint Chiefs confidently insisted that an invasion of Cuba could be undertaken without embarking on a "general war" with the Soviet Union; but Kennedy mistrusted them because he believed that they had misled him with the ill-prepared, poorly planned Bay of Pigs intervention. He was particularly uneasy with the air force chief of staff, General Curtis LeMay, who led a force that held 3,000 nuclear bombs, after hearing one of the general's bloodthirsty briefings about how to deal with America's enemies—bomb them back to the Stone Age. LeMay, in return, derided the president's fear that a miscalculation could end in a nuclear holocaust, stating that the president's concerns smacked of appeasement. The general's resolution of the strategic dilemma was simple: since the United States possessed overwhelming nuclear superiority, the Kremlin would not launch a nuclear conflict that it would likely lose. Kennedy, however, found it difficult to understand that the Soviets would just stand by and ignore the deaths of hundreds of their soldiers. "These brass hats have one great advantage in their favor," Kennedy said. "If we listen to them and do what they want us to do, none of us will be alive later to tell them that they were wrong."[37]

Kennedy's nationwide telecast on October 22 embodied the official assumption that the Soviet missiles endangered the hemisphere, and, unlike U.S. missiles in Europe, their mission was offensive, not defensive. He had gradually endorsed the Ex Com concept of a stop and search blockade or quarantine to isolate the Soviet forces in Cuba. The president's central warning was clear: "It shall be the policy of this Nation to regard any nuclear missile launched from Cuba against any nation in the Western Hemisphere as an attack by the Soviet Union on the United States, requiring a full retaliatory response upon the Soviet Union." In Europe, the alliance held firm as Britain, France, and West Germany pledged their support. In a display of common sense, Khrushchev agreed to withdraw his missiles, while Kennedy authorized removal of the obsolete U.S. Jupiter missiles from Turkey and pledged the United States would not invade Cuba. The resolution of the missile crisis, without a nuclear exchange, was a close-run affair. Shortly afterwards, President Kennedy and Chairman Khrushchev agreed to a limited nuclear test ban and a "hot line" to allow them to communicate with each other directly, instead of through intermediaries.

The U.S.-Soviet Quest for Détente

After the settlement of the Cuban missile crisis, the United States and the U.S.S.R. accepted the nuclear stalemate as a reality. The questions of Germany and Berlin were not settled, but Chancellor Adenauer's successors were less insistent on immediate German reunification, while the Soviets refrained from creating further crises over Berlin. Under these circumstances Presidents Lyndon B. Johnson (1963–1969), Richard M. Nixon (1969–1974), Gerald R. Ford (1974–1977), and Jimmy Carter (1977–1980) sought to improve relations with the Soviet Union and, as Johnson phrased it, to "build bridges" of trade and understanding with the smaller nations of Eastern Europe. The Vietnam War and the Arab-Israeli wars of 1967 and 1973 kept tensions alive between the superpowers. Moscow viewed the war in Vietnam as a "war of national liberation" and a war of U.S. "aggression" and "imperialism." The Soviets and Chinese provided war matériel to the armies of North Vietnam. Premier Alexei Kosygin, who together with Communist Party chief Leonid I. Brezhnev replaced Khrushchev in 1964, told the editors of *Life* (February 2, 1968) that "we [the Soviets], for our part will do all we can so that the U.S. does not defeat Vietnam." "American aggression," he added, "will be met with growing rebuff." Accordingly, attempts by both Johnson and Nixon to persuade Moscow and Beijing to assist in bringing Hanoi to accept United States peace terms provided, on the whole, limited results. President Nixon ended America's commitment to South Vietnam in 1973 with the signing of the Paris Peace Accords, but the North Vietnamese military successfully unified the country in 1975 as the Americans withdrew from Indochina. The superpowers were frequently drawn to conflicts in the Middle East, especially the Arab-Israeli wars, during which the Soviets established a large naval presence in the

Mediterranean, where it shadowed the movements of the American Sixth Fleet. These activities, and those of the Security Council, did little to resolve the persistent Arab-Israeli conflict.

Where the United States and the Soviet Union did succeed in reducing Cold War tensions was in their efforts to employ diplomacy and political agreements to slow the arms race and to dampen the impact of weapons of mass destruction. President Kennedy and Soviet Chairman Khrushchev initiated the process with the 1963 treaty banning of nuclear tests in the atmosphere that removed a threat to global health; however, it had not halted the proliferation of nuclear weaponry or the superpowers' quest for more sophisticated ones. "I am haunted," President Kennedy worried in 1963, "by the feeling that by 1970, unless we are successful, there may be 10 nuclear powers instead of four, and by 1975, 15 or 20." In addition to the original four nuclear weapons states—the United States, Britain, Russia, and France—six other states—China, Israel, India, Pakistan, North Korea, and South Africa—would develop nuclear weapons, the latter state scrapping its weapons and means of producing them. A number of states that at one time considered a nuclear weapons program, or even began one, subsequently halted their efforts.

President Johnson reenergized the diplomatic efforts to reduce the prospects of global proliferation of nuclear weaponry. Following the People's Republic of China's first nuclear test on October 16, 1964, Washington and Moscow responded to the UN General Assembly's 1965 call to prevent nuclear proliferation. Each cooperated with the Eighteen Nation Disarmament Committee that drafted the Non-Proliferation Treaty (NPT) of 1968 that drew widespread adherence. The nonnuclear countries argued that this pact must not divide the world into nuclear "haves" and "have-nots," but rather balance obligations. Nonnuclear weapons states pledged not to acquire nuclear weapons in exchange for access to peaceful nuclear technology and a pledge from the nuclear weapons states to pursue nuclear disarmament. The task of inspection was placed under the International Atomic Energy Agency (IAEA), which supervised the peaceful use of nuclear energy and the exchange of necessary technology. At the same time, Washington and Moscow reluctantly agreed "to pursue negotiations in good faith on effective measures relating to cessation of the nuclear arms race at an early date and to nuclear disarmament, and on a treaty on general and complete disarmament under strict and effective international control."

In time, the NPT emerged as the main component of a "regime": the IAEA; negotiations for a comprehensive nuclear test ban; and regional Nuclear-Weapons-Free Zones. Early proposals for the latter originated from the Polish foreign minister Rapacki, in 1957 and 1962, that sought to eliminate nuclear weapons from Poland, Czechoslovakia, West and East Germany, but they came to naught. The multilateral Antarctic Treaty of 1959 excluded a specific geographical area from major power competition and, at the same time, provided the confidence for future such pacts. The Treaty of Tlatelolco of 1967 to denuclearize Latin America was the first of several such agreements. The significant Outer Space Treaty of 1967, a UN-sponsored, multilateral pact, committed its signatories "not to place in orbit around the Earth any objects carrying nuclear weapons or any other kinds of weapons of mass destruction, install such weapons on celestial bodies, or station such weapons in outer space in any other manner." In addition, the article prohibited "the establishment of military bases, installations and fortifications, the testing of any type of weapons and the conduct of military maneuvers on celestial bodies." The Seabed Treaty of 1971 prevented installation of nuclear weapons on the ocean floor beyond national territorial waters.[38]

The first multilateral efforts sought to bring the entire range of nuclear weaponry under control—the Baruch Plan (1946)—and Soviet and American proposals for General and Complete Disarmament (1962) were unsuccessful. Following their embarrassment from a lack of offensive missiles during the "Cuban" missile crisis, the Soviets launched an intense effort to build a fleet of intercontinental ballistic missiles (ICBMs) to offset the United States' superiority. At the same time, both superpowers were in the early phase of developing defensive antiballistic missile (ABM) systems. In the United States, the Nixon administration constructed a primitive "light" ABM system, known as "Safeguard," for defense of missile sites; however, it was dismantled as obsolete shortly after becoming operational. To lessen the dangers of an unintentional nuclear conflict, the superpowers turned to diplomacy as they continued seeking more and better weapons.

The major stumbling block to any treaty limiting or reducing weaponry was Washington's insistence on "on-site inspection" to verify compliance. How could an adversary be reasonably confident that the other was faithfully honoring its agreements? After all, the increasingly sophisticated nuclear weapon systems fostered a mutual fear of a surprise attack, or "first strike." Early in the early 1950s, Presidents Harry Truman and Eisenhower were so desperate to gain information regarding Soviet military capabilities that they authorized the U.S. Air Force to overfly Soviet territory. Ignoring international law, Washington officials on one occasion sent its RB-47Es on 156 missions over Soviet territory from March 21 to May 10, 1956. With the intelligence-gathering missions completed, the Eisenhower administration dispatched a diplomatic note to Moscow expressing regret that navigational errors led to the intrusion into Soviet airspace. Subsequently, the United States employed the U-2 airplane to continue ferreting out and photographing Soviet military installations until 1960, when Francis Gary Powers was shot down.

Technology finally resolved the issue. An American "spy" satellite began operating on a regular basis, in August 1960, and the Soviet Union was employing its own space reconnaissance vehicles by 1962. Both superpowers now embraced the age of national technical verification—the Soviets perhaps less enthusiastically—that opened the way to arms control agreements on strategic weaponry. With the advent of modern electronics, photography, space vehicles, and other devices, "national technical means" added to the effectiveness of self-monitoring. Such devices could verify, with reasonable accuracy, both the quantitative and qualitative features of strategic weaponry, particularly the numbers and characteristics of ballistic missiles, providing information vital to negotiations and to the monitoring of actual agreements. In ironic fashion, the sophisticated technologies developed by the superpowers as part of their military competition had contributed greatly to progress in verification techniques. The "billions of dollars and rubles" that had been invested, according to Allan Krass, "gave each side a remarkably accurate picture of the military capabilities of its adversary." By early 1965, satellite cameras could count antiballistic missile systems, land-based strategic ballistic missiles, aircraft on the ground, and submarines in port with reasonable accuracy. Some minor evasions might take place, but a major violation would be detected as the Central Intelligence Agency proved that it could monitor Soviet missile deployments with a substantial degree of accuracy. In an October 1967 speech, Assistant Secretary of Defense Paul Warnke urged the Soviets to discuss limiting strategic weapons, stipulating that the United States would consider an agreement that would be verified by "our own unilateral capability" rather than on-site inspections.[39]

Having witnessed the difficulty of reaching a multilateral agreement, the superpowers shifted their focus to a series of bilateral agreements. From these negotiations gradually emerged limits on nuclear weapons systems and, much later, the reduction of them. The first was the 1972 Interim Agreement on Strategic Offensive Weapons (SALT I) that established, among other restrictions, a quantitative limit on both intercontinental ballistic missiles—the United States 1,054 ICBMs, the Soviets 1,618 ICBMs operational and under construction—and submarine-launched ballistic missiles (SLBMs). SALT I focused on the numbers of missile or launchers rather than on warheads, and allowed deployment of multiple independently targeted reentry vehicles (MIRVs) that eventually expanded greatly the number of warheads in both nation's arsenals. SALT I did not secure reductions, and its ceilings were higher than existing forces, thereby allowing the deployment of additional ballistic missiles. Article V of the SALT I pact declared that: "Each Party shall use national technical means of verification at its disposal in a manner consistent with generally recognized principles of international law;" that "Each Party undertakes not to interfere with the national technical means of verification of the other Party"; and that "Each Party undertakes not to use deliberate concealment measures which impede verification by national technical means." The 1972 Anti-Ballistic Missile Treaty, negotiated concurrently with SALT I, stipulated that each side could deploy up to 100 ABM interceptors at each of two sites, later reduced to one site. Although both parties had spent substantial funds to develop ABM systems, their efforts bore little fruit because of doubtful operational technology and the increasing numbers of warheads, especially on MIRVed missiles. The ABM Treaty also endorsed national technical means for verification purposes. Significantly, this was the first mention in any arms control treaty of prohibitions on hindering or limiting verification efforts. Noteworthy as well was the creation of the Standing Consultative Commission to quietly examine questions regarding the treaty's implementation. President Gerald Ford and General Secretary Brezhnev at Vladivostok, in November 1974, agreed to the formula for the SALT II that was eventually signed in Vienna on April 18, 1979. Negotiated by President Jimmy Carter, SALT II was a mix of an engineering document and a lawyer's brief—the text was extraordinarily complex, with extensive definitions and elaborate "counting rules" appended. The treaty limited each side to 2,400 ICBMs, SLBMs and heavy bombers, to be reached within six months after the treaty entered into force, followed by a further reduction to 2,250 strategic nuclear launch vehicles by 1981. Each side was limited within this ceiling to no more than 1,320 ICBMs, SLBMs, and long-range bombers equipped with MIRVs or multiple cruise missiles. The 78-page treaty required both parties to dismantle some systems to make room for new deployments and included an extensive list of qualitative restrictions.[40]

The Soviet-American negotiations produced several other agreements, some dealing with "arms control," a relatively new concept. Earlier, Kennedy and Khrushchev initiated the "hot line"—frequently modified—to directly connect the chiefs of state in Moscow and Washington to lessen the prospect of an unintended conflict. Several similar bilateral pacts followed, including: the Accidents Measures Agreement (1971) to improve the safety and security of each party's nuclear weapons; the High Seas Accord (1972) to regulate the "shadowing" of each other's warships; the Prevention of Nuclear War Accord (1973). The latter pact was instigated by Moscow's unsuccessful effort to obtain a U.S. commitment of "No-first-use" of nuclear weapons; the Soviets did make this pledge in 1982. Meanwhile, Nixon on November 25, 1969, reaffirmed the United States' chemical warfare "no-first-use" policy that dated from World War II, while he unilaterally renounced the United States' use of bacteriological or biological weapons, closed all facilities producing these offensive weapons, and ordered existing stockpiles of biological weapons and agents destroyed. In April 1972, the United States and the Soviet Union joined other nations in signing the Biological Convention. In 1974, the two countries also signed a Threshold Test Ban pact, limiting the yield of underground tests of nuclear weapons to the upper limits of 150 kilotons for single detonations. These agreements, together with progress in commercial and economic relations, peaceful uses of atomic energy, and cultural exchanges, seemed to augur well for Soviet-American relations.[41]

Nixon and Brezhnev, at the June 1973 Washington summit, regarded their agreements on arms limitation and the avoidance of nuclear war as the key achievements. Washington and Moscow understood the risks and costs of their perennial disagreements and the advantages of a stable relationship. The 1973 "Basic Principles of Relations" agreement, initiated by the Kremlin but largely ignored by America leadership, might have substantially reduced tensions between the superpowers if this effort to institutionalize détente had been better defined and realistically explained to the American public. Moscow thought that this pact could provide the basis for superpower cooperation in resolving basic differences. Thus, Soviet officials considered it "an important political declaration" that they wished, as Ambassador Anatoly Dobrynin recalled, would be the basis of a "new political process of *détente* in our relations." Moscow hoped the agreement would recognize the Soviet doctrine of peaceful coexistence (or détente) and acknowledge the "principle of equality as a basis for the security of both countries." However, the Soviets could not escape their ideological past and the expectations it placed on their actions. And the Nixon administration could not satisfy those Americans who believed the Soviet threat too immediate and pervading to permit any lasting agreements or relaxation of tension. Failure to develop détente's boundaries and to gain public acceptance for it would temporarily doom the idea.[42]

NATO and De Gaulle

NATO in its second and third decades had lost much of its cohesiveness and at least some of its importance. As the apparent danger of Soviet aggression declined, so did the bond that held the diverse members of the alliance together, and rifts appeared in the structure. Many of these were minor. Europeans, understandably, resented Washington's habit of making unilateral decisions on defense and other matters, while Americans, in turn, felt that the NATO nations of a newly prosperous Europe were carrying less than their share of the burden of common defense. Some Americans deplored the failure of most of the NATO allies to sympathize with, not to mention support, American policy in Vietnam, communist China, Cuba, and the Middle East. The United States, furthermore, found its neighbor to the north, Canada, less than cooperative in continental defense policy during the tenure of Prime Minister John Diefenbaker (1957–1963), though this trend reversed itself somewhat under Pierre Trudeau. Portugal resented its allies' faultfinding with its colonial policy in Africa and threatened to deny them the use of bases in the Azores. In the mid-1970s, Portugal's domestic upheavals caused the United States no small concern. Greece and Turkey continued to quarrel over Cyprus, thereby rendering NATO's right flank vulnerable. And Italy, which increasingly relied on the support of the Italian Communists to function,[43] caused NATO to worry about bringing local communists into policymaking with its classified material.

These misunderstandings and problems were of minor importance compared with the aftermath of France's defection. Assuming power in France in June 1958 after a succession of weak governments, Charles de Gaulle quickly restored stability to French political life and ended the exhausting colonial war in Algeria. But he was dissatisfied with France's relatively minor role in world politics compared with that of the "Anglo-Saxons." When President Eisenhower rejected his proposal for a three-power directorate—France, Britain, and the United States to guide the policies of NATO—de Gaulle repeatedly took positions antagonistic to the United States: recognizing communist China, condemning American policy in Vietnam, catering to anti-Americanism in Latin America, encouraging French separatism in Quebec, siding with the Arabs against Israel in the Six-Day War of 1967, and rebuffing the United States as well as England in temporarily barring the United Kingdom from the European Economic Community (Common Market).

More serious, however, was de Gaulle's nationalistic policy toward NATO. In opposition to American policy, he insisted that France must have, at great expense, its own independent nuclear force, or *force de frappe*. To justify the enormous costs involved, he warned the French people and their European allies that the United States probably would not sacrifice their cities to defend Western Europe in a nuclear exchange with the Soviet Union.[44] France would fulfill its obligations under the North Atlantic Treaty, but he rejected the idea of a unified command—a fundamental concept of NATO. Measures of partial withdrawal from the command structure—detachment of the French Mediterranean fleet, denial of base and air rights to nuclear-armed American planes, and so forth—climaxed in March 1966 when the French president declared that all NATO military installations, including its headquarters, must leave French soil by April 1, 1967. Even before that date, French officers were withdrawn from all of the headquarters' planning committees. NATO headquarters, civil as well as military, moved to Belgium. France continued as an ally and made no move to withdraw, but France's armed forces, the geographical and military keystone to the defense of Western Europe, could no longer be counted on to take orders from the Supreme Commander in the event of an attack from the East. De Gaulle's passing from the scene failed to improve matters, as his successors continued to pursue an independent nuclear force replete with atomic bombers, second-generation ICBMs, and a modest nuclear submarine fleet. Furthermore, the French made no secret that they would respond to a threat of Soviet invasion with the immediate use of tactical nuclear weapons in contrast to NATO's policy of "flexible response," which relied initially on conventional warfare rather than on nuclear weapons.[45]

By the late 1960s, other NATO nations followed France's example, not in detaching their forces but in reducing the number of forces readily available. The United States, where the maintenance of 350,000 troops in Europe contributed (with the war in Vietnam) to a chronic foreign exchange deficit, transferred 35,000 troops from Europe to American soil in 1967, though these troops were still committed to NATO and could be returned to Europe on short notice. Britain took similar action with 6,500 of its 51,000 troops on the continent. Canada, two years later in 1969, announced that it would cut its ground troops and air force in Europe by almost 50 percent. And West Germany reduced its projected contribution to NATO forces from 508,000 to 400,000 men.[46] Democratic Senate leader Mike Mansfield called year after year for a "substantial reduction" of American forces in Europe, a move successfully resisted by Johnson to Nixon. By mid-1976, and in the face of a new set of circumstances—the steady buildup of Soviet military power—the United States pledged to increase its army in Europe from 13 to 16 divisions.

The United States and Communist China

Although there was considerable evidence of the Sino-Soviet rift after 1960, the Kennedy and Johnson administrations made few attempts to reexamine the previous assumptions and policies regarding China. Officials in Washington continued to see a dangerous Moscow-Beijing axis. In practice, their anti-Beijing attitudes resulted in charges of misbehavior, nonrecognition, and trade restrictions. Richard Nixon, however, had early identified with the critics' arguments that the United States' China policies—to isolate 700 million Chinese diplomatically and economically—served no useful purpose and antagonized much of the world. Indeed, Nixon wrote in the October 1967 issue of *Foreign Affairs* that "any American policy toward Asia must come urgently to grips with the reality of China." As president, Nixon established the need to improve relations with China as one essential component of a new American foreign policy. "I was fully aware," he recalled, "of the profound ideological and political differences between our countries.... But I believed also that in this era we could not afford to be cut off from a quarter of the world's population. We had an obligation to try to establish contact ... and perhaps move on to greater understanding." Nixon understood that China posed a lesser danger than two decades of apocalyptic rhetoric had suggested.[47]

In 1969, the Nixon administration, working through third countries, opened some discussion with Beijing, but its initial efforts were largely unilateral—allowing Americans to purchase Chinese goods; validating passports after March 1970 for travel in China; and licensing, after April 1970, of certain nonstrategic American goods for export to China. During a visit to Rumania in October 1970, Nixon, for the first time, deliberately used Beijing's official title, the People's Republic of China. No American initiatives toward China would succeed unless they were received with some graciousness. When, in October 1970, President Yahya Khan of Pakistan carried a Nixon overture to Beijing, the Beijing government responded: "We welcome the proposal from Washington for face-to-face discussions. We would be glad to receive a high-level person for this purpose, to discuss withdrawal of American forces from Taiwan." Nixon welcomed the invitation, but could not accept the Chinese objective. During April 1971, in Nagoya, Japan, the Chinese ping-pong team invited the American team, competing for the world championships, to visit the Chinese mainland. Prime Minister Chou En-lai addressed the American team: "[W]ith your acceptance of our invitation, you have opened a new page in the relations of the Chinese and

American people." Then, on July 15, the president announced that earlier Kissinger and Chou had held secret talks in Beijing. The premier invited the president to visit China, and Nixon accepted the invitation.[48]

Washington's new opening to China culminated in the president's trip to Beijing in February 1972. Minutely prepared, the venture became one of the greatest media events of the decade. By acknowledging the legitimacy of the Chinese government—which four preceding administrations had refused to do—Nixon expected Beijing to accept the legitimacy of the existing international order and the limits of proper political and diplomatic conduct. Late in 1971, the Beijing government, facing only an adverse vote from the United States, replaced the Republic of China in the United Nations. In 1973, the United States established a permanent liaison office in Beijing. Nixon's informal recognition of the Beijing regime was met with the American people's almost universal approval.

Clearly, the Asia of the 1970s presented opportunities for new policies. Washington's initiatives toward Moscow and Beijing encouraged Japan to establish closer relations with both communist powers. Japan's influence in Asia expanded, with that country's trade and investment around the continent's eastern and southern rim. Everywhere the lines of East-West tension in Asia were receding. China and the U.S.S.R. were in direct confrontation across Asia. As early as 1969, Moscow offered defense pacts to the countries of Southeast Asia against an allegedly aggressive China. Beijing retaliated in 1972 by inviting the United States to maintain its bases in Southeast Asia as a guarantee against Soviet encroachment. Nothing dramatized more effectively the revolution in the U.S. perception of Asia than the president's recognition of a new regional balance of power. "We must remember," he declared in early 1972, "the only time in the history of the world that we have had any extended period of peace is when there has been a balance of power.... I think it will be a safer world and a better world if we have a strong, healthy United States, Europe, Soviet Union, China, Japan—each balancing the other." Thereafter, the new American outlook toward Asia set the stage for a limited, ordered relationship with China.[49]

Road to the Helsinki Accord

Weakening and revival of commitments to NATO were the result, actually, of fluctuating skepticism as to the reality of the danger of Soviet aggression. Such doubts grew as tension over Berlin relaxed, and the Soviet Union became more deeply involved in its quarrel with communist China in the 1960s. Western fears were reawakened, however, when

Soviet-led Warsaw troops intervened in Czechoslovakia in 1968 to suppress a liberalizing program in that communist state. In justification, General Secretary Brezhnev proclaimed, in what came to be known as the Brezhnev Doctrine, the "defense of proletarian internationalism," the right of the Soviet Union to intervene in any state of the communist bloc to preserve the integrity of the socialist system. More alarming than the Brezhnev Doctrine was the arrival on the Czechoslovak-West German frontier of five Russian divisions and a statement from Moscow that Articles 53 and 107 of the UN Charter gave the Soviet Union the right to intervene in West Germany, a former enemy state. Not surprisingly, the threat brought about a more cooperative attitude on the part of France and led the governments of France, Britain, and the United States to warn the Kremlin to keep hands off the German Federal Republic.

In March 1969 at Budapest, the Warsaw Pact powers proposed a European conference on security, the consequence of which would be an official endorsement of Soviet territorial gains from World War II, in exchange for a yet undetermined communist accommodation. Nothing came of the proposal, but in October the Warsaw Pact powers tried again, proposing Helsinki as a meeting place and suggesting that the United States and Canada might be included. The NATO governments replied that they were "receptive" to suggestions on "measures to reduce tension and promote cooperation in Europe," but stipulated that "prospects of concrete results" would be essential. Listed as such "concrete results" were free access to West Berlin, a working agreement between East and West Germany, and an agreement on reduction of armed forces in Europe.[50] While NATO hesitated, Chancellor Willy Brandt moved his own nation directly toward détente with the communist bloc. As foreign minister in Chancellor Kurt Georg Kiesinger's cabinet, he had refrained from pushing for reunification of Germany as an immediate goal and dropped the demand of the previous regime for access to nuclear weapons. He had also offered to recognize the Oder-Neisse line as Germany's eastern boundary, thus surrendering claims to the formerly German territory occupied since 1945 by Poland.

As chancellor, Brandt proposed to negotiate agreements renouncing the use or threat of force with the nations of Eastern Europe, agreements that would also guarantee mutual respect for the territorial integrity of the signers, thus, in effect, assuring Poland and Czechoslovakia against any German irredentist claims. While still unwilling to recognize East Germany as a sovereign state and insisting that all Germany was really one, Brandt stated his government's willingness to work for "contractually agreed cooperation" with East Germany and to abandon attempts to interfere with East Germany's economic and cultural relations with other nations.[51] Meetings between Chancellor Brandt and East German premier Willi Stoph, in March and May 1970, collapsed, but meanwhile Bonn's talks with Warsaw and Moscow were more productive. The Moscow talks reached a culmination on August 7, when the Soviet and West German foreign ministers initialed a treaty by which both governments renounced the use of force in their mutual relations and agreed to respect existing national boundaries. In accompanying notes, the Bonn government reserved the right to seek the unification of Germany by peaceful means and assured the Western Allies that the treaty in no way infringed their rights in Berlin. Three months later, in a treaty with Poland, West Germany accepted the Oder-Neisse line as Poland's border with Germany. And while treaties with Czechoslovakia and Hungary were expected to follow, Chancellor Brandt made it perfectly clear that neither the Soviet nor other treaties would be submitted to the Reichstag until East Germany agreed to relax tensions in Berlin and to ease restrictions on intercourse between Berlin and West Germany.

After 22 years, amicable discussions resumed in Berlin between delegates of the four occupying powers. Beginning in March 1970, these talks took place with increasing frequency, and on August 23, it was announced that a Quadripartite treaty had been agreed on. The heart of the treaty dealt with Western access to Berlin, the U.S.S.R. pledging to make traffic unimpeded between them and the Federal Republic of Germany. In the meantime, talks between East and West Germany on mutual relations, which had begun in November 1970, bore fruit in December 1971, with the conclusion of a number of agreements aimed at implementing the terms of the Quadripartite treaty. In January 1972, the two governments then proceeded to open negotiations with a view to concluding a traffic treaty between the two German states. Successfully concluded in April of that year, the treaty was signed in East Berlin on May 26. Thus, despite animosities that were never very far below the surface, the principals, in a changing attitude toward the Cold War, came to terms on what had once been the world's premier flashpoint.

On another front, and after lengthy negotiations, the heads of the 35 nations of Europe, plus the United States and Canada, came together in Helsinki in late summer 1975 to sign the so-called final act of the Conference on Security and Cooperation in Europe, known as the Helsinki Conference. The high-water mark of détente, the Helsinki Conference declared the current frontiers of Europe "inviolable," thereby endorsing the Soviet Union's postwar territorial gains and its hegemony in Eastern Europe, but not excluding the alteration of borders by "peaceful agreement."[52] This latter agreement thus left open the prospect of a future German reunification. In return, the NATO countries induced Moscow and the Warsaw powers to open themselves to a freer flow of ideas and people. The reduction of heavy communist censorship exposed the peoples of the Soviet satellites to Western ideas and material progress—a process that would within a decade and half end Soviet control of Central and Eastern Europe.

CHAPTER 15

The United States and Southeast Asia: Laos, Cambodia, and Vietnam

I don't think that unless a greater effort is made by the [South Vietnamese] Government to win popular support that the war can be won out there. In the final analysis, it is their war. They are the one who have to win it or lose it.... All we can do is help.
—President John F. Kennedy, interview with Walter Cronkite, CBS-TV, September 2, 1963

I made the decision to renew and increase the bombing of... North Vietnam. The bombing began on December 18, [1972]. It was a necessary step.... The bombing broke the deadlock in negotiations.... and on January 23, 1973, the long-awaited peace agreement was finally achieved.
—Richard M. Nixon, *The Real War* (New York: Warner Books, 1980), 113

The hostilities in Southeast Asia, into which the United States was gradually drawn during the 1960s, was, like the Korean War, a part of the program for containing Asiatic communism. Although Washington's concern were local communist insurgents in the region—such as Burma, Indonesia, Malaya, and the Philippines in the 1950s, and Thailand, Laos, Cambodia, and, of course, South Vietnam, in the 1960s—looming large in the background was the fear that the insurgents were strengthening the "Communist Monolith," the People's Republic of China and its then partnership with the Soviet Union. It was this fear that led U.S. leaders to subsidize France's unsuccessful effort to maintain its grip on Indochina and later to intervene militarily on behalf of South Vietnam. Washington, as former defense secretary Robert McNamara has noted, "viewed Indochina as a necessary part of our containment policy—an important bulwark in the Cold War.... We viewed these conflicts [guerrilla insurgencies] not as nationalist movements—as they largely appear in hindsight—but as signs of a unified Communist drive for hegemony in Asia."[1] This thinking led in April 1954 to President Dwight Eisenhower's widely accepted prediction that should Indochina fall to the communists, the rest of Southeast Asia would also follow like a "row of dominoes." He was convinced that: "The possible consequences of the loss are just incalculable to the free world." The United States, subsequent presidents argued, had promised protection to the government and people of South Vietnam; to ignore that promise would not only result in bloody reprisals, it would impair or destroy the United States' credibility in the eyes of its allies. But how was the United States to prevent insurgents in Laos, Cambodia, and South Vietnam—backed by North Vietnam and China—from winning? To Presidents Eisenhower, Kennedy, Johnson and Nixon, the Indochina problem would seem intractable.

After the division of Vietnam at the Geneva Conference of 1954, the noncommunist South's security was initially threatened, not by an invasion from the communist North, but from the Viet Cong (Vietnamese Communists) in the South that had fought against France. Vietnamese nationalism, as distinct from communism, played an important role in the resistance to France and later to the United States. Ho Chi Minh, who led the war against France and, until his death in 1969, against the United States, was a committed communist, but nationalism—his insistence on independence for Vietnam—seems to have been his major motivation at least in the struggle with France. Moreover, the dedication of his followers must certainly be ascribed in part to hatred of foreign domination, whether by Japan, France, or the United States. And in this struggle for a united independent Vietnam, Ho drew support from the Chinese and Soviets. The war in Southeast Asia formed a complex mosaic that was—for the American public and many of those who fought there—extraordinarily difficult to understand.

The French in Indochina

Vietnam, Laos, and Cambodia were known before World War II as French Indochina.[2] They had come under French rule by stages from the 1860s to the 1880s. On the eve of World War II, the Japanese occupied much of the area, with the reluctant consent of the Vichy French authorities. The Japanese took direct control of southern Vietnam (Cochin China) but returned Cambodia, Laos, and northern and central Vietnam (called by the French Tonkin and Annam) to their native rulers—in Vietnam to Bao Dai, Emperor of Annam. When the Japanese surrendered on August 14, 1945, President Franklin Roosevelt, a foe of colonialism, questioned Indochina being restored to France. He suggested that Indochina be put under trusteeship in preparation for independence.[3] After Roosevelt's death, however, his proposal was ignored; the Allied High Command designated Britain and China to receive the surrender of Japanese troops in southern and northern Indochina, respectively; subsequently, the British and Chinese withdrew in favor of the French. The French, however, met formidable resistance from the Viet Minh (Vietnam Independence League), a native nationalist organization headed by Ho Chi Minh. The Viet Minh at this stage was a united front of communists and other nationalist elements, whose common objective was an independent Vietnam. The Viet Minh leaders persuaded Emperor Bao Dai to abdicate, and on September 2, 1945, at Hanoi, Ho Chi Minh proclaimed the independence of the Democratic Republic of Vietnam.

Paris was determined to keep its prewar colonial empire for reasons of both economics and prestige, though modified to bear a distant resemblance to the British Commonwealth. Negotiations between French authorities and Ho Chi Minh led to an agreement on March 6, 1946, by which France recognized Vietnam as a "free state" within the French Union, on condition: (1) that Vietnam would be a member of an Indochinese federation, with Laos and Cambodia, which had again accepted the status of French protectorates; and (2) that a plebiscite in Cochin China should determine whether the latter would be included in Vietnam or constitute a separate "free state" in the Union. The agreement broke down primarily over Cochin China, the most highly developed and productive section of Indochina. So intent were the French authorities on keeping it in their hands that they ignored the provision for a plebiscite and set up a puppet "Cochin Chinese Republic." This and other disputes led to an outbreak of hostilities between the French and the Viet Minh in November 1946. The French set up a rival Vietnamese government, installed the former emperor Bao Dai as chief of state, and extended its authority over Cochin China. Britain and the United States recognized the Bao Dai government, but the Bao Dai regime had little appeal to nationalist Vietnamese.

The Viet Minh, meanwhile, abandoned Ho's united front policy, purged its noncommunist elements, and aligned itself with Beijing and Moscow from which the Democratic Republic of Vietnam gained recognition and some material support. In the words of one authority, however, it had "blundered across the no-man's land of the cold war into a position where it found itself confronted by the containment policy newly formulated by the United States."[4] France and the government of Bao Dai, as opponents of world communism, could now count on aid from the United States, aid that was stepped up once France joined NATO, the Korean War began, and the Cold War intensified. By 1954, the United States was bearing some 70 percent of the cost of the French military effort in Vietnam; yet the war went badly for the French. It reached a crisis in the spring of 1954 when a French and Vietnamese army of 20,000 men was surrounded and cut off by a superior force of Viet Minh troops in the frontier fortress of Dienbienphu. The French government, in appeals to Washington, warned that without direct military aid from the United States, Dienbienphu was doomed and that its fall might pave the way for communist conquest of all Indochina, perhaps all of Southeast Asia. To President Eisenhower, who agreed with the domino thesis, and even more to Secretary of State John Foster Dulles, such a challenge to the containment policy had to be met at almost any cost. When Congressional leaders indicated strong opposition to America's unilateral intervention, Dulles tried unsuccessfully to persuade the British government to join with the United States, France, and minor states in an alliance to save the French position in Vietnam and to contain communism in Southeast Asia. Since an international conference was about to meet in Geneva to deal with the problems of Korea and Indochina, the British were unwilling to take action that might prevent the success of the conference. Consequently, nothing was done to save Dienbienphu, which fell on May 7.

The Geneva Conference of 1954

The Geneva Conference from April 26 to July 21, 1954, having failed to reach agreement on Korea, turned to the Indochina crisis, where it had more success.[5] The United States, however, played little more than an observer's role at the conference. Dulles, reluctant to meet the Chinese delegate Chou En-lai (whose government the United States did not recognize) and to subscribe to the inevitable cession of territory to the communist Viet Minh, personally took little part in the conference. His deputy, Undersecretary Walter Bedell Smith, attended only intermittently, and, not surprisingly, the United States refused to sign the conference documents. Little did the administration, convinced that Ho was a puppet of Beijing and Moscow, understand Ho's bitterness toward China and the U.S.S.R. for pressuring him to agree to the division of Vietnam or the southern Viet Minh's bitterness on being "sold out." Armistice terms agreed on ending the fighting and dividing Vietnam at the 17th parallel of north latitude. The Viet Minh, officially the Democratic Republic of Vietnam, took the north, including the city of Hanoi and port of Haiphong. The State of Vietnam, soon to be known as South Vietnam, was to control all south of the line. The division, however, was expected to be temporary, with the country to be united following free general elections in July 1956. An international commission, composed of representatives of Canada, India, and Poland, would supervise carrying out the armistice terms.

The United States acquiesced in the terms of settlement and gave assurance that it would "refrain from the threat or use of force to disturb them" and would view attempts by others to do so as "seriously threatening international peace and security." The State of (South) Vietnam also withheld approval from the settlement and protested against many of its terms, including the provision for elections. Under a new premier, Ngo Dinh Diem, the South Vietnamese government acted independently of the French. Before the end of the year, in fact, France had agreed to the complete independence of all three states of Indochina.[5]

The SEATO Alliance

Since it appeared that only international action could prevent the further advance of communism, Secretary Dulles took the initiative in creating a Southeast Asia Treaty Organization (SEATO) to contain communism in the area, much the same as NATO served in Europe. Unfortunately, several of the most important nations of Southeast Asia—India, Burma, Ceylon, and Indonesia—would have no part in such an organization because of their declared neutrality in the Cold War. The terms of the Geneva armistice prevented Vietnam, Cambodia, and Laos from participation. The Nationalist Chinese government on Taiwan, unrecognized by Great Britain, could not be included, while disarmed Japan could make no contribution to a military-oriented organization. The delegates of Philippines, Thailand, and Pakistan, the only Asiatic nations to be counted on, met in Manila on September 6, 1954, with representatives of the United States, Great Britain, France, Australia, and New Zealand. Thus five of the eight participating governments were of the West (in culture if not in geography); four were of the English-speaking world.

Certain that communists would denounce their activities as "imperialist," the delegates sought to avoid such a stigma by adopting Philippine president Ramon Magsaysay's proposal for a "Pacific Charter." The signatories of this document affirmed their faith in "the principle of equal rights and self-determination of peoples" and promised to "strive by every peaceful means to promote self-government and to secure independence of all countries whose peoples desire it and are able to undertake its responsibilities." Then the eight delegations agreed on the "South-east Asia Collective Defense Treaty," signed on September 8, 1954. The treaty stated that an attack on one would be recognized as dangerous to the peace and safety of the others, and members would "act to meet the common danger in accordance with its constitutional processes." If any member were threatened with subversion, the treaty provided for consultation and collective action. To deal with military or other planning, the treaty established a council all parties.[6] To deter communist activities in Southeast Asia, SEATO was obviously dependent on the power and determination of the United States.

Washington accredited ambassadors to Cambodia, Laos, and South Vietnam and initiated economic and military aid programs deliberately supplanting the French in the three states, because, Dulles believed, the native people would not view Americans as "imperialist" masters. By replacing French influence in the area, Washington assumed, morally at least, responsibility for seeing that the Geneva terms were observed. Cambodia took an outspokenly neutralist position, seeming at times more suspicious of the West than of the communists, while Laos was in danger of being torn apart among leftist, neutralist, and rightist elements. South Vietnamese officials were uncompromisingly anticommunist and pro-Western. Ngo Dinh Diem, hitherto little known, had become premier in June 1954, nominally under the absentee emperor, Bao Dai. A Catholic Christian, a celibate, an ascetic, and a nationalist, he was uncompromising in his opposition to communism. It was he who, along with the United States' delegates, had refused to sign the Geneva agreement. Faced with apparently insuperable obstacles—other hostile armed factions at home, antagonism of the emperor, hostility of the French, and the problem of resettling nearly a million refugees from north of the 17th parallel—the premier overcame most of them, thanks partly to American aid but primarily to his own shrewdness and determination. When the emperor sought to remove him in October 1955, he held a plebiscite in which the South Vietnamese were asked to choose between him and Bao Dai. Victor by an enormous majority in an election allegedly "rigged" by his unscrupulous brother, Ngo Dinh Nhu, Diem declared the state a republic—henceforth the Republic of Vietnam—and himself president. By the end of the year, he seemed to have the political situation under control, but reliance on his family and his autocratic manner eventually would be his undoing.

Compromise in Laos

In Laos, the complicated political turbulence from 1954 to 1963 permits only summary treatment. The Geneva settlement left the communist Pathet Lao forces holding two northeastern provinces adjoining North Vietnam and communist China. Neutralist premier Prince Souvanna Phouma failed to integrate these forces and their political leaders into the Laotian army and government. Attempts by his right-wing successors to suppress the Pathet Lao led to armed resistance, supported, so the Laos government claimed, by North Vietnamese troops. Laos's 1959 appeal to the United Nations to stem such aggression led the Security Council, over Moscow's objection, to investigate, whereupon the rebellion subsided. In 1960, a renewed effort to come to terms with the Pathet Lao led to civil war between right and left with the United States, which had been training and supplying the Royal Laotian Army, aiding the right and the Soviet Union flying in military equipment for the communists. As the Royal Army proved unable to halt the communist offensive, Washington believed that only intervention from outside could preserve even a neutral Laos. The SEATO Council, meeting in Bangkok in March 1961, failed to take decisive action.[7] The co-chairmen (Britain and Russia) of the 1954 Geneva Conference reconvened the participants hoping to settle the Laotian muddle.

A 14-nation conference met at Geneva in May 1961.[8] It's efforts were stimulated by a June 4 statement from President John F. Kennedy and Premier Nikita Khrushchev reaffirming "their support of a neutral and independent Laos." The only neutralist solution for Laos, it was apparent, was a coalition government headed by neutralist Prince Souvanna Phouma and his rivals on the right and left, Princes Boun Oum and Souphanouvong, respectively. After a year of hard bargaining, the three princes reached an agreement, during which time a new communist offensive threatened to overflow into Thailand. The landing in Thailand of 1,800 U.S. Marines, followed by token forces from Great Britain, Australia, and New Zealand, headed off any such danger and perhaps expedited agreement on Laos.[9] On June 11, 1962, Souvanna Phouma became premier, Prince Souphanouvong and General Phoumi Nosavan (replacing Prince Boun Oum), deputy premiers. On questions of foreign policy, defense, and police, decisions were to be concurred in by the three. In a statement of July 9, the new government guaranteed its neutrality and renounced the protection of "any alliance or military coalition" (i.e., SEATO). The transaction was completed at Geneva on July 21, 1962, when rules were agreed to for the International Commission that would supervise the settlement.[10] Since the Commission (Canada, India, Poland), like the Laotian government, generally operated on the "troika" principle, its efficacy as a bulwark against further communist encroachment was dubious. Subsequent intermittent communist pressure on neutralist and rightist elements indicated that the Laotian settlement was at best only a shaky armistice.

Diem Confronts a Guerrilla War

Meanwhile, the United States found itself caught up in a crisis in South Vietnam. North Vietnam had never abandoned its intention to "liberate" the South and thus unify the country under communist rule. Ho Chi Minh expected to accomplish this peaceably through the July 1956 elections, and his prestige as a nationalist patriot provided good reason to believe that he would have carried a fair countrywide election. In Saigon, however, South Vietnam's Ngo Dinh Diem maintained that since no election in the communist north could be fair, and since neither he nor the Americans who backed this argument had agreed to the elections, he could rightfully refuse to hold the countrywide elections. In rejecting this part of the Geneva settlement, however, it has been argued that he forfeited any right to be protected by the armistice, another part of the same complex agreement. Diem's refusal to participate meant that no elections were held in 1956, and Ho Chi Minh's hope for a peaceful unification of Vietnam was frustrated. Here one reaches a controversial point: was the terrorist campaign that began in the south in 1957—chiefly the assassination of village officers, killing or kidnapping of schoolteachers, etc.—instigated by a frustrated Hanoi, or did it stem from local South Vietnamese grievances such as abolition of village elections, collection of back rent for absentee landlords, persecution of former Viet Minh and other opponents of the regime? The U.S. State Department consistently maintained that the campaign of subversion was, from the beginning, engineered from Hanoi. Some reputable scholars, both French and American, have concluded that the rebellion against Diem's government was indigenous to the south and that Hanoi came to its support only in 1960 when implored to do so by southern veterans of the former Viet Minh. If resolution to this question could be ascertained with certainty, it would have an obvious bearing on the character of the war. Was it a war of aggression of the North against the South? Or was it a civil war in the south with the north coming to the aid of one faction? American policy was based on the former hypothesis.[11]

By 1958, at any rate, Diem's government had a guerrilla war on its hands with the Viet Cong. Diem and his American military advisers, however, were slow in facing the facts. American military advisers were training the South Vietnam army for conventional warfare patterned after the Korean conflict, while political advisers failed to persuade Diem to adopt economic and social reforms needed to hold peasant loyalty. In December 1960, the formation of the National Liberation Front (NLF) of South Vietnam seems to have been inspired by Hanoi to provide the political arm for the Viet Cong forces. By 1961, Southern Vietnamese who had withdrawn to the North at the time of the partition returned and joined the resistance. At the end of that year, the Viet Cong exercised influence over perhaps 80 percent of the South Vietnamese countryside.

The United States Sends Advisers and Military Aid

President Kennedy had been in office only a short time when he received President Diem's appeal for increased military aid. In May 1961, Kennedy sent Vice President Lyndon B. Johnson on a fact-finding mission to Vietnam and elsewhere in Asia. Johnson, who as Senate leader had opposed intervention to save Dienbienphu in 1954, concluded that unless communism was defeated in Southeast Asia, "the United States, inevitably, must surrender the Pacific and take up our defenses on our own shores." The United States must decide whether "to attempt to meet the challenge of Communist expansion now in Southeast Asia by a major effort in support of the forces of freedom in the area, or throw in the towel." An affirmative decision would involve heavy costs "in terms of money, of effort, and of United States prestige" yet, Johnson added, "I recommend we proceed with a clear-cut and strong program of action."[12] President Diem had not yet asked for U.S. combat forces, but General Maxwell D. Taylor found that Diem would welcome American military personnel to assist in logistics and communications. In December 1961, Kennedy assured Diem that "the campaign of force and terror now being waged against your people and your Government is supported and directed from the outside by the authorities at Hanoi" and, as these activities violated the provisions of the Geneva settlement, the United States viewed such violations "with grave concern." The United States, said the president, would "promptly increase our assistance to your defense effort."[13]

Thus began a new phase of American aid to South Vietnam, which for the period 1955–1962 exceeded $2 billion and by 1963 cost nearly $500 million annually. A dramatic indicator of the new policy was the arrival at Saigon on December 12, 1961, of an American escort carrier bearing over 30 helicopters, four single-engine training planes, and operating and maintenance crews. This was a prelude to the "helicopter war," in which U.S. personnel during the next three years flew Vietnamese troops, sometimes successful, sometimes not, to detect and intercept units of the Viet Cong. In addition, the United States sought to train the Vietnamese army in counterinsurgency tactics and persuaded President Diem's government to launch a program of resettling the peasantry in fortified villages—a program the British found successful in fighting communist guerrillas in Malaya. The number of American forces in South Vietnam increased steadily, reaching some 16,500 before the end of 1963. Still, President Kennedy had not committed to full-scale intervention. "I don't think that unless a greater effort is made by the [South Vietnamese] Government to win popular support that the war can be won out there," he told Walter Cronkite of CBS-TV on September 2, 1963. "In the final analysis, it is their war. They are the one who have to win it or lose it.... All we can do is help." Technically, U.S. troops were engaged only in transportation, training, and advice, but these activities inevitably exposed them to combat conditions. By the end of May 1964, therefore, more than 200 Americans had been killed, about half of them in battle.[14]

The Fall of Diem

The American task in South Vietnam was rendered more difficult by a growing rift between President Diem and noncommunist elements in the population. He had become increasingly authoritarian and resentful of American suggestions for alleviating popular discontent. Members of his family, it was charged, exercised too much influence, especially his younger brother, Ngo Dinh Nhu, who was his principal adviser, and Nhu's attractive and outspoken wife. A Senate subcommittee, visiting Southeast Asia late in 1962, feared that sudden termination of aid "would open the region to upheaval and chaos" and probable Chinese domination. Yet they were concerned that the chaos in Vietnam might become "an American war, to be fought primarily with American lives." No interest of the United States in Vietnam justified such a war. Survival of South Vietnam should rest with its government and people.[15]

Dissatisfaction, both native and American, with the rule of the Ngo Dinh family reached the boiling point in the summer and fall of 1963. A basic cause of trouble was antagonism between the Catholic ruling family and the Buddhist majority (commonly stated at 70%) of the population.

A bloody suppression in May 1963 of a Buddhist procession in Hue—where a brother of Diem was the archbishop—led to a series of spectacular suicides by fire in Saigon, and to government raids on Buddhist pagodas and the imprisonment of scores of Buddhist monks. Native resentment became so intense that President Kennedy and his advisers became persuaded that without a change in policies, if not in personnel, the war against the Viet Cong would hopelessly bog down. A new U.S. ambassador, Henry Cabot Lodge, was unsuccessful in persuading Diem to part with his brother or to reform his administration. On November 1, a group of army officers, headed by General Duong Van Minh, carried out a carefully planned revolution, seized the royal palace, and captured the brothers Diem and Nhu—both of whom were killed. The military junta set up a civilian figurehead as premier, promised free elections, released political prisoners, declared the press free, and began to conduct the war more effectively. The United States promptly recognized the provisional government, hoping that it might save Washington from the dilemma of making the war in Vietnam "primarily American" or letting the Viet Cong take the country. In the months that followed, Hanoi encouraged the National Liberation Front to increase its political and military activities, while North Vietnamese matériel and forces moved to the south.

Escalating the War

The overthrow and death of President Diem was followed in less than three weeks by the assassination of President Kennedy. Lyndon B. Johnson, the new president, inherited a dangerous, unstable situation in Saigon, Johnson informed Lodge on November 24, 1963, that he wanted to win the war—put aside social reforms—win the war![16] But the stability and efficiency that had been hoped for from the new government failed to materialize, and victory never was in sight. Military coups followed one another at frequent intervals until June 1965, when General Nguyen Van Thieu became president, with Air Vice-Marshal Nguyen Cao Ky as vice president. The new constitution, with an elected Senate and House of Representatives, gave the appearance of a democracy, though opponents of the regime were denied political rights and often their liberty. Thieu and Ky proved cooperative and amenable to U.S. suggestions. Some progress was made in pacifying the villages and hamlets of the rural areas—winning their allegiance to the government and providing protection from further incursions of the Viet Cong. Yet, during the year and a half after Diem's fall, the overall war was going badly for the government.

The provocation that gave President Johnson authority to commit major U.S. forces to assist South Vietnam was an alleged attack by North Vietnamese PT-boats on American destroyers cruising in international waters in the Gulf of Tonkin on August 2, 1964, and again, so it was claimed, on August 4. The United States retaliated by bombing North Vietnamese naval stations, and Congress, at the president's request, approved a joint resolution authorizing the president "to take all necessary measures to repel any armed attack against the forces of the United States," or "to assist any member or protocol state" of the SEATO treaty "requesting assistance in defense of its freedom."[17] The Tonkin Gulf Resolution passed the House of Representatives unanimously, the Senate by a vote of 82 to 2. Described as "a functional equivalent of a declaration of war," it authorized President Johnson to escalate the war as he chose. Its passage was later bitterly regretted by some of its sponsors—and would be repealed by the Senate in June 1970. The Tonkin Gulf incident occurred during a presidential campaign in which the Republican candidate, Senator Barry Goldwater, urged more vigorous U.S. participation in the war, while Johnson repeatedly declared American boys would not be sent "nine or ten thousand miles away from home to do what Asian boys ought to be doing for themselves."[18]

By January 1965, there were some 23,000 U.S. troops in South Vietnam acting as "advisers." On February 7, however, at Pleiku, and three days later at Quinhon, attacks by Viet Cong on American barracks caused heavy casualties. Each time, the United States retaliated by bombing military targets in North Vietnam, but by summer of 1965 it had escalated to include oil installations at Hanoi and Haiphong, port facilities at Haiphong, ironworks and railroad yards, and the railroad from Hanoi to China to within 10 miles of the Chinese border. Bombing close to or within cities inevitably killed civilians, bringing charges of "war crimes" from critics abroad and at home.[19] The bombing continued until 1968, except for occasional pauses, during which it was hoped, in vain, that Hanoi would indicate a desire for peace negotiations. In the meantime, "American boys" were taking over an increasingly heavy share of the war on the ground. The United States put ashore two Marine battalions at Danang on May 6, 1965—the first American troops to be actually deployed for combat in Vietnam.

Hawks versus Doves

The conflict had become a major American war, and yet there had been no declaration of war by Congress. The Tonkin Gulf Resolution, apart from its assertion of the right to defend U.S. forces, found its basis in the SEATO treaty. The State Department contended that South Vietnam had become an independent state and that infiltration from North Vietnam across the cease-fire line constituted armed aggression, which called for action under the SEATO treaty and also justified it as "collective self-defense" under Article 51 of the UN Charter—the Tonkin Gulf Resolution had taken care of "constitutional processes."[20] Many opponents to the hostilities in Vietnam, however, saw the conflict as a civil war in which nationalist Vietnamese fought a reactionary and corrupt government; few gave any credence to the so-called "domino effect." The United States thus had no obligation to intervene under the SEATO treaty.[21] Furthermore, some critics held, the United States could not win but in the effort to do so, it was destroying the society that it professed to be saving. A North Vietnam victory, opponents conceded, might make all of Vietnam communist, but those who understood the historical relationships of the two countries knew that it would not be a puppet of China.

As scenes from the war appeared nightly on living room TVs, antiwar protests at home grew louder and divided the American people. American officials, both military and civilian, apparently failed to anticipate the vital role the "home front" would play in influencing Washington's Vietnam strategies. With a "silent majority" of Americans supporting the war, the debate went on, in Congress and out. The longer the war dragged on with no end in sight, the stronger grew the critics' appeal to a badly disillusioned public. In Washington and Saigon, public pronouncements and military briefings were frequently self-serving and inhibited the flow of information to the American public. Historians continue to dispute the significance of the media's role in presenting "the facts" about the fighting and the pressure of the antiwar movement's huge public rallies for "an end to the war." But eventually "public will," more than military or economic power, would determine America's final strategy—withdrawal.

The War a Stalemate

Despite the enormous American effort, supplemented by the operations of some 700,000 South Vietnamese troops and the smaller contingents from other allies, the war by 1968 had reached a stalemate. The Viet Cong and North Vietnamese troops could not drive the Americans out or destroy the Saigon government, but neither were the Americans and their allies' forces able to defeat their adversaries. Nor could they protect

South Vietnamese cities and villages. Yet in November 1967, General William C. Westmoreland, commander of U.S. troops in Vietnam, stated, "We are winning a war of attrition," predicting a slow withdrawal of U.S. forces beginning in two years with a progressively larger share of the security responsibility falling to the Vietnamese.[22] The Tet (Lunar New Year) offensive of January–February 1968 illustrated the vulnerability of South Vietnam. On January 31, Viet Cong and North Vietnamese forces simultaneously assaulted 26 or more unsuspecting provincial capitals and, as the *New York Times* reported, "uncounted numbers of district towns and American and Vietnamese air fields and bases."

The most dramatic episodes were the six-hour occupation by 20 Viet Cong of the American Embassy compound in Saigon and the capture of Hue, the old Annamese capital. Decimated Viet Cong forces were eventually expelled from all the towns and cities that they had seized, allowing President Johnson to proclaim the Tet offensive "a complete failure." It was in military terms, yet it had destroyed the optimism produced by Westmoreland, set back the pacification program, and largely ended talk of "victory." A negotiated peace became the declared objective.

The Search for Peace

The search for a negotiated end to hostilities in South Vietnam—sought by both sides—was thwarted by Washington's failure to understand Vietnamese nationalism and the Hanoi leadership's inability to grasp U.S. motives in Southeast Asia. As early as 1945–1949, Vietnamese communists seeking to establish a peaceful relationship with Washington, only to be ignored by an administration focused on European affairs, concluded the United States was opposed to them. Even when the United States supported the French during 1950–1954, the Vietnamese communists did not view the Americans as a hostile foe. Hanoi's Communist Party secretary Le Duan tried from May to August 1962 to interest the Kennedy administration in developing a neutralist coalition government for Vietnam to be staffed exclusively by southerners. French president Charles de Gaulle publicly supported a "neutral solution"; but Washington had serious doubts about neutralization based on the Laotian model because of what they believed to be serious Hanoi violations of it. Hanoi, moreover, failed to develop its views on how the coalition would function with the Americans because "(1) it feared appearing weak; and (2) it feared the wrath of the Chinese," who opposed negotiations with Washington. Even though the president's thinking was beginning to focus on "How do we get out," neither Kennedy nor his staff ever "probed or even carefully examined Hanoi's interest in a neutral solution."[23]

President Johnson stated the essence of America's peace terms at Johns Hopkins University on April 7, 1965: "an independent South Vietnam—securely guaranteed and able to shape its own relationships to all others—free from outside interference—tied to no alliance—a military base for no other country." If peace were assured, he added, the United States would be ready to invest a billion dollars in development of the Mekong River delta.[24] Hanoi responded next day with a four-point proposal: (1) complete withdrawal of all U.S. troops from South Vietnam and cancellation of the alleged U.S.-South Vietnam "military alliance"; (2) observation of the 1954 Geneva agreement pending the unification of Vietnam; (3) settlement of the internal affairs of South Vietnam by the people of South Vietnam in accordance with the program of the NLF; and (4) peaceful unification of Vietnam "to be settled by the Vietnamese people in both zones, without any foreign interference."[25] Later Hanoi imposed a fifth requirement or precondition—all bombing of North Vietnam must stop before negotiations could begin. Ho Chi Minh, Le Duan, and Prime Minister Pham Van Dong doubtless presumed they had designed flexibility in their proposal, especially point 3, which recognized the southern resistance for a neutral coalition government to last at least 10 years. Washington focused on point 4, however, declaring it would not negotiate on these terms because of the presumption the NLF was Hanoi's puppet. Johnson, under pressure at home and abroad to pave the way for negotiations, experimented with a bombing halt. A five-day cessation in May 1965 was criticized as being too short. Then from Christmas Eve 1965 to January 31, 1966, Johnson sent Vice President Hubert Humphrey, UN ambassador Arthur Goldberg, Ambassador-at-Large Averell Harriman, and others to 40 foreign capitals, seeking to enlist their aid in bringing Hanoi to the conference table. When this appeal failed, the bombing was resumed.

The bombing continued through 1966 and 1967, hitting targets in North Vietnam and along the Ho Chi Minh Trail in Laos that the Joint Chiefs of Staff sought to inhibit the movement of supplies and men from North Vietnam to the scene of fighting. Although Secretary of Defense Robert McNamara was skeptical about its efficacy, Johnson now took the position that he could not halt the bombing without some corresponding de-escalation. In a speech at San Antonio, Texas, on September 29, 1967, he set forth his "San Antonio formula": "The United States is willing to stop all aerial and naval bombing of North Vietnam when this will lead promptly to productive discussions. We, of course, assume that while discussions proceed, North Vietnam would not take advantage of the bombing cessation or limitation."[26] On November 2, UN ambassador Arthur Goldberg stated—and the State Department concurred—that the United States would not resist participation of the NLF as a party in a peace conference.

Hanoi's response was the Tet offensive, described above, which produced deep disillusionment with the war in the United States. Secretary of Defense Clark M. Clifford, who succeeded McNamara on March 1, 1968, became convinced that pressing for military victory in Vietnam was useless and that the bombing should be halted as a step toward a negotiated peace. His arguments ultimately prevailed. In a television address on March 31, 1968, Johnson announced that the bombing of North Vietnam would largely end on the following day. Then he announced that he would neither seek nor accept his party's renomination for the presidency.

Negotiations Begin

The Hanoi government responded by agreeing to negotiate. Eventually both sides met in Paris on May 10, 1968, with delegations headed by veteran diplomat W. Averell Harriman for the United States and Xuan Thuy for North Vietnam. The results were disappointing, though not surprising, for the North Vietnamese refused to discuss terms of settlement until all bombing of the North stopped. The United States had refused to stop bombing the supply routes that increased the peril to U.S. troops, yet on October 31, Johnson ended all bombing of North Vietnam. Now the Saigon government stalled, this time over the position of the NLF delegation at the talks. Finally, on January 16, 1969, the delegations agreed that the table should be round, signifying equality of all participants. Four days later, the new Republican administration of Richard M. Nixon took office. When the four delegations met on January 25, 1969, for an actual beginning of negotiations, Henry Cabot Lodge, who had replaced Averell Harriman, proposed as an eventual goal the withdrawal of all foreign (including North Vietnamese) troops from South Vietnam, but as an immediate objective the restoration of the neutralized character of the Demilitarized Zone (DMZ). Five days later, the North Vietnamese and NLF delegations rejected Lodge's proposal in a seven-hour session in which, as described by a *New York Times* reporter, "most of the proceedings were devoted to propaganda, recriminations and occasionally rough language."[27]

President Nixon, in March, endorsed secret talks with Hanoi, while at the same time President Thieu revealed a willingness to begin private talks with the NLF or Viet Cong.[28] On May 8, the NLF made public a 10-point peace proposal. Six days later President Nixon, in a television address to the nation, stated the American objectives.[29] A comparison of these two sets of proposals reveals the points of incompatibility that were for many months to stand in the way of any agreement. In a few words, President Nixon was demanding, as the Johnson administration had insisted, that Hanoi withdraw its troops from South Vietnam and leave the South Vietnamese people to settle their own affairs in peace. Hanoi refused and with the NLF were demanding the unilateral withdrawal of Allied troops and the creation of a South Vietnamese coalition government that excluded Thieu and Ky and their faction. Ho Chi Minh's death on September 3, 1969, failed to bring significant changes. Finally, on July 1, 1970, after the military campaign in Cambodia, Nixon replaced Lodge with David K. E. Bruce, a distinguished diplomat and a Democrat, as head of the American negotiating team in Paris with "great flexibility."[30]

Mme. Nguyen Thi Binh, the chief Viet Cong negotiator, returned to the peace table on September 17, 1970, bringing an eight-point formula. The new proposal, like those before it, called for the unilateral withdrawal of all American and allied troops. There were some concessions, including a possible cease-fire and a willingness to discuss exchange of prisoners prior to a general settlement. There was a sufficient degree of "give" here, thought the *New York Times*, to warrant exploration through submission of new proposals by the United States.[31] On October 7, Nixon presented a five-point plan for a "standstill" cease-fire, immediate exchange of prisoners, a widened peace conference to include Cambodia and Laos (tacit admission that the war had become an "Indochina war"), and a promise to withdraw all American troops as part of an overall settlement. Although the actual proposal did not repeat the insistence that withdrawal of troops be mutual, it became evident that this demand still stood.[32] If the new formula favorably impressed Nixon's former critics at home and abroad, the response from the enemy camp was disappointing. Moscow promptly described the offer as "a great fraud," while it was totally rejected by the Hanoi and Viet Cong negotiators in Paris.

"Vietnamizing" the War

While still hoping to end the war through negotiations, President Nixon attempted to quiet criticism at home by "Vietnamization" of the conflict—gradual withdrawal of U.S. forces and their replacement by better-trained and equipped South Vietnamese troops. An announcement on June 8, 1969, that 25,000 U.S. troops would be withdrawn during July, to be replaced by South Vietnamese, was followed a few days later by the hope that more than 100,000 could be withdrawn before the end of 1970. Then on September 16, it was announced that by the end of 1969 an additional 35,000 would be brought home. All U.S. combat ground forces, Nixon said on November 3, 1969, would be withdrawn from Vietnam and replaced by Vietnamese forces "on an orderly scheduled timetable." The rate of withdrawal depended on three variables: (1) progress of the peace negotiations, (2) "the level of enemy activity," and (3) progress in training the South Vietnamese forces. He warned Hanoi that any increase in violence would be met with "strong and effective measures."[33] The Vietnamization plan focused specifically on the withdrawal of U.S. ground combat forces, but other elements—air, logistics, and artillery—would presumably remain as needed to support Vietnamese forces.[34] Nixon's Vietnamization program added up to a reduction of 265,000 troops by the spring of 1971.

In spite of doubts, the president's plan appeared effective in quieting the antiwar clamor at home for a time. On December 2, the Democratic-controlled House of Representatives adopted by a vote of 333 to 55 a resolution supporting the president "in his efforts to negotiate a just peace in Vietnam." Nixon's promise to begin withdrawing American troops seemed to have taken the steam out of the antiwar movement until he announced on April 30, 1970, that American and South Vietnamese forces were carrying the war into Cambodia. The declared purpose of the intrusion into Cambodia was to capture the communist command headquarters for operations in South Vietnam and to destroy Viet Cong and North Vietnamese sanctuaries in areas adjoining South Vietnam, which for years had been used with the tacit consent of nominally neutralist Prince Norodom Sihanouk, Cambodia's chief of state. The United States had long tolerated this breach of neutrality rather than risk driving Sihanouk into the enemy camp. In March 1969, however, the U.S. Air Force began a series of secret, illegal bombing raids in eastern Cambodia that lasted until Sihanouk was ousted on March 18, 1970, by pro-West premier General Lon Nol. Described as long on ambition but short on ability, Lon Nol believed his country was threatened by the presence of North Vietnamese troops. Not only was the enemy threatening to take over Cambodia, Nixon declared, he was "concentrating his main forces in the sanctuaries where they are building up to launch massive attacks on our forces and those of South Vietnam." In view of this dual threat, the president argued it was necessary "to go to the heart of the trouble. That means cleaning out major North Vietnamese and Viet Cong-occupied sanctuaries which serve as bases for attacks on both

Cambodia and American and South Vietnamese forces in South Vietnam."[35]

The move into Cambodia produced a new, more intense round of demonstrations on some 1,350 college and university campuses, some turning violent. At Kent State University, the Ohio National Guard troop fired on demonstrators, killing 4 students and wounding 9, and at Jackson State University Mississippi, police shot 2 students and wounded 12. Senators introduced several resolutions designed to prevent the president from expanding the area of war without consent of Congress. Upon completion of the sweep on June 30, limited to 30 kilometers within Cambodia, the president issued a long report, claiming dubious successes for the operation, since the "key control center" of the communist command had not been found.[36] The American public had had enough. According to a Gallup poll taken in May 1971, 6 out of 10 Americans now thought it had been a mistake for the United States to get involved in Vietnam. This was a complete reversal of public opinion since August 1965, and the poll revealed that Republicans had changed their views of the war almost as drastically as Democrats.[37]

Fighting and Negotiating

In the November following the Cambodian invasion, the Nixon administration began increasingly to concern itself with a large buildup of supplies in North Vietnam, the problem being one of how to prevent them from moving southward. To meet the challenge and to test Vietnamization, in February 1971, two of South Vietnam's best divisions launched a major offensive (Lam Son 719) aimed at cutting the Ho Chi Minh trail in Laos. Without American advisers but with American air cover, the outmanned South Vietnamese were challenged by four veteran North Vietnamese divisions, resulting in a disaster for Saigon's forces. Thereafter, the intensified fighting of 1971 was met with increased U.S. bombing, albeit within the framework of continued American withdrawals. In the spring of 1972, perceiving that President Nixon's hands would be tied in an election year and persuaded of the vulnerability of the Thieu regime, Hanoi launched a major offensive in the south, this time abandoning its guerrilla tactics in favor of a conventional alignment led by Soviet-supplied T-54 tanks. Initial results were striking as entire South Vietnamese divisions panicked. In less than a month, Hanoi had captured the northern capital of Quantri and menaced Saigon itself, but did not destroy the South Vietnamese army. Although some southern units disintegrated, others fought well, but it was

U.S. airpower that played the decisive role in stopping the Easter Offensive. Despite his proposed trip to Moscow in May, Nixon ordered the heaviest bombing raids of the war thus far. Major facilities and installations were struck. Then the president authorized the mining of the entrances of North Vietnamese ports, thus setting the stage for a potentially direct confrontation with either the Soviet Union or China or both. But nothing of the sort happened. The war was again stalemated, but North Vietnamese forces held stronger positions in the south.[38]

Understandably anxious to secure peace before the coming presidential election in November, Nixon let it be known that he would accept a cease-fire in place rather than the complete withdrawal of North Vietnamese troops. With the American counteroffensive partially successful and in the face of a strengthened Thieu government, Hanoi opted for the peace table. Nixon suspended the bombing of North Vietnam, north of the 20th parallel. Negotiations took place at the formal meetings in Paris, but presidential adviser Henry Kissinger and North Vietnamese representative Le Duc Tho privately worked on preliminary terms of a final agreement. President Thieu balked, however, at the terms of the agreement and demanded that they be renegotiated. In the end, Nixon issued Thieu an ultimatum, and he acquiesced.[39] Meanwhile, when Hanoi began to stall, the president on December 18 resumed the bombing of the north with a vengeance. The North Vietnamese capital and Haiphong were bombed more heavily than at any previous stage of the conflict. In response to worldwide protests, Washington again restricted the bombing on December 30 to the area south of the 20th parallel and on January 15, 1973, ended all bombing of North Vietnam. Private talks between Kissinger and Le Duc Tho resumed in Paris on January 8 and, five days later, resulted in the conclusion of the elusive peace agreement signed on January 27.

The Paris cease-fire agreement, as it came to be called, provided, among other things, for a standstill cease-fire to take place immediately; the withdrawal of all U.S. forces from South Vietnam and the release of all American prisoners of war within 60 days; the formation of a four-party joint military commission to enforce these provisions; the establishment of an International Commission on Control and Supervision; the formation by agreement between the South Vietnamese parties of a National Council of National Reconciliation and Concord, which would set about the task of organizing general elections; and the holding of an international conference on Vietnam within 30 days of the signing of the agreement. American fighting on the ground terminated with the withdrawal of the last U.S. troops in March 1973, two months after the cease-fire and eight years after the first formal commitment of military forces. Thus ended, until then, the longest war in U.S. history.

American involvement in Vietnam was, by any standard, a most costly episode. The loss in national treasure and blood was staggering. According to Pentagon estimates, from 1961 until late April 1975, U.S. expenditures in Indochina came to more than $141 billion or, to put it another way, $7,000 for each of South Vietnam's 20 million people. The war produced many dubious precedents, including U.S. chemical operations, defoliation and crop destruction, that consumed some 5,229,484 acres; bombing tonnage (more than three times the total amount dropped in World War II); and the first known use of weather warfare, all of which left lasting ecological damage. The loss of life was equally staggering. From the 1961 death of Specialist 4 James Thomas Davis of Livingston, Tennessee, whom President Lyndon Johnson later called "the first American to fall in defense of our freedom in Vietnam," until the Paris Peace Accords of 1973, American casualties alone reached 350,000 with 59,000 killed (40,000 in combat). Casualty figures for Vietnamese (North and South), at best an estimate, may have reached a million deaths, including civilians, with more than 224,000 South Vietnamese combat deaths, and perhaps 660,000 combined North Vietnamese and Viet Cong combat deaths. Vietnam also had an impact at home: the "television war" turned napalm and "free-fire zones" into household words; severe inflation affected the economy as early as 1965; university campuses grew highly politicized; draft resisters fled to Canada and foreign lands; and presidents were made and unmade. Vietnam shaped and reshaped all who survived it—from political leaders and military chiefs to the proverbial man in the street.

The Collapse of American Policy

While the negotiated peace settlement allowed the United States an opportunity to extricate itself from Indochina with what the Nixon administration regarded as a semblance of "peace with honor," the reality of the situation was vastly different for those who remained behind. In view of the almost irreconcilable nature of the conflict between President Thieu and his opponents and the potential threat of 150,000 North Vietnamese regulars and Viet Cong poised on South Vietnamese soil, it seemed to most observers that it would be only a matter of time before the south would be overrun, perhaps as few as five years. As it turned out, it only required three years.

Hanoi was utterly undeterred by the peace agreement and soon set out to reunify the two Vietnams by force of arms. Correctly gauging the mood of the American public, the North Vietnamese General Staff, according to the most authoritative sources,[40] carefully laid the groundwork for the next offensive. In the spring of 1975, a combined North Vietnamese and Viet Cong attack proved too much for the poorly led South Vietnamese army. Saigon, renamed Ho Chi Minh City, fell on April 30.

The United States' covert activities in Laos were for years conducted by the Hmong, who were supplied and directed by the Central Intelligence Agency. Backed by U.S. airpower from 1962 to 1973 and by special Thai units, these mountain warriors, despite suffering very heavy casualties, conducted guerrilla operations that slowed the advance of Pathet Lao and North Vietnamese forces in Laos. The Vientiane Agreement of February 1973 ended U.S. bombing, required the withdrawal of Thai forces, and created a new coalition government. In December 1975, the Hanoi-backed Pathet Lao established the Lao People's Democratic Republic. The United States provided military support for Lon Nol's Cambodian regime from 1970 to 1973, especially channeling American airpower to help slow the advancing Khmer Rouge. After Congress halted aid shipments in late 1974, resistance collapsed the Khmer Rouge seized Phnom Penh on April 17, 1975, renamed Cambodia as Democratic Kampuchea, renounced ties with North Vietnam, and set about killing and torturing nearly 1 million Cambodians by the end of 1978.[41]

The collapse of South Vietnam, together with the defeat of the pro-Western forces in Laos and subsequently in Cambodia, marked the end of an American era in Southeast Asia.

The Legacy

An enduring legacy of the Vietnam War has been the extraordinary number of accounts by participants and critics of all sorts—a virtual cottage industry—that continue to present arguments without end. U.S. military officers, writing after the war, often felt that they had been denied victory. These professional soldiers usually held President Johnson responsible for refusing to mobilize the nation for war, for placing limitations on the forces in the field, for gradually escalating hostilities instead of launching a knockout aerial blow, and for not invading North Vietnam. However, as Pulitzer Prize–winning author Stanley Karnow points out, "such autopsies, like war games, often bear little resemblance to actual war. In reality, the communists were almost fanatical in their resolve to reunify Vietnam under their control. They saw the struggle against America and its South Vietnamese allies as another chapter in their nation's thousands of years of resistance to Chinese and, later, French rule. And they were prepared to accept unlimited losses to achieve their sacred objective." In pursuit of their paramount patriotic mission, the Vietnamese Communists obviously were willing to spend much more blood and treasure than was the United States to achieve its ill-defined, broadly conceived objective of staving off a possible domino debacle.

The Vietnam conflict, the only military defeat America had suffered, "had deflated its overweening belief in its supremacy." What exactly the American people wanted to know, went wrong? Walter Lippmann, the dean of American news commentators and long an opponent of the war, analyzed the matter. He found the war absurd: "Here we are, some 200 million of us, with the greatest armaments that any country has ever possessed, and there are the North Vietnamese, some 20 million of them, with a primitive industrial system. Yet we have been unable to make them do what we want them to do." Lippmann thought he knew why: "Because, armed peasants who are willing to die are a match for the mightiest power." Recognizing as legitimate the restraints implicit in unnecessarily drawing in China and the Soviet Union, the U.S. military, according to Lippmann, found itself with an impossible task: "Thus, our failure in Vietnam sprang from a great mistake. We asked the armed forces to do what it was not possible for them to do." This appears to be a fair assessment of the situation, and coming from the "father" of the critique of containment, it struck a responsive chord among a large section of the population.[42]

Consequently, the American public, baffled, sober, and ambivalent, demonstrated a distinct lack of enthusiasm to undertake another overseas military venture. They, much like the U.S. military leadership, were infected with the "Vietnam Syndrome." Out of this reluctance to send U.S. troops anywhere to engage in hostilities emerged the so-called Weinberger Doctrine. In a November 28, 1984, speech, President Reagan's secretary of defense, Caspar Weinberger, outlined six points that had to be met before the Pentagon would again recommend sending U.S. forces into combat:

(1) armed force would be used only to protect vital interests of the US or its allies;
(2) when the US commits itself to the use of force it must do so wholeheartedly, with the clear intention of winning;

(3) troops should be committed only in pursuit of clearly defined political and military objectives, and we should know in advance precisely how the forces committed can accomplish those clear objectives;
(4) the relationship between the forces committed—their size, composition, etc.—and the objectives must continually be reassessed and adjusted if necessary;
(5) before the US commits combat forces abroad, there must be some reasonable assurance we will have the support of the American people and their representatives in Congress; and
(6) the commitment of US armed force should be the last resort.[43]

The Vietnam Syndrome influenced the American public and the Pentagon until the United States' overwhelming military victory in the First Gulf War.

CHAPTER 16

Reagan, Bush, Gorbachev, and the End of the Cold War

Wars end in victory or defeat. One of the foremost authorities on communism in the world today has said we have ten years. Not ten years to make up our minds, but ten years to win or lose—by 1970 the world will be all slave or free.
—Ronald Reagan, Address, the Phoenix, Arizona, Chamber of Commerce, 1961

[The INF treaty] offers a big chance at last to get onto the road leading away from the threat of catastrophe. It is our duty... to move forward toward a nuclear-free world... [that is] without fear and without a senseless waste of resources on weapons of destruction.
—Mikhail Gorbachev, Washington Summit, December 8, 1987

Ronald Reagan entered the White House in January 1981 and, with his new administration, promptly launched what some historians have labeled "The Second Cold War." The Republican Party platform had detected "clear danger signals indicating that the Soviet Union was using Cuban, East German, and now Nicaraguan, as well as its own, military forces to extend its power to Africa, Asia and the Western Hemisphere." During the presidential campaign, Reagan condemned the Carter administration for the humiliation caused by Iran's seizure of American hostages, its failure to act while the Soviets intervened in Afghanistan, and for permitting the Soviet Union to gain military supremacy over the United States. "We're already *in* an arms race," Reagan replied to doubters, "but only the Soviets are racing."[1] Even though America's economic and military strength continued to stabilize a divided Europe, to Republicans the Carter administration failed to halt Soviet expansionism.

Yet nowhere did Reagan or these Cold Warriors urge the United States to militarily challenge the Soviet Union, neither did they propose with any precision solutions to the dilemmas they presented. There seemed to be little recognition that the Kremlin's successes in the Third World were largely due to tying itself to local nationalistic movements, movements that would shed Moscow's influence when Soviet interests conflicted with indigenous interests.

Long before the presidential campaign, Reagan had developed a well-crafted anticommunist litany in his trademark speech. Addressing the Phoenix, Arizona, Chamber of Commerce in 1961, he stated, "Wars end in victory or defeat. One of the foremost authorities on communism in the world today has said we have ten years. Not ten years to make up our minds, but ten years to win or lose—by 1970 the world will be all slave or free." Two decades later, Reagan still approached the Cold War much as other strident anticommunists: "We are faced with the most evil enemy mankind has known in his long climb from the swamp to the stars." After castigating American liberals for seeking agreements to limit strategic nuclear weapons, he insisted, "We are being asked to buy our safety from the threat of the Bomb by selling into permanent slavery our fellow human beings enslaved behind the Iron Curtain." Reagan charged his opponents with "encouraging them to give up their hope of freedom because we are ready to make a deal with their slave masters."[2] Reagan's "evil empire" speech, on March 8, 1983, to the National Association of Evangelicals—although it was not the first occasion he employed that term to describe the Soviet Union—represented the climax of his hostile rhetoric.

Fear of Soviet military power and global expansionism dominated the outlook of the Reagan administration. The president defined these dangers at a White House news conference in late January 1981: "From the time of the Russian revolution until the present, Soviet leaders have reiterated their determination that their goal must be the promotion of world revolution and a one world socialist or communist state.... They have openly and publicly declared that the only morality they recognize is what will further their cause; meaning they reserve unto themselves the right to commit any crime; to lie [and] to cheat in order to obtain that." Echoing this view, Secretary of State designate Alexander Haig at his confirmation hearings warned members of the Senate Foreign Relations Committee the years ahead would "be unusually dangerous. Evidence of that danger ... [was] everywhere." The nation needed to be vigilant and be prepared to expend the resources necessary to control future events. "Unchecked," he said, "the growth of Soviet military power must eventually paralyze Western policy altogether." Three months later, Haig declared that

Washington needed to concentrate its policies on the Soviet Union because the Kremlin was "the greatest source of international insecurity today.... Let us be plain about it: Soviet promotion of violence as the instrument of change constitutes the greatest danger to world peace."[3]

The Reagan administration, despite its rhetoric to the contrary, deliberately sought to distance itself from previous presidential efforts to employ diplomacy in seeking limits to the nuclear arms race. The president was on record opposing the 1963 Test Ban pact (Kennedy), the 1968 Non-Proliferation Treaty (Johnson), the 1972 Strategic Arms Limitation (SALT I) pact and the Anti-Ballistic Missile (ABM) agreements (Nixon), and the Helsinki Accords (Ford). He now insisted the SALT II treaty (Carter) was "fatally flawed." Indeed, he argued, SALT II allowed the Soviet Union a "window of vulnerability" through which its missile superiority would threaten U.S. long-range missile forces. Despite his anti-Soviet rhetoric, Reagan ultimately expected much improved relations with the Kremlin. His inaugural address emphasized the American people's desire for peace: "We will negotiate for it, sacrifice for it, [but] we will not surrender for it, now or ever." The new president, however, was determined to negotiate from strength, to build up before building down. His expanded military program, Reagan later explained, was aimed at gaining concessions from the Soviets. It was questionable, however, whether Reagan ever lacked the military strength to negotiate. Negotiation always consists of more than assessing existing power, whatever its magnitude, when it carries no serious sign of impending hostile action. Successful negotiation entails compromises needed to establish a satisfactory agreement grounded on mutual interests, whether dealing with territorial disputes or arms reductions.[4]

U.S. Military Buildup

During the presidential campaign, Reagan and his supporters repeatedly pledged to rebuild America's military forces to reverse what they perceived as a national malaise. Consequently, the new administration eventually set in motion the costliest defense program in the nation's peacetime history. Reagan's military advisers, pushing for higher levels of defense expenditures, ignored traditional review procedures and refused to reconsider the military utility of a project once authorized. Even Defense Secretary Caspar W. Weinberger, who had arrived with a well-earned reputation for cost cutting, endorsed the Pentagon's "wish list," with its requirement of nothing less than an annual 7 percent budget increase. Reagan agreed and included the inflated figure in his new budget, not recognizing that his staff had confused budget calculations and actually increased military expenditures by 10 percent per year. The fiscally conservative president consequently tripled the national debt—slightly under $1 trillion to more than $3 trillion by the end of the decade. With new, technologically advanced weapons Washington expected to deal from a position of greater strength, reassure allies, and perhaps force Moscow to agree to a disadvantageous reduction of its nuclear weaponry. The proposed expenditures—$1.6 trillion in five years—would be used to acquire new missile systems, especially the mobile MX; underwrite the nation's most ambitious naval program ever; update air force planes and facilities; and create a stronger, more mobile conventional force prepared for any global challenges. The immediate dilemma, not always resolved, required distinguishing weapons that were necessary, effective, and manageable from those that were merely expensive. Reiterating a long-held Pentagon truism, Secretary Weinberger nevertheless insisted that Soviet intervention in Afghanistan demonstrated the United States must always be ready to fight several conventional wars simultaneously. "We must be prepared for waging a conventional war that may extend to many parts of the world."[5]

The massive new military buildup was not without its critics. To informed observers the Reagan administration's claim of Soviet overwhelming military power was nothing more than a myth. According to James Fallows, symbols unquestionably play a part in international politics. "The Russians have derived incalculable mileage from the impression that they have built a world-conquering military force, an impression they have been fostering, overtly and covertly, since 1945. But why should we help them create that impression," he questioned, "when it is at such variance with the facts. . . . If the problem is the perception of American strength, why not assess that strength coolly rather that create exaggerated fears?" The administration's avoidance of readily available facts was evident. Christopher Paine pointed out in a fall 1982 edition of *Bulletin of the Atomic Scientists* that "85 percent of the Soviet submarine-launched ballistic missile force [is] usually in port on any given day," while only one-third of U.S. submarines were similarly in port. The *New York Daily News* reported in February 1982, "morale among Soviet troops stationed in East Germany is so bad that some units are close to mutiny."[6] Not surprisingly, overly generous annual assessments of the Soviet armed forces published by the Pentagon's public relations office, used to justify its budgets during the early Reagan years, ignored such data.

There were many businessmen, though, and even some Pentagon officials, who questioned whether the projected military spending exceeded the requirements of national security. Could Defense Secretary Weinberger reduce the military's wasteful habits, could the Pentagon be accountable—perhaps even balance its books? Congressmen, equally troubled by the perennial rise in the cost of national defense, had difficulty arguing that specific expenditures were excessive when the experts, with their control of essential information, insisted that they were not. (Moreover, most Congressional representatives benefited from the monies spent in their districts and recognized substantial reductions of defense expenditures would result in the loss of jobs at home.) There existed in Washington, in any case, a strange lack of concern for an effective distribution of allocated defense funds. Nonetheless, the expenditures themselves were somehow expected to send a message to the Kremlin.

Rhetoric versus Action

The president and his advisers expected far more than the perpetuation of the status quo from the country's costly defense efforts; indeed, some thought the higher levels of U.S. preparedness would bring about long-desired changes in Soviet behavior. "We have a right, indeed a duty," Secretary Haig echoed, "to insist that the Soviets support a peaceful international order, that they abide by treaties, and that they respect reciprocity." Another senior administration official announced that a Soviet withdrawal from Afghanistan and Angola was not sufficient as a precondition for moderating the United States' posture; he would demand nothing less than an extensive reduction in Soviet military spending. Others in Washington anticipated that when the United States achieved overwhelming nuclear supremacy, the Soviet Union would be coerced into accepting conditions that conformed to American design. In some measure, Reagan's approach to the U.S.S.R. was a reaffirmation of the Eisenhower administration's concept of massive retaliation, with its underlying assumption that the Soviets could not, in the long run, survive American competition.[7]

The administration would never link its fears of the Soviet Union with its actions, for the Reagan team never formulated policies that focused on fulfilling its self-proclaimed global goals. Foreign policy rhetoric spewed about during the administration's early months never determined policy, for the occasions when American force might be used was never defined with any precision. Shooting down two Libyan aircraft, in late 1981, that challenged an American naval presence inside the Gulf of Sidra was scarcely a defining moment. Raising questions about his policy of toughness, Reagan, in early April 1981, terminated Carter's embargo on grain shipments to the Soviet Union. Much like Carter, Reagan coexisted—often quietly employing the Central Intelligence Agency (CIA)—with the Soviet activities in Afghanistan, Africa, and the Arabian Peninsula. The Reagan rhetoric was meant, critics logically concluded, not to form the basis of the tougher policy toward Moscow, but rather to assuage a fearful American public.

Gradually, a chasm between official words and official actions aggravated differences between the administration's pragmatists and the ideologues. Because of the lack of clearly defined objectives, Reagan received conflicting policy proposals from Haig's State Department, Weinberger's Defense Department, Richard Allen's National Security Council, Jeane Kirkpatrick's UN office, and Republicans everywhere. Not surprisingly, bitter bureaucratic struggles sprang up, leading Haig to complain that the decision-making process was as "mysterious as a ghost ship; you heard the creak of the rigging and the groan of the timbers and even glimpsed the crew on deck. But which one of the crew was at the helm? It was impossible to know for sure."[8]

Central America

Reagan's new globalism obligated Washington to challenge Moscow's expansionist activities not only in Central America but elsewhere. Central America, specifically Nicaragua's radical Sandinista regime and El Salvadoran guerrillas, posed an immediate challenge to the Reagan administration. The Republican platform of 1980 had warned of the growing power of communism in Central America as demonstrated by the Marxist takeover of Nicaragua and Marxist attempts to destabilize El Salvador, Guatemala, and Honduras. "As a result," noted the platform, "a clear and present danger threatens the energy and raw material lifelines of the Western world." Kirkpatrick, the American ambassador to the UN, condemned President Carter's failure to assist Nicaragua's Anastasio Somoza, even if he was a dictator, because his pro-American government was a more acceptable ally. Since Somoza had created an efficient, urban political regime, she insisted Washington should have provided whatever support he needed to stay in power.[9]

Even before assuming office, Reagan had designated El Salvador as a focal point of Soviet-American confrontation. Since it was well known that Cuba and other Soviet-bloc countries supplied Salvadoran rebels with arms *via* Nicaragua, an administration counteroffensive supporting the right-wing-dominated government would not only reassert America's role in hemispheric defense, it could also do so without risking the introduction of

U.S. combat forces. The Carter administration's unsuccessful support of a moderate regime had hoped to blunt the communist-led insurgency, only to find that large landowners and the military employed "death squads" in a bloody repression that resulted in the murder of thousands. Americans suspected only of favoring insurgents did not escape the violence, as Salvadoran soldiers abducted, raped, tortured, and murdered four American churchwomen and buried them in a shallow grave.

Reagan resurrected the domino theory to emphasize the nature of the Soviet challenge. "What we're doing," he told newsmen, "is try to halt the infiltration into the Americas, by terrorists and by outside interference, and those who aren't just aiming at El Salvador but, I think, are aiming at the whole of Central America and possibly later South America and, I'm sure, eventually North America." Lawrence Eagleburger, Reagan's undersecretary of state for political affairs, worried: "[I]f the Sandinistas and the Salvadoran guerrillas are successful in overthrowing the Government in El Salvador, that's the beginning, not the end, of the problem. The Costa Ricans, the Hondurans and the Guatemalans are certainly going to face the same sort of threat. I can't even say that the Mexicans wouldn't have a problem." Secretary Haig insisted that the Kremlin must control its clients in Cuba, Nicaragua, and El Salvador or assume responsibility for their activities. El Salvador was merely a single item on "a priority target list—a hit list, if you will, for the ultimate takeover of Central America," he informed the House Foreign Affairs Committee in mid-March. If the spread of this Soviet-sponsored terrorism is not halted, the secretary warned, "[We] will find it within our own borders tomorrow." With Nicaragua already under Moscow's domination, El Salvador, Guatemala, and Honduras would surely follow.[10] To many observers, however, the administration had overplayed its hand. Administration officials were subsequently forced to recognize that the political realities of Central America were far more complex than Haig's hit list suggested. Critics questioned the notion that poverty-stricken and revolution-prone El Salvador somehow could be the keystone of hemispheric security.

Without warning, on October 25, 1983, U.S. military forces invaded the small island of Grenada in the eastern Caribbean with a population of 120,000. Ever since Maurice Bishop in a bloodless coup had seized control of the government in 1979 and established close ties with Cuba's Fidel Castro, Washington kept the island under close scrutiny. On a visit to the Caribbean in 1982, Reagan declared that the Soviet Union had brought Grenada, as well as Cuba and Nicaragua, under its influence in order to "spread the virus" of Marxism throughout the Caribbean.[23] Bishop, assisted by Venezuela, East Germany, North

Korea, and Canada created by 1983 a booming tourist trade. Cubans were brought in to construct a 12,000-foot airstrip, improve medical facilities and other public projects. In addition, Bishop imported large quantities of Cuban arms. The Reagan administration condemned the runway as one designed only for military use, although Barbados, the Bahamas, and Martinique all had longer airstrips to handle tourists. Bishop's verbal confrontation with Washington ended on October 19 with his assassination during a coup led by the deputy prime minister. In their success, the island's political extremists squandered whatever legitimacy Bishop's revolution possessed.

Fearing the possibility of chaos, most of the island's population welcomed the arrival of U.S. forces and the promises of order and democracy that they offered. American students at the local medical college enthusiastically greeted what the president termed a rescue mission. Grenada's new leadership announced an election in November 1984. If the American public overwhelmingly approved of the surprise invasion, as a military venture Operation Urgent Fury left much to be desired. The attacking U.S. force of 7,000 took three days to overwhelm the lightly armed Cuban construction hands. The lack of a unified command found army and navy personnel failing to attend the other's planning sessions, equipping their attacking units with incompatible radios, and, at least on one occasion, assaulting the other's positions. Nevertheless, the administration reveled in successfully preventing Grenada's incorporation into the Soviet-Cuban bloc and at limited cost. Much of the country seemed to agree.[11]

Reagan and Europe

Washington's relations with Europe were severely strained by the Reagan administration's opposition to the Soviets' proposed multibillion-dollar Yamal natural gas pipeline. The pipeline would convey 3 billion cubic meters of natural gas from the Yamal Peninsula, above the Arctic Circle, to West Germany, France, and Italy by 1984. The Europeans hailed the pipeline in 1980 as a means of providing much-needed energy, while Reagan offered coal and nuclear power. Having rejected détente, he had no desire to encourage closer ties between Europe and the Soviet Union. This project, he told a Western summit conference at Ottawa in July 1981, would provide Moscow a potential stranglehold over Western Europe's energy supplies. The Defense Department feared the $8 billion the Soviets earned annually would enhance the Soviet economy and provide for even greater military spending.[12] Washington's arguments did not play well in Western European capitals. European leaders preferred Moscow to reliance on the Middle East since natural gas would account for only 2 percent of their combined energy requirements. Moreover, with some 25 million unemployed in the West, the projected pipeline offered opportunities for much-needed jobs and commerce.

Undeterred, Reagan looked to bar American corporations from supplying materials for the construction of the pipeline; however, soon internal concerns surfaced. Would these economic sanctions seriously endanger the NATO alliance? Defense Secretary Weinberger and Pentagon officials, urging unilateral enforcement of a broad ban, were willing to risk alienating America's allies to prevent the Soviet Union from receiving funds from the pipeline. Ultimately, on June 18, 1982, the president, in defiance of international law, authorized sanctions on U.S. firms, their European subsidiaries, and foreign companies producing equipment under U.S. licenses. Worried about their economies, officials in Bonn, Rome, Paris, and London announced that they would honor their pipeline contracts. The president's action prompted some Europeans to question why, if so concerned about bringing economic pressure on the Kremlin, Washington had not canceled the sale of American grain to the Soviet Union. "We no longer speak the same language," France's foreign minister Cheysson complained. "The United States seems wholly indifferent to our problems."[13]

As the controversy heated up, European governments instructed firms operating within their borders to fulfill their contracts with the Soviet Union. To West German chancellor Schmidt, national sovereignty and the sanctity of contracts were at stake. The dispute, said *The Times* (London) had "torn a nasty hole in the Western Alliance." The *Daily Mail* added, "The Atlantic Alliance is a genuine partnership of free and independent nations, not a superpower plus a gaggle of satellites." Administration critics warned that strict application of the pipeline sanctions could bring about reprisals that would endanger U.S. investments in Europe. Reagan had stressed that unity of the Western alliance was vital to improve relations with Moscow. Now wasn't it also true, West Germany's Hans-Dietrich Genscher observed, that agreement within the alliance on policy toward Moscow was equally vital for coherent Western actions?[14] Without a face-saving retreat, Reagan abruptly terminated the sanctions in the fall of 1982.

Other disagreements continued to plague Washington and its Western European allies: Reagan policies toward the Third World, especially Central America, and his administration's approach to the emerging Polish crisis. Many European critics ridiculed the administration's claims that Soviet expansionism was the universal source of turmoil. "Americans see danger, revolution and terrorism everywhere," declared Germany's *Der Spiegel*, "and behind it all are the Russians." Why support a notoriously repressive government in El Salvador, send assistance to suppress the civil war there, and seek to overturn the government of Nicaragua? Some European writers, such as Robert Held of the *Frankfurter Allgemeine Zeitung*, did endorse Reagan's cause. "The Americans," he wrote, "simply cannot afford to let the land bridge to the South American continent become a hegemonical [sic] zone of the Soviet Union." Much like their American counterparts, European critics considered the political and social upheavals in Central America to be regional rather than global, indigenous rather than external. "President Reagan still sees in any Third World crisis the hand of the Soviet Union," complained Andre Fontaine, editor of Paris's *Le Monde*, in April 1982. "From here that appears ridiculous. You don't need Russians to create situations like Nicaragua and El Salvador."

The December 1981 unrest in Poland also became a divisive issue. When Warsaw's communist government announced a state of national emergency, established martial law, and called on its military to crack down on the popular union-led Solidarity movement, European leaders expressed relief that Soviet armed forces were not involved and sent shipments of food. Washington officials, in contrast, held Moscow responsible for crushing Solidarity's efforts to gain power. German foreign minister Hans-Dietrich Genscher, however, refused to consider the administration's proposed sanctions to be levied against the Kremlin. Undaunted by Europe's refusal to cooperate, Reagan, in late December, embargoed all shipments of American technology to the Soviet Union, suspended Aeroflot flights to the United States, restricted Soviet access to U.S. ports, and refused to renew exchange agreements in energy, science, and technology. Having failed to consult its allies cost the White House allied support for its initiative.[15]

A Second Cold War?

The Reagan administration's ideological crusade had inexcusably heightened tensions between Washington and Moscow. Writing in the *New Yorker* on October 3, 1983, Soviet expert George F. Kennan noted that public discussion of Soviet-American relations seemed to point to a military showdown. "Can anyone mistake, or doubt," he asked, "the ominous meaning of such a state of affairs? The phenomena just described... are the familiar characteristics, the unfailing characteristics, of a march toward war—that, and nothing else." This grim assessment suggested that America was bent on creating a second, more dangerous Cold War. Yet nowhere did the administration's alleged toughness result in diplomatic achievements that improved America's security. Reagan's ideological approach, Stanley Hoffmann argued in *Dead Ends*, "has turned out to be utterly deficient as a strategy because it fails to address many real problems, it aggravates others, it provides no priority other than the anti-Soviet imperative, and precious little guidance even in connection with the new Cold War."[16] The character of the Soviet power structure was irrelevant to the requirement of dealing openly and frankly with the Kremlin. "Like Mount Everest," wrote *Newsweek*'s Meg Greenfield, in September 1983, "the Russians are there. And, like Mount Everest, their features are not exactly a mystery. We need to stop gasping and sighing and exclaiming and nearly dying of shock every time something truly disagreeable happens. We have to grow up and confront them—as they are."

Meanwhile, on September 1, 1983, the Soviets shot down a Korean commercial airliner (KAL 007) that had strayed over Russian territory. To Washington officials, the incident was additional evidence of Soviet paranoia and unconcern for human life. While the State Department called the disaster "brutal and unprovoked," the president's statement for the media declared: "What can we think of a regime that so broadly trumpets its vision of peace and global disarmament and yet so callously and quickly commits *a terrorist act*? What can be said about *Soviet credibility* when they so *flagrantly lie about such a heinous act* [italics in original]?" In perhaps the most comprehensive and categorical top-level Soviet denunciation of any U.S. administration since the early Cold War, Soviet premier Yuri Andropov condemned Reagan's attitude on September 28. The president's ideological challenges risked the prospect of actual war, the Soviet leader declared. "To turn the battle of ideas into military confrontation would be too costly for the whole of mankind. But those who are blinded by anticommunism are evidently incapable of grasping this," Andropov continued. "Starting with the bogey of a Soviet military threat, they have now proclaimed a crusade against socialism as a social system."[17]

The reality of Andropov's warning came two months later. Without notifying the Warsaw Pact countries, NATO had scheduled a command post exercise, code-named Able Archer, for November 2–11, 1983, that involved Western leaders to test nuclear release procedures. Uncertain of the exercise's purpose, the Soviet Union went on a strategic intelligence alert. Days passed, and the attack did not come; the Soviets had apparently exaggerated the danger. Throughout the crisis—although they were aware of the turmoil in Moscow—Washington offered the Soviets no explanation. On November 16, Alexander Bovin, *Izvestia*'s political commentator, accused American leaders of ignoring the security interests of the Soviet Union and compelling the two countries to walk "the edge of the missile precipice." From mid-1983 into 1984, according to CIA reports, senior officials in Moscow took "very seriously" the threat of a U.S. preemptive nuclear attack. Former diplomat W. Averell Harriman warned Reagan on January 1, 1984, that his program of emphasizing military strength while denigrating diplomacy could lead to disaster. Blaming the Kremlin for the world's current instabilities was, he wrote, "not a strategy or a policy.... It will not reshape the Russian nation; it will not bring down the Iron Curtain; and, above all, it will not reduce the nuclear threat that hangs over every American."

Reagan was quite surprised to learn that "many people at the top of the Soviet hierarchy were genuinely afraid of America and Americans." Why would the Soviets have such fears," Reagan wondered naively: "I'd always felt that from our deeds it must be clear to anyone that Americans were a moral people who starting at the birth of our nation had always used our power only as a force of good in the world."[18]

Seeking Nuclear Limits

With its early emphasis on increasing America's nuclear armaments, its lack of interest in arms control, and its harsh anti-Soviet rhetoric, the administration and its supporters greatly aroused the anxieties of antinuclear movements from the United States across Western Europe. The administration's ardent anticommunists openly acknowledged the possibility of hostilities. Reagan's arms control chief, Eugene Rostow, noted, "We are living in a prewar and not a postwar world." Even Defense Secretary Weinberger, who believed nuclear wars were not winnable, nevertheless insisted: "We are planning to prevail if we are attacked." Echoing this opinion, White House adviser Thomas C. Reed, added, "Prevailing with pride is the principal new ingredient of American foreign policy."[19] In the spring of 1982, four distinguished Americans—McGeorge Bundy, George Kennan, Robert McNamara, and Gerard Smith—argued in *Foreign Affairs* that the United States, to limit the possibilities of nuclear war, should reverse its policy of three decades and promise never to use nuclear weapons first. It did not happen.

Of immediate concern was Moscow's deployment in Europe of SS-20s, a significantly upgraded intermediate missile carrying three nuclear-tipped warheads. The United States began planning in 1979 to counter with 108 Pershing II and 464 ground-launched cruise missiles (GLCMs) to West Germany, Belgium, Britain, the Netherlands, and Italy. Fear of a renewed nuclear arms race by the superpowers set off the powerful European peace movement of 1981, as over 2 million Europeans joined antinuclear, and largely anti-American, demonstrations. West Germans, at the potential center of any European firestorm, were understandably upset with the apparent nonchalance in Washington about the talk of fighting and winning a nuclear war. Pressure from antinuclear protesters in NATO countries and the nuclear freeze movement at home prompted the administration, in late 1981, to review the unsuccessful arms control negotiations. Attempting to pacify European demonstrators, the Reagan administration offered a "zero option" concept—the United States would cancel its deployment of intermediate-range missiles, scheduled for two year in the future, in exchange for the Soviets' prompt withdrawal of its deployed SS-20s carrying some 1,100 warheads. In May 1982, Reagan unveiled his two-phased proposal for the promised Strategic Arms Reduction Talks (START) that emphasized a "practical phased reduction" of strategic nuclear systems. This plan would require the Soviets to substantially reduce their force of land-based ICBMs— their most effective strategic weapons—and to reduce by almost two-thirds the aggregate throw weight of their missiles. Meanwhile, the United States would retain most of its land-based Minutemen, deploy a hundred new large MXs missiles, expand its cruise missiles, and modernize its submarine and bomber fleets. Knowledgeable observers found the START formula, like the earlier "zero option," so one-sided it was nonnegotiable. "This proposal is so stacked against the Soviets," the sponsor of the House's nuclear freeze resolution Congressman Edward J. Markey complained, "there is little chance they will accept it." Not surprisingly, Moscow ignored both of Washington's proposals.[20]

Neither beltway insiders nor Kremlin leaders were prepared for Reagan's March 23, 1983, proposal for a defense against nuclear-tipped ballistic missiles. After noting America's security currently depended on nuclear deterrence, he offered his vision of a better future to a television audience: "It is that we embark on a program to counter the awesome Soviet military threat with measures that are defensive." With little or no understanding of the technological challenges or the history of previous failures, Reagan called "upon the scientific community in this country, who gave us nuclear weapons... to give us the means of rendering these weapons impotent and obsolete." The official program was named the Strategic Defense Initiative (SDI) in January 1984, while critics quickly dubbed it "Star Wars." It mattered little that SDI ignored reality, for Reagan, although he never analyzed SDI's complicated problems, became emotionally and politically attached to it.[21]

If many U.S. military leaders and most scientists believed a successful Star Wars program lay far in the future, its existence initially posed problems to Moscow. Soviet leader Yuri Andropov viewed SDI as a program to bury the 1972 Anti-Ballistic Missile (ABM) treaty and unleash an arms race in offensive and defensive weapons. "Engaging in this is not just irresponsible, it is insane," Andropov charged in a March 27 *Pravda* interview, "Washington's actions are putting the entire world in jeopardy." The SDI project would raise questions about the status of the 1972 ABM Treaty and haunt future arms control negotiations.[22]

The Reagan Doctrine

In February 1985, Reagan's crusading efforts on behalf of anticommunist guerrillas blossomed into the "Reagan Doctrine." In his State of the Union address, the president declared: "We must not break faith with those who are risking their lives on every continent from Afghanistan to Nicaragua to defy Soviet-supported aggression and secure rights which have been ours from birth." Reversing the Truman Doctrine, which ultimately justified intervening to protect governments threatened by communists, the Reagan Doctrine proclaimed the right, indeed an obligation, to subvert existing communist regimes. Ignoring the Helsinki Agreement, Reagan told Polish Americans at the White House on August 17, 1984, that he rejected "any interpretation of the Yalta agreement" indicating "American consent for the division of Europe into spheres of influence." Cold warriors saw Reagan's doctrine as the antithesis of the Brezhnev Doctrine's assertion that Soviet gains were irreversible. To Charles Krauthammer, Reagan's doctrine rested on America's support of justice, necessity, and tradition: justice because anticommunist revolutionaries were fighting tyranny; necessity because any defeat for "freedom fighters" assigned a country irrevocably to Soviet dominance; and tradition because the United States had always supported the cause of freedom abroad.[23]

Critics pointed to Washington's usual habit of exaggerating the dangers posed by communist regimes, as well as available capacity to eliminate them. Robert Tucker questioned the doctrine's core tenet that all Marxist-Leninist governments lacked legitimacy and that the United States had a moral responsibility to support rebels who opposed them. The Nicaraguan government, he noted, served its people far better than several of those in Central America supported by the United States. "What the Reagan Doctrine requires, in theory," political scientist Kenneth Thompson warned, "is indiscriminate intervention to overturn

Communist regimes regardless of calculations of interest and power." In practice, the Reagan Doctrine unleashed limited war by proxy. It provided the rationale for Washington's economic and military assistance to the Mujahedeen resistance in Afghanistan, to rebel factions in Cambodia, and, following the repeal of the Clark Amendment in 1985, to Jonas Savimbi's guerrilla forces in Angola. Here the United States' contribution was the risk-free funding of low-cost mercenaries, whose devotion to democratic principles and prospects of success remained highly questionable.[24] But the doctrine's main thrust, of course, sought to justify Reagan's obsession with the Nicaraguan contras. "They are our brothers, these freedom fighters, and we owe them our help," he observed on March 1, 1985. "They are the moral equivalent of the Founding Fathers and the brave men and women of the French Resistance. We cannot turn away from them. For the struggle is not right versus left, but right versus wrong." Unfortunately, few contra leaders possessed democratic credentials; some ultimately faced trial and execution for murder and other crimes. When support in Congress stalled, Wyoming's Dick Cheney, anticipating his later position as vice president, criticized those who held back: "You can't have foreign policy carried out by 435 House members and 100 Senators. There are times when the president needs strong support, and debate has to stop at the water's edge."[25]

In practice, the administration endorsed notoriously oppressive authoritarian governments in Argentina, Chile, Guatemala, El Salvador, Haiti, and the Philippines. As repressive Washington-supported governments dissolved, however, the president decided in March 1986 to oppose all dictatorships, right and left. His decision, in effect, indicated a belated recognition that Third World struggles were indigenous and that the perpetuation of friendly governments was not vital for American security.

The so-called Iran-Contra affair not only embarrassed the administration and tarnished the president, it wrote the concluding chapter to Reagan's Central American crusade and confused Washington's intervention in the Iran-Iraq War. Iraq's invasion of Iran on September 22, 1980, went well until the Iranians regrouped. Fearing Iraq was in danger of losing the war, the United States, U.S.S.R., France, and England provided sophisticated military equipment and financial aid. Yet while the administration was openly assisting Iraq, it also secretly sold arms, especially antiaircraft weapons, to Iran in the hope of gaining funds to help the Nicaraguan contras and, at the same time, achieving the release of Americans held hostage by radical Islamist groups. After the Iran-Contra affair became public, Congressional investigations began, in May 1987, to focus on National Security Adviser John Poindexter and staff member Lieutenant Colonel Oliver North. Over initial objections by Secretary of State Shultz and Defense Secretary Weinberger, North directed a parallel, largely secret, foreign policy apparatus, with its own sources of funds, communications systems, secret envoys, leased ships and airplanes, and Swiss bank accounts. Testifying in July, decorated and unrepentant, Colonel North blamed Congress for the loss of Vietnam and the failure to confront enemy aggression in Central America. Similarly, Poindexter declared that the security of the United States was not safe in the hands of the State Department, the Defense Department, or Congress. Both men were convicted and later pardoned.[26]

But the fallout did not end there. The administration's long crusade to eliminate the Sandinistas and subdue the Salvadoran guerrillas was about to end. An independent Costa Rican peace process emerging in 1987 found more in common among the Marxist-oriented Sandinistas and the other Central American governments than in Washington's anti-Soviet crusade. The Reagan administration failed to recognize that Central Americans had minds, wills, and interests of their own. Nicaragua ceased to be an issue when, in 1990, a free election drove the Sandinistas from power.[27]

Reagan and Gorbachev

As early as February 12, 1983, Reagan lamented that he had not visited Moscow. After Secretary Shultz explained such trips needed significant improvement in Washington's relations with leaders of the communist powers, the president began exchanging messages with Soviet premier Andropov. In his July 11 letter, Reagan emphasized his long-held antipathy toward nuclear weapons and noted that both leaders shared "an enormous responsibility for the preservation of stability in the world." In October, Robert McFarlane, who had succeeded Clark as head of National Security Council, advised the president that it was time for the United States to exploit its military buildup by negotiating arms limitations with the Soviet Union. At Georgetown University on April 6, 1984, the president commented that the United States' increased military power paved the way for successful negotiations. "If the new Soviet leadership is devoted to building a safer and more humane world, rather than expanding armed conquests," he stated, "it will find a sympathetic partner in the West." Both countries should focus on reducing the risk of nuclear war because, he warned, "a nuclear war cannot be won and must never be fought."[28] Reagan ended his successful campaign for a second term determined to pursue closer ties with Moscow.

A youthful, rising star, Mikhail Gorbachev was destined to become head of the Soviet state, since Konstantin Chernenko, who had succeeded Andropov in February, was old and ill. When Gorbachev visited London in mid-December 1984, Prime Minister Margaret Thatcher detected in Gorbachev's predictable elevation new diplomatic opportunities. "I can do business with this man," she informed the press. Following Chernenko's death in March 1985, Gorbachev emerged as secretary general of the party, with a better grasp of the realities of international life than his predecessors. His basic challenges lay in maintaining the U.S.S.R.'s international status while rescuing it from its debilitating global role—especially in Afghanistan—and stimulating a stagnant economy. As Gorbachev, a dedicated socialist, struggled with the Kremlin's internal troubles, his "new thinking" on foreign affairs began to emerge. During 1985–1986, Gorbachev intensified military operations, installed a stronger Afghan leader, and sought to save "Soviet credibility" before withdrawing. If Gorbachev focused less on Third World issues, he nevertheless was annoyed by what he saw as Reagan's hypocrisy. In an April 23, 1985, speech, he pointed to Washington's protesting of Moscow's intervention in Afghanistan while claiming its "right to interfere" in Grenada and Nicaragua.[29]

By the summer of 1985, Reagan finally found someone in the Kremlin willing to discuss the possibility of curbing the nuclear arms race. Gorbachev believed that "the policy of total, military confrontation has no future," and that the "arms race, as well as nuclear war, cannot be won." Equally significant, Gorbachev saw "the task of building security appears to be a political task, and it can be resolved only by political means." This approach evoked criticism from veteran Soviet policymakers, one of whom grumbled, "Are you against force, which is the only language that imperialism understands?" Following eight months of long-range discussions, Reagan and Gorbachev finally prepared to meet at a Geneva Summit in November 1985. At this time, historian Raymond Garthoff noted, "a limited but interesting transformation occurred in [Reagan's] statements on the source and nature of the difficulties in American-Soviet relations." Departing for Geneva, the president hoped both nations would "seek to reduce the suspicions and mistrust that had led us to acquire mountains of strategic weapons." He even conceded that nuclear weapons, not an evil opponent, posed "the greatest threat in human history to survival of the human race."[30]

At Geneva, essentially a media event, Gorbachev pressed for limiting the Strategic Defense Initiative, maintaining SALT II, and new arms reductions, but found Reagan refusing to offer concessions on any contested point. The president, however, saw Gorbachev as one with whom he shared "a kind of chemistry." The most significant outcome of the summit undoubtedly was the growing rapport that developed between the two heads of state. In January 1986, Gorbachev offered the United Nations a grand plan for arms reductions. He would eliminate medium-range missiles altogether, set aside the issue of French and British nuclear forces, and cut strategic weapons by 50 percent, including the SS-18 heavy missiles. Gorbachev's ambitious economic modernization program, endorsed by the 27th Party Congress in February–March, required the reduced military spending that would follow arms reductions. The Soviet objective had become the attainment of mutual security at the lowest possible strategic balance.[31]

The president, in late May 1986, announced that the United States would no longer be bound by the SALT II formula at the end of the year unless the Kremlin undertook undefined "constructive steps." Critical European reaction followed. *Le Figaro* complained that Washington did not bother to ask Europe's opinion. "It's a disaster," fumed Helmut Kohl. *The Economist* noted that half the Britons polled distrusted Reagan's judgment and considered Americans equal to the Soviets as a threat to peace. In Washington, officials insisted that the president was justified in his action because of apparent Soviet cheating, but also conceded that they had not anticipated Europe's reaction. Gorbachev recognized Europe's anxiety and offered a series of new arms proposals, which Pentagon officials routinely rejected. *New York Times* columnist James Reston noted the preference for "ideological confrontation and warrior diplomacy ... at the Pentagon and the White House." To columnist Andrew J. Glass, "[T]he national security apparatus in the White House remains thoroughly fractionated. With so many hawks and pseudo-hawks flapping about in the Reagan aviary, it will muster all the administration's ability in diplomatic falconry merely to fashion a cogent response to the latest Soviet initiative." Meanwhile, Gorbachev topped European polls as the man of peace, while Reagan put aside a decision on the SALT II treaty until their October meeting.[32]

The two leaders met briefly at Reykjavik, Iceland, in October, with Gorbachev proposing to scrap all SS-20s in Europe while retaining 100 in Asia and allowing the United States 100 similar missiles in Alaska. At the final session, Reagan presented the "sweeping" U.S. proposals to eliminate all nuclear warheads by 2000, which his advisers were confident Gorbachev would reject. Startling everyone, the Soviet leader responded, "Yes." He would accept Reagan's proposal if the president agreed to limit SDI research to "laboratories" for at least five years. Reagan rejected

Gorbachev's counteroffer, declaring he would not compromise his missile defense project. Reagan had confused his priorities. For, when his long-held desire to eliminate nuclear weapons loomed, he clung to the Strategic Defense Initiative that as yet showed no evidence it would work and, if it eventually should, when it might be available. Thus, he rejected an opportunity that might have satisfied his frequently professed desire to eliminate the nuclear threat. Reagan and Gorbachev departed Reykjavik disappointed and exhausted. However, Western military strategists and political leaders—and most certainly Soviet marshals—were shaken by news of a near-agreement to abolish nuclear weapons. Prime Minister Margaret Thatcher hurried to Washington, warning Reagan that the nuclear deterrence strategy had been the bedrock of almost 40 years of U.S. and European security.[33]

If not everyone agreed, Gorbachev's strategy of ending the Cold War by reducing the nuclear threat found widespread popular approval. He surprised Pentagon hard-liners on February 28, 1987, by accepting their proposal to eliminate all intermediate-range nuclear missiles in Europe and, later, in Asia—the United States' "zero option." Secretary of State Shultz immediately accepted Gorbachev's offer. Negotiators subsequently agreed to destroy 2,611 intermediate-range missiles with flight ranges from 300 to 3,440 miles (500 to 5,000 kilometers), including U.S. Pershing IIs and cruise missiles and Soviet SS-4s, SS-12s, SS-20s, and SS-23s. When Defense Secretary Weinberger and other hard-liners demanded on-site inspections, Gorbachev agreed to an "intrusive verification" plan where each power would inspect the other's facilities to fulfill Intermediate Nuclear Force (INF) Treaty terms. Soviet enthusiasm for intrusive inspections gave pause to the Pentagon, the National Security Agency, and the CIA—all of whom had for decades made this a fundamental requirement for substantial reductions. Now they feared the prospect of Soviet inspectors prowling U.S. defense plants, nuclear-armed submarines, and missile sites. As Weinberger's replacement, Frank Carlucci, admitted, "[V]erification has proven to be more complex than we thought it would be. The flip side of the coin is its application to us. The more we think about it, the more difficult it becomes." The United States now desired less intrusive procedures. The Washington summit of December 1987 to sign the INF Treaty turned out to be a Reagan-Gorbachev triumph with hugely favorable media coverage. The Soviet leader and his wife were so enthusiastically greeted in the normally blasé capital that it prompted *Washington Post* columnist Tom Shales to observe the city was seized by "Gorby fever." When Gorbachev expressed concern about the criticism that Reagan was receiving from hard-liners, Shultz reassured him, "[T]he vast majority of Americans support what President Reagan is doing." "For the first time in history," Reagan declared when signing the INF treaty on December 8, "the language of 'arms control' was replaced by 'arms reduction' in this case, the complete elimination of an entire class of U.S. and Soviet nuclear missiles." The treaty offered "a big chance at last to get onto the road leading away from the threat of catastrophe," Gorbachev added. "It is our duty... to move forward toward a nuclear-free world... [that is] without fear and without a senseless waste of resources on weapons of destruction." Although the INF pact eliminated only 4 percent of the superpowers' nuclear arsenal, it would eventually launch other serious arms reductions.[34]

The INF treaty initially failed to spur the talks toward a strategic arms reduction treaty. Although the Soviets offered several concessions, interminable bureaucratic delays hampered Washington's attempts to modify its initial START proposal substantially—indeed an agreement would not be reached until 1991. Meanwhile, the intractability of various American bureaucracies over the specific terms was frequently more intense than the negotiations with Moscow. This bickering led an unhappy member of the National Security Council to suggest, "Even if the Soviets did not exist, we might not get a START treaty because of disagreements on our side." If the Soviets "came to us," another high-ranking U.S. official complained, "and said, 'You write it, we'll sign it,' we still couldn't do it."

The Kremlin's concern about Reagan's strategic missile defense program gradually dissipated. Russian scientist Andrei Sakharov persuaded Gorbachev there was no defense capable of stopping a barrage of intercontinental ballistic missiles carrying decoys and multiple warheads. He argued that SDI was a kind of "Maginot line in space," a line that could not defeat a concentrated missile attack any more than the French Maginot defense line stopped the German blitzkrieg in 1940. Soviet scientists recognized that the SDI program was a "fuss about nothing." As Roald Z. Sagdeyev, the head of the Soviet Institute for Space Research told Strobe Talbott, "We came to realize that we had not helped ourselves by screaming so much about SDI... we had overestimated how much damage SDI could do to strategic stability in the short run and even in the medium term."[35]

With the vast majority of the Senate favoring the INF treaty and Reagan's assurance that he was negotiating from strength, ratification came on May 29, 1988, as the president left for the Moscow summit. The significance of this triumphant meeting was the reintroduction of détente and the end of Reagan's ideological crusade. On Sunday, May 29, 1988, as Reagan received a warm welcome at the Kremlin, Gorbachev declared, "[H]istory has objectively bound our two countries by a common responsibility for the destinies of mankind." On Tuesday, as Reagan walked through Red Square, he commented publicly that the two leaders had "decided to talk to each other instead of about each other. It's working just fine." In the Kremlin, when asked by a reporter what became of the 1983 "evil empire," the president replied, "I was talking about another time, another era." Gorbachev and Reagan signed the INF ratification documents at the final ceremony.[36] If short on achievement, the summit had been long on goodwill.

Predictably, the neoconservatives once again criticized Reagan's actions, asserting that the Soviet Union, with its human rights violations, remained the evil empire. George Will's judgment of the Moscow summit served for most hawks: "Ronald Reagan's foreign policy has produced much surprise but little delight. His fourth and, one prays, final summit is a suitable occasion for conservatives to look back with bewilderment and ahead with trepidation." In his final White House years, as Will saw it, the president had ruined his earlier, superb foreign and military policy. Among anti-Soviet hard-liners, inside and outside Washington, the ultimate Reagan triumphs had emerged with the Reagan Doctrine, followed in 1986 by the vote for contra aid, the warm White House welcome for Angola's Jonas Savimbi, and the destructive bombing of Libyan targets in response to Qaddafi's alleged terrorist activities in Europe.

Despite criticism from the right, it seemed apparent that moderates were gaining the ascendancy in the administration's turf wars over foreign policy. Secretary of State Shultz had organized the State Department into an effective group for conducting negotiations with the Soviets. Together with Frank Carlucci as the new secretary of defense and General Colin L. Powell as national security adviser, the Reagan administration finally had three top advisers who were in general agreement. As one administration spokesman phrased it in March 1988, "Over the past three years we have established a broad, active, and quietly developing relationship, almost from a cold start in '85." For the president, the move toward moderation appeared to be a slow, pragmatic evolution of policy. The pragmatists understood that there was no choice but to coexist on the planet with the U.S.S.R. and regarded Gorbachev as a durable Soviet leader. They agreed with his December 7, 1988, address before the United Nations where he criticized the reliance on nuclear arms. Gorbachev, at this time, reached the high point of his global leadership by pledging the unilateral reduction of Soviet military forces by 500,000 men and withdrawing forces from Afghanistan.[37]

Leaving Washington hours after George H. W. Bush was inaugurated, Reagan declared flatly: "The Cold War is over." Weeks ahead of most policymakers, the American public had grasped that the Cold War was over after hearing Gorbachev's UN speech. Public opinion polls revealed that 54 percent of Americans now considered the Soviets to be either "no threat" or "only a minor threat," while 60-odd percent believed the Soviets now were essentially focused on their own security and only 28 percent thought they were still seeking world domination. Frances Fitzgerald summed it up best: "Gorbachev launched a political revolution in the Soviet Union. Few in Washington understood what he was doing or where he was going, and the Cold War was over before the American policy establishment knew it."[38]

Bush and Gorbachev

The transition from Reagan to George H. W. Bush was not as smooth as might have been expected. As vice president, Bush remained quiet about his personal dislike of Reagan's harsh anti-Soviet rhetoric and his concern that Reagan went too far in restoring a détente with Moscow based on a personal friendship with Gorbachev. The new president, determined to establish policies and programs that bore his own imprint, removed most of the "Reaganites" from the cabinet and other senior positions in his administration. George Bush entered the presidency in January 1989 unconvinced that the Cold War was receding; consequently, he and his senior staff insisted on a well-thought-out strategy before formally addressing Moscow.

A cautious man by nature, Bush rarely questioned conventional wisdom or was given to innovative actions. In February, even as Soviet forces left Afghanistan, the president warned: "It is important not to let these encouraging changes, political and military, lull us into a sense of complacency. Nor can we let down our guard against a worldwide threat. . . . Military challenges to democracy persist in every hemisphere." His national security adviser, General Brent Scowcroft, agreed. The administration must be wary of the "clever bear syndrome" that could lull the public into a false sense of security. In keeping with a long-held Washington theme, he insisted that "only when we've been scared to death" have the American people sustained their vigilance.[39] In concert with his old friend and now secretary of state James Baker, the president was determined not to be rushed into a summit with Gorbachev. In her normal direct manner, British prime minister and a solid friend of the United States Margaret Thatcher indicated to Secretary Baker her dissatisfaction with the slow-moving, relaxed manner with which Washington officials were approaching their policy review. "I'm sure," she added, "Mr. Gorbachev is, too."

The U.S. ambassador to Moscow, Jack Matlock, who witnessed the historical changes taking place in the Soviet Union, would later title his chapter on this initial period of the Bush administration, "Washington Fumbles." Gorbachev's adviser Anatoly Chernyaev was not so kind in calling the last chapter of his memoirs, "The Lost Year."[40]

To stir up Reagan's moribund START talks, the normally cautious Bush suggested going for broke—let's offer the Soviets a ban on all the threatening, vulnerable land-based MIRVed intercontinental missiles. When Secretary of Defense Dick Cheney and Pentagon officials learned of the proposed ban, an intramural struggle began, and soon the idea of a total MIRV ban was dropped. With modest progress, the Malta summit inched its way forward moving the arms limitations agenda. After eight and a half frustrating years, President Bush and Soviet president Gorbachev on July 31, 1991, finally signed a detailed 750-page START I treaty. Basically, it limited each side to the deployment of 1,600 ballistic missiles and long-range bombers, carrying 6,000 so-called accountable warheads, and established further sublimits. This was the first agreement that called on each side to make significant cuts in their strategic arsenals. Almost 50 percent of the nuclear warheads carried on ballistic missiles would be eliminated. Additionally, the agreement established a complex verification system that would satisfactorily serve future accords on strategic weaponry.[41]

Both nations had spent several trillions of dollars over four decades on their strategic arsenals and nuclear weapons. These growing nuclear arsenals had assumed an increasingly significant political role in the discussions between Moscow and Washington. Thus, diplomatic activity focusing on these weapons dominated negotiation between the superpowers from John Kennedy to George H. W. Bush. Indeed, arms control had been for years the primary if not the only area of political dialogue between the two powers. Former secretary of state Dean Rusk noted that even if these deliberations went badly, "they provided a forum in which Soviet and American officials sat across from each other at long tables, sipped mineral water and discussed military matters that used to be the stuff spies were paid and shot for. So in that sense, even . . . [the] disagreements were often salutary. The process was the product." An official in several presidential administrations and strident Cold Warrior, Paul H. Nitze, acknowledged that arms control endeavors had played a major role in negotiations between Moscow and Washington. "[G]iven the lack of diplomatic negotiations dealing with other basic political differences," he wrote, "arms control became the principal conduit for Soviet-American relations." Emphasizing their significant role as a political conduit during the Cold War, Nitze noted: "Even in times of [political] tension, arms control trudged ever on in some form."[42]

Who Ended the Cold War?

Ronald Reagan entered office in January 1981 committed to the enhancement of the country's security through tougher anticommunist rhetoric and massive military expansion. Even before Reagan's inauguration, the Soviet Union had entered its long, predictable disintegration that in 1985 produced Mikhail Gorbachev and the possibility of a genuine U.S.-Soviet détente, one that Reagan and Gorbachev achieved in their four summits from 1986 to 1988. Throughout their relationship Reagan clung to his conviction, much to the dismay of skeptical neoconservatives, that the Soviet leader's efforts at domestic reform and international cooperation were genuine. Moreover, he willingly met and negotiated with Gorbachev. By continuing to talk with Gorbachev, in spite of the abusive criticism of so many erstwhile supporters, historian Michael Beschloss placed Reagan in his pantheon of courageous presidents.[43]

Gorbachev provided the charismatic, imaginative leadership during the "crisis" of the mid-1980s that redirected the Kremlin's relations with the West, as well as a liberalization of his own domestic policies. What many American hard-liners failed to recognize was that the crisis also provided an opening for powerful reactionary forces that could have instituted repressive policies in the Soviet Union and prolonged the Cold War for at least a few more decades. Thus, Gorbachev was elected general secretary in March 1985 by an unorganized majority of conservatives. In restructuring Soviet policies the following year, a close observer noted that Gorbachev had "already decided, come what may, to end the arms race," because he was convinced "nobody is going to attack us even if we disarm completely." The subsequent unraveling of the Soviet empire was an unintended side effect of his reforms; termination of the Cold War was not. Though politically weakened, Gorbachev conceded nothing to U.S. military superiority. It was Gorbachev who concluded that the superpowers had become "mesmerized by ideological myths" that ruled out meaningful discussions of any possible political accommodation. He broke the Cold War's ideological straitjacket that had paralyzed Moscow and Washington's ability to resolve their differences.[44] In doing so, he faced great political, even physical, risks.

Yet professional Cold Warriors, with ideological blinders, refused to admit that the joint policies of Reagan, Bush, and Gorbachev, after they began cooperating, had brought the Cold War to an end. After 1991,

Robert Gates and Weinberger as well as such pundits as George Will and Irving Kristol argued that Ronald Reagan's military buildup and SDI program had played the dominant role in the collapse of the Soviet Union. If this myth received extensive publicity during the 1990s, respected scholars investigating U.S.-Soviet relations have since challenged these claims. They were, in Professor Robert English's considered assessment, "greatly oversimplified." He suggests the Reagan military buildup, coupled with the administration's aggressive rhetoric, actually "made the accession of genuine reformist leadership much more difficult. The effort to tilt the military balance sharply in the West's favor certainly heightened Soviet perceptions of deepening problems and a need for a change." The contention, however, that the military buildup and the Star Wars program caused the Soviet system to collapse, English argues, reflects "a lapse in basic counterfactual reasoning, if not an even more deterministic triumphalism."[45]

Reagan, and Bush much later, both deserve their share of the credit for recognizing the Soviet leader's sincerity and his determination to greatly alter earlier Kremlin policies. Yet, considering all of this, it is difficult to avoid the conclusion that without Gorbachev's determination and innovative policies, the end of the Cold War could have played out very differently and very dangerously. After nearly a half century, the Cold War had exited quietly, without ceremony.

CHAPTER 17

The United States and the Middle East: Israel, Lebanon, Iran, and Iraq

> An attempt by an outside force to gain control of the Persian Gulf region will be regarded as an assault on the vital interests of the United States of America, and such an assault will be repelled by any means necessary, including force.
> —President Jimmy Carter, January 1980, State of the Union Address

> Because of the real and psychological impact of a curtailment in the flow of oil from the Persian Gulf on the international economic system, we must assure our readiness to deal promptly with actions aimed at disrupting that traffic.
> —National Security Decision Directive 114, November 26, 1983

Relations between the Arab states and the United States since World War II have characteristically been shaped by competing and contradictory factors, often conditioned by the protracted Arab-Israel conflict. Washington officials initially confronted strategic Cold War concerns, sympathy for Israel as a homeland for the survivors of Nazi Germany's genocide, the political muscle of the American Jewish Lobby, access to Middle East oil, distaste for certain Arab regimes, and ambivalence toward Palestinian refugees and statehood. Not surprisingly, as different crises arose there was confusion as to how best to serve America's interests in the Middle East. The United States' increasingly strong support of Israel alienated most Arab publics and posed difficulties for Washington dealings with their leaders.

Origins of Arab-Israeli Conflict

The persistent Palestinian issue, central to the Arab-Israeli conflict, began with a statement regarding a Jewish homeland issued in November 1917 by Britain's foreign minister, Arthur James Balfour, during the dying days of World War I. Balfour stated his government favored "the establishment in Palestine of a national home for the Jewish people and will use the best endeavors to facilitate the achievements of that object, it being clearly understood that nothing shall be done which may prejudice the civil and religious rights of non-Jewish communities in Palestine."[1] After Britain evacuated its forces from Palestine in 1947–1948, Zionist leaders agreed to the UN partition plan for Palestine and in Palestine's Jewish sectors established the state of Israel. Because about two-thirds of Palestine's population was Arab, the Arab leaders rejected the partition plan, claiming that the Arab majority should rule an undivided state. President Harry S. Truman, facing serious opposition from many of his senior advisers, insisted in March 1948 that the United States should be the first country to formally recognize Israel's existence. According to Clark Clifford, who defended the president's case, Truman "has always supported the right of the Jews to have their own homeland. . . . He considers this to be a question about the moral and ethical considerations that are present in that part of the world." However, his secretary of state, George C. Marshall—along with Undersecretary of State Robert Lovett, future secretary of state Dean Acheson, head of State's Policy Planning Staff George F. Kennan, and the brilliant but erratic secretary of defense James V. Forrestal—stoutly opposed the decision, because it was likely to jeopardize access to the huge Mideast oil reserves and imperil the United States' strategic position. Clifford, in his memoirs, acknowledged that at the time he recognized that "oil, historic antagonisms, and numerical imbalances might create many of the problems Israel's opponents in Washington predicted. Many of their fears, in fact, came true; the Mideast remains today the single most volatile place on earth, a legacy, in part, of the events of 1948."[2] Consequently, in May 1948, hostilities broke out pitting Israel against Arab communities. Aided by the United States, Israeli forces seized lands that the UN partition plan had designated for Arabs, and about 700,000 Palestinian Arabs lost their homes and became refugees.

During the mid-1950s, the Eisenhower administration confronted several destabilizing events in the Middle East. In September 1955, the Cold War filtered into the region with the Egyptian-Soviet arms deal that rendered obsolete the Tripartite Agreement of 1950, by which the United

States, Britain, and France had sought to stabilize the region with balancing arms shipments to Israel and Arab states. In July 1956, Washington withdrew its proposed funding of Egypt's Aswan Dam, for President Dwight Eisenhower believed it would contribute to the "weakening of Nasser."[3] Instead, Gamel Abdul al-Nasser became an Arab hero when he defied Great Britain, in July 1956, and nationalized the Suez Canal. His reputation not only survived but was enhanced during the October 1956 military assault by Israel, Britain, and France to retake the canal by force. This episode found Washington and Moscow jointly supporting a UN Security Council resolution that gained a cease-fire. Tensions between the Arab states and Israel became more and more fraught with danger as both sides refused to compromise their differences and the Soviet Union sent arms to Egypt and Syria, while Israel clamored for more U.S. weapons. The June 1967 Israeli-Arab war became a turning point in modern Middle Eastern history. During a six-day period, beginning on June 5, Israeli armies conquered Syria's Golan Heights, moving close enough to Damascus to lob artillery shells into the city. Israel also defeated Jordanian forces and took control of the entire West Bank of the Jordan River and Jerusalem. At the same time, Israeli forces overran the Gaza Strip and the Sinai Peninsula, delivering a disastrous blow to Nasser's Soviet-supplied Egyptian army. Israel additionally occupied Jerusalem, which the United Nations had designated as an international city in the 1947 partition plan. Under pressure from Washington and Moscow, the Arab states and Israel accepted a UN cease-fire on June 11, but the Israeli government would not withdraw its forces from the occupied West Bank. This would continue to inflame Arab-Israeli relations and find the Arabs contemptuous of the United States.

The Egyptian army's surprise attack on Israel in October 1973 would have, before the decade was over, global consequences. Anwar Sadat, Egypt's new moderate leader, broke off relations with the Soviet Union and later sought the good offices of President Jimmy Carter to broker a peace agreement with Israel in 1978–1979. Egypt also obtained U.S. financial assistance aimed at building a stronger Egyptian economy. During the war, Egypt's army overran most of the Sinai Peninsula in the first week of battle, and an endangered Israel appealed to the United States for aid. On October 13, President Richard Nixon began a full-scale airlift of military equipment to Israel, while his close adviser Henry Kissinger urged Moscow not to intervene. In reaction, the Arab states decided to embargo oil shipments to the United States, Western Europe, and Japan. By October 21, Saudi Arabia, Kuwait, and other major Arab oil producers joined the embargo. Although Arab economic action failed to prevent Israel from counterattacking, the oil embargo caused a domestic crisis in the United States, as long lines of cars waited to purchase available gasoline. Israel's offensive regained the Sinai Peninsula before the belligerents agreed to a UN cease-fire on October 25. Nixon could not, however, prevent increases in gasoline prices at home; moreover, Arab oil producers recognized, in addition to gaining certain political leverage, they also could command higher prices. They cut production and raised prices from $3 per barrel in 1972 to $11.65 by the end of 1973. Members of the Organization of Petroleum Exporting Countries (OPEC), organized by Saudi Arabia in September 1960, grew to include most Third World oil-producing nations. After the 1973 war, OPEC members controlled oil production, established export quotas set for each nation, and raised prices and profits. By the end of the 1970s, OPEC's fixed prices ranged between $39 and $41 per barrel. In subsequent decades, the price of oil would fluctuate greatly, but eventually always higher.[4]

The 1967 and 1973 Arab-Israeli wars not only changed Egyptian and OPEC policies, but they also had been a blow to Baath Party moderates in Syria and Iraq. By 1972, Syria's General Hafez Assad had established strong military control over Syria. In Iraq, General Hassan al-Bakr and his assistant Saddam Hussein al-Takriti gained power in 1968. In 1979, Hussein assumed power in a coup d'état that underscored a predilection for eliminating anyone he perceived as a threat.[5]

Carter's Policies toward Iraq and Iran

Policies generated in Washington, Baghdad, and Tehran during three decades (1980–2010) were often grounded in misperceptions that resulted in unintended consequences. Although Saddam Hussein—who would be both an ally and a foe of the United States—seized control of the Iraqi government in July 1979, his appearance scarcely appeared on Washington's political radar because of other unsettling Middle Eastern events. The Iranian Revolution, earlier in January, displaced Shah Mohammad Reza Pahlevi, who had anchored Washington's strategic position in the Persian Gulf region. Ayatollah Ruhollah Khomeini's Islamic Revolution set in motion a series of unpleasant crises beginning with his insistence that the United States return the shah to Iran to answer for his crimes against the Persian people. After President Jimmy Carter refused to do so, on November 4, a group of Iranian militants seized control of the U.S. embassy in Tehran, taking 65 Americans as hostages, not to be released until Ronald Reagan's inauguration on January 20, 1981. Meanwhile, the Carter administration froze

Iranian assets in the United States and halted Iranian oil imports.[6] These episodes led to a disruption of American-Iranian relations that continued well into the twenty-first century.

While American officials were seeking a way to deal with Tehran, Moscow's decision to send military forces into Afghanistan in December 1979 to bolster that country's faltering communist government aroused fears in Washington for the security of Pakistan and Iran. Viewing the Soviet Union's intervention as a prelude to Moscow's attempt to dominate Middle Eastern oil supplies, President Carter reacted in muscular fashion. "An attempt by any outside force to gain control of the Persian Gulf region," Carter declared in his January 1980 State of the Union message, "will be regarded as an assault on the vital interests of the United States of America, and such an assault will be repelled by any means necessary, including military force."[7] To support the "Carter Doctrine," the administration proposed a record high peacetime military budget that designated supplies for the newly formed Rapid Deployment Joint Task Force designed to project a prompt military response to meet any Middle East crisis.

Saddam Hussein rejected Carter's declaration and on February 8 promulgated his "Pan-Arab Charter." In contrast to the Carter Doctrine, the "Hussein Doctrine" demanded that all foreign powers leave the Gulf region. Arab nations, Hussein declared, would collectively defend the Gulf from Western oppressors.[8] Although Carter had primarily directed his warning at Moscow, Hussein, who received aid from the Soviets, berated the Americans as imperialists that aided Israel and exploited Arabs. Thus, if Hussein's Doctrine was Cold War induced, it was directed essentially against the United States on behalf of Arab nationalism.

Reagan's Misadventure in Lebanon

Events in the Middle East during 1982 undermined President Ronald Reagan's declared anti-Soviet strategy for the region. Repeatedly, European officials had reminded Washington that a comprehensive peace between Israel and the Arab world, including a settlement of the Palestinian question, was more essential for regional stability than attempting to build a military arrangement to keep the Soviets out. Israel's annexation in late December 1981 of the Golan Heights, seized from Syria in the 1967 war, prompted Washington to suspend its newly signed strategic cooperation agreement with Tel Aviv. Prime Minister Menachem Begin immediately castigated the United States for treating Israel like a "banana republic."[9]

Israel exacerbated the already tense relationship between Washington and Tel Aviv during the spring and summer of 1982, especially by authorizing the construction of new Jewish settlements in the West Bank. Irritating Israel, the Palestine Liberation Organization (PLO), headquartered in Beirut, kept up its harassment from bases in the south of Lebanon. Seizing on the June 3 attempted assassination of its ambassador to London, Tel Aviv two days later sent its troops and tanks sweeping into southern Lebanon for the announced purpose of pushing back the PLO and, possibly with UN assistance, creating a neutral zone. Advancing beyond their initial objectives in the south, however, on June 13 Israeli forces encircled the PLO-occupied areas of Beirut and began subjecting the city to heavy aerial bombing and artillery barrages. The resulting civilian casualties and devastation—and not for the last time—dismayed a global audience.

In mid-September, Lebanese militia forces, with apparent Israeli encouragement, entered the Sabra and Shatila Palestinian refugee camps and slaughtered scores of men, women, and children. Shortly thereafter, Reagan announced he was sending U.S. Marines to join the multinational force. Their mission, he explained in late September 1982, was to join "with our allies, the French and the Italians, to give a kind of support and stability while the Lebanese Government seeks to reunite its people, which have been divided for several years, now into several [armed] factions, and bring about a unified Lebanon with a Lebanese army that will then be able to preserve order." The administration expected to accomplish these goals by supporting Amin Gemayel's new Lebanese government, removing Syrian influence, and persuading Israel to withdraw its forces. Unfortunately, Gemayel, buoyed by the peacekeeping forces, pressed his own agenda in defiance of the other political groups. In the subsequent bitter struggle, the marines were caught between the violent contending factions. While Congress worried that the position of U.S. forces in Lebanon was no longer simple or reassuring, it permitted the president to extend the Marines' stay 18 months.

The multinational force in Lebanon, including U.S. Marines, suffered serious losses in Beirut. On October 23, 1993, the French unit of the multinational force incurred the loss of 58 men to a suicide squad, while the same day, a suicide bomber drove a truck into the U.S. Marine barracks, killing 241 and wounding another 130. The Marines had accomplished little, for they did not have the capacity to bring stability to Lebanon. That was always the responsibility of the Lebanese. Affairs did not bode well for the Gemayel government despite the United States' continued verbal support. Syria moved some 50,000 troops into

Lebanon to protect Moslem dissidents, while the Soviets increased their presence in Syria. By early February 1984, American forces left Lebanon with the Syrians dominating affairs in Beirut. Perhaps the administration's most serious miscalculation was supporting the Lebanese government that could not bring the country's quarreling factions together. Israeli defense minister Sharon's overbearing attitude in Lebanon, however, contributed greatly to preventing a possible favorable settlement in September and October 1982. In the end, Tel Aviv gained little from its massive, costly invasion of Lebanon. The PLO had been transplanted, but the Palestinian issue remained. "Lebanon is a quagmire," Yitzhak Rabin told Secretary of State George Shultz in May 1983. "Anyone there will get drawn deeper and deeper into the engulfing morass."[10]

Reagan and the Iran-Iraq War

For several years, Washington had ignored border clashes involving Iraq and Iran forces. In 1979, these disputes revived the dormant Shatt al Arab waterway controversy. Iraq claimed the 200-kilometer channel up to the Iranian shore as its territory, while Iran insisted that the line running down the middle of the waterway, negotiated in 1975, was the recognized border. On February 11, 1979, Khomeini further inflamed tensions between Baghdad and Tehran, declaring: "We will export our revolution to the four corners of the world because our revolution is Islamic." He also launched a personal attack on Saddam Hussein, proclaiming him un-Islamic and his followers as the "infidel Baath Party" and a "chief enemy of Islam."[11] Hussein responded with equally vitriolic personal attacks. He and other Sunni Arab leaders became apprehensive that Khomeini would encourage domestic fundamentalist Islamic believers to challenge their leadership. As tensions heightened between Tehran and Baghdad, Hussein, in September 1980, decided to invade Iran—with an army of 190,000, supported by 2,200 tanks and 450 aircraft—expecting to remove Khomeini and occupy disputed territory.

Hussein's surprise attack on September 22 enabled the Iraqi armies to occupy the disputed territory by the end of the year. Tehran rejected Saddam's settlement offer, and its forces counterattacked in 1981, regaining the lost territory. Saddam had miscalculated the appeal of Khomeini's fundamental nationalism to recruit volunteers willing to die in a holy war against Iraq. In July 1982, Revolutionary Guard forces and the untrained People's Army volunteers, ranging in age from 9 to over 50, launched "human wave" assaults that brought them near the key Iraqi cities of Basra, Baghdad and Fao. The Iranians sustained immense casualties and succeeded in threatening Iraq's survival, which persuaded Saudi Arabia, Kuwait, Egypt, Jordan, and the Gulf emirates to respond to Iraq's appeal for help. Meanwhile, the UN Security Council called for a cease-fire and asked member nations not to aid the combatants. Initially, the Soviets opposed the war and cut off aid to both sides, but in 1982, Moscow resumed arms shipments to Iraq. Iran's military, stocked with U.S.-made weaponry purchased during the shah's reign, could not buy replacement parts directly from American producers. They had to depend on a broad spectrum of third-party suppliers, including European countries and Israel. According to a November 1980 cable from the U.S. embassy at Ankara, Turkey, Israel was selling matériel to both "Islamic belligerents."[12]

The United States had terminated its arms sales to Tehran after the shah fell and in 1980 broke off diplomatic relations with Iran because of the hostage crisis. Much earlier, Baghdad had ended formal ties with Washington during the 1967 Arab-Israeli war. Although President Carter remained neutral toward the belligerents, his secretary of defense, Harold Brown, and National Security Adviser Zbigniew Brzezinski believed that "Iraq provided a counterbalance to the Iranians and we should cultivate that." This assessment ignored U.S. intelligence reports that portrayed Saddam Hussein as "ruthless and dangerous." Despite warnings by Middle East experts, Brown and Brzezinski thought Hussein was "a man you could do business with," an attitude that Presidents Ronald Reagan and George H. W. Bush would follow until August 2, 1990. President Reagan, while publically acknowledging the policy of neutrality, gradually tilted U.S. policy toward Iraq. "The temptation was to stand by and watch this dictatorial pair of countries pound each other to pulp," Secretary of State Shultz recalled. Yet he believed, as Brown and Brzezinski had earlier, that if Iraq collapsed, it "could not only intimidate but inundate our friends in the Gulf and be a strategic disaster for the United States."[13]

Reagan's National Security Decision Directive (NSDD) 114 of November 26, 1983, revised the administration's priorities. It called for greater regional military cooperation to defend oil facilities, improvement of U.S. military capabilities in the Persian Gulf, and directed the secretaries of state and defense and the Joint Chiefs of Staff to respond to critical situations in the area. "Because of the real and psychological impact of a curtailment in the flow of oil from the Persian Gulf on the international economic system," the directive read, "we must assure our readiness to deal promptly with actions aimed at disrupting that traffic." Soon thereafter, presidential envoy Donald Rumsfeld—having served in the Nixon and Ford administrations—visited Baghdad in December 1983.

Rumsfeld and Saddam's discussion of regional issues and mutual interests the State Department regarded as a "positive milestone." The department announced in December that there "should no longer be an impediment to [U.S. Export-Import Bank] financing for U.S. sales to Iraq" despite questions about that country's credit. Washington thought this action should "go far to show our support for Iraq in a practical, neutral context," while gaining a foothold in the potentially large Iraqi market.[14] The United States' quiet assistance largely consisted of battlefield intelligence and weaponry. Many details of the aid to Iraq surfaced after the First Gulf War, with the most controversial issue being to what extent did Washington officials turn a blind eye toward Iraq's use of chemical weapons while at the same time the U.S. government officially condemned their employment.

America's issues with Tehran mounted significantly during the mid-1980s. Washington blamed the Iranians for the truck bombing of a U.S. barracks in October 1983 by Lebanese Shia militants (Hezbollah), and the administration listed Iran, in January 1984, as a nation that supported international terrorism, subjecting Tehran to even more restrictive export regulations. The abduction of William Buckley, the CIA station chief in Beirut, followed on March 16, and two months later the pro-Iranian militants held five American hostages. A June 1985 hijacking by pro-Iranian Shias of a Trans-World Airways resulted in a 17-day standoff at the Beirut airport during which the hijackers killed a U.S. navy diver. American public and official hostility toward Tehran increased significantly. Trying to get Iran to release U.S. hostages held in Lebanon, Reagan permitted a secret arms-for-hostage deal with Iran—involving U.S. Hawk antiaircraft weapons and 2008 TOW antitank missiles. Disclosure during the winter of 1986–1987 resulted in the administration's Iran-Contra scandal. It also lessened America's credibility with the Arab states.[15]

Hostilities gradually involved Persian Gulf shipping and directly challenged U.S. interests. To counter Iran's offensive successes, in 1984, the Iraqis struck at Iran's oil tankers and oil facilities. Iran soon retaliated, often hitting Kuwaiti or Saudi Arabian shipping because Iraq usually exported its oil either in these ships or through Turkey and Saudi Arabia pipelines. By late 1986, after Iran's army thrust into southern Iraq, capturing the city of Fao, Iraq increased its air assaults on Iran's cities and its Gulf shipping, often inadvertently threatening Kuwaiti and Saudi Arabian oil exports to Europe and Japan, thus raising insurance rates on oil tankers. In December 1986, Kuwait asked both Washington and Moscow to protect Kuwaiti ships by permitting them to carry their flag. The Soviets accepted, agreeing to lease Soviet ships to Kuwait, and four days later, on March 7, 1987, Reagan announced that Kuwaiti ships could fly the U.S. flag.

In addition to Soviet and American protection for Kuwaiti shipping, other nations sent an armada of naval vessels to the Gulf, including minesweepers and escort naval ships. Among the many Gulf military incidents during 1987–1988, two were most notable. On May 17, 1987, an Iraqi jet plane launched a French Exocet missile that damaged the U.S. frigate, U.S.S. *Stark*, killing 37 U.S. sailors. Iraq apologized for the accident, and Reagan told reporters that Iran was to blame because it refused to end the Gulf War.

If Reagan's reaction to the *Stark* incident reflected his support for Hussein, the second incident, on July 3, 1988, demonstrated American feelings against Iran. As an Iranian commercial airliner flew in an air corridor across the Gulf of Hormuz to Dubai, a U.S. Navy cruiser, the U.S.S. *Vincennes*, mistook the Airbus for an Iranian combat plane and shot it down. The disaster killed 209 passengers and crew. Although U.S. public opinion rejected paying compensation to the deceased families, in July 1989, the George H. W. Bush administration offered to compensate each family of the 290 victims the sum of $250,000.[16]

Until 1987, Iran seemed to be on the road to victory, but the tide turned because Iraq, with loans from Saudi Arabia, Kuwait, and other Arab oil states, purchased new conventional military equipment; bought materials for nuclear, biological, and chemical weapons; and created the world's fourth-largest army in 1988. One military expert estimated that Saddam spent $42.8 billion on armaments between 1982 and 1989, and that the Soviet Union provided about 40 percent of the arms, China 13 percent, and Western Europe, the United States, and Latin America about 47 percent.[17] The military buildup and aerial bombing of Iranian cities persuaded Iran, in July 1988, to accept the UN-sponsored cease-fire. On August 20, the two countries agreed to terminate the nearly eight-year war. When the hostilities ended, they left two dissatisfied countries with war-weary populations and battered economies. One source placed the casualties suffered by the belligerents at 400,000–600,000 Iranians and 300,000 Iraqi killed and 1 million Iranian and 800,000 Iraqi wounded.

Origins of First Gulf War

By August 1990, Saddam Hussein had become frustrated with the wealthy Arab leaders of the Gulf States who failed to condemn what he perceived as a U.S.-Israeli conspiracy designed to keep Arab states divided.

Although some Arab leaders supported Hussein's charges, moderate Arab officials did not believe that Iraq should lead the Arab cause against Israel and the West. When Hussein met with U.S. ambassador April Glaspie on July 25, he criticized America's economic actions against Iraq. Specific examples were obvious. On April 12, 1990, the United States expelled an Iraqi diplomat and canceled a U.S. trade mission to Baghdad. Later, on May 21, the U.S. Commerce Department delayed a $500 million food commodity credit for Iraq's purchase of American wheat. Finally, on July 27, Congress voted to place trade and loan restrictions on Iraq and to withdraw a $700 million loan guarantee to expedite food sales to Iraq. While Hussein fumed about these economic rebuffs, he deplored even more Washington's persistent pro-Israeli leanings. On April 24, many Arabs joined Hussein in condemning a Congressional resolution that urged the president to recognize Jerusalem as Israel's capital, thus contradicting the UN's 1947 Partition Plan that set aside Jerusalem as an international city for all religious faiths. Israel occupied Jerusalem during the Six Day War of 1967 and in 1980 moved its government from Tel Aviv to Jerusalem. The Carter, Reagan, and Bush administrations joined other nations in rejecting Israel's unilateral action. In early 1990, the American Jewish lobby pressured Congress to approve the nonbinding resolution, yet President Bush refused to recognize Jerusalem as Israel's capital. Nevertheless, on May 7, the United States vetoed Arab proposals condemning Israel for building more Jewish settlements in the occupied territory, and on May 31, the United States vetoed a Security Council proposal to send a UN observer team to the occupied Palestinian territories after a deranged Israeli soldier had killed seven Palestinians. When Israel prime minister Yitzhak Shamir called on the United States to halt its talks with the PLO, Bush complied on June 20, 1990, ending the discussions that had begun in December 1988. Once heralded as a means of moving toward peace, Bush abandoned Washington's most recent attempt to get a PLO-Israeli settlement.[18]

America's support of Israel probably angered Hussein less than the unwillingness of wealthy Arab states to help Iraq's struggling economy. He wanted moderate Arab leaders to forgive the 1981 to 1988 wartime loans, to extend Iraq reconstruction money, and to raise oil prices to $25 per barrel. Hussein reportedly asked Kuwait privately for $27 million and raised the matter of OPEC quota violations by the United Arab Emirates that lowered oil prices, costing Iraq billions of desperately needed dollars. (World oil prices had fallen from $39–$40 per barrel in 1980 to $18–$20 by 1988. This was partly due to Britain's North Sea oil production, but also due to OPEC quota violations. In early 1990, some spot oil prices reached $12, prices that benefitted the Americans and Israelis.) The communiqué of the Arab League's May 1990 summit blamed the United States for encouraging Israeli terrorism and expansion. It also threatened economic "measures" against nations that recognized Jerusalem as Israel's capital, without mentioning what the sanctions should be or how they could be enforced. Finally, Arab League members backed Iraq's search for sophisticated technology, saying that nations that interfered with this committed "acts of aggression."[19] Iraqi officials subsequently visited Kuwait and the other Arab emirates seeking more money for economic rehabilitation, but received few satisfactory commitments. For example, they asked Kuwait for $10 billion, but Kuwait only offered Iraq $300 million over three years, an amount Saddam Hussein believed was insulting.

President Hussein also sought to rectify the Kuwait-Iraq boundary where oil fields overlapped. Since the 1920s, when Britain drew up the Iraq-Kuwait boundaries, there had been disputes about the north-south border and Kuwait's acquisition of the two islands of Warba and Bubiyan. The north-south border became critical after 1938 when oil explorers found the 50-mile-long Rumalia oil fields crossing the border, about 90 percent of the fields being in Iraq. During the Iran-Iraq War, Kuwait used slant-drilling in the Rumalia sector, a tactic that enabled Kuwait to "steal" several million dollars' worth of Iraqi oil. After 1988, however, Kuwait rejected Hussein's claim to these windfall profits and would not repay Iraq for the disputed oil. Additionally, Hussein wanted to buy or lease all or part of Warba and Bubiyan Islands to construct a secure Iraqi naval base at Umm Qasr. Since 1975, Iraq had planned a new naval base there, but in 1989, Kuwait again rejected the request. According to G. Henry Schuler, the CIA may have encouraged Kuwait's refusal to make Iraqi border changes and to stop Iraq from building a naval base, citing an Iraqi-released report taken from Kuwait's Foreign Ministry file that described CIA Director William Webster asking Kuwaiti officials to pressure Iraq to recognize Kuwait's existing borders. Although the CIA denied Iraq's report, Schuler's information may explain why Jordanian officials told Milton Viorst of the *New Yorker* that Kuwaiti officials had acted "very cocky" in dealing with Iraq. Kuwaitis told the Jordanians "the United States would intervene if there was trouble with Iraq."[20]

Hussein Seizes Kuwait/U.S. Response

On August 2, 1990, Hussein ordered his armed forces to seize the small, neighboring Emirate of Kuwait. Because he had been denying any intention to attack, the invasion was unexpected, but the outcome for Kuwait was predictable. In four hours, Iraq's 300 Soviet-made T-72 tanks reached Kuwait City. With the world's fourth-largest army, Iraq easily overran Kuwait's army of 20,300 men. Although correctly anticipating his success in Kuwait, Hussein had seriously miscalculated the world's response to the assault. He never expected that Kuwait's Emir Sheik Jaber al-Ahmed al-Sabah would successfully call for American help. Or that soon after King Fahd of Saudi Arabia would ask for, and receive, American forces. Or that Bush could rally the United Nations, including Iraq's former patron, the Soviet Union to condemn the invasion, to demand Iraq's withdrawal from Kuwait, and to support that demand with military force.

American policy toward Iraq underwent an immediate revolution after Saddam Hussein attacked Kuwait. On the same day of Iraq's invasion, the UN Security Council unanimously called on Iraq to withdraw. With the Soviet Union joining the United States in opposing Iraq's aggression and President George H. W. Bush rallying UN members, an American-led multinational force moved into Saudi Arabia. Simultaneously, the UNSC levied economic sanctions against Iraq on August 29 and on November 29 approved a resolution fixing January 15, 1991, as the deadline for Iraq to withdraw or risk attack. Although Saddam Hussein gained some Arab support by comparing Iraq's occupation of Kuwait to Israel's occupation of Palestinian land, he never anticipated that Saudi Arabia and other Arab nations would allow stationing of Western military forces on their territory. Nevertheless, Saddam stubbornly held on to Kuwait, believing either that his strong defenses could withstand an attack or that America would not be able to bring a dominating military force to liberate Kuwait. But again Hussein miscalculated, for after the invasion, Bush hastened to form a global alliance to thwart Iraq's aggression.

After news of Iraq's invasion reached Washington, Bush and his advisers quickly issued a statement condemning Iraq and asked the Treasury Department to freeze the financial assets of Kuwait and Iraq held in the United States. Other nations also condemned Iraq, and the UN Security Council by a vote of 14–0 approved Resolution 660, which demanded the immediate and complete withdrawal of Iraqi forces.

President Bush immediately requested detailed information from four key advisers: National Security Director Brent Scowcroft, Defense Department Secretary Dick Cheney, State Department Secretary James Baker, and Chairman of the Joint Chiefs of Staff Colin Powell. The four concluded that there was a clear need to defend Saudi Arabia from possible attack. An oil man from Texas, Bush knew that Iraq's control of Kuwait gave it 20 percent of the world's oil resources, and if Saudi

Arabia fell, Iraq would control over 60 percent of the world's oil.[21] Because no Arab leader would permit U.S. bases on their soil, the United States had built air and naval bases outside the Arab Gulf states. Between 1980 and 1983, Congress approved $435 million for the rapid deployment force, and by 1990, prepositioned ships in the Persian Gulf waters could provide arms for over 300,000 army troops, a marine brigade, and high-tech equipment for the U.S. Army and Air Force. Because Saudi Arabia objected to placing American bases on their soil, the U.S. Army Corps of Engineers developed "military cities" at Al-Batin, Tabuq, and Khamis Mishayt. Because the Israeli lobby stopped U.S. sales of arms to the Saudis, Great Britain became the principal source for Saudi arms to go with the "facilities" the U.S. Corps of Engineers built. Most important, General Norman Schwarzkopf's Central Command had deployment plans ready before August 1990, and prior U.S. and British activity had established an infrastructure to defend Saudi Arabia or other Gulf states. Moreover, General Schwarzkopf's Central Command had practiced war games in July 1990 for a Persian Gulf War similar to the one developed in August.[22]

Bush Seeks Support for War

President Bush soon committed himself to forcing Iraq's withdrawal from Kuwait. British prime minister Margaret Thatcher, it is suggested, persuaded Bush that a strong military response was essential. After Bush returned from meeting Thatcher, he told reporters that Iraq's "naked aggression" could not stand and described Hussein as an "Adolf Hitler" whose aggression would continue to expand if the United States did not act. On August 3, Bush decided to seek Saudi Arabia's invitation to have U.S. troops protect them. On August 6, U.S. advisers headed by Defense Secretary Cheney visited King Fahd in Riyadh, where General Schwarzkopf presented satellite photos indicating that three Iraqi armored divisions were on their way toward the Saudi border. Fahd promptly requested U.S. protection. He also asked the United States to invite Arab forces such as those of Egypt, Morocco, and other Gulf States to join the defensive coalition. In addition to the 55,000-man force sent by the Gulf States of Qatar, Oman, Bahrain, and the United Arab Emirates, Egypt sent 40,000 and Syria sent 21,000 while other Muslim states such as Pakistan, Senegal, and Bangladesh sent token forces.[23]

On August 8, as the first U.S. F-15 fighter planes, AWAC planes, and 2,300 paratroopers began arriving at Saudi bases, President Bush said the U.S. troops would deter Iraq from expanding its conquests until it withdrew from Kuwait under pressure of UN sanctions. He described the U.S. mission—titled Desert Shield—as "wholly defensive." Throughout the next three months, the United States and its allies assembled over 200,000 soldiers, plus high-tech aircraft and other modern weaponry in Saudi Arabia, the Persian Gulf, the Red Sea, the Mediterranean Sea, and Turkey. While Bush's Hitler analogy appealed to the older generations of Americans, he promised the younger generation this would not be another Vietnam, because the United States would employ its full power. He found that the use of the United Nations served the interests of the Arab states, Britain, and the Soviet Union, who would have had difficulty in backing U.S. unilateral decisions.[24]

The Bush administration pressed for a Security Council resolution that established a deadline for Iraq to withdraw or face the UN coalition. Bush justified his claim for action by pointing to Iraq's nuclear potential. In a scenario echoed a decade later by his son, Bush argued that experts "who would measure the time table for Hussein's atomic program in years may be seriously underestimating the reality of that situation and the gravity of that threat." Each day "brings Saddam one step closer to realizing his goal of a nuclear arsenal." (U.S. scientists, however, thought Iraq needed 2 to 10 years to obtain the most basic type of A-bomb.) Security Council Resolution 678, passed on November 29, 1990, set a deadline of January 15 for Hussein to withdraw from Kuwait, or the UN coalition would "use all means necessary" to evict Iraqi forces. At home, the deadline escalated debate between proponents of war and advocates of continuing economic sanctions until Hussein withdrew. After Bush announced an expanded military buildup on November 8, these discussions took place throughout the nation. The principal stage was Capitol Hill, where Congressional committees aired the pros and cons of "Bush's War" from late November until the debate reached the floor of Congress, just before the January 15 deadline. Although the administration initially claimed that the sanctions were effective, once an offensive buildup began, Bush insisted that sanctions alone would not get Iraq out of Kuwait. Once the withdrawal ultimatum was set, the administration's only concession to the peace process was to inform Iraqi leaders that unconditional surrender was necessary and that the coalition would definitely launch its attack after the deadline.[25]

On December 5–6, Secretary of State James Baker and Defense Secretary Dick Cheney told the House Committee on Foreign Affairs that sanctions had some negative effects on Iraq but that Kuwait's people were suffering from the occupation. Sanctions injured coalition allies, Cheney said. In similar fashion, Baker told the Senate Foreign Relations

Committee "nobody can tell you that sanctions alone will ever be able to impose a high enough cost on Saddam Hussein to get him to withdraw.... I am personally pessimistic that they will." Former chairmen of the Joint Chiefs Admiral William S. Crowe and General David C. Jones supported the sanctions before the Senate Committee and advocated more time for them to work. Crowe thought 12 to 18 months of sanctions might be required. "It is curious that some expect our military to train soldiers to face hostile fire," Crowe observed, "but doubt its ability to train them to occupy ground and wait patiently." Jones's testimony generally agreed with Crowe's assessment. Former secretary of defense James Schlesinger thought the probability of sanctions persuading Iraq to leave Kuwait was "very, very high if we stick with the original objectives," rather than seeking the destruction of Iraq's military power as Prime Minister Margaret Thatcher desired.

Bush hoped to avoid asking Congress to declare war, but public opinion polls in December showed two-thirds of Americans wanted the legislators to examine the issue. The so-called Weinberger Doctrine, enunciated by Reagan's defense secretary Caspar Weinberger, warned that a president should obtain legislative approval before undertaking military action abroad, so a later domestic political crisis, such as over Vietnam, could not be repeated. Consequently, Bush sent a letter to Congress on January 8, 1991, requesting the authority to employ American forces after January 15 should Hussein choose to ignore the UN deadline. From January 10 to 12, Congress debated resolutions to restrict or permit the president's right to launch an attack. "For the first time in anyone's memory," Pamela Fessler noted, "the U.S. Congress was debating openly and extensively whether the president should be authorized to take the country unprovoked by direct attack, into war." On January 12, Congress approved a resolution authorizing the president to use force after January 15 "if necessary." The House vote was 250 to 136 in favor; the Senate vote was 52 to 47. The vote was the closest margin of support for war since June 1812 when Congress divided on President James Madison's request for war against Great Britain. (In 1812, the vote was 79 to 49 in favor in the House and 19 to 13 in the Senate.) Unlike 1812, when Federalist opponents continued to oppose war, opposition Democrats in 1991 endorsed Senator Sam Nunn of Georgia, who declared: "We may disagree in this chamber but when the vote is over... we are going to stand united."[26]

Bush Goes to War

On November 30, President Bush offered to talk with the Iraqis largely to show the American public that he had "gone the last mile" for peace, but his offer did not include any suggestion of a possible compromise. The only direct U.S.-Iraq talks before the deadline took place in Geneva on January 9 between Secretary Baker and Iraqi foreign minister Aziz. Aziz insisted that the invasion of Kuwait was a defensive act against "an alliance among the United States, Israel and the former rulers of Kuwait to destroy Iraq." He sought to link the invasion to the Israel and Palestinian dispute, but Baker responded, "no one in the world would buy your explanation" that you "acted in self-defense."[27] The same day, Hussein told a meeting of the Baath Party that Iraq was ready to do battle. "If the Americans are involved in a Gulf conflict," he boasted, "you will see, we will make them swim in their blood." The hostilities opened with 38 days of intensive aerial assault by cruise missiles, bombers, and later attack helicopters as the campaign moved with great success from targeting Iraq's "center of gravity," to its armored battalions, highways, bridges, and defense networks. Hussein responded with several unorthodox tactics. Beginning on January 18, Iraq launched Scud ballistic missiles with conventional bombs at Israeli cities even though Israel was not a member of the UN coalition, in hopes of enticing Israel to retaliate, thus gaining it support of Arab states. Then Iraqi forces reportedly began spilling some oil from Kuwaiti pipelines into the Persian Gulf and later began to torch Kuwait's oil facilities. By the time Kuwait was liberated, 732 oil wells were on fire; the last fire was not extinguished until November 1991. As the aerial assault was under way, Moscow sought to persuade Hussein to withdraw. On February 17, Mikhail Gorbachev met in Moscow with Iraq's Foreign Minister Aziz but accomplished nothing. After consulting with French, British, and Arab leaders, Bush gave Iraq until noon of February 23 to withdraw, and if the withdrawal did not begin by that date, allied forces would move to liberate Kuwait. Hussein replied by calling Bush's ultimatum "shameful" and refused to order a withdrawal.

The ground war itself lasted 100 hours, from February 24 to 28. General Schwarzkopf deployed 200,000 British and American forces along the Saudi-Iraq border up to 300 miles from the Gulf. When the invasion began, the forces furthest from the Gulf made a wide left-hook movement north and east into Iraq, some of them ending up near Basra. The sweep prevented Iraqi reinforcements and supplies from coming down the highways from Baghdad to support Iraqi troops in Kuwait. At the same time, American and British armored units struck just north of the Kuwaiti border with Iraq while the main allied forces moved directly across the Kuwait-Saudi border. Two U.S. Marine divisions and a U.S. Army brigade drove through the heavily defended border while Saudi and Pan-Arab troops struck up the Gulf coast from the south. Other Arab divisions from Egypt and Syria moved across Kuwait's northwest border. In the Persian Gulf, Allied warships pounded the coastal defenses. The allies breached Iraq's defenses more easily than anticipated, largely because many of the Iraqis were sick, thirsty, or starving. On February 27, Kuwait City was liberated, while allied troops reached Basra and the northern border of Kuwait, where one of the war's extensive firefights ensued with 800 American tanks defeating 300 Iraqi tanks of the Republican Guard. On February 28, President Bush declared a cease-fire, unilaterally ordered the suspension of hostilities and offered to halt the conflict. Saddam Hussein accepted the offer and approved the signing of formal terms on March 3, 1991. The final terms were decided when the UN Security Council approved Resolution 687 on April 3, 1991, that reaffirmed Iraq must comply with the 13 resolutions passed between August 2 and November 29, 1990. The new demands of Resolution 687 called for the destruction of Iraq's chemical, biological, and nuclear weapons, along with its missiles and launchers with a range over 90 miles. UN inspection teams would oversee the fulfillment of these actions and conduct regular future inspections.

There was a great differential in the casualties. Iraqi losses were very difficult to determine; the Pentagon estimated that 100,000 Iraqi soldiers died, but said the margin of error was about 50 percent, and about 300,000 were wounded. The Pentagon's final count of American casualties was 148 combat deaths, 458 wounded, 120 noncombat deaths, 11 female combat deaths, 4 female noncombat deaths, and 13 additional deaths after February 28. Of these totals, 35 deaths and 72 wounded resulted from friendly fire, largely due to the speed and mobility of high-tech weapons.[28]

Bush's decision to halt military operations without destroying Iraq's military forces, seizing Baghdad, or removing Saddam Hussein became a topic of debate for the next decade. Schwarzkopf revealed his inclination was first to destroy Iraq's military power. "We were 150 miles from Baghdad," he said, "and nothing stood in our way." Yet he agreed the president had made a courageous and "very humane decision." Chairman of the Joint Chiefs General Powell stated that the international coalition had been charged with a defined mission—the liberation of Kuwait—and it had been accomplished. Furthermore, Powell notes, the Arab states did not want Iraq invaded, resulting in its dismemberment. U.S. ambassador to Saudi Arabia Charles Freeman had warned of the geopolitical consequences of military action. "For a range of reasons," Freeman wrote, "we cannot pursue Iraq's unconditional surrender and occupation by us. It is not in our interest to destroy Iraq or weaken it to the point that Iran and/or Syria are not constrained by it." Nor would it enhance Middle Eastern stability, Powell commented in his memoirs, "to have Iraq fragmented into separate Sunni, Shia, and Kurd political entities." Yet, he wrote, it was "hard to drive a stake through the charges that the job was left unfinished."[29]

Bush Calls for a New World Order

In his victory speech on March 6, President Bush prescribed a new order enabling the United Nations to fulfill its historic vision based on principles of justice and fair play, with the strong protecting the weak. In particular, he outlined an American program to stabilize the Middle East by seeking an Arab-Israeli peace process, creating shared security arrangements, fostering economic development in the Gulf region, and preventing the proliferation of weapons of mass destruction. Of these four proposals, only one was advanced, when a Middle East Peace process was initiated by an international conference at Madrid, Spain, on October 30, 1991. The other three objectives achieved mixed or no success. Secretary of State Baker adopted an incremental approach in which the Madrid Conference would host the first of a series of discussions so that subsequently there would be agendas on a nation-to-nation basis. It took him eight months to persuade Israel and the various Arab nations to talk with each other.

The Madrid Conference met from October 30 to November 3, 1991, with the best public performance coming from the Palestine delegates. After Syria's Foreign Minister Farouk al-Sharaa made a harsh, unyielding attack on Israel and Shamir replied in kind, Palestine's Haidar Abdul-Shafi and Mrs. Mikhail-Ashrawi were conciliatory and made the only substantive concessions during the three days at Madrid. They said they would accept a limited Palestinian self-rule in the occupied territories as a means to later independence, an offer the PLO previously rejected. Baker's attempt at an incremental series of conferences lasted until the summer of 1992, but faded, as did Bush's grand design, because of PLO-Israel differences over Jewish settlements on the West Bank.[30]

Clinton and Containing Iraq

Presidents Bush and Bill Clinton faced postwar problems with Iraq ranging from disarming Iraq under a UN mandate to maintaining "no-fly" zones for the protection of Iraq's northern Kurds and southern Shiites who had rebelled against Hussein's rule. After placing economic and military sanctions against Iraq until it fulfilled all the peace terms, the United Nations ordered Hussein to admit inspectors from the International Atomic Energy Agency (IAEA) and the UN Special Commission (UNSCOM) to supervise the destruction of certain weapons. While IAEA inspectors dealt with nuclear weapons materials, UNSCOM teams sought out chemical and biological weapons as well as SCUD missiles capable of carrying a warhead beyond 90 miles. On their initial search, the inspectors uncovered detailed documents that indicated Iraq's destructive weapons stockpile had been 10 times larger than prewar U.S. intelligence estimates.

U.S. bombers failed to destroy Iraq's hidden underground nuclear complexes where Iraqi scientists used outmoded equipment that could only produce atomic bombs similar to those America dropped in 1945, powerful but much less destructive than modern hydrogen warheads. Iraqis moreover had focused on ballistic missiles to deliver their bombs. IAEA teams found and supervised the destruction of Iraq's largest nuclear complex at al-Atheer and another complex at al-Hateem. UN inspectors estimated Iraq might have completed a "crude explosive device" within 12 months, but would have needed two to three years to construct a nuclear arsenal and the missiles to carry them. Clearly, Israel's bombing of Hussein's nuclear facility at Osirak on June 7, 1981—officially condemned by the Reagan administration—had accomplished little, even perhaps accelerating efforts.[31]

As soon as the inspections began in 1991, the teams faced a growing pattern of deliberate confrontations: denial of the existence of documentation, being barred from visiting certain facilities, and periodically being ousted from Iraq on Hussein's orders. Yet the inspectors had made considerable progress using information garnered from defectors that led to the discovery of missile molds and dies, and crates of hidden documents. As the decade lengthened, friction among the allies grew, with France, Russia, and China urging an end to all of the United Nations' increasingly ineffective economic sanctions and irritating inspections. (Later it became known that Iraq, with the collusion of Western companies, was circumventing the oil sanctions.) Meanwhile, UN inspection teams had made considerable progress despite Iraq's obstructionist tactics. Inspector Scott Ritter argued that UN inspectors had accounted for, destroyed, or removed 90 to 95 percent of Iraq's weapons of mass destruction, leaving Hussein with nothing but "documents and scraps of material, and seed stock" for any future "reconstitution effort." Hussein's continued defiance of Security Council resolutions, however, aroused the suspicion that he was hiding dangerous weaponry.[32]

After withdrawing from northern Iraq in September 1991, the United States, France, and Britain established a no-fly zone above the 36th parallel that allowed allied aircraft to shoot down any Iraqi aircraft attacking the Kurds. Later, on August 26, 1992, Bush announced a no-fly zone below the 32nd parallel that allowed allied aircraft to protect the Shiites. After becoming president in January 1993, Bill Clinton continued Bush's policy of joining Britain and France in patrolling Iraq's two no-fly zones. Clinton's first attack on Iraq was an air raid on June 26, 1993, in response to Hussein's complicity in an attempted assassination of his predecessor during an April visit to Kuwait.[33]

In December 1998, citing Iraq's obstructionist tactics and ignoring previous Security Council resolutions, Clinton and British prime minister Tony Blair bombed Iraq from December 16 to 18. American and British aircraft launched Operation Desert Fox, striking Iraq's military targets, transportation agencies, Basra's oil refinery complex, secret palaces, and Baath Party headquarters. Clinton's critics were harsh in their evaluations, even as late as 2004, frequently denigrating his policies as a sham and the bombings as destroying empty buildings. Later interviews with leading Iraqis, however, indicated that the bombing had forced Iraqi officials to realize that large programs, such as missiles that required testing, could easily be identified by aerial surveillance. After Desert Fox, the Clinton administration became involved in three foreign interventions. First, from February to June 1999, Clinton, Blair and NATO focused on a bombing campaign against Serbia's repressive activity in Kosovo. Second, U.S. and U.K. aircraft continued to shoot down Iraqi aircraft and destroy Iraq's antiaircraft batteries in no-fly zones of northern and southern Iraq. From January to May 1, 1999, the U.S.-U.K. flights destroyed 70 Iraqi tanks. The third U.S. efforts revived activities by Iraqi exile groups opposed to Hussein. Saddam Hussein, meanwhile, continued to flaunt UN sanctions and revived trade relations with France, Russia, China, and other nations who opposed economic sanctions.[34]

When Bill Clinton left the White House in January 2011, the Iraqi challenge to the United Nations had spanned a full decade. His administration had bombed Iraqi targets in retaliation for Hussein's defiance of weapons inspections. The United Nations had no power to enforce its resolutions, and, except as they applied to Iraq, Washington could not have cared less. Israel defied far more resolutions aimed at it than did Iraq, and did so with the complete approval of the United States. Critics had long condemned as pointless, if not immoral, the continuing U.S.-British air campaign against Iraq, as well as the death and havoc produced by the ongoing UN sanctions. UN action in both the Korean (1950) and Gulf (1991) crises followed Washington's commitment to military responses against clear international aggressions. But Saddam had refrained from embarking on another military aggression. There would, therefore, be no military action against Saddam Hussein unless Washington could build a case for its necessity and, with or without UN support, launch an invasion of Iraqi.

Almost imperceptibly, a crusade to eliminate the Saddam Hussein regime had been building for almost a decade. In November 1993, Ahmad Chalabi, leader of the Iraqi National Congress (INC) devoted to Saddam's overthrow, presented to the Clinton administration a detailed plan of action, with a request for money. Chalabi launched his insurrection in 1995; it failed dramatically. Within a year, the Iraqi army had driven Chalabi's operation out of Iraq. Nonetheless, anti-Saddam forces in the United States were well prepared to support the Iraqi cause. In June 1997, former U.S. officials such as Donald Rumsfeld, Dick Cheney, I. Lewis (Scooter) Libby, Zalmay Khalilzad, Norman Podhoretz, and Elliott Abrams established the Project for the New American Century, calling for a policy to "promote the cause of political and economic freedom abroad." In February 1998, 18 signers of an open letter to President Clinton, including members of the same group, declared that Saddam ruled by terror and thus was vulnerable to overthrow. "Iraq today," the letter concluded, "is ripe for a broad-based insurrection." The letter advised the recognition of the INC as the provisional government of Iraq. The Clinton administration offered no response. Four months later, the signers condemned the president's refusal to act as an "incalculable blow to American leadership and credibility." Finally, in the fall of 1998, Congress passed and Clinton signed the Iraq Liberation Act that allocated $97 million for training and equipping the Iraq opposition. While Clinton refused to spend the funds, no candidate in the 2000 presidential campaign could afford to ignore the mounting issue of Iraq.[35]

CHAPTER 18

Twenty-First-Century Challenges

> States like these [North Korea, Iran, and Iraq] and their terrorist allies constitute an axis of evil, arming to threaten the peace of the world. By seeking weapons of mass destruction, these regimes pose a grave and growing danger.
>
> —George W. Bush, January 29, 2002

> Some argue that the spread of these weapons cannot be stopped, cannot be checked.... Such fatalism is a deadly adversary, for if we believe that the spread of nuclear weapons is inevitable, then in some way we are admitting to ourselves that the use of nuclear weapons is inevitable.
>
> —Barack Obama, April 5, 2009

Concerns with terrorism, nuclear proliferation, and war dominated America's first decade of the twenty-first century. The nation's worldview was conditioned by the threat of global terrorism and fear of weapons of mass destruction in the hands of Iraq, Iran, and North Korea. President George W. Bush rallied the country after 9/11, helped develop an international network to thwart terrorist threats, and invaded Afghanistan and Iraq—the latter with the hope of spreading democracy throughout the Middle East. In dealing with Iran and North Korea, he engaged in various economic sanctions and antimissile systems designed to destroy incoming ballistic missiles. His missile defense program, however, was seen in Moscow and Beijing as being put in place to diminish their deterrent forces. Upon his departure from office, American military and foreign affairs were in considerable disarray.

President Barack Obama inherited tense relationships with both China and Russia, a need to negotiate a new treaty with Moscow reducing nuclear-tipped missiles, review the antimissile system, withdraw forces from Iraq, and bolster Afghanistan's inept government. Then, too, he faced other dilemmas: what to do with an Iranian government that might be building a nuclear weapon? How does one deal with a nuclear-endangered South Asia? And what position should the United States take during the Arab Spring?

Focus on Iraq

Presidential campaigns during 2000 set the stage for renewed conflict with Iraq. Vice President Albert Gore, the Democratic nominee, defended the Clinton record on Iraq, but added: "I want to go further. I want to give robust support to the groups that are trying to overthrow Saddam Hussein." George W. Bush, the Republican nominee, declared, if as president he found Saddam manufacturing weapons of mass destruction, he would "take him out." Later, he warned on TV's *Jim Lehrer News Hour*: "If we catch him developing weapons of mass destruction in any way, shape, or form, I'll deal with that in a way that he won't like." Republican vice-presidential candidate Richard (Dick) Cheney warned that if Saddam considered possessing weapons of mass destruction, "we'd have to give very serious consideration to military action to stop that activity."[1] The Republican platform strongly endorsed the Iraq Liberation Act. Some State Department officials favoured new sanctions, but nowhere did the 2000 campaign resolve the question of Saddam's future. But George W. Bush's election would.

Many in the new Bush administration shared the muscular and unilateralist vision of the country's leading neoconservative pundits who advocated expanding the world's democratic arena with displays of U.S. power. Charles Krauthammer, columnist for the *Washington Post*, demanded a "new unilateralism" that sought to "strengthen American power and unashamedly deploy it on behalf of self-defined global ends." Among those who dominated the new administration were self-defined neoconservatives such as Paul Wolfowitz, deputy secretary of defense; Douglas Feith, undersecretary of defense; Richard Armitage, undersecretary of state; and Condoleezza Rice, national security adviser. The administration's dominant spokesmen, Vice President Cheney and Secretary of Defense Rumsfeld, were not neocons, but rather assertive nationalists driven by perceptions of danger to U.S. security. What rendered such distinctions irrelevant was the general agreement within the new administration that Washington pursue an aggressive foreign policy against the world's unacceptable regimes, based on incontestable military power and a readiness to use it. Only Colin Powell, the new secretary of state, was reluctant to endorse the administration's assertive outlook on world affairs.[2]

As the curtain opened on the new administration, Iraq held center stage. At the initial meeting of the new National Security Council on January 30, 2001, there was a high degree of agreement that Saddam needed to go. Leading the anti-Saddam crusade were Wolfowitz, Rumsfeld, and Cheney. Critics noted the failure to uncover any Iraqi weapons program—the sole rational of the demand for action. But toppling Saddam found no consensus in the vast majority of the American people, no less than the world, generally. Iraq largely remained a dead issue.

9/11 Terrorist Attacks and Afghanistan Invasion

Plans to remove Saddam's regime were interrupted by the September 11, 2001, terrorist attacks on New York and Washington. The president declared that: "Those who make war on the United States have chosen their own destruction.... We will find those who did it. We will smoke them out of their holes. We'll get them running, and we'll bring them to justice." Even Russia's President Vladimir Putin condemned the attacks, defining them as "a blatant challenge to humanity." Britain's prime minister Tony Blair declared mass terrorism the new evil in world society, one "utterly indifferent to the sanctity of human life." Some Europeans hoped that the United States, in its pursuit of vengeance, would not push the world into a spiral of uncontrolled violence. Throughout much of the Undeveloped World, however, the reaction to the 9/11 attacks was unsympathetic, for they understood that Arab hatred toward the United States had driven the attacks. To many Arabs, the United States was an alien, oppressive, and corrupting influence throughout the Middle East. But most of the hatred flowed from the perennial U.S. support of Israel. For Bush, however, Arab hatred of the United States lay not in what America did, but in what it was. "They hate our freedoms," he told a joint session of Congress on September 20, "our freedom of religion, our freedom of speech, our freedom to vote and assemble and disagree with each other." Recognizing only American values as an explanation of terrorist action, the president relieved himself and his administration from any obligation to reassess the role of U.S. power and behavior in Middle Eastern affairs.[3]

Following 9/11, Cheney and Rumsfeld proposed that the United States attack Iraq as well as al Qaeda in Afghanistan; but Powell opposed an immediate invasion of Iraq because it would inflame America's Middle Eastern Arab allies. The chairman of the Joint Chiefs of Staff, General Henry B. Shelton, agreed, arguing that action against the Afghan terrorists be completed before launching other military strikes. Bush accepted their advice and delayed plans to attack Iraq. In contemplating his opening move against terrorism, the president revealed that al Qaeda, a loosely affiliated terrorist organization, with its leader Osama bin Laden, had planned the attack. As bin Laden and his supporters resided in Afghanistan under the protection of that country's Taliban regime, Washington demanded that the Taliban government turn over al Qaeda leaders or face a U.S. invasion.

With the Taliban's refusal, Washington, on October 7, launched its war against terrorism in Afghanistan. NATO had invoked Article 5 to provide military assistance, but the Pentagon preferred to act without major European support. It limited U.S. forces to 60,000, with half retained in the Gulf region, relying heavily on 15,000 Afghan Northern Alliance fighters and, after October, an equal number of Pashtuns in the south. Again, the American war centered heavily on precision bombing from aircraft, flying thousands of sorties, largely from carriers. The initial conflict was brief, and U.S. casualties few. The Taliban, along with al Qaeda leaders, retreated eastward to the cave complexes in the mountains bordering Pakistan. American-led forces seized control of Kabul by December 2001 and made Hamid Karzai head of Afghan's interim government. Bush's main problems were the failure to capture Osama bin Laden and to neutralize the Taliban—the latter would require nothing less than nation-building. Unless reconstituted, the country would again become a haven for terrorists, but the fighting had rendered the entire region unstable. What the Afghan war achieved for America's war against terrorism remained tenuous.[4]

Its losses in Afghanistan deprived al Qaeda of its base, but it did not prevent the scattering of its leaders to Western Europe and throughout the Middle East, with less money and logistical support, but still active. The thousands of men who had passed through the al Qaeda training camps in Afghanistan had returned to their homes around the world. After celebrating the Afghan victory in his State of the Union message on January 29, 2002, Bush said: "What we found in Afghanistan confirms that, far from ending there, our war against terror is only beginning." Americans must be patient in shutting down terrorist camps, disrupting their plans, and bringing them to justice. We must also prevent attacks by terrorist regimes "who seek chemical, biological or nuclear weapons" to threaten "the United States and the world." After citing

North Korea, Iran, and Iraq as nations exporting terrorism and having weapons of mass destruction (WMD), Bush concluded: "States like these and their terrorist allies, constitute an axis of evil, arming to threaten the world." The United States "can't stop short—leaving terror camps intact and terror[ist] nations unchecked."[5] The administration's focus again was on Hussein.

To the Bush Doctrine

Earlier, on November 21, President Bush had signed top-secret instructions to plan military options for an invasion of Iraq. At the same time, the president addressed Rumsfeld: "What kind of a war plan do you have for Iraq? How do you feel about the war plan for Iraq?"[6] With the overthrow of the Taliban, the Washington hawks demanded that the United States close in on Iraq. These demands prompted sharp differences over how to deal with Iraq, with Cheney and Rumsfeld claiming UN sanctions and weapons inspections had failed to remove or damage Saddam's regime for over 10 years and diplomacy was a waste of time and money. In contrast, Powell said the Security Council's newly approved sanctions would weaken Saddam's control in Iraqi, because they would not only restrict Iraq's weapon's imports but also would help retain U.S alliances with Arab nations. He wanted to sponsor a Security Council resolution requiring Iraq to admit UNMOVIC inspectors, which Saddam had opposed since 1999. Meanwhile, the Bush administration sought European support for a more aggressive policy toward Saddam. During a February 2002 NATO Conference on Security Policy at Munich, Republican senator John McCain of Arizona declared: "The next front is apparent and we should not shrink from acknowledging it. A terrorist resides in Baghdad with the rich resources of the entire state" and is "proud of a decade-long record of falsifying the international community's demands that he come clean on his programs to develop weapons of mass destruction." The American's hawkish position shocked European delegates. House of Commons member Menzies Campbell said Britain supported a stronger position against Iraq, but London "would require incontrovertible evidence in order to justify" a military operation. A member of the German Parliament (Reichstag), Gert Weisskirchen, wanted a "multilateral approach in U.S. policy" toward Iraq, arguing America must involve its allies in planning and executing any battles ahead.[7]

Bush and British prime minister Blair met in March 2002, where Bush insisted that Iraq must permit intrusive inspections of all its weaponry.

A "Secret Downing Street Memo" dated July 23, 2002, made public in June 2005, summarized the status of Blair's partnership with Bush. It declared recent talks in Washington had concluded: "Military action was now seen as inevitable. Bush wanted to remove Saddam through military action, justified by the conjunction of terrorism and WMD. But the intelligence and facts were being fixed around the policy. The NSC had no patience with the UN route and no enthusiasm for publishing material on the Iraqi regime's record. There was little discussion of the aftermath of military action." Since Britain's attorney general had indicated that the desire for regime change "was not a legal base for military action," the memo continued, there remained "three possible legal bases: self-defence, humanitarian intervention, or UNSC authorisation." The prime minister added that if Saddam Hussein refused to admit UN inspectors, this could provide legal grounds for action. During a July 23 session, British principals concluded they would assume the United Kingdom would take part in any military action once American planning was known. In addition, they would begin British military planning, check on the role of UN inspectors, seek out the positions of Turkey and EU members, and obtain a complete intelligence update on Iraq.[8]

Inasmuch as Saddam would never provide Washington with an overt excuse for intervention, an Iraqi war would be a matter of choice. The administration found the elusive legitimacy for a U.S. invasion in the doctrine of preemption, granting the United States the right to defend itself from an impending attack. At West Point, on June 1, President Bush advanced the doctrine of preemption by declaring deterrence and containment obsolete. He argued that "new threats" required "new thinking.... We must take the battle to the enemy, disrupt his plans and confront the worst threats before they emerge.... Our security will require all Americans... to be ready for preemptive action when necessary to defend our liberty and to defend our lives." Finally he said: "We will not leave the safety of America at the mercy of a few mad terrorists and tyrants."[9] While he did not mention Iraq, most observers correctly concluded Bush was ready to attack Iraq—his preemptive war concepts became policy on September 20, 2002, as part of U.S. National Security Strategy. Here, Bush warned: "We will maintain the forces sufficient to support our obligations, and to defend freedom. Our forces will be strong enough to dissuade potential adversaries from pursuing a military buildup in hopes of surpassing, or equaling, the power of the United States." The country would seek international support, he acknowledged, but it would not "hesitate to act alone, if necessary, to exercise [its] right to self-defence by acting preemptively." The document was ultimately a defense of American unilateralism, based on the supposition that the United States was sufficiently powerful enough to eliminate, alone, anything unacceptable in world politics.[10]

The preemption option was not new. (Every president since Harry Truman understood that he possessed it, but they refrained from emphasizing or employing it.) The rules regarding preemptive war had long been embedded in international law and practice. What defined and justified its acceptable exercise was that the danger be clear and imminently threatening based on specific and incontrovertible evidence. The danger had to be critical and unacceptable. Finally, it had to exceed the possibility of control by peaceful means. Such rules could always be open to questioning, but they were sufficiently stringent and precise to rule out most claims for the right of preemption. Henry Kissinger declared in an attack on preemption: "It cannot be in either the American national interest or the world's interest to develop principles that grant every nation an unfettered right of pre-emption against its own definition of threats to its security."[11] Preemptive war, launched in advance of any visible threat, simply had no standing in international law.

The Administration Prevails

During the spring of 2002, the Bush administration confirmed its decision to convert the war against terrorism into a preemptive strike against Iraq. In March, Vice President Cheney observed that it was no longer a question of if, but of when, the United States would attack Iraq. British intelligence, like that of the United States, could find no evidence of Saddam's alleged weapons program or his connection with al Qaeda. On July 23, Sir Richard Dearlove, the head of British intelligence, reported to Prime Minister Tony Blair that the president had decided on war to remove Saddam Hussein: "Military action was now seen as inevitable. Bush wanted to remove Saddam through military action, justified by the conjunction of terrorism and WMD. But the intelligence and facts were being fixed around policy." Rice declared in a BBC interview of August 15 that the United States and other nations had no choice but to seek the removal of Saddam Hussein. Her arguments were moral as well as strategic. "This is an evil man," she averred, "who, left to his own devices, will wreak havoc again on his own population, his neighbours and, if he gets weapons of mass destruction and the means to deliver them, on all of us." She noted that Saddam was close to acquiring nuclear weapons, had used chemical weapons against his neighbors and his own people, and, after 1998, barred UN inspectors from his country—all enough to make Iraq a prime case for preemption. "History," she argued, "is littered with cases of inaction that led to very grave consequences for the world. [Past experience revealed] how many dictators who ended up being a tremendous global threat and killing thousands and, indeed, millions of people, we should have stopped in their tracks." How exactly Saddam presented such a danger she failed to explain.[12]

"There is no doubt," Cheney declared on August 26, "that Saddam Hussein now has weapons of mass destruction. There is no doubt he is amassing them to use against our friends, against our allies and against us." In the hands of a "murderous dictator," Cheney warned, weapons of mass destruction are "as grave a threat as can be imagined. The risks of inaction are far greater than the risk of action." This nation, he assured his listeners, "will not live at the mercy of terrorists or terror regimes." The vice president concluded that, in facing such a determined antagonist, weapons inspections were futile. "A return of inspectors," he said, "would provide no assurance whatsoever of his compliance with UN resolutions."[13] Cheney's speech was harsh and unilateralist. He found, however, during his visit to a dozen Middle Eastern countries little support for Washington's unilateralist approach. Beyond eliminating Iraq's weapons of mass destruction, the administration adopted, under the preachments of Cheney and others, the broader and more ambitious object of creating a thriving democracy in Iraq as a model for all Arab and Muslim nations.

Although Powell accepted the notion of preemptive war, he believed the president should seek international support available only through the United Nations. Cheney, Rumsfeld, and other hawks argued that the United Nations, not the United States, should be the issue, especially its failure to enforce its Iraqi resolutions. Cheney and Rice agreed that the United Nations was becoming irrelevant, reduced in large measure to a debating society. But at the August 16 meeting of the National Security Council, the members agreed unanimously to give the UN another chance to perform before Washington would advocate war. Former advisers to George H. W. Bush, Brent Scowcroft and James Baker opposed a new war with Iraq. Former NSC advisor Scowcroft argued there was "scant evidence to tie Saddam to terrorist organizations" because Saddam has little in common with terrorists. He opposed an Iraqi war that would divert American military activity "from our war on terrorism." About the same time, former secretary of state James Baker conceded a military attack could force Saddam out of office, but insisted "unless we do it the right way, there will be costs to other American foreign policy interests, including our relations with practically all Arab countries," as well as "our top foreign policy priority, the war on terrorism." Baker wanted "a simple and straightforward" Security Council resolution demanding intrusive inspections in Iraq with authorization to use "all necessary means to enforce it." Both Scowcroft and Baker opposed the use of military force unless the "Big Five" permanent Security Council members approved as in 1990.[14]

On September 7 at Camp David, Britain's Tony Blair announced that new evidence revealed activity at Iraq's nuclear sites. Bush confirmed Blair's revelation, "I don't know what more evidence we need." On September 8, Cheney claimed that: "We do know, with absolute certainty, that [Saddam] is using his procurement system to acquire the equipment he needs in order to enrich uranium to build a nuclear weapon." That same day Rice warned that Saddam was "actively pursuing a nuclear weapon" and that the tubes, described in U.S. intelligence reports as dual-use items, were "only really suited for nuclear weapons programs." She acknowledged that there would always be some uncertainty about how quickly Iraq could acquire nuclear weapons but, she added, "We don't want the smoking gun to be a mushroom cloud." Others took up the theme of the mushroom cloud. On September 28, Bush told members of Congress: "The danger to our country is grave.... The Iraqi regime possesses biological and chemical weapons.... [It]'s seeking a nuclear bomb, and with fissile material, could build one within a year." At Cincinnati, on October 7, he averred that Saddam possessed a "stockpile of biological weapons, thousands of tons of chemical agents, [and was] reconstituting his nuclear weapons program.... Facing clear evidence of peril," he added, "we cannot wait for the final proof—the smoking gun—that could come in the form of a mushroom cloud."

On October 10–11, Congress authorized the president to order an invasion of Iraq whenever he might choose to do so. That crucial decision came without serious debate; the outcome was preordained. The administration had captured Congress and the public. (Without any evidence of links between Saddam and al Qaeda, a Pew Research poll of October found that 66 percent of Americans surveyed believed that Saddam helped the terrorists in the 9/11 attacks.) The vote in the House was 296 to 133, with 126 Democrats voting against it. The Senate vote was 77 to 23. Resolution 114 granted the president the power to "use the Armed Forces of the United States as he determines to be necessary and appropriate in order to defend the national security of the United States against the continuing threat posed by Iraq." The president need not consult Congress for a formal declaration of war. Critics deplored Congress's desertion of its constitutional role in governing such powers.[15]

Bush Goes to War

After Security Council Resolution 1441 was approved on November 8, 2002, the UN Monitoring, Verification and Inspections Commission (UNMOVIC) headed by Hans Blix and the International Atomic Energy Agency (IAEA) led by Mohamand ElBaradei resumed inspection of Iraq. During the first week, the UN Commission and IAEA made 20 inspections and failed to find any Iraqi biological or chemical weapons. CIA personnel monitored the inspectors' activity because their findings were vital to any decision on war. Moreover, Bush, Cheney, and Rice feared Blix was not aggressively pressing the search for weapons. On January 9, 2003, Blix reported that his inspectors had found no "smoking gun" to show Iraq had any proscribed weapons.[16]

Soon after, Defense Secretary Rumsfeld informed Bush that the essential U.S. and U.K. troops were deployed in the Gulf region and ready for war. Meanwhile, Bush met with Iraqi exiles on January 10th and told them if Saddam doesn't disarm "we will remove him." One of the delighted exiles declared the "people will greet troops with flowers and sweets." On January 11, Cheney, Rumsfeld, and chairman of the Joint Chiefs of Staff General Richard Myers asked Saudi Arabia's Ambassador Prince Bandar bin Sultan to allow U.S. soldiers and planes to move through Saudi territory on their way into Iraq as in 1991; this time they promised Saddam would be removed. Subsequently, Bandar obtained approval for the United States to use Saudi Arabia's Prince Sultan Air Base to direct the coalition's air command and control facilities over Iraq, but the Saudis denied U.S. and coalition forces the use of their seaports, territory, or air bases for combat operations. British prime minister Blair met with Bush on January 31, 2003. According to a memo by David Manning, Blair's foreign policy adviser, an attack on Iraq would begin on March 10 with the bombing of Iraqi targets. The two leaders believed there would be a quick victory, and Bush thought "it was unlikely there would be internecine warfare between the different religious and ethnic groups."[17] This was a monumental miscalculation.

Meanwhile, the inspectors provided the Security Council with a second report on January 27, 2003, after IAEA teams had inspected 230 sites and UNMOVIC teams had searched over 300 sites. Blix indicated inspectors did not know whether or not Iraq had biological, chemical, or nuclear weapons, but they lacked evidence that Iraq did. He thought there were "strong indications" Iraq produced more anthrax than declared, but there was no compelling evidence that Iraq desired to activate anthrax. Finally, he said Iraq had tested Samoud-2 missiles with a range of more than the permitted range of 90 miles (150 km) set by the 1991 UNSC resolution. IAEA teams found no evidence that Iraq had an active nuclear weapons program. Finally, Blix concluded, UNMOVIC and IAEA investigators would continue their search with approval from the Security Council, a view both chief inspectors shared as "a valuable investment in peace."[18]

What quickly undermined any hope for avoiding war through inspections was the escalation of U.S. threats against Iraq during January and February. The administration's move toward war was increasingly apparent, rendering inspections irrelevant. Washington's continuing effort to produce the intelligence needed to underwrite its rationale for war culminated in Colin Powell's television address, of February 5, before the UN Security Council and the world. Powell began with the assurance: "What we are giving you are facts and conclusions based on solid intelligence." Then followed a multimedia slide show; with photographs of secret Iraqi weapons factories, tapes of intercepted telephone conversations among Iraqi officials, and charts revealing clandestine links between Baghdad and al Qaeda operatives. The message was clear and graphic: Iraq was guilty of denial, deception, and failure to disarm. World leaders found the speech unconvincing. Powell's portrayal of the Iraqi danger came under immediate examination that revealed only fragments to be accurate.[19] Yet for the administration, Powell's speech achieved its purpose—public opposition to an Iraqi war began to melt.

Members of the administration became increasingly contemptuous of opinions not their own. The president declared that he owed no one an explanation of his policy preferences. Rice declared that the failure of the United Nations to support the United States in Iraq mattered little; the United States alone would "act to defend...the world and the United States." Such bellicose rhetoric emanating from Washington placed the Bush administration totally at odds with many of its historic European allies. France and Germany, joined by Russia, had long established themselves as Washington's primary opponents in its effort to obtain European support for an Iraqi war. Polls revealed that 8 out of 10 Europeans agreed with the Franco-German opposition. Joseph Joffe, editor of the German political weekly *Die Zeit*, observed that Europe's opposition was less concerned with Saddam than with the need to inhibit the United States. "This," he concluded, "is about controlling American power." What underwrote much of Europe's fear of the United States was Washington's assertion that no nation be allowed to challenge America's global power and primacy. Secretary Rumsfeld warned France and Germany that they were facing diplomatic isolation in their opposition to war. The secretary faced biting rebuttals from French, German, and Russian officials, with warnings that the United States was in danger of overreaching badly. Rumsfeld noted that Poland, the Czech Republic, and Hungary supported President Bush. He termed the supportive states of Eastern Europe the "New" Europe, in contrast to the "Old" Europe of Germany and France, long reduced, he said, to a harmless tourist attraction—France with its vanity and pride, Germany stubborn and wrongheaded.[20]

The United States, Britain, and Spain, on February 24, 2003, submitted a resolution to the Security Council declaring that Iraq had missed its final opportunity to disarm peacefully, and now faced the consequences. Immediately, Germany, France, and Russia circulated an alternative plan to pursue the peaceful disarmament of Iraq through strengthened inspections extended over another five months. French President Jacques Chirac warned that France would veto any resolution that opened the way for war. No UN resolution emerged. As the administration moved toward war, it repeatedly warned of Saddam's weapons of mass destruction and their intended use. As Secretary Rumsfeld expressed: "Any country on the face of the Earth, with an active intelligence program, knows that Iraq has weapons of mass destruction." Speaking on March 17, the president again warned: "Intelligence gathered by this and other governments leaves no doubt that the Iraq regime continues to possess and conceal some of the most lethal weapons ever devised." Vice President Cheney offered even more frightening news: "We believe [Hussein] has, in fact, reconstituted nuclear weapons." To the end, Saddam's alleged weapons comprised the sole and most terrifying rationale for war. Yet Hans Blix observed that those who purported to know with certainty that Iraq had weapons could never identify their locations. The inspectors, he declared, had found no prohibited weapons at any site suggested by intelligence agencies.[21]

What enhanced the appeal of an Iraqi war was the conviction that a regime change in Baghdad would transform the entire Arab world. The president, in late February, declared that the liberation of Iraq would not only lead to a new regime for all Iraqis, but also unleash the spread of democratic values throughout the Arab world. When questioned by members of Congress, secretaries Powell and Rumsfeld offered sweeping assurances that postwar Iraq would have a representative government "that would help transform the region around it." For the administration, the creation of a thriving Iraqi democracy would become a model for all Arab and Muslim nations; the new moderation would become contagious and assure a peaceful settlement of the Palestinian question. On March 16, Cheney declared that the Iraqis want "to get rid of Saddam Hussein and they will welcome as liberators the United States when we come to do that." Washington apparently hoped to imitate in Iraq the successes of the U.S. occupations in post-1945 Germany, Italy, and Japan, in establishing an exemplary democratic regime. Unfortunately, these three countries scarcely served as a model for Iraq since they possessed all the essential materials for democratic reconstruction: educated and industrious populations, surviving infrastructures, modern industrial experience, and no large, restive minorities. Iraq was an artificial country of many faiths, tribes, and ethnic groups, including Sunnis, Shiites, and Kurds. Nowhere was it apparent how the United States could transform the country, divided essentially by its historic rivalries, into a united liberal-democratic state.[22]

Bush Goes to War

On March 17, 2003, the president gave Saddam 48 hours to quit Iraq. American security, he said, demanded no less. Two days later, from the Oval Office, he announced his decision for war, declaring again that Saddam constituted a grave danger. "We will meet that threat now," he said, "so we do not have to meet it later... on the streets of our cities." An ABC News-*Washington Post* poll found American overwhelmingly in agreement with the decision. The subsequent invasion of Iraq predictably encountered no weapons of mass destruction; nor were they expected. Those weapons, always elusive, were the rationale for the war, not the reason.[23]

Perhaps the Iraqi war produced the easiest victory in U.S. history. Precision bombing eliminated the anticipated, potentially costly but limited struggle for Baghdad. So unequal was the contest that some U.S. soldiers wondered why the Iraqis would throw themselves away against such impossible odds. American pilots were equally dismayed by the total lack of sophistication in the Iraqi air defenses. No one had predicted that the initial defeat of the Iraqi forces would be so easy. Aboard the U.S.S. *Abraham Lincoln*, on May 1, President Bush declared victory with the assurance that "major combat operations in Iraq have ended." Behind him a banner proclaimed "MISSION ACCOMPLISHED." The United States, he declared, had eliminated its Iraqi enemies, disposed of an ally of al Qaeda, and liberated the Iraqi people. It was in control of events in Iraq and set to rebuild Iraqi society, with Iraqis celebrating the U.S. presence. Rice added that the United States had achieved a "special opportunity to advance a positive agenda for the Middle East that will strengthen security in the region and throughout the world."[24] Winning the war against terrorism demanded no less.

The official anticipation was that the easy military victory in Iraq would leave no problems in its trail. Rumsfeld believed that the mere presence of a small occupying force would be adequate to establish order. "We continue to feel," he declared in mid-April, "that there's no need for a broader conflict if the Iraq leaders act to save themselves." Consequently, he rejected consideration of the State Department's postwar plan, convinced that American forces would turn over control to new Iraq authorities and leave. Consequently, when the fighting ended in April, the Pentagon was not prepared for the collapse of Iraqi society or the destruction of the country's infrastructures through looting and sabotage. Washington had received repeated warnings that the elimination of the Iraqi military could unleash massive looting of Baghdad's famed National Museum, the National Library, the Religious Endowment Library, and other such institutions with their priceless antiquities. The administration did nothing to protect them. The cultural losses were staggering. By May, the looting had run its course, with military buildings, palaces, and many factories and stores stripped bare. The looting then shifted to robbing, abducting, and harassing. This was merely a dramatic portent of what was to come. Pentagon planners believed their forecasts so completely that they failed to prepare for the collapse of Iraq's social, economic, and political infrastructure. This left a security and administrative vacuum that the U.S. military was totally unprepared to fill. American forces lacked the personnel to secure the streets, tackle the crime, restore a sense of public order, or recreate the necessary governing apparatus. Basic necessities, especially electricity, water, and gasoline, were almost nonexistent. An American official lamented, "The planning was ragged and the execution was worse."[25]

The Protracted Occupation

By July 2003, U.S. forces were facing dozens of assaults daily. The postwar deaths began to exceed the number killed in the war itself, with far greater numbers wounded, many seriously. Almost every night C-17 transport jets arrived at Andrews Air Force base outside Washington on medical evacuation missions. That month General Tommy Franks, commander of U.S. forces in Iraq, acknowledged that the dangers facing American security forces in Iraq were likely to persist. By the late months of 2003, almost every day bought reports of deadly roadside bombs directed against U.S. combat patrols and supply convoys. The U.S. military played down the attacks as insignificant and as having no effect on day-to-day operations. As late as November, the president proclaimed: "We are not only containing the terrorist threat, we are turning it back." President Bush and his advisers continued to link the war in Iraq with the war on terror, and thus any U.S. retreat from Iraq would seriously threaten the nation's security. He defined the danger on August 26, 2003: "Our military is confronting terrorists in Iraq and Afghanistan and other places so our people will not have to confront terrorist violence in New York and St. Louis or Los Angeles." Henry Kissinger, who often conferred with the president, warned in the *Washington Post* of August 12, 2005: "Victory over the insurgency is the only meaningful exit strategy." There must be no withdrawal of U.S. forces. Vice President Cheney warned that any retreat from Iraq would expose the country to increased terrorist attacks.[26] The administration remained in a state of denial—there would be no "victory," only exit.

Obama and Nuclear Weapons

In addition to Middle East issues, especially Iraq and Afghanistan, President Barack Obama inherited a need to negotiate a new treaty with Moscow reducing nuclear weaponry, to contend with nuclear proliferation (especially in Iran and South Asia), and to review Bush's antimissile system. Even after the collapse of the Soviet Union in 1991, one prolonged episode after another arose involving critical events. Senior civilian and military leaders in Washington and Moscow—as well as in Washington and Beijing—never quite seemed to shed the trappings of the Cold War's environment despite moments of good feelings. In otherwise polite speeches, these unreconciled attitudes frequently arose during the dealing with post–Cold War strategic nuclear weaponry. These symptoms could be found in Washington's continuing insistence on deploying missile defense systems that Moscow, and to some extent Beijing, questioned as threatening their deterrent forces. Yet there was recognition of certain mutual interests as found in the Cooperative Threat Reduction program and Global Threat Reduction Initiative aimed at securing stocks of dangerous nuclear material scattered around the former Soviet Union and elsewhere in the world. Then, too, former adversaries cooperated in the functioning of such unofficial international agencies as the Nuclear Suppliers Group that sought to control the export of material, equipment, and facilities that if diverted from peaceful uses could contribute to nuclear weapons or creating other weapons of mass destruction.

The Obama administration needed to act promptly to replace the expiring 1991 bilateral Strategic Arms Reduction Treaty (START I) since both the United States and Russia used its verification system to monitor each other's strategic nuclear weaponry. The Russians objected to

George W. Bush's proposed expansion of U.S. missile defenses—a program of dubious value—to Europe, which were needed, according to the administration, to counter a possible missile threat from Iran. But, Russian officials protested, this system could be used to counter their missile force as well. Bush's other missile defense system was located primarily in Alaska to intercept any missiles from North Korea; but Beijing viewed it as having been developed to counter their missiles. Both Moscow and Beijing were convinced the United States was attempting to negate their missile forces designed to deter a U.S. nuclear strike. Although neither opponent was placated by American denials, the Russians did agree in 2010 to a New START Treaty that replaced START I and led to a significant reduction in nuclear warheads.[27]

At Prague on April 5, 2009, President Obama outlined a path toward "a world without nuclear weapons." He directed attention to elements of the nonproliferation regime "to cut off the building blocks needed for a bomb." Working together, he said, "we will strengthen the nuclear Non-Proliferation Treaty as a basis for cooperation." Various nations had been persuaded to give up their nuclear weapons programs—South Korea, Taiwan, Brazil, Argentina, South Africa, Libya, and the former Soviet republics—the question was could the programs of North Korea, Iran, India, Pakistan, and Israel be restrained? The hope of abolishing nuclear weapons was raised much earlier at the United Nations, in June 1988, by India's prime minister, Rajiv Gandhi, who warned that nuclear war "will mean the extinction of four thousand million: the end of life as we know it on our planet earth." Yet Indian officials viewing China's nuclear program as threatening ultimately developed their own nuclear weapons and missiles. New Delhi's program, while providing a deterrence strategy vis-à-vis China, aroused fears in Pakistan sufficient for its officials to develop nuclear and missile programs. With few means to influence events, Americans must watch the competition between India and Pakistan and worry it could erupt in hostilities with potentially disastrous results that would reach far beyond their borders.[28]

North Korea's nuclear ambitions presented a more complex set of circumstances: the desire for additional security vis-à-vis the United States and greater international recognition of their status. Perceived American nuclear threats, according to Michael Mazarr in *North Korea and the Bomb*, "have pervaded North Korean strategic thoughts and actions since the Korean War, and may have played a decisive role in stimulating North Korean leaders to embark on their own nuclear weapons program." Responding to numerous North Korean violations of the armistice, the United States sent nuclear-capable artillery shells, rockets, cruise missiles, and land mines to bolster the defense of South Korea. During the Clinton administration the United States and South Korea sought to entice the North Koreans to cooperate with IAEA inspections at suspected nuclear weapons facilities. Washington worked out a pact with North Korea on October 16, 1994, known as the Agreed Framework; it subsequently floundered because of a continuing aura of mistrust. George W. Bush's labeling North Korea as one of the "axis of evil" and, in 2002, Secretary of State Colin Powell's demand for controls on North Korea's missile program essentially terminated meaningful negotiations. Pyongyang tested two nuclear devices, in 2006 and 2009, with varying degrees of success and began developing and testing missiles as possible delivery vehicles. Many foreign observers believed the otherwise desperate, hungry population (and failing regime?) that make up North Korea was best symbolized by its nuclear and missile programs, which gave rise to the basic question, What are the programs intended to provide offensive weapons: defensive ones or symbols of status? In spite of the prolonged diplomatic negotiations with Pyongyang officials over the past two decades, the question of motivation remains elusive.[29]

For several years, Western nations and, of course, Israel have viewed Iran as posing twin threats: the construction of enhanced nuclear enrichment facilities as a first step in obtaining nuclear warheads and an ambitious missile program. In Washington, officials first began worrying about Iran's interest in nuclear weaponry during the 1970s. A 1975 State Department memorandum suggested "uncertainty" over Iran's "long-term objectives despite its NPT status." Indeed, a Central Intelligence Agency's 1988 report asserted that Tehran had undertaken nuclear weapons "design work" prior to the 1979 Islamic revolution and that the revolutionary government had initially halted the program only to reinstitute it three years later. By 1985, A National Intelligence Council report identified Iran as a potential "proliferation threat" and declared that the new regime was "interested in developing facilities that ... could eventually produce fissile material that could be used in a [nuclear] weapon." It was estimated that it would take at least a decade for Tehran to produce a weapon. An International Atomic Energy Agency investigation, together with information supplied by Tehran after an October 2003 agreement, suggested "Iran had engaged in a variety of clandestine nuclear-related activities." The election of President Mahmoud Ahmadinejad in 2005 resulted in Iranian intransigence regarding restrictions on their nuclear activities. Yet Supreme Leader Ayatollah Ali Khamene'i declared on June 3, 2008, that Iran was opposed to nuclear weapons "based on religious and Islamic beliefs as well as based on logic and wisdom." Even

President Ahmadinejad asserted on April 9, 2009, "those who accumulate nuclear weapons are backwards in political terms." Unconvinced Western leaders turned to the UN Security Council for economic sanctions, found in Resolutions 1803 (2006), 1747 (2007), 1696 (2006), and 1929 (2010), intended to halt or regulate Iran's nuclear enrichment programs and allow its facilities to be inspected by the International Atomic Energy Agency.

With diplomacy and sanctions, the West and the United States, particularly, continued seeking to persuade or coerce Iran not to join the nuclear weapons club. For example, the U.S. Nuclear Posture Review Report in April 2010 stated: "We seek to bolster the nuclear non-proliferation regime and its centerpiece, the NPT, by reversing the nuclear ambitions of North Korea and Iran, strengthening International Atomic Energy Agency safeguards and enforcing compliance with them." By late 2011, diplomatic activity and sanctions appeared unable to achieve the United Nations and IAEA's desired goals. Additionally, intermittent diplomatic activities were caught up in a basic contradiction: how to acknowledge Iran's sovereign rights and yet deny it the right to nuclear weaponry. No previous attempt was ever made to apply this contradictory policy—not to the acknowledged nuclear weapons states, including Israel, Pakistan, and India.[30]

Back to the Middle East

President Barack Obama presided over the withdrawal of U.S. forces from Iraq, confronted new tensions in the Middle East with the rise of "Arab Spring," and bolstered Afghanistan's inept government. The United States left Iraq not certain of the legacy left behind. In late December 2011, the United States lowered its flag in Baghdad as the U.S. military mission in Iraq came officially to an end. The low-key ceremony stood in sharp contrast to America's 2003 invasion. Americans at first had no clear idea as to whether they were to be liberators or occupiers. Consequently, the resilience and effectiveness of the insurgents caught civilian and military officials in Baghdad and Washington unprepared for the bloody years that followed.

Contributing to the insurgency was General Franks and Rumsfeld's failure to grasp the force requirements for internal security, the resources needed for reconstruction, or a plan for establishing a new governing structure for Iraq. Not until August 5, 2004, was a plan for Iraq finally issued calling for controlling insurgent attacks, training Iraqi security forces, rehabilitating the economy, persuading the Sunnis by coercion and cooperation to stop supporting the violence, and developing a counterinsurgency program. These actions only gradually disarmed local militias and slowed insurgent attacks on civilians and coalition forces—between 2003 and 2010 there were over 1,000 suicide bombings, with, Iraqi civilians suffering heavy losses. On September 7, 2006, the United States "formally" turned over control of Iraq's armed forces to Prime Minister Nouri al-Maliki's government, and the next year Iraqi officials began demanding Washington set a date for withdrawal of American forces. In November 2008, a Status of Forces Agreement was signed stipulating that all U.S. forces would be completely out of Iraq by December 31, 2011. Almost nine years after the U.S. invasion of the country, the withdrawal was completed on December 16.

The costs of the Iraqi misadventure in blood and treasure were considerable. Coalition troops suffered a total of 4,804 fatalities—4,486 U.S., 179 British, and 139 other—and some 32,000 U.S. wounded. Estimates of Iraqi fatalities ranged from 100,000 to 600,000, while tens of thousands fled the country. Direct financial costs as of withdrawal reached more than $800 billion, but ongoing medical treatment, replacement of vehicles, and so on will push the cost to $4 trillion or more. (The national debt increased from $5.7 to $10.6 trillion during Bush's presidency.) It is most difficult to assess what was accomplished, other than the hanging of Saddam Hussein, as bombings attributed to the Sunnis have continued to kill and injure mostly Shiites.[31]

The popular protests and rebellions in various Moslem countries—beginning in Egypt, spreading to Libya, Syria, and the Gulf emirates—also took American policymakers by surprise, causing some to applaud what was seen as a move toward democracy. In May 2011, Obama stated that America had four essential interests at stake in the Middle East: the security of Israel, ensuring the flow of the Persian Gulf's oil and gas, combating terrorism, and halting the proliferation of weapons of mass destruction. Iran, clearly, threatened each of these vital interests, but was deterred by the U.S. 5th Fleet, based in the Gulf. If the pre-Arab Spring policies, based on a partnership with stable autocracies in the region, were adequate, by 2011 the United States found itself connected to the least democratic regimes. Attempting to assess these uprisings prompted some to view them as a "cold war" between Saudi Arabia and Iran, others as a struggle between revolutionary and traditionalist regimes. In either case, it has been difficult for the United States to choose sides, especially based on earlier assumptions. Infrequently now, according to Columbia University's Andrew Exum, "do U.S. interests in the region lead to clear policy preferences. Often, in fact, it is unclear how U.S. interests are best served in the long run. And more often than not,

U.S. interests actually compete against one another, forcing policymakers to prioritize ruthlessly." The region is changing, and U.S. policymakers will necessarily assume some risk, but what may well meet short-range objectives may carry long-term dangers.[32]

Meanwhile, the United States had been trying to deal with the resurgence of the Taliban in Afghanistan brought on by shifting Washington's attention to Iraq and starving operations aimed at creating a strong, stable Afghan government. Thus, as American forces were withdrawn from Iraq, Washington called on its NATO partners and Pakistan to meet the mounting Taliban insurgency. Unfortunately, U.S. military operations over the border impaired its relations with Pakistan and raised questions about that nation's ability to deal with terrorists and the security of its nuclear weapons. Since 2007, the Taliban and other insurgents have increasingly employed mines and improvised explosive devices (IEDs) as they expanded their operations. From 2001 to 2011, the United States spent more than $467 billon, and coalition forces suffered 2,847 military fatalities—the majority (1,864) being American.

On May 2, 2012, the U.S.-Afghan strategic partnership agreement, signed by President Obama and Afghan president Hamid Karzai, confirmed 2014 for the planned withdrawal of all U.S. combat troops, but pledged the United States would not abandon Afghanistan. The agreement, though not legally binding, demonstrated that by applying three key historic lessons, the Obama administration avoided the pitfalls that plagued Bush officials in Iraq. It recognized Afghan sovereignty, did not demand American military immunity, and, in separate understandings, defused such sensitive issues as detention facilities and special operations.

Rogue States and Stateless Rogues

American officials during the next decades, it seems evident, will find the nation's security challenged by rogue states arming themselves with weapons of mass destruction (WMD) and by stateless rogues inspired, individually or in groups, to commit terrorist acts. What policies will officials devise to meet these challenges? Will they understand that superior military capabilities cannot always dictate favorable outcomes? What past experiences will they draw on? In dealing with complex, worldwide threats, should not Washington emphasize international cooperation in policy and practice to obtain mutual goals? "Disinclined to rely on multinational regimes and institutions that were seen as cumbersome and lacking decisiveness," as the distinguished academic commentator Lawrence Scheinman delicately phrased it, "the [George W.] Bush administration chose to counter" the perceived threats of rogue states and terrorists "by unilateral means or, where necessary or appropriate, non-institutionalized multilateral arrangements."[33] Buried in the history of American relations with foreign states there has always lingered an urge for unilateral action when tangled affairs challenged domestic desires. The same may be said of Washington's enthusiasm for international law—it was often applied when politically useful, ignored when it was not.

Another serious observer reviewing past U.S. policies urged Americans not to assume the superiority of their institutions and values. Reviewing Washington's policies in Iraq, correspondent Robert Kaiser, who had served in Vietnam, lamented that Americans had apparently learned little. "We twice took a huge risk in the hope that we could predict and dominate events in a nation whose history we did not know, whose language few of us spoke, whose rivalries we didn't understand, whose expectations for life, politics and economics were all foreign to Americans."[34] Few disagreed.

Notes

Chapter 1

1. Colin G. Galloway, *The Scratch of a Pen: 1763 and the Transformation of America* (New York: Oxford University Press, 2006).
2. Fred Anderson, *Crucible of War: The Seven Years' War and the Fate of Empire in British North America, 1754–1766* (New York: Alfred A. Knopf, 2000).
3. Thomas Paine, *Common Sense* (London: Penguin Classics, 1982), 86.
4. See Felix Gilbert, *To the Farewell Address: Ideas of Early American Foreign Policy* (Princeton, NJ: Princeton University Press, 1970); James H. Hutson, "Intellectual Foundations of Early American Diplomacy," *Diplomatic History* 1 (1972): 1–19; David M. Fitzsimons, "Tom Paine's New World Order: Idealistic Internationalism in the Ideology of Early American Foreign Relations, *Diplomatic History* 19 (1995): 569–82.
5. Gilbert, *To the Farewell Address*, 28.
6. Orville T. Murphy, "The View from Versailles: Charles Gravier Comte de Vergennes's Perceptions of the American Revolution," in Ronald Hoffman and Peter J. Albert, eds., *Diplomacy and Revolution: The Franco-American Alliance of 1778* (Charlottesville: University Press of Virginia, 1981), 107–49.
7. See S. F. Bemis, *The Diplomacy of the American Revolution* (New York: Appleton-Century-Crofts, 1965), 93.
8. Jonathan R. Dull, "Franklin the Diplomat: the French Mission," *Transactions of the American Philosophical Society* 72 (1982): 33.
9. Gregg L. Lint, "John Adams on the Drafting of the Treaty Plan of 1776," *Diplomatic History* 2 (1978): 313–20.
10. John Adams, *The Works of John Adams, Second President of the United States: with a Life of the Author, Notes and Illustrations, by His Grandson Charles Francis Adams* (Boston: Little, Brown, 1856). 10 vols. vol. 9., chap: TO JOHN WINTHROP. Accessed from http://oll.libertyfund.org/title/2107/161330/2838396 on 2010–07–01.

11. Jonathon R. Dull, *The French Navy and American Independence: A Study of Arms and Diplomacy, 1774–1787* (Princeton, NJ: Princeton University Press, 1975); Chris Tudda, " 'A Messiah That Will Never Come': A New Look at Saratoga, Independence, and Revolutionary War Diplomacy," *Diplomatic History* 32 (2008): 779–810.

12. The Royal Instructions to the Peace Commission of 1778 are conveniently printed in S. E. Morison, ed., *Sources and Documents Illustrating the American Revolution, 1764–1788* (Oxford: Clarendon Press, 1923), 186–203.

13. Copies of the treaties are available through the Avalon Project—the Treaty of Amity and Commerce is available at: http://avalon.law.yale.edu/18th_century/fr1788-1.asp and the Treaty of Alliance at: http://avalon.law.yale.edu/18th_century/fr1788-2.asp.

14. See Lawrence S. Kaplan, "The Treaties of Paris and Washington, 1778 and 1949: Reflections on Entangling Alliances," in Ronald Hoffman and Peter J. Albert, eds., *Diplomacy and Revolution: The Franco-American Alliance of 1778* (Charlottesville: University Press of Virginia, 1981), 107–49.

15. Jonathon R. Dull, *A Diplomatic History of the American Revolution* (New Haven: Yale University Press, 1985), 109.

16. Bemis, *Diplomacy of the American Revolution*, 34.

17. Dull, *Diplomatic History of the American Revolution*, 110–11.

18. Gregg L. Lint, "Preparing for Peace: The Objectives of the United States, France, and Spain in the War of the American Revolution," in Ronald Hoffman and Peter J. Albert, eds., *Peace and the Peacemakers: The Treaty of 1783* (Charlottesville: University Press of Virginia, 1986), 30–51.

19. Esmond Wright, "The British Objectives, 1780–1783: 'If Not Dominion Then Trade," in Ronald Hoffman and Peter J. Albert, eds., *Peace and the Peacemakers: The Treaty of 1783* (Charlottesville: University Press of Virginia, 1986), 3–29.

20. James H. Hutson, "The American Negotiators: The Diplomacy of Jealousy," in Ronald Hoffman and Peter J. Albert, eds., *Peace and the Peacemakers: The Treaty of 1783* (Charlottesville: University Press of Virginia, 1986), 52–69.

Chapter 2

1. Doris Kearns Goodwin, *Team of Rivals: The Political Genius of Abraham Lincoln* (Camberwell, VIC: Penguin, 2009).

2. Alexander DeConde, *Entangling Alliance: Politics & Diplomacy under George Washington* (Durham, NC: Duke University Press, 1958), 68–73; Albert Hall Bowman, *The Struggle for Neutrality: Franco-American Diplomacy during the Federalist Era* (Knoxville: University of Tennessee Press, 1974), 34–36.

3. Charles D. Hazen, *Contemporary American Opinion of the French Revolution* (Baltimore: Johns Hopkins Press, 1897).

4. Stanley Elkins and Eric McKitrick, *The Age of Federalism* (New York: Oxford University Press, 1993), 336–41.

5. Harry Ammon, *The Genet Mission* (New York: W. W. Norton, 1973).

6. Eugene R. Sheridan, "The Recall of Edmond Charles Genet: A Study in Transatlantic Politics and Diplomacy" *Diplomatic History* 18:4 (1994): 463–88.

7. Elkins and McKitrick, *The Age of Federalism*, 388–91.

8. E. A. Cruikshank, ed., *The Correspondence of Lieut. Governor John Graves Simcoe, with Allied Documents Relating to His Administration of the Government of Upper Canada* (Toronto: Ontario Historical Society, 1923–1931), vol. 2, 149–50.

9. Bemis, *Jay's Treaty*, 298.

10. Joseph Charles, "The Jay Treaty: The Origins of the American Party System," *William and Mary Quarterly* 12:4 (1955): 581–630.

11. Todd Estes, "Shaping the Politics of Public Opinion: Federalists and the Jay Treaty Debate," *Journal of the Early Republic* 20 (2000): 393–422; Todd Estes, *The Jay Treaty Debate, Public Opinion, and the Evolution of Early American Political Culture* (Amherst: University of Massachusetts Press, 2006).

12. Samuel Flagg Bemis, *Pinckney's Treaty: America's Advantage from Europe's Distress, 1783–1800* (New Haven, Yale University Press, 1960).

13. Bradford Perkins, *The First Rapprochement: England and the United States, 1795–1805* (Philadelphia: University of Pennsylvania Press, 1955).

14. Quoted in Bowman, *The Struggle for Neutrality*, 277.

15. Samuel Flagg Bemis, "Washington's Farewell Address: A Foreign Policy of Independence," *American Historical Review* 39 (1934): 250–68.

16. A copy of Washington's Farewell Address can be found in Thomas G. Paterson and Dennis Merril, *Major Problems in American Foreign Relations, Volume I: To 1920* (Lexington, MA: D. C. Heath, 1995), 75–78.

17. Alexander DeConde, *The Quasi-War: The Politics and Diplomacy of the Undeclared War with France 1797–1801* (New York: Charles Scribner's Sons, 1966), 41.

18. William Stinchcombe, *The XYZ Affair* (Westport, CT: Greenwood Press, 1980).

19. Thomas A. Ray, "'Not One Cent for Tribute': The Public Addresses and American Popular Reaction to the XYZ Affair, 1798–1799," *Journal of the Early Republic* 3 (1983): 389–411.

20. Perkins, *The First Rapprochement*, 96–98.

21. Quoted in DeConde, *The Quasi-War*, 95.

22. See Richard C. Rohrs, "The Federalist Party and the Convention of 1800," *Diplomatic History* 12:3 (1988): 237–60.

23. Thomas Jefferson to James Monroe, Washington, November 24, 1801, in Barbara B. Oberg, ed., *The Papers of Thomas Jefferson*, vol. 35 (Princeton, NJ: Princeton University Press, 2008), 719.

24. Thomas Jefferson to William C. C. Claiborne, Washington, July 13, 1801, *The Papers of Thomas Jefferson*, vol. 34, 560.

25. Alexander DeConde, *This Affair of Louisiana* (New York: Charles Scribner's Sons, 1976), 91–105.

26. Tim Matthewson, "Jefferson and Haiti," *Journal of Southern History* 61:2 (1995): 209–48.

27. Quoted in Robert W. Tucker and David C. Hendrickson, *Empire of Liberty: The Statecraft of Thomas Jefferson* (Oxford: Oxford University Press, 1990), 131.

28. To the United States Minister in France (Robert E. Livingston), Washington, April 18, 1802, in Albert Ellery Bergh, ed., *The Writings of Thomas Jefferson*, vol. 10 (Washington, DC: Thomas Jefferson Memorial Association, 1907), 311–16.

29. Quoted in Albert H. Bowman, "Pichon, the United States and Louisiana," *Diplomatic History* 1:3 (1977): 266.

30. For the Louisiana Purchase Treaty, April 30, 1803, see the Avalon Project of the Lillian Goldman Law Library of Yale Law School: http://avalon.law.yale.edu/19th_century/louis1.asp.

31. Quoted in DeConde, *This Affair of Louisiana*, 174.

32. Tucker and Hendrickson, *Empire of Liberty*, 137–44.

Chapter 3

1. Bradford Perkins, *Prologue to War: England and the United States, 1805–1812* (Berkeley: University of California Press, 1961), 91.

2. Thomas Jefferson to James Monroe, Washington, November 24, 1801, in Barbara B. Oberg, ed., *The Papers of Thomas Jefferson*, vol. 35 (Princeton, NJ: Princeton University Press, 2008), 719.

3. Quoted in Thomas S. Martin, "Nemo Potest Exuere Patriam: Indelibility of Allegiance and the American Revolution," *American Journal of Legal History* 35:2 (1991): 218.

4. Paul A. Varg, *Foreign Policies of the Founding Fathers* (Baltimore: Penguin, 1970), 173.

5. Robert E. Cray Jr., "Remembering the USS Chesapeake: The Politics of Maritime Death and Impressment," *Journal of the Early Republic* 25:3 (2005): 446.

6. W. A. Phillips and A. H. Reede, *The Napoleonic Period*, vol. 2 of *Neutrality: Its History, Economics and Law*, 4 vols. (New York: Columbia University Press, 1935–1936), 226–30, 234.

7. See Anthony Steel, "Impressment in the Monroe-Pinckney Negotiation, 1806–1807," *American Historical Review* 57:2 (1952): 352–69.

8. Marshall Smelser, *The Democratic Republic, 1801–1815* (New York: Harper & Row, 1968), 148.

9. Quoted in Cray, "Remembering the USS Chesapeake," 456.

10. See Jeffrey A. Frankel, "The 1807–1809 Embargo against Great Britain," *The Journal of Economic History* 42:2 (1982): 291–308.

11. Quoted in Roger H. Brown, *The Republic in Peril: 1812* (New York: Columbia University Press, 1964), 23.
12. Robert Allen Rutland, *The Presidency of James Madison* (Lawrence: University Press of Kansas, 1990), 64.
13. James Madison, State of the Union Address, November 5, 1811. Available at: http://www.presidentialrhetoric.com/historicspeeches/madison/stateoftheunion.1811.html.
14. Roger H. Brown, *The Republic in Peril: 1812* (New York: Columbia University Press, 1964). On the war hawks see articles by Roger H. Brown and Reginald Horsman, with comments by Alexander DeConde and Norman K. Risjord, in *Indiana Magazine of History* 60:2 (June 1964): 119–58.
15. Marshall Smelser, "Tecumseh, Harrison and The War of 1812," *Indiana Magazine of History* 65:1 (1969): 25–44.
16. Quoted in J. C. A. Stagg, "James Madison and the Coercion of Great Britain: Canada, the West Indies, and the War of 1812," *William and Mary Quarterly*, Third Series, 38:1 (1981): 4.
17. Perkins, *Prologue to War*, 431.
18. Donald R. Hickey, *The War of 1812: A Forgotten Conflict* (Urbana: University of Illinois Press, 1989), 42.
19. Hickey, *The War of 1812*, 132–135, 190–193; Jon Latimer, *1812: War with America* (Cambridge, MA: Belknap Press, 2007), 181–84, 354–60.
20. James A. Carr, "The Battle of New Orleans and the Treaty of Ghent," *Diplomatic History* 3 (1979): 273–82.
21. Quoted in Samuel Flagg Bemis, *John Quincy Adams and the Foundations of American Foreign Policy* (New York: Knopf, 1949), 197.
22. See Fred L. Engelman, *The Peace of Christmas Eve* (New York: Harcourt, Brace and World, 1962).
23. John Sugden, *Tecumseh: A Life* (New York: Henry Holt, 1997), 369–401.
24. Robert V. Remini, *Andrew Jackson and the Course of American Empire, 1716–1821* (New York: Harper & Row, 1977), 207–33.
25. The British government never formally abandoned the right of impressment, but never again practiced it against American ships. By a convention of 1870, however, it abandoned the principle of indelible allegiance, thus recognizing American naturalization laws.
26. Bradford Perkins, *The Cambridge History of American Foreign Relations*, vol. 1, *The Creation of a Republican Empire, 1776–1865* (Cambridge: Cambridge University Press, 1993), 146.
27. Henry Clay, "On the Direct Tax, and the State of the Nation after the Close of the War with Great Britain, in the House of Representatives, January, 1816," in *The Life and Speeches of the Hon. Henry Clay*, vol. 1 (New York: Robert P. Bixby, 1843), 276; "Henry Adams, *A History of the United States*, vol. 9 (New York, 1891), 220.

28. The Rush-Bagot Agreement, April 28, 1818, in Henry Steele Commager, ed., *Documents of American History* (New York: Appleton-Century-Crofts, 1958), vol. 1, 213.

29. C. P. Stacey, "The Myth of the Unguarded Frontier, 1815–1871," *American Historical Review* 56 (1950): 1–18.

30. The Webster-Ashburton Treaty, August 9, 1842, in Commager, *Documents of American History*, vol. 1, 298–300.

31. Grace P. Morris, "Development of Astoria, 1811–1850," *Oregon Historical Quarterly* 38:4 (1937): 413–24.

32. More precisely, from a line drawn due north or south—south as it turned out to be—from the most northwestern point of the Lake of the Woods to its intersection with the 49th parallel.

33. Remini, *Andrew Jackson*, 347–49.

34. William Earl Weeks, "John Quincy Adams's "Great Gun" and the Rhetoric of American Empire," *Diplomatic History* 14:1 (1990): 25–42.

35. William Earl Weeks, *John Quincy Adams and American Global Empire* (Lexington: University Press of Kentucky, 1992), 147–54.

36. Florida Treaty, February 22, 1819, in Commager, *Documents of American History*, vol. 1, 223–24.

37. J. C. A. Stagg, *Borderlines in Borderlands: James Madison and the Spanish-American Frontier, 1776–1821* (New Haven, CT: Yale University Press, 2009), 202–5.

Chapter 4

1. Mark T. Gilderhaus, "The Monroe Doctrine: Meanings and Implications," *Presidential Studies Quarterly* 36:1 (2006): 5–16.

2. An Address to the Senate, January 22, 1917, in Arthur S. Link, ed., *The Papers of Woodrow Wilson*, vol. 40 (Princeton, NJ: Princeton University Press, 1966–1994), 536.

3. T. R. Schellenberg, "Jeffersonian Origins of the Monroe Doctrine," *The Hispanic American Historical Review* 14:1 (February 1934): 1–31.

4. Washington's Farewell Address can be found in Thomas G. Paterson and Dennis Merrill, *Major Problems in American Foreign Relations*, vol. 1, *To 1920* (Lexington, MA: D. C. Heath, 1995), 75–78.

5. A Letter to Alexander von Humboldt December 6, 1813, in Helmut de Terra, "Alexander von Humboldt's Correspondence with Jefferson, Madison, and Gallatin," *Proceedings of the American Philosophical Society* 103:6 (1959): 793.

6. The Monroe Doctrine: Extracts from President Monroe's Seventh Annual Message to Congress, December 2, 1823, in Henry Steele Commager, ed., *Documents of American History* (New York: Appleton-Century-Crofts, 1958), vol. 1, 236. [italics added]

7. Frederick Merk, *Albert Gallatin and the Oregon Problem, A Study in Anglo-American Diplomacy* (Cambridge, MA: Harvard University Press, 1950), 28.

8. The ukase actually forbade all non-Russian ships to come within 100 *Italian* miles of the American coast north of that latitude. Italian miles were slightly shorter than the standard American mile. See Irby C. Nicoles Jr., "The Russian Ukase and the Monroe Doctrine: A Re-Evaluation," *Pacific Historical Review* 36 (1967): 13–26; Irby C. Nicoles Jr. and Richard A. Ward, "Anglo-American Relations and the Russian Ukase: A Reassessment," *Pacific Historical Review* 41 (1972): 444–59.

9. *Memoirs of John Quincy Adams, Comprising Portions of His Diary from 1795–1848*, edited by Charles Francis Adams, vol. 6 (Philadelphia: J. B. Lippincott, 1875), 163.

10. See Nikolai N. Bolkhovitinov, "Russia and the Declaration of the Noncolonization Principle: New Archival Evidence," *Oregon Historical Quarterly* 72 (1971): 101–26.

11. Dexter Perkins, *A History of the Monroe Doctrine* (Boston: Little, Brown, 1963), 32.

12. The Quadruple Alliance is often confused with the Holy Alliance. The Holy Alliance treaty, which was originated by Czar Alexander I of Russia, was a benign declaration to the effect that the signatory sovereigns would be guided by Christian principles in their relations with one another and with their subjects. It was signed by all the sovereigns of Europe except the Pope, the Sultan of Turkey, and the British Prince Regent. The United States was invited to adhere but sent a polite declination. Since the Czar, the Emperor of Austria, and the King of Prussia were also members of the Quadruple Alliance, it is not surprising that contemporary writers and later historians have confused the two alliances.

13. Speech in Congress, May 10, 1820, *Annals of Congress*, 16th Congress, 1st Session, p. 2727.

14. Thomas Jefferson to Gouverneur Morris, Philadelphia, November 7, 1792, in John Catanzariti, ed., *The Papers of Thomas Jefferson*, vol. 24 (Princeton, NJ: Princeton University Press, 1990), 593.

15. Thomas Jefferson to Thomas Pinckney, Philadelphia, December 30, 1792, in Catanzariti, *The Papers of Thomas Jefferson*, vol. 24, 803.

16. Speech in the House of Representatives, March 24, 1818, reproduced in *Niles' Weekly Register*, April 18, 1818, 127.

17. Adams to Monroe, August 24, 1818, in Worthington Ford, ed., *Writings of John Quincy Adams*, vol. 6 (New York: Macmillan, 1916), 442.

18. John Quincy Adams, Secretary of State, to Baptis Irvine, Special Agent of the United States to Venezuela, Washington, January 31, 1818, in William R. Manning, ed., *Diplomatic Correspondence of the United States Concerning the Independence of the Latin American Nations*, vol. 1 (New York: Oxford University Press, 1925), 55.

19. Letter from George Canning to Richard Rush, August 20, 1823, reproduced in Harold Temperley, *The Foreign Policy of Canning, 1822–1827: England, the Neo-Holy Alliance, and the New World* (London: Frank Cass, 1966), 110–13.

20. George Dangerfield, *The Era of Good Feelings* (New York: Harcourt, Brace & World, 1952), 291–292, 319.

21. Richard Rush, United States Minister to Great Britain, to John Quincy Adams, Secretary of State of the United States, London, August 18, 1823, in William R. Manning, ed., *Diplomatic Correspondence of the United States Concerning the Independence of the Latin American Nations*, vol. 3 (New York: Oxford University Press, 1925), 1484.

22. Bradford Perkins, *Castlereagh and Adams: England and America, 1812–1823* (Berkeley: University of California Press, 1964), 321–23.

23. John Quincy Adams's Account of the Cabinet Meeting of November 7, 182,3 in *Memoirs of John Quincy Adams, Comprising Portions of His Diary from 1795–1848*, ed. by Charles Francis Adams, vol. 6 (Philadelphia: J. B. Lippincott, 1875), 179.

24. Adams's first draft of the answer to Canning, prepared November 17, and the amendments made by Monroe, November 20, reproduced in Worthington Chauncey Ford, "John Quincy Adams and the Monroe Doctrine," *American Historical Review* 8:1 (1902): 33–38.

25. This point is well developed in G. W. McGee, "The Monroe Doctrine—A Stopgap Measure," *Mississippi Valley Historical Review* 38 (1951): 223–50.

26. *Memoirs of John Quincy Adams, Comprising Portions of His Diary from 1795–1848*, edited by Charles Francis Adams, vol. 6 (Philadelphia: J. B. Lippincott, 1875), 197–98.

27. The Polignc Conference and Memorandum (October 3–9, 1823) in Temperley, *Foreign Policy of Canning, 1822–1827*, 114–18.

28. Dexter Perkins, *The Monroe Doctrine, 1823–1826* (Cambridge, MA: Harvard University Press, 1927), chap. 4.

29. George Canning's Address on the King's Message Respecting Portugal, December 12, 1826, in Temperley, *The Foreign Policy of Canning, 1822–1827*, 379–81.

Chapter 5

1. Thomas Jefferson to James Monroe, Washington, November 24, 1801, in Barbara B. Oberg, ed., *The Papers of Thomas Jefferson*, vol. 35 (Princeton, NJ: Princeton University Press, 2008), 719.

2. Robert J. Loewenberg, "Creating a Provisional Government in Oregon: A Revision," *Pacific Northwest Quarterly* 68:1 (1977): 13–24.

3. M. C. Jacobs, *Winning Oregon: A Study of an Expansionist Movement* (Caldwell, ID: Caxton Printers, 1938), 124–39, 169–76.

4. Democratic Party Platform of 1844, May 27, 1844, available at John T. Woolley and Gerhard Peters, *The American Presidency Project* [online]. Santa Barbara, CA. Available from World Wide Web: http://www.presidency.ucsb.edu/ws/?pid=29573.

5. Edwin A. Miles, "'Fifty-four Forty or Fight'—An American Political Legend," *Mississippi Valley Historical Review* 44 (1957): 291–309; Hans Sperber, "'Fifity-Four Forty or Fight': Facts and Fictions," *American Speech* 32 (1957): 5–11.

6. Inaugural Address, March 4, 1845, in John J. Farrell, ed., *James K. Polk, 1795–1849: Chronology, Documents, Bibliographical Aids* (Dobbs Ferry, NY: Oceana, 1970), 25–34.

7. Ibid., 35–48, this quote and two quotes above come from this message.

8. Diary entry, January 4, 1846, in Milo Milton Quaife, ed., *The Diary of James K. Polk During His Presidency, 1845 to 1849*, vol. 1 (Chicago: A. C. McClurg, 1910), 155.

9. Quoted in Stuart Anderson, "British Threats and the Settlement of the Oregon Boundary Dispute," *Pacific Northwest Quarterly* 66:4 (1975): 159.

10. John Bassett Moore, ed., *The Works of James Buchanan: Comprising His Speeches, State Papers, and Private Correspondence*, vol. 6, 1844–1846 (Philadelphia: J. B. Lippincott, 1909), 377–87.

11. J. W. Pratt, "The Origin of 'Manifest Destiny,'" *American Historical Review* 32 (1927): 795–98; "John L. O'Sullivan and Manifest Destiny," *New York History* 45 (1933): 213–34.

12. *Oregon: The Cost and the Consequences*, by "a Disciple of the Washington School" (Philadelphia: J. C. Clark's Bookstore, 1846).

13. George Lockhart Rives, *The United States and Mexico, 1821–1848: A History of the Relations between the Two Countries from the Independence of Mexico to the Close of the War with the United Sates*, vol. 2 (New York: Charles Scribner's Sons, 1918), 20.

14. Frederick Merk, *The Oregon Question: Essays in Anglo-American Diplomacy and Politics* (Cambridge, MA: Harvard University Press, 1967), chap. 8.

15. The Oregon Treaty, June 15, 1846, in Henry Steele Commager, ed., *Documents of American History* (New York: Appleton-Century-Crofts, 1958), vol. 1, 311.

16. N. A. Graebner, *Empire on the Pacific: A Study in American Continental Expansion* (New York: Ronald Press Company, 1955), emphasizes commercial interest in Pacific harbors.

17. William L. Marcy to Taylor, July 30, 1845, in George Lockhart Rives, *The United States and Mexico, 1821–1848; A History of the Relations between the Two Countries from the Independence of Mexico to the Close of the War with the United States* (New York, C. Scribner's Sons, 1913), 137.

18. James Schouler, *History of the United States of America under the Constitution*, rev. ed., 7 vols. (New York: Dodd, Mead, 1894–1913), 4: 498.

Bancroft to Schouler February 1887: Schouler says the conversation between Polk and Bancroft is "still preserved." This may mean that Bancroft had preserved a contemporary memorandum of the conversation.

19. Quoted in Robert Glass Cleland, "The Early Sentiment for the Annexation of California: An Account of the Growth of American Interest in California from 1835 to 1846," *Southwestern Historical Quarterly*, 18:1 (July 1914): 144.

20. Moore, *The Works of James Buchanan*, vol. 6, 275–78.

21. Polk seemed to restrict the noncolonization principle to the Northern hemisphere; see Dexter Perkins, *The Monroe Doctrine, 1826–1867* (Baltimore: Johns Hopkins Press, 1933), chap. 2.

22. First Annual Message, December 2, 1845, in Farrell, *James K. Polk, 1795–1849*, 35–48.

23. Mr. Peña y Peña to Mr. Black, Mexico, October 15, 1845, reproduced in *Niles' National Register*, May 30, 1846, 204–5.

24. Under the minimum proposal, the line would follow the Rio Grande from mouth to source, thus depriving Mexico of the eastern portion of New Mexico, including Santa Fe and Taos, and thence run due north to the 42nd parallel.

25. Slidell to Buchanan, March 15, 1846, in Jesse S. Reeves, *American Diplomacy under Tyler and Polk* (Baltimore: Johns Hopkins, 1907), 284.

26. Diary entry of February 17, 1846, in Quaife, *The Diary of James K. Polk*, vol. 1, 234.

27. Diary entry of May 9, 1846, in Quaife, *The Diary of James K. Polk*, 385.

28. Message to Congress on War with Mexico, May 11, 1846, in Farrell, *James K. Polk, 1795–1849*, 49–52.

29. See N. A. Graebner, "The Mexican War: A Study in Causation," *Pacific Historical Review* 49 (1980): 405–26.

30. An excellent analysis of the debate on the war resolutions in Charles Sellers, *James K. Polk, Jacksonian, 1795–1843*, 2 vols. (Norwalk, CT: Easton Press, 1987), 416–21.

31. Mackenzie's report on his conversations with Santa Anna, dated June 7, 1846, in Reeves, *American Diplomacy under Tyler and Polk*, 299–307.

32. Buchanan to the Mexican Minister of Foreign Affairs, July 27, 1846, in Moore, *The Works of James Buchanan*, vol. 7, 40; September 26, 1846, ibid., 88.

33. Diary entry of May 13, 1846, in Quaife, *The Diary of James K. Polk*, vol. 1, 398.

34. Andrew Rolle, "Exploring an Explorer: Psychohistory and John Charles Frémont," *Pacific Historical Review* 51 (1982): 145–163; Richard R. Stenberg, "Polk and Fremont, 1845–1846," *Pacific Historical Review* 7 (September 1938): 211–27; George Tays, "Fremont Had No Secret Instructions," *Pacific Historical Review* 9 (June 1940): 157–72.

35. The best defense of Trist is still L. M. Sears, "Nicholas P. Trist, a Diplomat with Ideals," *Mississippi Valley Historical Review* 11 (1924): 85–98.

36. For excellent analysis see Frederick Merk, *Manifest Destiny and Mission in American History: A Reinterpretation* (New York: Alfred A. Knopf, 1963), chaps. 5–8; *The United States Democratic Review* 21:112 (October 1847), 291.

37. Third Annual Message, December 7, 1847, Farrell, *James K. Polk, 1795–1849*, 63–72.

38. *The Works of Daniel Webster*, vol. 5 (Boston: Little, Brown, 1881), 294.

Chapter 6

1. Patrick Sowle, "A Reappraisal of Seward's Memorandum of April 1, 1861, to Lincoln," *Journal of Southern History* 33:2 (1967): 234–39.

2. Quoted in Amanda Foreman, *A World on Fire: An Epic History of Two Nations Divided* (London: Allen Lane, 2010), 85.

3. Frank Lawrence Owsley, *King Cotton Diplomacy: Foreign Relations of the Confederate States of America* (Chicago: University of Chicago Press, 1931), chaps. 2, 19.

4. Philip S. Foner, *British Labor and the American Civil War* (New York: Holmes & Meir, 1981); R. J. M. Blackett, *Divided Hearts: Britain and the American Civil War* (Baton Rouge: Louisiana State University Press, 2001).

5. Ivor Debenham Spencer, *The Victor and the Spoils: A Life of William L. Macy* (Providence, RI: Brown University Press, 1959), 381–86.

6. Quoted in Ephraim Douglas Adams, *Great Britain and the American Civil War* (New York: Russell & Russell, 1958), 143.

7. Department of State, *Policy of the United States toward Maritime Commerce in War*, prepared by Carlton Savage, 2 vols. (Washington, DC: U.S. Government Printing Office, 1934–1936), vol. 1: 416–19, 432–35.

8. C. S. Alden and Allan Westcott, *The United States Navy: A History* (New York: J. B. Lippincott, 1943), 144.

9. Russell to Lyons, February 15, 1862, quoted in D. P. Crook, *The North, the South and the Powers, 1861–1865* (New York: John Wiley, 1974), 177.

10. J. P. Baxter, "The British Government and Neutral Rights, 1861–1865," *American Historical Review* 34:1 (1928): 9–29.

11. Hamilton Cochran, *Blockade Runners of the Confederacy* (New York: Bobbs-Merrill, 1958).

12. J. W. Pratt, "The British Blockade and American Precedent," *U.S. Naval Institute Proceedings* 46 (1920), 1789–1802; Simeon E. Baldwin, "The 'Continuous Voyage' Doctrine during the Civil War, and Now," *American Journal of International Law* 9:4 (1915): 793–801.

13. Charles Francis Adams Jr., "The Trent Affair," *American Historical Review* 17 (April 1912): 547.

14. Charles M. Hubbard, *The Burden of Confederate Diplomacy* (Knoxville: University of Tennessee Press, 2000), 61–71.

15. Gordon H. Warren, *Fountain of Discontent: The Trent Affair and Freedom of the Seas* (Boston: Northeastern University Press, 1981).

16. John Wheeler-Bennett, *A Wreath to Clio: Studies in British, American and German Affairs* (New York: St. Martin's Press, 1967), 110–27.

17. Seward to Lord Lyons, Department of State, Washington, December 26, 1861, in Montague Bernard, *A Historical Account of the Neutrality of Great Britain during the American Civil War* (London: Longmans, Green, Reader and Dyer, 1870), 205–13.

18. Ibid., 212.

19. Howard Jones, *Blue & Gray Diplomacy: A History of Union and Confederate Foreign Relations* (Chapel Hill: University of North Carolina Press, 2010), 110.

20. Quoted in Adams, *Britain and Civil War*, 243.

21. Frank J. Merli, *Great Britain and the Confederate Navy, 1861–1865* (Bloomington: Indiana University Press, 1970).

22. Mr. Adams to Earl Russell, Legation of the United States, London, September 5, 1863, *Correspondence concerning claims against Great Britain, transmitted to the Senate of the United States in answer to the resolutions of December 4 and 10, 1867, and of May 27, 1868* (Washington, DC: U.S. Government Printing Office, 1870), vol. 2: 365.

23. Merli, *Great Britain and the Confederate Navy*, 195–217; Warren F. Spencer, *The Confederate Navy in Europe* (University, AL: University Alabama Press, 1983), 93–126.

24. Adrian Cook, *The Alabama Claims: American Politics and Anglo-American Relations, 1865–1872* (Ithaca, NY: Cornell University Press, 1975), 73–102; Charles Sumner, *The Alabama Claims. Speech of the Honorable Charles Sumner, Delivered in Executive Session of the United States Senate, on Tuesday, April 13th, 1869 against the Ratification of the Johnson-Clarendon Treaty for the Settlement of the Alabama and Other Claims* (London: Stevens Brothers, 1869).

25. The Treaty of Washington, May 8, 1871, in Henry Steele Commager, *Documents of American History* (New York: Appleton-Century-Crofts, 1958) vol. 2, 67–68.

26. Cook, *The Alabama Claims*, 233–40.

Chapter 7

1. Richard H. Immerman, *Empire for Liberty: A History of American Imperialism from Benjamin Franklin to Paul Wolfowitz* (Princeton, NJ: Princeton University Press, 2010), 98–127.

2. Charles Callan Tansill, *The Purchase of the Danish West Indies* (Gloucester, MA.: Peter Smith, 1966), 5–153; Halvdan Koht, "The Origin of Seward's Plan to Purchase the Danish West Indies," *American Historical Review* 50:4 (July 1945): 762–67.

3. Andrew Johnson, "Fourth Annual Message," December 9, 1868. Online, Gerhard Peters and John T. Woolley, *The American Presidency Project.* http://www.presidency.ucsb.edu/ws/?pid=29509.

4. Robert David Johnson, *The Peace Progressives and American Foreign Relations* (Cambridge, MA: Harvard University Press, 1995), 23–24; Harold T. Pinkett, "Efforts to Annex Santo Domingo to the United States, 1866–1871," *Journal of Negro History* 26:1 (1941): 12–45.

5. Convention for the Cession of the Russian Possessions in North America to the United States, concluded March 30, 1867, ratifications exchanged, June 20, 1867, in Henry Steele Commager, *Documents of American History*, vol. 2 (New York: Appleton-Century-Crofts, 1958), 42–43.

6. Arthur Power Dudden, *The American Pacific: From the Old China Trade to the Present* (New York: Oxford University Press, 1992), 22–23; N. N. Bolkhovitinov, "The Sale of Alaska in the Context of Russian American Relations in the Nineteenth Century," in Arthur Power Dudden, ed., *American Empire in the Pacific: From Trade to Strategic Balance* (Aldershot: Ashgate, 2004), 155–70; Paul F. Sharp, "Three Frontiers: Some Comparative Studies of Canadian, American, and Australian Settlement," *Pacific Historical Review* 24:4 (1955): 369–77.

7. Treaty with Russia, March 30, 1867, in George P. Sanger, ed., *The Statues at Large, Treaties, and Proclamations of the United States of America from December 1867 to March 1869*, vol. 15 (Boston: Little, Brown, 1869), 539–44.

8. David McCullough, *The Path between the Seas: The Creation of the Panama Canal, 1870–1914* (New York: Simon & Schuster, 1977), 22–59.

9. Rutherford B. Hayes: "Special Message," March 8, 1880, Gerhard Peters and John T. Woolley, *The American Presidency Project.* http://www.presidency.ucsb.edu/ws/?pid=68534; Ari Hoogenboom, *The Presidency of Rutherford B. Hayes* (Lawrence: University Press of Kansas, 1988), 184–92.

10. Lawrence A. Clayton, "The Nicaragua Canal in the Nineteenth Century: Prelude to American Empire in the Caribbean," *Journal of Latin American Studies* 19:2 (1987): 323–52.

11. Stuart Anderson, "'Pacific Destiny' and American Policy in Samoa, 1872–1899," *Hawaiian Journal of History* 12 (1978): 45–60.

12. Seward to Cook [Confidential], Department of State, Washington, September 12, 1867, *Foreign Relations of United States, 1894, Affairs in Hawaii* (Washington, DC: U.S. Government Printing Office, 1894), Appendix II, 143.

13. John Patterson, "The United States and Hawaiian Reciprocity, 1867–1870," *Pacific Historical Review* 7:1 (1938): 14–26; Donald Marquand Dozer "The Opposition to Hawaiian Reciprocity, 1876–1888," ibid. 14:2 (1945): 157–83.

14. Richard D. Weigle, "Sugar and the Hawaiian Revolution," *Pacific Historical Review* 16:1 (1947): 41–58; William A. Russ, Jr., "The Role of Sugar in Hawaiian Annexation," ibid. 12:4 (1943): 339–50; Merze Tate, *The United*

States and the Hawaiian Kingdom: A Political History (New Haven, CT: Yale University Press, 1965), 60–110.

15. Tate, *The United States and the Hawaiian Kingdom*, 190; United States Legation, Honolulu, February 1, 1893, *FRUS, 1894, Affairs in Hawaii*, Appendix II, 402.

16. Alfred L. Castle, "Tentative Empire: Walter Q. Gersham, U.S. Foreign Policy, and Hawaii, 1893–1895," *Hawaiian Journal of History* 29 (1995): 83–96.

17. Otto Schoenrich, "The Venezuela-British Guiana Boundary Dispute," *American Journal of International Law* 43:3 (1949): 523–30.

18. Walter LaFeber, *The New Empire: An Interpretation of American Expansion, 1860–1898* (Ithaca, NY: Cornell University Press, 1963), 195; William L. Scruggs, *British Aggressions in Venezuela, or, The Monroe Doctrine on Trial* (Atlanta: Franklin Printing, 1895), 26.

19. Mr. Olney to Mr. Bayard. Department of State, Washington, July 20, 1895. United States Department of State, *FRUS, with the annual message of the president, transmitted to Congress December 2, 1895*, Part I (Washington, DC: U.S. Government Printing Office, 1895), 558, 561–62.

20. N. M. Blake, "Background of Cleveland's Venezuelan Policy," *American Historical Review* 47 (1942): 259–77; Walter LaFeber, "The Background of Cleveland's Venezuelan Policy: A Reinterpretation," *American Historical Review* 66 (1961): 947–67; Grover Cleveland: "Special Message," December 17, 1895, Gerhard Peters and John T. Woolley, *The American Presidency Project*. http://www.presidency.ucsb.edu/ws/?pid=70729.

21. John A. S. Grenville, and George Berkeley Young, *Polities, Strategy, and American Diplomacy: Studies in Foreign Policy, 1873–1917* (New Haven, CT: Yale University Press, 1966), 167; Joseph J. Mathews, "Informal Diplomacy in the Venezuela Crisis of 1896," *Mississippi Valley Historical Review* 50 (1963): 195–212.

22. Nelson M. Blake, "The Olney-Pauncefote Treaty of 1897," *American Historical Review* 50:2 (1945): 228–43.

23. John King Fairbank, *Trade and Diplomacy on the China Coast: The Opening of the Treaty Ports, 1842–1854* (Stanford, CA: Stanford University Press, 1969), 3–39.

24. John W. Swift, P. Hodgkinson, and Samuel W. Woodhouse, "The Voyage of the Empress of China," *Pennsylvania Magazine of History and Biography* 63:1 (1939), 24–36; Tyler Dennett, *Americans in Eastern Asia* (New York: Macmillan, 1922), 74.

25. Fairbank, *Trade and Diplomacy on the China Coast*, 84–113.

26. Treaty of Peace, Amity, and Commerce between the United States and China: 1844, in Ruhl J. Bartlett, ed., *The Record of American Diplomacy: Documents and Readings in the History of American Foreign Relations* (New York: Knopf, 1964), 260–261; Ping Chia Kuo, "Caleb Cushing and the Treaty of Wanghia, 1844." *Journal of Modern History* 5:1 (1933): 34–54.

27. Shunzo Sakamaki, *Japan and the United States, 1790–1853* (*The Transactions of the Asiatic Society of Japan*, second series, vol. 18, Tokyo, 1939), 50–55.

28. Instructions to Commodore Perry, Department of State, Washington, November 5, 1852, in Bartlett, *The Record of American Diplomacy*, 268–69.

29. Arthur Walworth, *Black Ships off Japan: The Story of Commodore Perry's Expedition* (New York: Knopf, 1946), 71; Treaty of Peace, Amity and Commerce between the United States and Japan: 1854, in Bartlett, *The Record of American Diplomacy*, 272–73.

30. Walter LaFeber, *The Clash: U.S.-Japanese Relations throughout History* (New York: W. W. Norton, 1997), 3–31; William L. Neuman, *American Encounters Japan: From Perry to MacArthur* (Baltimore: Johns Hopkins Press, 1963), 19–35; Paul H. Clyde, "Our Concern for the Integrity of China," *Annals of the American Academy of Political and Social Science* 215 (May 1941): 66–73.

31. J. W. Pratt, ed., "Our First 'War' in China: The Diary of William Henry Powell, 1856," *American Historical Review* 53 (1948): 776–86.

32. Chester A. Bain, "Commodore Matthew Perry, Humphrey Marshall, and the Taiping Rebellion," *Far Eastern Quarterly* 10:3 (May 1951): 258–70; Burlingame to Seward, Legation of the United States, Peking, April 18, 1863, *FRUS*, 1863, vol. 2: 927–28.

33. LaFeber, *The Clash*, 19; Treaty between the United States and Japan, signed on July 29, 1858, in W. G. Beasley, ed., *Select Documents on Japanese Foreign Policy 1853–1868* (London: Oxford University Press, 1960), 183–89.

34. John Schrecker, "'For the Equality of Men—For the Equality of Nations': Anson Burlingame and China's First Embassy to the United States, 1868," *Journal of American-East Asian Relations* 17:1 (2010): 9–34.

35. Erika Lee, "The Chinese Exclusion Example: Race, Immigration, and American Gatekeeping, 1882–1924," *Journal of American Ethnic History* 21:3 (2002): 36–62; Andrew Gyory, *Closing the Gate: Race, Politics, and the Chinese Exclusion Act* (Chapel Hill: University of North Carolina Press, 1998).

36. Michael H. Hunt, *The Making of a Special Relationship: The United States and China to 1914* (New York: Columbia University Press, 1983), 125–32.

37. S. C. M. Paine, *The Sino-Japanese War of 1894–1895: Perceptions, Power, and Primacy* (Cambridge, UK: Cambridge University Press, 2003), 247–94.

38. David S. Muzzey, *James G. Blaine: A Political Idol of Other Days* (Port Washington, NY: Kennikat Press, 1963), 437–58; "U.S. Tariff Commission, *Reciprocity and Commercial Treaties* (Washington, DC: U.S. Government Printing Office, 1919), 153–55; *Literary Digest*,15 (December 11,1897), 964.

39. William P. Black, "Tariff Bargains," *North American Review* 238:2 (1934): 160; Alfred E. Eckes Jr., *Opening America's Market: U.S. Foreign Trade Policy Since 1776* (Chapel Hill: University of North Carolina Press, 1995), 75–82.

Chapter 8

1. A collected volume, A. T. Mahan, *The Interest of America in Sea Power, Present and Future* (Boston: Little, Brown, 1897).

2. A. T. Mahan, *The Influence of Sea Power upon History, 1660–1783* (Boston: Little, Brown, 1890), 83.

3. Mahan, *The Interest of America in Sea Power*, 102–3.

4. Edward P. Crapol, *James G. Blaine: Architect of Empire* (Lanham, MD: Rowman & Littlefield, 2000), 122.

5. Richard Hofstadter, "Manifest Destiny and the Philippines," in Daniel Aaron, ed., *America in Crisis: Fourteen Crucial Episodes in American History* (New York: Knopf, 1952), 173–200. See F. J. Turner, *The Frontier in American History* (New York: Henry Holt, 1920), 1–38; also Walter LaFeber, *The New Empire: An Interpretation of American Expansion, 1860–1898* (Ithaca, NY: Cornell University Press, 1963), 80–85.

6. H. C. Lodge, "Our Blundering Foreign Policy," *The Forum* 19 (1895), 8–17.

7. See Harold and Margaret Sprout, *The Rise of American Naval Power, 1776–1918* (Princeton, NJ: Princeton University Press, 1939), chaps. 12, 13; G. T. Davis, *A Navy Second to None* (New York: Harcourt Brace & World, 1940), chaps. 3–6.

8. Julius W. Pratt, *Expansionists of 1898* (Baltimore: Johns Hopkins Press, 1936).

9. John J. Offner, "McKinley and the Spanish-American War," *Presidential Studies Quarterly* 34 (2004): 50.

10. Julius W. Pratt, "American Business and the Spanish-American War," *Hispanic American Historical Review* 14 (1934): 163–201.

11. Pratt, *Expansionists of 1898*.

12. William McKinley, *Messages of the President... on the relations of the United States to Spain: and also transmitting consular correspondence respecting the condition of the reconcentrados in Cuba, the state of the war in that island, and the prospects of the projected autonomy* (Washington, DC: U.S. Government Printing Office, 1898).

13. Lewis L Gould, *The Presidency of William McKinley* (Lawrence: Regents Press of Kansas, 1980), 73.

14. H. G. Rickover, *How the Battleship Maine Was Destroyed* (Washington, DC: Naval History Division, 1976).

15. *Literary Digest* 16 (1898), 367.

16. Senate speech on conditions in Cuba, March 17, 1898, *Congressional Record*, 55th Congress, vol. 37, 2917.

17. *Wall Street Journal*, March 19, 1898, quoted in Pratt, *Expansionists of 1898*, 246.

18. Quoted in Walter LaFeber, *The American Search for Opportunity, 1865–1913* (New York: Cambridge University Press, 1993), 143.

19. John L. Offner, *An Unwanted War: the Diplomacy of the United States and Spain over Cuba, 1895* (Chapel Hill: University of North Carolina Press, 1992), 159–76.

20. McKinley's War Message, April 11, 1898, in Henry Steele Commager, *Documents of American History*, vol. 2 (New York: Appleton-Century-Crofts, 1958), 182–85.

21. Thomas J. McCormick, *China Market: America's Quest for Informal Empire, 1893–1901* (Chicago: Quadrangle Books, 1967), 107–8.

22. J. A. S. Grenville and G. B. Young, *Politics, Strategy, and American Diplomacy* (New Haven, CT: Yale University Press, 1966), 269–78.

23. John Offner, "The United States and France: Ending the Spanish-American War," *Diplomatic History* 7 (1983): 1–21.

24. R. H. Miller, ed., *American Imperialism in 1898: The Quest for National Fulfillment* (New York: John Wiley, 1970), 10.

25. Pratt, *Expansionists of 1898*, 231.

26. Quoted in Pratt, "American Business and the Spanish-American War," 191.

27. Winthrop S. Hudson, "Protestant Clergy Debate the Nation's Vocation, 1898–1899," *Church History* 42 (1973): 110–18.

28. See T. A. Bailey, "Dewey and the Germans at Manila Bay," *American Historical Review* 45 (1935), 59–81; L. B. Shippee, "Germany and the Spanish-American War," ibid., 33 (1925), 754–77.

29. Treaty of Peace with Spain is in Commager, *Documents of American History*, vol. 2: 187–89.

30. Christopher Lasch, "The Anti-Imperialists, the Philippines, and the Inequality of Man," *Journal of Southern History* 24 (1958): 319–331.

31. *Downes v. Bidwell*, 182 U.S. 244 (1901); see also J. W. Pratt, *America's Colonial Experiment* (Englewood Cliffs, NJ: Prentice-Hall, 1950), 157–64.

32. Paul E. Coletta, *William Jennings Bryan*, 3 vols. (Lincoln: University of Nebraska Press, 1964–1970), vol. 1, 233–36.

33. See Pratt, *Expansionists of 1898*, 317–26.

34. Dirk H. R. Spennemann, "The United States Annexation of Wake Atoll, Central Pacific Ocean," *Journal of Pacific History* 33 (1998): 239–47.

35. F. H. Harrington, "The Anti-Imperialist Movement in the United States, 1898–1900," *Mississippi Valley Historical Review* 22 (1935), 211–30; R. L. Beisner, *Twelve against Empire: The Anti-Imperialists, 1898–1900* (New York: McGraw-Hill, 1968).

36. Thomas. A. Bailey, "Was the Presidential Election of 1900 a Mandate on Imperialism?" *Mississippi Valley Historical Review* 24 (1937): 43–52.

Chapter 9

1. G. T. Davis, *A Navy Second to None* (New York; Harcourt, Brace & World, 1940), chaps. 8, 9.

2. Bradford Perkins, *The Great Rapprochement: England and the United States, 1895–1914* (New York: Atheneum, 1968).

3. United States Department of State, *Papers relating to the foreign relations of the United States, with the annual message of the president transmitted to Congress December 5, 1898* (Washington, DC: U.S. Government Printing Office, 1898), vols. 49–96 Hereafter referred to as *FRUS*.

4. Walter LaFeber, *The Panama Canal: The Crisis in Historical Perspective* (New York: Oxford University Press, 1978).

5. The Hay-Pauncefote Treaty, November 18, 1901, in Henry Steele Commager, *Documents of American History* (New York: Appleton-Century-Crofts, 1958), vol. 2: 200–1.

6. C. D. Ameringer, "The Panama Canal Lobby of Philippe Bunau-Varilla and William Nelson Cromwell," *American Historical Review* 68 (January 1963): 346–63.

7. D. C. Miner, *The Fight for the Panama Route: The Story of the Spooner Act and the Hay-Herrán Treaty* (New York: Columbia University Press, 1940).

8. John Major, "Who Wrote the Hay-Bunau-Varilla Convention," *Diplomatic History* 8 (1984): 115–23.

9. Theodore Roosevelt, *An Autobiography* (New York: Echo Library, 2006), 330; James F. Vivian, "The 'Taking' of the Panama Canal Zone: Myth and Reality," *Diplomatic History* 4:1 (1980): 95–100.

10. J. F. Rippy, *The Capitalists and Colombia* (New York: Vanguard Press, 1931), 103–21.

11. Charles. C. Tansill, *The Purchase of the Danish West Indies* (Baltimore: Johns Hopkins Press, 1932).

12. Convention between the United States and the Republic of Panama for the Construction of a Ship Canal to Connect the Waters of the Atlantic and Pacific Oceans (1904), *FRUS, 1932. The American Republics* (Washington, DC: U.S. Government Printing Office, 1932), vol. 5: 543.

13. Lejeune Cummins, "The Formulation of the Platt Amendment," *The Americas* 23 (1967): 370–89.

14. "The Origin and Purpose of the Platt Amendment," *American Journal of International Law* 8 (1914): 585–591; Pedro Capo-Rodriguez, "The Platt Amendment," *American Journal of International Law* 17 (1923): 761–65.

15. T. P. Wright Jr., "United States Electoral Intervention in Cuba," *Inter-American Economic Affairs* 13 (Winter 1959): 50–71; Louis A. Pérez, *Cuba under the Platt Amendment, 1902–1934* (Pittsburgh, PA: University of Pittsburgh Press, 1991).

16. Serge Ricard, "The Roosevelt Corollary," *Presidential Studies Quarterly* 36 (2006): 17–26.

17. Cyrus Veeser, "Inventing Dollar Diplomacy: The Gilded Age Origins of the Roosevelt Corollary to the Monroe Doctrine," *Diplomatic History* 27 (2003): 301–26.

18. J. Fred Rippy, "The Initiation of the Customs Receivership in the Dominican Republic," *Hispanic American Historical Review* 17 (1937): 419–57.

19. Dana Gardner Munro, "Dollar Diplomacy in Nicaragua, 1909–1913," *Hispanic American Historical Review* 38 (1958): 209–34.

20. Philip Marshall Brown, "Costa Rica v. Nicaragua," *American Journal of International Law* 11 (1917): 156–60.

21. Burton J. Hendrick, ed., *The Life and Letters of Walter H. Page*, 2 vols. (London: Heinemann, 1922), vol. 1: 204–5.

22. Dana G. Munro, *Intervention and Dollar Diplomacy in the Caribbean, 1900–1921* (Princeton, NJ: Princeton University Press, 1964), 351–52.

23. For Madero's regime and Huerta's coup d'état, see C. C. Cumberland, *Mexican Revolution: Genesis under Madero* (Austin: University of Texas Press, 1952).

24. A. S. Link, *Woodrow Wilson and the Progressive Era, 1910–1917* (New York: Harper & Row, 1954), 109.

25. R. S. Baker, *Woodrow Wilson, Life and Letters*, 8 vols. (Garden City, NY: Doubleday, 1927–1939), vol. 4: 245.

26. Baker, *Woodrow Wilson*, vol. 8: 195.

27. James A. Sandos, "Pancho Villa and American Security: Woodrow Wilson's Mexican Diplomacy Reconsidered," *Journal of Latin American Studies* 13 (1981): 293–311.

28. Thomas. J. McCormick, *China Market: America's Quest for Informal Empire, 1893–1901* (Chicago: Quadrangle Books, 1967), 128, 141–45.

29. The notes to Great Britain, Germany, and Russia were dated September 6, 1899; others were not sent till November.

30. Tyler Dennett, *John Hay, from Poetry to Politics* (New York: Dodd, Mead, 1933), 293.

31. *FRUS, 1900* (Washington, DC: U.S. Government Printing Office, 1902), 304, 316, 317, 324, 328, 344, 345, 359.

32. Tsing Hua College, designed to prepare Chinese students for American universities, was instituted and supported largely from Boxer indemnity funds. W. W. Willoughby, *Foreign Rights and Interests in China*, 2 vols. (Baltimore: Johns Hopkins Press, 1927), vol. 2: 986–87, 1012–17.

33. McCormick, *China Market*, 179.

34. The Anglo-Japanese alliance was renewed in 1905 and again for 10 years in 1911.

35. E. E. Morison, ed., *The Letters of Theodore Roosevelt*, 8 vols. (Cambridge, MA: Harvard University Press, 1951–1954), vol. 4: 1284.

36. Morison, *Letters*, vol. 4: 1315; also see H. L. Stoddard, *It Costs to Be President* (New York: Harper & Row, 1938), 148–52.

37. *New York Times*, September 6, 1905, 2. For his role in ending the war, Roosevelt received the Nobel Peace Prize.

Chapter 10

1. Philip C. Jessup, *Elihu Root*, 2 vols. (New York: Dodd, Mead, & Co., 1938), vol. 2: 313.
2. Quoted in Joseph M. Siracusa, "Wilson's Image of the Prussian Menace: Ideology and *Realpolitik,*" *The German Empire and Britain's Pacific Dominions, 1871–1919*, edited by John A. Moses and Christopher Pugsley (Claremont, CA: Regina Books, 2000), 68.
3. Walter Lippmann, *U.S. Foreign Policy, Shield of the Republic* (Boston: Little, Brown, 1943), 33–39; also see Siracusa, "Wilson's Image of the Prussian Menace," 51–89.
4. See "A Communication" from Charles A. Beard," *New Republic* 87 (June 17, 1936): 177.
5. R. S. Baker and W. E. Dodd, eds. *The Public Papers of Woodrow Wilson: The New Democracy*, 2 vols. (New York: Harper & Row, 1926), vol. 2: 282.
6. The Germans had begun laying mines in the North Sea. The British had asserted the right to retaliate, and on November 2, 1914, had proclaimed the entire North Sea to be a "war area," which merchant vessels would enter at their own risk. C. C. Tansill, *America Goes to War* (Boston: Little, Brown, 1938), 176–77.
7. E. M. Borchard and W. P. Lage, *Neutrality for the United States*, 2nd ed. (New Haven, CT: Yale University Press, 1940), 87–88, 136–37, 77–83.
8. Tansill, *America Goes to War*, chaps. 13–14.
9. Ibid, 491.
10. Arthur S. Link, *Woodrow Wilson and the Progressive Era, 1910–1917* (New York: Harper & Row, 1954), 219–22.
11. Arthur S. Link, *Wilson: Campaigns for Progressivism and Peace* (Princeton, NJ: Princeton University Press, 1965), 221–25.
12. Wilson and Henry Cabot Lodge had spoken to this effect to the League to Enforce Peace, in Washington, May 27, 1916.
13. In hearings on the treaty in 1919, Wilson was asked: "Do you think that if Germany had committed no act of war or no act of injustice against our citizens that we would have gotten into this war?" He replied: "I do think so." *Peace Treaty Hearings*, Senate Document 106, 66 Congress 1 sess., 536. This later opinion is contradicted in Link, *Wilson: Campaigns*, 277–81.
14. Wilson was particularly indignant because von Bernstorff had been permitted to communicate with his government in cipher through the State Department and the American embassy in Berlin. British Intelligence, having possession of the German code, caught the communication from the cable and also as sent by wireless. R. S. Baker, *Woodrow Wilson, Life and Letters*, 8 vols. (Garden City, NY: Doubleday, 1927–1939), vol. 6: 470–79; Hendrick, *The Life and Letters of Walter H. Page*, 3.
15. Samuel R. Spencer Jr., *Decision for War, 1917* (Peterborough, NH: Richard R. Smith, 1953), chap. 2.

16. Daniel M. Smith and Joseph M. Siracusa, *The Testing of America: 1914–1945* (St. Louis: Forum Press, 1979), chap. 2.

17. Joseph M. Siracusa, *Diplomacy: A Very Short Introduction* (Oxford: Oxford University Press, 2010), 42–44.

18. See Thomas A. Bailey, *Woodrow Wilson and the Lost Peace* (New York: Macmillan, 1944), 297–98. The later addresses in R. S. Baker and W. E. Dodds, eds., *The Public Papers of Woodrow Wilson: War and Peace*, 2 vols. (New York: Harper & Row, 1927).

19. Most secret agreements are in H. W. V. Temperley, ed., *A History of the Peace Conference of Paris*, 6 vols. (London: Henry Frowde and Hodder & Stoughton, 1920–1924).

20. Really six more, for two additional senators signed later.

21. Siracusa, *Diplomacy*, 48–53.

22. The German counterproposals and the Allied reply are in *Foreign Relations of the United States: The Paris Peace Conference*, 13 vols. (Washington, DC: U.S. Government Printing Office, 1942–1947), vol. 6: 800 ff. See also J. T. Shotwell, *At the Paris Peace Conference* (New York: Macmillan, 1937), chap. 4; Temperley, *A History of the Peace Conference of Paris*, 2: 1–20.

23. The treaty with Germany took effect—but not for the United States—on January 10, 1920. Treaties with the other Central Powers were signed as follows: with Austria at St. Germain-en-Laye, September 10, 1919; with Bulgaria at Neuilly-sur-Seine, November 27, 1919; with Hungary at the Trianon, June 4, 1920. A treaty with Turkey was signed at Sevres, August 10, 1920.

24. H. C. Lodge, *The Senate and the League of Nations* (New York: Charles Scribner's Sons, 1925), 209. For an opposite view, see D. F. Fleming, *The United States and World Organization, 1920–1933* (New York: Columbia University Press, 1938), 19–25; also D. F. Fleming, *The United States and the League of Nations, 1918–1920* (New York: G. P. Putnam's Sons, 1932), 475–87.

25. Lodge, *Senate and the League of Nations*, 164.

26. The liberals' break with Wilson is in Selig Adler, *The Isolationist Impulse: Its Twentieth Century Reaction* (New York: Abelard-Schulman, 1957), chap. 3.

27. Lodge, *Senate and the League of Nations*, 151.

28. Kurt Wimer, "Woodrow Wilson Tries Conciliation: An Effort That Failed," *The Historian* 25 (August 1963), 419–38. Wilson's speaking tour is appraised in Thomas. A. Bailey, *Woodrow Wilson and the Great Betrayal* (New York: Macmillan, 1945), chaps. 6–7.

29. On the third reservation, declaring that the United States should accept no mandate without consent of Congress, see Lodge, *Senate and the League of Nations*, 185.

30. Wilson and Hitchcock's reservations are in Bailey, *Wilson and the Great Betrayal*, 393–94.

31. Lodge, *Senate and the League of Nations*, 194. Also see C. O. Johnson, *Borah of Idaho* (New York: Longmans, Green, 1936), 246–48.

32. Norman A. Graebner and Edward M. Bennett, *The Versailles Treaty and Its Legacy: The Failure of the Wilsonian Vision* (New York: Cambridge University Press, 2011), 65–66.

Chapter 11

1. Robert H. Ferrell, *American Diplomacy in the Great Depression: Hoover-Stimson Foreign Policy, 1929–1933* (New Haven, CT: Yale University Press, 1957), 278.
2. Akira Iriye, *After Imperialism: The Search for a New Order in the Far East, 1921–1931* (Cambridge, MA: Harvard University Press, 1965); Emily O. Goldman, *Sunken Treaties: Naval Arms Control Between the War* (University Park: Pennsylvania State University Press, 1994), 156, 173, 178–80.
3. Dorothy Borg, *The United States and the Far Eastern Crisis of 1933–1938* (Cambridge, MA: Harvard University Press, 1964).
4. Ferrell, *American Diplomacy in the Great Depression*, 35–43.
5. Robert Dallek, *Franklin D. Roosevelt and American Foreign Policy, 1932–1945* (New York: Oxford University Press, 1979), and Warren F. Kimball, *The Juggler* (Princeton, NJ: Princeton University Press, 1991).
6. Wayne S. Cole, *Roosevelt and the Isolationists, 1932–45* (Lincoln: University of Nebraska Press, 1983).
7. Donald F. Drummond, "Cordell Hull," in Norman A. Graebner, ed. *An Uncertain Tradition: American Secretaries of State in the Twentieth Century* (New York: McGraw-Hill, 1961), 184–209; Richard Dean Burns, "Cordell Hull and American Interwar Internationalism," in N. A. Graebner, ed. *American Diplomacy, 1865–1945* (Lanham, MD: University Press of America, 1985), 137–60.
8. Irwin Gellman, *Secret Affairs: Franklin Roosevelt, Cordell Hull, and Sumner Welles* (Baltimore: Johns Hopkins University Press, 1995).
9. Ferrell, *American Policy in the Great Depression*, 194.
10. Burns, "Cordell Hull and American Interwar Internationalism," 141–42.
11. Joan Hoff Wilson, *Ideology and Economics: U.S. Relations with the Soviet Union, 1918–1933* (Columbia: University of Missouri Press, 1974).
12. Donald G. Bishop, *The Roosevelt-Litvinov Agreements* (Syracuse, NY: Syracuse University Press, 1965).
13. Bryce Wood, *The Making of the Good Neighbor Policy* (New York: Columbia University Press, 1961); and Irwin Gellman, *Good Neighbor Diplomacy* (Baltimore: Johns Hopkins University Press, 1979).
14. Allen Guttmann, *The Wound in the Heart: America and the Spanish Civil War* (New York: Free Press, 1962).
15. Dorothy Borg, "Notes on Roosevelt's 'Quarantine' Speech," *Political Science Quarterly* 72:3 (1957): 405–33.
16. Richard Dean Burns and Warren A. Dixon, "Foreign Policy and the 'Democratic Myth': The Debate on the Ludlow Amendment," *Mid-America* 47:4 (1972): 288–306.

17. David Wyman, *Paper Walls: America and the Refugee Crisis, 1938–1941* (Amherst: University of Massachusetts Press, 1968), and *Abandonment of the Jews* (New York: Pantheon Press, 1986).
18. Quoted in Cyrus Adler and Aaron M. Margalith, *With Firmness in the Right* (New York: American Jewish Committee, 1946), 381.
19. Arnold A. Offner, *American Appeasement: United States Foreign Policy and Germany, 1933–1938* (Cambridge, MA: Harvard University Press, 1969).

Chapter 12

1. Winston S. Churchill, *Their Finest Hour*, vol. 2 of *The Second World War* (Boston: Houghton Mifflin, 1949), 404.
2. Joseph M. Siracusa and David G. Coleman, *Depression to Cold War: A History of America from Herbert Hoover to Ronald Reagan* (Westport, CT: Praeger, 2002), 73.
3. S. E. Morison, *The Battle of the Atlantic, History of United States Naval Operations in World War II*, vol. 1 (Boston: Little, Brown, 1947), 46, 47; Winston S. Churchill, *The Grand Alliance*, vol. 3 of *The Second World War* (Boston: Houghton Mifflin, 1950), 137–38; Maurice Matloff and E. M. Snell, *Strategic Planning for Coalition Warfare, 1941–1942* in *United States Army in World War II: The War Department* (Washington, DC: Department of the Army, 1953), chap. 3.
4. E. W. McInnis, *The Unguarded Frontier: A History of American-Canadian Relations* (Garden City, NY: Doubleday, 1942), 355–56.
5. Churchill, *The Grand Alliance*, 427.
6. Joseph M. Siracusa, *The American Diplomatic Revolution: A Documentary History of the Cold War, 1941–1947* (Port Washington, NY: Kennikat, 1977), 7–9.
7. Churchill, *The Grand Alliance*, 444.
8. Ibid., 140.
9. E. J. King and W. M. Whitehill, *Fleet Admiral King: A Naval Record* (New York: W. W. Norton, 1952), 343 (italics inserted).
10. The bill passed Congress, 50 to 37 in the Senate, 212 to 194 in the House.
11. Joseph C. Grew, *Turbulent Era: A Diplomatic Record of Forty Years, 1904–1945*, 2 vols. (Boston: Houghton Mifflin, 1952), vol. 2: 1211–12.
12. Herbert, Feis, *The Road to Pearl Harbor: The Coming of the War between the United States and Japan* (Princeton, NJ: Princeton University Press, 1950), 114, 120.
13. Feis, *Road to Pearl Harbor*, 111–17.
14. Grew, *Turbulent Era*, vol. 2: 1259–66.
15. Ibid.: 1307.
16. John H. Boyle, "The Drought-Walsh Mission to Japan," *Pacific Historical Review* 34 (May 1965): 141–61. See also R. J. C. Butow, "The Hull-Nomura Conversations: A Fundamental Misconception," *American Historical*

Review 65 (July 1960): 822–36, and W. L. Langer and S. E. Gleason, *The Undeclared War, 1940–1941* (New York: Harper & Row, 1953), 314–15, 321.

17. See Alvin D. Coox, *Nomonhan: Japan against Russia, 1939*, 2 vols. (Stanford, CA: Stanford University Press, 1985); U.S. Naval Intelligence's intercepts of Tokyo's instructions to diplomatic representatives abroad informed Washington and London not only of the plan against Indochina but also of proposed further moves against British and Dutch possessions. F. C. Jones, *Japan's New Order in East Asia: Its Rise and Fall, 1937–1945* (New York: Oxford University Press, 1954), 263.

18. Langer and Gleason, *The Undeclared War*, 670–677, 694–695; Churchill, *The Grand Alliance*, 440, 446.

19. Toshikazu Kase, *Journey to the Missouri* (New Haven, CT: Yale University Press, 1950), 46–64; for the Emperor's role, see Herbert P. Bix, *Hirohito and the Making of Modern Japan* (New York: HarperCollins, 2000). On the attitude of the Navy, see Peter Mauch, *Sailor Diplomat: Nomura Kichisaburo and the Japanese-American War* (Cambridge, MA: Harvard University Press, 2010).

20. Jones, *Japan's New Order*, 304.

21. Dexter Perkins, *The American Approach to Foreign Policy* (Cambridge: Harvard University Press, 1952), 138–39.

22. In addition to the Atlantic Conference of August 1941 and the "Arcadia" Conference, meetings of the president and the prime minister occurred as follows: Washington, June 1942; Casablanca, January 1943; Washington, May 1943 ("Trident"); Quebec, August 1943 ("Quadrant"); Cairo, November 1943 (with Chiang Kai-shek); Tehran, November–December 1943 (with Stalin); Cairo, December 1943; Quebec, September 1944; Yalta, February 1945 (with Stalin).

23. Robert E. Sherwood, *Roosevelt and Hopkins: An Intimate History* (New York: Harper & Row, 1948), 656.

24. The Molotov-Ribbentrop Pact of 1939 had assigned Lithuania to the German sphere of influence; it was later shifted to the Russian sphere.

25. Hull, *Memoirs*, vol. 2: 967. Also see Siracusa, *The American Diplomatic Revolution*, 9–10.

26. *Documents on American Foreign Relations*, 30 vols. (New York: Simon & Schuster for the Council on Foreign Relations, 1939–1970), vol. 4: 216.

27. Ibid., vol. 5: 527–30.

28. Norman A. Graebner, Richard Dean Burns, and Joseph M. Siracusa, *America and the Cold War, 1941–1991*, 2 vols. (Santa Barbara, CA: Praeger, 2010), vol. 1: 14–15.

29. H. L. Stimson and McGeorge Bundy, *On Active Service in Peace and War* (New York: Harper & Row, 1948), 568–83 (the memorandum is on 576–77); and Henry Morgenthau Jr., *Germany Is Our Problem* (New York: Harper & Row, 1945).

30. See Joseph M. Siracusa, "The Night Stalin and Churchill Divided Europe," *Review of Politics* 3 (1981): 381–409.

31. Churchill, *Triumph and Tragedy*, 235–43.

32. Feis, *The China Tangle*, 232–33.

33. For a discussion of Yalta, including the various agreements reached, see Graebner, Burns, and Siracusa, *America and the Cold War*, vol. 1: 37–64.

34. See also Toshikazu Kase, *Journey to the Missouri* (New Haven, CT: Yale University Press, 1950), chaps. 6–11; Grew, *Turbulent Era*, 2: chap. 36; Stimson and Bundy, *On Active Service in Peace and War*, chap. 23; and Richard. N. Current, *Secretary Stimson: A Study in Statecraft* (New Brunswick, NJ: Rutgers University Press, 1954), 220–37.

35. E. M. Zacharias, *Secret Mission: The Story of an Intelligence Officer* (New York: G. P. Putnam's Sons, 1946), chap. 31.

36. *Documents on American Foreign Relations*, vol. 8: 105–6.

37. Herbert Feis, *The Atomic Bomb and the End of World War II* (Princeton, NJ: Princeton University Press, 1960), 107–10.

38. Sadao Assada, "The Shock of the Atomic Bomb and Japan's Decision to Surrender: A Reconsideration," *Pacific Historical Review* 67 (1998): 477–513; and Joseph M. Siracusa, *Nuclear Weapons: A Very Short Introduction* (Oxford: Oxford University Press, 2008).

Chapter 13

1. Early predictions of Soviet expansionism included Joseph C. Grew, *Turbulent Era: A Diplomatic Record of Forty Years, 1904–1945*, Walter Johnson, ed. (Boston: Houghton Mifflin, 1952), vol. 2: 1446; Mark Ethridge's memorandum on Bulgaria and Rumania, December 7, 1945, *Foreign Relations of the United States, Diplomatic Papers* (hereafter *FRUS*), 1945 (Washington, DC: U.S. Government Printing Office, 1967), vol. 5: 637; John D. Hickerson to James Byrnes, December 10, 1945, ibid. (Washington, 1968), vol. 4: 407; Joint Chiefs of Staff quoted in Melvyn P. Leffler, *A Preponderance of Power* (Stanford, CA: Stanford University Press, 1992), 50.

2. Joseph and Stewart Alsop, "Tragedy of Liberalism," *Life* 20 (May 20, 1946): 69.

3. Edwin G. Wilson to Byrnes, March 18, 1946, *FRUS*, 1946 (Washington, DC: U.S. Government Printing Office, 1969), vol. 7: 818–19; George Lewis Jones to Loy Henderson, August 9, 1946, ibid., 830; Acheson to Byrnes, August 15, 1946, ibid., 840–41.

4. R. E. Sherwood, *Roosevelt and Hopkins: An Intimate History* (New York: Harper & Row, 1948), 359–360.

5. Cordell Hull, The *Memoirs of Cordell Hull*, 2 vols. (New York: Macmillan, 1948), vol. 2: 1651.

6. Sumner Welles, *Where Are We Heading?* (New York: Harper & Row, 1946), 24–25

7. It was agreed at Yalta to include France as one of the permanent members of the council.

8. See Joseph M. Siracusa, *Nuclear Weapons: A Very Short Introduction* (Oxford: Oxford University Press, 2008), 27–39.

9. Lawrence Badash, *Scientists and the Development of Nuclear Weapons: From Fission to the Limited Test Ban Treaty, 1939–1963* (Atlantic Highland, NJ: Humanities Press, 1995), 69–70; Barton Bernstein, "The Quest for Security: American Foreign Policy and International Control of Atomic Energy, 1942–1946," *Journal of American History* 60 (March 1974): 1044.

10. For Kennan's Long Telegram of February 22, 1946, see George F. Kennan, *Memoirs: 1925–1950* (Boston: Little, Brown, 1967), 547–59.

11. On the fears of U.S. officials, see John Lewis Gaddis, *The United States and the Origins of the Cold War, 1941–1947* (New York: Columbia University Press, 1972), 319; John Foster Dulles, "Thoughts on Soviet Foreign Policy and What to Do about It," *Life* (June 3, 1946): 113–26; (June 10, 1946): 119–20.

12. The Clifford-Elsey Report, "American Relations with the Soviet Union," in Arthur Krock, *Memoirs: Sixty Years on the Firing Line* (New York: Funk & Wagnalls, 1968), 427, 431.

13. Winston S. Churchill, *Triumph and Tragedy*, vol. 6 of *The Second World War* (Boston: Houghton Mifflin, 1953), 456.

14. Ibid., 573.

15. At the end of May, Truman sent Harry Hopkins to Moscow to seek agreement on Poland. Stalin consented to the admission of Mikolajczyk and other noncommunist Poles to the Provisional Government of National Unity, recognized by the United States and the United Kingdom.

16. Finland, defeated and having lost part of her territory by Russia in 1939–1940, had joined Germany in the war against the Soviets after June 1941.

17. *Documents on American Foreign Relations*, vol. 8: 210–18. This was a startling offer in the light of President Roosevelt's statement to Stalin that American troops would remain in Europe no longer than two years.

18. *U.S. in World Affairs, 1947–1948*, 78.

19. Authorship of the "containment" policy is attributed to George F. Kennan, a Foreign Service officer who became head of the new Policy Planning Staff in the State Department in the spring of 1947. Kennan expounded "containment" in an anonymous article (signed "X"), "The Sources of Soviet Conduct," in *Foreign Affairs* 25 (July 1947): 566–82; republished in G. F. Kennan, *American Diplomacy, 1900–1950* (Chicago: University of Chicago Press, 1951), 107–28; he and his staff also played a part in the Marshall Plan. See George. F. Kennan, *Memoirs, 1925–1950* (Boston: Atlantic Monthly Press, 1967), chs. 14–15; Joseph M. Jones, *The Fifteen Weeks (February 21–June 5, 1947)* (New York: Viking Press, 1955), 154–55, 255; Dean Acheson, *Present at the Creation: My Years in the State Department* (New York: W. W. Norton, 1969), chs. 24–26.

20. *Documents on American Foreign Relations*, vol. 11: 10.

21. *Documents on American Foreign Relations*, vol. 10: 106–27.

22. Adam B. Ulam, *Expansion and Coexistence: The History of Soviet Foreign Policy, 1917–1967* (New York: Praeger, 1968), 404.

23. *Documents on American Foreign Relations*, vol. 10: 302; A. H. Vandenberg Jr., ed., *The Private Papers of Senator Vandenberg* (Boston: Houghton Mifflin, 1952), 403–11.

24. The 12 original signers were the United States, Canada, Iceland, the United Kingdom, France, Belgium, the Netherlands, Luxembourg, Denmark, Norway, Portugal, and Italy.

25. Dean Acheson, *Present at the Creation*, 375–77, 752–53. Also see Joseph M. Siracusa, "NSC 68: A Reappraisal," *Naval War College Review* 33 (1980): 4–14.

26. For a different view, see Norman A. Graebner, Richard Dean Burns, and Joseph M. Siracusa, *America and the Cold War, 1941–1991: A Realist Interpretation*, 2 vols. (Santa Barbara, CA: Praeger, 2010), vol. 1: 194–209.

27. The treaty was open to other nations for signature, and 124 states had acceded to it by 2003. Richard Dean Burns, *The Evolution of Arms Control: From Antiquity to the Nuclear Age* (Santa Barbara, CA: Praeger, 2009), 125.

Chapter 14

1. Herbert Feis, *The China Tangle: The American Effort in China from Pearl Harbor to the Marshall Mission* (Princeton, NJ: Princeton University Press, 1953), 284–89, 309–12.

2. The texts in *United States Relations with China*, Department of State Publication 3573. (Washington, DC: Department of State, 1949), 585–96.

3. Feis, *The China Tangle*, chap. 37; *U.S. Relations with China*, 607–9.

4. *U.S. Relations with China*, 686–89.

5. Ibid., 814. The text of Wedemeyer's report, in *ibid*., 764–814.

6. *U.S. Relations with China*, 299–300.

7. *Documents on American Foreign Relations*, vol. 12: 431–32.

8. U.S. Congress, Senate, *The United States and the Korean Problem: Documents, 1943–1953*, Senate Document 74, 83 Cong. 1 sess. (Washington, DC: U.S. Government Printing Office, 1953).

9. S. L. A. Marshall, *The River and the Gauntlet: The Defeat of the Eighth Army by the Chinese Communist Forces* (New York: William Morrow, 1953).

10. *Military Situation in the Far East* (Hearings before the Committee on Armed Service and the Committee on Foreign Relations, United States Senate, 82 Cong. 1 sess. In five parts. Washington, DC: U.S. Government Printing Office, 1951); R. H. Rovere and A. M. Schlesinger Jr., *The General and the President* (New York: Farrar, Straus and Young, 1951).

11. Dwight D. Eisenhower, *The White House Years: Mandate for Change, 1953–1956* (New York: Doubleday, 1963), 178–91.

12. William Stueck, *The Korean War: An International History* (Princeton, NJ: Princeton University Press, 1995), 362.

13. *New York Times*, December 23, 1968, 1–2; Lloyd M. Bucher, U.S.N., *Bucher: My Story* (Garden City, NY: Doubleday, 1970).

14. *New York Times*, September 5, 1976, 6.

15. Francis Gary Powers and Curt Gentry, *Operation Overflight: The Story of U-2 Sky Pilot Francis Gary Powers* (New York: Holt, Rinehart and Winston, 1970).

16. *Documents on American Foreign Relations, 1961*, 137–41.

17. The note of July 17 and the broadcast of July 25 are printed in *Documents on American Foreign Relations, 1961*, 1411–49 and 95–105.

18. "Address... for Members of Congress and for the Diplomatic Corps of the Latin American Republics," March 13, 1961, in Woolley and Peters, *The American Presidency Project*: http://www.presidency.ucsb.edu/ws/?pid=8531; see also Teodoro Moscoso, "Progress Report on the Alliance for Progress," *New York Times Magazine* (August 12, 1962): 11, 59–63; Jerome Levinson and Juan de Onís, *The Alliance That Lost Its Way* (Chicago: Quadrangle Books, 1970), 77–87, 166.

19. See Peter Wyden, *Bay of Pigs: The Untold Story* (New York: Simon & Schuster, 1979).

20. Paul H. Nitze, *From Hiroshima to Glasnost: At the Center of Decision—A Memoir* (New York: Grove Weidenfeld, 1989), 183–84.

21. Lawrence Freedman, *Kennedy's Wars: Berlin, Cuba, Laos, and Vietnam* (New York: Oxford University Press, 2000), 134–35.

22. Wyden, *Bay of Pigs*, chs. 5–7.

23. Quoted in ibid, 8.

24. *New York Times*, September 9, 1962; "Address Before the American Society of Newspaper Editors," April 20, 1961, in Woolley and Peters, *The American Presidency Project*: http://www.presidency.ucsb.edu/ws/?pid=8076

25. "Lessons of Cuba," *New York Times*, September 9, 1962.

26. Taylor Branch and George Crile III, "The Kennedy Vendetta: How the CIA Waged a Silent War against Cuba," *Harper's* 251 (August 1975): 49–63; see "Mongoose," in Freedman, *Kennedy's Wars*, 153–60.

27. Quoted in Nitze, *From Hiroshima to Glasnost*, 184.

28. Joseph S. Tulchin, "The Promise of Progress: U.S. Relations with Latin America during the Administration of Lyndon B. Johnson," in Warren I. Cohen and Nancy Bernkopf Tucker, eds., *Lyndon Johnson Confronts the World: American Foreign Policy, 1963–1968* (New York: Cambridge University Press, 1994), 211, 229; Tad Szulc, *Twilight of the Tyrants* (New York: Holt, 1959).

29. Levinson and de Onís, *The Alliance That Lost Its Way*, 87–88.

30. Tulchin, "The Promise of Progress," 218, 227.

31. Ibid., 228–31.

32. Ibid., 235–36.

33. Quoted in Peter Felten, "Yankee, Go Home and Take Me with You: Lyndon Johnson and the Dominican Republic," in H. W. Brands, ed., *The Foreign Policies of Lyndon Johnson: Beyond Vietnam* (College Station: Texas A&M University Press, 1999), 103.

34. Philip Geyelin, *Lyndon B. Johnson and the World* (New York: Praeger, 1966), 238, 257–58.

35. Tulchin, "The Promise of Progress," 240–42.

36. See Michael Dobbs, *One Minute to Midnight: Kennedy, Khrushchev, and Castro on the Brink of Nuclear War* (New York: Knopf, 2008); Lester H. Brune, *The Cuba-Caribbean Missile Crisis of October 1962* (Claremont, CA: Regina Books, 1996); Michael Beschloss, *The Crisis Years: Kennedy and Khrushchev, 1960–63* (New York: HarperCollins, 1991); James G. Blight and David A. Welch, *On the Brink: Americans and Soviets Reexamine the Cuban Missile Crisis* (New York: Noonday, 1989); A. A. Fursenko and Timothy J. Naftali, *One Hell of a Gamble: Khrushchev, Castro, and Kennedy, 1958–1964* (New York: Norton, 1997).

37. Dobbs, *One Minute to Midnight*, 26–30, 109, 125, 179, 249, 282–84; McNamara quoted in Ned Lebow and Janice Gross Stein, *We All Lost the Cold War* (Princeton, NJ: Princeton University Press, 1994), 98; Freedman, *Kennedy's Wars*, 127–46, 171.

38. William Epstein, "The Non-Proliferation Treaty and the Review Conferences, 1965–," in Richard Dean Burns, ed. *Encyclopedia of Arms Control and Disarmament*, 3 vols. (New York: Scribners, 1993), vol. 2: 855ff; John R. Redick, "Nuclear Weapons-Free Zones," in ibid., vol. 2: 1079–92; also see Burns, *The Evolution of Arms Control: From Antiquity to the Nuclear Age* (Santa Barbara, CA: Praeger, 2009), chs. 2, 4.

39. Burns, *The Evolution of Arms Control*, ch. 8; David F. Winkler, *Cold War at Sea: High-Seas Confrontation between the United States and the Soviet Union* (Annapolis, MD: Naval Institute Press, 2000), 20; Allan S. Krass, *The United States and Arms Control: The Challenge of Leadership* (Westport, CT: Praeger, 1997), 14–15.

40. Joseph M. Siracusa, *Nuclear Weapons: A Very Short Introduction* (Oxford: Oxford University Press, 2008), 112–15; John Newhouse, *Cold Dawn: The Story of SALT* (New York: Holt, Rinehart & Winston, 1973); Gerard C. Smith, *Doubletalk: The Story of SALT I* (Garden City, NY: Doubleday, 1980); Strobe Talbott, *Endgame: The Inside Story of SALT II* (New York: Harper & Row, 1979), ch. 5.

41. Charles C. Flowerree, "Chemical and Biological Weapons and Arms Control," in Burns, *Encyclopedia of Arms Control and Disarmament*, vol. 2: 1005; also see Thomas Graham Jr. *Disarmament Sketches: Three Decades of Arms Control and International Law* (Seattle: University of Washington Press, 2002), ch. 2.

42. Henry Kissinger, *White House Years* (Boston: Little, Brown, 1979), 1132, 1150–51; Anatoly Dobrynin, *In Confidence: Moscow's Ambassador to America's Six Cold War Presidents* (New York: Random House, 1995), 251–52.

43. See Vincent P. DeSantis's "Italy and the Cold War," in *The Impact of the Cold War: Reconsiderations*, edited by Joseph M. Siracusa and Glen Barclay (Port Washington, NY: Kennikat Press, 1977), 26–39.

44. "Today, in the world of freedom, the proudest boast is '*Ich bin ein Berliner.*' " *The Kennedy Years*, ed. Joseph M. Siracusa (New York: Facts on File, 2004), 592–93.

45. *New York Times*, December 23, 1973.

46. *U.S. in World Affairs*, 1967, 201–4; *New York Times*, September 20, 1969, 1, 4.

47. Richard M. Nixon, "Asia after Viet Nam," *Foreign Affairs* (October 1967): 121; Richard Nixon, *RN: The Memoirs of Richard Nixon* (New York: Grosset & Dunlap, 1978), 344.

48. Nixon, *RN*, 545, 548; Marvin Kalb and Bernard Kalb, *Kissinger* (Boston: Little, Brown, 1974), 239–40, 251.

49. Richard Nixon, *Third Annual Report to Congress...* (Washington, DC: February 8, 1972).

50. *New York Times*, December 6, 1969, 1, 14. Brzezinski, "Detente in the 70s," *New Republic*, January 3, 1970, 17–18.

51. *New York Times*, October 29, 1969, 10.

52. *New York Times*, August 2, 1975; Graebner, Burns, and Siracusa, *America and the Cold War, 1941–1991*, vol. 2, 385–87.

Chapter 15

1. Robert S. McNamara, *In Retrospect: The Tragedy and Lessons of Vietnam* (New York: Times Books, 1995), 31.

2. Vietnam under French rule was divided into, from north to south, Tonkin, Annam, and Cochin China. Cochin China, comprising the Mekong Delta and Saigon, was a colony. Annam, Tonkin, Laos, and Cambodia were protectorates with native rulers guided by French advisers.

3. See Joseph M. Siracusa, "The United States, Vietnam, and the Cold War: A Reappraisal," *Journal of Southeast Asian Studies* 5 (1974): 82–101; and *Into the Dark House: American Diplomacy and the Ideological Origins of the Cold War* (Claremont, CA: Regina Books, 1998), 95–101.

4. Ellen J. Hammer, *The Struggle for Indochina* (Stanford, CA: Stanford University Press, 1954), 247; Gary R. Hess, "The First American Commitment in Indochina: The Acceptance of the 'Bao Dai Solution,' 1950," *Diplomatic History* 2 (1978): 331–50.

5. Participants were the United States, the U.S.S.R., Britain, France, Communist China, Cambodia, Laos, the Democratic Republic of (North) Vietnam, and the State of (South) Vietnam.

6. *Documents on American Foreign Relations, 1954* (Boston: World Peace Foundation, 1954), 283–318.

7. Ibid., 318–23. The United States was to act against communist aggression only but also agreed to consult with other signers "in the event of other aggression or armed attack."

8. *Documents on American Foreign Relations, 1961* (Boston: World Peace Foundation, 1961), 296–99.

9. The governments taking part were Burma, Cambodia, Canada, Communist China, France, India, Laos, Poland, Thailand, the U.S.S.R., the United Kingdom, the United States, North Vietnam, and South Vietnam.

10. *U.S. in World Affairs, 1962*, 197.

11. *New York Times*, June 12, 1, 14; June 13, 3; July 10, 4; July 22, 1, 14, 1962.

12. U.S. State Department White Paper *Aggression from the North*, Department of State Publication 7839 (Washington, DC: Government Printing Office, 1965).

13. Rowland Evans and Robert Novak, *Lyndon B. Johnson: The Exercise of Power* (New York: New American Library, 1966), 321–23.

14. Graebner, Burns, and Siracusa, *America and the Cold War*, vol. 2: 317–24; McNamara, *In Retrospect*, 61–62.

15. *Viet Nam and Southeast Asia*. Report of Senator Mike Mansfield et al. to the Senate Committee on Foreign Relations (Washington, DC: Government Printing Office, 1963), 3–9; *New York Times*, November 3, 1962, Sec. 4, 1; November 15, 1963, 13.

16. Memorandum for the Record of a Meeting, November 24, 1963, U.S. Department of State, *Foreign Relations of the United States, 1961–1963* (Washington, DC: Government Printing Office, 1980), vol. 4: 635–37.

17. *Documents on American Foreign Relations, 1964*, 216–17; Joseph C. Goulden, *Truth Is the First Casualty: The Gulf of Tonkin Affair—Illusion and Reality* (Chicago: Rand McNally, 1969); *The Gulf of Tonkin, The 1964 Incidents*, Hearing before the Committee on Foreign Relations, United States Senate, 90th Cong., 2d sess., February 20, 1968 (Washington, DC: Government Printing Office, 1968). On June 24, 1970, the Senate voted 81 to 10 to repeal the Tonkin Gulf Resolution. The House of Representatives later concurred, and President Nixon signed it on January 12, 1971. *New York Times*, June 25, 26 (editorial), 1970.

18. Quoted in A. M. Schlesinger Jr., *The Bitter Heritage: Vietnam and American Democracy, 1941–1966* (Boston: Houghton Mifflin, 1967), 29.

19. *U.S. in World Affairs*, 1966, 94.

20. *Aggression from the North, U.S. in World Affairs, 1967*, 375.

21. England, France, and Pakistan denied any such obligation. Australia, New Zealand, and Thailand sent small military contingents, and Thailand supplied air bases for American planes. The Philippines sent a 2,000–man construction battalion (paid for by the United States). The only nation that sent significant military support (some 50,000 troops) was South Korea, not a member of SEATO.

22. *New York Times*, November 26, 1967, Sec. 4, 2.

23. Robert S. McNamara, et al., *Argument without End: In Search of Answers to the Vietnam Tragedy* (New York: Public Affairs, 1999), 99, 403.

24. Department of State *Bulletin* 52 (April 26, 1965): 606–10.

25. M. G. Raskin and B. B. Fall, eds., *The Viet-Nam Reader: Articles and Documents of American Foreign Policy and the Viet-Nam Crises* (New York: Vintage Books, 1965), 342–43. Matters included in the NLF program and not mentioned in that of Hanoi were removal of the Saigon government, agrarian and educational reform, improved living conditions, and equal treatment of the minorities in Vietnam. Text in ibid., 216–21.

26. *New York Times*, September 30, 1967, 8.

27. Ibid., January 26, 31, 1969, 1.

28. Ibid., March 26, 1969, 3. See also Henry A. Kissinger, "The Viet Nam Negotiations," *Foreign Affairs* (January 1969): 211–234.

29. *New York Times*, May 9, 1969. 1, 6; May 15, 1969, 16.

30. Ibid., July 2, 1970, 1, 14; John Osborne, "Why Cambodia?" *New Republic*, June 11, 1970, 7–9.

31. *New York Times*, September 18, 1970, 2; September 27, 1970 (sec. 4), 14.

32. Ibid., October 8, 1970, 1, 18; *The New Republic* (October 17, 1970): 5, 6.

33. *New York Times*, November 4, 1969, 16. The President's address on Vietnamization came 19 days after a nationwide peaceful demonstration at which hundreds of thousands of people called for an "immediate" pullout of all U.S. forces in Vietnam. For Vietnamization efforts, see James H. Willbanks, *Abandoning Vietnam: How America Left and South Vietnam Lost Its War* (Lawrence: University Press of Kansas, 2004).

34. *New York Times*, January 11, 1970, Sec. 4, 5.

35. Ibid., May 1, 1970, 1–2.

36. Ibid., May 31, 1970 (sec. 4), 3; see Tom Wells, *The War Within: America's Battle over Vietnam* (New York: Holt, 1994).

37. Ibid., June 6, 1971. Publication of the "Pentagon Papers" later reinforced the American public's belief that the war indeed had been a mistake. *New York Times*, June 13, 1971, 1, 35–38. This was the first in a series of articles.

38. See Dale Andradé, *Trial by Fire: The 1972 Easter Offensive, America's Last Vietnam Battle* (New York: Hippocrene Books, 1995).

39. President Nixon's letter of proposal for postwar support to Thieu came to light after the fall of South Vietnam, ibid., May 1, 1975, 1, 16.

40. Hanoi's chief of staff, General Van Tien Dung, candidly recounted these and subsequent events of the war's final battles in two official North Vietnamese newspapers, excerpts of which are found in *New York Times*, April 26, 1976, 16.

41. See Timothy N. Castle, *At War in the Shadow of Vietnam: United States Military Aid to the Royal Lao Government, 1955–1975* (New York: Columbia University Press, 1993) and William Shawcross, *Sideshow: Kissinger, Nixon and the Destruction of Cambodia* (New York: Simon & Schuster, 1979).

42. Stanley Karnow, *Vietnam: A History*, rev. ed. (New York: Penguin Books, 1991), 15; Lippmann in *New York Times*, May 1, 1970, 1–2. Also see

Michael Lind, *Vietnam, the Necessary War: A Reinterpretation of America's Most Disastrous Military Conflict* (New York: Free Press, 1999).

43. "Excerpts from Address of Weinberger," *New York Times*, November 29, 1984, A5.

Chapter 16

1. *Newsweek* (September 1, 1980): 18.

2. Frances Fitzgerald, *Way Out in the Blue: Reagan, Star Wars and the End of the Cold War* (New York: Simon & Schuster, 2000), 27–31.

3. Reagan quoted in *Newsweek*, February 9, 1981, 45; Opening Statement at Confirmation Hearings, January 9, 1981, U.S. Department of State, Bureau of Public Affairs, *Current Policy No. 257*; *New York Times*, May 3, 1981.

4. *Public Papers of the Presidents: Ronald Reagan, 1981* (Washington, DC: Government Printing Office, 1981), vol. 1: 957, 958; also see Joseph M. Siracusa and David G. Coleman, *Depression to Cold War: A History of America from Herbert Hoover to Ronald Reagan* (Westport, CT: Praeger, 2002), 249–50.

5. Richard Rhodes, *Arsenals of Folly: The Making of the Nuclear Arm Race* (New York: Knopf, 2007), 148–49; Drew Middleton, *New York Times*, June 21, 1981, January 3, 1982, February 14, 1982; Richard Halloran, *New York Times*, April 11, 1982.

6. James M. Fallows, *National Defense* (New York: Random House, 1981), 70–71, 163; Christopher Paine, "A False START," *Bulletin of the Atomic Scientists* 38 (August/September 1982): 13; *New York Daily News*, "Report from Munich," February 20, 1982, 6.

7. U.S. Department of State, Bureau of Public Affairs, *Current Policy No. 275*, 2; Seweryn Bialer and Joan Afferica, "Reagan and Russia," *Foreign Affairs* 61 (Winter 1982–83): 71; "Promoting Democracy and Peace," U.S. Department of State, Bureau of Public Affairs, *Current Policy No. 399*, 3–5.

8. James Reston, *New York Times*, July 17, 1981; Alexander M. Haig Jr., *Caveat, Realism, Reagan and Foreign Policy* (New York: Macmillan, 1984).

9. Walter LaFeber, *Inevitable Revolutions: The United States and Central America* (New York, 1983), 240; *New York Times*, March 23, 1980, 8; July 13, 1980, 14; ibid., April 2, 1981, 3.

10. Reagan quoted in Alexander Cockburn, *Wall Street Journal*, March 12, 1981; other quotes in Siracusa and Coleman, *Depression to Cold War*, 260, 261–64; Karen de Young, *Washington Post*, March 8, 1981; *Newsweek*, March 16, 1981, 34–38; March 30, 1981, 20–21.

11. J. Thomas, *New York Times*, October 30, 1983; Bernard Gwertzman, *New York Times*, October 30, 1983, 1; Nicholas von Hoffman, "Terrestrial Wars," *The Spectator* (April 13, 1985): 8–9; Norman A. Graebner, "The Uses and Misuses of Power: The 1980s." *Dialogue: A Magazine of International Affairs* 1:1 (March 1988): 29.

12. For the Ottawa Conference, see Leslie H. Gelb, *New York Times*, July 19, 26, 1981.

13. For the debate within the administration, see Bernard Gwertzman, *New York Times*, February 21, 1982; For the Reagan announcement and the bitter European reaction, see *World Press Review* 29 (August 1982): 4; Flora Lewis, *New York Times*, June 27, 1982.

14. Steven Ratner, *New York Times*, August 29, 1982; Hans-Dietrich Genscher, "Toward an Overall Western Strategy for Peace, Freedom, and Progress," *Foreign Affairs* 61 (Fall 1982): 42.

15. Quotes in *World Press Review* 29 (April 1982): 12; *Newsweek*, March 22, 1982, 42; *Times Herald Record*, December 24, 1981; *Manchester Guardian* in *World Press Review* 29 (February 1982): 14; Ronald Steel, *New York Times*, January 3, 1982.

16. Lawrence T. Caldwell and Robert Legvold, "Reagan through Soviet Eyes," *Foreign Policy* 52 (Fall 1983): 5. Stanley Hoffmann, *Dead Ends: American Foreign Policy in the New Cold War* (Cambridge, MA: Ballinger, 1983), 154–55.

17. Reagan's Address to Congress, September 5, 1983, *American Foreign Policy: Current Documents, 1983* (Washington, DC: Government Printing Office, 1985), 544–47; Strobe Talbott, *The Russians and Reagan* (New York: Vintage, 1984), 122, appendix.

18. Alexander Bovin quoted in *World Press Review* 31 (January 1984): 53; for the impact of "Able Archer," see Gates, *From the Shadows*, 270–73; *New York Times*, January 1, 1984, E13; Ronald Reagan, *Ronald Reagan: An American Life* (New York: Pocket Books, 1990), 588–589.

19. Richard J. Barnet, *New Yorker* (October 17, 1982): 153; Christopher Paine, "A False START," *Bulletin of the Atomic Scientists* 38 (August/September 1982): 14; see also Douglas C. Waller, *Congress and the Nuclear Freeze* (Amherst: University of Massachusetts Press, 1987).

20. Barnet, *New Yorker*, 156; Fitzgerald, *Way Out There in the Blue*, 83–96; Waller, *Congress and the Nuclear Freeze*, 14; Thomas Graham Jr., *Disarmament Sketches: Three Decades of Arms Control and International Law* (Seattle: University of Washington Press, 2002), 103; Waller, *Congress and the Nuclear Freeze*, 94–97, 99; Lou Cannon, "Dealings with the Soviets Raise Uncomfortable Questions," *Washington Post*, July 2, 1984, A13.

21. Edward Reiss, *The Strategic Defense Initiative* (New York: Cambridge University Press, 1992); McGeorge Bundy, *Danger and Survival: Choices about the Bomb in the First Fifty Years* (New York: Random House, 1988), 571; Reagan, *An American Life*, 571–72; Rhodes, *Arsenals of Folly*, 178–80; also see Richard Dean Burns, *The Missile Defense Systems of George W. Bush: A Critical Assessment* (Santa Barbara, CA: Praeger, 2010), chs. 1 & 2.

22. John Tirman, "The Politics of Star Wars," in John Tirman, ed., *The Empty Promise: the Growing Case against Star Wars* (Boston: Beacon, 1986); Union of Concerned Scientists, *The Fallacy of Star Wars* (New York: Vintage, 1984); and Burns, *The Missile Defense Systems of George W. Bush*, 34–35.

23. George P. Shultz, "Shaping American Foreign Policy: New Realities and New Ways of Thinking," *Foreign Affairs* (Spring 1985): 713; George Will, *Washington Post*, December 12, 1985, A19.

24. Robert W. Tucker, "Intervention and the Reagan Doctrine," *Intervention and the Reagan Doctrine* (New York: The Council on Religion and International Affairs, 1985), 16–17.

25. Christopher Dickey, *With the Contras: A Reporter in the Wilds of Nicaragua* (New York: Simon & Schuster, 1987), 10–11; *The Sandinista Military Build-Up*, Inter-American Series 119 (Washington, DC: Department of State, 1985); and *The Soviet-Cuban Connection in Central America and the Caribbean* (Washington, DC: Department of State and Department of Defense, 1985); Cheney quoted in Steven V. Roberts, *New York Times*, May 25, 1986, E1.

26. Michael T. Klare, "Fueling the Fire: How We Armed the Middle East, *Bulletin of the Atomic Scientists* 47 (January/February1991): 19–26; Theodore Draper, *A Very Thin Line: The Iran-Contra Affairs* (New York: Hill and Wang, 1991), 333, 344–45.

27. George Black, *The Good Neighbor: How the United States Wrote the History of Central America and the Caribbean* (New York: Pantheon Books, 1988), 179–80.

28. State of the Union Address, January 25, 1984, *American Foreign Policy: Current Documents, 1984* (Washington, DC: Government Printing Office, 1986), 28; Address at Georgetown University, April 6, 1984, *American Foreign Policy*, 8; Address on U.S.-Soviet Relations, January 16, 1984, *Public Papers of the Presidents: Ronald Reagan, 1984*, vol. 1 (Washington, DC: Government Printing Office, 1986), 42; John Newhouse, "Annals of Diplomacy: The Abolitionist—II," *New Yorker* (January 9, 1989): 51.

29. For Gorbachev in London, *New York Times*, December 16, 1984, 1, 5; see Robert D. English, *Russia and the Idea of the West: Gorbachev, Intellectuals & the End of the Cold War* (New York: Columbia University Press, 2000), esp. ch. 6, and Vladislav M. Zubok, *A Failed Empire: The Soviet Union in the Cold War from Stalin to Gorbachev* (Chapel Hill: University of North Carolina, 2007), 278–84.

30. Gorbachev quoted in Zubok, *A Failed Empire*, 286; Reagan in Shultz, *Turmoil and Triumph*, 598; Raymond L. Garthoff, *The Great Transition: American-Soviet Relations and the End of the Cold War* (Washington, DC: Brookings Institution, 1994), 235–38.

31. See Shultz, *Turmoil and Triumph*, 596–607; Matlock, *Reagan and Gorbachev*, ch. 6; English, *Russia and the Idea of the West*, 206; Philip Taubman, *New York Times*, April 6, 1986.

32. On compliance, see John Newhouse, *New Yorker* (January 9, 1989): 59–61; James Reston, *New York Times*, April 6, 1986, E23; Michael R. Gordon, *New York Times*, June 7, 1987, 7; *New York Times* August 29, 1986.

33. Garthoff, *The Great Transition*, 252–67; Shultz, *Turmoil and Triumph*, 751–755; Mikhail Gorbachev, *Reykjavik: Results and Lessons* (Madison, CT:

Sphinx Press, 1987); also see "The Reykjavik File: Previously Secret Documents from U.S. and Soviet Archives on the 1986 Reagan-Gorbachev Summit," posted October 13, 2006, by the National Security Archive, George Washington University, at http://www.nsarchive.org; on Thatcher see David K. Shipler, "The Week in Review," *New York Times*, October 26, 1986, E1.

34. Garthoff, *Transition*, 327, n. 64; Shultz, *Turmoil*, 1009–15; Newhouse, *New Yorker* (January 9, 1989): 65–66; Lou Cannon, *President Reagan: The Role of a Lifetime* (New York: Public Affairs, 1991), 694; Fitzgerald, *Way Out There in the Blue*, 426, 444–45.

35. Fitzgerald, *Way Out There in the Blue*, 445; Andrei Sakarov, *Moscow and Beyond* (New York: Alfred A. Knopf, 1991), 21–42; Strobe Talbott, *Master of the Game: Paul Nitze and the Nuclear Peace* (New York: Alfred A. Knopf, 1988), 306.

36. Lou Cannon and Gary Lee, *Washington Post*, May 30, 1988, A1, A21; Don Oberdorfer, *Washington Post*, June 1, 1988, A1.

37. Will in *Washington Post*, June 7, 1988, A23; ibid., May 29, 1988, C7; *New York Times*, July 10, 1988, E30; see David K. Shipler, ibid., May 29, 1988, E1, E3.

38. Fitzgerald, *Way Out There in the Blue*, 17–18, 466–71.

39. *Newsweek* (May 15, 1989): 22; Department of State *Bulletin* 89 (April 1989): 4–5; *Washington Post*, February 13, 1990, A1, A9; Michael R. Beschloss and Strobe Talbott, *At The Highest Levels: The Inside Story of the End of the Cold War* (Boston: Little, Brown, 1993), 12–13, 17–19.

40. George Bush and Brent Scowcroft, *A World Transformed* (New York: Knopf, 1998), 40–41; Thatcher quoted in Beschloss and Talbott, *At the Highest Levels*, 29; Jack F. Matlock Jr., *Autopsy on an Empire* (New York: Random House, 1995), 177; Anatoly Chernyaev, *My Six Years with Gorbachev* (University Park: Penn State University Press, 2000), 201.

41. Jeffrey A. Larsen and James M. Smith, *Historical Dictionary of Arms Control and Disarmament* (Lanham, MD: Scarecrow Press, 2005), 204–5.

42. George Bush and Brent Scowcroft, *A World Transformed* (New York: Knopf, 1998), xi; Rusk quoted in Strobe Talbott, *Endgame: The Inside Story of SALT II* (New York: Harper & Row, 1979), 19–20; Paul H. Nitze, "Foreword," in Aleksandr' G. Savel'yev and Nikolay N. Detinov, *The Big Five: Arms Control Decision-Making in the Soviet Union* (Westport, CT: Praeger, 1995), xi-xii.

43. See Michael Beschloss, *Presidential Courage: Brave Leaders and How They Changed America, 1789–1989* (New York: Simon & Schuster, 2007).

44. English, *Russia and the Idea of the West*, 206, 212, 217, 241.

45. Ibid., 33–34.

Chapter 17

1. Lester H. Brune and Richard Dean Burns, *Chronological History of U.S. Foreign Relations*, 3 vols. (New York: Routledge, 2003) vol. 1: 396.

2. Clark Clifford with Richard Holbrooke, *Counsel to the President: A Memoir* (New York: Random House, 1991), 4–8.

3. Candace Karp, *Missed Opportunities: U.S. Diplomatic Failures and the Arab-Israel Conflict, 1947–1967* (Claremont, CA: Regina Books, 2005), 149.

4. On the 1973 War, see Raymond L. Garthoff, *Détente and Confrontation* (Washington, DC: Brookings Institution, 1985), 306–408; on OPEC, see Daniel Yergin, *The Prize* (New York: Simon & Schuster, 1991), 588–652.

5. Marion Farouk-Slugett and Peter Slugett, *Iraq since 1958: From Revolution to Dictatorship* (London: I. B. Tauris, 1987), 107–122; 203–5, and 255–57.

6. Zbigniew Brzezinski, *Power and Principle: Memoirs of the National Security Adviser, 1977–1981* (New York: Farrar, Straus, Giroux, 1983), 444, 456, 477.

7. Jimmy Carter, *Keeping Faith: A Memoir* (New York: Bantam Books, 1982), 326–412; Cyrus Vance, *Hard Choices: Critical Years in America's Foreign Policy* (New York: Simon & Schuster, 1983): 226–31.

8. Marion Farouk-Slugett and Peter Slugett, *Iraq since 1958: From Revolution to Dictatorship* (London: I.B. Tauris, 1987): 107–122; 203–205.

9. Peter Jay, "Europe and America: Europe's Ostrich and America's Eagle," *Atlantic Community Quarterly* 18 (Summer 1980): 141–42; Robert Lacey, "How Stable Are the Saudis?" *New York Times Magazine* (November 8, 1981): 35–38, 118–121.

10. George P. Shultz, *Turmoil and Triumph: My Years As Secretary of State* (New York: Scribners, 1993), 110–111, 227–228, 233; Thomas J. Friedman, "America's Failure in Lebanon," *New York Times Magazine* (April 8, 1984): 32–33.

11. Dilip Hiro, *The Longest War: The Iran-Iraq Military Conflict* (New York: Routledge and Kegan Paul), 30–34.

12. Doc. 1 in Joyce Battle, ed. "Shaking Hands with Saddam Hussein: The U.S. Tilts toward Iraq, 1980–1984," National Security Archive *Electronic Briefing Book No. 82* (February 25, 2003).

13. Doc. 3, "Military Equipment for Iran and Iraq," ibid. (February 16, 1981); Shultz, *Turmoil and Triumph*, 235, 236.

14. Docs. 26, 27, 31, 32, 33, 40 in Battle, ed. "Shaking Hands with Saddam Hussein."

15. Jonathan Marshall, et al., *The Iran-Contra Connection: Secret Teams and Cover Operations in the Reagan Era* (Boston: South End Press, 1987), 7–166; Jim Mann, *Rise of the Vulcans: The History of Bush's War Cabinet* (New York: Penguin, 2004), 150–56; John K. Cooley, *Payback: America's Long War in the Middle East* (New York: Brassey's, 1991), 22–46.

16. James H. Noyes, "Through the Gulf Labyrinth: Naval Escorts and U.S. Policy," *American Arab Affairs* 29 (Summer 1989): 1–19; Anthony Cordesman, "The Attack on the U.S.S. Stark: The Tragic Cost of Human Error," *Armed Forces* (London) 6:10 (October 1987): 447–50; George C. Wilson, "Navy Missiles Down Iranian Jetliner over Gulf" *Washington Post* (July 4, 1988): A-1.

17. Anthony Cordesman, *The Gulf and the West: Strategic Relations and Military Realities* (Boulder, CO: Westview, 1988).

18. Efraim Karsh and Inari Rautsu, *Saddam Hussein, A Political Biography* (New York: Free Press), 198–216; Phyllis Bennis and Michel Moushabeck, eds. *Beyond the Storm: A Gulf Crisis Reader* (Brooklyn, NY: Interlink Publishing, 1991), 391–96.

19. Text of Arab summit, *Foreign Broadcast Information Service, Near East-South Asia* 90–105 (May 31, 1990), 1–5.

20. G. Henry Schuler, "Congress Must Take a Hard Look at Iraq's Charges against Kuwait," *Los Angeles Times*, December 2, 1990, M-4, 8; Milton Viorst, "The House of Hashem (Jordan)," *New Yorker* 66 (January 7, 1991): 32–37ff; Pierre Salinger and Eric Laurent, *Secret Dossier: The Hidden Agenda behind the Gulf War* (New York: Penguin, 1991), 235–41.

21. Bob Woodward, *The Commanders* (New York: Simon and Schuster, 1991), 35–42.

22. Joseph W. Twiman, "Controversial Arms Sales to Saudi Arabia: An American Tragedy in Possibly Four Acts," *American Arab Affairs* 29 (Summer 1989): 47–55; Roger Cohen and Claudio Gatti, *In the Eye of the Storm: The Life of General H. Norman Schwarzkopf* (New York: Farrar, Straus, and Giroux, 1991), 185; H. Norman Schwarzkopf, *It Doesn't Take a Hero* (New York: Linda Grey, 1992), 291–94.

23. Woodward, *Commanders*, 240–73; Salinger and Laurent, *Secret Dossier*, 96–114, 136–47; Viorst, "The House of Hashem," 32–52; Norman Friedman, *Desert Victory* (Annapolis, MD: United States Naval Institute, 1991), 287–92.

24. Friedman, *Desert Victory*, 50–51, 87–107; Otto Friedrich, ed. *Desert Storm* (Boston: Little, Brown, 1991): 12, 27, and 125–27; Richard A. Falk, "Twisting the U.N. Charter to U.S. Ends," in Hamid Mowlana et. al. eds., *Triumph of the Image* (Boulder, CO: Westview Press, 1992), 175–80.

25. George Bush and Brent Scowcroft, *A World Transformed* (New York: Knopf, 1998), 411–12; Richard Wilson, "Nuclear Proliferation and the Case of Iraq," *Journal of Palestine Studies* 20:3 (Spring 1991): 5–15; James A. Baker, III, *Politics of Diplomacy: Revolution, War & Peace, 1989–1992* (New York: Putnam's, 1995), 325–28; Woodward, *Commanders*, 333–35; Elaine Sciolino, "An Arbitrary Diplomatic Deal Becomes an Eminent Threat," *New York Times* (January 15, 1991): A-10.

26. "Administration Makes Its Case but Fails to Sway Skeptics," *Congressional Quarterly Weekly Report* 48 (December 8, 1990): 4082–85, 4113–16; Richard Sobol, *The Impact of Public Opinion on U.S. Foreign Policy since Vietnam* (New York: Oxford University Press, 2001), 148–57; Pamela Fessler, "Members Solemn over Crucial Choice...." *Congressional Quarterly Weekly Report* 49 (January 12, 1991): 66; "Even Votes of Conscience Follow Party Lines," ibid. 49 (January 12, 1991): 135–37, 190–204.

27. Baker, *Politics of Diplomacy*, 355–65.

28. See H. Norman Schwarzkopf, *Doesn't Take a Hero: An Autobiography* (New York: Linda Grey-Bantam, 1992) and Dilip Hiro, *Desert Shield to Desert Storm* (New York: Routledge, 1992).

29. Schwarzkopf, *Doesn't Take a Hero*, 447–500; Bush and Scowcroft, *Transformed*, 484–90; Colin Powell, *My American Journey* (New York: Ballantine, 1995), 509–15.

30. Baker, *Politics of Diplomacy*, 443–69, 487–515; Dennis Ross, *The Missing Peace: The Inside Story of the Fight for Middle East Peace* (New York: Farrar, Straus and Giroux, 2004), 46–78; Yossi Beilin, *Touching Peace: From the Oslo Accords to a Final Agreement*. (London: Weidenfeld & Nicolson, 1999), 42–46.

31. Rolf Ekeus, "Unearthing Iraq's Arsenal," *Arms Control Today* 22 (April 1992): 6–9; Mahdi Obeidi, *The Bomb in My Garden: Secrets of Saddam's Nuclear Mastermind* (Hoboken, NJ: Wiley, 2004), 6–8, 144–54; for UNSCOM and IAEA inspections, see David Albright and Mark Hibbs's reports in *The Bulletin of Atomic Scientists*, vols. 47 & 48.

32. Scott Ritter, *Endgame: Solving the Iraq Problem—Once and For all* (New York: Simon & Schuster, 1999), 181–82.

33. On Kurds, see Clyde Haberman, "The Kurds in Flight Once Again," *New York Times Magazine* (May 15, 1991): 33–36ff; on Shiites, see Patrick Tyler, "Contradictions in U.S. Policy," *New York Times*, March 31, 1991, A-1, 3; on no-fly zones, see Dilip Hiro, *Iraq in the Eye of the Storm* (New York: Thunder's Mouth Press, 2002), 45–49.

34. See Hans Blix, *Disarming Iraq* (New York: Pantheon, 2004) and Geoff Simons *Targeting Iraq: Sanctions and Bombing in US Policy* (London: Saqi Books, 2002).

35. Seymour M. Hersh, "The Iraq Hawks," *New Yorker*, December 24 & 31, 2001, 58–59.

Chapter 18

1. Nicholas Lemann, "The Iraq Factor," *New Yorker*, January 22, 2001, 34.

2. See C. G. Ryn, "The Ideology of American Empire," *Orbis* 47:3 (Summer 2003): 383; James Mann offers brief biographies of Rumsfeld, Cheney, Powell, Rice, Wolfowitz, and Armitage in *Rise of the Vulcans*.

3. *Public Papers of President George W. Bush*, "Remarks in a Meeting with the National Security Team and an Exchange with Reporters at Camp David, Maryland," September 15, 2001; *The Economist* (London) 350 (September 15, 2001): 15; Carlyle Murphy, "The Roots of Hatred," *Washington Post National Weekly Edition*, September 24–30, 2001, 29; ibid., September 21, 2001, A24; see also *World Press Review* 48 (November 2001).

4. For Afghan war, see Bob Woodward's *Plan of Attack* (New York: Simon & Schuster, 2004) and *Bush at War* (New York: Simon & Schuster, 2002).

5. *Public Papers of George W. Bush*, "State of the Union Address," January 29, 2002.

6. Woodward, *Plan of Attack*, 1.

7. Rubin, "NATO Unconvinced on Iraq," *Associated Press*, February 3, 2002.

404 Notes

8. Woodward, *Plan of Attack*, 177–79; Mark Danner, *The Secret Way to War: The Downing Street Memo and the Iraq War's Buried History* (New York: New York Review of Books, 2006), 87–127.

9. Elisabeth Bumiller, "U.S. Must Act First to Battle Terror, Bush Tells Cadets," *New York Times*, June 2, 2002, 1, 6.

10. *The National Security: Strategy of the United States of America*, September 17, 2002, 29–30; Philip Zelikow, "The Transformation of National Security," *The National Interest* 71 (Spring 2003), 17–28.

11. Paul W. Schroeder, "Iraq: The Case against Pre-emptive War," *The American Conservative* 1:2 (October 21, 2002): 3.

12. Mark Danner, "The Secret Way to War," *The New York Review*, June 9, 2005, 70–71; Glenn Kessler, "Rice Lays Out Case for War in Iraq," *The Washington Post*, August 16, 2002, A1, A20.

13. Bob Woodward, "A Struggle for Heart and Mind," *Washington Post National Weekly*, December 2–8, 2002, 7.

14. Woodward, *Plan of Attack*, 163–66, 180–185; Micah Sifry and Christopher Cerf, *Iraq War Reader: History, Documents and Opinions* (New York: Touchstone, 2003), 295–300; Baker, "The Right Way to Change a Regime," *New York Times*, August 25, 2002, WK-9.

15. Woodward, *Bush at War*, 351; Talbot Brewer, "We the People, We the Warriors," *The Washington Post National Weekly*, September 2–8, 2002, 26.

16. Hans Blix, *Disarming Iraq* (New York Pantheon, 2004), 111–14. 232–33.

17. Woodward, *Plan of Attack*, 228–31 ff.

18. Blix, *Disarming Iraq*, 117–18, 139–41.

19. "The Case against Iraq," *Washington Post National Weekly*, February 10–16, 2003, 9; Glenn Kessler and Walter Pincus, "A Flawed Argument for War," ibid., February 9–15, 2004, 6.

20. *Washington Post*, February 9, 2003, A1, A25, March 10, 2003, A15; Robert G. Kaiser, "The United States Risks Isolation and a Loss of Key Allies," *Washington Post National Weekly*, March 24–30, 2003, 9; Lewis Lapham, *Harper's* 306 (April 2003), 38.

21. For the Rumsfeld quotation, see Mortimer B. Zuckerman's editorials in *U.S. News & World Report*, December 23, 2002, 56; ibid., January 27/February 3, 2003, 76; *The Nation*, 277 (July 21/28, 2003), 6.

22. Arnaud de Borchgrave, *The American Conservative* 1:4 (November 18, 2002), 20.

23. *The Economist*, 366 (March 22, 2003), 27; Richard Morin and Claudia Deane, "Rallying 'Round the President," *Washington Post National Weekly*, March 24–30, 2003, 34.

24. Condoleezza Rice, "Transforming the Middle East," *Washington Post National Weekly*, August 11–17, 2003, 26.

25. David Rieff, "Blueprint for a Mess," *New York Times Magazine*, November 2, 2003, 28–29; Rajiv Chandrasekaran, "Ties to GOP Trumped

Know-How Among Staff Sent to Rebuild Iraq," *Washington Post*, September 17, 2006, A1, A24–A25.

26. Robert G. Kaiser, "Iraq and Vietnam, Rhyme and Reason," *Washington Post National Weekly*, January 5–14, 2004, 21; Peter Baker and Kim Vande Hei in ibid., September 4–10, 2006, 13.

27. See Richard Dean Burns, *The Missile Systems of George W. Bush: A Critical Assessment* (Santa Barbara, CA: Praeger, 2010); Steven Pifer, "New START: Good News for U.S. Security," *Arms Control Today* (May 2010): 8–14.

28. Cole Harvey, "Obama Calls for Nuclear Weapons-Free World," *Arms Control Today* 39 (May 2009): 28–30; George Perkovich, *India's Nuclear Bomb: The Impact on Global Proliferation* (Berkeley: University of California Press, 2001), 139–42.

29. Michael J. Mazarr, *North Korea and the Bomb: A Case Study in Nonproliferation* (London: Macmillan, 1995), 17–21, 32; see also Charles L. Pritchard, *Failed Diplomacy: The Tragic Story of How North Korea Got the Bomb* (Washington, DC: Brookings Institution Press, 2007), ch. 1; Bruce W. Bennett, *Uncertainties in the North Korean Nuclear Threat* (Santa Monica, CA: RAND, National Defense Research Institute, 2010), 14.

30. Paul K. Kerr, "Iran's Nuclear Programs: Status," *CRS Report for Congress*, RL34544 (Washington, DC: Congressional Research Service, September 18, 2009), 1–3; see also William Burr, "A Brief History of U.S.-Iranian Nuclear Negotiations," *Bulletin of the Atomic Scientists* (January/February 2009); Kenneth Katzman, "Iran Sanctions," *CRS Report for Congress*, RS20871 (Washington, DC: Congressional Research Service, June 23, 2010), 1–10.

31. David R. Francis, "Iraq War Will Cost More Than World War II," *Christian Science Monitor*, October 25, 2011.

32. Andrew Exum, "No Binary Choices for U.S. in the Middle East," *World Politics Review* (April 25, 2012).

33. Lawrence Scheinman, "Disarmament: Have the Five Nuclear Powers Done Enough?" *Arms Control Today* 35 (January/February 2005), 6–11.

34. Robert G. Kaiser, "Trapped by Hubris, Again," *Washington Post National Weekly*, January 22–28, 2007), 22.

Selected Bibliography

Needless to say, there is a vast literature on the many and various aspects of the politics and history of the American diplomatic experience examined in our study. The publications listed below represent only the tip of the iceberg and include some of the most useful studies in English. Constraints of space have made it necessary to omit many excellent and otherwise important works in the field.

General Themes

Adler, S. *The Isolationist Impulse: Its Twentieth Century Reaction.* New York: Abelard-Schulman, 1957.
Bemis, S. F., ed. *The American Secretaries of State and Their Diplomacy.* 10 vols. New York: Cooper Square Publishers, 1963–.
Bemis, S. F. *A Diplomatic History of the United States.* 5th ed. New York: Holt, Rinehart and Winston, 1965.
Cole, W. S., *An Interpretive History of American Foreign Relations.* 2nd ed. Homewood, IL: Dorsey, 1974.
Eckes, A. E., Jr. *Opening America's Market: U.S. Foreign Trade Policy since 1776.* Chapel Hill: University of North Carolina Press, 1995.
Ferrell, R. H. *American Diplomacy: A History.* 3rd ed. New York: Norton, 1975.
Flanagan, J. C. *Imagining the Enemy: American Presidential War Rhetoric from Woodrow Wilson to George Walker Bush.* Claremont, CA: Regina Books, 2009.
Gilbert, F. *To the Farewell Address: Ideas of Early American Foreign Policy.* Princeton, NJ: Princeton University Press, 1970.
Graebner, N. A. *Ideas and Diplomacy: Readings in the Intellectual Tradition of American Foreign Policy.* New York: Oxford University Press, 1964.

Immerman, R. H. *Empire for Liberty: A History of American Imperialism from Benjamin Franklin to Paul Wolfowitz,* Princeton, NJ: Princeton University Press, 2010.
May, E. R., *"Lessons" of the Past: The Use and Misuse of History in American Foreign Policy.* New York: Oxford University Press, 1973.
McInnis, E. W. *The Unguarded Frontier: A History of American-Canadian Relations.* Garden City, NY: Doubleday, 1942.
Merli F. J. and T. A. Wilson, eds. 2 vols. *Makers of American Diplomacy: From Benjamin Franklin to Henry Kissinger.* New York: Scribners, 1974.
Paterson T. G. and D. Merrill. *Major Problems in American Foreign Relations,* 2 vols. Lexington, MA: D. C. Heath, 1995.
Siracusa, J. M. and D. G. Coleman. *Depression to Cold War: A History of America from Herbert Hoover to Ronald Reagan.* Westport, CT: Praeger, 2002.
Smith, D. M. *The American Diplomatic Experience.* Boston: Houghton Mifflin, 1972.
Ulam, A. B. *Expansion and Coexistence: The History of Soviet Foreign Policy, 1917–1973.* 2nd ed. New York: Praeger, 1974.

Pacific and East Asia

Dennett, T. *Americans in Eastern Asia.* New York: Macmillan, 1922.
Dudden, A. P., ed. *American Empire in the Pacific: From Trade to Strategic Balance.* Aldershot, UK: Ashgate, 2004.
Dudden, A. P. *The American Pacific: From the Old China Trade to the Present.* New York: Oxford University Press, 1992.
Fairbank, J. K. *Trade and Diplomacy on the China Coast: The Opening of the Treaty Ports, 1842–1854.* Stanford, CA: Stanford University Press, 1969.
Grew, J. C. *Turbulent Era: A Diplomatic Record of Forty Years, 1904–1945,* 2 vols. Boston: Houghton Mifflin, 1952.
LaFeber, W. *The Clash: U.S.-Japanese Relations throughout History.* New York: W. W. Norton, 1997.
McCormick, T. J. *China Market: America's Quest for Informal Empire, 1893–1901.* Chicago: Quadrangle Books, 1967.
Neumann, W. L. *America Encounters Japan: From Perry to MacArthur.* Baltimore: Johns Hopkins Press, 1963.
Paine, S. C. M. *The Sino-Japanese War of 1894–1895: Perceptions, Power, and Primacy.* Cambridge: Cambridge University Press, 2003.
Tate, M. *The United States and the Hawaiian Kingdom: A Political History.* New Haven, CT: Yale University Press, 1965.
Walworth, A. *Black Ships off Japan: The Story of Commodore Perry's Expedition* New York: Alfred A. Knopf, 1946.

Central and Latin America

Ettinger, A. A. *The Mission to Spain of Pierre Soule, 1853–1855: A Study in the Cuban Diplomacy of the United States.* New Haven, CT: Yale University Press, 1932.
Foner, P. S. *A History of Cuba and Its Relations with the United States*, 2 vols. New York: International Publishers, 1963.
Guggenheim, H. F. *The United States and Cuba: A Study in International Relations.* New York: Macmillan, 1934.
Hunt, M. H. *The Making of a Special Relationship: The United States and China to 1914.* New York: Columbia University Press, 1983.
LaFeber, W. *The Panama Canal: The Crisis in Historical Perspective.* New York: Oxford University Press, 1978.
McCullough, D. *The Path between the Seas: The Creation of the Panama Canal, 1870–1914.* New York: Simon & Schuster, 1977.
Munro, D. G. *Intervention and Dollar Diplomacy in the Caribbean, 1900–1921.* Princeton, NJ: Princeton University Press, 1964.
Parks, E. T. *Colombia and the United States, 1765–1934.* Durham, NC: Duke University Press, 1935.
Rives, G. L. *The United States and Mexico, 1821–1848: A History of the Relations between the Two Countries from the Independence of Mexico to the Close of the War with the United Sates*, 2 vols. New York: Charles Scribner's Sons, 1918.
Scraggs, W. O. *Filibusters and Financiers: The Story of William Walker and his Associates.* New York: Macmillan, 1916.
Skaggs, J. M. *The Great Guano Rush: Entrepreneurs and American Overseas Expansion.* New York: St. Martin's Press, 1994.
Williams, M. W. *Anglo-American Isthmian Diplomacy, 1815–1915.* New York: Russell & Russell, 1965.

Specialized Topics

Burns, R. D. *The Evolution of Arms Control: From Antiquity to the Nuclear Age.* Santa Barbara, CA: Praeger, 2009.
Hilderbrand, R. C. *Power and the People: Executive Management of Public Opinion in Foreign Affairs, 1897–1921.* Chapel Hill, NC: University of North Carolina Press, 1981.
Johnson, R. D. *The Peace Progressives and American Foreign Relations.* Cambridge, MA: Harvard University Press, 1995.
Kennan, G. F. *American Diplomacy, 1900–1950.* Chicago: University of Chicago Press, 1951.
Kennan, G. F. *Memoirs, 1925–1950.* Boston: Atlantic Monthly Press, 1967.
Merk, F. *Manifest Destiny and Mission in American History: A Reinterpretation.* New York: Alfred A. Knopf, 1963.

Perkins, D. *The American Approach to Foreign Policy*. Cambridge: Harvard University Press, 1952.
Perkins, D. *A History of the Monroe Doctrine*. Boston: Little, Brown, 1963.
Siracusa, J. M. *Diplomacy: A Very Short Introduction*. Oxford: Oxford University Press, 2010.
Siracusa, J. M. *Nuclear Weapons: A Very Short Introduction*. Oxford: Oxford University Press, 2008.
Soulsby, H. G. *The Right of Search and the Slave Trade in Anglo-American Relations, 1814–1862*. Baltimore: Johns Hopkins Press, 1933.

From Revolution to Mexican War

Anderson, F. *Crucible of War: The Seven Years' War and the Fate of Empire in British North America, 1754–1766*. New York: Alfred A. Knopf, 2000.
Bemis, S. F. *John Quincy Adams and the Foundations of American Foreign Policy*. New York: A. A. Knopf, 1949.
Dangerfield, G. *The Era of Good Feelings*. New York: Harcourt, Brace & World, 1952.
Graebner, N. A., R. D. Burns, and J. M. Siracusa. *Foreign Affairs and the Founding Fathers: From Confederation to Constitution, 1776–1787*. Santa Barbara, CA: Praeger, 2011.
Remini, R. V. *Andrew Jackson and the Course of American Empire, 1716–1821*. New York: Harper & Row, 1977.
Stagg, J. C. A. *Borderlines in Borderlands: James Madison and the Spanish-American Frontier, 1776–1821*. New Haven, CT: Yale University Press, 2009.
Tucker, R. W. and D. C. Hendrickson. *Empire of Liberty: The Statecraft of Thomas Jefferson*. Oxford: Oxford University Press, 1990.

American Revolution to Constitution

Ammon, A. *The Genet Mission*. New York: W. W. Norton, 1973.
Bemis, S. F. *Jay's Treaty: A Study in Commerce and Diplomacy*. New Haven, CT: Yale University Press, 1962.
Bemis, S. F. *Pinckney's Treaty: America's Advantage from Europe's Distress, 1783–1800*. New Haven, CT: Yale University Press, 1960.
DeConde, A. *Entangling Alliance: Politics & Diplomacy under George Washington*. Durham, NC: Duke University Press, 1958.
Dull, J. R. *A Diplomatic History of the American Revolution*. New Haven, CT: Yale University Press, 1985.
Dull, J. R. *The French Navy and American Independence: A Study of Arms and Diplomacy, 1774–1787*. Princeton: Princeton University Press, 1975.

Estes, T. *The Jay Treaty Debate, Public Opinion, and the Evolution of Early American Political Culture*. Amherst: University of Massachusetts Press, 2006.
Galloway, Colin G. *The Scratch of a Pen: 1763 and the Transformation of America*. New York: Oxford University Press, 2006.
Varg, P. A. *Foreign Policies of the Founding Fathers*. Baltimore: Penguin, 1970.

To the War of 1812

Bowman, A. H. *The Struggle for Neutrality: Franco-American Diplomacy during the Federalist Era*. Knoxville: University of Tennessee Press, 1974.
Brown, R. H. *The Republic in Peril: 1812*. New York: Columbia University Press, 1964.
DeConde, A. *The Quasi-War: The Politics and Diplomacy of the Undeclared War with France 1797–1801*. New York: Charles Scribner's Sons, 1966.
DeConde, A. *This Affair of Louisiana*. New York: Charles Scribner's Sons, 1976.
Hickey, D. R. *The War of 1812: A Forgotten Conflict*. Urbana: University of Illinois Press, 1989.
Latimer, J. *1812: War with America*. Cambridge, MA: Belknap Press, 2007.
Perkins, B. *Castlereagh and Adams: England and America, 1812–1823*. Berkeley: University of California Press, 1964.
Perkins, B. *The First Rapprochement: England and the United States, 1795–1805*. Philadelphia: University of Philadelphia Press, 1955.
Perkins, B. *Prologue to War: England and the United States, 1805–1812*. Berkeley: University of California Press, 1961.
Stinchcombe, W. *The XYZ Affair*. Westport, CT: Greenwood Press, 1980.
Sugden, J. *Tecumseh: A Life*. New York: Henry Holt, 1997.

Mexican War to World War I

Cook, A. *The Alabama Claims: American Politics and Anglo-American Relations, 1865–1872*. Ithaca, NY: Cornell University Press, 1975.
Crapol, E. P. *James G. Blaine: Architect of Empire*. Lanham, MD: Rowman & Littlefield, 2000.
Gambrell, H. *Anson Jones: The Last President of Texas*. Garden City, NY: Doubleday, 1948.
Graebner, N. A. *Empire on the Pacific: A Study in American Continental Expansion*. New York: Ronald Press, 1955.
LaFeber, W. *The American Search for Opportunity, 1865–1913*. New York: Cambridge University Press, 1993.
LaFeber, W. *The New Empire: An Interpretation of American Expansion, 1860–1898*. Ithaca, NY: Cornell University Press, 1963.

Temperley, H. *The Foreign Policy of Canning, 1822–1827: England, the Neo-Holy Alliance, and the New World.* London: Frank Cass, 1966.

To the Mexican War

Price, G. W. *Origins of the War with Mexico: The Polk-Stockton Intrigue.* Austin: University of Texas Press, 1967.
Quaife, M. M., ed. *The Diary of James K. Polk during his Presidency, 1845 to 1849,* vol. 1. Chicago: A. C. McClurg, 1910.
Weeks, W. E. *John Quincy Adams and American Global Empire.* Lexington: University Press of Kentucky, 1992.

To the Civil War

Adams, E. D. *Great Britain and the American Civil War.* New York: Russell & Russell, 1958.
Blackett, R. J. M. *Divided Hearts: Britain and the American Civil War.* Baton Rouge: Louisiana State University Press, 2001.
Crook, D. P. *The North, the South and the Powers, 1861–1865.* New York: John Wiley & Sons, 1974.
Foner, P. S. *British Labor and the American Civil War.* New York: Holmes and Meir, 1981.
Garber, P. N. *The Gadsden Treaty.* Philadelphia: Press of the University of Pennsylvania, 1924.
Goodwin, D. K. *Team of Rivals: The Political Genius of Abraham Lincoln.* Camberwell, VIC: Penguin, 2009.
Hubbard, C. M. *The Burden of Confederate Diplomacy.* Knoxville: University of Tennessee Press, 2000.
Jones, H. *Blue & Gray Diplomacy: A History of Union and Confederate Foreign Relations.* Chapel Hill: University of North Carolina Press, 2010.
Merli, F. J. *Great Britain and the Confederate Navy, 1861–1865.* Bloomington: Indiana University Press, 1970.
Offner, J. L. *An Unwanted War: The Diplomacy of the United States and Spain over Cuba, 1895.* Chapel Hill: University of North Carolina Press, 1992.
Owsley, F. L. *King Cotton Diplomacy: Foreign Relations of the Confederate States of America.* Chicago: University of Chicago Press, 1931.
Sellers, C. *James K. Polk, Continentalist, 1843–1846.* Princeton, NJ: Princeton University Press, 1966.
Spencer, W. F. *The Confederate Navy in Europe.* University, AL: University Alabama Press, 1983.

To the Spanish-American War

Gould, L. L. *The Presidency of William McKinley.* Lawrence: Regents Press of Kansas, 1980.

Grenville J. A. S. and G. B. Young. *Polities, Strategy, and American Diplomacy: Studies in Foreign Policy, 1873–1917*. New Haven, CT: Yale University Press, 1966.
Gyory, A. *Closing the Gate: Race, Politics, and the Chinese Exclusion Act*. Chapel Hill: University of North Carolina Press, 1998.
Merk, F. *Albert Gallatin and the Oregon Problem: A Study in Anglo-American Diplomacy*. Cambridge, MA: Harvard University Press, 1950.
Miller, R. H., ed. *American Imperialism in 1898: The Quest for National Fulfillment*. New York: John Wiley and Sons, 1970.
Pérez, L. A. *Cuba under the Platt Amendment, 1902–1934*. Pittsburgh, PA: University of Pittsburgh Press, 1991.
Pletcher, D. M. *The Awkward Years: American Foreign Relations under Garfield and Arthur*. Columbia: University of Missouri Press, 1962.
Pratt, J. W. *America's Colonial Experiment*. Englewood Cliffs, NJ: Prentice-Hall, 1950.
Pratt, J. W. *Expansionists of 1898*. Baltimore: Johns Hopkins Press, 1936.
Reckner, J. R. *Teddy Roosevelt's Great White Fleet*. Annapolis MD: Naval Institute Press, 1988.
Reeves, J. S. *American Diplomacy under Tyler and Polk*. Baltimore: Johns Hopkins, 1907.
Rickover, H. G. *How the Battleship Maine Was Destroyed*. Washington, DC: Naval History Division, 1976.
Spencer, D. S. *Louis Kossuth and Young America: A Study of Sectionalism and Foreign Policy 1848–1852*. Columbia: University of Missouri Press, 1977.
Spencer, I. D. *The Victor and the Spoils: A Life of William L. Macy*. Providence, RI: Brown University Press, 1959.
Warren, G. H. *Fountain of Discontent: The Trent Affair and Freedom of the Seas*. Boston: Northeastern University Press, 1981.
Wiltse, C. M. *John C. Calhoun, Sectionalist, 1844–1850*. Indianapolis: Bobbs-Merrill, 1951.

World War I through World War II

Bailey, T. A. *Woodrow Wilson and the Lost Peace*. New York: Macmillan, 1944.
Dando-Collins, S. *Tycoon's War: How Cornelius Vanderbilt Invaded a Country to Overthrow America's Most Famous Military Adventurer*. Cambridge, MA: Da Capo Press, 2008.
Feis, H. *The China Tangle: The American Effort in China from Pearl Harbor to the Marshall Mission*. Princeton, NJ: Princeton University Press, 1953.
Feis, H. *Churchill, Roosevelt, Stalin: The War They Waged and the Peace They Sought*. 2nd ed. Princeton, NJ: Princeton University Press, 1967.
Feis, H. *The Road to Pearl Harbor: The Coming of the War between the United States and Japan*. Princeton, NJ: Princeton University Press, 1950.
Fleming, D. F. *The United States and the League of Nations, 1918–1920*. New York: G. P. Putnam's Sons, 1932.

Graebner, N. A. and E. M. Bennett. *The Versailles Treaty and Its Legacy: The Failure of the Wilsonian Vision*. New York: Cambridge University Press, 2011.
Hart, L., *History of the First World War*. London: Weidenfeld and Nicolson, 1970.
Joll, J. and G. Martel. *The Origins of the First World War*. 3rd ed. Oxford: Oxford University Press, 2006.
Knock, Thomas J. *To End All Wars: Woodrow Wilson and the Quest for a New World Order*. Princeton, NJ: Princeton University Press, 1995.
Langer, W. L. and S. E. Gleason. *The Undeclared War, 1940–1941*. New York: Harper & Row, 1953.
Link, A. S. *Wilson: Campaigns for Progressivism and Peace*. Princeton, NJ: Princeton University Press, 1965.
Link, A. S. *Woodrow Wilson and the Progressive Era, 1910–1917*. New York: Harper & Row, 1954.
Lodge, H. C. *The Senate and the League of Nations*. New York: Charles Scribner's Sons, 1925.
Mauch, P. *Sailor Diplomat: Nomura Kichisaburo and the Japanese-American War*. Cambridge, MA: Harvard University Press, 2010.
McNeill, W. H. *America, Britain, and Russia: Their Cooperation and Conflict, 1941–1946*. London: Oxford University Press for Royal Institute of International Affairs, 1953.
Miscamble, W. D. *From Roosevelt to Truman: Potsdam, Hiroshima, and the Cold War*. New York: Cambridge University Press, 2007.
Pratt, J. W. *Challenge and Rejection: The United States and World Leadership, 1900–1921*. New York: Macmillan, 1967.
Sherwood, R. E. *Roosevelt and Hopkins: An Intimate History*. New York: Harper & Row, 1948.
Snell, J. L. *The Meaning of Yalta: Big Three Diplomacy and the New Balance of Power*. Baton Rouge: Louisiana State University Press, 1956.
Tansill, C. C. *America Goes to War*. Boston: Little, Brown, 1938.

Cold War

Acheson, D. *Present at the Creation: My Years in the State Department*. New York: W. W. Norton, 1969.
Bacevich, A. J. *The Long War: A New History of U.S. National Security Policy since World War II*. New York: Columbia University Press, 2007.
Boyle, P. G. *American-Soviet Relations: From the Revolution to the Fall of Communism*. New York: Routledge, 1993.
Cohen, W. I. *America in the Age of Soviet Power, 1945–1991*. Vol. 4: *The Cambridge History of American Foreign Relations*. New York: Cambridge University Press, 1993.
Eisenhower, D. D. *The White House Years: Mandate for Change, 1953–1956*. New York: Doubleday, 1963.

Foreman, A, *A World on Fire: An Epic History of Two Nations Divided*. London: Allen Lane, 2010.
Gaddis, J. L. *We Now Know: Rethinking Cold War History*. New York: Oxford University Press, 1997.
Garthoff, R. L. *Détente and Confrontation: American Relations from Nixon to Reagan*. Rev. ed. Washington, DC: Brookings Institution Press, 1994.
Goulden, J. C. *Truth Is the First Casualty: The Gulf of Tonkin Affair—Illusion and Reality*. Chicago: Rand McNally, 1969.
Graebner, N. A., R. D. Burns, and J. M. Siracusa. *America and the Cold War, 1941–1991: A Realist Interpretation*. 2 vols. Santa Barbara, CA: Praeger 2010.
Graebner, N. A., R. D. Burns, and J. M. Siracusa. *Reagan, Bush, Gorbachev: Revisiting the End of the Cold War*. Westport, CT: Praeger, 2008.
Hammer, E. J. *The Struggle for Indochina*. Stanford, CA: Stanford University Press, 1954.
Hogan, M. J. *A Cross of Iron: Harry S. Truman and the Origins of the National Security State, 1945–1954*. New York: Cambridge University Press, 1998.
Jones, J. M. *The Fifteen Weeks (February 21–June 5, 1947)*. New York: Viking Press, 1955.
LaFeber, W. *America, Russia, and the Cold War, 1945–2000*. 9th ed. New York: McGraw-Hill, 2002.
Larson, D. W. *Anatomy of Mistrust: U.S.-Soviet Relations during the Cold War*. Ithaca, NY: Cornell University Press, 1997.
Leffler, M. P. *For the Soul of Mankind: The United States, the Soviet Union, and the Cold War*. New York: Hill & Wang, 2007.
Lind, M. *Vietnam, the Necessary War: A Reinterpretation of America's Most Disastrous Military Conflict*. New York: Free Press, 1999.
McCormick, T. J. *America's Half Century: United States Foreign Policy in the Cold War and After*. 2nd ed. Baltimore: Johns Hopkins University Press, 1995.
Paterson, T. G. *Meeting the Communist Threat: Truman to Reagan*. New York: Oxford University Press, 1988.
Rovere R. H. and A. M. Schlesinger, Jr. *The General and the President*. New York: Farrar, Straus and Young, 1951.
Schlesinger, A. M., Jr. *The Bitter Heritage: Vietnam and American Democracy, 1941–1966*. Boston: Houghton Mifflin, 1967.
Siracusa, J. M. *Into the Dark House: American Diplomacy and the Ideological Origins of the Cold War*. Claremont, CA: Regina Books, 1998.
Siracusa, J. M. and G. Barclay, eds. *The Impact of the Cold War: Reconsiderations*. Port Washington, NY: Kennikat Press, 1977.
Smith, T. *America's Mission: The United States and the Worldwide Struggle for Democracy in the Twentieth Century*. Princeton, NJ: Princeton University Press, 1994.
Stueck, W. *The Korean War: An International History*. Princeton, NJ: Princeton University Press, 1995.

Wittner, L. *Cold War America: From Hiroshima to Watergate.* New York: Praeger, 1974.
Zubok, V. M. *A Failed Empire: The Soviet Union in the Cold War from Stalin to Gorbachev.* Chapel Hill: University of North Carolina Press, 2007.

Post–Cold War

Ash, T. G. *Free World: America, Europe, and the Surprising Future of the West.* New York: Random House, 2004.
Bacevich, A. J. *The New American Militarism: How Americans Are Seduced by War.* New York: Oxford University Press, 2005.
Bamford, J. *A Pretext for War: 9/11, Iraq, and the Abuse of America's Intelligence Agencies.* New York: Doubleday, 2004.
Battersby, P., J. M. Siracusa, and S. Ripilsoki. *Crime Wars: The Global Intersection of Crime, Violence, and International Law.* Santa Barbara, CA: Praeger, 2011.
Battersby, P., and J. M. Siracusa. *Globalization and Human Security.* Lanham, MD: Rowman & Littlefield, 2009.
Beck, S., and M. Downing. *The Battle for Iraq.* Baltimore. MD: Johns Hopkins University Press, 2003.
Brune, L. *The United States and Two Gulf War: Prelude & Aftermath.* Claremont, CA: Regina Books, 2007.
Clark, R. *Against All Enemies: Inside America's War on Terror.* New York: Free Press, 2006.
Clark, W. *Winning Modern Wars: Iraq, Terrorism and the American Empire.* New York: Public Affairs, 2003.
Coleman, D. G. and J. M. Siracusa. *Real-World Nuclear Deterrence: The Making of International Strategy.* Westport, CT: Praeger Security International, 2006.
Cordesman, A. H. *The War after the War: Strategic Lessons of Iraq and Afghanistan.* Washington, DC: Center for Strategic Studies Press, 2004.
Dallder, I. and J. M. Lindsay. *America Unbound: The Bush Revolution in Foreign Policy.* Washington, DC: Brookings Institution Press, 2003.
Gaddis, J. *Surprise, Security and the American Experience.* Cambridge, MA: Harvard University Press, 2004.
Hoffmann, S. *Gulliver Unbound: America's Imperial Temptation and the War in Iraq.* Lanham, MD: Rowman & Littlefield, 2004.
Kagan, R. *Of Paradise and Power: America and Europe in the New World Order.* 2nd ed. New York: Vintage Books/Random House, 2001.
Leffler, M. and J. Legro, eds. *In Uncertain Times: American Foreign Policy after the Berlin Wall and 9/11.* Ithaca, NY: Cornell University Press, 2011.
Lodal, J. *The Price of Dominance: The New Weapons of Mass Destruction and Their Challenge to American Leadership.* New York: Council on Foreign Relations Press, 2001.

Makiya, K. *Cruelty and Silence: War, Tyranny, Uprising, and the Arab World.* New York: W. W. Norton, 1993.
Mann, J. *Rise of the Vulcans: The History of Bush's War Cabinet.* New York: Viking, 2004.
Mockaitis, T. R. *The Iraq War: A Documentary and Reference Guide.* Santa Barbara, CA: Praeger Security International, 2012.
The 9/11 Commission Report. New York: W. W. Norton, 2004.
Ross, D. *The Missing Peace: The Inside Story of the Fight for Middle East Peace.* New York: Farrar, Straus and Giroux, 2004.
Schlesinger, A. M., Jr. *War and the American Presidency.* New York: W. W. Norton, 2004.
Weeks, A. *The Choice of War: The Iraq War and the Just War Tradition.* Westport, CT: Praeger Security International, 2009.
Woodward, Bob. *Bush at War.* New York: Simon & Schuster, 2003.

Reference Works

Bartlett, R. J., ed. *The Record of American Diplomacy: Documents and Readings in the History of American Foreign Relations.* New York: Alfred A. Knopf, 1964.
Beisner, R. L. ed. *American Foreign Relations since 1600: A Guide to Literature.* 2 vols. 2nd ed. Santa Barbara, CA: ABC-CLIO, 2003.
Brune, Lester, comp., and R. D. Burns, ed. *Chronology of the Cold War, 1917–1992.* New York: Routledge, 2006.
Burns, R. D, ed. *Encyclopedia of Arms Control and Disarmament.* 3 vols. New York: Scribners, 1993.
Burns, R. D. and J. M. Siracusa, *Historical Dictionary of the Kennedy-Johnson Era.* Lanham, MD: Scarecrow, 2007.
Commager, H. S., ed. *Documents of American History.* 2 vols. New York: Appleton-Century-Crofts, 1958.
DeConde, A., et al., eds. *Encyclopedia of American Foreign Policy,* 3 vols. 2nd ed. New York: Scribners, 2002.
Link, A. S., ed. *The Papers of Woodrow Wilson.* 69 vols. Princeton, NJ: Princeton University Press, 1966–1994.
Matray, J. I., ed. *East Asia and the United States: An Encyclopedia of Relations since 1784.* 2 vols. Westport, CT: Greenwood Press, 2002.
Siracusa, J. M., ed. *The American Diplomatic Revolution: A Documentary History of the Cold War, 1941–1947.* Port Washington, NY: Kennikat Press, 1977.
U.S. Department of State. [Papers Relating to the] *Foreign Relations of the United States.* Washington, DC: GPO, 1861–.
U.S. President. *Public Papers of the Presidents of the United States.* Washington, DC: GPO, 1961–.

Index

ABC News-*Washington Post* poll, 355
Abdul-Shafi, Haidar, 339
Aberdeen, Lord, 60, 62
Able Archer military exercise, 305
ABM (Anti-Ballistic Missile) Treaty, 262, 297, 308
Abrams, Elliott, 342
Accidents Measures Agreement, 263
Acheson, Dean, 212, 231, 240–42, 243, 322
Act of Bogota, 252
Adams, Charles Francis, 82, 83–84
Adams, Henry, 37
Adams, John: as diplomat, 7–8, 10; election of, 23; on neutrality, 1; peace negotiations, 9; Plan of Treaties of 1776, 4; Vergennes and, 6
Adams, John Quincy: on Canning's proposal, 53; noncolonization principle, 47–48; noninterference principle, 54; recognition policy, 50–51, 56; as secretary of state, 37; Spain and, 40–42; speech to House of Representatives, 45
Adenauer, Konrad, 228
Advisers, in South Vietnam, 279–80

Advisory Committee on Problems of Foreign Relations, 212–13
Afghanistan, 309, 325, 345–47, 362
Afghan Northern Alliance, 346
AFL (American Federation of Labor), 169
Agency for International Development, 255
Agreed Framework, 359
Aguinaldo, Emilio, 119, 121
Ahmadinejad, Mahmoud, 359–60
Alabama (Confederate cruiser), 83–86
Alaska, 89–91
Albania, 181–82
Albert, the Prince Consort, 81
Alexander I, Czar, 371n12
Alexandra, 84
Allen, Richard, 300
Alliance for Progress, 251–52, 254, 255
Allied Control Committee, 208
Allied Council, 237–38
"All-Mexico" movement, 71, 72
All Quiet on the Western Front (Remarque), 173
Al Qaeda, 346
Alsop, Joseph, 212
Alsop, Stewart, 212

Amelia Island, 41
America Goes to War (Tansill), 174
American Communist Party, 180
American Expeditionary Force, 153
American Federation of Labor (AFL), 169
American Legion, 169
American Revolution, diplomacy of: alliance with France, 2–5; Constitution, 14; European rivalries and, 6–7; introduction to, 1–2; objectives, 7–8; peace negotiations, 8–9; problems of independence, 10–11; Spain and, 3, 5–6; stakes of, 7–8; trade, 11–12; treaty, 10; western frontier, 12–14
Ampudia, Pedro de, 67
Andropov, Yuri, 305, 308
Anglo-Japanese alliance, 141, 383n34
Angola, 309
Antarctic Treaty of 1959, 260
Anti-Ballistic Missile (ABM) Treaty, 262, 297, 308
Antiballistic missile systems, 260
Anti-Chinese riots, 102
Anticommunism, 218–19, 295–97. *See also* Cold War
Anti-Imperialist League, 119
Antiwar sentiment: Vietnam War, 283, 288–89, 396n33; World War II, 173–74
Arab-Israeli conflict: Cold War and, 258–59; H. W. Bush and, 331; origins of, 322–24; Reagan and, 325–27; Six-Day War of 1967, 264
Arab League, 332
Arab Spring, 360–62
Arcadia Conference, 198–200
Argentina, 49, 56, 172, 216
Armistice, World War I, 155–56
Armitage, Richard, 344
Arms control, 259–62, 306–8, 311–15, 317–18, 357–58
Arms race, 234–35

Articles of Confederation, 11, 13
Asia: Hoover and, 166–67; Japan and Harris, 101–2; "Old China Trade," 97–98; opening of Japan, 98–100; Tientsin treaties, 100–101; U.S. commercial agents in, 96–97. *See also* China; Japan
Assad, Hafez, 324
Astor, John Jacob, 39
Astoria, 39
Aswan Dam, 323
Atlantic Charter, 188–89, 198, 201, 213
Atocha, A. J., 67
Atomic energy, international control of, 217–18
Atomic Energy Commission, UN, 217
Atomic weapons. *See* Nuclear weapons
Attlee, Clement, 208, 221
Australia, 395n21
Austria, 49, 180, 223
Austria-Hungary, 145, 153, 155–56
Autobiography (T. Roosevelt), 127
Axis of evil speech (G. W. Bush), 343, 346–47
Aziz, Tariq, 337

Bagot, Charles, 37–38
Baker, James, 316, 333, 335–37, 339, 350–51
Al-Bakr, Hassan, 324
"Balance of terror," 234
Balfour, Arthur James, 322
Bancroft, Edward, 3
Bancroft, George, 67
Bao Dai, 273–74, 276
Barnes, Harry Elmer, 173–74
Baruch, Bernard, 217–18
Baruch Plan, 217, 260
"Basic Principles of Relations" agreement, 263
Baton Rouge, 28
Battle of Fallen Timbers, 19, 21

Battle of Horseshoe Bend, 37
Battle of Tippecanoe, 34
Bayard, Thomas, 88
Bay of Pigs invasion, 252–53
Bear Flag revolt, 69
Beaumarchais, Caron de, 3
Begin, Menachem, 325
Belgium, 186, 307
Belligerent rights, 76, 77–80
Bemis, Samuel Flagg, 5
Benton, Thomas Hart, 58
Berlin, 237, 269
Berlin airlift, 229
Berlin crisis, 249–51
Bermuda, 80
Bernstein, Barton, 218
Beschloss, Michael, 318
Bethmann-Hollweg, Theobald von, 151
Bevin, Ernest, 221
Big Four summit, 250
Bikini Atoll, 217
Bin Laden, Osama, 346
Bin Sultan, Prince Bandar, 352
Biological Convention, 263
Bishop, Maurice, 301–2
Black Hand, 145
Blacklist, Great Britain's, 150–51
Blaine, James G., 104, 109
Blair, Tony, 341, 345, 347–49, 351, 352
Blitzkrieg (lightning war), 186
Blix, Hans, 352–53, 354
Bolivia, 172
Bolshevik revolution, 153
Bonaparte, Napoleon, 23–24, 25–27, 32, 33
Borah, William E., 160–61, 169, 173, 183
Bosch, Juan, 255
Boston (U.S. cruiser), 92
Boun Oum, 277
Bovin, Alexander, 306
Boxer Rebellion, 139–41

Bradley, Omar N., 244
Brandt, Willy, 268–69
Brazil, 56
Brezhnev, Leonid I., 258, 262, 263, 268
Brezhnev Doctrine, 268, 308
Bright, John, 77
British Aggressions in Venezuela, or the Monroe Doctrine on Trial (Scruggs), 94
British East India Company, 96
British Guiana, 93–94
British Malaya, 192
British Trade Journal, 94
"Broken voyage," 31–32
Brooks Island. *See* Midway Island
Browder, Earl, 180
Brown, Harold, 328
Brown, Jacob, 35
Bruce, David K. E., 287
Brussels Conference, 178
Brussels Pact alliance, 233
Bryan, William Jennings, 121, 123, 132–34, 147–49, 164
Bryan-Chamorro Treaty, 133
Brzezinski, Zbigniew, 328
Buchanan, James, 59–62, 67, 68, 70–71
Buckley, William, 329
Buddhist monks, suppression of, 281
Bulganin, Nikolai A., 247
Bulgaria: indemnities, 222; Soviet Union and, 204, 221, 223, 228; World War I, 145–46, 153
Bull, John, 60, 95
Bulletin of the Atomic Scientists, 298
Bullitt, William C., 162
Bulloch, James D., 82–83
Bunau-Varilla, Philippe, 127
Bundy, McGeorge, 254, 306
Bunker, Ellsworth, 255
Burgoyne, John, 4
Burlingame, Anson, 101

Bush, George H. W.: election of, 315; end of the Cold War, 319; First Gulf War, seeking support for, 333, 334–36; First Gulf War policies, 336–39; Gorbachev and, 316–18; Iranian commercial airline incident, 330; "new world order," 339

Bush, George W.: axis of evil speech, 343, 346–47; Bush Doctrine, 347–49; on Hussein, 344, 347; Iraq War, events leading to, 349–51; Iraq War linked with war on terror, 356–57; Iraq War policies, 352–56; missile defense program, 343; North Korea and, 359; occupation of Iraq, 356–57; on September 11, 2001, terrorist attacks, 345

Bush Doctrine, 347–49

Byrnes, James, 208–9, 222, 224

Caceres, Ramon, 134–35
Cairo Declaration, 208
Calhoun, John C., 34, 61, 71
California, 64–66, 69
Cambodia, 273, 276, 287–89, 292, 309
Campbell, Menzies, 347
Camp David meeting, 249–50
Canada, 34, 36, 172, 188, 264
Canning, George, 51–56
Cardenas, Lazaro, 172
Caribbean Danger Zone, 254
Caribbean protectorates, 126–29
Carlucci, Frank, 313, 315
Carranza, Venustiano, 136–37
Carter, Jimmy: Central America, 300–301; Iran-Iraq War, 328; Middle East and, 323–25; Panama Canal and, 255; policies toward Iraq and Iran, 324–25; Reagan and, 299–300; SALT II, 262; Soviet Union and, 258; State of the Union address, 321, 325
Carter Doctrine, 325

Casablanca conference, 202
Castlereagh, Lord, 39
Castro, Cipriano, 130
Castro, Fidel, 252–54, 301
Catherine II of Russia, 6
Central America: Carter, Jimmy, 300–301; Cold War in, 251–55, 300–302, 309–10; Reagan and, 300–302, 309–10
Central American Court of Justice, 133
Central Europe, Cold War and, 220–22
Central Intelligence Agency (CIA), 261, 292, 300, 359
Central Powers, World War I, 145–46
Chalabi, Ahmad, 342
Chamberlain, Neville, 180–82
Chamber of Commerce speech (Reagan), 296
Cheney, Dick: as Defense Secretary, 317, 333, 334, 335; on Hussein, 344–45, 347; Iraq War, 349–50, 352, 354–55; linking Iraq War with war on terror, 357; Project for the New American Century, 342; on the role of Congress in foreign policy, 309
Chernenko, Konstantin, 311
Chernyaev, Anatoly, 317
Chesapeake (American frigate), 31
Chiang Kai-shek, 166, 179, 193, 203–4, 207–8, 238–39
Chiari, Roberto, 254
Chile, 49, 56
China: Boxer Rebellion, 139–41; civil war, 238–41; commercial expansion, 96–98, 102–4; Communist China, 266–67; communist takeover, 238–41; conflict over Manchuria, 166; Declaration of Four Nations on General Security, 203; France and, 100–101, 104; F. Roosevelt and,

198–99; Germany and, 103, 141; Great Britain and, 98, 100–101, 104, 141; immigration from, 102; Japanese invasion of, 177–79; Korea and, 102–3, 243–45; in negotiations with Japan, 193; nuclear weapons and, 358; "Old China Trade," 97–98; Open Door policy, 104, 137–39; People's Republic of China, 231, 240; Russia and, 100–101, 103–4; Seward and, 102; Shufeldt and, 103; war with Japan, 103
Chinese exclusion, 102
Chinese People's Consultative Conference, 240
Chirac, Jacques, 354
Chou En-lai, 266–67, 274
Christian Front, 180
Churchill, Winston: on colonial holdings, 199; F. Roosevelt and, 188–89, 198–200, 202, 388n22; on international organization, 213; Iron Curtain speech, 211, 225; on Japan, 194; on the Morgenthau Plan, 202–3; on a second front, 201; on Soviet expansionism, 220; Tehran conference, 203–4; on transfer of destroyers to Great Britain, 185, 187; visit to Moscow, 204–5; Yalta conference, 205–7
CIA (Central Intelligence Agency), 261, 292, 300, 359
Civil War diplomacy: belligerent rights, 76, 77–80; introduction to, 75–77; neutral obligations, 76, 82–86; *Trent* affair, 80–82
Claiborne, W. C. C., 27–28
Clark Amendment, 309
Clay, Henry, 29, 34, 37, 50–51, 56
Clayton-Bulwer Treaty, 90–91, 126
Clemenceau, Georges, 155, 157–58, 160
Cleveland, Grover, 93, 95, 112

Clifford, Clark, 219, 286, 322
Clinton, Bill, containment of Iraq, 339–42
Cochin China, 273, 394n2
Cockburn, Alexander, 86
Cold War: arms control, 259–62, 306–8, 311–14, 317–18, 357; arms race, 234–35; Bush and Gorbachev, 316–18; Central America, 251–55, 300–302, 309–10; Central and Eastern Europe, 220–22; Chinese civil war, 238–41; collective defense agreements, 229–34; containment policy, 225–27, 229–31, 248–49, 272, 390n19; Cuban Missile Crisis, 234, 255–58; détente, 247–51, 258–63; Eastern Europe, 220–22; end of, 315–16, 318–19; ideological origins of, 218–19; Korean conflict, 231–32, 241–47; Latin America, 251–55; NATO, 264–65; occupation of Germany, 220–21, 223–24; occupation of Japan, 237–38; overview of later years, 295–97; Quadripartite Treaty, 267–70; Reagan and Europe, 302–4; Reagan and Gorbachev, 310–16; Reagan Doctrine, 308–10, 315; Reagan's approach to, 304–6; rhetoric vs. action, 299–300; satellite treaties, 222–23; Second Cold War, 295; U.S. military buildup, 297–99; U.S.-Soviet quest for détente, 258–63; West German republic, 227–29
Collective defense agreements, 229–34
Colombia, 49, 56, 90, 127–28
Combined Chiefs of Staff, 200
Cominform (Communist Information Bureau), 228
Comintern, 201

Commercial expansionism: in Asia, 96–97; China, Korea, and Japan, 96–98, 102–4; commercial reciprocity, 104–5; foreign markets, 88–89; Hawaii, 91–92; introduction to, 87–89; Japan, 98–100, 101–2; "Old China Trade," 97–98; Tientsin treaties, 100–101
Commercial reciprocity, 104–5
Common Sense (Paine), 1, 2
Communist Information Bureau (Cominform), 228
Conference of American Foreign Ministers, 189
Conference on Security and Cooperation in Europe. *See* Helsinki Accord
Congressional Record, 161
Connally Resolution, 213
Constitution, U.S., 11, 14
Containment policy, 225–27, 229–31, 248–49, 272, 390n19. *See also* Cold War
"Continental Democrats," 71
Continuous voyage, doctrine of, 80
Contras, 309
Convention of 1818, 40
Convention of Aranjuez, 5, 6
Cooperative Threat Reduction program, 357
Costa Rica, 133, 310
Council of Foreign Ministers, 221–22, 224, 225
Covenant of the League of Nations, 158–59, 161
Creek Confederacy, 37, 41
Cronkite, Walter, 271, 280
Crowe, William S., 336
Cuba: American intervention, 112–14, 252–54; American investments in, 111; Cuban Missile Crisis, 234, 255–58; insurgency against Spain, 110–12; McKinley on, 129; Platt Amendment, 129–30, 171; as U.S. protectorate, 128. *See also* Spanish-American War
Cuba Convention, 129
Cuban Missile Crisis, 234, 255–58
Curzon Line, 204–5
Cushing, Caleb, 98
Czech Legion, 155
Czechoslovakia, 180–81, 228, 268
Czechoslovak National Council, 156

Daladier, Édouard, 180–81
Daughters of the American Revolution, 169
Davie, William R., 23
Davis, James Thomas, 291
Dawson, Thomas C., 131
Dead Ends, 305
Deane, Silas, 3
Dearlove, Richard, 349
Declaration by the United Nations, 197–98, 201
Declaration of Four Nations on General Security, 203, 213
Declaration of Paris, 37, 78–79
De Gaulle, Charles, 198, 264–65, 284
Demilitarized zone (DMZ), 245–46, 286
Democratic Kampuchea, 292. *See also* Cambodia
Democratic Party: F. Roosevelt and, 187; imperialism debate, 122; League of Nations negotiations, 161–62; territorial expansion, 59
Democratic People's Republic of Korea, 241
Democratic Republic of Vietnam, 273–75. *See also* Vietnam War
Democratic Review, 61, 71
Denmark, 6, 88, 186, 216
Dennett, Tyler, 98
Détente, 247–51, 258–63
Detroit, 19, 35

Dewey, George, 116, 118
Dias, Adolfo, 132
Diaz, Porfirio, 135
Diefenbaker, John, 264
Diem, Ngo Dinh, 278–79, 280–81
Dienbienphu, 274, 279
Dieppe Raid, 199
Dies, Martin, 180
Dies Committee, 180
Die Zeit, 353
Dingley tariff, 104–5
DMZ (demilitarized zone), 245–46, 286
Dobrynin, Anatoly, 263
Dodd, William E., 175
Dole, Sanford B., 93
Dollar diplomacy, 131–33
Dominican Republic, 128, 131–35, 255. *See also* Santo Domingo
Domino effect, 212, 272, 283, 301
Dorchester, Lord, 19
Dos Passos, John, 173
Draft law, 230
Dudley, William, 180
Dulles, John Foster, 219, 232–33, 249, 274, 275–76
Dumbarton Oaks Proposals, 213–14, 216
Duong Van Minh, 281
DuPont de Nemours, Pierre Samuel, 26
Dutch East Indies, 191, 192–93

EAC (European Advisory Commission), 203, 220
Eagleburger, Lawrence, 301
Early Republic: Jay's Treaty, 19–21; Louisiana Purchase, 24–28; neutrality in European conflicts, 16–18; Pinckney's Treaty, 21–22; "Quasi-War" with France, 22–24; tensions with Great Britain, 18–19
Eastern Europe, Cold War and, 220–22

Easter Offensive, 289–90
East Germany, 229, 268–69
The Economist, 312
Economy, 11–12, 147–48. *See also* Trade
EDC (European Defense Community), 232
Eden, Anthony, 203, 247
Egypt, 323–24
Eighteen Nation Disarmament Committee, 259
Eighth Pan American Conference, 172
Einstein, Albert, 175
Eisenhower, Dwight: on advance to Berlin, 220–21; Camp David meeting, 249–50; De Gaulle and, 264; domino effect, 272; Geneva summit, 247–48; Hungary and, 248–49; Korea and, 244; Middle East and, 322–23; overflying the Soviet Union, 260–61; as Supreme Commander of NATO, 232; U-2 incident, 250
ElBaradei, Mohamand, 352
Ellsworth, Oliver, 23
El Salvador, 133, 300–301
Elsey, George, 219
Embargo Act, 33
Empire: Boxer Rebellion, 139–41; creation of, 115–19; dollar diplomacy, 131–33; introduction to, 125–26; Open Door policy, 104, 137–39; Panama Canal and Caribbean protectorates, 126–29; Platt Amendment, 129–30, 171; popular opinion of, 122–23; Roosevelt Corollary, 131–33, 170; Russo-Japanese War, 141–42; Wilson's Latin American interventionism, 133–37
Empress of China, 97
Englebrecht, Helmuth C., 173
English, Robert, 319

Eritrea, 222
Erving, George, 42
Essex (American merchant ship), 31–32, 79
Estonia, 200
Ethiopia, 175, 182, 222
Europe: Iraq War, 353–54; League of Armed Neutrality, 6; postwar economic situation, 226; Reagan and, 302–4. *See also specific nations*
European Advisory Commission (EAC), 203, 220
European Defense Community (EDC), 232
European Economic Community (Common Market), 264
European Economic Cooperation, committee of, 227
European Recovery Program, 226–27
European rivalries, American Revolution and, 6–7
Evil empire speech (Reagan), 296
Ex Com (Executive Committee of the National Security Council), 256–57
Expansionism, 89–93. *See also* Empire
Export-Import Bank, 192
Exum, Andrew, 361–62

Fahd, King, 333, 334
Fallows, James, 298
Far East Commission, 238
Faure, Edgar, 247
Federalists, 16
Feith, Douglas, 344
Ferdinand, Archduke Francis, 145
Ferdinand VII, King, 42–43, 49
Fessler, Pamela, 336
"Fifty-four forty or fight," 59–62
Le Figaro, 312
Fillmore, Millard, 99
Finland, 154, 168, 200, 222–23, 228, 390n16

First Gulf War: Bush seeks support for, 333, 334–36; Bush's policies during, 336–39; casualties, 338; Hussein seizes Kuwait, 332–34; origins of, 330–32
Fish, Hamilton, 85, 86, 88
Fishing rights, 40, 96
Five Year Plan, 169
Fletcher, Henry P., 137
Florida, 5–6, 10, 26–27, 41–42
Florida (Confederate cruiser), 83–84, 86
FOA (Foreign Operations Administration), 227, 232
Foch, Ferdinand, 156
Fontaine, Andre, 304
Ford, Gerald, 247, 258, 262
Ford Motor Company, 169
Foreign Affairs, 266, 306
Foreign Enlistment Act of 1819, 82, 86
Foreign markets, and commercial expansionism, 88–89
Foreign Operations Administration (FOA), 227, 232
Foreign Relations Committee (Senate), 85, 161–63, 176, 215, 335–36
Formosa (Taiwan), 240–41, 244, 275
Forrestal, James V., 212, 322
Fort George, 39
Fort Ross, 47
Fort Sumter, 75
Foster, John W., 110
Four Nations' Declaration. *See* Declaration of Four Nations on General Security
Four-Power Control Council, 223
Fourteen Points, 153–54, 156
Fourth Neutrality Law, 185–86
France: alliance with during American Revolution, 2–5; Big Four summit, 250; Canning and, 54–55; China

and, 100–101, 104; Geneva Convention of 1954, 274–75; German invasion of, 186; in Indochina, 272–74; Iraq no-fly zone, 341; League of Nations negotiations, 159; Louisiana Purchase, 25–27; NATO and, 264–65; Panama Canal, 90; "Quasi-War" with, 22–24; recognition of American independence, 10; in Russia, 155; Spain and, 5; Suez crisis, 323; U.S. Civil War and, 76; Vietnam War, 395n21; World Disarmament Conference, 168; World War I, 145–46, 156, 157; World War II, 181–82, 183; Yalta conference, 389n7
Franco, Francisco, 176
Frankfurter Allgemeine Zeitung, 304
Franklin, Benjamin, 3–4, 7, 8–9
Franks, Tommy, 356, 360
Freeman, Charles, 338–39
Free silver movement, 123
Frémont, John C., 65, 69
French and Indian War, 1–2
French Indochina. *See* Cambodia; Indochina; Laos; Vietnam War
French Revolution, 16
Frick, Henry Clay, 161
Frontier thesis, 109
Fulbright, J. William, 253
Fulbright Resolution, 213
Fur seal dispute, 96

Gallatin, Albert, 39, 40
Gallup Poll, 174, 184, 289
Galvez, Bernardo de, 6
Gandhi, Rajiv, 358
Gardoqui, Don Diego de, 10, 14
Garthoff, Raymond, 311
Gates, Robert, 319
Gemayel, Amin, 326
General and Complete Disarmament, 260

General Assembly, UN, 243, 249–50, 259
General Electric, 169
Genesis of the World War (Barnes), 174
Genet, Edmond, 16–18
Geneva Convention of 1954, 272, 274–75
Geneva summit, 247–48, 311
Genscher, Hans-Dietrich, 303, 304
German-American Bund, 180
German Democratic Republic. *See* East Germany
German People's Government, 156
Germany: annexation of Austria and part of Czechoslovakia, 180; *Blitzkrieg* (lightning war), 186; China and, 103, 141; defiance of the Versailles Treaty, 175; invasion of Poland, 184; invasion of Soviet Union, 200; occupation of, 220, 221, 223–24; as priority of U.S. and Great Britain, 198–99; reparations, 159–60, 206, 221–22, 224; Spanish Civil War and, 176; submarine warfare, 148–50, 151–53, 189–90; Treaty of Versailles, 157–60, 175; Tripartite Pact, 179, 191–92, 193; Venezuela and, 130; "war guilt" clause, 160; World Disarmament Conference, 168; World War I, 145–46, 151, 156; World War II, 180–84, 207–9; Yalta conference, 205–6. *See also* Hitler, Adolf
Gerry, Elbridge, 23
Gibraltar, 5
Gillespie, Archibald, 69
Glaspie, April, 331
Glass, Andrew J., 312
GLCMs (ground-launched cruise missiles), 306–7
Global Threat Reduction Initiative, 357
Goebbels, Joseph, 203

Golan Heights, 325
Goldberg, Arthur, 285–86
Goldwater, Barry, 282
Goluchowski, Count, 104–5
Gomulka, Wladyslaw, 248
Good Neighbor policy, 170–73
Goodwin, Doris Kearns, 15
Gorbachev, Mikhail: arms control, 311–15; background, 311; end of the Cold War, 318–19; First Gulf War, 337; George H. W. Bush and, 316–18; on the INF Treaty, 295; Reagan, 310–16
Gore, Albert, 344
Grand Alliance, 197–200, 202–5
Grant, Ulysses S., 87, 88, 90, 91
Gray, Robert, 39
Great Britain: accommodation of U.S. in Western Hemisphere, 126; belligerent rights, 77–78; Big Four summit, 250; blacklist, 150–51; building of ships for the Confederacy, 82–86; Canning and, 51–54; China and, 98, 100–101, 104, 141; class divisions over U.S. Civil War, 77; Clayton-Bulwer Treaty, 90–91, 126; cooperation with in the Far East, 138; Dunkirk, 186; F. Roosevelt and, 186–87; impressment issue, 18, 30–31, 32, 36, 369n25; Iraq no-fly zone, 341; Iraq War, 347–48; Jay's Treaty, 19–21; League of Nations negotiations, 159; management of colonies, 1–2; Monroe Doctrine and, 54–56; Native Americans and, 34; noncolonization principle and, 48; Nootka Sound, 15–16; nuclear weapons and, 307; Oregon question, 58–62; Quadruple Alliance, 49; recognition of American independence, 10; Soviet Union and, 183; Suez crisis, 323; tensions with during Early Republic, 18–19; transfer of destroyers to, 187; *Trent* affair, 81; Turkey and Greece, 226; U.S. Civil War and, 76–77; Venezuela and, 130; Venezuelan Crisis, 94–96; Vietnam War, 395n21; on the western frontier, 12–13; Wilson and, 150–51; World War I, 145–46, 149, 156; World War II, 181–82, 186. *See also* Blair, Tony
Great Depression, 165–66
Greater East Asia Co-prosperity Sphere, 190–91, 192
Great Lakes, 35, 37–38
Greece, 182, 204–5, 225–26
Greenfield, Meg, 305
Greenland, 189
Greer (destroyer), 189
Grenada, 301–2
Gresham, Walter Q., 94
Grew, Joseph C., 190, 192
Grey, Edward, 150
Ground-launched cruise missiles (GLCMs), 306–7
Guam, 119, 122
Guantanamo Bay, Cuba, 129–30
Guatemala, 132, 300

Haig, Alexander, 296–97, 299, 300, 301
Hainan, 190
Haiti, 128, 133–34, 171
Hamilton, Alexander, 15–17
Harper, John A., 34
Harriman, Averell, 200, 207, 285, 286, 306
Harris, Townsend, 99, 101–2
Harrison, Benjamin, 92–93, 109–10
Harrison, William Henry, 34
Hawaii, 91–93, 121–22
Hay, John, 119, 138–41
Hayes, Rutherford B., 90, 102
Hearst, William R., 111, 168
Held, Robert, 304

Index   429

Helsinki Accord, 267–70, 297, 308
Hemingway, Ernest, 173
Herrera, José Joaquín de, 66–67
Herter, Christian A., 250
High Seas Accord, 263
Hiroshima, bombing of, 208
Hitchcock, Gilbert M., 163–64
Hitler, Adolf: death of, 207; opinion of the U.S., 181; rise of, 165, 174–75; speech in the Reichstag, 165; World Disarmament Conference, 168. *See also* Germany; World War II
Hmong people, 292
Hoar, George F., 120
Hoare-Laval plan, 175
Ho Chi Minh, 272, 273, 278, 285, 287
Hoffmann, Stanley, 305
Hofstadter, Richard, 109
Holy Alliance, 371n12
Honduras, 132, 300
Hong Kong, 98, 100
Hoover, Herbert, 163, 166–67, 171
Hopkins, Harry, 200, 390n15
Hotze, Henry, 82
House, Edward M., 147, 150, 153–54, 156, 163
House Committee on Foreign Affairs, 215, 335
House Committee on Un-American Activities, 180
House of Representatives, U.S., 20–21
Hudson's Bay Company, 58, 62
Huerta, Victoriano, 135–36
Hull, Cordell: anticolonialism, 199; approach to foreign policy, 167–68; on German invasion of Soviet Union, 200; on international organization, 203; Japan and, 179, 191, 193–97; Latin America and, 171–72; on the Morgenthau Plan, 202; neutrality legislation, 175, 183; Reciprocal Trade Agreement Act, 168; on Soviet revolutionary activities, 170; Soviet Union and, 203; Spanish Civil War and, 176; United Nations, 212–13, 215
Humphrey, Hubert, 285
Hungary, 181, 222, 228, 248
Hussein, Saddam: First Gulf War, 330–32, 337–38; George W. Bush and, 344, 347; Hussein Doctrine, 325; Iran-Iraq War, 327–30; rise of, 324; seizure of Kuwait, 332–34; weapons inspections, 340, 341, 348
Hussein Doctrine, 325

IAEA (International Atomic Energy Agency), 259, 340, 352–53, 359–60
ICBM (intercontinental ballistic missiles), 234, 256, 260, 261–62
Immigration, from China, 102
Imperialism, 89–90, 119–21, 122–23. *See also* Expansionism
Import-Export Bank, 172
Impressment issue, 18, 30–31, 32, 36, 369n25
INC (Iraqi National Congress), 342
Independence, 2–3, 10–11
India, 358
Indiana (battleship), 110
Indirect claims, 85–86
Indochina, 193, 272–75. *See also* Cambodia; Laos; Vietnam War
INF (Intermediate Nuclear Force) Treaty, 313–15
The Influence of Sea Power upon History, 1660–1783 (Mahan), 108
Inter-American Development Bank, 255
Intercontinental ballistic missiles (ICBM), 234, 256, 260, 261–62
Intermediate Nuclear Force (INF) Treaty, 313–15

Intermediate-range ballistic missiles (IRBM), 234
International Atomic Development Authority, 217
International Atomic Energy Agency (IAEA), 259, 340, 352–53, 359–60
International Commission on Control and Supervision, 290
International Court of Justice, 216
International Harvester, 169
International Labor Organization, 168
International police power doctrine, 135
Inter-oceanic Canal Commission, 90
Iowa (battleship), 110
Iran, 324–25, 329–30, 359–60. *See also* Iran-Iraq War
Iran-Contra affair, 309–10, 329
Iran hostage crisis, 324–25
Iranian commercial airline incident, 330
Iranian Revolution, 324
Iran-Iraq War, 309, 327–30
Iraq, 324–25, 328–30, 339–42, 344–45. *See also* First Gulf War; Iran-Iraq War; Iraq War
Iraqi National Congress (INC), 342
Iraq Liberation Act, 342, 344
Iraq War: Bush's policies during, 352–56; costs and casualties of, 361; end of, 360–61; Europe, 353–54; events leading to, 349–51; Great Britain, 347–48; insurgency, 360–61; linked with war on terror, 356–57; occupation, 356–57
IRBM (intermediate-range ballistic missiles), 234
Iron Blood and Profits (Seldes), 173
Iron Curtain speech (Churchill), 211, 225
Israel, 322–26, 331. *See also* Arab-Israeli conflict
Isthmian Canal Act, 127

Italian miles, 371n7
Italian Somaliland, 222
Italy: indemnities, 222; invasion of Ethiopia, 175; League of Nations negotiations, 159; nuclear weapons and, 307; occupation of Albania, 181–82; Spanish Civil War and, 176; Tripartite Pact, 191; World War I, 146, 156, 157. *See also* Mussolini, Benito
Izvestia, 306

Jackson, Andrew, 35–36, 37, 41–42
Jackson State University, 289
"Jacobins Clubs," 16
Japan: commercial expansionism, U.S., 98–100, 101–2; commercial expansion of, 97, 102–4; conflict over Manchuria, 166; deterioration of relations with, 190–94; embargoes against, 192; German and Italian pacts with, 175; Harris and, 101–2; Hull and, 179, 191, 193–97; invasion of China, 177–79; Korea and, 102–3, 243–45; League of Nations negotiations, 159; negotiations with prior to Pearl Harbor attack, 192–94, 195–97; "New Order," 179, 190; occupation of, 237–38; opening of, 98–100; Russo-Japanese War, 141–43; in Siberia, 155; southern expansion, 194–95; surrender of, 208–9; Tripartite Pact, 191–92; Vietnam and, 272; war with China, 103; World War I, 146, 157
Japanese-American commercial treaty of 1911, 179
Jay, John, 5, 7, 8–9, 14, 19–21
Jay's Treaty, 19–21
Jay Treaty, 38, 96
Jefferson, Thomas: on America's separation from Europe, 46; on

expansionism, 57; First Inaugural Address, 15; on French Revolutionary wars, 16–17; Louisiana Purchase, 24–28; neutral rights and, 32; "peaceable coercion," 33; on recognition of newly independent nations, 50; as secretary of state, 15–16
Jeffersonian Republicans, 16
Jerusalem, 331
Jiang Jieshi. *See* Chiang Kai-shek
Jim Lehrer News Hour, 344
Joffe, Joseph, 353
Johnson, Andrew, 88
Johnson, Hiram, 169
Johnson, Lyndon: arms control, 259; Latin America, 254–55; peace negotiations, 285; San Antonio formula, 285–86; Soviet Union and, 258; Vietnam War, 279, 281–82, 284, 291, 292
Johnson Act, 168
Johnson-Clarendon convention, 84–85
Joint Defense Production Committee, 188
Jones, David C., 336
Joseph II, Emperor, 6
J. P. Morgan, 148

Kadar, Janos, 248
Kaiser, Robert, 363
Kalakaua, King, 92
Karnow, Stanley, 292–93
Karzai, Hamid, 346, 362
Katsura, Count, 143
Kearny (destroyer), 189–90
Kearny, Stephen W., 69
Kearsarge, U.S.S., 83
Kellogg-Briand Pact, 178
Kennan, George F., 165, 219, 304–5, 306, 322, 390n19
Kennedy, John F.: Alliance for Progress, 251–52, 254, 255; assassination of, 254, 281; Bay of Pigs invasion, 252–53; Cronkite interview, 271; Cuban Missile Crisis, 234, 256–58; Khrushchev and, 250–51; Laos and, 277; Limited Test Ban Treaty, 234–35, 259; Vietnam and, 279–80; in West Berlin, 237
Kennedy, Robert, 253
Kent State University, 289
Khalilzad, Zalmay, 342
Khamene'i, Ayatollah Ali, 359
Khan, Yahya, 266
Khmer Rouge, 292
Khomeini, Ayatollah Ruhollah, 324, 327
Khrushchev, Nikita: Berlin crisis, 249–51; Cuban Missile Crisis, 234, 255–58; Geneva summit, 247–48; Kennedy and, 250–51; Laos and, 277; Limited Test Ban Treaty, 234–35, 259
Kiesinger, Kurt Georg, 268
Kimball, William W., 116
Kim Il Sung, 241, 245–47
King, E. J., 189
King, Ernest, 198
King, Mackenzie, 188
King Cotton, 76–77
Kingdom of the Two Sicilies, 6
Kirkpatrick, Jeane, 300
Kissinger, Henry, 246, 267, 290, 323, 349, 357
Knox, Frank, 187
Knox, Henry, 16–17
Knox, Philander C., 132
Koenitz, Karl, 207
Kohl, Helmut, 312
Korea: commercial airliner incident, 305; commercial expansion, 97, 102–4; conflict in, 231–32, 241–47; relations with China and Japan, 102–3, 243–45; Russia and,

103, 142. *See also* North Korea; South Korea
Kosygin, Alexei, 258
Krass, Allan, 261
Krauthammer, Charles, 308, 344
Kristallnacht, 181
Kristol, Irving, 319
Kruger, Paul, 95
Kuang Hsu, 139
Kurusu, Saburo, 195–96
Kuwait, 329–34, 337–38

Laconia, sinking of, 152
Laird Brothers, 83
Lake Champlain, 35, 37–38
Lake Huron, 38
Lake of the Woods, 38, 370n32
Lake Ontario, 37–38
Lansdale, Edward, 252–53
Lansing, Robert, 133, 146–50, 154–55, 162
Laos, 273, 275, 276, 277–78, 287, 292
Larkin, Thomas O., 65, 69
Latin America: Alliance for Progress, 251–52, 254, 255; Cold War in, 251–55; Good Neighbor policy, 170–73; Wilson's interventionism, 133–37. *See also* Monroe Doctrine
Latvia, 200
League of Armed Neutrality, 6
League of Nations: debates over, 160–64; Italian invasion of Ethiopia, 175; Japan and, 166; on the Japanese invasion of China, 178; vs. Monroe Doctrine, 45, 159, 163–64; opposition to, 161; United Nations, 213; Wilson and, 158–59
League of Nations Commission, 159
League to Enforce Peace, 384n12
Lebanon, 325–27
Le Duan, 284, 285
Le Duc Tho, 290
Lee, Arthur, 3

LeMay, Curtis, 257
Lend-lease program, 187–88, 191–92, 200–201
Leopard (British frigate), 31
Lesseps, Ferdinand de, 90
Lewis and Clark explorations, 39
Liaison Conference, 191
Libby, I. Lewis (Scooter), 342
Libya, 222, 315
Life magazine, 212, 219, 258
Li Hung-chang, 103
Liliuokalani, Queen, 92–93
Limited Test Ban Treaty, 234–35, 259
Limited war by proxy, 309
Lincoln, Abraham, 75, 78–80
Lippmann, Walter, 293
Lithuania, 154, 200, 388n24
Litvinov, Maxim, 169–70, 183
Liverpool, Lord, 53
Livingston, Robert R., 25–26
Lloyd George, David, 145, 151, 157–58, 159
Lodge, Henry Cabot: on Cuba, 111; on expansionism, 109; on the League of Nations, 158, 161, 163–64, 385n29; Mahan and, 108; Spanish-American War, 117; Vietnam and, 281, 286–87
Lome, Dupuy de, 112
London Daily Mail, 303
London Times, 82, 303
Long Telegram (Kennan), 219
Lon Nol, 288, 292
Louisiana, 13
Louisiana Purchase, 24–28
Louisville Courier-Journal, 107
Louis XVI, King, 3, 16
Louis XVIII, King, 49
L'Ouverture, Toussaint, 25
Lovett, Robert, 322
Ludlow Amendment, 179–80
Lusitania, sinking of, 149–50
Lyons, Lord, 81

MacArthur, Douglas, 198, 237, 238, 242–44
Machado, Gerardo, 171
Macon's Bill No. 2, 33
Madero, Francisco I., 135
Madison, James, 27, 29, 33, 53
Madrid Conference, 339
Magsaysay, Ramon, 275
Mahan, Alfred Thayer, 107, 108–9
Maine (battleship), 112–13, 114
Malik, Yakov A., 242, 244
Al-Maliki, Nouri, 361
Manchuria, 166, 238–39
Mandate System, 215
Manifest Destiny: "all-Mexico" movement, 71; California, 64–66; Mexican American War, 66–73; new, 108–10; Oregon, 58–59; origins of, 61; Republican Party and, 88, 107–8; Texas, 59–62; Texas annexation, 62–64
Mann, Thomas C., 254, 255
Manning, David, 352
Mansfield, Mike, 265
Mao Tse-tung, 239, 240
Marcy, William, 78
Marines, U.S., in Lebanon, 326
Maritime Canal Company, 90, 126
Markey, Edward J., 307
Marquis of Rockingham, 7
Marshall, George C., 198, 224, 226, 239–40, 322
Marshall, John, 23
Marshall Plan, 226–27, 228
Martin, Edwin A., 252
Masaryk, Thomás, 155
Mason, James M., 80–82, 84
Massachusetts (battleship), 110
Massive retaliation, 299
Matlock, Jack, 317
Matsuoka, Yosuke, 167, 191, 193–94
Maumee River, 19
Mazarr, Michael, 358
McAdoo, William G., 148

McCain, John, 347
McFarlane, Robert, 310
McKinley, William: Cuba and, 112–14, 129; election of 1900, 123; foreign policy, 110; Panama Canal, 126; Spanish-American War, 114–19
McNamara, Robert, 257, 271–72, 285, 306
Meiji Restoration, 102
Mellon, Andrew W., 161
Merchant marine, 11, 30, 190
Merchants of Death (Englebrecht), 173
Metternich, Prince, 49, 55
Mexican American War, 67–73
Mexico: California and, 65; claims of American citizens against, 63, 64; expropriation of foreign-owned property, 172; independence of, 49, 56; movement for annexation of, 71, 72; Polk and, 62–63, 66–67; reasons for war with, 63; Texas and, 62–63; Wilson and, 135–37; Zimmermann and, 152
Middle East: Arab Spring, 360–62; Carter's policies toward Iraq and Iran, 323–25; Clinton and containing Iraq, 339–42; Eisenhower and, 322–23; introduction to, 321; origins of Arab-Israeli conflict, 322–24; Reagan and Lebanon, 325–27; Reagan and the Iran-Iraq War, 327–30. *See also* First Gulf War
Middleton, Henry, 48
Midway Island, 89, 90, 122
Mikolajczyk, Stanislaw, 205
Military aid, to South Vietnam, 279–80
Military Armistice Commission, 245
Military Staff Committee, 216
MIRVs (multiple independently targeted reentry vehicles), 262

Mississippi River, 5, 7, 9–10, 13–14, 21
Mobile, Alabama, 28
Modus vivendi, 131–32
Molotov, Vyacheslav M., 183, 203, 222
Molotov-Ribbentrop Pact of 1939, 388n24
Le Monde, 304
Monroe, James: on Canada, 34; Canning's proposal and, 53–54; Florida and, 41; Louisiana Purchase, 26; message to Congress, 45, 46; as minister to Britain, 32; noninterference principle, 46–47; recognition policy, 49–51; as secretary of state, 33; Treaty of Ghent, 36. *See also* Monroe Doctrine
Monroe Doctrine: Canning and Monroe, 51–54; as collective defense system, 172; French canal project and, 90; F. Roosevelt and, 171; Great Britain and, 54–56; introduction to, 45–47; Latin American view of, 170; League of Nations and, 159, 163–64; noncolonization, 46, 47–48, 56; noninterference, 46–47, 48–49, 54, 94–95, 171; Platt Amendment, 130; Polk's reference to, 66; reception of, 54–56; recognition of Spanish colonies, 49–51; Roosevelt Corollary, 128–31, 133; Venezuelan Crisis, 93–96
Montreux Convention, 225
Morgenthau, Henry Jr., 202
Morgenthau Plan, 202
Morocco, 10
Moscow conference, 203, 205, 225
Most-favored-nation status, 98, 99, 100, 102, 138
Muhlenberg, Frederick, 20–21

Multiple independently targeted reentry vehicles (MIRVs), 262
Munger, William, 89
Munich agreement, 180–82
Munitions sales, 147–48
Mussolini, Benito, 165, 174, 180–81
Mutual deterrence, 234
Mutual Security Agency, 232
Myers, Richard, 352

Nagasaki, bombing of, 208
Nagy, Imre, 248
Napoleon III, 76
Al-Nasser, Gamel Abdul, 323
National Association of Evangelicals, 296
National Council of National Reconciliation and Concord, 290
National Intelligence Council, 359
Nationalism, 272, 284, 325
Nationalist Chinese. *See* Chiang Kai-shek
National Liberation Front (NLF), 279, 281, 286–87, 396n25
National Security Council, 350
National Security Decision Directive 114, 321, 328
National Security Strategy, U.S., 348
National Socialist Party. *See* Nazi Party
Native Americans, 18–19, 34, 36–37, 41
NATO (North Atlantic Treaty Organization), 230–33, 264–65, 305–6
Naturalization laws, 30, 369n25
Naval battles, 35, 37–38
Naval blockades, 32, 78–80
Naval building programs, 166–67
Naval Intelligence, 195, 388n17
Navy, U.S., 90, 115–16, 125–26, 135, 189
Navy Department, creation of, 23
Nazi Party, 175

Index   **435**

Neoconservatives, 315, 344
Neo-imperialism, European, 109
Netherlands, 10, 186, 307
Netherlands East Indies. *See* Dutch East Indies
Neutrality: Adams on, 1; during Early Republic, 16–18; in French Revolutionary wars, 16–18; move away from in World War II, 186–90; neutrality legislation after World War I, 173–77; neutral obligations during the Civil War, 82–86
Neutrality Acts, 174–75, 176–77, 182–83, 185–86
Neutral obligations, 76, 82–86
Neutral rights, 32–33
New Granada, 90
New Manifest Destiny, 108–10
"New Order" (Japan), 179, 190
New Orleans, 21–22, 24, 25–26, 35–36
New Panama Canal Company, 127
Newsweek, 305
"New world order," 339
New York Daily News, 298
New Yorker, 304, 332
New York Herald, 71, 111–12
New York Journal, 111–12, 113
New York Journal of Commerce, 111–12, 117–18
New York Morning News, 61
New York Sun, 71, 111–12
New York Times, 111–12, 284, 286, 287, 312
New York Tribune, 111–12
New York World, 111–12
New Zealand, 395n21
Ngo Dinh Diem, 275, 276, 278–81
Ngo Dinh Nhu, 276, 280
Nguyen Cao Ky, 281
Nguyen Thi Binh, 287
Nguyen Van Thieu, 281, 286–87, 290, 396n39

Nicaragua, 90, 126–28, 132–33, 171, 300, 309–10
Nine Power Pact, 178
Nitze, Paul, 253, 317–18
Nixon, Richard: on bombing of North Vietnam, 271; Brezhnev and, 263; Cambodia and, 288–89; China and, 266–67; Middle East and, 323–24; North Korea and, 246; Soviet Union and, 258; Vietnamization, 287–89, 396n33; Vietnam War, 286–87, 289–90
NLF (National Liberation Front), 279, 281, 286–87, 396n25
Nobel Peace Prize, 383n37
No-fly zones, 339–40, 341
Nomura, Kichisaburo, 193, 194–95
Nonaggression pacts, 183–84, 200
Noncolonization principle, 46, 47–48, 56
Noninterference principle, 46–47, 48–49, 54, 94–95, 171
Non-Proliferation Treaty (NPT), 259, 297, 358
Nootka Sound, 15
Norodom Sihanouk, Prince, 288
North, Oliver, 310
North Atlantic Council, 232, 233
North Atlantic Treaty, 5, 230–31
North Atlantic Treaty Organization (NATO), 230–33, 264–65, 305–6
North Korea, 358–59
North Korea and the Bomb (Mazarr), 358
North Sea, 384n6
North Vietnam, bombing of, 285–86, 290. *See also* Vietnam War
North West Company of Montreal, 39
Northwest Territory, 18–19
Norway, 186
NPT (Non-Proliferation Treaty), 259, 297, 358
NSC 68, 231–32

Nuclear arms control, 306–8
Nuclear Suppliers Group, 357
Nuclear Test Ban Treaty, 297
Nuclear weapons: arms control, 306–8, 357–58; arms race, 234–35; China and, 358; inspections of, 340, 341, 348, 352–53, 359–60; international control of, 217–18; Iran and, 359–60; Iraq and, 351, 354; North Korea and, 358–59; Obama and, 357–60; proliferation, 343; Soviet Union and, 231, 251; test ban, 259–60; use of in Japan, 208
Nuclear-Weapons-Free Zones, 259–60
Nunn, Sam, 336
Nuremberg Laws, 175
Nye, Gerald P., 174
Nye Committee Hearings, 174

OAS (Organization of American States), 172, 255
Obama, Barack: Afghanistan, 362; Arab Spring, 360–62; arms control, 357–58; Middle East interests, 361; on nuclear weapons, 343; nuclear weapons and, 357–60
Offner, John, 110
Oil embargo, 324
"Old China Trade," 97–98
Olney, Richard, 94–95, 112
Onis, Don Luis de, 41–42
On-site inspections, 260, 261
OPEC (Organization of Petroleum Exporting Countries), 324, 331–32
Open Door policy, 104, 137–39
Operation Crossroads, 217
Operation Desert Fox, 341
Operation Desert Shield, 335
Operation Magic, 195, 388n17
Operation Mongoose, 253
Operation Overlord, 199, 204
Operation Torch, 199

Operation Urgent Fury, 302
Opium War of 1839–1842, 98
Orders-in-Council, 32–33, 34
Ordinance of 1787, 19
Oregon, 39–40, 58–62
Oregon (battleship), 110
Oregon Provisional Government, 58
Organization of American States (OAS), 172, 255
Organization of Petroleum Exporting Countries (OPEC), 324, 331–32
Orlando, Vittorio, 157–58
O'Sullivan, John L., 61
Oswald, Richard, 7, 8–9
Outer Space Treaty, 260

Page, Walter H., 147
Pago Pago harbor, 91
Pahlevi, Shah Mohammad, 324
Paine, Christopher, 298
Paine, Thomas, 1, 2
Pakistan, 275, 362, 395n21
Palestine Liberation Organization (PLO), 326, 327
Palmerston, Viscount, 77
Panama, 127, 128
Panama Canal, 90, 126–29, 171, 254–55
Panama Canal Company, 126–27
Pan-Arab Charter, 325
Panay incident, 178–79
Panic of 1873, 102
Panic of 1893, 94
"Paper blockades," 32
Paredes, Mariano, 66, 68
Paris cease-fire agreement, 290
Paris Peace Accords, 258, 291
Pathet Lao, 277, 292
Patterson, Robert, 212
"Peaceable coercion," 33
Peace Corps, 252
Peace movements, 173
Peace negotiations: American Revolution, 8–9; Vietnam War,

284–87, 289–91; World War I, 156–57
Peace of Amiens, 25
Pearl Harbor, 92, 179, 190–91
Peña y Peña, Manuel de la, 66, 70
People's Republic of China, 231, 240. *See also* China
Perkins, Bradford, 34, 37, 126
Perkins, Dexter, 48
Perkins, Francis, 168
Permanent Joint Board of Defense, 188
Perry, Matthew, 99–100
Pershing, John J., 137, 153
Peterhoff, 80
Pew Research poll, 351
Pham Van Dong, 285
Philippines, 116, 117, 118–29, 133, 275
Phoumi Nosavan, 277
Pichon, Louis-Andre, 22, 26
Pierce, Franklin, 99
Pinckney, Charles C., 22–23
Pinckney, Thomas, 21–22
Pinckney's Treaty, 21–22
Pinkney, William, 32
Pittman, Key, 176
Plan of Treaties of 1776, 4, 18
Platt, Orville H., 120–21, 129
Platt Amendment, 129–30, 171
PLO (Palestine Liberation Organization), 326, 327
Podhoretz, Norman, 342
Poindexter, John, 309–10
Poland, 154, 181–84, 186, 204, 206, 216, 228, 304, 390n15
Polignac, Prince de, 54–55
Polish Provisional Government of National Unity, 206
Political isolationism, 173–75
Polk, James: California, 62–63, 64–66; Mexico and, 62–63, 66–67; Monroe Doctrine, 66; Oregon, 59–62; Texas, 63–64; Trist and, 72; war with Mexico, 57, 66–71
Polk corollary, 66
Popular Front strategy, 180
Porter, Peter B., 34
Portugal, 6, 264
Post–World War I era: F. Roosevelt's approach to foreign policy, 167–69; Good Neighbor policy, 170–73; Hoover and the Far East, 166–67; introduction to, 165–66; Japanese invasion of China, 177–79; neutrality legislation, 173–77; Soviet Union and diplomacy, 169–70
Potsdam conference, 221–22
Potsdam Declaration, 208
Powell, Colin L., 315, 333, 338–39, 345–46, 347, 350, 353, 354, 359
Powers, Francis Gary, 250, 261
Pravda, 217, 308
Preemption, doctrine of, 348–49
Prevention of Nuclear War Accord, 263
Princip, Gavrilo, 145
Prisoners of war, 244–45
Privateering, 78
Proclamation of 1763, 1
Proctor, Redfield, 113
Project for the New American Century, 342
Protectorates, 128
Prussia, 6, 10, 49
Public opinion: of empire, 122–23; on German invasion of Poland, 184; on Iraq and the 9/11 attacks, 351; on Iraq War, 353–54, 355; on neutrality, 174; on the prospect of World War II, 179–80; on the Spanish Civil War, 176; Vietnam War, 289; on World War I, 147
Pueblo incident, 246
Puerto Rico, 116, 118, 119, 128, 133
Pulitzer, Joseph, 111

Punch, 76
Punitive expedition, 137
Putin, Vladimir, 345

Quadripartite Treaty, 267–70
Quadruple Alliance, 49, 55, 371n12
"Quarantine Speech" (F. Roosevelt), 178
"Quasi-War" with France, 22–24
Quebec Act, 8

Rabin, Yitzhak, 327
Raccoon (British sloop), 39
Radio Free Europe, 249
Randolph, Edmund, 16–17
Rapid Deployment Joint Task Force, 325
Reagan, Ronald: arms control, 311–15; Carter and, 299–300; Central America and, 300–302, 309–10; Chamber of Commerce speech, 296; critics of, 304–6, 308–9, 315; election of, 295; end of the Cold War, 315–16, 318–19; Europe and, 302–4; evil empire speech, 296; Gorbachev and, 310–16; ideological approach to Cold War, 304–6; introduction to, 295–97; Iran-Contra affair, 309–10, 329; Iran-Iraq War, 327–30; Iraq and, 328–30; Lebanon, 325–27; military buildup, 297–99; Reagan Doctrine, 308–10, 315; rhetoric vs. action, 299–300; Strategic Arms Reduction Talks (START), 307; on wars, 295
Reagan Doctrine, 308–10, 315
The Real War (Nixon), 271
Reciprocal Trade Agreement Act, 168
Reciprocity, 104–5
Reciprocity treaty with Hawaii, 91–92
Recognition policy, 49–51, 56, 171, 240

Reconcentration policy in Cuba, 110–11
Red Scare, 155
Reed, Thomas B., 123
Reed, Thomas C., 306
Religion, public opinion on the Soviet Union and, 169–70
Remarque, Erich, 173
"Remember the Maine," 113
Reparations, Germany and, 159–60, 206, 221–22, 224
Reparations Commission, 160
Republican Party, 88, 107–8, 122, 161, 295
Republic of Korea, 241–42, 245. *See also* Korea
Republic of Vietnam. *See* South Vietnam
Resolution 687, 338
Reston, James, 312
Reuben James (destroyer), 189–90
Revisionist history, 173–74
Reykjavik summit, 312–13
Rhee, Syngman, 244, 245. *See also* Korea
Ribbentrop, Joachim von, 184
Rice, Condoleezza, 344, 349–50, 351, 353, 355
"Right of deposit," 21–22
Right of extraterritoriality, 98, 101
Rio Pact, 230
Ritter, Scott, 340
Rockhill, W. W., 138
"Rocking chair doctrine," 255
Rogue states, 362–63
Rome-Berlin Axis, 175
Roosevelt, Franklin D.: address to Hitler and Mussolini, 182–83; anticolonialism, 199; approach to foreign policy, 167–69; Canada and, 172; Churchill and, 188–89, 198–200, 202, 388n22; death of, 207; Declaration by the United Nations, 198; Good Neighbor

policy, 171; Great Britain and, 186–87; Indochina and, 273; on international organization, 213; Japan and, 179; negotiations with Hitler, 180–81; neutrality legislation, 174–75, 183, 185–86, 190; on postwar occupations, 390n17; public isolationist position, 177; "Quarantine Speech," 178; reaction to Tripartite Pact, 191–92; Spanish Civil War and, 176; Tehran conference, 203–4; war preparations, 186; Yalta conference, 205–7

Roosevelt, Theodore: Dominican Republic, 131–32; election of 1900, 123; international police power doctrine, 135; Mahan and, 108; naval power, 125–26; Nobel Peace Prize, 383n37; Panama Canal, 127; Platt Amendment, 129–30; Roosevelt Corollary, 128–33, 170; Russo-Japanese War, 142–43; Samoa, 122; Spanish-American War, 115–16, 117; State of the Union address, 125; on Wilson, 157

Roosevelt Corollary, 128–33, 170
Root, Elihu, 125, 129, 146
Rostow, Eugene, 306
Rule of 1756, 79
Rumania: indemnities, 222; Soviet Union and, 221, 223, 228; World War I, 146; World War II, 182, 183, 204–5
Rumsfeld, Donald, 329, 342, 344–45, 347, 352, 353–54, 356, 360
Rush, Richard, 37–38, 39, 40, 48, 52–53, 54
Rush-Bagot agreement, 38
Rusk, Dean, 317
Russell, Earl, 77, 79, 81, 82, 83–84
Russell, John, 75

Russia: Allied intervention in, 154–55; Bolshevik revolution, 153; China and, 100–101, 103–4; claims in the Pacific Northwest, 47–48; Fourteen Points and, 153–54; Korea and, 103, 142; League of Armed Neutrality, 6; noncolonization principle and, 56; Quadruple Alliance, 49; Russo-Japanese War, 141–43; sale of Alaska, 89; World War I, 145, 157. *See also* Soviet Union
Russian American Company, 47
Russo-German War, 193–94
Russo-Japanese War, 141–43

Al-Sabah, Jaber al-Ahmed, 333
Sabra and Shatila refugee camps, 326
SAC (Strategic Air Command), 234
Sadat, Anwar, 323
Sagdeyev, Roald Z., 314
Sakharov, Andrei, 314
Salisbury, Lord, 95–96
SALT I (Strategic Arms Limitation) Treaty, 261–62, 297
SALT II, 262, 297, 311–12
Samoa, 91, 109, 121–22
Sampson, William T., 116
San Antonio formula, 285–86
Sandinistas, 310
San Domingo Improvement Company of New York, 131
San Francisco Conference, 215–16
San Jacinto (U.S. cruiser), 80
Santa Anna, Antonio López de, 67, 68, 69–70
Santo Domingo, 25, 88, 131, 255. *See also* Dominican Republic
Satellite treaties, 222–23
Saudi Arabia, 324, 333–34, 352
Savimbi, Jonas, 309, 315
Scheinman, Lawrence, 362–63
Schlesinger, James, 336
Schley, Winfield Scott, 116

Schmidt, Helmut, 303
Schomburgk, Robert, 94
Schuler, G. Henry, 332
Schurz, Carl, 88, 110
Schwarzkopf, Norman, 334, 337
Scott, Winfield, 35, 70
Scowcroft, Brent, 316, 333, 350 51
Scruggs, William L., 94
SDI (Strategic Defense Initiative), 307–8, 311, 313
Seabed Treaty, 260
Sea power, 108–9
SEATO (Southeast Asia Treaty Organization), 275–76
SEATO Council, 277
Second Cold War, 295
"Secret Downing Street Memo," 348
Secret treaties (World War I), 157
Sectional tensions, over Oregon, 61–62
Security Council, UN: creation of, 214–15; First Gulf War, 333, 335, 338; Iran and, 360; Iran-Iraq War, 328; Iraq and, 347, 351, 352, 353–54; Korean conflict, 242; Laos, 277; purpose of, 216; Suez crisis, 323
Seldes, George, 173
Selective service law, 230
Self-determination, 156–57, 199
Seminoles, 41
Senate, U.S.: imperialism debate, 119–21; League of Nations, 158–59, 160–62, 163–64; UN Charter, 216. *See also* Foreign Relations Committee (Senate)
September 11, 2001, terrorist attacks, 345–47
Serbia, 145
Seventh Congress of the Comintern, 170
Seventh Pan American Conference, 171
Seven Years' War, 1–2

Seward, William H., 76; Alaska, 89; China and, 102; Great Britain and, 78–79; Hawaii, 91; Manifest Destiny, 88; treaty with Nicaragua, 90; *Trent* affair, 81–82
Shafter, W. R., 116
Shales, Tom, 313
Shamir, Yitzhak, 331
SHAPE (Supreme Headquarters, Allied Powers in Europe), 232, 233
Al-Sharaa, Farouk, 339
Shelburne, Lord, 7, 9
Shelton, Henry B., 346
Shenandoah, 83–84, 86
Sherman, John, 110
Shipping, interference with, 18, 19–20, 31–32
Shufeldt, Robert, 103
Shultz, George, 310, 313–14, 315, 327, 328
"The Significance of the Frontier in American History" (Turner), 109
Silver Shirts, 180
Sinai Peninsula, 323–24
Sino-Japanese War, 103
Sino-Soviet treaty, 238–39
Six-Day War of 1967, 264, 323, 331
Slave revolts, 25
SLBM (submarine-launched ballistic missiles), 234, 261–62
Slidell, John, 66–67, 69, 80–82
Sloat, John D., 69
Smelser, Marshall, 32
Smith, Gerard, 306
Smith, Walter Bedell, 274
Social Democrats, 224
Socialist Unity Party, 224
Solidarity movement, 304
Somoza, Anastasio, 300
Sorensen, Theodore C., 253
Souphanouvong, 277
Southeast Asia: French intervention in Indochina, 272–74; Geneva Convention of 1954, 274–75;

Index **441**

introduction to, 271–72; Laos, 277–78; SEATO Alliance, 275–76; South Vietnam, 275, 276, 278–86, 291–92. *See also* Vietnam War
South-east Asia Collective Defense Treaty, 276
Southeast Asia Treaty Organization (SEATO), 275–76
South Korea, 395n21
South Manchuria Railway, 143
South Vietnam, 275, 276, 278–86, 291–92. *See also* Vietnam War
Souvanna Phouma, 277
Soviet Union: Atlantic Charter, 201; Baruch Plan, 217; Carter and, 258; Central and Eastern Europe, 220–22; conflict over Manchuria, 166; Czechoslovakia and, 268; diplomacy and, 169–70; expansionism, 211–12; France and, 183; German invasion of, 200; Hungary and, 248; ideological expansionism, 218–19; invasion of Afghanistan, 325; Iraq and, 328; joining war against Japan, 206–7, 208; Korea and, 241–42; Korean commercial airliner incident, 305; on the Marshall Plan, 228; nonrecognition of, 169; nuclear weapons, 231; occupation of Germany, 224, 229; on occupation of Japan, 222; postwar disagreement over atomic weapons, 217–18; relations with during World War II, 200–202; on reparations, 224; satellite nations, 228; support of sought by France and Great Britain, 183; U.S. overflights, 260–61; U.S.-Soviet quest for détente, 258–63; Warsaw Pact, 233–34; West Germany and, 268–69; Yamal natural gas pipeline, 302–3. *See also* Russia; Stalin, Josef

Spain: American Revolution and, 3, 5–6; Cuba and, 110–12, 113–14; Florida and, 10; Louisiana Purchase, 24–28; Nootka Sound, 15–16; Pinckney's Treaty, 21–22; recognition of independence, 10; recognition of rebellious colonies, 49–51; Transcontinental Treaty, 40–43; on the western frontier, 12–14. *See also* Spanish-American War
Spanish-American War: American intervention in Cuba, 112–14; annexation of Hawaii, 121–22; Cuban insurgency against Spain, 110–12; decision for war, 114–15; empire, creation of, 115–19; imperialism debate, 119–21
Spanish Civil War, 176
Spheres of interest, 97, 137–39, 220
Der Spiegel, 304
Springbok, 80
Sputnik, 234
Spy satellites, 261
Stalin, Josef: China and, 238–39; death of, 247; Five Year Plan, 169; nonaggression pact with Germany, 183–84; Poland and, 390n15; postwar policies, 225; rise of, 165; on a second front, 201–2; Tehran conference, 203–4; United Nations, 214–15; Yalta conference, 205–7. *See also* Soviet Union
Standard Oil Company, 172, 178
Standing Consultative Commission, 262
Standing Group on Cuba, 254
Stark, U.S.S., 330
START (Strategic Arms Reduction Talks), 307, 314, 317, 357–58
Star Wars. *See* Strategic Defense Initiative (SDI)
Stateless actors, 362–63
Status of Forces Agreement, 361

442 Index

St. Croix River, 38
Stettinius, Edward R., Jr., 215
Stevens, John L., 92–93
Stimson, Henry L., 166–67, 187, 196, 202
St. Lawrence River, 38
Stockton, Robert F., 69
Stoeckel, Baron, 89
Stoph, Willi, 269
Strategic Air Command (SAC), 234
Strategic Arms Limitation (SALT I) Treaty, 261–62, 297
Strategic Arms Reduction Talks (START), 307, 314, 317, 357–58
Strategic Defense Initiative (SDI), 307–8, 311, 313
Submarine-launched ballistic missiles (SLBM), 234, 261–62
Submarine warfare, 148–50, 151–53, 189–90
Suez crisis, 323
Sullivan and Cromwell law firm, 127
Sumner, Charles, 85, 89
Sun, 71
Supreme Court, U.S., 79–80
Supreme Headquarters, Allied Powers in Europe (SHAPE), 232, 233
Sussex, sinking of, 150, 152
Suzuki, Kantaro, 208
Sweden, 6, 10
Syria, 324, 326–27

Taft, William H., 132, 143, 163
Taiping Rebellion, 100–101
Talbott, Strobe, 314
Taliban, 346, 362
Talleyrand-Périgord, Charles Maurice de, 23, 26–27
Tansill, C. C., 174
Taylor, Maxwell D., 279
Taylor, Zachary, 63–64, 67–69
Technical Assistance program, 227
Tecumseh, 34
Tehran conference, 203–4

Teller, Henry M., 115
Teller Amendment, 116–17, 118
Temporary Commission on Korea, 241
Ten Years' War, 110
Territorial expansionism: Alaska, 89–91; Hawaii, 91–93; introduction to, 87–89; in the Pacific, 89–91; Samoa, 91. *See also* Expansionism
Tet Offensive, 284, 286
Texas, 59, 62–64
Thailand, 275, 395n21
Thatcher, Margaret, 311, 313, 316, 334, 336
The *Spectator*, 87
Thompson, Kenneth, 308–9
Threshold Test Ban pact, 263
Tientsin treaties, 100–101
Tito, Marshal, 248
Tojo, Hideki, 195, 238
Tonkin Gulf Resolution, 282–83
Tracy, Benjamin F., 109–10
Trade, 11–12, 31–32, 108–9, 117–18, 169–70. *See also* Economy
Transcontinental railroad, 87, 90
Transcontinental Treaty, 40–43
Trans-Siberian Railway, 141, 155
Trans-World Airways hijacking, 329
Treaty of 1915, 134
Treaty of Aigun, 100
Treaty of Alliance, 4–5
Treaty of Amity and Commerce, 4
Treaty of Berlin, 91
Treaty of Brest-Litovsk, 154
Treaty of Ghent, 35, 36–37, 38
Treaty of Guadalupe Hidalgo, 72
Treaty of Kanagawa, 99
Treaty of Nanking, 98
Treaty of Paris, 1, 9, 10
Treaty of San Lorenzo, 21–22
Treaty of Shimonoseki, 103
Treaty of Tlatelolco, 260
Treaty of Versailles, 157–60, 175

Treaty of Wanghia, 98
Treaty of Washington, 85–86
Trent affair, 80–82
Tripartite Agreement of 1950, 322–23
Tripartite Pact, 179, 191–92, 193
Triple Entente powers, 146
Trist, Nicholas P., 70–72
Trist's Treaty, 71–72
Trudeau, Pierre, 264
Truman, Harry S.: aid for Greece and Turkey, 225–26; Berlin airlift, 229; China and, 239–41; Korea and, 242; MacArthur and, 242–44; Marshall Plan, 227; overflying the Soviet Union, 260; postwar draft, 230; Potsdam conference, 221; Potsdam Declaration, 208; recognition of Israel, 322; Soviet Union and, 390n15; Truman Doctrine, 211, 226, 308; on unconditional surrender, 185; withdrawal of troops from Berlin, 221
Truman Doctrine, 211, 226, 308
Tsing Hua College, 383n32
Tucker, Robert, 308
Turkey, 145–46, 153, 212, 225–26, 256, 258
Turner, Frederick Jackson, 109
Tutuila, 121, 122
Tuyll, Baron, 47–48
Twenty-first century challenges: Arab Spring, 360–62; Bush Doctrine, 347–49; introduction to, 343–44; invasion of Afghanistan, 345–47; Iraq policy, 344–45; Iraq War, 349–57; Obama and nuclear weapons, 357–60; rogue states and stateless actors, 362–63; September 11, 2001, terrorist attacks, 345–47. *See also* Iraq War
Two-Ocean Naval Act, 179

Tyler, John, 58, 63, 98
Tzu His, 139

U-2 incident, 250, 261
Ukase, 371n7
Ukraine, 154
UNCIO (United Nations Conference on International Organization), 215
Unconditional surrender, 202, 208
Undeveloped World, 345
Unequal treaties, 98, 101
"Unguarded frontier," 38
Unilateral vs. multilateral actions, 362–63
"United Action for Peace" plan, 243
United Nations: General Assembly, 243, 249–50, 259; international control of atomic energy, 217–18; Korea and, 241–45, 246; origins of, 205, 211, 212–15; partition plan, 322; San Francisco Conference, 215–16. *See also* Security Council, UN
United Nations Charter, 214
United Nations Conference on International Organization (UNCIO), 215
United Provinces of Rio de la Plata, 49
UN Monitoring, Verification and Inspections Commission (UNMOVIC), 352–53
UN Special Commission (UNSCOM), 340
U.S. Atomic Energy Act, 233
U.S. News and World Report, 254
U.S. Nuclear Posture Review Report, 360

Vandenberg, Arthur, 215
Vandenberg Resolution, 230
Vans Murray, William, 23
Van Tien Dung, 396n40
Varg, Paul, 30

444 Index

V-E Day, 207–8
Venezuelan Crisis, 93–96, 130, 172
Veracruz, occupation of, 136
Vergennes, Comte de, 3–4, 6
Vichy France, 191, 194
Victor Emmanuel III, King, 181
Victoria, Queen, 114
Vientiane Agreement, 292
Viet Cong, 279, 282, 283–84
Viet Minh (Vietnam Independence League), 273–75
Vietnam, divisions of under French rule, 394n2
Vietnamization, 287–89, 396n33
Vietnam Syndrome, 293–94
Vietnam War: antiwar sentiment, 283, 288–89, 396n33; bombing of North Vietnam, 285–86, 290; collapse of American policy, 291–92; costs and casualties of, 291; Diem and guerrilla war, 278–79; domestic debate, 282–83; Easter Offensive, 289–90; escalation of, 281–82; fall of Diem, 280–81; legacy of, 292–94; media's role in, 283; military aid and advisers, 279–80; Paris cease-fire agreement, 290; Paris Peace Accords, 291; as part of the Cold War, 258; peace negotiations, 284–87, 289–91; as a stalemate, 283–84; Tet Offensive, 284, 286; Tonkin Gulf Resolution, 282–83; Vietnamization, 287–89, 396n33. *See also* South Vietnam
Villa, Francisco, 137
Vincennes, U.S.S., 330
Viorst, Milton, 332
Virgin Islands, 88, 128
Voice of America, 249
Von Bernstorff, Johann Heinrich, 149–50, 151–52, 384n14

Wachusett, U.S.S., 83
Wake Island, 122
Waldorf-Astoria Hotel, 170
Walker, Robert J., 70–71
Wall Street Journal, 113
"War guilt" clause, 160
War hawks, 34
Warnke, Paul, 261
War of 1812: American commerce, 31–32; demilitarization and arbitration, 37–38; drift into, 34–35; impressment issue, 30–31; as indecisive, 35–36; Jefferson's "peaceable coercion," 33; northern boundary and Oregon, 39–40; Transcontinental Treaty with Spain, 40–43; Treaty of Ghent, 36–37
War of the First Coalition, 16
Warsaw Pact, 233–34, 248–49
Washington, George: called out of retirement, 23; Farewell Address, 15, 22, 46; French Revolutionary wars and, 16–18; Jay's Treaty, 21; presidency of, 15–16
Washington, U.S.S., 134
Washington Conference, 166
Washington Post, 107, 313, 344, 357
Watterson, Henry "Marse," 107
Wayne, "Mad" Anthony, 19
Weapons inspections, 340, 341, 348, 352–53, 359–60
Weapons of mass destruction (WMD), 347, 348, 349, 362
Webster, Daniel, 72
Webster, William, 332
Webster-Ashburton Treaty, 38, 58
Weinberger, Caspar, 293–94, 297–99, 300, 303, 306, 310, 313, 319, 336
Weinberger Doctrine, 293–94, 336
Weisskrichen, Gert, 347
Welles, Sumner, 171
Western European Union, 233

Western frontier, American Revolution, 12–14
West Germany, 227–29, 232–33, 268–69, 307
Westmoreland, William C., 284
Weyler, Valeriano, 110–11, 112
Wilkes, Charles, 64–65, 80–81, 122
Wilkinson, James, 14
Will, George, 315, 319
Willis, Albert S., 93
Willkie, Wendell L., 187
Wilmot Proviso, 71
Wilson, Henry Lane, 135
Wilson, Woodrow: on Bolshevik Russia, 154–55; dollar diplomacy, 132–33; Fourteen Points, 153–54; on German submarine warfare, 148–49, 152; Great Britain and, 150–51; health of, 162–63; Latin American interventionism, 133–37; League of Nations, 162–63; on Lodge, 163–64; Mexico and, 135–37; on the Monroe Doctrine, 45; peace negotiations, 156–57, 384n13; proclamation of neutrality, 146; tour in support of the League of Nations, 162–63; war message, 145; World War I peace negotiations, 150–52
Wilson-Gorman tariff, 104
WMD (Weapons of mass destruction), 347, 348, 349, 362
Wolfowitz, Paul, 344–45
Wood, Leonard, 129
Woodford, Stewart L., 114
Workingmen of Manchester, 75
World Court, 216
World Disarmament Conference, 168
World War I: Allied intervention in Russia, 154–55; American economy and, 147–48; armistice, 155–56; declaration of war, 153; Fourteen Points, 153–54; German submarine warfare, 148–50; introduction to, 145–47; League of Nations, 160–63; peace negotiations, 156–57; submarine warfare, 151–53; Treaty of Versailles, 157–60; Wilson's relationship with the British, 150–51
World War II: end of, 207–9; events leading to, 180–84; events leading to Pearl Harbor attack, 190–91; Grand Alliance, 197–200, 202–5; introduction to, 185–86; Japanese southern expansion, 194–95; lend-lease program, 191–92; move away from neutrality, 186–90; negotiations with Japan, 192–94, 195–97; occupation of Germany, 220, 221, 223–24; public opinion and the prospect of, 179–80; relations with Soviet Union, 200–202; strategy decisions, 198–99, 202–5; Yalta conference, 205–7

Xuan Thuy, 286

Yalta conference, 204, 205–7, 214, 389n7
Yamal natural gas pipeline, 302–3
Yellow journalism, 111
Yugoslavia, 204–5, 222–23, 228

Zaibatsu, 238
Zapata, Emiliano, 137
Zelaya, Jose Santos, 132
"Zero option," 307, 313
Zimmermann, Arthur, 152

About the Authors

RICHARD DEAN BURNS is Professor Emeritus of History at California State University, Los Angeles. He is the author/coeditor of 13 books, including *The Evolution of Arms Control* (Praeger Security International, 2009); *The Missile Defense Systems of George W. Bush* (Praeger Security International, 2010); and *Reagan, Bush, Gorbachev: Revisiting the End of the Cold War* (with Norman A. Graebner and Joseph M. Siracusa, Praeger, 2008).

JOSEPH M. SIRACUSA is Professor of Human Security and International Diplomacy, Royal Melbourne Institute of Technology, Melbourne, Australia. He is internationally known for his writings on international nuclear weapons, diplomacy, and the Cold War. He has written numerous books including *Nuclear Weapons* (Oxford University Press, 2008); *Diplomacy* (Oxford University Press, 2010); and *America and the Cold War, 1941–1991* (with Norman A. Graebner and Richard Dean Burns, Praeger, 2010)

JASON C. FLANAGAN is Assistant Professor in International Studies at the University of Canberra, Australia. He has published on American foreign policy and presidential politics, including *Imagining the Enemy: American Presidential War Rhetoric from Woodrow Wilson to George W. Bush* (Regina, 2009).